Seeing & Writing 4

Seeing &

Writing 4

Donald McQuade
University of California, Berkeley

Christine McQuade
Queens College, City University of New York

Bedford/St. Martin's
Boston & New York

For Bedford/St. Martin's

Developmental Editor: Abby Bielagus
Senior Production Editor: Karen S. Baart
Senior Production Supervisor: Nancy Myers
Marketing Manager: Molly Parke
Editorial Assistant: Erin McGhee
Production Assistant: David Ayers
Copyeditor: Alice Vigliani
Photo Editor: Elissa Curtis
Senior Art Director: Anna Palchik
Text and Cover Design: 2x4, Inc.
Composition: NK Graphics
Printing and Binding: RR Donnelley and Sons

President: Joan E. Feinberg
Editorial Director: Denise B. Wydra
Editor in Chief: Karen S. Henry
Director of Marketing: Karen R. Soeltz
Director of Editing, Design, and Production:
    Marcia Cohen
Assistant Director of Editing, Design, and Production:
    Elise S. Kaiser
Managing Editor: Elizabeth M. Schaaf

Library of Congress Control Number: 2009928934

For information, write: Bedford/St. Martin's,
75 Arlington Street, Boston, MA 02116
(617-399-4000)

ISBN-10: 0–312–47604–3
ISBN-13: 978-0-312-47604-5

Acknowledgments

Introduction
Verbal Texts
Robert Frost. "In White." From *The Dimensions of Robert Frost* by Reginald L. Cook. Copyright © 1958 by Reginald L. Cook. Reprinted by permission of Henry Holt & Company, LLC. "Design." From *The Poetry of Robert Frost* edited by Edward Connery Latham. Copyright © 1964 by Lesley Frost Ballantine, 1936 by Robert Frost, 1969 by Henry Holt & Company. Reprinted by permission of Henry Holt & Company, LLC.

David Ignatow. "My Place." From *Against the Evidence.* Copyright © 1993 by David Ignatow. Reprinted by permission of Wesleyan University Press.
Visual Texts
Untitled drawings. Peter Arkle. © Peter Arkle, 2005.
Subway Passengers, New York, NY, 1938. Walker Evans. The Metropolitan Museum of Art, Gift of Arnold H. Crane, 1971 (1971.646.18) © Walker Evans Archive, The Metropolitan Museum of Art.
Image of Homelessness. Mark Peterson. Courtesy of Mark Peterson / Redux Pictures.
American Gothic. Gordon Parks. Courtesy Gordon Parks / Corbis.
Overhead View of a Cloverleaf. Getty Images.
Dean College, *Prepare for What's Next.* Courtesy of Dean College, Franklin, MA.
Migrant Mother, Nipomo, California series. Dorothea Lange. Courtesy The Dorothea Lange collection, Oakland Museum of California.
12-23-97 5:09 p.m.; 2-21-00 4:38 p.m. Richard Misrach. Courtesy of Fraenkel Gallery, San Francisco; Pace-MacGill, New York and Marc Selwyn Fine Arts, Los Angeles.
Natural Resources, 2005. Reprinted with permission by Cagle Cartoons, Inc.
Mountain Lakes, New Jersey, 1977. Courtesy of Arno Rafael Minkkinen.
Down and Out in Discount America cover by *The Nation* magazine, January 3, 2005. Reprinted with permission from the issue of *The Nation.* http://www.thenation.com
The Black Panthers' Newsletter back cover, 1972. Malik. *Poverty is a Crime and Our People are the Victims (after Migrant Mother, Nipomo, California), c. 1972* © The Dorothea Lange Collection, Oakland Museum of California, City of Oakland. Gift of Paul S. Taylor.
Warren Avenue at 23rd Street, Detroit, Michigan, October 1993. Joel Sternfeld. Courtesy of the artist and Luhring Augustine, New York.

For Susanne and Marc

Preface for Instructors

As with previous revisions of *Seeing & Writing*, we began our work on this fourth edition by engaging in a series of conversations with people who know the book best – the teachers and students who have used it. Their thoughtful responses and imaginative suggestions have helped us develop an even more effective teaching tool.

Through these conversations we learned a great deal about the current state of composition classrooms and reaffirmed our conviction that *Seeing & Writing* should be grounded in a simple pedagogical premise: to invite students to give words and images equal attention. This premise informs the book's three goals: (1) to provide opportunities for composition students to think critically about visual and verbal aspects of American culture, (2) to help students write effectively about the way they perceive themselves, especially in relation to the images and words that compete for their attention, and (3) to give instructors the flexibility to work with these materials in ways that best suit their students' interests and abilities.

Our decades of experience on both sides of the instructional desk convince us that instructors ought to start where students are able – and with the myriad visual elements of contemporary American experience, material with which most students are thoroughly familiar, although often in a passive and uncritical way. We believe that undergraduates are sufficiently conversant with the subjects and strategies of a wide range of visual images (including advertisements, photographs, paintings, and comic art) and nonfiction prose, short stories, and poems to want to write about them – and the issues they raise – in original, coherent, and convincing terms. We believe that enabling students to move fluently within and among visual and verbal worlds will improve their analytic and compositional skills.

Numerous instructors have told us that a significant percentage of their students are reading far beyond the materials assigned in

Seeing & Writing, and that their students are not only exploring each text more critically but also thinking more incisively about the compositional and cultural context within which each text operates. Such increased understanding has improved their ability to write thoughtfully and convincingly about visual and verbal texts – and appreciably so.

Throughout the revision process, we were also encouraged by reports from instructors across the nation that *Seeing & Writing* generates lively classroom discussions. In this fourth edition we have assembled a first-rate collection of engaging verbal and visual texts; these teachable materials encourage students to see, think, and write with increasing clarity and conviction.

A frequent refrain in our dialogue with instructors is their appreciation for our efforts to present outstanding teaching material in a flexible manner, thereby accommodating multiple teaching styles. We have been diligent about maintaining this instructional flexibility throughout *Seeing & Writing 4*.

As we prepared this edition, we continued to work closely with Michael Rock, Georgie Stout, and their colleagues at the widely acclaimed design firm 2x4. We wanted our colleagues to recapture a sense of seeing the book for the first time, so through a close collaboration we have streamlined the design for *Seeing & Writing 4*. The simplified look and feel will help instructors and students to focus even more productively on the interrelatedness of reading and writing. Open and clean-looking pages allow students a chance to slow down and become absorbed in the photograph or essay at hand. Stunning images are centered and framed, with only a few bleeding off the page – to allow students to pause, reflect, and engage in critical inquiry. Texts all follow a one-column format for easier close, critical reading. The more "composed" and accessible text facilitates students' efforts to analyze both visual and verbal texts. We aimed for elegance and simplicity rather than embellishment, for strategic placement and focus rather than saturation.

Although the design has changed, the features that make the book an engaging tool for the composition classroom remain. **Pairs** that present a striking image with a poem or short prose piece ask students to think and write about the relationship between visual and verbal composition strategies; **Portfolios** display collections of paintings, photographs, or mixed-media texts by a single artist and allow students to consider style, theme, and vision; **Retrospects** provide visual timelines to the changing look of the advertisements we see, the movies we watch, and the magazines we read; **Looking Closer** units present a targeted collection of visual and verbal texts and challenge students to dig deep into one topic within each chapter's larger theme.

New to This Edition

We preserved *Seeing & Writing*'s core strengths and made the text an even more productive instructional tool by focusing this revision on the following features:

- A new, graphic-novel treatment of the writing process is the first thing students see as they open the book. Eight pages of illustrations by celebrated artist Peter Arkle fold out to tell a story of one student and the development of his essay. The student, his teacher, and his peers reappear in each chapter to explain the challenges associated with writing, in voices that are both engaging and instructive.

- Sixty-five new selections include photographs, advertisements, poems, essays, short stories, and screen shots. We chose them for their rhetorical variety, their strength as models for student writers, and the diverse occasions for writing they represent. For example:

  In stunning photographs and startling facts, Peter Menzel and Faith D'Aluisio expose the compelling international relationship between people and food.

  Yang Liu, with her stark graphics, highlights differences in philosophy between East and West.

  Barbara Ehrenreich and Steven Johnson provide provocative essays about,

respectively, class in the United States and a favorite pastime – watching television.

- The apparatus makes connections between and among texts, and it includes more writing assignments that encourage students to consult a variety of outside sources. Additional **Responding Visually** assignments offer new opportunities for students to create visual compositions.

- Student voices are more prevalent, as they talk about their experiences with college writing in quotations sprinkled throughout the chapters. The quotations are paired with similar quotations from professional writers – to show that college and professional writers respond in similar ways to the same challenges when putting ideas on the page.

- This new edition offers a wider range of visual compositions with more interconnections. We have juxtaposed classic and contemporary works of art (photographs, paintings, sculpture, and graphic art) with cultural artifacts (web sites, ads, movie posters and stills, and icons) to expand teaching possibilities.

Teaching SEEING & WRITING 4

A comprehensive instructor's manual – *Teaching SEEING & WRITING 4* – offers suggestions on how to teach the material in this new edition, paying respectful attention to different institutional settings and instructional purposes. A hands-on manual, it includes the voices of several dozen teachers who have used *Seeing & Writing* successfully. These accomplished instructors share their syllabi and their most effective assignments as well as snapshots of themselves, their schools, and their students.

Each chapter of this "field-tested" compendium of teaching resources includes generous helpings of the following elements:

- **Sure-Fire Classes and Assignments:** Sure-fire methods, from instructors around the country, for working with the images and verbal texts in *Seeing & Writing 4*.

- **Generating Class Discussion and In-Class Writing:** A thorough guide for how to work productively with each text to stimulate discussion and in-class writing. This classroom work increases students' motivation to write engaging, coherent, and convincing essays about the texts, issues, and themes articulated in the book.

- **Additional Writing Topics:** A group of additional topics for each selection that includes informal and personal writing, descriptive and narrative essays, expository and argumentative papers, and research assignments.

- **Connections with Other Texts:** Activities that link each selection to other texts in the chapter or book, along with suggestions for encouraging students to discover these interconnections on their own.

- **Suggestions for Further Reading, Thinking, and Writing:** Examples of supplemental material designed for classroom use — including print, video, audio, and digital sources — along with recommendations on how to use them to reinforce instructional goals.

Additionally, the **Seeing & Writing Student Center** is a book-related web site with guided exercises on reading visual images; web-based research activities; annotated research links to sources about the artists, writers, and thematic and compositional issues in the book; and doorways to visual resources, virtual museums, and much more. Our premium digital content is gathered into a collection for composition called *Re:Writing Plus*, a resource that can be packaged with *Seeing & Writing*.

Acknowledgments

From its inception to this fourth edition, *Seeing & Writing* has been the product of pleasant and productive conversations and collaborations — with each other, our colleagues, our families and friends, the Bedford/St. Martin's team, the design firm 2x4, and a growing community of instructors and students.

The genesis of the book can be traced to innumerable conversations over more than twenty years between Don McQuade and Charles H. Christensen, the now-retired founder of Bedford/St. Martin's and an extraordinary patron and developer of teaching ideas. Throughout this long collaboration and friendship, Chuck and Don talked about creating a book that draws on undergraduates' familiarity with the visual dimensions of American culture to develop their skills as readers, thinkers, and writers.

When Chuck Christensen, Joan Feinberg (now president of Bedford/St. Martin's), and Don McQuade began to talk seriously about bringing this vision to fruition in 1996, Don initiated a series of dinner-table conversations with his family — his wife, Susanne, and their children, Christine and Marc — about relationships between the visual and the verbal in the writing classroom and in contemporary American culture. Christine had returned for the holidays from New York City, where she had completed the fall season dancing with the STREB modern dance company. Marc was home from the University of California, Berkeley, where he had finished his first semester as an architecture major. We batted around questions like these: Which has a more powerful impact on people — an image or a word? What place do images have in a writing classroom? How is writing visual? How do nonverbal learners learn to write?

Those early conversations, and Marc's thoughts on the relationship between word and image in particular, were the central impetus for developing the book. We were immediately struck by the value of a cross-generational conversation about an interdisciplinary subject.

Having studied American popular culture as a history major and having served as a writing tutor at Berkeley's Student Learning Center, Christine was eager to investigate the teaching of writing in a visual age. Her ideas about reading visual and verbal texts drew her father's attention and encouragement, and she was eager to apprentice with him in the craft of creating textbooks.

Our collaboration began spontaneously and grew organically. We would like to take this opportunity, more than a decade later, to thank each other for the continuing conversation.

Our work together is only one part of the collaborative effort behind *Seeing & Writing*. In preparing this fourth edition, we once again relied on instructors from around the country who took time from busy schedules to meet with us and share their experiences teaching with previous editions. Many others generously offered critiques during its development. We are enormously grateful for their insight, enthusiasm, and honesty. Those conversations guided our planning for this revision; they also revealed a growing community of passionate instructors who share our commitment to starting where students are able and to improving their analytical and compositional skills through exploring the visual and verbal dimensions of American culture. We hope that we have responded effectively to their suggestions for improving the book's pedagogical strengths.

For their many thoughtful and helpful recommendations, we would like to thank the following:

Ann L. Avery, Central Wyoming College
Kelly Bradbury, The Ohio State University
Elizabeth Byrne, Shaw University
Jeff E. Cravello, California State Polytechnic University
Amy E. Dayton-Wood, University of Alabama
Stephanie Dowdle, Salt Lake Community College
Melina Draper, Northern Essex Community College
Cathleen Galitz, Shoshoni High School
Stephanie B. Gibson, University of Baltimore
Kim Haimes-Korn, Southern Polytechnic State University
Charles Hood, Antelope Valley College
Glenn Hutchinson, University of North Carolina
JoAnne Juett, University of Wisconsin
Kevin S. Knight, University of North Carolina, Wilmington
Melissa Korber, Las Positas College
Patricia Leaf, Ball State University
Jon K. Lindsay, Southern Polytechnic State University
Kara Lybarger-Monson, Moorpark College
Ben McCorkle, The Ohio State University
Johanna Movassat, San Jose State University
Suzanne Nielsen, Minneapolis College of Art and Design
Brian Oliu, University of Alabama
Scott Orme, Spokane Community College
Ann Parker, Southern Polytechnic State University
Stephanie Pippin, Washington University
Amy M. Pointer, University of Baltimore
Valerie A. Reimers, Oklahoma State University
Rhonda Schlatter, Mesa Community College
Leah Schweitzer, High Point University
Suzanne Scott, George Mason University
Dianna Rockwell Shank, Southwestern Illinois College
Jason Stupp, West Virginia University
Fritz Swanson, University of Michigan
Kathryn Sweney, University of North Dakota
Brooke Taylor, Washington University in St. Louis
Jason Thompson, University of Arizona
Rebecca Todd, Xavier University
Beverly Wall, Trinity College
James M. Wilson, Flagler College
Joseph P. Wood, University of Alabama

We would also like to acknowledge – and express our gratitude to – our students at UC Berkeley and at Queens College for their thoughtful engagement with the pedagogy of *Seeing & Writing* and for their innumerable contributions to strengthening this edition.

Behind this collaborative effort also stand a number of friends and colleagues who generously allowed us into their already crowded lives to seek advice, encouragement, and assistance since the first edition. We would like to underscore our gratitude to Elizabeth Abrams of the University of California, Santa Cruz; Tom Ahn; Austin Bunn; Eileen O'Malley Callahan; Beth Chimera; Mia Chung; Lee Dembart; Duncan Faherty of Queens College, CUNY; Kathy Gin; Sandra and Yuen Gin; Justin Greene; Anne-Marie Harvey; Eli Kaufman; Aileen Kim; Laura Lanzerotti; Joel Lovell; Greg Mullins of Evergreen College; Barbara Roether; Anjum Salam; Shayna Samuels; Elizabeth Streb and the dancers of STREB. We remain grateful to Andrew Beahrs, whose superb reading skills and admirable sensitivity to teaching matters strengthened earlier editions of the book. We would also like to acknowledge Dr. Darryl Stephens, who brings inestimable intelligence, writing skill, sensitivity to cultural nuance, and pedagogical care to his reading and to the questions following many selections in *Seeing & Writing*.

It quickly became clear that the book would need an especially sophisticated designer's eye. We remain grateful to Irwin Chen for introducing us to the design firm 2x4. Michael Rock and Katie Andresen – and more recently Georgie Stout, Erica Deahl, and Fabienne Hess – have been invaluable in helping us not only to expand our imagination of how this book could look and function, but also to sharpen our own abilities to think visually. During the preparation of the fourth edition, Georgie Stout and Erica Deahl joined with Michael Rock in turning a seemingly chaotic collection of materials into an elegant and useful instructional tool.

It has been a special pleasure to continue to work with Peter Arkle, a brilliant illustrator whose art provides fascinating portraits and social commentary on contemporary American life. We are delighted that Peter accepted our invitation to continue our collaboration, accentuating the relationship between seeing and writing in engaging and memorable ways. His eight-page foldout on the composing process, his humorous drawings on pages 2, 4, 13, and 16 of the introduction, and his renderings of student and faculty characters in each chapter are eminently teachable materials in their own right. Those interested in seeing more of Peter's work can explore his web site at *peterarkle.com*.

We remain grateful to Esin Goknar, Naomi Ben-Shahar, and Sally McKissick for opening new vistas in photography and other visual media in previous editions of *Seeing and Writing* – and for their respect for teaching and learning. We especially thank Elissa Curtis for her superb work on this fourth edition. Not only is she delightful to work with, but she demonstrates repeatedly that she has an admirable sensitivity to the pedagogical possibilities of visual materials. *Seeing & Writing 4* is a much stronger book because of her thoroughly professional approach, and we are grateful for all she has taught us about seeing carefully.

We would like to call special attention to the first-rate companion volume, *Teaching SEEING & WRITING 4*, prepared by Kim Haimes-Korn, an outstanding teacher and writer, and a professor of English and director of the Composition Program at Southern Polytechnic State University. We are honored that she has joined us in exploring the most effective ways to strengthen students' reading and writing skills as they work with the book's visual and verbal texts. Stefanie Wortman also deserves our thanks for her able assistance in this endeavor. Instructors interested in improving their teaching repertoire will be well rewarded by reading Professor Haimes-Korn's imaginative suggestions.

We would also like to acknowledge Dan Keller, Professor of Rhetoric and Composition at Ohio State University, Newark, for his invaluable collaboration on earlier editions of *Teaching SEEING & WRITING*. His understanding of the practical applications of the book's vision, as well as his insight into what works well in the classroom, made earlier editions far more than a successful companion volume to *Seeing & Writing*.

We once again extend special thanks to the kind people at Bedford/St. Martin's. Alice Vigliani copyedited the manuscript with exceptional skill as well as unfailing sensitivity to, and respect for, our pedagogical purposes. The quality of her work prompted us to look forward to her notations and queries. Anyone who can edit that well understands, appreciates, and helps produce effective writing.

We also thank Erin McGhee for her exemplary editorial assistance. Susan Doheny and Sandy Schechter once again managed with great skill and determination the complex responsibility of securing permissions to reprint the visual and verbal materials in the book. We are especially indebted to Karen Baart for her remarkable editorial skill and attentiveness, as well as her personal kindness and generous spirit, as production editor. Karen was never at a loss for an imaginative solution to a seemingly intractable editorial problem, and she managed the logistics of producing this fourth edition with an admirable blend of intelligence, imagination, common sense, patience, and good will. Thanks as well to David Ayers, who assisted with production in countless essential ways. We also thank marketing manager Molly Parke and the superb sales representatives of Bedford/St. Martin's for their insights about the pedagogical strengths and weaknesses of the third edition of *Seeing & Writing*. These colleagues also were central in helping us to discover – and to make more visible in *Teaching SEEING & WRITING* – the community of teachers who have found working with *Seeing & Writing* both enjoyable and effective.

We continue to be indebted to Joan Feinberg, a perceptive, encouraging, and compelling voice of reason and impeccable judgment. Her vision of the book's potential and her critiques of our work stand as models of professional integrity. Chuck Christensen offered wise and energizing support well beyond his retirement. His thoughtful counsel and confidence in us and what we seek to achieve in *Seeing & Writing* has made each sentence easier to write.

Genevieve Hamilton Day and Alanya Harter served with great skill and sensitivity as the editors of earlier editions of *Seeing & Writing*, and we celebrate their continued presence in this new edition. Abby Bielagus took responsibility for editing *Seeing & Writing 4*, and from our first conversation she unfailingly demonstrated intelligence, a keen editorial eye, good judgment, rigorousness, gracious encouragement, patience, sensitivity to pedagogical responsibility, and tireless dedication to the project. She has earned our deep admiration. Abby strengthened *Seeing & Writing 4* in countless ways, and we are grateful for her steadfast support in improving this teaching tool. We consider ourselves most fortunate to have worked with such a succession of outstanding editors. Their patience, clear-mindedness, professionalism, intellectual integrity, and good humor have created the kinds of supportive conditions in which every writer and teacher can thrive.

From the first edition of *Seeing & Writing* to the fourth, our work has coincided – and delightfully so – with the birth of a child. One edition saw the birth of Alanya's daughter, and another welcomed Genevieve's daughter. This edition is no exception, as Christine McQuade gave birth to her daughter, Sky Liang Hsu, this past winter. Her grandfather can now look forward to the satisfactions of introducing yet another generation to the sustaining pleasures of writing about reading and writing!

Special thanks to Michael Hsu for reading and rereading our drafts and for giving encouragement and support. His generous and rigorous intelligence, and his energy and patience, along with his care of Sky Liang Hsu, have made it possible for us to complete this revision. We also continue to learn from the example of his first-rate prose.

Finally, we would like to acknowledge Susanne and Marc McQuade. This project would never have been possible without their questions, ideas, encouragement, and most important, their inspiring intellectual curiosity.

Merci vu mou!
Donald McQuade and Christine McQuade

How This Book Works

Each of the selections and exercises in this book asks students to take a closer look at the objects, people, places, identities, ideas, and experiences that make up the varied expressions of American culture — to pay closer attention to, interpret, and then write about what they see.

The chapters in the book are filled with images and words that will help students think critically and write convincingly about increasingly complex themes and issues: observing "ordinary" objects, exploring what makes a space a place, considering the ways in which we record personal and public memories, how we embody and express sex and sexuality, and how race figures in our personal and public Americas. An entirely new chapter has been added that explores how class informs identity. The last chapter has been heavily revised to focus on argument; challenging texts and images address complex questions that require students to take a stand.

Generally we have designed each chapter to progress from the concrete to the abstract, from shorter to longer texts, and from works with a limited and readily accessible frame of reference to works that are complex. The overall organization of the book reflects a similar progression — from practicing skills of observation and inference, to working with description and narration, and then to applying exposition, argumentation, and other rhetorical forms. Yet, because each chapter is self-contained and begins with an exercise in observation and inference, instructors can sequence subjects and themes to best address their own instructional needs as well as the interests and backgrounds of their students.

Accompanying each selection is a headnote that provides background information about the writer or artist and text as well as suggested questions for "Seeing" and for "Writing." Seeing questions help students generate careful observations and think through — and beyond — their initial response; writing questions help them identify compositional issues such as how the author or artist has chosen to assemble the elements of the piece. "Responding Visually" prompts offer opportunities to create visual compositions in response to certain selections.

On the facing page are thumbnails of the special features and sample selections in the book. A brief description of each recurring feature runs below its thumbnail. These give students a sense of the pedagogical, visual, and textual architecture that underpins *Seeing & Writing 4* — each page of which, we hope, will reward their closer attention.

PORTFOLIOS

A provocative collection of images opens each chapter, and images by a single artist or on a single theme later in the chapter ask students to consider style, theme, and vision.

PAIR

Images juxtaposed with a poem or short prose piece ask students to think about the relationship between verbal and visual strategies.

RETROSPECT

Visual timelines graphically show students how time has changed the face of the ads we're shown, the movies we see, and the magazines we read.

VISUALIZING COMPOSITION

Key concepts for writers – such as tone, structure, purpose, and audience – are given concrete shape.

CONTEXT

Cultural and historical documents and images give additional context for challenging readings.

LOOKING CLOSER

A sharply targeted collection of visual and verbal texts invites students to focus attention on a specific aspect of each chapter's larger topic.

Contents

INTRODUCTION

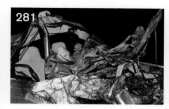

399

404

434

Seeing & Writing 4

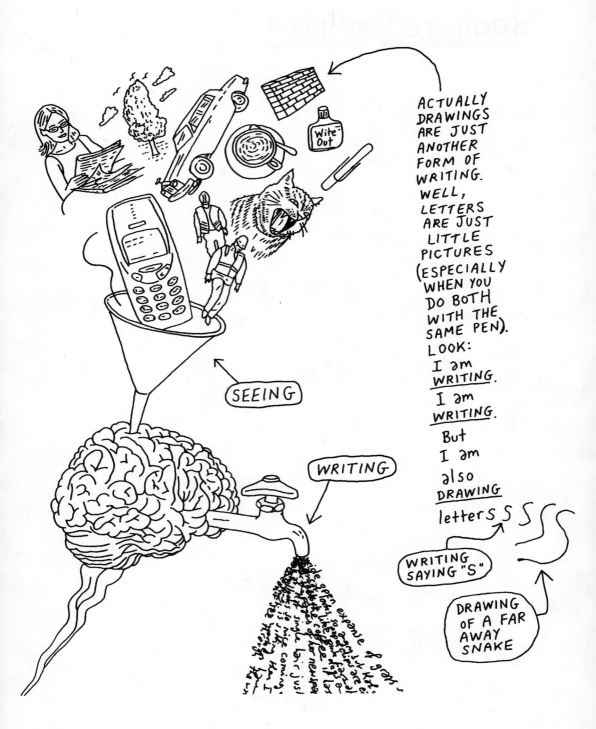

WRITING MATTERS

"The real voyage of discovery consists not in seeking new landscapes but in having new eyes." —Marcel Proust

What does seeing have to do with writing? You may be asking this question as you begin working with this book. Seeing and writing seem – on the surface – to have very little to do with each other. We tend to regard seeing as an effortless, reflex-level activity. Think of common phrases such as *take a quick glance* or *give something a look-see*. They suggest speed, lightness, and ease. Writing, on the other hand, is more frequently associated with careful thought, weight, and labor. The idiom *writer's block* is an example: Think of the classic image of a writer staring at a blank page, crumpled papers overflowing a nearby trash can. Few writers of any age or level of experience have not lived through some version of this frustration.

In this book we will show you that seeing and writing have more in common than you might think. They are inextricably bound: Learning to see more carefully will help you write more easily and successfully. The more your eyes are open and alert, the more you will have to write about and the more you will write with conviction and clarity.

This book provides you with opportunities to sharpen your perception and develop your ability to write with clarity and insight. In the following pages you will find a wide range of visual and verbal "snapshots" from contemporary culture: words, pictures, and combinations of the two taken from our increasingly multimedia world. You will be invited to pay as much attention to, say, an advertisement for the latest T-Mobile Google phone as to the more traditional essays and arguments you will read and write in most of your college courses.

We hope you will consider virtually everything around you to be a potential text for serious reading, discussion, and writing – from a movie poster for the latest box-office hit to a wall with graffiti scrawled on it; from an advertisement for building a stronger body to an essay about immigrating to the United States from Puerto Rico; from the clothes you buy to the jingles you hear on television commercials. Some may be familiar, some unfamiliar. Some might inspire, others unsettle. Our hope is that you will use these selections to draw on your own experience with contemporary culture and to recognize – and practice – your skills as an effective thinker and writer.

We believe that anyone interested in becoming an articulate and confident writer needs to "cross-train," to learn from the different ways in which serious thinkers see the world and express their distinct perspectives on it. The strategies artists and photographers employ to capture and direct the viewer's attention, make a point, or create an effect are not very different from the strategies writers use to achieve the same effects, albeit in a different medium. For example, you might think of a writer's choice of word as akin to a painter's brushstroke.

A dot of bright color (say, red), like a single word (say, *smash*), doesn't do much on its own: It's the combination of different elements, the composition of a text, that gives the audience something to read, respond to, admire, and remember.

Thinking carefully about visual and verbal strategies will improve your own skills as a reader and writer. We want to help you become more aware of – and develop more practiced confidence in – the skills identified with both verbal and visual literacy. These skills will enable you to learn, recognize, understand, and create compelling and convincing messages for audiences within and beyond the halls of higher education. You are already a member of several distinct communities; mastering the skills of critical reading and writing will enable you to contribute your ideas – to make your voice heard – in these and other communities with which you choose to associate.

Whatever your field of study in college, you will be asked to make observations and draw inferences about what you read, and you will be expected to formulate these inferences as assertions about an idea or a text. And you will be expected to support your claims with evidence. Such moves – from observation to inference, from concrete to abstract – form the cornerstone of all academic inquiry. This book provides you with opportunities to practice these fundamental skills.

This introduction offers you a set of concrete intellectual tools to help you practice the skills of seeing more clearly and writing more effectively about the world around you – the people, objects, images, events, ideas, and commercial appeals that compete for your attention and seek to gain your endorsement and loyalty.

"Stare. It is the way to educate your eye, and more. Stare, pry, listen, eavesdrop. Die knowing something. You are not here long."
–Walker Evans

"Seeing comes before words."
–John Berger

"No method nor discipline can supersede the necessity of being forever on the alert. What is a course of history, or philosophy, or poetry, or the most admirable routine of life, compared with the discipline of looking always at what is to be seen? Will you be a reader, a student merely, or a seer?"
–Henry David Thoreau

Walker Evans
Subway Passengers, New York, NY, 1938

Making Observations

A useful place to begin with any text – visual or verbal – is to jot down your first impressions. Answer these questions: What details do I notice? What parts of the text stand out to me more than others? It is important to allow yourself to react "purely" to a text before you begin analyzing it. What are your initial instincts about the text?

Whenever you read anything, you bring to that activity the sum total of your experience and your identity – how you define yourself in terms of race, class, gender, sexuality, and politics. You should also acknowledge your predispositions to, or prejudices about, the text in question.

Once you've attended to your first impressions, look again and write down a set of more careful observations about the text. An observation is a neutral, nonjudgmental, and verifiable statement.

Making notes on what you observe involves recording the obvious. Observations are concrete; they describe things that everyone can see in a text. It's easy to make assumptions about something you're looking at or reading without taking the time to base your statements on what you can actually see.

Making initial observations when responding to a text will enable you to build confidence in your ability to read it carefully and insightfully. Reading with an eye toward making observations also best prepares you to write effectively about what you see in a text.

We urge you to write down as many statements as possible about whatever you are observing. Whenever you encounter a new text, always begin by writing out or typing your thoughts.

observation: 1. (a) The act, practice, or power of noticing. (b) Something noticed. 2. (a) The fact of being seen or noticed; the act or practice of noting and recording facts and events, as for some scientific study. (b) The data so noted and recorded. 3. A comment or remark based on something observed.

"The best writing advice I've ever received is: 'Facts are eloquent.'"
– Norrie Epstein

"I always wanted to be somebody. I should have been more specific."
– Lily Tomlin

Exercise
Take a few moments to write down as many
observations as possible about this photograph by Mark Peterson. What exactly do
you notice?

Mark Peterson
Image of Homelessness, 1994 (p. 169)

Drawing Inferences

One of the most productive ways to approach understanding and appreciating any text involves a two-step process: Make observations, and then draw reasonable and verifiable inferences from those observations. This pattern of observing and inferring — what we regard as the cornerstone skills of careful reading and writing — can be applied to any question you ask about a text in terms of its purpose, structure, audience, metaphor, point of view, and tone, or the context within which it was written or produced.

How can you know whether the inferences you have drawn from your observations are reasonable? What makes an inference reasonable is whether specific evidence in the text warrants the intellectual leap you've made. When drawing an inference, be careful not to rush to judgment and formulate a conclusion, even a provisional one, before you have carefully examined the details of the evidence under consideration.

Remember to verify each interpretive claim you make with *specific details* from the text. Providing ample, detailed evidence to support each of your assertions also ensures that you don't develop the habit of believing that you can say whatever you want about a text, that you can read, as one student put it, "almost anything into a text."

Observation and inference are the fundamental building blocks of academic inquiry. Anytime you write an essay, carry out a scientific experiment, or investigate an historical question, you must make observations and draw inferences, find evidence and make assertions. Observations and inferences provide the basic material you need to write an essay. Essays are pieces of writing that support the assertions they make. Assertions are articulated in a thesis, and your evidence forms the body of the essay. In the next section we explore the process of moving from note-taking to drafting an essay.

inference: An intellectual leap from what one sees to what those details might suggest.

Exercise
What inferences can you draw about Mark Peterson's photograph (p. 7) based on your observations? Now think about how you might apply the same process of making careful observations and drawing inferences to a verbal text. Take a few moments to read the poem by David Ignatow on the next page. Then write down as many observations and inferences as possible.

MY PLACE
David Ignatow

I have a place to come to.
It's my place. I come to it
morning, noon and night
and it is there. I expect it
5 to be there whether or not
it expects me — my place
where I start from and go
towards so that I know
where I am going and what
10 I am going from, making me
firm in my direction.

I am good to talk to,
you feel in my speech
a location, an expectation
15 and all said to me in reply
is to reinforce this feeling
because all said is towards
my place and the speaker
too grows his
20 from which he speaks to mine
having located himself
through my place.

Observations and Inferences: One Student's Responses

We've reprinted a series of observations and inferences one student made about Mark Peterson's photograph and David Ignatow's poem. How do they compare with your own findings? those of your classmates?

Observations

1. I notice that there are cardboard boxes strapped to a sidewalk bench with three different kinds of twine or fabric.

2. I notice a Burger King sign in the top left of the image.

3. I notice that there are pieces of cardboard boxes on the ground.

4. I notice that there are dead leaves on the ground.

5. I notice that there are four people in the background.

6. I notice that the words HANDLE WITH CARE are written on the box in the bottom left corner of the photograph.

7. I notice that there is a pillow and at least two blankets visible through the opening of the box.

8. I notice that the diagonal line of the fence behind the bench divides the image in two.

9. I notice that the background street scene is blurry but that the foreground bench part is in focus.

Inferences

1. Based on the observations I made, I infer that this is a place where someone has set up a place to sleep.

2. The way the photographer framed this shot helps emphasize the juxtaposition between the life of a homeless person and the rest of bustling city life in New York City.

3. Based on the photograph's subject, the way it is framed or cropped, and the prominent inclusion of the Burger King sign and the text HANDLE WITH CARE, I infer that Peterson is making an ironic statement about the severity of the homelessness problem.

MY PLACE
David Ignatow

I have a place to come to.
It's my place. I come to it
morning, noon and night
and it is there. I expect it
5 to be there whether or not
it expects me — my place
where I start from and go
towards so that I know
where I am going and what
10 I am going from, making me
firm in my direction.

I am good to talk to,
you feel in my speech
a location, an expectation
15 and all said to me in reply
is to reinforce this feeling
because all said is towards
my place and the speaker
too grows his
20 from which he speaks to mine
having located himself
through my place.

Observations

1. I notice that the word *place* is repeated five times in this poem, in addition to the title.

2. I notice that Ignatow uses *I,* the first person.

3. I notice that this poem is made up of two parts, or stanzas.

4. I notice that there are eleven lines in both parts of the poem.

5. I notice that the longest line in the poem is six words long.

6. I notice that Ignatow uses simple, relatively short words in this poem.

7. I notice that the first stanza is made up of two sentences; the second stanza is made up of one sentence.

Inferences

1. Based on the observations I made, I infer that Ignatow is not referring to an actual, physical place in this poem but rather to an idea of place.

2. Ignatow's use of simple words, short lines, and stanzas of equal length helps reinforce the simplicity of the poem's message.

3. The balanced form of the poem helps convey an overall feeling of being centered, or "at home."

Drafting

Composing is a <u>recursive</u> process of seeing and writing. Taking a closer look around you not only gives you subjects and ideas to write about (which are the initial ingredients in writing) but also leads to effective writing. Careful seeing is an intellectual equivalent of breathing in; writing is a form of intellectual exhaling—expressing an idea in clear, convincing, and memorable terms. Writing, in turn, can also help you see and understand your subject more clearly.

Writing rarely proceeds neatly from one phase to the next. Rather the phases often overlap, making the process somewhat messy. Many writers revise what they have written as soon as they see the word or sentence on the page. Others wait until they have a complete draft and only then go back through it. Each writer participates in the writing process in a different way, at a different pace, and with a different result.

The term *draft* is used across disciplines to describe a first take, a first focused and sustained effort at completing a piece of writing or artwork. In the first phase of the writing process a writer usually chooses a subject to write about (or one may be assigned), identifies a purpose for writing about that subject, develops observations and inferences about the text(s) in question, generates a thesis—a controlling idea—about the subject, considers the audience to be addressed, and then expands that idea in brainstorming or freewriting exercises, in an outline, or in some other form that provides the basis for a first draft of the essay.

Exercises like brainstorming and freewriting help writers search for and then decide on a subject to write about. These exercises are excellent confidence builders, especially if you are a relatively inexperienced writer, because they can help you produce a great deal of writing in a short time. They also enable you to see rather quickly just how much you have to say about a subject while resisting the urge to edit your work prematurely.

We believe that there is no single way to write, no fail-proof formula to produce successful essays. Anyone who is seriously interested in learning to write can benefit not only from listening carefully to what other writers and artists have to say about the challenges and pleasures of the composing process, but also, and more importantly, from a willingness to practice the skills regularly.

Writing is, after all, a skill; and skills develop over time with frequency of practice. Like throwing the perfect pitch, drawing a portrait, or playing a piano sonata, writing with clarity and ease requires daily practice. Making writing a habitual, daily activity reduces the anxiety and tension about whether you're writing correctly. Too many people focus on writing to avoid making mistakes rather than on articulating the ideas they want to convey. The best method to build confidence as a writer starts out with seeing carefully.

recursive: From the Latin *recursus*, "a return, a coming back." A term used to describe a process in writing in which the writer loops back to a preceding point in order to move forward with an idea.

"When you sit down to write, tell the truth from one moment to the next and see where it takes you."
– David Mamet

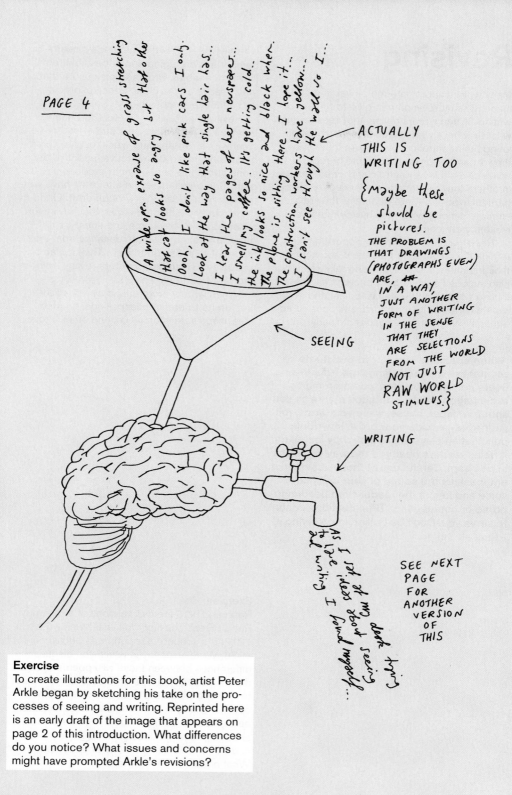

PAGE 4

A wide open expanse of grass stretching
that cat looks so angry but that other
Oooh, I don't like pink cars I only
Look at the way that single hair has...
I hear the pages of her newspaper...
I smell my coffee. It's getting cold...
the ink looks so nice and black when...
The phone is sitting there. I hope it...
The construction workers have yellow...
I can't see through the wall so I...

→ ACTUALLY
THIS IS
WRITING TOO

{Maybe these
should be
pictures.
THE PROBLEM IS
THAT DRAWINGS
(PHOTOGRAPHS EVEN)
ARE,
IN A WAY,
JUST ANOTHER
FORM OF WRITING
IN THE SENSE
THAT THEY
ARE SELECTIONS
FROM THE WORLD
NOT JUST
RAW WORLD
STIMULUS.}

← SEEING

WRITING ↙

SEE NEXT
PAGE
FOR
ANOTHER
VERSION
OF
THIS

Exercise
To create illustrations for this book, artist Peter
Arkle began by sketching his take on the processes of seeing and writing. Reprinted here
is an early draft of the image that appears on
page 2 of this introduction. What differences
do you notice? What issues and concerns
might have prompted Arkle's revisions?

Revising

Many writers appreciate the power and permanence that revision can give to the act of writing. When writers revise, they reexamine what they have written with an eye to strengthening their control over ideas. As they revise, they expand or delete, substitute or reorder. In some cases they revise to clarify or emphasize. In others they revise to tone down or reinforce particular points. More generally, they revise either to simplify what they have written or to make it more complex.

Revising gives writers an opportunity to rethink their essays, to help them accomplish their intentions more clearly and fully. Revising also includes such larger concerns as determining whether the essay is logical and consistent, whether its main idea is supported adequately, whether it is organized clearly, and whether it satisfies the audience's needs or demands in engaging and accessible terms. Revising enables writers to make sure that their essays are as clear, concise, precise, and effective as possible.

Revising also allows writers to distance themselves from their work and to see more clearly its strengths and weaknesses. This helps them make constructive, effective decisions about the best ways to produce a final draft. Some writers revise after they have written a very quick and very rough draft. Once they have something on paper, they revise for as long as they have time and energy. Still other writers require more distance from their first draft to revise effectively. Thinking about an audience also helps writers revise, edit, and proofread their essays.

When writers proofread, they reread their final drafts to detect misspellings, omitted lines, inaccurate information, and other errors.

"When speaking aloud, you punctuate constantly—with body language. Your listener hears commas, dashes, question marks, exclamation points, quotation marks as you shout, whisper, pause, wave your arms, roll your eyes, wrinkle your brow. In writing, punctuation plays the role of body language. It helps readers hear you the way you want to be heard. Careful use of those little marks emphasizes the sound of your distinctive voice and keeps the reader from becoming bored or confused. . . . [Punctuation] exists to serve you. Don't be bullied into serving it."
– Russell Baker

Exercise
Reprinted here are two versions of a poem by Robert Frost. The first, "In White," was written in 1912; the second, "Design," was published in 1936. Write an essay in which you discuss the differences between these two poems. How does the speaker's tone of voice lead the reader to respond differently to each poem? Point to specific changes in diction and metaphor that help characterize the change in voice the second poem has undergone. See pages 21 and 22 for definitions of tone and metaphor. What happens in the revision?

IN WHITE
Robert Frost

A dented spider like a snow drop white,
On a white Heal-all, holding up a moth
Like a white piece of lifeless satin cloth—
Saw ever curious eye so strange a sight?—
5 Portent in little, assorted death and blight
Like the ingredients of a witches' broth?—
The beady spider, the flower like a froth,
And the moth carried like a paper kite.

What had that flower to do with being white,
10 The blue prunella every child's delight.
What brought the kindred spider to that height?
(Make we no thesis of the miller's plight.)
What but design of darkness and of night?
Design, design! Do I use the word aright?

DESIGN
Robert Frost

I found a dimpled spider, fat and white,
On a white heal-all, holding up a moth
Like a white piece of rigid satin cloth—
Assorted characters of death and blight
5 Mixed ready to begin the morning right,
Like the ingredients of a witches' broth—
A snow-drop spider, a flower like a froth,
And dead wings carried like a paper kite.

What had that flower to do with being white,
10 The wayside blue and innocent heal-all?
What brought the kindred spider to that height,
Then steered the white moth thither in the night?
What but design of darkness to appall?—
If design govern in a thing so small.

Composition Toolkit

All texts and images are composed. By *composition* we mean both the process of creating a text and the way in which a text is put together. This section will help you sharpen your understanding and appreciation of the compositional techniques used by the authors and artists you encounter. The more confident you become in your own capabilities as a writer, the more you will exercise compositional strategies and techniques in your own prose. We encourage you to think about the following seven features of composition in particular. As you look closely at an image or text, you should establish a wider lens for viewing and looking at the overall composition of the text, on how the details and the elements of the work are put together to form a whole.

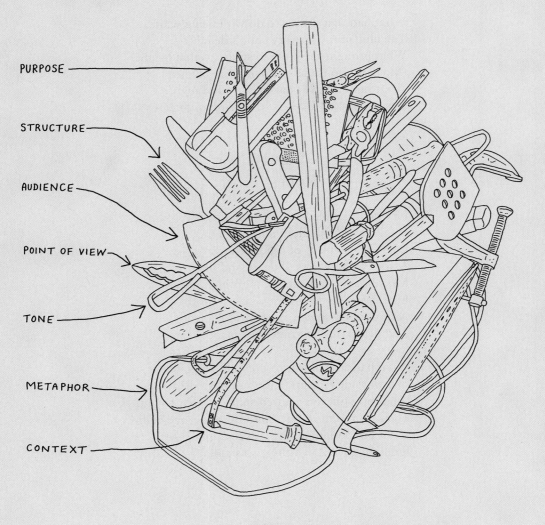

PURPOSE

STRUCTURE

AUDIENCE

POINT OF VIEW

TONE

METAPHOR

CONTEXT

Purpose

Determining your purpose means making decisions about what to say and how to say it. The first of these concerns establishes the general content and overall goal of the essay. The second focuses on the writer's style, on choices in aspects of writing such as structure, diction, and tone. For many writers, the principal purpose can be as simple as wanting to narrate or describe an experience, recall a concert, remember a family story, advocate a certain social cause, argue on behalf of freedom of speech, or recount the pleasure of reading a book or seeing a film or a play. Just as there is no surefire way to succeed at writing, there is no single definition of an appropriate subject or purpose in writing.

When you read a text, try to determine the author's or producer's purpose by asking the following questions: What compositional purpose does this particular text serve? Does it explain? describe? tell a story? entertain? convince me of an argument? persuade me to engage in an action? move me to laughter or tears? do something else? These questions may be difficult to answer quickly, and you will no doubt need to work closely with details in the text and then infer reasonable answers. Likewise, when you sit down to write your own text, we hope that you'll be motivated to draft a paper with a clear purpose in mind, something other than earning a good grade.

Exercise

How would you describe the compositional purpose of this photograph by Gordon Parks?

Gordon Parks
American Gothic, 1942 (p. 525)

Structure

Every text has a shape of its own. Images are built through subject, color, texture, light, line, and focus, or patterns of color or shape, to name just a few structural variables. Written texts use ideas, words, details, voice, and other tools as their structural building blocks. The most polished texts are hard to pull apart. If you're having trouble describing the structure of a text, make a list of the work's constituent parts and only then think about how they contribute to the whole.

When you are working carefully with an image, begin by breaking the image into visual fields. Find its horizontal or diagonal line. Some-times this line is self-evident, as in the image below, where the highway forms diagonal lines that divide the frame. Lines like these direct the viewer's attention up or down or across; they also provide smooth movement within an image, which is important for the visual percep-tion of most viewers. Familiar objects offer excellent picture possibilities and a chance to exercise your imagination.

Exercise
What structure do you see in the photograph below? How do the highway lines divide the frame? Where is your eye drawn?

Getty Images, *Overhead View of a Cloverleaf*

Audience

Audience refers to the reader(s) you have in mind when you write an essay or create a visual text. Most first-year college writers assume—mistakenly—that they are writing *solely* for their instructors rather than a larger audience beyond their classroom. Identifying the audience for a specific text is important because certain audiences have certain expectations. Consider, for example, television shows. *Gossip Girl* is written and performed for one group of people, and *The NewsHour with Jim Lehrer* is produced for a different group.

Trying to picture the intended audience helps writers articulate what they want to say and how to say it. Writers usually ask some version of the following questions: Who is my reader? What do I have to do to help that person understand what I want to say about my subject? The first question addresses the knowledge, background, and predispositions of the reader toward the subject. The second points to the kind of information or appeal to which the reader is most likely to respond.

Thinking about their readers helps writers make decisions about appropriate subjects, the kinds of examples to include, the type and level of diction and tone to use, and the overall organization of the essay. Every writer wants to be clear and convincing.

Exercise

What audience did the creator of this ad have in mind? What choices in imagery and language did the creator employ to "speak" to the intended audiences?

Dean College
Dean College Takes You as Far as You Want to Go

Point of View

Point of view is a term used to describe the angle of vision, the vantage point from which the writer or artist presents a story or a description or makes a point. The term also applies to the way in which the writer or artist presents readers with material.

As you think about how writers use point of view, consider the following questions: How is the image or text framed? What's included within the frame? What's been left out? What is the point of view from which the subject is seen? It can be difficult to determine what is not included in an image or an essay, but occasionally what is excluded can be more important than what you see.

You should consider point-of-view choices when you read a verbal text as well as a visual one. For example, if you are reading a class-mate's essay about going to college that talks about the friendship she developed with her roommate, you might reasonably ask how using this event to describe her university days – rather than, say, the classes she took or what she learned in them – contributes to the overall effect of the essay.

Exercise

Consider Dorothea Lange's famous photograph of a migrant mother and her children. Notice what happens when the same subject is framed in a different way. What are the effects of Lange's decision to focus on the faces of her subjects rather than to take their picture from farther away? How do these framing choices change Lange's point of view?

Dorothea Lange
Migrant Mother, Nipomo, California, 1936, three views (pp. 574, 560, and 566)

Tone

Tone is a widely used term that has slightly different meanings in different disciplines. In its simplest sense, *tone* refers to the quality or character of sound. As such, tone usually describes the sound of one's voice, what Robert Frost called "the hearing imagination." Frost was talking about our natural ability to detect the tone of voice a person is using in a conversation, even if that conversation is going on behind closed doors and we are not able to hear precisely what is being said.

In music, *tone* refers to sound; in art, *tone* indicates the general effect of light in a painting or photograph. In everyday language, the word also can evoke images of the muscles in the body. In speaking and writing, *tone* is the feeling—joy, anger, skepticism—the writer uses to convey his or her expression. It also describes the degree of formality in a written work.

Exercise
The point of view in these two photographs of the Golden Gate Bridge in San Francisco Bay by the photographer Richard Misrach is consistent; the only variation is the day and time. How would you describe the tone of each of these images?

Richard Misrach
12-23-97 5:09 p.m.

Richard Misrach
2-21-00 4:38 p.m.

Metaphor

In writing, a metaphor is a word or phrase meaning one thing that is used to describe something else in order to suggest a likeness or analogy. *She's drowning in money* uses a metaphor of money as water to suggest an infinite quantity; it's far more descriptive than simply saying *She has more money than she needs.*

Metaphor can work in visual texts as well. Here the artist uses an image that we accept as having one meaning in a way that suggests a likeness to something completely different. Many symbolic images, or icons, in our culture have shared meaning: the American flag, Elvis Presley, the bar code. When we see these images in a context we recognize – the flag flying over the White House for example, or the bar code on the back of this book – most of us would agree that it means something in particular: a symbol for the United States; a code that marks commercial products, tracks inventory, and denotes prices. But if these symbols are used to describe something else, as in *Man Turning into a Bar Code,* they suggest something completely different (the loss of individuality in a consumer culture). When you read verbal and visual texts, pay close attention to the way the texts use symbolic language or imagery to suggest relationships.

Exercise
Look carefully at the three images below. What metaphors are being used in these images? What kind of relationship is suggested in each?

Nerilicon
Natural Resources, 2005

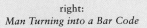

Arno Rafael Minkkinen
Mountain Lakes, New Jersey, 1977

right:
Man Turning into a Bar Code

Context

Visual and verbal texts are not composed and published in a vacuum. As you practice reading and writing about texts, we encourage you to consider the various contexts within which they function. Gather information about the circumstances behind the original composition: Who created the text? Who was the intended audience? Where was it originally published? For what purpose? To what extent does this contextual information deepen your reading of the text?

To widen your perspective on a text, consider the larger cultural and historical context in which it was created. What cultural assumptions do you think the artist or author relied on? Asking questions about the larger cultural context of a particular text or image means recognizing the assumptions that are made about a shared body of knowledge on the part of the audience. You as a reader — with your own set of assumptions, values, knowledge, and experience — are also part of every text's larger context. What value(s) and code(s) of conduct does the writer of the text encourage you to adopt?

Context is an essential aspect of both understanding and practicing the art of composition. Asking questions about the relationship between a text and its context — or the relationship of a part to the whole — is another way to see clearly and write well.

Exercise

Dorothea Lange's *Migrant Mother* is one of the recognizable images in American history. What observations and inferences can you make about the context of each of the three images below? What is the bigger picture behind the three uses of the same image? For more information on Lange's *Migrant Mother,* see pages 578–79.

Dorothea Lange
Migrant Mother, 1936 (p. 560)

Cover of *The Nation*
January 3, 2005 (p. 576)

Back cover of
The Black Panthers' Newsletter
December 7, 1972

Exercise

Take a moment to practice the skills of seeing
and writing discussed in this introduction.
What do you notice first about this photograph
by Joel Sternfeld? What initial observations
and inferences can you make? Now consider
the compositional strategies used: How would
you describe the structure of the image? the
photographer's point of view? the use of
metaphor? Read the biographical note about
Sternfeld on page 140 for contextual information on the artist. Then write the first draft of an
essay in which you make an assertion about
the overall impact of this photograph based on
your observations of Sternfeld's compositional
strategies. Make sure to support your assertions with detailed evidence from the image.

"Malice Green dropped off a friend
in front of this suspected crack
house right before he was stopped
by two police officers. After Green
was asked to produce his driver's
license and registration, a struggle
ensued and the officers beat him to
death with three-pound flashlights.
The beating continued even after
Green had been handcuffed and an
ambulance had been flagged down.

Larry Nevers was found guilty
of second-degree murder and
sentenced to twelve to twenty-five
years in prison. Walter Budzyn,
convicted of the same crime, was
given eight to eighteen years."
– Joel Sternfeld

Joel Sternfeld
Warren Avenue at 23rd Street, Detroit, Michigan, October 1993

1
OBSERVING THE ORDINARY

Imagine the following scene: It's Thanksgiving, well into the second night of a long holiday weekend. You have two papers due on Monday and an exam on Tuesday. It's been only two hours since you savored the delights of a home-cooked alternative to dorm food. Yet for the third time tonight, you stand at the refrigerator door and stare blankly inside.

What, exactly, are you doing? You are looking without actually noticing. That's the kind of attention many of us give to the ordinary in our lives. Staring into the refrigerator is a common example of what might be called *passive looking* – seeing without recognizing, looking without being aware of what we're looking at. How accurately, for example, can you describe the objects most familiar to you: a penny? your favorite pair of shoes? the blanket on your bed? the food you ate this morning for breakfast? Most of us need to have things physically in front of us to describe them in detailed and accurate terms. Even if we all had the same object before us, our descriptions would likely be different, depending on our backgrounds, the perspective from which we view the object, and the details we find important in it. If we practice examining commonplace objects with both attention to and an awareness of what makes every individual's perspective unique, we can begin to characterize who we are for ourselves and others. By *actively seeking* the details of the ordinary, we hone our skills of observation. This is the first step toward becoming a confident writer.

Observing the ordinary with fresh eyes sharpens our descriptive skills and develops our ability to draw inferences, to make discoveries about the seemingly commonplace. Reasonable inferences only come from accurate and careful observations.

Consider, for example, the food we eat. The opening portfolio of images for this chapter presents what a "full plate" (a full week's worth of food) looked like in different parts of the world in 2005. These images by Peter Menzel, along with a summary by Faith D'Aluisio, provide an opportunity to make observations and to draw reasonable inferences from the different kinds of food that are available in different places. The portfolio also provides an opportunity to compare and contrast the socioeconomic circumstances and the fascinating cultural and culinary differences that inform eating choices and habits on different continents. Some people take eating breakfast, lunch, and dinner for granted; for others, three square meals a day is not the normal routine. What objects and activities that you view as ordinary might some other people see as exceptional?

Each of the selections in this chapter presents the ordinary in some extraordinary way. The work of Peter Menzel, Matthew Pillsbury, Tracey Baran, and Gueorgui Pinkhassov conveys the clarity of attention a photographer gives the ordinary through the lens of a camera; the installation by Pepón Osorio shows what can result when high art meets mundane subjects; and the essays by Annalee Newitz, Larry Woiwode,

Tillie Olsen, Brian Doyle, K. C. Cole, and Annie Dillard demonstrate how writing can make us see something clearly that we would probably not otherwise notice at all.

As you practice your own writing and mindfully describe what is extraordinary in your everyday life, you'll also be practicing active seeing. To be an effective thinker and writer, you need to bring all of your sight – and insight – to bear on what is around you. Observing the ordinary is both the simplest skill to start exercising as a writer and a practical means of training yourself to think and write analytically. If you notice and attend to the ordinary, if you devote focused and sustained attention to it, you increase the likelihood of becoming someone on whom, as the novelist Henry James once said, "nothing is lost."

Peter Menzel
The Mendoza Family of Guatemala, 2007

Peter Menzel
The Fernandez Family of the United States, 2004

(pp. 30–31)

GUATEMALA / THE MENDOZAS OF TODOS SANTOS

The Mendoza family and a servant in their courtyard in Todos Santos, Cuchumatán, Guatemala, with a week's worth of food. Between Fortunato Pablo Mendoza, 50, and Susana Pérez Matias, 47, stand (left to right) Ignacio, 15, Cristolina, 19, and a family friend (standing in for daughter Marcelucia, 9, who ran off to play). Far right: Sandra Ramos, 11, live-in helper. Not present: Xtila, 17, and Juan, 12. Cooking methods: gas stovetop, wood stove. Food preservation: refrigerator.

One Week's Food in November

Grains & Other Starchy Foods: $11.49**
Corn (yellow and white mixed),* 48 lb; potatoes, 20 lb; masa (corn tortilla dough), 8 lb; Inti pasta, 4.4 lb; corn tortillas, 4 lb; Quaker Avena Mosh (oat breakfast cereal), 1.1 lb; rice,‡ 1 lb.

Dairy: $2.25
Milk, powdered, 14.1 oz.

Meat, Fish & Eggs: $7.93
Chickens, 4.4 lb, two other chickens in the photograph are for the All Saints Day celebration; eggs, 30.

Fruits, Vegetables & Nuts: $34.75
Yellow bananas, 7.4 lb; pineapples, 6.4 lb; zapote (brown-colored fruit), 5 lb; passion fruit, 3.9 lb; anona (custard apples), 3.2 lb; oranges, 2.6 lb; lemons, 2.2 lb; black beans, dried, 13.2 lb; green squash, 12 lb; tomatoes, 10 lb; carrots, 7.8 lb; avocados, 5 lb; white onions, 5 lb; cauliflower, 3 heads; green beans, 4.4 lb; cucumbers, 3.5 lb; chayote squash, 3.2 lb; green onions, 3 lb; cabbage, 1 head; red chili peppers, 1.5 lb; green chili peppers, 8.8 oz.

Condiments: $8.85
Oil, 3.2 qt; herbs, assorted, fresh, 1 bunch; white sugar, 5 oz; Malher black pepper, 3 oz; Malher garlic salt, 3 oz; Malher onion salt, 3 oz; Malher salt, 3 oz; cinnamon, 2 sticks.

Snacks: $3.96
Chocolate, hand-pressed, 1 lb; Azteca tortilla chips, 5 bags.

Prepared Food: $0.79
Malher chicken bouillon, 3 oz.

Beverages: $5.68
Bottled water, 5 gal, for drinking only; Corazon de Trigio (wheat drink), 1.1 lb; Incasa coffee, 8 oz.

**Market value of homegrown foods, if purchased locally: $4.12*

Homegrown; ‡Not in photo

Except during holidays, most families in Todos Santos eat meat less than once a week. Three times a day they eat rice, beans, potatoes, eggs, and tortillas, in one combination or another. "We don't have fish as we live so far from the sea," says Susana. Her daughter Cristolina, 19, tells us that they don't eat candies and cakes. "If we want a postre [dessert], we have a banana," she says, her smile revealing beautifully white, cavity-free teeth. Although soft drinks are available in the village, and in fact the Mendozas sell them in their new bar, the family drinks only water, a wheat drink, and instant coffee.

The Mendozas eat fruits and vegetables when they are in season—not before or after—because local stores don't have the refrigeration and transportation necessary to stock out-of-season items. Though potatoes are plentiful in the village, when Cristolina was studying in another part of Guatemala, five hours away, she didn't eat potatoes. "The price was incredible," she exclaims, "twice the cost of potatoes here, and very small." Did she miss eating potatoes? "Oh yes," she says.

Food Expenditure for One Week:
573 quetzales/$75.70

(pp. 32–33)

UNITED STATES / THE FERNANDEZES OF TEXAS

The Fernandez family in the kitchen of their San Antonio, Texas home with a week's worth of food – Lawrence, 31, and wife Diana, 35, standing, and Diana's mother, Alejandrina Cepeda, 58, sitting with her grandchildren Brian, 5, and Brianna, 4. Cooking methods: electric stove, microwave, toaster oven, outdoor BBQ. Food preservation: refrigerator-freezer. Favorite foods – Diana: shrimp with Alfredo sauce. Lawrence: barbecue ribs. Brian and Brianna: pizza. Alejandrina: chicken mole.

One Week's Food in March

Grains & Other Starchy Foods: $19.28
Potatoes, 5 lb; homemade tortillas, 1.6 lb; Kellogg's Special K cereal with red berries, 1.5 lb; Nature's Own honey wheat bread, 1 loaf; Quaker masa harina, 1.3 lb; Gold Medal all-purpose flour, 1 lb; H-E-B (store brand) French-style bread, 1 lb; white rice, 1 lb; Cream of Wheat cereal, 14 oz; Quaker oatmeal, 13.5 oz; dinner rolls, 13 oz; Post Cocoa Pebbles cereal, 13 oz; H-E-B fettuccine, 5.3 oz; Q&Q vermicelli, 5 oz.

Dairy: $17.72
Borden Kid Builder milk, 1% low-fat, high-calcium, 1 gal; Oak Farms Skim Deluxe milk, 1 gal; Blue Bell ice cream, 1 qt; Dannon Danimals, Swingin' Strawberry Banana and Rockin' Raspberry drinkable yogurt, 25.2 fl oz; Yoplait piña colada yogurt, 1.5 lb; Yoplait blueberry yogurt, 12 oz; Kraft Colby & Monterey Jack cheese, 8 oz; Frigo Cheese Heads string cheese, 6 oz.

Meat, Fish & Eggs: $42.10
Hill Country Fare chicken drumsticks, 3 lb; Hill Country Fare jumbo eggs, 18; H-E-B rotisserie chicken, original flavor, 2.5 lb; Sanderson Farms chicken thigh fillets, boneless & skinless, 1.5 lb; Gorton's Original Tenders fish sticks, frozen, 1.1 lb; H-E-B extra-lean beef, ground, 1 lb; H-E-B turkey breast, ground, 1 lb; Oscar Mayer turkey cotto salami, 1 lb; shrimp, frozen, 1 lb; Butterball turkey variety pack, sliced, 12 oz; H-E-B beef, top round cubes, 12 oz; Tyson fun nuggets, frozen chicken, 12 oz; Hill Country Fare smoked chicken, sliced, 5 oz.

Fruits, Vegetables & Nuts: $33.05
Grapefruit, 5 lb; Dole bananas, 2.5 lb; Granny Smith apples, 1.3 lb; green grapes, 1.3 lb; Coastal strawberries, 1 lb; Key limes, 1 lb; red apples, 12.8 oz; Hass avocados, 4; Hunt's tomato sauce, 2.5 lb; Green Giant green beans, canned, 2 lb; Green Giant corn, frozen, 1.6 lb; tomatoes, 1.3 lb; La Sierra refried pinto beans, 15 oz; iceberg lettuce, 1 head; Fresh Express Italian salad mix, 8.8 oz; yellow onions, 8.6 oz; Fresh Express coleslaw, 8 oz; mini carrots, 8 oz; mushrooms, sliced, 8 oz; jalapeño peppers, 4 oz; garlic, 2 oz; Planter's honey-roasted peanuts, 12 oz.

Condiments: $16.05
Great Value vegetable oil, 2.1 qt; Hill Country Fare BBQ sauce, 1.1 lb; International Delight coffee creamer, 16 fl oz; I Can't Believe It's Not Butter spread, 15.8 oz; Aunt Jemima Butter Lite syrup, 12 oz; Hill Country Fare ketchup, 9 oz; Clover Burleson's honey, 8 oz; H-E-B roasted pepper salsa picante, 8 oz; Season All seasoned salt, 8 oz; Wish Bone Classic Ranch Up! dressing, 6 oz; peanut butter, 4 oz; pepper, ground, 1 oz; salt, 0.5 oz.

Snacks & Dessert: $23.33
H-E-B Texas-shaped corn chips, 1 lb; pretzels, 1 lb; Dreyers whole-fruit bar popsicles, 16.5 fl oz; Oreo cookies, 9 oz; Ritz whole wheat crackers, 7.5 oz; Pepperidge Farm Goldfish Colors crackers, 6.6 oz; Ritz Sticks crackers, 6.3 oz; Pringles potato chips, 6 oz; General Mills Fruit Gushers snacks, 5.4 oz; Kellogg's Special K blueberry bars, 4.9 oz; Kellogg's Special K peaches & berry bars, 4.9 oz; Orville Redenbacher's Smart Pop microwave popcorn, 3.7 oz; Barnum's animal crackers, 2.1 oz.

Prepared Food: $18.16
Prego spaghetti sauce, 1 lb; La Sierra refried beans with cheese, 15 oz; Ranch Style beans with jalapeño peppers, 15 oz; Pioneer Brand buttermilk pancake mix, 10.7 oz; Bertolli creamy alfredo sauce, 8 oz; Zatarain's black beans and rice, 7 oz; Zatarain's gumbo mix, 7 oz; Pioneer brown gravy mix, nonfat, 2.8 oz; Pioneer Country gravy mix, nonfat, 2.8 oz; Knorr Suiza chicken broth, 2 oz; Diana at work, 5 cafeteria meals, variety of main courses available. Lawrence grabs a salad or a slice of pizza at work.

Fast Food: $11.81
McDonald's: 3 Happy Meals; 4 Mountain Blast ice cream drinks; 1 vanilla ice cream cone.

Restaurants: $42.11
Fire Mountain Buffet: dinner for 5, assorted items, sold by the pound, 3.8 lb; Cici's Pizza: large beef pizza, large white pizza, large meat lover's pizza, 3 salads.

Beverages: $18.87
Hill Country Fare natural spring water, 8 gal; Tree Top apple juice, 1 gal; Capri Sun Mountain Cooler, 10 6.8-fl-oz pkgs; Capri Sun orange drink, 10 6.8-fl-oz pkgs; Dole pineapple-orange-banana juice, 8 6-fl-oz cartons; Hill Country Fare iced tea mix, 1.7 lb; Wylers Light pink lemonade, powdered mix, 1.2 lb; H-E-B Café Ole coffee, 3 oz; Ovaltine malted instant drink mix, 3 oz; Kool-Aid, sugar-free grape, powdered mix, 1.2 oz.

Food Expenditure for One Week: $242.48

Peter Menzel
The Ukita Family of Japan, 2007

Peter Menzel
The Aboubakar Family of Chad, 2004

(pp. 36–37)

JAPAN / THE UKITAS OF KODAIRA CITY

The Ukita family—Sayo Ukita, 51, and her husband, Kazuo Ukita, 53, with children Maya, 14 (holding chips) and Mio, 17—in their dining room in Kodaira city, Japan, with one week's worth of food. Cooking methods: gas stove, rice cooker. Food preservation: small refrigerator-freezer. Favorite foods—Kazuo: sashimi. Sayo: fruit. Mio: cake. Maya: potato chips.

One Week's Food in May

Grains & Other Starchy Foods: $31.55
Koshihikari rice, 5.5 lb; potatoes, 5.3 lb; Danish white bread, sliced, 1 loaf; white flour, 1.3 lb; sato imo (Japanese yam), peeled, 1.1 lb; udon noodles, 1.1 lb; somen noodles, 14.1 oz; white sandwich bread, 12.4 oz; Nippn macaroni, 10.6 oz; soba noodles, 10.6 oz; FryStar7 bread crumbs, 8.1 oz.

Dairy: $2.26
Whole milk, 25.4 fl oz; Haruna yogurt, 12 oz; butter,‡ 8.8 oz.

Meat, Fish & Eggs: $99.80
Rainbow trout, 2.6 lb; ham, 2.2 lb; eggs, 10; sardines, large, 1.3 lb; clams, 1.1 lb; octopus, 1.1 lb; Spanish mackerel, 1.1 lb; pork loin, 1 lb; tuna, sashimi, 15.5 oz; horse mackerel, 14.8 oz; saury (fish), 13.5 oz; Japanese smelt (fish), 13.1 oz; eel, 12.7 oz; albacore, sashimi, 11.9 oz; Hagoromo tuna, canned, 11.3 oz; pork, cubed, 11.3 oz; beef, 10.8 oz; pork, minced, 10.6 oz; pork, sliced, 10.6 oz; pork, thin sliced, 10.3 oz; bacon, 7.8 oz; beef korokke (beef and potato patties), frozen, 7.4 oz, used for children's lunch; sea bream, sashimi, 3.6 oz; Nozaki's new corned beef (mix of horse and beef meat), canned, 3.5 oz.

Fruits, Vegetables & Nuts: $81.43
Watermelon, 9.9 lb; cantaloupe, 4.4 lb; yellow bananas, 2.8 lb; red apples, 2.4 lb; white grapefruit, 2.2 lb; strawberries, 1.7 lb; cherries, canned, 7 oz; yellow onions, 4.8 lb; green peppers, 4 lb; cucumbers, 3.5 lb; daikon, 3.3 lb; bitter gourd,‡ 2.8 lb; soft tofu, 2.2 lb; tomatoes, 2 lb; carrots, 1.2 lb; green peas, in pods, 1.1 lb; broccoli, 1 lb; lettuce, 1 head; spinach, fresh, 1 lb; edamame, frozen, 14.1 oz; asparagus, 10.6 oz; green beans, frozen, 10.6 oz; mixed vegetables, frozen, 10.6 oz; bamboo shoots, 8.8 oz; white asparagus, canned, 8.8 oz; scallions, 8 oz; daikon sprouts, 6 oz; shitake mushrooms, 6 oz; wakame (seaweed), fresh, 5.6 oz; bean curd, fried, 1.8 oz; nori (seaweed), dried, 1.8 oz; wakame,‡ dried, 1.8 oz.

Condiments: $28.28
White sugar, 15.6 oz; Ebara BBQ sauce, 9.9 oz; white miso, 9.9 oz; margarine,‡ 8.8 oz; Honen salad oil, 8.5 fl oz; sesame oil, 7.1 oz; bean sauce, 6 fl oz; ginger, 6 oz; Tea Time Mate sugar, 28 .2-oz pks; Kyupi mayonnaise, 5.6 oz; Hinode cooking sake, 4.7 fl oz; Hinode mirin (low-alcohol rice wine for cooking), 4.7 fl oz; soy sauce, 4.7 fl oz; Sudo orange marmalade, 4.7 fl oz; Sudo strawberry jam, 4.7 fl oz; vinegar, 4.7 fl oz; Fuji oyster sauce, 4.2 oz; Bull Dog tonkatsu sauce, 3.4 fl oz; Captain Cook coffee creamers, 20 .2-fl-oz pks; salt, 3.5 oz; Chinese spicy sauce, 2.9 oz, used on tofu; Kagome ketchup, 2.7 fl oz; sesame seeds,‡ whole, 2.6 oz; honey, 2.5 oz; Pokka Shokutaku lemon juice, 2.4 fl oz; Momoya kimchi paste, 2.2 fl oz; soy sauce salad dressing, 2 fl oz; Ajinomoto olive oil, 1.8 oz; S&B hot mustard, 1.5 oz; S&B wasabi, 1.5 oz; white sesame, ground, 1.4 oz; black pepper,‡ 0.7 oz.

Snacks & Desserts: $15.33
Small cakes, 4; coffee break cookies, 1 lb; cream buns, 10 oz; Koikeya potato chips, 8.8 oz; Pasco cream rings, 8.8 oz; chiffon chocolate cake, 5.3 oz.

Prepared Food: $21.78
Nissin cup of noodles, instant, 1.5 lb; Sapporo Ichiban noodles, instant, 1.1 lb; Showa pancake mix, 12.4 oz; Mama pasta meat sauce, canned, 10.4 oz; Oh My pasta meat sauce, canned, 10.4 oz; seaweed salad, dehydrated, 8.8 oz, add water to reconstitute; S&B golden hayashi sauce mix (Japanese style beef bouillon cubes), 8.8 oz; Chinese dumplings,‡ frozen, 8.5 oz, used for children's lunches; Ajinomoto hondashi soup base, bonito (fish) flavor, 5.3 oz; soup, instant, 2.7 oz; yaki fu (baked rolls of wheat gluten, wheat powder, and rice powder), 2.7 oz, eaten in soup; vegetable and seaweed rice ball mix, 1.3 oz; Riken seaweed ball mix, 1.2 oz; Kyowa egg drop soup, instant, 0.9 oz.

Beverages: $28.40
Kirin beer, 6 12-fl-oz cans; Coca-Cola, 2.1 qt; Nacchan orange soda, 2.1 qt; Suntory C.C. lemon joyful vitamin C soda, 2.1 qt; Ban Shaku sake, 1.8 qt; Coffee Break instant coffee, 2.5 oz; green tea, 2.1 oz; Alpha wheat tea, 2 oz; Afternoon Tea darjeeling black tea, 1.8 oz; tap water for drinking and cooking.

Miscellaneous: $8.42
Mild Seven super-light cigarettes, 4 pks, smoked by Kazuo.

‡Not in photo

Food Expenditure for One Week: 37,699 yen/$317.25

Food Expenditure for One Week:
685 CFA francs (Communauté
Financière Africaine)/$1.23

(pp. 38–39)

CHAD / THE ABOUBAKARS OF BREIDJING CAMP

The Aboubakar family of Darfur province, Sudan, in front of their tent in the Breidjing Refugee Camp, in eastern Chad, with a week's worth of food. D'jimia Ishakh Souleymane, 40, holds her daughter Hawa, 2; the other children are (left to right) Acha, 12, Mariam, 5, Youssouf, 8, and Abdel Kerim, 16. Cooking method: wood fire. Food preservation: natural drying. Favorite food–D'jimia: soup with fresh sheep meat.

One Week's Food in November

Grains & Other Starchy Foods:**
Sorghum ration, unmilled, 39.3 lb; corn-soy blend ration (CSB), 4.6 lb.

Dairy:
Not available to them.

Meat, Fish & Eggs: $0.58**
Goat meat, dried and on the bone, 9 oz; fish, dried, 7 oz. Note: Periodically, such as at the end of Ramadan, several families collectively purchase a live animal to slaughter and share. Some of its meat is eaten fresh in soup and the rest is dried.

Fruits, Vegetables & Nuts: $0.51**
Limes, small, 5; pulses ration, 4.6 lb, the seeds of legumes such as peas, beans, lentils, chickpeas, and fava beans. Red onions, 1 lb; garlic, 8 oz; okra, dried, 5 oz; red peppers, dried, 5 oz; tomatoes, dried, 5 oz.

Condiments: $0.13**
Sunflower oil ration, 2.1 qt; white sugar ration, 1.4 lb; dried pepper, 12 oz; salt ration, 7.4 oz; ginger, 4 oz.

Beverages:
Water, 77.7 gal, provided by Oxfam, and includes water for all purposes.

Rations organized by the United Nations with the World Food Programme.

**Market value of food rations, if purchased locally: $24.37*

Peter Menzel & Faith D'Aluisio

The husband and wife team of Peter Menzel (b. 1948) and Faith D'Aluisio (b. 1957) are internationally recognized for their photojournalistic books about the everyday lives of people across the world. They first collaborated on *Material World: A Global Family Portrait* (1995), which provided vivid portraits taken by sixteen renowned photographers of "statistically average" families and their possessions in thirty different countries. This groundbreaking look beneath the surface of everyday family life set the stage for the team's subsequent collaborations, with Menzel as photographer and D'Aluisio as writer, producing books such as *Women in the Material World* (1996), *Man Eating Bugs: The Art and Science of Eating Insects* (1998; winner of the James Beard Foundation Award for best culinary book), and *Hungry Planet: What the World Eats* (2005).

Hungry Planet offers insights into the seemingly ordinary subject of food through portraits of thirty families worldwide with their week's supply of groceries. Surprisingly, the book shows how prepackaged foods are becoming widely available even in poor, developing countries and obesity rates are increasing. Unsurprisingly, the book reveals deep inequalities in the quantity and quality of food available to average families in each country. According to the authors, "There's so much to learn from other people around the world. And sometimes we learn more from mistakes than from good examples. This book is full of both, and we should be able to recognize them and pick and choose and change ourselves just a little bit, in order to make our lives better."

In 2008, Menzel and D'Aluisio published a children's version of *Hungry World,* entitled simply *What the World Eats;* they are working on another book of photojournalism focused on world food consumption. They live in Napa Valley, California, with their children.

SEEING

1. How would you describe Peter Menzel's photographic portraits of ordinary people's food in different parts of the world to someone who has not seen them? What specific words and phrases would you use to characterize what you see in the photographs? Which details — for example, textures, colors, objects, shapes, and setting — stand out the most to you? Choose one of Menzel's photographs. What reasonable inferences can you draw from the observations you have made about this photograph? What story (or stories) does the photograph suggest to you? In what specific ways is your understanding and appreciation of each photograph enhanced by Faith D'Aluisio's accompanying summary?

2. Choose two of Menzel's photographs, and compare and contrast your observations about each and the inferences you draw from these observations. How do different foods represent a "full plate" in these photographs? By highlighting different physical settings and sociocultural contexts? different economic conditions? In what specific ways are the scenes and contexts similar? In which instance do you find D'Aluisio's text more informative and insightful? Explain why.

WRITING

1. Choose one of Peter Menzel's photographs, and treat it as an artistic statement of a family's <u>values</u>. Choose two or three words or phrases that you think accurately describe what this photograph is communicating. Write a descriptive paragraph on each of these words or phrases, using evidence from the photograph to illustrate your choices. How would seeing this image in a different context — for example, in an advertisement for one or more of the products — change the way you read it?

2. Look through a popular magazine, and make notes about the kinds of ordinary objects and experiences presented in its advertising and prose content. What images of the ordinary do you find there? How are the images of these objects and experiences presented, and for what purpose? Choose one presentation, and compare and contrast it with Menzel's photograph (and, if you find it helpful, D'Aluisio's prose text). Write an expository essay comparing and contrasting the magazine's methods with those used by Menzel (and D'Aluisio) to analyze the experience of observing the ordinary.

<u>values: The ideals, customs, and institutions of a society toward which its people have an emotional reaction. These values may be positive (such as cleanliness, freedom, or education) or negative (such as cruelty, crime, or blasphemy).</u>

MY LAPTOP
Annalee Newitz

My laptop computer is irreplaceable, and not just for all the usual reasons. It's practically a brain prosthesis. Sometimes I find myself unable to complete a thought without cracking it open and accessing a file of old notes, or hopping online and Googling a fact or two.

Besides, I love it. I would recognize the feel of its keyboard under my fingers in a darkened room. I have worn two shiny spots on it where the palms of my hands rest when I'm not typing. I carried it on my back all over England, Cuba, Canada, and the United States. When I use it in bed, I remember to keep the blankets from covering its vents so it doesn't overheat. I've taken it completely apart, upgraded its RAM, and replaced its original operating system with Linux. It doesn't just belong to me; I also belong to it.

I'm hardly alone in my infatuation. When I was fifteen, my friends and I would often stay up late into the night, chatting online over a multiuser chat system called WizNet. Using online aliases, we spent hours talking about science fiction, movies, computers, and sex. My alias was Shockwave Rider, a reference to a science fiction novel about some guy who hacked phone systems. I was the only girl in the group, although you wouldn't have known it. Like everybody else, I was just a command line full of glowing green letters.

Matthew Pillsbury
Penelope Umbrico (with Her Daughters), Monday, February 3, 2003, 7–7:30 p.m.

Annalee Newitz

A self-professed and proud geek, Annalee Newitz (b. 1969) grew up in Irvine, California, where she was an early devotee of *Star Trek, Wonder Woman,* and books by science fiction novelist Ursula K. Le Guin, Marxist literary critic Frederic Jameson, and pioneering popular cultural critic Susan Sontag. Newitz began publishing articles and books prior to receiving a PhD in English and American Studies from the University of California – Berkeley in 1999, and she continues to write and publish tirelessly today. In addition to contributing to print and online periodicals such as *Salon.com, Popular Science,* the *New York Times, Nerve,* and *New Scientist,* she has co-edited *White Trash: Race and Class in America* (1997) and *She's Such a Geek: Women Write about Science, Technology, and Other Nerdy Stuff* (2007), authored *Pretend We're Dead: Capitalist Monsters in American Pop Culture* (2006), and contributes to numerous blogs, including her own *Techsploitation.com* and the recently launched *i09.*

Speaking about her new blog, Newitz said, "What drew me to the blog is the chance to talk about how our fantasies about the future affect what we do to build that future. . . . I'm standing in the middle between fantasies and application." As "My Laptop," her contribution to *Evocative Objects: Things We Think With* (2007, edited by Sherry Turkle) reveals, Newitz has always gained satisfaction from making use of technology, from investigating the everyday, and from imagining how technology will impact the future.

Matthew Pillsbury

Born in Neuilly, France, in 1973, photographer Matthew Pillsbury quickly gained a notable reputation after obtaining his master's degree in fine arts from New York's School of Visual Arts in 2004. Based almost solely on his haunting series Screen Lives, Pillsbury was named one of *Photo District News*'s top thirty emerging artists for 2005. Since then he has been exhibited internationally, has won the prestigious HSBS Foundation for Photography Prize (2007), and has seen his work enter the permanent collections of the Museum of Modern Art in New York, the Whitney Museum, the Guggenheim Museum, and the Los Angeles County Museum of Art, among others.

In addition to the sense of possibility he shares with Annalee Newitz when considering everyday technological objects, Pillsbury explores a darker side to our daily interaction with technology in the Screen Lives series. By means of long black and white exposures, the photographer depicts ghostlike figures working at their computers, using hand-held devices, or watching television, while the technological objects and the surrounding spaces remain crystal clear. In *Penelope Umbrico (with Her Daughters), Monday, February 3, 2003, 7–7:30 p.m.,* reproduced here, not only are the three figures spectral, but their heads remain bowed toward their computer screens, as if each figure is unaware of the other two. According to the artist, "The photographs . . . allow viewers to address a conundrum that technology has interjected into our lives; at the same time that we have been given the possibility of instant global communication, we find ourselves increasingly isolated from each other physically."

SEEING

1. As you study Matthew Pillsbury's photograph *Penelope Umbrico (with Her Daughters), Monday, February 3, 2003, 7–7:30 p.m.,* where are your eyes first drawn? On what specific aspects of laptop use does Pillsbury focus his attention? With what effect(s)? After examining his photograph carefully, in what specific ways is your overall understanding of the photograph different from your initial impression?

2. One of the most memorable aspects of Annalee Newitz's essay "My Laptop" is the skillful and imaginative way in which she transforms her laptop into a character. What compositional techniques does she use to achieve this effect? Compare and contrast the effectiveness of Pillsbury's compositional choices in creating his photograph with Newitz's use of language. According to Pillsbury and Newitz, what role does the laptop play in contemporary society? What judgment does each artist offer about the importance of the laptop? Which artistic vision do you find more appealing? Why?

WRITING

1. One way to gain important new awareness is to look at objects that we take for granted. Pillsbury's photograph and Newitz's prose account of the laptop offer two perspectives on one of the most commonplace objects in contemporary experience. Choose another ordinary object – a ballpoint pen, a stapler, a cell phone, for example – and write the first draft of an essay about the object. Then use your description as a basis for drawing inferences about the object's distinctive character.

2. Pillsbury and Newitz use different artistic techniques to focus their audience's attention on the role of the laptop. What artistic tools are available to Pillsbury in his photograph that are not available to Newitz in her prose account? After you have analyzed these differences, write an expository essay in which you compare and contrast the different results produced by a photograph and an essay.

Responding Visually

Choose an ordinary object that has significance for you, and create a visual/verbal composition in the style of this pair. Limit your composition to two pages; one page should feature a visual representation of your object and the other a description of its meaning to you.

ODE TO AN ORANGE
Larry Woiwode

Oh, those oranges arriving in the midst of the North Dakota winters of the forties—the mere color of them, carried through the door in a net bag or a crate from out of the white winter landscape. Their appearance was enough to set my brother and me to thinking that it might be about time to develop an illness, which was the surest way of receiving a steady supply of them.

"Mom, we think we're getting a cold."

"*We?* You mean, you two want an orange?"

This was difficult for us to answer or dispute; the matter seemed moved beyond our mere wanting.

5   "If you want an orange," she would say, "why don't you ask for one?"

"We want an orange."

"'We' again. '*We want an orange.*'"

"May we have an orange, please."

"That's the way you know I like you to ask for one. Now, why don't each of you ask for one in that same way, but separately?"

10   "Mom . . ." And so on. There was no depth of degradation that we wouldn't descend to in order to get one. If the oranges hadn't wended their way northward by Thanksgiving, they were sure to arrive before the Christmas season, stacked first in crates at the depot, filling that musty place, where pews sat back to back, with a springtime acidity, as if the building had been rinsed with a renewing elixir that set it right for yet another year. Then the crates would appear at the local grocery store, often with the top slats pried back on a few of them, so that we were aware of a resinous smell of fresh wood in addition to the already orangy atmosphere that foretold the season more explicitly than any calendar.

And in the broken-open crates (as if burst by the power of the oranges themselves), one or two of the lovely spheres would lie free of the tissue they came wrapped in—always purple tissue, as if that were the only color that could contain the populations of them in their nestled positions. The crates bore paper labels at one end—of an orange against a blue background, or of a blue goose against an orange background—signifying the colorful otherworld (unlike our wintry one) that these phenomena had arisen from. Each orange, stripped of its protective wrapping, as vivid in your vision as a pebbled sun, encouraged you to picture a whole pyramid of them in a bowl on your dining room table, glowing in the light, as if giving off the warmth that came through the windows from the real winter sun. And all of them came stamped with a blue-purple name as foreign as the otherworld that you might imagine as their place of origin, so that on Christmas day you would find yourself digging past everything else in your Christmas stocking, as if tunneling down to the country of China, in order to reach the rounded bulge at the tip of the toe which meant that you had received a personal reminder of another state of existence, wholly separate from your own.

The packed heft and texture, finally, of an orange in your hand — this is it! — and the eruption of smell and the watery fireworks as a knife, in the hand of someone skilled, like our mother, goes slicing through the skin so perfect for slicing. This gaseous spray can form a mist like smoke, which can then be lit with a match to create actual fireworks if there is a chance to hide alone with a match (matches being forbidden) and the peel from one. Sputtery ignitions can also be produced by squeezing a peel near a candle (at least one candle is generally always going at Christmastime), and the leftover peels are set on the stove top to scent the house.

And the ingenious way in which oranges come packed into their globes! The green nib at the top, like a detonator, can be bitten off, as if disarming the orange, in order to clear a place for you to sink a tooth under the peel. This is the best way to start. If you bite at the peel too much, your front teeth will feel scraped, like dry bone, and your lips will begin to burn from the bitter oil. Better to sink a tooth into this greenish or creamy depression, and then pick at that point with the nail of your thumb, removing a little piece of the peel at a time. Later, you might want to practice to see how large a piece you can remove intact. The peel can also be undone in one continuous ribbon, a feat which maybe your father is able to perform, so that after the orange is freed, looking yellowish, the peel, rewound, will stand in its original shape, although empty.

The yellowish whole of the orange can now be divided into sections, usually about a dozen, by beginning with a division down the middle; after this, each section, enclosed in its papery skin, will be able to be lifted and torn loose more easily. There is a stem up the center of the sections like a mushroom stalk, but tougher; this can be eaten. A special variety of orange, without any pits, has an extra growth, or nubbin, like half of a tiny orange, tucked into its bottom. This nubbin is nearly as bitter as the peel, but it can be eaten, too; don't worry. Some of the sections will have miniature sections embedded in them and clinging as if for life, giving the impression that babies are being hatched, and should you happen to find some of these you've found the sweetest morsels of any.

15   If you prefer to have your orange sliced in half, as some people do, the edges of the peel will abrade the corners of your mouth, making them feel raw, as you eat down into the white of the rind (which is the only way to do it) until you can see daylight through the orangy bubbles composing its outside. Your eyes might burn; there is no proper way to eat an orange. If there are pits, they can get in the way, and the slower you eat an orange, the more you'll find your fingers sticking together. And no matter how carefully you eat one, or bite into a quarter, juice can always fly or slip from a corner of your mouth; this happens to everyone. Close your eyes to be on the safe side, and for the eruption in your mouth of the slivers of watery meat, which should be broken and rolled fine over your tongue for the essence of orange. And if indeed you have sensed yourself coming down with a cold, there is a chance that you will feel it driven from your head—your nose and sinuses suddenly opening—in the midst of the scent of a peel and eating an orange.

And oranges can also be eaten whole—rolled into a spongy mass and punctured with a pencil (if you don't find this offensive) or a knife, and then sucked upon. Then, once the juice is gone, you can disembowel the orange as you wish and eat away its pulpy remains, and eat once more into the whitish interior of the peel, which scours the coating from your teeth and makes your numbing lips and tip of your tongue start to tingle and swell up from behind, until, in the light from the windows (shining through an empty glass bowl), you see orange again from the inside. Oh, oranges, solid o's, light from afar in the midst of the freeze, and not unlike that unspherical fruit which first went from Eve to Adam and from there (to abbreviate matters) to my brother and me.

"Mom, we think we're getting a cold."

"You mean, you want an orange?"

This is difficult to answer or dispute or even to acknowledge, finally, with the fullness that the subject deserves, and that each orange bears, within its own makeup, into this hard-edged yet insubstantial, incomplete, cold, wintry world.

Larry Woiwode

Born in 1941, Larry Woiwode grew up in North Dakota and attended college at the University of Illinois. After moving to New York City in his twenties, he began to publish poems and stories in prestigious magazines such as *The New Yorker, The Atlantic,* and *Harper's.* Among his early successes were the highly acclaimed novels *What I'm Going to Do, I Think* (1969) and *Beyond the Bedroom Wall* (1975), which was nominated for the National Book Award. Since his relocation back to North Dakota in 1978, Woiwode has continued to build his reputation as a renowned novelist, essayist, and poet. Recently he has focused on writing memoirs, including the critically acclaimed *What I Think I Did* (2001) and its follow-up, *A Step from Death* (2008).

Woiwode uses precise observation and a sense of place in all of his work, and he writes in a simple, accessible style. According to the author, "For some reason the purest and simplest sentences permit the most meaning to adhere to them. In other words, the more specific a simple sentence is about a place in North Dakota, let us say, the more someone from outside that region seems to read universality into it."

Although the essay "Ode to an Orange," which originally appeared in *The Paris Review* in 1985, focuses on an object rather than a place, the same principle applies. In engagingly expressive prose, Woiwode remembers specific experiences and evokes a universal romance with an ideal orange.

SEEING

1. Larry Woiwode lingers on the special qualities of what most of us would view as an ordinary piece of fruit. What impression of an orange does Woiwode create? When, how, and why does he draw on each of the five senses to create this overall effect?

2. In addition to description, what other techniques does Woiwode use to evoke such a vibrant orange? What does he mean when he says that the oranges of his youth signified "the colorful otherworld" (para. 11)? What range of associations do the oranges of his youth evoke in Woiwode now? He was a child in the 1940s and 1950s, the same time that labels like "Have One" (p. 52) were used to promote the fruit. If you consider the essay and the crate label together, does the way you see each one change? Why or why not?

Page 52

HAVE ONE

WRITING

1. Consider Woiwode's title: "Ode to an Orange." How does his essay satisfy the expectations usually associated with the word ode? Write your own ode to a piece of fruit. The goal is to evoke longing in your readers.

2. Woiwode uses each of the five senses — touch, sound, sight, smell, and taste — to convey the appeal of an orange. Imagine that only four senses were available to you. Which sense would you give up? Write the first draft of an essay explaining your choice and using examples from Woiwode's work to support your argument.

ode: A formal lyric poem, usually written in an elevated style and voice, usually praising a person or thing.

Top: Sequoia Citrus Association, *Have One,* 1920s
Bottom: California Orange Growers, *Orange Crate Labels,* early 20th century

Sequoia Citrus Association

From the late 1880s through the 1950s, California citrus growers and farmers relied on colorful paper labels to promote the fruits and vegetables they shipped in wooden crates throughout the United States. Designed primarily to attract wholesale buyers in distant markets, these distinctive examples of commercial art also helped to promote an idealized image of California and to lure seekers of sunshine and fortune. Many early labels accentuated the image of California as a land of plenty, innocence, and beauty. Pastoral images and allegorical scenes soon yielded to the accelerated pace and more sophisticated look of urban life: bolder typography, darker colors, and the billboard-like graphics associated with automobile advertisements.

The use of paper labels ended when corporate interests overshadowed individual and family enterprises, when small private groves were consumed by cooperatives or turned into sites for tract-home communities, and when cardboard cartons replaced wooden crates.

The orange crate label for the Have One brand, which appeared in the 1920s, and the other labels reprinted here from the early twentieth century offer striking examples of the graphics and themes used to identify brand names through easily remembered images.

SEEING

1. The label used by the Sequoia Citrus Association to identify its oranges looks simple: a hand, an orange, a brand name. But as you examine the label more carefully, do you notice anything that makes the image more complicated? What about the hand makes it distinct? How does its placement reinforce – or subvert – the invitation to have an orange? What are the advantages – and the disadvantages – of using an imperative in the headline ("Have One")? Is anything being sold here besides an orange?

2. Look at each of the graphic elements in the label. What do you notice about the placement of the forearm and hand? What effects does the artist achieve by superimposing the forearm and hand on the image? What aspects of the fruit does the artist highlight to call attention to the orange? What other graphic elements help focus the viewer's attention on the orange and its succulence? In what ways does the typography used in the name of the brand reinforce or detract from the effectiveness of this graphic design?

have: (1) to possess a thing or a privilege, as in *to have permission;* (2) to receive, as in *I had some news;* (3) to feel an obligation to do, as in *to have a deadline;* (4) to aquire or get possession of a person or thing, as in *I had him where I wanted him;* (5) to be characterized by a certain quality, as in *I have blue eyes;* (6) to use or exercise a quality, as in *to have pity;* (7) to trick or fool, as in *I was had;* (8) to be forced to do something, as in *I have to go.*

WRITING

1. Cryptic advertising imperatives that never explicitly name the product they are promoting (e.g., "Just do it" or "Enjoy the ride") are used in many contemporary ads and commercials. Which is more effective in these ads – the image or the language? Choose a cryptic ad or commercial for any product, and write an expository essay about why you think the ad or commercial does or does not work.

Working with Sources

2. What products are most often identified with the community in which you live or attend college? Choose one product that interests you, and conduct preliminary research on its earliest commercial representations. (You might check the holdings in the periodical and rare-book sections of your library, or you might visit the local historical society.) Focusing on one example of commercial art used to promote this product, write an analytical essay in which you show how the graphic elements and language borrow from or help reinforce the identity of this particular community.

WITHIN THE REACH OF MILLIONS

THE most valuable things on earth are the commonest things. Gifts of Mother Nature—air, rain, sunlight and colors in the sky, grass underfoot and foliage overhead. Gifts of human nature — love, loyalty, handclasps and friendly speech.

Then, of material things, some of the most useful are the commonest and cheapest. These we take almost for granted. There is no way to reckon their actual worth.

It is a great tribute to the value of the telephone that within a few short generations it has come to be ranked among these common things. Its daily use is a habit of millions of people. It speeds and eases and simplifies living. It extends the range of your own personality. It offers you gayety, solace, security — a swift messenger in time of need.

Daily it saves untold expense and waste, multiplies earning power, sweeps away confusion. Binds together the human fabric. Helps the individual man and woman to triumph over the complexities of a vast world.

You cannot reckon fully the worth of so useful and universal a thing as the telephone. You can only know that its value may be infinite.

AMERICAN TELEPHONE AND TELEGRAPH COMPANY

1933

Family far away?

It's fun to talk by telephone

When you telephone the folks back home, you can almost *hear* them smile. An out-of-town call is warm . . . personal . . . and enjoyable. The cost is small. And you don't have to hurry your call. Why not telephone your family right now?

BELL TELEPHONE SYSTEM
Call by Number. It's Twice as Fast.

1958

Those first steps just walked into a couple of hearts a thousand miles away. And the next thing you know, out of that endless string of gibberish will come something that sounds like "grandma" or "grandpa," especially to grandma or grandpa. Magic times. Times worth sharing. Remember, no matter how far away your family or family of friends may be, you can always reach out and touch them. **Bell System**

Reach out and touch someone.

1980

Don't Be Bound By Convention

The Sony

Cordless Telephone…

…technology that sets you

free with an elegance of

design that expresses

your individuality.

© 1991 Sony Corporation of America.
All rights reserved. Sony is a trademark of Sony.

SONY

1992

2008

My earliest memories of reading are of those in school when my teacher would make us read every day after lunch. I found it so relaxing after running around for an hour to just lay my head on my cool desk and read a book of my choice.

Lizet Gaytan, student at Moorpark College

A writer is a reader who is moved to emulation.

Saul Bellow, Nobel Prize–winning writer

Tracey Baran
Mom Ironing, 1997

Tracey Baran

Born in Bath, New York, in 1975, Tracey Baran moved to New York City in 1993 to study at the School of Visual Arts. Shortly thereafter, in 1999, Baran won critical renown with her photographic series Give and Take.

The series, which includes *Mom Ironing*, focuses on the literal and emotional landscape of Baran's childhood. When asked how she came to photograph her family life, she explained, "I was trying to figure out myself and how I reacted to certain things. I noticed my reactions were like my parents'. It's all pretty much based on my family life in upstate New York. Studying them was like studying myself. I just wanted to show the relationships between each family member and how people live and the care they give to themselves and things that are important to them."

Over the past decade, Baran's photographs have been featured in museums and galleries in New York, London, and Busan, Korea. Through photographic series such as Still (2001), Red (2004), See through Me (2006), and Note to Self (2007), Baran has created an ongoing visual autobiography that captures both the beauty and the ordinariness of everyday life.

SEEING

1. Tracey Baran's *Mom Ironing* illustrates her remarkable ability to portray ordinary activities and scenes as engaging and enduring subjects for artistic expression. What, in your view, happens to a commonplace activity such as ironing when it is captured in Baran's photograph? What do you notice about the activity presented here? Carefully examine the context within which the ironing occurs. What do you notice about the scene captured in this photograph? How would you characterize the relationship between and among the objects and people depicted in this photograph? Given what you see in this image, what is the likelihood of effective communication between the older woman and the younger woman? What details in the photograph prompt you to draw your inferences?

2. Imagine yourself in a museum viewing Baran's *Mom Ironing*. How would seeing the photograph as part of an exhibit change your understanding and appreciation of it? How would Baran's attitude influence your reading of her artistic purpose? What do you think Baran "says" in this image? On what grounds could you argue that *Mom Ironing* is a work of art? How would you defend that argument?

WRITING

1. Make a list of commonplace activities, ones that you've performed so often that you seldom think carefully about them. Choose one, and write an expository essay in which you focus your attention – and your readers' – on the details of this everyday activity or ritual. In what ways do you personalize this otherwise commonplace activity?

2. Make a list of specific similarities and differences between the scenes and relationships depicted in this photograph and in Tillie Olsen's story "I Stand Here Ironing" (p. 62). After you have reread the photograph and story carefully, several times, write the first draft of an essay in which you compare and contrast the aesthetic appeal – and effectiveness – of the photograph and story.

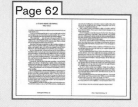
Page 62

I STAND HERE IRONING
Tillie Olsen

I stand here ironing, and what you asked me moves tormented back and forth with the iron.

"I wish you would manage the time to come in and talk with me about your daughter. I'm sure you can help me understand her. She's a youngster who needs help and whom I'm deeply interested in helping."

"Who needs help." . . . Even if I came, what good would it do? You think because I am her mother I have a key, or that in some way you could use me as a key? She has lived for nineteen years. There is all that life that has happened outside of me, beyond me.

And when is there time to remember, to sift, to weigh, to estimate, to total? I will start and there will be an interruption and I will have to gather it all together again. Or I will become engulfed with all I did or did not do, with what should have been and what cannot be helped.

5 She was a beautiful baby. The first and only one of our five that was beautiful at birth. You do not guess how new and uneasy her tenancy in her now-loveliness. You did not know her all those years she was thought homely, or see her poring over her baby pictures, making me tell her over and over how beautiful she had been — and would be, I would tell her — and was now, to the seeing eye. But the seeing eyes were few or nonexistent. Including mine.

I nursed her. They feel that's important nowadays. I nursed all the children, but with her, with all the fierce rigidity of first motherhood, I did like the books then said. Though her cries battered me to trembling and my breasts ached with swollenness, I waited till the clock decreed.

Why do I put that first? I do not even know if it matters, or if it explains anything.

She was a beautiful baby. She blew shining bubbles of sound. She loved motion, loved light, loved color and music and textures. She would lie on the floor in her blue overalls patting the surface so hard in ecstasy her hands and feet would blur. She was a miracle to me, but when she was eight months old I had to leave her daytimes with the woman downstairs to whom she was no miracle at all, for I worked or looked for work and for Emily's father, who "could no longer endure" (he wrote in his good-bye note) "sharing the want with us."

I was nineteen. It was the pre-relief, pre-WPA world of the depression. I would start running as soon as I got off the streetcar, running up the stairs, the place smelling sour, and awake or asleep to startle awake, when she saw me she would break into a clogged weeping that could not be comforted, a weeping I can hear yet.

10   After a while I found a job hashing[1] at night so I could be with her days, and it was better. But it came to where I had to bring her to his family and leave her.

It took a long time to raise the money for her fare back. Then she got chicken pox and I had to wait longer. When she finally came, I hardly knew her, walking quick and nervous like her father, looking like her father, thin, and dressed in a shoddy red that yellowed her skin and glared at the pockmarks. All the baby loveliness gone.

She was two. Old enough for nursery school they said, and I did not know then what I know now—the fatigue of the long day, the lacerations of group life in the kinds of nurseries that are only parking places for children.

Except that it would have made no difference if I had known. It was the only place there was. It was the only way we could be together, the only way I could hold a job.

And even without knowing, I knew. I knew the teacher that was evil because all these years it has curdled into my memory, the little boy hunched in the corner, her rasp, "why aren't you outside, because Alvin hits you? that's no reason, go out, scaredy." I knew Emily hated it even if she did not clutch and implore "don't go Mommy" like the other children, mornings.

15   She always had a reason why we should stay home. Momma, you look sick. Momma, I feel sick. Momma, the teachers aren't there today, they're sick. Momma, we can't go, there was a fire there last night. Momma, it's a holiday today, no school, they told me.

But never a direct protest, never rebellion. I think of our others in their three-, four-year-oldness—the explosions, the tempers, the denunciations, the demands—and I feel suddenly ill. I put the iron down. What in me demanded that goodness in her? And what was the cost, the cost to her of such goodness?

The old man living in the back once said in his gentle way: "You should smile at Emily more when you look at her." What *was* in my face when I looked at her? I loved her. There were all the acts of love.

It was only with the others I remembered what he said, and it was the face of joy, and not of care or tightness or worry I turned to them—too

---

1. hashing: Working as a short-order cook; literally, chopping meat and potatoes. [Eds.]

late for Emily. She does not smile easily, let alone almost always as her brothers and sisters do. Her face is closed and somber, but when she wants, how fluid. You must have seen it in her pantomimes, you spoke of her rare gift for comedy on the stage that rouses a laughter out of the audience so dear they applaud and applaud and do not want to let her go.

Where does it come from, that comedy? There was none of it in her when she came back to me that second time, after I had had to send her away again. She had a new daddy now to learn to love, and I think perhaps it was a better time.

20   Except when we left her alone nights, telling ourselves she was old enough.

"Can't you go some other time, Mommy, like tomorrow?" she would ask. "Will it be just a little while you'll be gone? Do you promise?"

The time we came back, the front door open, the clock on the floor in the hall. She rigid awake. "It wasn't just a little while. I didn't cry. Three times I called you, just three times, and then I ran downstairs to open the door so you could come faster. The clock talked loud. I threw it away, it scared me what it talked."

She said the clock talked loud again that night I went to the hospital to have Susan. She was delirious with the fever that comes before red measles, but she was fully conscious all the week I was gone and the week after we were home when she could not come near the new baby or me.

She did not get well. She stayed skeleton thin, not wanting to eat, and night after night she had nightmares. She would call for me, and I would rouse from exhaustion to sleepily call back: "You're all right, darling, go to sleep, it's just a dream," and if she still called, in a sterner voice, "Now go to sleep, Emily, there's nothing to hurt you." Twice, only twice, when I had to get up for Susan anyhow, I went in to sit with her.

25   Now when it is too late (as if she would let me hold and comfort her like I do the others) I get up and go to her at once at her moan or restless stirring. "Are you awake, Emily? Can I get you something?" And the answer is always the same: "No, I'm all right, go back to sleep, Mother."

They persuaded me at the clinic to send her away to a convalescent home in the country where "she can have the kind of food and care you can't manage for her, and you'll be free to concentrate on the new baby." They still send children to that place. I see pictures on the society page of sleek young women planning affairs to raise money for it, or dancing at the affairs, or decorating Easter eggs or filling Christmas stockings for the children.

They never have a picture of the children so I do not know if the girls still wear those gigantic red bows and the ravaged looks on the every other

Sunday when parents can come to visit "unless otherwise notified"—as we were notified the first six weeks.

Oh it is a handsome place, green lawns and tall trees and fluted flower beds. High up on the balconies of each cottage the children stand, the girls in their red bows and white dresses, the boys in white suits and giant red ties. The parents stand below shrieking up to be heard and the children shriek down to be heard, and between them the invisible wall "Not To Be Contaminated by Parental Germs or Physical Affection."

There was a tiny girl who always stood hand in hand with Emily. Her parents never came. One visit she was gone. "They moved her to Rose Cottage" Emily shouted in explanation. "They don't like you to love anybody here."

30   She wrote once a week, the labored writing of a seven-year-old. "I am fine. How is the baby. If I write my leter nicly I will have a star. Love." There never was a star. We wrote every other day, letters she could never hold or keep but only hear read—once. "We simply do not have room for children to keep any personal possessions," they patiently explained when we pieced one Sunday's shrieking together to plead how much it would mean to Emily, who loved so to keep things, to be allowed to keep her letters and cards.

Each visit she looked frailer. "She isn't eating," they told us.

(They had runny eggs for breakfast or mush with lumps, Emily said later, I'd hold it in my mouth and not swallow. Nothing ever tasted good, just when they had chicken.)

It took us eight months to get her released home, and only the fact that she gained back so little of her seven lost pounds convinced the social worker.

I used to try to hold and love her after she came back, but her body would stay stiff, and after a while she'd push away. She ate little. Food sickened her, and I think much of life too. Oh she had physical lightness and brightness, twinkling by on skates, bouncing like a ball up and down up and down over the jump rope, skimming over the hill; but these were momentary.

35   She fretted about her appearance, thin and dark and foreign-looking at a time when every little girl was supposed to look or thought she should look a chubby blond replica of Shirley Temple. The doorbell sometimes rang for her, but no one seemed to come and play in the house or be a best friend. Maybe because we moved so much.

There was a boy she loved painfully through two school semesters. Months later she told me how she had taken pennies from my purse to buy him candy. "Licorice was his favorite and I brought him some every day, but he still liked Jennifer better'n me. Why, Mommy?" The kind of question for which there is no answer.

School was a worry to her. She was not glib or quick in a world where glibness and quickness were easily confused with ability to learn. To her overworked and exasperated teachers she was an overconscientious "slow learner" who kept trying to catch up and was absent entirely too often.

I let her be absent, though sometimes the illness was imaginary. How different from my now-strictness about attendance with the others. I wasn't working. We had a new baby, I was home anyhow. Sometimes, after Susan grew old enough, I would keep her home from school, too, to have them all together.

Mostly Emily had asthma, and her breathing, harsh and labored, would fill the house with a curiously tranquil sound. I would bring the two old dresser mirrors and her boxes of collections to her bed. She would select beads and single earrings, bottle tops and shells, dried flowers and pebbles, old postcards and scraps, all sorts of oddments; then she and Susan would play Kingdom, setting up landscapes and furniture, peopling them with action.

40   Those were the only times of peaceful companionship between her and Susan. I have edged away from it, that poisonous feeling between them, that terrible balancing of hurts and needs I had to do between the two, and did so badly, those earlier years.

Oh there are conflicts between the others too, each one human, needing, demanding, hurting, taking—but only between Emily and Susan, no, Emily toward Susan that corroding resentment. It seems so obvious on the surface, yet it is not obvious. Susan, the second child, Susan, golden- and curly-haired and chubby, quick and articulate and assured, everything in appearance and manner Emily was not; Susan, not able to resist Emily's precious things, losing or sometimes clumsily breaking them; Susan telling jokes and riddles to company for applause while Emily sat silent (to say to me later: that was *my* riddle, Mother, I told it to Susan); Susan, who for all the five years' difference in age was just a year behind Emily in developing physically.

I am glad for that slow physical development that widened the difference between her and her contemporaries, though she suffered over it. She was too vulnerable for that terrible world of youthful competition, of preening and parading, of constant measuring of yourself against every other, of envy, "If I had that copper hair," "If I had that skin. . . ." She tormented herself enough about not looking like the others, there was enough of the unsureness, the having to be conscious of words before you speak, the constant caring—what are they thinking of me? without having it all magnified by the merciless physical drives.

Ronnie is calling. He is wet and I change him. It is rare there is such a cry now. That time of motherhood is almost behind me when the ear is not one's own but must always be racked and listening for the child cry, the child call. We sit for a while and I hold him, looking out over the city spread in charcoal with its soft aisles of light. "*Shoogily,*" he breathes and curls closer. I carry him back to bed, asleep. *Shoogily.* A funny word, a family word, inherited from Emily, invented by her to say: *comfort.*

In this and other ways she leaves her seal, I say aloud. And startle at my saying it. What do I mean? What did I start to gather together, to try and make coherent? I was at the terrible, growing years. War years. I do not remember them well. I was working, there were four smaller ones now, there was not time for her. She had to help be a mother, and house-keeper, and shopper. She had to set her seal. Mornings of crisis and near hysteria trying to get lunches packed, hair combed, coats and shoes found, everyone to school or Child Care on time, the baby ready for transporta-tion. And always the paper scribbled on by a smaller one, the book looked at by Susan then mislaid, the homework not done. Running out to that huge school where she was one, she was lost, she was a drop; suffering over her unpreparedness, stammering and unsure in her classes.

45   There was so little time left at night after the kids were bedded down. She would struggle over books, always eating (it was in those years she developed her enormous appetite that is legendary in our family) and I would be ironing, or preparing food for the next day, or writing V-mail[2] to Bill, or tending the baby. Sometimes, to make me laugh, or out of her despair, she would imitate happenings or types at school.

I think I said once: "Why don't you do something like this in the school amateur show?" One morning she phoned me at work, hardly under-standable through the weeping: "Mother, I did it. I won, I won; they gave me first prize; they clapped and clapped and wouldn't let me go."

Now suddenly she was Somebody, and as imprisoned in her differ-ence as she had been in her anonymity.

She began to be asked to perform at other high schools, even in col-leges, then at city and statewide affairs. The first one we went to, I only recognized her that first moment when thin, shy, she almost drowned her-self into the curtains. Then: Was this Emily? The control, the command,

---

2. V-mail: Special forms used to communicate with soldiers serving overseas at the end of World War II. These forms were photographed, put on film, and shipped to the soldier's location, cutting down on the time and space a normal letter would take. [Eds.]

the convulsing and deadly clowning, the spell, then the roaring, stamping audience, unwilling to let this rare and precious laughter out of their lives.

Afterwards: You ought to do something about her with a gift like that—but without money or knowing how, what does one do? We have left it all to her, and the gift has as often eddied inside, clogged and clotted, as been used and growing.

50 She is coming. She runs up the stairs two at a time with her light graceful step, and I know she is happy tonight. Whatever it was that occasioned your call did not happen today.

"Aren't you ever going to finish the ironing, Mother? Whistler painted his mother in a rocker. I'd have to paint mine standing over an ironing board." This is one of her communicative nights and she tells me everything and nothing as she fixes herself a plate of food out of the icebox.

She is so lovely. Why did you want me to come in at all? Why were you concerned? She will find her way.

She starts up the stairs to bed. "Don't get *me* up with the rest in the morning." "But I thought you were having midterms." "Oh, those," she comes back in, kisses me, and says quite lightly, "in a couple of years when we'll all be atom-dead they won't matter a bit."

She has said it before. She *believes* it. But because I have been dredging the past, and all that compounds a human being is so heavy and meaningful in me, I cannot endure it tonight.

55 I will never total it all. I will never come in to say: She was a child seldom smiled at. Her father left me before she was a year old. I had to work her first six years when there was work, or I sent her home and to his relatives. There were years she had care she hated. She was dark and thin and foreign-looking in a world where the prestige went to blondness and curly hair and dimples; she was slow where glibness was prized. She was a child of anxious, not proud, love. We were poor and could not afford for her the soil of easy growth. I was a young mother, I was a distracted mother. There were the other children pushing up, demanding. Her younger sister seemed all that she was not. There were years she did not let me touch her. She kept too much in herself, her life was such she had to keep too much in herself. My wisdom came too late. She has much to her and probably little will come of it. She is a child of her age, of depression, of war, of fear.

Let her be. So all that is in her will not bloom—but in how many does it? There is still enough to live by. Only help her to know—help make it so there is cause for her to know—that she is more than this dress on the ironing board, helpless before the iron.

Tillie Olsen

Born in Omaha, Nebraska, Tillie Olsen (ca. 1913–2007) was the second of six children of Jewish immigrants who had escaped czarist Russia. Olsen followed in the footsteps of her working-class parents: She married young, had four children, and worked at various low-paying jobs. She also took up writing. At age nineteen, influenced by Rebecca Harding Davis's *Life in the Iron-Mills,* Olsen began what would be her only novel, *Yonnondio.* (The title, drawn from a Walt Whitman poem, means "a lament for the lost.") Olsen wrote *Yonnondio* during the Great Depression and published it forty years later (1974), despite the fact that she never completed it.

Olsen became a pioneer among American writers, giving eloquent voice to the struggles of everyday people. "I Stand Here Ironing" is drawn from her widely acclaimed short story collection, *Tell Me a Riddle* (1961). One critic summarized the significance of Olsen's work as her ability to find "characters who could fully embody her vision of hope with hopelessness, of beauty in the midst of ugliness."

Olsen received many awards during her lifetime for her fiction and nonfiction, including *Silences* (1979) and *Mothers and Daughters* (1987). When Olsen died in 2007, the world lost a pioneering voice – one that not only articulated the struggles of women and the poor, but also expressed the common humanity of us all.

SEEING

1. Characterize the <u>narrator</u> in this story. To whom does she seem to be speaking? Why is this person so interested in Emily? Does it seem to you that he or she understands Emily better than the speaker does? Why or why not? What does Emily's mother think about the way she has raised her daughter? In what ways would she have raised Emily differently? What are some of the ways she thinks Emily's upbringing went wrong? Who or what is responsible for what happened? What does this suggest about the mother's attitude toward her own life? Does Emily's mother think her daughter has found happiness, now that she is a popular performer? Why or why not?

2. Olsen's story ends with a dramatic appeal: "Only help her to know – help make it so there is cause for her to know – that she is more than this dress on the ironing board, helpless before the iron" (para. 56). What is the nature – and the significance – of the image here? To what extent does the speaker wish someone could have helped her know the same thing earlier in her life? To what extent does she seem "helpless before the iron" herself? How do you think Olsen wants us to react to the mother? to the daughter? What, specifically, prompts your response?

<u>narrator: The person telling a story.</u>

WRITING

1. Imagine yourself in the role of one of your parents. Write the first draft of a personal essay about your life from either your father's or your mother's <u>point of view</u>. What went wrong, and what went right, in your upbringing? What mistakes do you think your parents made? What are the effects of your upbringing on the way you are now? You may want to talk with your parents before writing your story, and you may want to address it to someone outside your family who knows you but not too well.

2. Olsen builds her story around an ordinary object and an ordinary activity. She uses these simple devices as a way to develop a story that is far more than a string of excuses for the mother's failure – because of ignorance and circumstances – to give her daughter the upbringing that she needed. Choose an ordinary object, and use it as the central image for creating a story that defines the relationship between a parent and a child.

<u>point of view: The perspective, or angle of vision, from which a story is told.</u>

As a reader, I would describe myself as an addict with no intentions of recovering.

Nii Martey Codjoe, student at
Southern Polytechnic State University

The greatest gift is
the passion for reading.
It is cheap, it consoles,
it distracts, it excites,
it gives you knowledge
of the world and
experience of a wide kind.
It is moral illumination.

Elizabeth Hardwick, literary critic and novelist

VISUALIZING COMPOSITION:
SLOWED-DOWN READING

Let's talk about Brian Doyle's essay, "Joyas Volardores."

What did you notice about it?

I found all the details about hummingbirds really interesting.

There's something really beautiful about the essay. It took my breath away.

I think he's saying something about the vulnerability of the human heart.

Okay, now that you've offered your **initial impressions,** let's go back for a second, more **careful reading** of the first four sentences.

This time, don't focus on what the sentences mean, instead **focus on what observations** you can make about the text.

Each contains the word "hummingbird."

Each is roughly the same length.

Each sentence has a kind of even rhythm.

Yes! You're making *observations* about the compositional choices Doyle made. **Why** might he have made those choices? **What effects** does each of these choices produce?

He's asking readers to "consider the hummingbird for a long moment." And in repeating the word "hummingbird" so many times, I think he forces us to do exactly that. It seems like the rhythm of those first sentences *sounds* like the quick repetitive heart beat of a **hummingbird.**

These are terrific examples of careful reading. You may feel that there's a lot of pressure on you to leap into focusing on what a text **"means."** But first concentrate instead on asking yourself simple questions, such as "What do I notice about the text?"

If you SLOW DOWN your reading, you'll be able to make **informed** observations about any text, which will lead to reasonable inferences. SLOWING DOWN YOUR READING in order

to notice, to understand, and to appreciate the choices a writer makes will enable you to read not only more effectively, but also with greater satisfaction.

The most ENGAGED readers are often the most ENGAGING writers.

Gueorgui Pinkhassov
Pregame Prayer, Billy Ryan High School, Denton, Texas

Gueorgui Pinkhassov
Salat-ul-Zuhr (Noon) Prayers, Mardigian Library, University of Michigan–Dearborn

Gueorgui Pinkhassov
Day of Miracles Ceremony, Land of Medicine Buddha, Soquel, California

Gueorgui Pinkhassov
Satnam Waheguru Prayer, Minar's Taj Palace, New York

Gueorgui Pinkhassov

Born in Russia in 1952, Gueorgui Pinkhassov first became interested in photography as a teenager. He went on to study cinematography at the Institute of Cinematography in Moscow (VGIK), and later he worked as a member of the camera crew and as a film-stills photographer at Mosfilm Studios. Today Pinkhassov is considered one of the world's finest color photographers. He joined the prestigious Magnum group in 1986.

In 1985 Pinkhassov moved to Paris, where he still resides today. He travels the world for his photographic reporting, covering historical events for the *New York Times Magazine, Geo,* and *Le Figaro Magazine.* His first book, *Sightwalk* (1998), is a series of photographs of Tokyo, accompanied by Pinkasshov's own haiku.

Most recently, Pinkhassov was one of ten photographers who participated in The Image to Come, a photographic collaboration between Magnum Photos and the Cinemathèque Français on the subject of the relationship between motion pictures and photography. The results were published in 2007. Pinkhassov, a valuable contributor to the project due to his cinematic style and background in the Russian film industry, created a series of images in response to the films of Andrei Tarkovsky, one of Russia's most celebrated directors.

The images in this portfolio are taken from a 2003 award-winning *New York Times Magazine* photo essay, Moment of Silence. The photographs record the multiplicity of faiths practiced in the United States and the variety of venues, from libraries to football fields, in which Americans pray.

SEEING

1. What did you notice first when you examined Pinkhassov's portfolio of photographs? Which photograph attracted your attention first? Why? Which image held your attention longest? Why? With which image do you feel most comfortable? With which image do you feel least comfortable? Explain your answers.

2. Look again at Pinkhassov's photographs. What elements — beyond the act of praying — do the images share? How is each photograph unique? Point to similarities and differences in the way the photographer depicts the scene in each photograph. What reasonable inferences can you draw from your observation of Pinkhassov's subjects?

WRITING

1. Each of Pinkhassov's photographs is a narrative: It tells the story of how and, in several cases, why the subjects pray. Sort through your own photographs, and choose one that tells a story. Then write an essay that describes both the moment depicted in the image and the circumstances that led up to it. Your goal is to re-create for your readers the immediacy of the moment captured in the photograph.

2. To which of Pinkhassov's photographs are you most drawn? Examine that image carefully, until you are reasonably confident that you understand and appreciate how it works to elicit specific responses from its audience. Then write the first draft of a fictional narrative that sets the context for – and leads up to – the scene depicted in the photograph.

narrative: A verbal or graphic account of events.

JOYAS VOLARDORES
Brian Doyle

Consider the hummingbird for a long moment. A hummingbird's heart beats ten times a second. A hummingbird's heart is the size of a pencil eraser. A hummingbird's heart is a lot of the hummingbird. *Joyas volardores,* flying jewels, the first white explorers in the Americas called them, and the white men had never seen such creatures, for hummingbirds came into the world only in the Americas, nowhere else in the universe, more than three hundred species of them whirring and zooming and nectaring in hummer time zones nine times removed from ours, their hearts hammering faster than we could clearly hear if we pressed our elephantine ears to their infinitesimal chests.

Each one vists a thousand flowers a day. They can dive at sixty miles an hour. They can fly backwards. They can fly more than five hundred miles without pausing to rest. But when they rest they come close to death: On frigid nights, or when they are starving, they retreat into torpor, their metabolic rate slowing to a fifteenth of their normal sleep rate, their hearts sludging nearly to a halt, barely beating, and if they are not soon warmed, if they do not soon find that which is sweet, their hearts grow cold, and they cease to be. Consider for a moment those hummingbirds who did not open their eyes again today, this very day, in the Americas: bearded helmet-crests and booted racket-tails, violet-tailed sylphs and violet-capped wood-nymphs, crimson topazes and purple-crowned fairies, red-tailed comets and amethyst woodstars, rainbow-bearded thornbills and glittering-bellied emeralds, velvet-purple coronets and golden-bellied star-frontlets, fiery-tailed awlbills and Andean hillstars, spatuletails and pufflegs, each the most amazing thing you have never seen, each thunderous wild heart the size of an infant's fingernail, each mad heart silent, a brilliant music stilled.

Hummingbirds, like all flying birds but more so, have incredible enormous immense ferocious metabolisms. To drive those metabolisms they have race-car hearts that eat oxygen at an eye-popping rate. Their hearts are built of thinner, leaner fibers than ours. Their arteries are stiffer and more taut. They have more mitochondria in their heart muscles — anything to gulp more oxygen. Their hearts are stripped to the skin for the war against gravity and inertia, the mad search for food, the insane idea of flight. The price of their ambition is a life closer to death; they suffer heart attacks and aneurysms and ruptures more than any other living creature. It's expensive to fly. You burn out. You fry the machine. You melt the engine. Every creature on earth has approximately two billion heartbeats to spend in a lifetime. You can spend them slowly, like a tortoise, and live to be two hundred years old, or you can spend them fast, like a hummingbird, and live to be two years old.

The biggest heart in the world is inside the blue whale. It weighs more than seven tons. It's as big as a room. It *is* a room, with four chambers. A child could walk around in it, head high, bending only to step through the valves. The valves are as big as the swinging doors in a saloon. This house of a heart drives a creature a hundred feet long. When this creature is born it is twenty feet long and weighs four tons. It is waaaaay bigger than your car. It drinks a hundred gallons of milk from its mama every day and gains two hundred pounds a day and when it is seven or eight years old it endures an unimaginable puberty and then it essentially disappears from human ken, for next to nothing is known of the mating habits, travel patterns, diet, social life, language, social structure, diseases, spirituality, wars, stories, despairs, and arts of the blue whale. There are perhaps ten thousand blue whales in the world, living in every ocean on earth, and of the largest mammal who ever lived we know nearly nothing. But we know this: The animals with the largest hearts in the world generally travel in pairs, and their penetrating moaning cries, their piercing yearning tongue, can be heard underwater for miles and miles.

5   Mammals and birds have hearts with four chambers. Reptiles and turtles have hearts with three chambers. Fish have hearts with two chambers. Insects and mollusks have hearts with one chamber. Worms have hearts with one chamber, although they may have as many as eleven single-chambered hearts. Unicellular bacteria have no hearts at all; but even they have fluid eternally in motion, washing from one side of the cell to the other, swirling and whirling. No living being is without interior liquid motion. We all churn inside.

So much held in a heart in a lifetime. So much held in a heart in a day, an hour, a moment. We are utterly open with no one, in the end—not mother and father, not wife or husband, not lover, not child, not friend. We open windows to each but we live alone in the house of the heart. Perhaps we must. Perhaps we could not bear to be so naked, for fear of a constantly harrowed heart. When young we think there will come one person who will savor and sustain us always; when we are older we know this is the dream of a child, that all hearts finally are bruised and scarred, scored and torn, repaired by time and will, patched by force of character, yet fragile and rickety forevermore, no matter how ferocious the defense and how many bricks you bring to the wall. You can brick up your heart as stout and tight and hard and cold and impregnable as you possibly can and down it comes in an instant, felled by a woman's second glance, a child's apple breath, the shatter of glass in the road, the words *I have something to tell you,* a cat with a broken spine dragging itself into the forest to die, the brush of your mother's papery ancient hand in the thicket of your hair, the memory of your father's voice early in the morning echoing from the kitchen where he is making pancakes for his children.

Brian Doyle

Essayist Brian Doyle (b. 1956) is the editor of *Portland,* published quarterly by the University of Portland in Oregon and ranked among the ten best university magazines in America. Doyle is widely known for his essays on Catholicism and spirituality, and his work has appeared in *The American Scholar, The Atlantic, Orion, Commonweal, Georgia Review,* and *Harper's,* among other periodicals. His essays have also been reprinted in *The Best American Essays* anthologies of 1998 and 1999 and in *The Best Spiritual Writing* of 1999, 2001, and 2002.

Numerous collections of Doyle's essays have been published, including: *Two Voices: A Father and Son Discuss Family and Faith* (1996, with Jim Doyle, his father), *Credo* (1999), *Saints Passionate & Peculiar* (2002), *Leaping: Revelations & Epiphanies* (2003), *Spirited Men* (2004), *The Wet Engine* (2005), *The Grail: A Year Ambling and Shambling through an Oregon Vineyard in Pursuit of the Best Pinot Noir Wine in the Whole Wild World* (2006), and *Epiphanies & Elegies* (2007). He also is the editor of the annual anthology *The Best Catholic Writing.* Doyle and his wife, an artist and illustrator, have three children. He has said in an interview, "On my gravestone I'd be proud if it read A GOOD DAD. Everything else is second."

"Joyas Volardores" first appeared in 2004 in *The American Scholar,* a magazine published by the Phi Beta Kappa Society. The essay combines Doyle's interests in the scientific observation of nature and the spiritual dimensions of love.

SEEING

1. Brian Doyle uses the simple act of observing a hummingbird to organize an insightful essay. What other organizing devices help structure Doyle's thoughts in this essay? What overarching themes tie his reflections together? For example, what do the hummingbird and the blue whale have in common? In what specific ways do you think the comparison between the hummingbird and the whale is effective? How is Doyle's essay more than a paean to creatures large and small? What larger points does Doyle make in the essay?

2. To what extent does Doyle's use of metaphor strengthen the points he makes in the essay? Which <u>metaphor</u> do you find most effective? Why? Which do you judge least effective? Why? Some might argue that Doyle's use of metaphor distracts from the impact of his work. Do you find that argument convincing? Why or why not?

<u>metaphor: A word or phrase meaning one thing that is used to describe something else in order to suggest a relationship between the two; an implied comparison.</u>

WRITING

1. One way to gain new insight into the ordinary is to examine it closely, as Doyle does the hummingbird. Choose an ordinary object or an animal – something you see so often that you don't really see it at all – and study it. Then write an essay in which you use detailed description to uncover the significance of the object or animal.

2. Both <u>K. C. Cole's "A Matter of Scale"</u> and Doyle's "Joyas Volardores" devote considerable time to observing – and then drawing inferences from – the world of nature. Compare and contrast the way in which both authors write about their subjects.

Page 85

A MATTER OF SCALE
K. C. Cole

How would you suspend 500,000 pounds
of water in the air with no visible means of support?
(Answer: build a cloud.)
−Bob Miller, artist

There is something magically seductive about an invitation to a world where everything measures much bigger or smaller than ourselves. To contemplate the vast expanse of ocean or sky, to look at pond scum under a microscope, to imagine the intimate inner life of atoms, all cast spells that take us far beyond the realm of everyday living into exotic landscapes accessible only through the imagination. What would it be like to grow as big as a giant? As small as a bug? Alice ate a mushroom and puffed up like a Macy's Thanksgiving Day balloon, bursting out of her house; she ate some more and shrank like the Incredible Shrinking Woman, forever in fear of falling down the drain. From Stuart Little to King Kong, from *Honey, I Shrunk the Kids* to Thumbelina, the notion of changing size seems to have a powerful pull on our psyches.

There are good reasons to think a world that's different in scale will also be different in kind. More or less of something very often adds up to more than simply more or less; quantitative changes can make huge qualitative differences.

When the size of things changes radically, different laws of nature rule, time ticks according to different clocks, new worlds appear out of nowhere while old ones dissolve into invisibility. Consider the strange situation of a giant, for example. Big and strong to be sure, but size comes with distinct disadvantages. According to J. B. S. Haldane in his classic essay, "On Being the Right Size," a sixty-foot giant would break his thighbones at every step. The reason is simple geometry. Height increases only in one dimension, area in two, volume in three. If you doubled the height of a man, the cross section, or thickness, of muscle that supports him against gravity would quadruple (two times two) and his volume— and therefore weight—would increase by a factor of eight. If you made him ten times taller, his weight would be a thousand times greater, but the cross section of bones and muscles to support him would only increase by a factor of one hundred. Result: shattered bones.

To bear such weight would require stout, thick legs—think elephant or rhino. Leaping would be out of the question. Superman must have been a flea.

5   Fleas, of course, perform superhuman feats routinely (which is part of the science behind the now nearly extinct art of the flea circus). These puny critters can pull 160,000 times their own weight, and jump a hundred times their own height. Small creatures have so little mass compared to the area of their muscles that they seem enormously strong. While their muscles are many orders of magnitude weaker than ours, the mass they have to push around is so much smaller that it makes each ant and flea into a superbeing. Leaping over tall buildings does not pose a problem.[1]

Neither does falling. The old saying is true: The bigger they come, the harder they fall. And the smaller they come, the softer their landings. Again, the reason is geometry. If an elephant falls from a building, gravity pulls strongly on its huge mass while its comparatively small surface area offers little resistance. A mouse, on the other hand, is so small in volume (and therefore mass) that gravity has little to attract; at the same time, its relative surface area is so huge that it serves as a built-in parachute.

A mouse, writes Haldane, could be dropped from a thousand-yard-high cliff and walk away unharmed. A rat would probably suffer enough damage to be killed. A person would certainly be killed. And a horse, he tells us, "splashes."

The same relationships apply to inanimate falling objects—say, drops of water. The atmosphere is drenched with water vapor, even when we can't see it in the form of clouds. However, once a tiny particle begins to attract water molecules to its sides, things change rapidly. As the diameter of the growing droplet increases by a hundred, the surface area increases by ten thousand, and its volume a millionfold. The larger surface area reflects far more light—making the cloud visible. The enormously increased volume gives the drops the gravitational pull they need to splash down to the ground as rain.

According to cloud experts, water droplets in the air are simultaneously pulled on by electrical forces of attraction—which keep them herded together in the cloud—and gravity, which pulls them down. When the drops are small, their surface area is huge compared to volume; electrical (molecular) forces rule and the drops stay suspended in midair. Once the drops get big enough, however, gravity always wins.

---

1. According to Exploratorium physicist Tom Humphrey, all animals jump to the same height, roughly speaking. Both fleas and humans can jump about a meter off the ground — an interesting invariant. [All notes are Cole's.]

10   Pint-size objects barely feel gravity—a force that only makes itself felt on large scales. The electrical forces that hold molecules together are trillions of times stronger. That's why even the slightest bit of electrical static in the air can make your hair stand on end.

These electrical forces would present major problems to flea-size Superman. For one thing, he'd have a hard time flying faster than a speeding bullet, because the air would be a thick soup of sticky molecules grasping him from all directions; it would be like swimming through molasses.

Flies have no problem walking on the ceiling because the molecular glue that holds their feet to the moldings is stronger than the puny weight pulling them down. The electrical pull of water, however, attracts the insects like magnets. As Haldane points out, the electrical attraction of water molecules makes going for a drink a dangerous endeavor for an insect. A bug leaning over a puddle to take a sip of water would be in the same position as a person leaning out over a cliff to pluck a berry off a bush.

Water is one of the stickiest substances around. A person coming out of the shower carries about a pound of extra weight, scarcely a burden. But a mouse coming out of the shower would have to lift its weight in water, according to Haldane. For a fly, water is as powerful as flypaper; once it gets wet, it's stuck for life. That's one reason, writes Haldane, that most insects have a long proboscis.

In fact, once you get down to bug size, almost everything is different. An ant-size person could never write a book: The keys to an ant-size typewriter would stick together; so would the pages of a manuscript. An ant couldn't build a fire because the smallest possible flame is larger than its body.

15 Shrinking down to atom size alters reality beyond recognition, opening doors into new and wholly unexpected vistas. Atom-size things do not behave like molecule-size things or human-size things. Atomic particles are ruled by the probabilistic laws of quantum mechanics. Physicists have to be very clever to lure these quantum mechanical attributes out in the open, because they simply don't exist on the scales of human instrumentation. We do not perceive that energy comes in precisely defined clumps or that clouds of electrons buzz around atoms in a permanent state of probabilistic uncertainty. These behaviors become perceptible macroscopically only in exotic situations—for example, superconductivity—a superordered state where pairs of loose electrons in a material line up like a row of Rockettes. With electrons moving in lockstep, electricity can flow through superconductors without resistance.

Scale up to molecule-size matter, and electrical forces take over; scale up further, and gravity rules. As Philip and Phylis Morrison point out in the classic *Powers of Ten,* if you stick your hand in a sugar bowl, your fingers will emerge covered with tiny grains that stick to them due to electrical forces. However, if you stick your hand into a bowl of sugar cubes, you would be very surprised if a cube stuck to your fingers—unless you purposely set out to grasp one.

We know that gravity takes over in large-scale matters because everything in the universe larger than an asteroid is round or roundish—the result of gravity pulling matter in toward a common center. Everyday objects like houses and mountains come in every old shape, but mountains can only get so high before gravity pulls them down. They can get larger on Mars because gravity is less. Large things lose their rough edges in the fight against gravity. "No such thing as a teacup the diameter of Jupiter is possible in our world," say the Morrisons. As a teacup grew to Jupiter size, its handle and sides would be pulled into the center by the planet's huge gravity until it resembled a sphere.

Add more matter still, and the squeeze of gravity ignites nuclear fires; stars exist in a continual tug-of-war between gravitational collapse and the outward pressure of nuclear fire. Over time, gravity wins again. A giant star eventually collapses into a black hole. It doesn't matter whether the star had planets orbiting its periphery or what globs of gas and dust went into making the star in the first place. Gravity is very democratic. Anything can grow up to be a black hole.

Even time ticks faster in the universe of the small. Small animals move faster, metabolize food faster (and eat more); their hearts beat faster; their life spans are short. In his book *About Time,* Paul Davis raises the interesting question: Does the life of a mouse feel shorter to a mouse than our life feels to us?

20   Biologist Stephen Jay Gould has answered this question in the negative. "Small mammals tick fast, burn rapidly, and live for a short time; large mammals live long at a stately pace. Measured by their own internal clocks, mammals of different sizes tend to live for the same amount of time."

We all march to our own metronomes. Yet Davis suggests that all life shares the same beat because all life on Earth relies on chemical reactions—and chemical reactions take place in a sharply limited frame of time. In physicist Robert Forward's science fiction saga *Dragon's Egg,* creatures living on a neutron star are fueled by nuclear reactions; on their world, everything takes place millions of times faster. Many generations could be born and die before a minute passes on Earth.

And think how Earth would seem if we could slow our metabolism down. If our time ticked slowly enough, we could watch mountains grow and continental plates shift and come crashing together. The heavens would be bursting with supernovas, and comets would come smashing onto our shores with the regularity of shooting stars. Every day would be the Fourth of July.

An artist friend likes to imagine that if we could stand back far enough from Earth, but still see people, we would see enormous waves sweeping the globe every morning as people stood up from bed, and another huge wave of toothbrushing as people got ready to bed down for the night—one time zone after another, a tide of toothbrushing waxing and waning, following the shadow of the Sun across the land.

We miss a great deal because we perceive only things on our own scale. Exploring the invisible worlds beneath our skin can be a terrifying experience. I know because I tried it with a flexible microscope attached to a video camera on display at the Exploratorium in San Francisco. The skin on your arm reveals a dizzy landscape of nicks, creases, folds, and dewy transparent hairs the size of redwood trees—all embedded with giant boulders of dirt. Whiskers and eyelashes are disgusting—mascara dripping off like mud on a dog's tail. It is rather overwhelming to look through your own skin at blood cells coursing through capillaries. It's like looking at yourself without clothes. We forget the extent to which our view of the world is airbrushed, that we see things through a shroud of size, a blissfully out-of-focus blur.

25   An even more powerful microscope would reveal all the creatures that live on your face, dangling from tiny hairs or hiding out in your eyelashes. Not to mention the billions that share your bed every night and nest in your dish towels. How many bacteria can stand on the pointy end of a pin? You don't want to know.[2]

We're so hung up on our own scale of life that we miss most of life's diversity, says Berkeley microbiologist Norman Pace. "Who's in the ocean? People think of whales and seals, but 90 percent of organisms in the ocean are less than two micrometers."

In their enchanting journey *Microcosmos,* microbiologist Lynn Margulis and Dorion Sagan point out the fallacy of thinking that large beings are somehow supreme. Billions of years before creatures composed of cells with nuclei (like ourselves) appeared on Earth, simple bacteria transformed the surface of the planet and invented many high-tech processes that humans are still trying to understand—including the transformation

---

2. For an eye-opening view, read *The Secret House,* by David Bodanis.

of sunlight into energy with close to a 100 percent efficiency (green plants do it all the time). Indeed, they point out that fully 10 percent of our body weight (minus the water) consists of bacteria—most of which we couldn't live without.

Zoom in smaller than life-size, and solid tables become airy expanses of space, with an occasional nut of an atomic nucleus lost in the center, surrounded by furious clouds of electrons. As you zoom in, or out, the world looks simple, then complex, then simple again. Earth from far enough away would be a small blue dot; come in closer and you see weather patterns and ocean; closer still and humanity comes into view; closer still and it all fades away, and you're back inside the landscape of matter—mostly empty space.

So complexity, too, changes with scale. Is an egg complex? On the outside, it's a plain enough oval, like Jupiter's giant red spot. On the inside, it's white and yolk and blood vessels and DNA and squawking and pecking order and potential chocolate mousse or crème caramel.

30   The universe of the extremely small is so strange and rich that we can't begin to grasp it. No one said it better than Erwin Schrödinger himself:

> As our mental eye penetrates into smaller and smaller distances and shorter and shorter times, we find nature behaving so entirely differently from what we observe in visible and palpable bodies of our surroundings that no model shaped after our large-scale experiences can ever be "true." A complete satisfactory model of this type is not only practically inaccessible, but not even thinkable. Or, to be precise, we can, of course, think of it, but however we think it, it is wrong; not perhaps quite as meaningless as a "triangular circle," but more so than a "winged lion."

K. C. Cole

After graduating from Columbia University, K. C. Cole was pursuing an interest in Eastern European affairs when she "stumbled upon the Exploratorium" – a hands-on science museum in San Francisco – and soon thereafter began a career as a science and health writer. Cole has commented that her "writing career has changed gear many times." "A Matter of Scale" is one of a series of essays in *The Universe and the Teacup: The Mathematics of Truth and Beauty* (1998). In that book, Cole speaks to the relevance of mathematics to everyday life and on the ways in which math provides insight into social, political, and natural phenomena.

Awarded the American Institute of Physics Award for Best Science Writer in 1995, Cole writes regularly about science for the *Los Angeles Times.* She also teaches at the University of Southern California – Annenberg, contributes regularly to well-known publications such as *The New Yorker, Esquire, Discover,* and *Newsweek,* and provides radio commentary on science issues for KPCC-FM in California.

SEEING

1. "A Matter of Scale" is a masterful exercise in observing and drawing inferences from the natural world. What does Cole find "magically seductive" about observing "a world where everything measures much bigger or smaller than ourselves" (para. 1)? She writes that "We miss a great deal because we perceive only things on our own scale" (para. 24). What did Cole's essay show you that you had missed before? Which new facts will change the way you think? For example, how will knowing that liquid sticks to insects change the way you feel about a fly that becomes stuck in your soup? Which new facts will not change the way you think? Why not?

2. Why do you suppose Cole ends her essay by quoting another author? How would the essay have changed if she had paraphrased Schrödinger instead? What, for example, would be the effect(s) if Cole had ended her essay with the paragraph's first sentence and footnoted Schrödinger? As you develop a response, please review the way Cole weaves different authors into her essay. Where does she summarize, quote, or footnote, and why?

WRITING

1. At four weeks of age, the time when the brain begins to develop, the human body measures about 0.2 inches and weighs 0.001 ounces. Write a short story that traces the way physical forces affected you as you grew. For example, describe what falling was like as a baby, a child, and now. Imagine what having less mass and surface area felt like. How has scaling up in height and weight changed your perspective? What do you see and feel now that you did not before? What experiences are closed to you now at your present scale?

Working with Sources
2. As you reread Cole's essay, choose two of her claims and then conduct the research necessary to prove whether or not they are accurate. For example, will a mouse really survive a 1,000-yard fall? Are there really creatures living in your eyelashes? Before you begin, think carefully about what evidence you will use and from what sources you will gather it. Which types of evidence are more, or less, convincing? Why would proof drawn from an online source, such as Wikipedia, be better or worse than proof drawn from a book, a teacher, a friend, or your imagination?

Pepón Osorio

"My principal commitment as an artist is to return art to the community," says installation and video artist Pepón Osorio. Born in Santurce, Puerto Rico, in 1955, Osorio studied at the Universidad Inter-Americana in Puerto Rico; Lehman College, City University of New York; and Columbia University. From his experience as a social worker and his collaborations with avant-garde performance artist and choreographer Merián Soto, Osorio brings a social and artistic conscience to his art. The range of materials he uses to construct his installations—found objects, video, silkscreen, photography, and sound—are as rich as the experiences he draws on for inspiration.

Osorio created *Son's Bedroom* as one section of an artistic installation entitled *Badge of Honor. Son's Bedroom* is a fabricated rendition of the bedroom of a fifteen-year-old boy named Nelson Jr. The image on the right wall is a video screen that plays a twenty-two-minute tape of the son talking to his father, Nelson Sr.

Osorio's work has been shown in galleries and museums around the United States and Puerto Rico. He was awarded a prestigious MacArthur Fellowship in 1999 and was featured in the PBS series *art:21* in 2001. Osorio currently lives and works in Philadelphia, and his most recent installation, *Trials and Turbulence,* focuses on the American foster care system.

found objects: Ordinary objects, originally not intended as art, that are incorporated into a work of art by the artist.

SEEING

1. Pepón Osorio has fabricated the bedroom of a teenage boy. When you examine this image, what do you see first? Which objects draw your attention? What do you notice about each one? What cultural references does Osorio draw on to create this scene? What reasonable inferences can you make about this teenager's interests? Based on the details in this ordinary scene, what generalizations can you make about Osorio's style?

2. How successful has Osorio been at capturing the look of a teenage boy's bedroom? Point to specific examples to support your answer. Which aspects of Osorio's depiction of the bedroom strike you as based more on fiction or fantasy than on fact? Why? What criteria would you use to help someone understand the differences between fiction and fantasy?

style: The poet Robert Frost defined style as "the way [a person] carries himself [herself] toward his [her] ideas and deeds." In effect, style is the way in which something is said, done, performed, or expressed.

WRITING

1. Imagine yourself standing in the doorway to your bedroom at home or on campus. Compose a verbal picture of what you see as you examine the bedroom. Which aspects of the room would you want to tell others about? Which aspects would you rather not mention? Write the first draft of a descriptive essay in which you convey—in as much detail as possible—what you think someone would see in your bedroom.

2. Consider the differences between the look of your bedroom at home and that of your room on campus. Other than the size of the rooms, what differences do you notice in the ways you organize your space in the two locations? Write a comparison/contrast essay in which you discuss how these differences reflect different styles of presenting yourself at home and on campus.

(previous pages) Pepón Osorio
Badge of Honor, 1995 (detail)

Pepón Osorio
Badge of Honor, 1995

Context is an essential aspect of both understanding and practicing the art of composition—whether what is being composed is an essay, a painting, a photograph, or a film. In its simplest sense, context refers to the circumstances, or the setting, within which an event occurs. Context is also the part of a text or statement that surrounds a particular word, passage, or image and helps determine its meaning. Analyzing the relationship between a text and its context—or the relationship of a part to the whole—is an effective way to appreciate and master the complexity and effectiveness of seeing clearly and writing well.

We presented the teenager's bedroom on pages 92–93 outside its original context; this image is one-half of a large work titled *Badge of Honor,* created by installation artist Pepón Osorio. The full work, shown in the photograph above, consists of the teenager's crowded bedroom and the place his father sleeps, a stark prison cell. In each of these two fabricated rooms is a video screen. The father's image appears on the screen in the cell; the son's, on the screen in the bedroom. If you were standing in front of *Badge of Honor,* you would be able to hear father and son engaged in a twenty-two-minute conversation through the wall that separates their rooms.

Does seeing the entire work change your response to *Badge of Honor*? How? Describe the visual differences between the two rooms. How does the context of each room determine what you expect to find present in—and absent from—each room? To what do you think the title of the piece refers?

Go to *www.seeingandwriting.com* for an online interview with Pepón Osorio as well as a review of the installation by Joseph Jacobs.

SEEING
Annie Dillard

When I was six or seven years old, growing up in Pittsburgh, I used to take a precious penny of my own and hide it for someone else to find. It was a curious compulsion; sadly, I've never been seized by it since. For some reason I always "hid" the penny along the same stretch of sidewalk up the street. I would cradle it at the roots of a sycamore, say, or in a hole left by a chipped-off piece of sidewalk. Then I would take a piece of chalk, and, starting at either end of the block, draw huge arrows leading up to the penny from both directions. After I learned to write I labeled the arrows: SURPRISE AHEAD or MONEY THIS WAY. I was greatly excited, during all this arrow-drawing, at the thought of the first lucky passer-by who would receive in this way, regardless of merit, a free gift from the universe. But I never lurked about. I would go straight home and not give the matter another thought, until, some months later, I would be gripped again by the impulse to hide another penny.

It is still the first week in January, and I've got great plans. I've been thinking about seeing. There are lots of things to see, unwrapped gifts and free surprises. The world is fairly studded and strewn with pennies cast broadside from a generous hand. But—and this is the point—who gets excited by a mere penny? If you follow one arrow, if you crouch motionless on a bank to watch a tremulous ripple thrill on the water and are rewarded by the sight of a muskrat kit paddling from its den, will you count that sight a chip of copper only, and go your rueful way? It is dire poverty indeed when a man is so malnourished and fatigued that he won't stoop to pick up a penny. But if you cultivate a healthy poverty and simplicity, so that finding a penny will literally make your day, then, since the world is in fact planted in pennies, you have with your poverty bought a lifetime of days. It is that simple. What you see is what you get.

I used to be able to see flying insects in the air. I'd look ahead and see, not the row of hemlocks across the road, but the air in front of it. My eyes would focus along that column of air, picking out flying insects. But I lost interest, I guess, for I dropped the habit. Now I can see birds. Probably some people can look at the grass at their feet and discover all the crawling creatures. I would like to know grasses and sedges—and care. Then my least journey into the world would be a field trip, a series of happy recognitions. Thoreau, in an expansive mood, exulted, "What a rich book might be made about buds, including, perhaps, sprouts!" It would be nice to think so. I cherish mental images I have of three per-fectly happy people. One collects stones. Another—an Englishman, say—watches clouds. The third lives on a coast and collects drops of seawater which he examines microscopically and mounts. But I don't see what the specialist sees, and so I cut myself off, not only from the total picture, but from the various forms of happiness.

Unfortunately, nature is very much a now-you-see-it, now-you-don't affair. A fish flashes, then dissolves in the water before my eyes like so much salt. Deer apparently ascend bodily into heaven; the brightest oriole fades into leaves. These disappearances stun me into stillness and con-centration; they say of nature that it conceals with a grand nonchalance, and they say of vision that it is a deliberate gift, the revelation of a dancer who for my eyes only flings away her seven veils. For nature does reveal as well as conceal: now-you-don't-see-it, now-you-do. For a week last September migrating red-winged blackbirds were feeding heavily down by the creek at the back of the house. One day I went out to investigate the racket; I walked up to a tree, an Osage orange, and a hundred birds flew away. They simply materialized out of the tree. I saw a tree, then a whisk of color, then a tree again. I walked closer and another hundred blackbirds took flight. Not a branch, not a twig budged: The birds were apparently weightless as well as invisible. Or, it was as if the leaves of the Osage orange had been freed from a spell in the form of red-winged blackbirds; they flew from the tree, caught my eye in the sky, and van-ished. When I looked again at the tree the leaves had reassembled as if nothing had happened. Finally I walked directly to the trunk of the tree and a final hundred, the real diehards, appeared, spread, and vanished. How could so many hide in the tree without my seeing them? The Osage orange, unruffled, looked just as it had looked from the house, when three hundred red-winged blackbirds cried from its crown. I looked down-stream where they flew, and they were gone. Searching, I couldn't spot one. I wandered downstream to force them to play their hand, but they'd crossed the creek and scattered. One show to a customer. These appear-ances catch at my throat; they are the free gifts, the bright coppers at the roots of trees.

5   It's all a matter of keeping my eyes open. Nature is like one of those line drawings of a tree that are puzzles for children: Can you find hid-den in the leaves a duck, a house, a boy, a bucket, a zebra, and a boot? Specialists can find the most incredibly well-hidden things. A book I read when I was young recommended an easy way to find caterpillars to rear: You simply find some fresh caterpillar droppings, look up, and there's your caterpillar. More recently an author advised me to set my mind at

ease about those piles of cut stems on the ground in grassy fields. Field mice make them; they cut the grass down by degrees to reach the seeds at the head. It seems that when the grass is tightly packed, as in a field of ripe grain, the blade won't topple at a single cut through the stem; instead, the cut stem simply drops vertically, held in the crush of grain. The mouse severs the bottom again and again, the stem keeps dropping an inch at a time, and finally the head is low enough for the mouse to reach the seeds. Meanwhile, the mouse is positively littering the field with its little piles of cut stems into which, presumably, the author of the book is constantly stumbling.

If I can't see these minutiae, I still try to keep my eyes open. I'm always on the lookout for antlion traps in sandy soil, monarch pupae near milkweed, skipper larvae in locust leaves. These things are utterly common, and I've not seen one. I bang on hollow trees near water, but so far no flying squirrels have appeared. In flat country I watch every sunset in hopes of seeing the green ray. The green ray is a seldom-seen streak of light that rises from the sun like a spurting fountain at the moment of sunset; it throbs into the sky for two seconds and disappears. One more reason to keep my eyes open. A photography professor at the University of Florida just happened to see a bird die in midflight; it jerked, died, dropped, and smashed on the ground. I squint at the wind because I read Stewart Edward White: "I have always maintained that if you looked closely enough you could see the wind—the dim, hardly-made-out, fine débris fleeing high in the air." White was an excellent observer, and devoted an entire chapter of *The Mountains* to the subject of seeing deer: "As soon as you can forget the naturally obvious and construct an artificial obvious, then you too will see deer."

But the artificial obvious is hard to see. My eyes account for less than one percent of the weight of my head; I'm bony and dense; I see what I expect. I once spent a full three minutes looking at a bullfrog that was so unexpectedly large I couldn't see it even though a dozen enthusiastic campers were shouting directions. Finally I asked, "What color am I looking for?" and a fellow said, "Green." When at last I picked out the frog, I saw what painters are up against: The thing wasn't green at all, but the color of wet hickory bark.

The lover can see, and the knowledgeable. I visited an aunt and uncle at a quarter-horse ranch in Cody, Wyoming. I couldn't do much of anything useful, but I could, I thought, draw. So, as we all sat around the kitchen table after supper, I produced a sheet of paper and drew a horse. "That's one lame horse," my aunt volunteered. The rest of the family joined in: "Only place to saddle that one is his neck"; "Looks like we better shoot the poor thing, on account of those terrible growths." Meekly, I slid the pencil and paper down the table. Everyone in that family, including my three young cousins, could draw a horse. Beautifully. When the paper came back it looked as though five shining, real quarter horses had been corraled by mistake with a papier-mâché moose; the real horses seemed to gaze at the monster with a steady, puzzled air. I stay away from horses now, but I can do a creditable goldfish. The point is that I just don't know what the lover knows; I just can't see the artificial obvious that those in the know construct. The herpetologist asks the native, "Are there snakes in that ravine?" "Nosir." And the herpetologist comes home with, yessir, three bags full. Are there butterflies on that mountain? Are the bluets in bloom, are there arrowheads here, or fossil shells in the shale?

Peeping through my keyhole I see within the range of only about thirty percent of the light that comes from the sun; the rest is infrared and some little ultraviolet, perfectly apparent to many animals, but invisible to me. A nightmare network of ganglia, charged and firing without my knowledge, cuts and splices what I do see, editing it for my brain. Donald E. Carr points out that the sense impressions of one-celled animals are *not* edited for the brain: "This is philosophically interesting in a rather mournful way, since it means that only the simplest animals perceive the universe as it is."

10   A fog that won't burn away drifts and flows across my field of vision. When you see fog move against a backdrop of deep pines, you don't see the fog itself, but streaks of clearness floating across the air in dark shreds. So I see only tatters of clearness through a pervading obscurity. I can't distinguish the fog from the overcast sky; I can't be sure if the light is direct or reflected. Everywhere darkness and the presence of the unseen appall. We estimate now that only one atom dances alone in every cubic meter of intergalactic space. I blink and squint. What planet or power yanks Halley's Comet out of orbit? We haven't seen that force yet; it's a question of distance, density, and the pallor of reflected light. We rock, cradled in the swaddling band of darkness. Even the simple darkness of night whispers suggestions to the mind. Last summer, in August, I stayed at the creek too late.

Where Tinker Creek flows under the sycamore log bridge to the tear-shaped island, it is slow and shallow, fringed thinly in cattail marsh. At this spot an astonishing bloom of life supports vast breeding populations of insects, fish, reptiles, birds, and mammals. On windless summer evenings I stalk along the creek bank or straddle the sycamore log in absolute stillness, watching for muskrats. The night I stayed too late I was hunched on the log staring spellbound at spreading, reflected stains of lilac on the water. A cloud in the sky suddenly lighted as if turned on by a switch; its reflection just as suddenly materialized on the water upstream, flat and floating, so that I couldn't see the creek bottom, or life in the water under the cloud. Downstream, away from the cloud on the water, water turtles smooth as beans were gliding down with the current in a series of easy, weightless push-offs, as men bound on the moon. I didn't know whether to trace the progress of one turtle I was sure of, risking sticking my face in one of the bridge's spider webs made invisible by the gathering dark, or take a chance on seeing the carp, or scan the mudbank in hope of seeing a muskrat, or follow the last of the swallows who caught at my heart and trailed it after them like streamers as they appeared from directly below, under the log, flying upstream with their tails forked, so fast.

But shadows spread, and deepened, and stayed. After thousands of years we're still strangers to darkness, fearful aliens in an enemy camp with our arms crossed over our chests. I stirred. A land turtle on the bank, startled, hissed the air from its lungs and withdrew into its shell. An uneasy pink here, an unfathomable blue there, gave great suggestion of lurking beings. Things were going on. I couldn't see whether that sere rustle I heard was a distant rattlesnake, slit-eyed, or a nearby sparrow kicking in the dry flood debris slung at the foot of a willow. Tremendous action roiled the water everywhere I looked, big action, inexplicable. A tremor welled up beside a gaping muskrat burrow in the bank and I caught my breath, but no muskrat appeared. The ripples continued to fan upstream with a steady, powerful thrust. Night was knitting over my face an eyeless mask, and I still sat transfixed. A distant airplane, a delta wing out of nightmare, made a gliding shadow on the creek's bottom that looked like a stingray cruising upstream. At once a black fin slit the pink cloud on the water, shearing it in two. The two halves merged together and seemed to dissolve before my eyes. Darkness pooled in the cleft of the creek and rose, as water collects in a well. Untamed, dreaming lights flickered over the sky. I saw hints of hulking underwater shadows, two pale splashes out of the water, and round ripples rolling close together from a blackened center.

At last I stared upstream where only the deepest violet remained of the cloud, a cloud so high its underbelly still glowed feeble color reflected from a hidden sky lighted in turn by a sun halfway to China. And out of that violet, a sudden enormous black body arced over the water. I saw only a cylindrical sleekness. Head and tail, if there was a head and tail, were both submerged in cloud. I saw only one ebony fling, a headlong dive to darkness; then the waters closed, and the lights went out.

I walked home in a shivering daze, up hill and down. Later I lay open-mouthed in bed, my arms flung wide at my sides to steady the whirling darkness. At this latitude I'm spinning 836 miles an hour round the earth's axis; I often fancy I feel my sweeping fall as a break-neck arc like the dive of dolphins, and the hollow rushing of wind raises hair on my neck and the side of my face. In orbit around the sun I'm moving 64,800 miles an hour. The solar system as a whole, like a merry-go-round un-hinged, spins, bobs, and blinks at the speed of 43,200 miles an hour along a course set east of Hercules. Someone has piped, and we are dancing a tarantella until the sweat pours. I open my eyes and I see dark, muscled forms curl out of water, with flapping gills and flattened eyes. I close my eyes and I see stars, deep stars giving way to deeper stars, deeper stars bowing to deepest stars at the crown of an infinite cone.

15   "Still," wrote van Gogh in a letter, "a great deal of light falls on every-thing." If we are blinded by darkness, we are also blinded by light. When too much light falls on everything, a special terror results. Peter Freuchen describes the notorious kayak sickness to which Greenland Eskimos are prone. "The Greenland fjords are peculiar for the spells of completely quiet weather, when there is not enough wind to blow out a match and the water is like a sheet of glass. The kayak hunter must sit in his boat without stirring a finger so as not to scare the shy seals away. . . . The sun, low in the sky, sends a glare into his eyes, and the landscape around moves into the realm of the unreal. The reflex from the mirror-like water hypnotizes him, he seems to be unable to move, and all of a sudden it is as if he were floating in a bottomless void, sinking, sinking, and sinking. . . . Horror-stricken, he tries to stir, to cry out, but he can-not, he is completely paralyzed, he just falls and falls." Some hunters are especially cursed with this panic, and bring ruin and sometimes starvation to their families.

Sometimes here in Virginia at sunset low clouds on the southern or northern horizon are completely invisible in the lighted sky. I only know one is there because I can see its reflection in still water. The first time I discovered this mystery I looked from cloud to no-cloud in bewilder-ment, checking my bearings over and over, thinking maybe the ark of the covenant was just passing by south of Dead Man Mountain. Only much later did I read the explanation: Polarized light from the sky is very much weakened by reflection, but the light in clouds isn't polarized. So invisible clouds pass among visible clouds, till all slide over the moun-tains; so a greater light extinguishes a lesser as though it didn't exist.

In the great meteor shower of August, the Perseid, I wail all day for the shooting stars I miss. They're out there showering down, committing hara-kiri in a flame of fatal attraction, and hissing perhaps at last into the ocean. But at dawn what looks like a blue dome clamps down over me like a lid on a pot. The stars and planets could smash and I'd never know. Only a piece of ashen moon occasionally climbs up or down the inside of the dome, and our local star without surcease explodes on our heads. We have really only that one light, one source for all power, and yet we must turn away from it by universal decree. Nobody here on the planet seems aware of this strange, powerful taboo, that we all walk about carefully averting our faces, this way and that, lest our eyes be blasted forever.

Darkness appalls and light dazzles; the scrap of visible light that doesn't hurt my eyes hurts my brain. What I see sets me swaying. Size and distance and the sudden swelling of meanings confuse me, bowl me over. I straddle the sycamore log bridge over Tinker Creek in the summer. I look at the lighted creek bottom: Snail tracks tunnel the mud in quavering curves. A crayfish jerks, but by the time I absorb what has happened, he's gone in a billowing smokescreen of silt. I look at the water: minnows and shiners. If I'm thinking minnows, a carp will fill my brain till I scream. I look at the water's surface: skaters, bubbles, and leaves sliding down. Suddenly, my own face, reflected, startles me witless. Those snails have been tracking my face! Finally, with a shuddering wrench of the will, I see clouds, cirrus clouds. I'm dizzy, I fall in. This looking business is risky.

Once I stood on a humped rock on nearby Purgatory Mountain, watching through binoculars the great autumn hawk migration below, until I discovered that I was in danger of joining the hawks on a vertical migration of my own. I was used to binoculars, but not, apparently, to balancing on humped rocks while looking through them. I staggered. Everything advanced and receded by turns; the world was full of unexplained foreshortenings and depths. A distant huge tan object, a hawk the size of an elephant, turned out to be the browned bough of a nearby loblolly pine. I followed a sharp-shinned hawk against a featureless sky, rotating my head unawares as it flew, and when I lowered the glass a glimpse of my own looming shoulder sent me staggering. What prevents the men on Palomar from falling, voiceless and blinded, from their tiny, vaulted chairs?

20   I reel in confusion; I don't understand what I see. With the naked eye I can see two million light-years to the Andromeda galaxy. Often I slop some creek water in a jar and when I get home I dump it in a white china bowl. After the silt settles I return and see tracings of minute snails on

the bottom, a planarian or two winding round the rim of water, round-worms shimmying frantically, and finally, when my eyes have adjusted to these dimensions, amoebae. At first the amoebae look like muscae volitantes, those curled moving spots you seem to see in your eyes when you stare at a distant wall. Then I see the amoebae as drops of water congealed, bluish, translucent, like chips of sky in the bowl. At length I choose one individual and give myself over to its idea of an evening. I see it dribble a grainy foot before it on its wet, unfathomable way. Do its unedited sense impressions include the fierce focus of my eyes? Shall I take it outside and show it Andromeda, and blow its little endoplasm? I stir the water with a finger, in case it's running out of oxygen. Maybe I should get a tropical aquarium with motorized bubblers and lights, and keep this one for a pet. Yes, it would tell its fissioned descendants, the universe is two feet by five, and if you listen closely you can hear the buzzing music of the spheres.

Oh, it's mysterious lamplit evenings, here in the galaxy, one after the other. It's one of those nights when I wander from window to window, looking for a sign. But I can't see. Terror and a beauty insoluble are a ribband of blue woven into the fringes of garments of things both great and small. No culture explains, no bivouac offers real haven or rest. But it could be that we are not seeing something. Galileo thought comets were an optical illusion. This is fertile ground: Since we are certain that they're not, we can look at what our scientists have been saying with fresh hope. What if there are *really* gleaming, castellated cities hung upside-down over the desert sand? What limpid lakes and cool date palms have our caravans always passed untried? Until, one by one, by the blindest of leaps, we light on the road to these places, we must stumble in darkness and hunger. I turn from the window. I'm blind as a bat, sensing only from every direction the echo of my own thin cries.

I chanced on a wonderful book by Marius von Senden, called *Space and Light.* When Western surgeons discovered how to perform safe cataract operations, they ranged across Europe and America operating on dozens of men and women of all ages who had been blinded by cataracts since birth. Von Senden collected accounts of such cases; the histories are fascinating. Many doctors had tested their patients' sense perceptions and ideas of space both before and after the operations. The vast majority of patients, of both sexes and all ages, had, in von Senden's opinion, no idea of space whatsoever. Form, distance, and size were so many meaningless syllables. A patient "had no idea of depth, confusing it with roundness." Before the operation a doctor would give a blind patient a cube and a sphere; the patient would tongue it or feel it with his hands, and name it correctly. After the operation the doctor would show the same objects to the patient without letting him touch them; now he had no clue whatsoever what he was seeing. One patient called lemonade "square" because it pricked on his tongue as a square shape pricked on the touch of his hands. Of another postoperative patient, the doctor writes, "I have found in her no notion of size, for example, not even within the narrow limits which she might have encompassed with the aid of touch. Thus when I asked her to show me how big her mother was, she did not stretch out her hands, but set her two index-fingers a few inches apart." Other doctors reported their patients' own statements to similar effect. "The room he was in . . . he knew to be but part of the house, yet he could not conceive that the whole house could look bigger"; "Those who are blind from birth . . . have no real conception of height or distance. A house that is a mile away is thought of as nearby, but requiring the taking of a lot of steps. . . . The elevator that whizzes him up and down gives no more sense of vertical distance than does the train of horizontal."

For the newly sighted, vision is pure sensation unencumbered by meaning: "The girl went through the experience that we all go through and forget, the moment we are born. She saw, but it did not mean anything but a lot of different kinds of brightness." Again, "I asked the patient what he could see; he answered that he saw an extensive field of light, in which everything appeared dull, confused, and in motion. He could not distinguish objects." Another patient saw "nothing but a confusion of forms and colours." When a newly sighted girl saw photographs and paintings, she asked, "'Why do they put those dark marks all over them?' 'Those aren't dark marks,' her mother explained, 'those are shadows. That is one of the ways the eye knows that things have shape. If it were not for shadows many things would look flat.' 'Well, that's how things do look,' Joan answered. 'Everything looks flat with dark patches.'"

But it is the patients' concepts of space that are most revealing. One patient, according to his doctor, "practiced his vision in a strange fashion; thus he takes off one of his boots, throws it some way off in front of him, and then attempts to gauge the distance at which it lies; he takes a few steps toward the boot and tries to grasp it; on failing to reach it, he moves on a step or two and gropes for the boot until he finally gets hold of it." "But even at this stage, after three weeks' experience of seeing," von Senden goes on, "'space,' as he conceives it, ends with visual space, i.e., with color-patches that happen to bound his view. He does not yet have the notion that a larger object (a chair) can mask a smaller one (a dog), or that the latter can still be present even though it is not directly seen."

25   In general the newly sighted see the world as a dazzle of color-patches. They are pleased by the sensation of color, and learn quickly to name the colors, but the rest of seeing is tormentingly difficult. Soon after his operation a patient "generally bumps into one of these color-patches and observes them to be substantial, since they resist him as tactual objects do. In walking about it also strikes him—or can if he pays attention—that he is continually passing in between the colors he sees, that he can go past a visual object, that a part of it then steadily disappears from view; and that in spite of this, however he twists and turns—whether entering the room from the door, for example, or returning back to it—he always has a visual space in front of him. Thus he gradually comes to realize that there is also a space behind him, which he does not see."

The mental effort involved in these reasonings proves overwhelming for many patients. It oppresses them to realize, if they ever do at all, the tremendous size of the world, which they had previously conceived of as something touchingly manageable. It oppresses them to realize that they have been visible to people all along, perhaps unattractively so, without their knowledge or consent. A disheartening number of them refuse to use their new vision, continuing to go over objects with their tongues, and lapsing into apathy and despair. "The child can see, but will not make use of his sight. Only when pressed can he with difficulty be brought to look at objects in his neighborhood; but more than a foot away it is impossible to bestir him to the necessary effort." Of a twenty-one-year-old girl, the doctor relates, "Her unfortunate father, who had hoped for so much from this operation, wrote that his daughter carefully shuts her eyes whenever she wishes to go about the house, especially when she comes to a staircase, and that she is never happier or more at ease than when, by closing her eyelids, she relapses into her former state of total blindness." A fifteen-year-old boy, who was also in love with a girl at the asylum for the blind, finally blurted out, "No, really, I can't stand it any more; I want to be sent back to the asylum again. If things aren't altered, I'll tear my eyes out."

Some do learn to see, especially the young ones. But it changes their lives. One doctor comments on "the rapid and complete loss of that striking and wonderful serenity which is characteristic only of those who have never yet seen." A blind man who learns to see is ashamed of his old habits. He dresses up, grooms himself, and tries to make a good impression. While he was blind he was indifferent to objects unless they were edible; now, "a sifting of values sets in . . . his thoughts and wishes are mightily stirred and some few of the patients are thereby led into dissimulation, envy, theft and fraud."

On the other hand, many newly sighted people speak well of the world, and teach us how dull is our own vision. To one patient, a human hand, unrecognized, is "something bright and then holes." Shown a bunch of grapes, a boy calls out, "It is dark, blue and shiny. . . . It isn't smooth, it has bumps and hollows." A little girl visits a garden. "She is greatly astonished, and can scarcely be persuaded to answer, stands speechless in front of the tree, which she only names on taking hold of it, and then as 'the tree with the lights in it.'" Some delight in their sight and give themselves over to the visual world. Of a patient just after her bandages were removed, her doctor writes, "The first things to attract her attention were her own hands; she looked at them very closely, moved them repeatedly to and fro, bent and stretched the fingers, and seemed greatly astonished at the sight." One girl was eager to tell her blind friend that "men do not really look like trees at all," and astounded to discover that her every visitor had an utterly different face. Finally, a twenty-two-year-old girl was dazzled by the world's brightness and kept her eyes shut for two weeks. When at the end of that time she opened her eyes again, she did not recognize any objects, but, "the more she now directed her gaze upon everything about her, the more it could be seen how an expression of gratification and astonishment overspread her features; she repeatedly exclaimed: 'Oh God! How beautiful!'"

I saw color-patches for weeks after I read this wonderful book. It was summer; the peaches were ripe in the valley orchards. When I woke in the morning, color-patches wrapped round my eyes, intricately, leaving not one unfilled spot. All day long I walked among shifting color-patches that parted before me like the Red Sea and closed again in silence, transfigured, wherever I looked back. Some patches swelled and loomed, while others vanished utterly, and dark marks flitted at random over the whole dazzling sweep. But I couldn't sustain the illusion of flatness. I've been around for too long. Form is condemned to an eternal danse macabre with meaning: I couldn't unpeach the peaches. Nor can I remember ever having seen without understanding; the color-patches of infancy are lost. My brain then must have been smooth as any balloon. I'm told I reached for the moon; many babies do. But the color-patches of infancy swelled as meaning filled them; they arrayed themselves in solemn ranks down distance which unrolled and stretched before me like a plain. The moon rocketed away. I live now in a world of shadows that shape and distance color, a world where space makes a kind of terrible sense. What gnosticism is this, and what physics? The fluttering patch I saw in my nursery window—silver and green and shape-shifting blue—is gone; a row of Lombardy poplars takes its place, mute, across the distant lawn. That humming oblong creature pale as light that stole along the walls of my room at night, stretching exhilaratingly around the corners, is gone, too, gone the night I ate of the bittersweet fruit, put two and two together and puckered forever my brain. Martin Buber tells this tale: "Rabbi Mendel once boasted to his teacher Rabbi Elimelekh that evenings he saw the angel who rolls away the light before the darkness, and mornings the angel who rolls away the darkness before the light. 'Yes,' said Rabbi Elimelekh, 'in my youth I saw that too. Later on you don't see these things any more.'"

30   Why didn't someone hand those newly sighted people paints and brushes from the start, when they still didn't know what anything was? Then maybe we all could see color-patches too, the world unraveled from reason, Eden before Adam gave names. The scales would drop from my eyes; I'd see trees like men walking; I'd run down the road against all orders, hallooing and leaping.

Seeing is of course very much a matter of verbalization. Unless I call my attention to what passes before my eyes, I simply won't see it. It is, as Ruskin says, "not merely unnoticed, but in the full, clear sense of the word, unseen." My eyes alone can't solve analogy tests using figures, the ones which show, with increasing elaborations, a big square, then a small square in a big square, then a big triangle, and expect me to find a small triangle in a big triangle. I have to say the words, describe what I'm seeing. If Tinker Mountain erupted, I'd be likely to notice. But if I want to notice the lesser cataclysms of valley life, I have to maintain in my head a running description of the present. It's not that I'm observant; it's just that I talk too much. Otherwise, especially in a strange place, I'll never know what's happening. Like a blind man at the ball game, I need a radio.

When I see this way I analyze and pry. I hurl over logs and roll away stones; I study the bank a square foot at a time, probing and tilting my head. Some days when a mist covers the mountains, when the muskrats won't show and the microscope's mirror shatters, I want to climb up the blank blue dome as a man would storm the inside of a circus tent, wildly, dangling, and with a steel knife claw a rent in the top, peep, and, if I must, fall.

But there is another kind of seeing that involves a letting go. When I see this way I sway transfixed and emptied. The difference between the two ways of seeing is the difference between walking with and without a camera. When I walk with a camera I walk from shot to shot, reading the light on a calibrated meter. When I walk without a camera, my own shutter opens, and the moment's light prints on my own silver gut. When I see this second way I am above all an unscrupulous observer.

It was sunny one evening last summer at Tinker Creek; the sun was low in the sky, upstream. I was sitting on the sycamore log bridge with the sunset at my back, watching the shiners the size of minnows who were feeding over the muddy sand in skittery schools. Again and again, one fish, then another, turned for a split second across the current and flash! the sun shot out from its silver side. I couldn't watch for it. It was always just happening somewhere else, and it drew my vision just as it disappeared: flash, like a sudden dazzle of the thinnest blade, a sparking over a dun and olive ground at chance intervals from every direction. Then I noticed white specks, some sort of pale petals, small, floating from under my feet on the creek's surface, very slow and steady. So I blurred my eyes and gazed toward the brim of my hat and saw a new world. I saw the pale white circles roll up, roll up, like the world's turning, mute and perfect, and I saw the linear flashes, gleaming silver, like stars being born at random down a rolling scroll of time. Something broke and something opened. I filled up like a new wineskin. I breathed an air like light; I saw a light like water. I was the lip of a fountain the creek filled forever; I was ether, the leaf in the zephyr; I was flesh-flake, feather, bone.

35   When I see this way I see truly. As Thoreau says, I return to my senses. I am the man who watches the baseball game in silence in an empty stadium. I see the game purely; I'm abstracted and dazed. When it's all over and the white-suited players lope off the green field to their shadowed dugouts, I leap to my feet; I cheer and cheer.

But I can't go out and try to see this way. I'll fail, I'll go mad. All I can do is try to gag the commentator, to hush the noise of useless interior babble that keeps me from seeing just as surely as a newspaper dangled before my eyes. The effort is really a discipline requiring a lifetime of dedicated struggle; it marks the literature of saints and monks of every order East and West, under every rule and no rule, discalced and shod. The world's spiritual geniuses seem to discover universally that the mind's muddy river, this ceaseless flow of trivia and trash, cannot be dammed, and that trying to dam it is a waste of effort that might lead to madness. Instead you must allow the muddy river to flow unheeded in the dim channels of consciousness; you raise your sights; you look along it, mildly, acknowledging its presence without interest and gazing beyond it into the realm of the real where subjects and objects act and rest purely, without utterance. "Launch into the deep," says Jacques Ellul, "and you shall see."

The secret of seeing is, then, the pearl of great price. If I thought he could teach me to find it and keep it forever I would stagger barefoot across a hundred deserts after any lunatic at all. But although the pearl may be found, it may not be sought. The literature of illumination reveals this above all: Although it comes to those who wait for it, it is always, even to the most practiced and adept, a gift and a total surprise. I return from one walk knowing where the killdeer nests in the field by the creek and the hour the laurel blooms. I return from the same walk a day later scarcely knowing my own name. Litanies hum in my ears; my tongue flaps in my mouth Ailinon, alleluia! I cannot cause light; the most I can do is try to put myself in the path of its beam. It is possible, in deep space, to sail on solar wind. Light, be it particle or wave, has force: You rig a giant sail and go. The secret of seeing is to sail on solar wind. Hone and spread your spirit till you yourself are a sail, whetted, translucent, broadside to the merest puff.

When her doctor took her bandages off and led her into the garden, the girl who was no longer blind saw "the tree with the lights in it." It was for this tree I searched through the peach orchards of summer, in the forests of fall and down winter and spring for years. Then one day I was walking along Tinker Creek thinking of nothing at all and I saw the tree with the lights in it. I saw the backyard cedar where the mourning doves roost charged and transfigured, each cell buzzing with flame. I stood on the grass with the lights in it, grass that was wholly fire, utterly focused and utterly dreamed. It was less like seeing than like being for the first time seen, knocked breathless by a powerful glance. The flood of fire abated, but I'm still spending the power. Gradually the lights went out in the cedar, the colors died, the cells unflamed and disappeared. I was still ringing. I had been my whole life a bell, and never knew it until at that moment I was lifted and struck. I have since only very rarely seen the tree with the lights in it. The vision comes and goes, mostly goes, but I live for it, for the moment when the mountains open and a new light roars in spate through the crack, and the mountains slam.

Annie Dillard

Born Annie Doak in Pittsburgh in 1945, Annie Dillard changed her name when she married her writing instructor, Richard Dillard. She attended Hollins College, where she studied English, theology, and creative writing and earned a master's degree with her thesis on Henry David Thoreau.

Before publishing her first book of prose, *Pilgrim at Tinker Creek* (1974), Dillard spent four seasons living near Tinker Creek in the Blue Ridge Mountains of Virginia and filled more than twenty volumes of journals with notes about her experiences and thoughts on the violence and beauty of nature, often in religious terms. Fearing that a work of theology written by a woman would not be successful, she was reluctant to publish the book. But she did, and it won the Pulitzer Prize in 1975.

In the intervening years Dillard has published poetry, fiction, essays, memoirs, literary criticism, and autobiography, returning repeatedly to themes of the mysteries of nature, the quest for meaning, and religious faith. *The Annie Dillard Reader,* a collection of her writing, was published in 1994. Her long-awaited latest work, *The Maytrees,* was published in 2007.

"Seeing" is taken from *Pilgrim at Tinker Creek.* It speaks to Dillard's concern that a writer be "careful of what he reads, for that is what he will write . . . careful of what he learns, because that is what he will know."

SEEING

1. Near the end of her essay Annie Dillard observes, "Seeing is of course very much a matter of verbalization" (para. 31). Reread "Seeing," and make a list of every idiom the author uses to talk about seeing "truly." Consider, for example, the last line of paragraph 2: "What you see is what you get." Identify other idiomatic expressions, and explain how Dillard plays with the literal and figurative dimensions of each. What does she mean when she says, "This looking business is risky" (para. 18)? One of the strongest elements of Dillard's style is her use of metaphor. Identify two or three especially striking examples of metaphor in the essay, and explain the effects of each.

2. Near the end of paragraph 6, Dillard quotes the naturalist Stewart Edward White on seeing

deer: "As soon as you can forget the naturally obvious and construct an artificial obvious, then you too will see deer." Dillard immediately observes, "But the artificial obvious is hard to see" (para. 7). What does "the artificial obvious" mean here? How do people construct it? Why is it "hard to see"? Later, Dillard describes another kind of seeing, "a letting go" (para. 33). What does she mean when she says, "When I see this second way I am above all an unscrupulous observer" (para. 33)?

WRITING

1. Many of us at one time or another have succumbed to the impulse to hide something and then either to lead people to it or to make it as difficult as possible for others to locate. Recall one such impulse that you had, and develop detailed notes about not only the circumstances but also the consequences of your yielding to the impulse. Draft an essay in which you recount this story and then use it as a harbinger of other, more important events or behaviors in your life.

2. Reread Larry Woiwode's "Ode to an Orange" (p. 48). What do you think he would say about the nature of seeing? Using Woiwode's piece or another work in this chapter, write an essay in which you compare the author's philosophy about seeing with Dillard's — and argue that one is more compelling than the other.

Page 48

LOOKING CLOSER — Unpacking Our Stuff

We are surrounded by a dizzying amount of stuff. The array of ordinary objects that are a part of our lives – from lucky charms and keepsakes to cell phones and cars – speaks volumes about our needs, habits, and values. Yet the personal and collective stories behind our stuff are rarely articulated. What, in fact, does our stuff say about us?

Each of the texts and images on the following pages invites us to examine the personal and collective stories of our stuff. The excerpt from Pablo Neruda's "Ode to Things" and Siri Hustvedt's "Unknown Keys" shed light on the ways in which we imbue the objects around us with meaning. Akiko Busch's introduction to *The Uncommon Life of Common Objects* explores the question "What gives ordinary objects their value?" *GOOD* magazine's *This is Daphne and those are her things* provides a snapshot of one American's stuff. And Annie Leonard unpacks the implications of the production and consumption processes behind our ever-increasing amount of material possessions.

Each of us might relate to an ordinary object – a toothbrush, a coffee cup, a pencil – in different ways, yet such ordinary objects in American culture are likely to share at least some attributes of public significance. We all invest ordinary objects with private and public meanings.

From
ODE TO THINGS
Pablo Neruda

many things conspired
to tell me the whole story.
Not only did they touch me,
or my hand touched them:
5 they were
so close
that they were a part
of my being,
they were so alive with me
10 that they lived half my life
and will die half my death.

UNKNOWN KEYS
Siri Hustvedt

My father was a supremely organized man. After he died, my three sisters and I read through countless letters, papers, and documents he had filed, according to one lucidly explicated category or another, and then decided what to keep and what to discard. One day while I was working in the room alone, I came across a small green box. In it was a metal ring with seven keys of various sizes. Attached to the ring was a small chain with a label, on which my father had written in his unmistakable hand: "Unknown Keys." I now work with these unknown keys near me. They have become not only a reminder of my father—the man who is no longer there—but a sign of the act of writing itself. These keys to phantom doors, suitcases, safes, and diaries are linked in my mind to making stories. Now orphaned, they serve only as literal doubles of the imaginary keys that unlock nameless interiors: the peculiar dream spaces of fiction.

Introduction to

THE UNCOMMON LIFE OF
COMMON OBJECTS
Akiko Busch

Like most children, my sons went through a period when they were enchanted by magic tricks, and they prized their collection of two-headed nickels, knotted scarves, metal hoops that seemed to connect and disconnect at will, and assorted other props of deception. But among their favorites was a small, flat wooden box with the picture of a house on it. The box had a small slot, which contained a drawer with a thin disc, just big enough to hold a quarter, carved in its surface. Depending upon how the box was held and its drawer maneuvered, the quarter could appear, or disappear, giving the box its value or, in turn, taking it away. And for months, practicing this trick was a cherished exercise. Sometimes the little box had value, sometimes it had none, and its worth seemed to come and go, by pure chance. To the viewer, the selection appeared random and impossible to predict, but to the child, the logic of the trick, though secret, was clear, explicable, precise.

I couldn't help but think of this little wooden box with its two drawers as my boys grew older and started to prize their *things*—first action figures and basketball cards, then later their snowboards, backpacks, cameras. And the questions kept coming up: What gives ordinary objects their value? Where is the quarter hidden this time? Who has put the coin in the drawer, and what is its value?

How we assign merit to things often seems motivated by the vagaries of human impulse; the process is improvisational and at times comic. As a writer, I have often been given objects for articles and essays I have written. Over the years, I have been given a brass umbrella stand, a small red clock, a blue canvas bag, a tablecloth, a crystal shot glass, a martini pitcher. I accepted them all. Notwithstanding the conversational journalistic ethos of not taking favors and gifts from the subjects of one's stories, I accepted these things because I am charmed and intrigued by the impulse of such exchanges. I don't know that these are even exchanges, but I don't know that in this particular realm there is such a thing as an even exchange. The list of items I have been given has no particular logic, which is probably as it should be; there isn't much logic in trying to match objects to words. Still, I put a high value on the effort *anyone* makes to try to make such matches. And so I think, maybe that's it: a tablecloth is worth five hundred words; an umbrella stand is worth a thousand words; a martini pitcher, two thousand. All of these seem as good a place to start as any.

I don't think I am the only one curious about how we assign value to things. What is known as the American collectibles market generates over $10 billion annually. Auction houses selling the clothes, the furniture, the vast archives of memorabilia that once belonged to such public figures as Jackie Onassis, the Princess of Wales, Marilyn Monroe, and Leonard Bernstein routinely clear double and triple the anticipated amounts. Who could have known, the auctioneers ask. But if other people's things hold out an allure, so do our own. Each week, Americans across the country exhibit what may—or may not—be their treasures on *Antiques Roadshow,* displaying everything from scrimshaw mourning jewelry, a piece of South Pacific painted bark cloth, a Confederate bowie knife to gold Etruscan Revival earrings, a 1913 magnifying glass commemorating the Romanov dynasty, a 1953 All-Star baseball, a Beatles album cover, a John LaFarge drawing, all retrieved from their attics and garages, old cabinets, trunks, and forgotten drawers. "My grandmother kept this in her dining room cabinet for years," we hear, or "My great uncle left this in the attic when he got married and moved, and we've had it ever since."

5   And then we are told that such an object is scarcely worth the weight of the Styrofoam it has been packed in, or that it is worth tens of thousands of dollars, and in both cases the discussion between owners and appraisers considers both monetary and sentimental value. Certainly the drama of the exchange lies in part in finding that an ordinary ceramic bowl or turned table of little known value will now secure a comfortable retirement. But I would guess that an equal amount of drama lies in the narrative, the sure sense of theater created by the breathless anticipation of the owners, the academic dryness of the appraisers as the conversation progresses from where the item was made and how and by whom, to who then found it or bought it and saved it and loved it. Or didn't. And will it be kept or sold? It is difficult not to be captivated by these tales of ordinary things.

It is hard to watch such a program and not come away with a belief in the opera of the inanimate—the quiet fatigue of an old quilt, the spiritual conviction in a perfectly woven Navajo rug, the solid persistence of an eighteenth-century wooden spoon. I once saw an exhibition of paintings by John Singer Sargent that came to this point in a different way. Sargent was the most celebrated portrait painter of his time, yet as the curators suggested, in many of his works the action resides almost completely in the objects; a woman is sleeping on the grass in the garden, but the larger part of the canvas is taken up by her skirt's voluminous folds, creased almost violently. Or the languor of an afternoon tea party is undercut by the cloth that lies awry on the table. The artist seemed to be familiar with the idea that sometimes objects tell stories more eloquently than people.

Certainly those stories have a new resonance at a time when the ephemeral accosts us from all sides; physical objects engage us in a different way today. With our cell phones, e-mail, and assorted forms of wireless communication, the elusive corridors of cyberspace have whetted our appetite for what we can touch, hold, taste, see. In the virtual age, the sorcery of the physical has intensified. We become attached to objects out of sentiment, perhaps, or for their symbolic value—a wedding ring, a grandmother's quilt, an old fountain pen, all of which may commemorate personal history. We seem to accept the idea that things have a life of their own. And that acceptance is the beginning of having an emotional relationship with inanimate objects. Whether the object of one's affection is Marilyn Monroe's chipped kitchen table or a birch plywood table by Alvar Aalto, we seem to have developed a psychic intimacy with our stuff.

But objects make their emotional appeal to us on a much broader cultural level as well. I am certain that their narratives have some tangential connection to our contemporary design literacy. We live in a time when what is called "design" has achieved a certain market status. In *The Substance of Style,* Virginia Postrel argues that the ubiquity of town design review boards, Starbucks coffee, Alessi toilet brushes, and the styling of everything from sneakers to kitchen appliances to computers suggest that design is newly available not just to the elite, but to all of us. Certainly there is no arguing an increased attentiveness to design, but the actual meaning of design seems to vary.

One general and reductive way to define design has simply been to say it is about communication. Another conventional notion of design is that it is where technology, art, and culture converge to solve the problems of everyday life. In the late 1990s and early 2000s, Chrysler sponsored annual design awards, selecting objects for their recognition of color, technology, and craft. Design, the copy for the competition read, is "where form and function meet. The perfect marriage of passion and precision. Memorable designs are those whose very appearance exposes their excellence. And whose performance and engineering only intensify it." Postrel goes a little further in suggesting that emotional content is also essential to how something is designed: "Design provides pleasure and meaning as well as function, and the increasing demand for aesthetic expertise reflects a desire not for more function but for more pleasure—for the knowledge and skill to delight our senses." Even the *Harvard Business Review* recently went so far as to suggest that businesses are realizing that "emotionally compelling" objects and services are what will distinguish their offerings today.

10 As a citizen in an age of design literacy, as we all seem to be, I am interested in these assorted definitions, these phrases and verbal wranglings intended to capture the meaning of something obscure. It seems long overdue that the emotional content of objects, of buildings, of places be considered part of the equation. Because at the same time that I have been writing about design—about why mattresses are getting larger although we all seem to sleep less, why vintage rotary phones are finding a new market, or why skateboards can be an accessory to urban experience— I have also watched my two sons grow from infancy through childhood and adolescence through their teenage years. Witnessing the way in which they take ownership of their things has shaped the way I think about design. I have been reading about smart refrigerators for years, and about how what today are called "infopliances" will reinvent the way we not only prepare meals but also communicate with one another. But when my son Luc used the refrigerator as a place to store his dog's fur, it inevitably recast the way I thought about the function of this appliance. When his brother, Noel, came home from school one afternoon with the news that he had been taught how to apologize in a class called Home Careers, it shifted my thinking about how kids learn about domestic tasks. And this is just the kitchen.

Because such moments in the domestic life of my own family encouraged me to investigate how ordinary things are shaped and used, it gave me all the more pleasure to realize that the same quotidian family life, at times, causes things to be the way they are: A vegetable peeler takes new form because a man is trying to help his wife, who has arthritis; a lawn chair comes into being because another man wanted a place for his family to sit outdoors; and a father improvises a little snowboard so his daughter can slide down a snowy hill. A divorced, middle-aged woman suggests that housewives will buy brightly colored plastic food containers if they are sold at parties, and Tupperware enters the American kitchen. More and more, I found that the ideas, uses, and functions that came up time and again in our domestic life, whether they involved a backpack, camera, or phone, were rarely the same ideas I encountered in design theory or literature, much less in the marketing material purporting to make these objects appealing, necessary, desirable. How they are actually used and the details of how they inhabit our lives often follows a separate narrative.

More and more, that material narrative seemed worth following. Do the concerns of an engineer at GE who is designing a smart fridge ever intersect with those of a child who is considering how to store his pet's fur? Medicine cabinets are a common domestic object that has been growing in recent years, and the shape and size they take reflect values about home security, healthcare, and how we take care of ourselves. At the same time, the medicine cabinet is a potent symbol for contemporary artists like Damien Hirst, who constructed an entire pharmacy of imagined remedies. Is this pure coincidence, or do his reflections on the cabinet share anything with those of houseware designers who are producing their super-sized versions? And in this age of streamlined, accelerated communications, why did my neighbor John Scofield build a FedEx delivery box in the form of a Roman temple? If one is interested in design and in how things take their shape in the physical world, these narratives seem worth following.

In the end, it would be preposterous, of course, to draw grand and universal conclusions from the experience of two boys growing up in the Hudson Valley. Yet at the same time, it is difficult not to admit that their things tell a story not only about them, but also about the rooms, the landscape they inhabit. The strollers and cereal boxes, phones and cameras, and all manner of other ordinary domestic objects that have been their accomplices in everyday life compose a profile of their lives and time. The backpacks my kids use today have a universal appeal to middle-class American teenagers; they are accessories to their way of life, a form of psychic prosthetic for an entire generation. It would never occur to them to use tote bags made in the shape of AK-47 automatic rifles, though such bags are sometimes used in South Africa, where the murder rate is ten times that of the U.S. Such are the revelations of simple things. Our objects signal who we are.

But in recent history, it's not the catalogue of specialized backpacks, nor the volume of goods sold on eBay, nor the revelations of *Antiques Roadshow,* nor pictorial essays on ethnic curiosities that have said the most about our emotional engagement with the inanimate. Rather, it is something that occurred in winter 2004. A minor scandal broke in New York City when it was discovered that several FBI agents had taken an assortment of physical objects from the Staten Island landfill that held the debris from the World Trade Center. Some of the agents had spent long, painful months sifting through the rubble in an effort to collect further evidence of the particulars of the towers' collapse, and as mementos they took such varied objects as a globe paperweight, pieces of metal and concrete, an American flag. Outrage from some of the families followed, the sentiment being that the agents at best were removing evidence from a crime scene, and at worst, robbing graves.

15   The anger seems misplaced. It is only human to look upon objects and artifacts, though they may be inanimate, as witnesses to human experience. And it is not difficult to understand the agents' desire to have a small, physical piece of the debris. Only a few miles away at the New York Historical Society, an exhibition titled *Recovery* seemed to operate with a motive similar to that of the FBI agents. On display were objects found in the 1.8 million tons of debris at the Fresh Kills site—jewelry, coins, photographs, bits of demolished fire trucks, pieces from the planes, keys, a plaque for an elevator door, a piece of an airline seatbelt, all of them souvenirs of catastrophe. The items were selected with the utmost deliberation. Would it be sensationalizing to include bits of aluminum from a hijacked plane? In the end, Mark Schaming, the director of exhibitions and programs at the New York State Museum, wrote that "the staff at Fresh Kills began to see museums as a way to preserve not only the objects, but this story as well. Museums were giving something back—their work as documented history. . . . These objects will speak to generations about the World Trade Center."

Both the curators of the exhibition and the agents have been called souvenir hunters, but I would imagine Pablo Neruda's observation that many things conspire to tell the whole story applies equally to their enterprises. The desire to preserve tragedy through objects seems less exploitative than an effort to assimilate unfathomable disaster through the familiar. Why else would Amadou Diallo's[1] bullet-riddled doorway be auctioned on eBay? Why else would a man in Mississippi amass a large collection of artifacts related to slavery, an inventory of our inhumanity that includes shackles, whips, branding irons, and sales deeds? While such enterprises may be charged with sensationalizing tragedy, it seems more likely that they reflect the common impulse to observe human history through a culture's objects. The resonant narrative of physical objects elicits a universal response. To be a souvenir hunter is to be human.

The red glazed terra-cotta vases of fifth-century-B.C. Athens are prized not only for their graceful shape and the technical skill that went into their painting, but also for their figurative decoration, which tells us volumes about the way those early Greeks lived—everything from how they ate and conducted themselves in the rituals of ordinary life to how

---

1. Amadou Bailo Diallo (1975–1999): An immigrant to the United States from Guinea who was shot on February 4, 1999, by four New York City Police Department plainclothed officers, who fired a total of forty-one rounds, killing the unarmed Diallo. The circumstances and the number of shots fired provoked widespread controversy within—and beyond—New York City.

they fought their wars and worshipped their gods. As there are few written historical documents from that time, the red figure pots are the vital evidence. Today our books, photographs, films, magazines, and all types of digital technology record our time. But it seems clear that despite all of these, the resonance of simple domestic objects persists. They, too, are witnesses to their time. Whether it is a smashed messenger's bicycle from Fresh Kills or a horse with a spear in its side inscribed on a red clay pot twenty-five hundred years ago, both convey the fragments of a story. The impulse to measure human experience through the things we can touch, see, and hold comes naturally. We are all part of the market for collectibles.

Like my sons maneuvering the wooden box in their hands, we demand participation from *things*. We ask them to be our witnesses and accomplices. I am certain this is at the heart of design. How things are designed may well be about "performance" or "engineering" or "excellence" or "communication." But I think most of all that the way things take shape, form, size, color gives us a sense of measure in the physical world; it assures us that the world accommodates us and that we, in turn, can accommodate it and what it brings. That mutual reassurance can be at work in the way a backpack folds into one's shoulders and back, the way a comfortable desk offers a view of the world, or the way the handle of a vegetable peeler conforms to the human grip.

If there is a message, it is that things in this world can find a fit—the way the coin fits in the drawer, the drawer fits in the little wooden box, and the box itself fits into a child's hand, allowing him to believe in the transformative power of the physical world because we can make it a place where mystery, logic, and pleasure coincide. And I wonder if this is the hidden coin, the ability and inclination we have to persuade inanimate objects to be our partners in experience.

George Skelcher
Magic Money Boxes, 2004

This is Daphne

NAME	Daphne Chen
AGE	31
LOCATION	Los Angeles, California
HOMETOWN	Bedford, Texas
OCCUPATION	Violinist, string arranger, studio musician, and member of The Section Quartet

TIED TO FORM I can't remember not playing. When I was a kid my mom drove me four hours from Dallas to Houston every Saturday for a two-hour lesson. For orchestra performances I had the big pouffy dresses. I told a friend in high school, "I can't be in a band, I'm a violin player."

BREAKING STRINGS I went to USC to learn the rules; at CalArts, I learned how to break them. I joined The Section Quartet five years ago. I draw from my experience—the textures of classical, the weirdness of avant-garde music—and apply it to these more accessible songs. I've always wanted to arrange [David Bowie's] "Space Oddity."

and those are her things

1. Concert violin: "This was made in 1892 in Rome by Antonio Sgarbi. I recorded *Fuzzbox* on it." **2.** Retired ashtray and adjacent gum replacement: "I stopped smoking the day of the record release in New York, August 21st. Well, the day after." **3.** French and electrified German violins: "I used this one while playing in an experimental tango band. The blond's name is Hermon." **4.** Corset: "I had this made for me at the Trashy Lingerie store for when we played Coachella 2006." **5.** Sun painting: "My mom made this in the sixties." **6.** Photograph with Linda Martinez: "This is a picture of me with a friend who recently passed away: musical genius, my mentor, and cheerleader—I wouldn't be who I am today with out her." **7.** Feather headpiece: "My friend Emily made this for Section's L.A. release of the album at The Troubadour." **8.** Theremin: "You play this without touching it. It makes the sound you hear in horror films." **9.** First violin: "I've had it since I was five."

PHOTOS by Trujillo-Paumier

Photos by Trujillo-Paumier

Looking Closer / 123

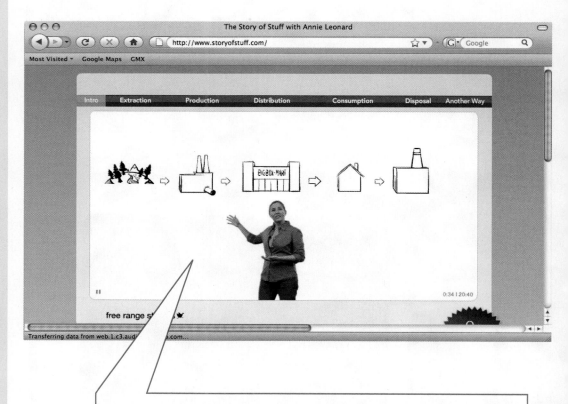

"Do you have one of these? [eds. note: holding an iPod.] I got a little obsessed with mine. In fact, I got a little obsessed with all of my stuff. Have you wondered where all the stuff we buy comes from and where it goes when we throw it out? I couldn't stop wondering about that, so I looked it up. And what the textbook said is that stuff moves through a system from extraction to production to distribution to consumption to disposal. Altogether, it's called the materials economy. Well, I looked into it a little bit more. In fact I spent ten years traveling the world tracking where our stuff comes from and where it goes. And you know what I found out? That is not the whole story. There is a lot missing from this explanation."

Pablo Neruda

One of the twentieth century's greatest poets, Pablo Neruda was born Neftali Ricardo Reyes Basoalto in the small town of Parral, Chile, in 1904. Inspired by his friendship with renowned poet Gabriela Mistral, Neruda began writing at a young age and published his first book of poetry while still a teenager. His second published collection, *Veinte Poemas de Amor y Una Cancion Desesperada* (*Twenty Love Poems and a Song of Despair,* 1924) is considered one of his masterworks. Neruda's long literary career resulted in other acclaimed works such as *Residencia en la Tierra* (*Residence on Earth,* 1935), *Canto General* (*General Study,* 1950), and *Cien Sonetos de Amor* (*One Hundred Love Sonnets,* 1960). In 1971, two years before his death, Neruda was awarded the Nobel Prize for literature.

Despite the prolific poet's success, he was unable to support himself exclusively through his art and relied on his second career as a diplomat and politician. His often controversial political career included a lifelong commitment to communism, several periods of exile from Chile, and alignment with the dictatorships of Josef Stalin, Fidel Castro, and Salvador Allende. Neruda's poetry was also controversial for its exploration of eroticism and political themes. But it is his ability to write beautifully about the ordinary and the sublime that will be remembered above all else.

Siri Hustvedt

Acclaimed novelist, occasional poet, and art critic Siri Hustvedt (b. 1955) is known primarily for her surrealist novels that tell dreamlike tales, based loosely on personal experiences. Her critically acclaimed first novel, *The Blindfold* (1992), relates the exploits of a graduate student, Iris (Siri spelled backwards), in New York and is based in part on Hustvedt's own experiences as a Columbia University graduate student. *The Enchantment of Lily Dahl* (1996) is a stylized exploration of the years Hustvedt spent as a teen living in a small Minnesota town. Over the last decade Hustvedt has written two celebrated novels, *What I Loved* (2003) and *The Sorrows of an American* (2008), and has also proved herself an accomplished essayist with her collections *Yonder* (1998), *A Plea for Eros* (2005), and *Being a Man* (2006). She is married to novelist Paul Auster, and the literary power couple live in Brooklyn with their daughter, Sophie.

In "Unknown Keys," an essay from the collection *How I Write: The Secret Lives of Writers* (edited by Dan Crowe and Philip Oltermann, 2007), Hustvedt describes how a set of her father's keys help to unlock her imagination when she writes.

Akiko Busch

Born in Japan and raised in the Hudson Valley, New York (where she still lives), Akiko Busch has long been fascinated by everyday objects. While growing up she took an interest in the unusual juxtaposition of items that filled her parents' home: Her mother's Asian art collection resided alongside English furniture that her father had inherited. Busch's attraction to design developed into a successful writing career.

In addition to writing many articles for publications such as *Metropolitan Home, House and Garden, Travel & Leisure,* the *New York Times,* and *Architectural Record,* Busch was a contributing editor at *Metropolis* magazine for twenty years, chaired the University of Hartford's school of art, and has written numerous books in which she discusses design and architecture in a cultural context. Among her most popular books are *Design is . . . Words, Things, People, Buildings, and Places at Metropolis* (2001), *Geography of Home: Writings on Where We Live* (2003), and *The Uncommon Life of Common Objects: Essays on Design and the Everyday* (2005), excerpted here, in which she explores the emotional connection between people and everyday objects as seemingly mundane as a mailbox or a vegetable peeler. Busch's most recent book, *Nine Ways to Cross a River: Midstream Reflections on Swimming and Getting There from Here* (2007), describes her recent pastime of swimming in rivers and the relationship she has formed with the natural world.

George Skelcher

British-born commercial artist George Skelcher (b. 1962) enrolled in London's Chelsea School of Art in 1981 and then "by mutual agreement" left to experience New York's thriving nightclub scene in 1983, taking a job at the hip Danceteria club. Returning to London to finish his degree, he found work in the then-new music video industry. By 1986, back in New York (where he still lives), Skelcher found himself increasingly involved with music video – the hip-hop scene provided him with steady work as art director on videos for such old-school luminaries as De La Soul, Public Enemy, Big Daddy Kane, and Eric B and Rakim. He also occasionally worked on rock videos for a variety of artists, including the Rolling Stones.

Later, while working on advertising campaigns for Target and Neiman Marcus, Skelcher scored a major commercial success when he designed a purse based on the familiar "We Are Happy to Serve You" coffee cups that many panhandlers in New York use to hold change. Instantly popular and now manufactured for international sale, the purse design has enabled Skelcher to concentrate on his fine art – for instance, the elegant pencil illustrations of simple objects (three of which are reprinted on p. 121) that accompany Akiko Busch's prose in *The Uncommon Life of Common Objects*.

Trujillo-Paumier

Not one person but two, Trujillo-Paumier is the photographer team of Joaquin Trujillo (b. 1976) and Brian Paumier (b. 1973). Both men received their undergraduate degrees at the Art Center College of Design in Pasadena, California, and joined forces in 2001. Trujillo is the photography editor at *GOOD* magazine, in which "This is Daphne" originally appeared, and Paumier is a U.S. Army specialist who has photographed tours of duty. As a team, Trujillo-Paumier have photographed for a wide variety of publications, including *Newsweek,* the *New York Times Magazine,* the *Los Angeles Times Magazine,* and *Travel & Leisure.* They have also exhibited at photography fairs and galleries, and they have received several awards, including a nomination for the prestigious Aperture West Book Prize for their body of work, Hot Cakes.

The photographs for "This is Daphne" demonstrate the artists' interest in capturing the essence of violinist Daphne Chen by presenting some of the most important everyday objects in her life, including a retired ashtray, a painting by her mother, a photograph of a friend who passed away, and, of course, her violins.

Annie Leonard

After spending two decades visiting the factories where products are made and the dumping grounds where products end up, Annie Leonard developed what she calls a healthy "neurosis" in environmental affairs. Currently the coordinator for the Funders Workgroup for Sustainable Production and Consumption, Leonard has spent her career working to raise awareness about the impact of everyday objects on the environment. In 1992 she testified before the U.S. Congress about the common practice of waste trafficking to third world countries.

Her most recent project, the twenty-minute web-based video presentation *The Story of Stuff,* allows anyone with access to the Internet a free, easy-to-understand lesson in production consumption patterns. The video is a call to action for others to join Leonard in "thinking about where all of this stuff in our life comes from, where it goes, and how we . . . are paying the price for our excessive consumerism."

SEEING

1. Akiko Busch begins her introduction to *The Uncommon Life of Common Objects* with the question, "What gives ordinary objects their value?" (para. 2). What answers does Busch provide – and elaborate on – in her essay? Reread the essay, and make a list of each of her arguments. Discuss your list with your classmates. Which of Busch's points do you find the most convincing? Which resonate most with your own experiences? Explain why. What perspective(s) on your individual and collective relationships to ordinary objects has Busch omitted?

Working with Sources

2. In "The Story of Stuff," Annie Leonard imagines the extraction, production, and consumption process that allowed her to buy a radio at Radio Shack for a mere $4.99. Choose an object, and research its story. What raw materials are used in the object's production? Where was it manufactured? How is it distributed? Leonard argues that we're not actually paying for our products; that the true costs of production and environmental and human impact are hidden to the consumer. To what extent does the story of your own object support or refute her claim?

WRITING

1. Siri Hustvedt describes the meaning of a set of her father's keys in "Unknown Keys." Choose an object that has special significance for you. Draft an essay in which you describe your subject in rich detail and illustrate its meaning in your life.

2. *GOOD* magazine's "This is Daphne" provides a rich cultural document for testing Akiko Busch's assertion that "Our objects signal who we are" (para. 13). Following *GOOD* magazine's approach, interview someone in or outside of your class, and create a list of his or her prized possessions. Draft an essay in which you describe this person's possessions and make an assertion concerning what those objects signal about your subject's backgrounds, habits, and beliefs.

Page 122   Page 114

Responding Visually

Represent your findings from Writing question 2 in a multimedia format of your choice. For example, you might arrange and photograph your subject's possessions, as *GOOD* magazine has done. Or you may choose to create a PowerPoint presentation, a video, or some other graphic presentation using visual images of your subject and his or her stuff as evidence for your thesis.

2

COMING TO

TERMS WITH

PLACE

"Where are you from?" This question invariably arises when two Americans meet for the first time, especially when traveling. "I'm from the South"; "I'm from L.A."; "I'm from Cody, Wyoming" – each response conjures different cultural assumptions and associations. In fact, the meaning we attribute to these responses suggests that growing up in a particular place leaves a deep, if not indelible, mark on a person's character. As the popular saying goes, "You can take the kid out of Brooklyn, but you can't take Brooklyn out of the kid." Place is a fundamental component of everyday life, the "where" that locates each event and experience in our lives. Place in this sense evokes public identity, the characteristics that inform our accents, our clothes, and our behavior.

Think of a place: a town, a city, America itself. If you were asked to describe that place, what comes immediately to mind: the people? the buildings? the landscape? landmarks? a feeling? Americans often classify people by where they are from, and in this we are encouraged by the settings for many film and television programs. Consider, for example, *Sex and the City*, *The Hills*, *CSI: Miami*.

Even as Americans invest meaning in our geographical roots, fewer of us remain in the same place for long. According to the U.S. Census Bureau, 46 percent of the American public changed their state of residence between 1995 and 2000. Indeed, answering the question "Where are you from?" has become increasingly difficult for many Americans, given the number of places where they have lived. Airplanes, mass transit, and highways reduce the distances between places. And when we arrive at our destinations, we realize that American places look increasingly alike. Few communities across the nation are without familiar fast-food chains and shopping malls. Likewise, the borders between regions continue to dissolve. Consider the number of restaurants in different parts of the country, each boasting authentic regional cuisine. No matter where you find yourself, you can probably enjoy down-home Cajun cooking, Chicago pizza, New York bagels, or New England clam chowder.

Our sense of place is no longer limited to the physical realm. The Internet offers a digital landscape, a virtual world in which we form social networks and communities around sites. Advertisers try to convince us that we can reach any place in the real or virtual world within seconds, without leaving "the privacy of your own home."

In contemporary American culture, the centuries-old distinctions between "place" and "space" seem to be disappearing. Jerry Brown, a former governor of California and candidate for president, and now the attorney general of California, drew the following distinction between place and space:

> People don't live in place, they live in space. The media used to accuse me of that — living in space. But it wasn't true. Now too many people just live in their

minds, not in communities. They garage themselves in their homes and live in market space. It's an alienated way for human beings to live. It's the difference between a native and an immigrant. A native lives in place, not space.

For most people, coming to terms with place is ultimately a personal matter. It can mean the smell of chicken roasting in the oven, the sound of traffic or a certain song, the sight of a familiar stretch of land. In many respects, place is also about relationships, both among people and between us and our associations with a particular time and space.

The essays and images in this chapter represent an attempt to map different ways we connect socially and culturally with others; they can help us understand how geographical location, or a sense of place, shapes who we are and our outlook on the world.

"In 1868 the federal government deeded millions of acres in the Black Hills of South Dakota to the Great Sioux Nation. Nine years later, when gold was discovered in the area, Congress broke the treaty and took the land back.

"In the 1920s the state of South Dakota, eager to attract tourists, commissioned a sculptor to carve a colossal monument into Mount Rushmore. The Sioux considered the Black Hills their own sacred land.

"In 1980 the Supreme Court awarded the Sioux $17 million plus interest accrued since 1877 as compensation. The award is now valued at nearly $300 million, but the Sioux continue to refuse the money and to seek title to their land."

Joel Sternfeld
Mount Rushmore National Monument, Black Hills National Forest, South Dakota, August 1994

Courtesy of the artist and Luhring Augustine, New York

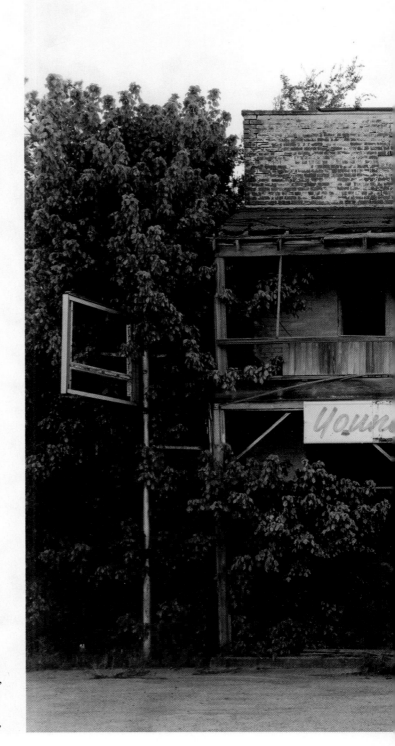

"In 1955 Emmett Till, a fourteen-year-old boy from Chicago, was visiting relatives near Money, Mississippi. Anxious to show new friends that he knew how to talk to white women, Till said, 'Bye, baby,' to Carolyn Bryant as he left this store.

"Three days later, Bryant's husband, Roy, and his half-brother, J. W. Milam, kidnapped, tortured, and killed Till. Milam and Bryant were found not guilty by an all-male, all-white jury. The deliberations lasted a little over an hour."

Joel Sternfeld
The Former Bryant's Grocery, Money, Mississippi, June 1994

Opening Portfolio / 135

"In 1942 the United States Army, searching for a place to manufacture plutonium for the atomic bomb, selected Hanford, a remote farming community in central Washington. Fewer than two thousand people occupied the half-million acres around the town. The Army took over the land and built the world's first large-scale nuclear reactor. Throughout the cold war, Hanford produced much of the raw material for America's nuclear arsenal.

"More than 440 billion gallons of chemical and radioactive waste were poured into the ground at Hanford, including enough plutonium to build two dozen nuclear bombs. Airborne radiation was deliberately released to test the effects of iodine 131 on the surrounding area and its residents, who were not warned of dangers to their health.

"Hanford's plutonium production facility was shut down in 1988. A massive cleanup effort is underway."

It's the Nature of O

Joel Sternfeld
Hanford Reservation, Hanford, Washington, August 1994

"Yetta M. Adams froze to death
sitting upright in this bus shelter
across from the Department of
Housing and Urban Development in Washington, D.C., on
November 29, 1993. The forty-
three-year-old mother of three
grown children had reportedly
been turned away from a homeless shelter the night before."

Joel Sternfeld
Metro Bus Shelter, 7th Street at E Street, Southwest, Washington, D.C., April 1995

Joel Sternfeld

Born in New York City in 1944, Joel Sternfeld began to take photographs after graduating from Dartmouth College. His photographs have been exhibited at New York's Museum of Modern Art, the Art Institute of Chicago, Portugal's LisboaPhoto, and Switzerland's Foto Museum, among other well-known venues. In addition, Sternfeld has received two Guggenheim fellowships, a Prix de Rome, and the Citigroup Photography Prize, one of the most prestigious international photography awards.

Like celebrated photographers Walker Evans and Robert Frank before him, Sternfeld explores the meaning of modern American identity. In his full-color portraits Sternfeld links memory and place with Americans and their way of life. His first book, *American Prospects* (1987), documented Sternfeld's eight years traveling across the United States.

The images and captions collected here first appeared in *On This Site: Landscape in Memoriam* (1996), for which Sternfeld photographed fifty seemingly ordinary sites, each the scene of a tragic event. As he explains, "The landscape contains meaning, contains clues. . . . The place itself becomes very important in so many of these events. . . . Having that one bit of certainty allows you to have your emotions in a way that all of the verbiage doesn't." *On This Site* underscores the artist's interest in irony, whether he photographs landscapes, places, or people.

Aside from *American Prospects* and *On This Site*, Sternfeld's many books include *Stranger Passing* (2001), *Walking the High Line* (2001), *Treading on Kings* (2002), *Sweet Earth* (2006), and *When It Changed* (2007). The latter two books reveal Sternfeld's interest in environmental matters. Sternfeld has taught photography at Sarah Lawrence College since 1985.

SEEING

1. Look at each of the photographs in this portfolio separately. What do you see first in each image? What is the range of vision – the perspective – the photographer allows us to view? Consider the structure and layout of each photograph. Comment on the effects of scale and distance. What does Sternfeld gain – and lose – by his choice of framing? What reasonable inferences can you draw from your observations of the individual images? of these photographs as a group?

2. Carefully examine the captions Sternfeld prepared to accompany his photographs. To what extent do his words increase your understanding and appreciation of the scene presented in each photograph? How would you characterize Sternfeld's tone of voice in the captions? Explain how his tone of voice compares with other elements of the photographs. Comment on Sternfeld's use of light, shade, and color to enhance the impact of these photographs. These are ordinary places. What makes them so extraordinary?

Responding Visually

The images in Joel Sternfeld's portfolio capture ordinary sites where extraordinary events occurred. Choose a local site that meets this criterion, photograph it, and then write a brief caption that offers the viewer a clear sense of what makes the site extraordinary. Model both your visual composition and your text composition on Sternfeld's work.

WRITING

1. One of the most prominent photographers of the Vietnam War, Nick Ut, has said that the role of photojournalism is to search for "the right moment that captures essentially the whole essence of the time and the place." How would you define *photojournalism*? Write an essay in which you define the term and apply it to one of Sternfeld's photographs. Given your definition, explain how the image is – or is not – an example of photojournalism.

Working with Sources
2. Each photograph in this series relates to a larger social issue: the land rights of Native Americans, racial violence, pollution, or homelessness. Choose one of the images, and research both the place it depicts and the event Sternfeld describes in the caption. Then write the first draft of an essay in which you explain the significance of the site, elaborate on the social issue at stake, and discuss the particular point of view Sternfeld's work provides on the issue.

EDWARD HOPPER
AND THE
HOUSE BY THE RAILROAD (1925)
Edward Hirsch

Out here in the exact middle of the day,
This strange, gawky house has the expression
Of someone being stared at, someone holding
His breath underwater, hushed and expectant;

5 This house is ashamed of itself, ashamed
Of its fantastic mansard rooftop
And its pseudo-Gothic porch, ashamed
Of its shoulders and large, awkward hands.

But the man behind the easel is relentless;
10 He is as brutal as sunlight, and believes
The house must have done something horrible
To the people who once lived here

Because now it is so desperately empty,
It must have done something to the sky
15 Because the sky, too, is utterly vacant
And devoid of meaning. There are no

Trees or shrubs anywhere—the house
Must have done something against the earth.
All that is present is a single pair of tracks
20 Straightening into the distance. No trains pass.

Now the stranger returns to this place daily
Until the house begins to suspect
That the man, too, is desolate, desolate
And even ashamed. Soon the house starts

25 To stare frankly at the man. And somehow
The empty white canvas slowly takes on
The expression of someone who is unnerved,
Someone holding his breath underwater.

And then one day the man simply disappears.
30 He is a last afternoon shadow moving
Across the tracks, making its way
Through the vast, darkening fields.

This man will paint other abandoned mansions,
And faded cafeteria windows, and poorly lettered
35 Storefronts on the edges of small towns.
Always they will have this same expression.

The utterly naked look of someone
Being stared at, someone American and gawky,
Someone who is about to be left alone
40 Again, and can no longer stand it.

Edward Hopper
House by the Railroad, 1925

Edward Hirsch

The poet, critic, and teacher Edward Hirsch was born in 1950 in Chicago and attended Grinnell College and the University of Pennsylvania. A professor of creative writing at the University of Houston, Hirsch has published poems and reviews in *The New Yorker*, *The Nation*, the *New York Times Book Review*, and other leading journals. He has published six volumes of poetry, including *Wild Gratitude* (1986), which won the National Book Critics Circle Award, and *Lay Back the Darkness* (2003). His 1999 book *How to Read a Poem and Fall in Love with Poetry* was a national best seller. Currently he serves as president of the Guggenheim Memorial Foundation and writes a poetry column for the *Washington Post Book World*.

Hirsch edited *Transforming Vision: Writers on Art* (1994), the responses—in prose and verse—of a number of prominent writers to works on display at the Art Institute of Chicago. In that book he argues that "the proper response to a work of visual art may well be an ode or an elegy, a meditative lyric, a lyrical meditation" because poetic descriptions of art "teach us to look and look again more closely" and "dramatize with great intensity the actual experience of encounter." "Edward Hopper and the House by the Railroad (1925)" dramatizes Hirsch's own encounter with Hopper's famous painting.

Edward Hopper

In virtually all of his paintings—a wide array of American scenes ranging from rural landscapes and seascapes to street scenes, isolated buildings, and domestic interiors—Edward Hopper (1882–1967) masterfully expressed the isolation, boredom, and vacuity of modern life. Even his most colorful, luminous scenes are stripped of joy through the extreme spareness of composition and detail. His Depression-era work in particular evokes the mood of that time. However, Hopper claimed that his work expressed personal rather than national truths: "I don't think I ever tried to paint the American scene," he once said; "I'm trying to paint myself."

Hopper grew up in Nyack, New York, and received his training in New York City and in Europe. He was still a young man when his work was included in the Armory Show of 1913, a New York City exhibition that featured what would become known as modernist paintings. But despite his critical success, Hopper had to work as a commercial illustrator to support himself. His career turned around when, in his forties, he married the artist Josephine Nivison (1883–1968). Through several decades of an emotionally turbulent but artistically productive relationship, Hopper created his most memorable paintings.

SEEING

1. In *House by the Railroad*, where does Hopper direct your attention? What details do you notice about the house? its structure? its relationship to the railroad track and the sky? Where does your eye linger as you study the painting more carefully? How does each aspect of its presentation reinforce the overall effect of the painting?

2. On what features of Hopper's painting does Edward Hirsch focus in his poem? What effects does Hirsch create through <u>personification</u> of the house? Explain how his repetition of words, phrases, and structural elements reinforces – or detracts from – the overall impression or mood created in the poem. In what ways does Hirsch's poem change or enhance your initial reactions to Hopper's painting?

<u>personification: Attributing human qualities to an object or an idea; often used as a poetic device.</u>

WRITING

1. Write a page – in any form you prefer – in which you dramatize your encounter with Hopper's *House by the Railroad*. Do you agree with Hirsch that the house has the look of "someone American and gawky" (l. 38)?

2. Reread "Edward Hopper and the House by the Railroad (1925)" several times, until you feel comfortable describing and characterizing Hirsch's shifts in subject and tone. Based on your rereading of the poem, would you agree – or disagree – with the assertion that Hirsch seems more interested in Hopper the artist than in the scene he paints? How is the artist characterized in the poem? With what effects? At what point do the terms used to characterize house and artist seem to merge? What characteristics do the house and the artist share? What overall impression does Hirsch create in this comparison? Write the first draft of an essay in which you use evidence from the poem and the painting to validate your own response to the assertion that Hirsch is far more interested in Hopper as artist than in the art he has created.

Eudora Welty
Storekeeper, 1935

THE LITTLE STORE
Eudora Welty

Two blocks away from the Mississippi state Capitol, and on the same street with it, where our house was when I was a child growing up in Jackson, it was possible to have a little pasture behind your backyard where you could keep a Jersey cow, which we did. My mother herself milked her. A thrifty homemaker, wife, mother of three, she also did all her own cooking. And as far as I can recall, she never set foot inside a grocery store. It wasn't necessary.

For her regular needs, she stood at the telephone in our front hall and consulted with Mr. Lemly, of Lemly's Market and Grocery downtown, who took her order and sent it out on his next delivery. And since Jackson at the heart of it was still within very near reach of the open country, the blackberry lady clanged on her bucket with a quart measure at your front door in June without fail, the watermelon man rolled up to your house exactly on time for the Fourth of July, and down through the summer, the quiet of the early-morning streets was pierced by the calls of farmers driving in with their plenty. One brought his with a song, so plaintive we would sing it with him:

> "Milk, milk,
> Buttermilk,
> Snap beans — butterbeans —
> Tender okra — fresh greens . . .
> And buttermilk."

My mother considered herself pretty well prepared in her kitchen and pantry for any emergency that, in her words, might choose to present itself. But if she should, all of a sudden, need another lemon or find she was out of bread, all she had to do was call out, "Quick! Who'd like to run to the Little Store for me?"

I would.

5   She'd count out the change into my hand, and I was away. I'll bet the nickel that would be left over that all over the country, for those of my day, the neighborhood grocery played a similar part in our growing up.

Our store had its name — it was that of the grocer who owned it, whom I'll call Mr. Sessions — but "the Little Store" is what we called it at home. It was a block down our street toward the capitol and half a block further, around the corner, toward the cemetery. I knew even the sidewalk to it as well as I knew my own skin. I'd skipped my jumping-rope up and down it, hopped its length through mazes of hopscotch, played jacks in its islands of shade, serpentined along it on my Princess bicycle, skated it backward and forward. In the twilight I had dragged my steamboat by its string (this was homemade out of every new shoebox, with candle in the bottom lighted and shining through colored tissue paper pasted over windows scissored out in the shapes of the sun, moon, and stars) across every crack of the walk without letting it bump or catch fire. I'd "played out" on that street after supper with my brothers and friends as long as "first-dark" lasted; I'd caught its lightning bugs. On the first Armistice Day (and this will set the time I'm speaking of) we made our own parade down that walk on a single velocipede—my brother pedaling, our little brother riding the handlebars, and myself standing on the back, all with arms wide, flying flags in each hand. (My father snapped that picture as we raced by. It came out blurred.)

As I set forth for the Little Store, a tune would float toward me from the house where there lived three sisters, girls in their teens, who ratted their hair over their ears, wore headbands like gladiators, and were considered to be very popular. They practiced for this in the daytime; they'd wind up the Victrola, leave the same record on they'd played before, and you'd see them bobbing past their dining-room windows while they danced with each other. Being three, they could go all day, cutting in:

"Everybody ought to know-oh
How to do the Tickle-Toe
   (how to do the Tickle-Toe)" —

They sang it and danced to it, and as I went by to the same song, I believed it.

A little further on, across the street, was the house where the principal of our grade school lived—lived on, even while we were having vacation. What if she would come out? She would halt me in my tracks — she had a very carrying and well-known voice in Jackson, where she'd taught almost everybody—saying, "Eudora Alice Welty, spell OBLIGE." OBLIGE was the word that she of course knew had kept me from making 100 on my spelling exam. She'd make me miss it again now, by boring her eyes through me from across the street. This was my vacation fantasy, one good way to scare myself on the way to the store.

Down near the corner waited the house of a little boy named Lindsey. The sidewalk here was old brick, which the roots of a giant chinaberry had humped up and tilted this way and that. On skates, you took it fast, in a series of skittering hops, trying not to touch ground anywhere. If the chinaberries had fallen and rolled in the cracks, it was like skating through a whole shooting match of marbles. I crossed my fingers that Lindsey wouldn't be looking.

10   During the big flu epidemic he and I, as it happened, were being nursed through our sieges at the same time. I'd hear my father and mother murmuring to each other, at the end of a long day, "And I wonder how poor little *Lindsey* got along today?" Just as, down the street, he no doubt would have to hear his family saying, "And I wonder how is poor *Eudora* by now?" I got the idea that a choice was going to be made soon between poor little Lindsey and poor Eudora, and I came up with a funny poem. I wasn't prepared for it when my father told me it wasn't funny and my mother cried that if I couldn't be ashamed for myself, she'd have to be ashamed for me:

> There was a little boy and his name was Lindsey.
> He went to heaven with the influinzy.

He didn't, he survived it, poem and all, the same as I did. But his chinaberries could have brought me down in my skates in a flying act of contrition before his eyes, looking pretty funny myself, right in front of his house.

Setting out in this world, a child feels so indelible. He only comes to find out later that it's all the others along his way who are making themselves indelible to him.

Our Little Store rose right up from the sidewalk; standing in a street of family houses, it alone hadn't any yard in front, any tree or flowerbed. It was a plain frame building covered over with brick. Above the door, a little railed porch ran across on an upstairs level and four windows with shades were looking out. But I didn't catch on to those.

Running in out of the sun, you met what seemed total obscurity inside. There were almost tangible smells — licorice recently sucked in a child's cheek, dill-pickle brine that had leaked through a paper sack in a fresh trail across the wooden floor, ammonia-loaded ice that had been hoisted from wet croker sacks and slammed into the icebox with its sweet butter at the door, and perhaps the smell of still-untrapped mice.

Then through the motes of cracker dust, cornmeal dust, the Gold Dust of the Gold Dust Twins that the floor had been swept out with, the realities emerged. Shelves climbed to high reach all the way around, set out with not too much of any one thing but a lot of things — lard, molasses, vinegar, starch, matches, kerosene, Octagon soap (about a year's worth of octagon-shaped coupons cut out and saved brought a signet ring addressed to you in the mail. Furthermore, when the postman arrived at your door, he blew a whistle). It was up to you to remember what you came for, while your eye traveled from cans of sardines to ice cream salt to harmonicas to flypaper (over your head, batting around on a thread beneath the blades of the ceiling fan, stuck with its testimonial catch).

15   Its confusion may have been in the eye of its beholder. Enchantment is cast upon you by all those things you weren't supposed to have need for, it lures you close to wooden tops you'd outgrown, boy's marbles and agates in little net pouches, small rubber balls that wouldn't bounce straight, frazzly kitestring, clay bubble-pipes that would snap off in your teeth, the stiffest scissors. You could contemplate those long narrow boxes of sparklers gathering dust while you waited for it to be the Fourth of July or Christmas, and noisemakers in the shape of tin frogs for somebody's birthday party you hadn't been invited to yet, and see that they were all marvelous.

You might not have even looked for Mr. Sessions when he came around his store cheese (as big as a doll's house) and in front of the counter looking for you. When you'd finally asked him for, and received from him in its paper bag, whatever single thing it was that you had been sent for, the nickel that was left over was yours to spend.

Down at a child's eye level, inside those glass jars with mouths in their sides through which the grocer could run his scoop or a child's hand might be invited to reach for a choice, were wineballs, all-day suckers, gumdrops, peppermints. Making a row under the glass of a counter were the Tootsie Rolls, Hershey Bars, Goo-Goo Clusters, Baby Ruths. And whatever was the name of those pastilles that came stacked in a cardboard cylinder with a cardboard lid? They were thin and dry, about the size of tiddly-winks, and in the shape of twisted rosettes. A kind of chocolate dust came out with them when you shook them out in your hand. Were they chocolate? I'd say rather they were brown. They didn't taste of anything at all, unless it was wood. Their attraction was the number you got for a nickel.

Making up your mind, you circled the store around and around, around the pickle barrel, around the tower of Cracker Jack boxes; Mr. Sessions had built it for us himself on top of a packing case, like a house of cards.

If it seemed too hot for Cracker Jacks, I might get a cold drink. Mr. Sessions might have already stationed himself by the cold-drinks barrel, like a mind reader. Deep in ice water that looked black as ink, murky shapes that would come up as Coca-Colas, Orange Crushes, and various flavors of pop, were all swimming around together. When you gave the word, Mr. Sessions plunged his bare arm in to the elbow and fished out your choice, first try. I favored a locally bottled concoction called Lake's Celery. (What else could it be called? It was made by a Mr. Lake out of celery. It was a popular drink here for years but was not known universally, as I found out when I arrived in New York and ordered one in the Astor bar.) You drank on the premises, with feet set wide apart to miss the drip, and gave him back his bottle.

20   But he didn't hurry you off. A standing scales was by the door, with a stack of iron weights and a brass slide on the balance arm, that would weigh you up to three hundred pounds. Mr. Sessions, whose hands were gentle and smelled of carbolic, would lift you up and set your feet on the platform, hold your loaf of bread for you, and taking his time while you stood still for him, he would make certain of what you weighed today. He could even remember what you weighed the last time, so you could subtract and announce how much you'd gained. That was goodbye.

Is there always a hard way to go home? From the Little Store, you could go partway through the sewer. If your brothers had called you a scarecat, then across the next street beyond the Little Store, it was possible to enter this sewer by passing through a privet hedge, climbing down into the bed of a creek, and going into its mouth on your knees. The sewer—it might have been no more than a "storm sewer"—came out and emptied here, where Town Creek, a sandy, most often shallow little stream that ambled through Jackson on its way to the Pearl River, ran along the edge of the cemetery. You could go in darkness through this tunnel to where you next saw light (if you ever did) and climb out through the culvert at your own street corner.

I was a scarecat, all right, but I was a reader with my own refuge in storybooks. Making my way under the sidewalk, under the street and the streetcar track, under the Little Store, down there in the wet dark by myself, I could be Persephone entering into my six-month sojourn underground—though I didn't suppose Persephone had to crawl, hanging onto a loaf of bread, and come out through the teeth of an iron grating. Mother Ceres would indeed be wondering where she could find me, and mad when she knew. "Now am I going to have to start marching to the Little Store for *myself*?"

I couldn't picture it. Indeed, I'm unable today to picture the Little Store with a grown person in it, except for Mr. Sessions and the lady who helped him, who belonged there. We children thought it was ours. The happiness of errands was in part that of running for the moment away from home, a free spirit. I believed the Little Store to be a center of the outside world, and hence of happiness—as I believed what I found in the Cracker Jack box to be a genuine prize, which was as simply as I believed in the Golden Fleece.

But a day came when I ran to the store to discover, sitting on the front step, a grown person, after all—more than a grown person. It was the Monkey Man, together with his monkey. His grinding-organ was lowered to the step beside him. In my whole life so far, I must have laid eyes on the Monkey Man no more than five or six times. An itinerant of rare and wayward appearances, he was not punctual like the Gipsies, who every year with the first cool days of fall showed up in the aisles of Woolworth's. You never knew when the Monkey Man might decide to favor Jackson, or which way he'd go. Sometimes you heard him as close as the next street, and then he didn't come up yours.

25   But now I saw the Monkey Man at the Little Store, where I'd never seen him before. I'd never seen him sitting down. Low on that familiar doorstep, he was not the same any longer, and neither was his monkey. They looked just like an old man and an old friend of his that wore a fez, meeting quietly together, tired, and resting with their eyes fixed on some place far away, and not the same place. Yet their romance for me didn't have it in its power to waver. I wavered. I simply didn't know how to step around them, to proceed on into the Little Store for my mother's emergency as if nothing had happened. If I could have gone in there after it, whatever it was, I would have given it to them—putting it into the monkey's cool little fingers. I would have given them the Little Store itself.

In my memory they are still attached to the store — so are all the others. Everyone I saw on my way seemed to me then part of my errand, and in a way they were. As I myself, the free spirit, was part of it too.

All the years we lived in that house where we children were born, the same people lived in the other houses on our street too. People changed through the arithmetic of birth, marriage, and death, but not by going away. So families just accrued stories, which through the fullness of time, in those times, their own lives made. And I grew up in those.

But I didn't know there'd ever been a story at the Little Store, one that was going on while I was there. Of course, all the time the Sessions family had been living right overhead there, in the upstairs rooms behind the little railed porch and the shaded windows; but I think we children never thought of that. Did I fail to see them as a family because they weren't living in an ordinary house? Because I so seldom saw them close together, or having anything to say to each other? She sat in the back of the store, her pencil over a ledger, while he stood and waited on children to make up their minds. They worked in twin black eyeshades, held on their gray heads by elastic bands. It may be harder to recognize kindness—or unkindness, either—in a face whose eyes are in shadow. His face underneath his shade was as round as the little wooden wheels in the Tinker Toy box. So was her face. I didn't know, perhaps didn't even wonder: Were they husband and wife or brother and sister? Were they father and mother? There were a few other persons, of various ages, wandering singly in by the back door and out. But none of their relationships could I imagine, when I'd never seen them sitting down together around their own table.

The possibility that they had any other life at all, anything beyond what we could see within the four walls of the Little Store, occurred to me only when tragedy struck their family. There was some act of violence. The shock to the neighborhood traveled to the children, of course; but I couldn't find out from my parents what had happened. They held it back from me, as they'd already held back many things, "until the time comes for you to know."

30   You could find out some of these things by looking in the unabridged dictionary and the encyclopedia—kept to hand in our dining room—but you couldn't find out there what had happened to the family who for all the years of your life had lived upstairs over the Little Store, who had never been anything but patient and kind to you, who never once had sent you away. All I ever knew was its aftermath: They were the only people ever known to me who simply vanished. At the point where their life overlapped into ours, the story broke off.

We weren't being sent to the neighborhood grocery for facts of life, or death. But of course those are what we were on the track of, anyway. With the loaf of bread and the Cracker Jack prize, I was bringing home the intimations of pride and disgrace, and rumors and early news of people coming to hurt one another, while others practiced for joy— storing up a portion for myself of the human mystery.

Eudora Welty

In short stories and novels, Eudora Welty (1909–2001) explored the frailty and strength of human character in her native Mississippi. A keen observer of behavior and social relations, she crafted fictional worlds that evoke compelling portraits of people and places.

Born in Jackson, Mississippi, Welty published her first story in 1936. In the years following she received many awards, including a Pulitzer Prize for the novel *The Optimist's Daughter* (1972), the American Book Award for *The Collected Stories of Eudora Welty* (1980), and the National Book Critics Circle Award for her autobiographical essays in *One Writer's Beginnings* (1984). Welty started her post-college career as a photographer for the Works Progress Administration during the Great Depression. Although she chose to focus on her writing, she continued to take photographs throughout her life, eventually publishing two collections: *Photographs* (1989) and *One Time, One Place* (1996).

"The Little Store" (1975) draws on personal experience. Remembering experience, she said, helped her craft fiction out of "the *whole* fund of my feelings, my responses to the real experiences of my own life, to the relationships that formed and changed it, that I have given most of myself to."

SEEING

1. What principles of selection and order does Eudora Welty use to organize her reminiscences of running errands to the local grocery store? Reread the opening paragraphs in which she affectionately recounts some of the games she played as a child. How do these moments express her feelings toward the store? What are the effects of presenting these paragraphs before she describes the store? To which senses does she appeal in describing the Little Store? What techniques does she use to reinforce the childlike perspective of the essay? In each instance, point to specific evidence to verify your point.

2. Welty was an accomplished photographer as well as a renowned writer. She hoped to capture "the moment in which people reveal themselves." After examining the photograph of the storekeeper, what do you think he reveals about himself? Note as many details of the photograph as you can. What, for example, do you notice about the man's stance? body language? facial expression? How does the lighting affect your impression of him? How has Welty chosen to frame her subject? What has she included in the photograph? What has she omitted?

WRITING

1. In an interview about her photography, Welty suggested that both the writer and the photographer must learn "about accuracy of the eye, about observation and about sympathy toward what is in front of you." Consider the meaning of each of the three components of her statement, and list the ways in which you can apply them to writing and to taking photographs. Write an essay in which you explore Welty's statement about the similarities between writing and taking pictures, using her own verbal and visual takes on similar subjects to support your points.

2. When Welty observed that in her photographs, she tries to capture "the moment in which people reveal themselves," what assumptions is she making about photography and spontaneity? Draft an analytical essay in which you defend or challenge the assertion that the subject's awareness of the photographer precludes the possibility of capturing a spontaneous moment. Whichever side you argue, support your claims with evidence and anticipate – and rebut – the arguments of the other side.

I'm not very eloquent about things like this, but I think that writing and photography go together. I don't mean that they are related arts, because they're not. But the person doing it, I think, learns from both things about accuracy of the eye, about observation and about sympathy toward what is in front of you. It's about trying to see into the essence of reality. It's about honesty, or truth telling, and a way to find it in yourself, how to need it and learn from it.

I still go back to a paragraph of mine from *One Time, One Place* as the best expression I was ever able to manage about what I did or was trying to do in both fields. It's still the truth:

> I learned quickly enough when to click the shutter, but what I was becoming aware of more slowly was a story-writer's truth: The thing to wait on, to reach for, is the moment in which people reveal themselves. . . . I learned from my own pictures, one by one, and had to; for I think we are the breakers of our own hearts.

— Eudora Welty, from "Storekeeper, 1935"

December 1977

January 1980

March 1990

September 1992

August 2001

April 2003

December 1983

November 1988

March 1994

June 1997

February 2004

May 2008

NO PLACE LIKE HOME
On the Manicured Streets
of a Master-Planned Community
David Guterson

To the casual eye, Green Valley, Nevada, a corporate master-planned community just south of Las Vegas, would appear to be a pleasant place to live. On a Sunday last April—a week before the riots in Los Angeles and related disturbances in Las Vegas—the golf carts were lined up three abreast at the upscale "Legacy" course; people in golf outfits on the clubhouse veranda were eating three-cheese omelets and strawberry waffles and looking out over the palm trees and fairways, talking business and reading Sunday newspapers. In nearby Parkside Village, one of Green Valley's thirty-five developments, a few homeowners washed cars or boats or pulled up weeds in the sun. Cars wound slowly over clean broad streets, ferrying children to swimming pools and backyard barbecues and Cineplex matinees. At the Silver Springs tennis courts, a well-tanned teenage boy in tennis togs pummeled his sweating father. Two twelve-year-old daredevils on expensive mountain bikes, decked out in Chicago Bulls caps and matching tank tops, watched and ate chocolate candies.

Green Valley is as much a verb as a noun, a place in the process of becoming what it purports to be. Everywhere on the fringes of its 8,400 acres one finds homes going up, developments going in (another twenty-one developments are under way), the desert in the throes of being transformed in accordance with the master plan of Green Valley's designer and builder, the American Nevada Corporation. The colors of its homes are muted in the Southwest manner: beiges, tans, dun browns, burnt reds, olive grays, rusts, and cinnamons. Its graceful, palm-lined boulevards and parkways are conspicuously devoid of gas stations, convenience stores, and fast-food restaurants, presenting instead a seamless facade of interminable, well-manicured developments punctuated only by golf courses and an occasional shopping plaza done in stucco. Within the high walls lining Green Valley's expansive parkways lie homes so similar they appear as uncanny mirror reflections of one another—and, as it turns out, they are. In most neighborhoods a prospective homeowner must choose from among a limited set of models with names like "Greenbriar," "Innisbrook," and "Tammaron" (or, absurdly, in a development called Heartland, "Beginnings," "Memories," and "Reflections"), each of which is merely a variation on a theme: Spanish, Moorish, Mexican, Territorial,

Mediterranean, Italian Country, Mission. Each development inhabits a planned socioeconomic niche—$99,000, $113,900, $260,000 homes, and on into the stratosphere for custom models if a wealthy buyer desires. Neighborhoods are labyrinthine, confusing in their sameness; each block looks eerily like the next. On a spring evening after eight o'clock it is possible to drive through miles of them without seeing a single human being. Corners are marked with signs a visitor finds more than a little disconcerting: WARNING, they read, NEIGHBORHOOD WATCH PROGRAM IN FORCE. WE IMMEDIATELY REPORT ALL SUSPICIOUS PERSONS AND ACTIVITIES TO OUR POLICE DEPARTMENT. The signs on garages don't make me feel any better. WARNING, they read, YOUR NEIGHBORS ARE WATCHING.

I'd come to Green Valley because I was curious to meet the citizens of a community in which everything is designed, orchestrated, and executed by a corporation. More and more Americans, millions of them—singles, families, retirees—are living in such places. Often proximate to beltway interchanges and self-contained office parks of boxy glass buildings, these communities are everywhere now, although far more common in the West than elsewhere: Its vast terrain, apparently, still lends itself to dreamers with grand designs. Irvine, California—the master-planned product of the Irvine Company, populated by 110,000 people and one of the fastest-growing *cities* in America—is widely considered a prototype, as are Reston, Virginia, and Columbia, Maryland, two early East Coast versions. Fairfield Communities, Inc., owns fourteen "Fairfield Communities": Fairfield in the Foothills, Fairfield's La Cholla, Fairfield's River Farm, and so forth. The Walt Disney Co. has its entry—Celebration—under way not far from Florida's Disney World. Las Colinas, Inc., invented Las Colinas, Texas, "America's Premier Master Planned Community," "America's Premier Development," and "America's Corporate Headquarters." The proliferation of planned communities is most visible in areas of rapid growth, which would certainly include the Las Vegas valley, the population of which has nearly doubled, to 799,381, since 1982.

That Sunday afternoon I made my way along peaceful boulevards to Green Valley's civic center, presumably a place where people congregate. A promotional brochure describes its plaza as "the perfect size for public gatherings and all types of social events," but on that balmy day, the desert in bloom just a few miles off, no one had, in fact, gathered here. The plaza had the desultory ambience of an architectural mistake—deserted, useless, and irrelevant to Green Valley's citizens, who had, however, gathered in large numbers at stucco shopping centers not far off—at Spotlight

Video, Wallpaper World, Record City, and Bicycle Depot, Rapunzel's Den Hair Salon, Enzo's Pizza and Ristorante, A Basket of Joy, and K-Mart.

5   Above the civic center, one after another, flew airplanes only seconds from touching down at nearby McCarran International Airport, which services Las Vegas casinogoers. Low enough that the rivets in their wings could be discerned, the planes descended at sixty-second intervals, ferrying fresh loads of gamblers into port. To the northeast, beyond a billboard put up by a developer—WATCH US BUILD THE NEW LAS VEGAS—lay a rectangle of desert as yet not built upon but useful as a dumping ground: Scraps of plastic, bits of stucco, heaps of wire mesh and lumber ends were all scattered in among low creosote bush. The corporate master plan, I later learned, calls for hauling these things away and replacing them with, among other things, cinemas, a complex of swimming pools, restaurants, and substantially more places to shop.

Inside the civic center were plenty of potted palms, walls of black glass, and red marble floors, but again, no congregating citizens. Instead, I found the offices of the Americana Group Realtors; Lawyer's Title of Nevada, Inc.; RANPAC Engineering Corporation; and Coleman Homes, a developer. A few real estate agents were gearing up for Sunday home tours, dressed to kill and shuffling manila folders, their BMWs parked outside. Kirk Warren, a marketing specialist with the Americana Group, listened patiently to my explanation: I came to the civic center to talk to people; I wanted to know what brought them to a corporate-planned community and why they decided to stay.

"It's safe here," Warren explained, handing me a business card with his photograph on it. "And clean. And nice. The schools are good and the crime rate low. It's what buyers are looking for."

Outside the building, in the forlorn-looking plaza, six concrete benches had been fixed astride lawns, offering citizens twenty-four seats. Teenagers had scrawled their graffiti on the pavement (DARREN WAS HERE, JASON IS AWESOME), and a footlight beneath a miniature obelisk had been smashed by someone devoted to its destruction. Someone had recently driven past on a motorcycle, leaving telltale skid marks.

The history of suburbia is a history of gradual dysfunction, says Brian Greenspun, whose family owns the American Nevada Corporation (ANC), the entity that created Green Valley. Americans, he explains, moved to the suburbs in search of escape from the more undesirable aspects of the city and from undesirable people in particular. Time passed and undesirables showed up anyway; suburbia had no means to prevent this. But in the end, that was all right, Greenspun points out, because master planners recognized the problem as an enormously lucrative market opportunity and began building places like Green Valley.

10   Rutgers history professor Robert Fishman, author of *Bourgeois Utopias: The Rise and Fall of Suburbia*, would agree that suburbia hasn't worked. Suburbia, he argues, appeared in America in the middle of the nineteenth century, offering escape from the squalor and stench of the new industrial cities. The history of suburbia reached a climax, he says, with the rise of Los Angeles as a city that is in fact one enormous suburb. Today, writes Fishman, "the original concept of suburbia as an unspoiled synthesis of city and countryside has lost its meaning." Suburbia "has become what even the greatest advocates of suburban growth never desired—a new form of city." These new suburb-cities have, of course, inevitably developed the kinds of problems—congestion, crime, pollution, tawdriness—that the middle class left cities to avoid. Now, in the nineties, developers and corporate master planners, recognizing an opportunity, have stepped in to supply the middle class, once again, with the promise of a bourgeois utopia.

As a product of the American Nevada Corporation, Green Valley is a community with its own marketing logo: the letters G and V intertwined quite cleverly to create a fanciful optical illusion—two leaves and a truncated plant stem. It is also a community with an advertising slogan: ALL THAT A COMMUNITY CAN BE. Like other master-planned communities in America, it is designed to embody a corporate ideal not only of streets and houses but of image and feeling. Green Valley's crisp lawns, culs-de-sac, and stucco walls suggest an amiable suburban existence where, as an advertising brochure tells us, people can enjoy life *more than they ever did before*. And, apparently, they do enjoy it. Thirty-four thousand people have filled Green Valley's homes in a mere fourteen years—the place is literally a boomtown. . . .

On weekday mornings, familiar yellow buses amble through Green Valley toward public schools built on acreage set aside in a 1971 land-sale agreement between ANC and Henderson, a blue-collar town just south of Vegas that was initially hostile to its new upscale neighbor but that now willingly participates in Green Valley's prosperity. Many parents prefer to drive their children to these schools before moving on to jobs, shopping, tennis, or aerobics classes. (Most Green Valley residents work in Las Vegas, commuting downtown in under twenty minutes.) The characteristic Green Valley family—a married couple with two children under twelve—has an average annual income of $55,000; about one in five are members of the Green Valley Athletic Club, described by master planners as "the focal point of the community" (family initiation fee: $1,000). The club's lavish swimming pools and air-conditioned tennis courts are, I was told, especially popular in summer, when Green Valley temperatures can reach 115 degrees and when whole caravans of Porsches and BMWs make their way toward its shimmering parking lots.

Inside is a state-of-the-art body-sculpting palace with Gravitron Upper Body Systems in its weight room, $3.99 protein drinks at its Health Bar, complimentary mouthwash in its locker rooms (swilled liberally by well-preserved tennis aficionados primping their thinning hair at mirrors before heading upstairs to Café Brigette Deux), and employees trained "to create an experience that brings a smile to every Member at every opportunity." I was given a tour by Jill Johnson, a membership service representative, who showed me the Cybex systems in the weight room, the Life-Circuit computerized resistance equipment, the aerobics studio, and the day-care center.

Upstairs, the bartender mixed an "Arnold Schwarzenegger" for an adolescent boy with a crisp haircut and a tennis racket: yogurt, banana, and weight-gain powder. Later, in the weight room, I met a man I'll call Phil Anderson, an accountant, who introduced me to his wife, Marie, and to his children, Jason and Sarah. Phil was ruddy, overweight, and sweat-soaked, and had a towel draped over his shoulders. Marie was trim, dressed for tennis; the kids looked bored. Phil had been playing racquetball that evening while Marie took lessons to improve her serve and the children watched television in the kids' lounge. Like most of the people I met in Green Valley, the Andersons were reluctant to have their real names used ("We don't want the reaction" was how some residents explained it, including Marie and Phil). I coaxed them by promising to protect their true identities, and the Andersons began to chat.

15   "We moved here because Jase was getting on toward junior high age," Marie explained between sets on a machine designed to strengthen her triceps. "And in San Diego, where we lived before, there were these . . . *forces*, if you know what I mean. There were too many things we couldn't control. Drugs and stuff. It wasn't healthy for our kids."

"I had a job offer," Phil said. "We looked for a house. Green Valley was . . . the obvious place—just sort of obvious, really. Our real estate agent sized us up and brought us out here right away."

"We found a house in Silver Springs," Marie said. "You can go ahead and put that in your notes. It's a big development. No one will figure it out."

"But just don't use our names, okay?" Phil pleaded. "I would really appreciate that."

"We don't need problems," Marie added.

20 Master planners have a penchant not just for slogans but for predictable advertising strategies. Their pamphlets, packets, and brochures wax reverent about venerable founding fathers of passionate vision, men of foresight who long ago—usually in the fifties—dreamed of building cities in their own image. Next comes a text promising an upscale pastoral: golf courses, blissful shoppers, kindly security guards, pleasant walkways, goodly physicians, yeomanly fire fighters, proficient teachers. Finally— invariably—there is culture in paradise: an annual arts and crafts festival, a sculpture, a gallery, Shakespeare in the park. In Las Colinas's Williams Square, for example, a herd of bronze mustangs runs pell-mell across a plaza, symbolizing, a brochure explains, a "heritage of freedom in a free land." Perhaps in the interstices of some sophisticated market analysis, these unfettered mustangs make perfectly good sense; in the context of a community whose dominant feature is walls, however, they make no sense whatsoever.

Walls are everywhere in Green Valley too; they're the first thing a visitor notices. Their message is subliminal and at the same time explicit; controlled access is as much metaphor as reality. Controlled access is also a two-way affair—both "ingress" and "egress" are influenced by it; both coming and going are made difficult. The gates at the thresholds of Green Valley's posher neighborhoods open with a macabre, mechanical slowness; their guards speak firmly and authoritatively to strangers and never smile in the manner of official greeters. One of them told me to take no pictures and to go directly to my destination "without stopping to look at anything." Another said that in an eight-hour shift he felt constantly nervous about going to the bathroom and feared that in abandoning his post to relieve himself he risked losing his job. A girl at the Taco Bell on nearby Sunset Road complained about Clark County's ten o'clock teen curfew—and about the guard at her neighborhood's gate who felt it was his duty to remind her of it. A ten-year-old pointed out that his friends beyond the wall couldn't join him inside without a telephone call to "security," which meant "the policeman in the guardhouse." Security, of course, can be achieved in many ways, but one implication of it, every time, is that security has insidious psychological consequences for those who contrive to feel secure.

"Before I built a wall," wrote Robert Frost, "I'd ask to know what I was walling in or walling out, and to whom I was like to give offense." The master planners have answers that are unassailably prosaic: "lot owners shall not change said walls in any manner"; "perimeter walls are required around all single family residential projects"; "side yard walls shall conform to the Guidelines for intersecting rear property walls." Their master plan weighs in with ponderous wall specifics, none of them in any way actionable: location, size, material, color, piers, pillars, openings. "Perimeter Project Walls," for example, "shall be made of gray colored, split face concrete masonry units, 8" by 16" by 6" in size, with a 4" high gray, split face, concrete block. . . . The block will be laid in a running bond pattern. . . . No openings are allowed from individual back yard lots into adjoining areas."

All of Green Valley is defined in this manner, by CC&Rs, as the planners call them—covenants, conditions, and restrictions embedded in deeds. Every community has some restrictions on matters such as the proper placement of septic tanks and the minimum distance allowed between homes, but in Green Valley the restrictions are detailed and pervasive, insuring the absence of individuality and suppressing the natural mess of humanity. Clotheslines and Winnebagos are not permitted, for example; no fowl, reptile, fish, or insect may be raised; there are to be no exterior speakers, horns, whistles, or bells. No debris of any kind, no open fires, no noise. Entries, signs, lights, mailboxes, sidewalks, driveways, rear yards, side yards, carports, sheds—the planners have had their say about each. All CC&Rs are inscribed into books of law that vary only slightly from development to development: the number of dogs and cats you can own (until recently, one master-planned community in Newport Beach, California, even limited the *weight* of dogs) as well as the placement of garbage cans, barbecue pits, satellite dishes, and utility boxes. The color of your home, the number of stories, the materials used, its accents and trim. The interior of your garage, the way to park your truck, the plants in your yard, the angle of your flagpole, the size of your address numbers, the placement of mirrored glass balls and birdbaths, the grade of your lawn's slope, and the size of your FOR SALE sign should you decide you want to leave.

"These things," explained Brad Nelson, an ANC vice president, "are set up to protect property values." ANC owner Greenspun put it another way: "The public interest and ANC's interest are one." . . .

25 As a journalist, I may have preferred a telling answer to my most frequent question—why do you live here?—but the people of Green Valley, with disconcerting uniformity, were almost never entirely forthcoming. ("I moved here because of my job," they would say, or "I moved here because we found a nice house in Heartland.") Many had never heard of the American Nevada Corporation; one man took me for a representative

of it and asked me what I was selling. Most had only a vague awareness of the existence of a corporate master plan for every detail of their community. The covenants, conditions, and restrictions of their lives were background matters of which they were cognizant but about which they were yawningly unconcerned. It did not seem strange to anyone I spoke with that a corporation should have final say about their mailboxes. When I explained that there were CC&Rs for nearly everything, most people merely shrugged and pointed out in return that it seemed a great way to protect property values. A woman in a grocery store checkout line explained that she'd come here from southern California because "even the good neighborhoods there aren't good anymore. You don't feel safe in L.A."

What the people of Green Valley want, explained a planner, is safety from threats both real and imagined and control over who moves in beside them. In this they are no different from the generation that preceded them in search of the suburban dream. The difference this time is that nothing has been left to chance and that everything has been left to the American Nevada Corporation, which gives Green Valley its contemporary twist: To achieve at least the illusion of safety, residents must buy in to an enormous measure of corporate domination. Suburbia in the nineties has a logo.

But even Eden—planned by God—had serpents, and so, apparently, does Green Valley. Last year a rapist ran loose in its neighborhoods; police suspected the man was a resident and responsible for three rapes and five robberies. George Hennard, killer of twenty-three people in a Killeen, Texas, cafeteria in October 1991, was a resident of Green Valley only months before his rampage and bought two of his murder weapons here in a private transaction. Joseph Weldon Smith, featured on the television series *Unsolved Mysteries*, strangled to death his wife and two stepdaughters in a posh Green Valley development called The Fountains.

The list of utopia's outrages also includes a November 1991 heist in which two armed robbers took a handcuffed hostage and more than $100,000 from a Green Valley bank, then fled and fired military-assault-rifle rounds at officers in hot pursuit. The same week police arrested a suspected child molester who had been playing football with Green Valley children and allegedly touching their genitals.

"You can run but you can't hide," one Green Valley resident told me when I mentioned a few of these incidents. "People are coming here from all over the place and bringing their problems with them." Perhaps she was referring to the gangs frequenting a Sunset Road fast-food restaurant—Sunset Road forms one fringe of Green Valley—where in the summer of 1991, according to the restaurant's manager, "the dining room was set on fire and there were fights every weekend." Perhaps she had talked to the teenagers who told me that LSD and crystal meth are the narcotics of choice at Green Valley High School, or to the doctor who simply rolled his eyes when I asked if he thought AIDS had arrived here.

30   Walls might separate paradise from heavy industry, but the protection they provide is an illusion. In May 1991 a leak at the nearby Pioneer Chlor Alkali plant spread a blanket of chlorine gas over Green Valley; nearly a hundred area residents were treated at hospitals for respiratory problems. The leak came three years after another nearby plant—this one producing rocket-fuel oxidizer for the space shuttle and nuclear missiles—exploded powerfully enough to register on earthquake seismographs 200 miles away. Two people were killed, 210 injured. Schools were closed and extra police officers called in to discourage the looting of area homes with doors and windows blown out.

And, finally, there is black comedy in utopia: A few days after Christmas last year, police arrested the Green Valley Community Association president for allegedly burglarizing a model home. Stolen items included pictures, cushions, bedspreads, and a gaudy brass figurine—a collection with no internal logic. A local newspaper described the civic leader running from the scene, dropping his loot piece by piece in his wake as he was chased by police to his residence. At home he hid temporarily in his attic but ultimately to no avail. The plaster cracked and he fell through a panel into the midst of the arresting officers.

Is it a coincidence that the one truly anomalous soul I met roams furtively the last unpaved place in Green Valley, a short stretch of desert called Pittman Wash?

Pittman Wash winds through quiet subdivisions, undeveloped chiefly because it is useful for drainage and unbuildable anyway. Lesser washes have been filled in, built on, and forgotten, but Pittman remains full of sand and desert hollyhock, a few tamarisks, some clumps of creosote bush. Children prefer it to the manicured squares of park grass provided for them by the master planners; teenagers drink beer here and write graffiti on the storm-drain access pillars buried in the wash's channel: FUCK HENDERSON PK. DSTC. and the like. Used condoms, rusting oil filters, a wind-whipped old sleeping bag, a rock wren, a yellow swallowtail butterfly.

Here I met nine-year-old Jim Collins, whose name has been changed—at his fervent request—on the off chance his mother reads these words and punishes him for playing in Pittman Wash again. Jim struck me as a lonesome, Huck Finn sort, brown-skinned and soft-spoken, with grit beneath his nails and sun-bleached hair. I found him down on his dirty knees, lazily poking a stick into a hole.

35   "Lizards," he explained. "I'm looking for lizards. There's rattlers, chipmunks, coyote, mountain lion, black widows, and scorpions too." He regaled me with stories of parents in high dudgeon over creatures of the wash brought home. Then, unsolicited, he suddenly declared that "most of the time I'm bored out of my guts . . . the desert's all covered up with houses—that sucks."

He insisted, inexplicably, on showing me his backyard, which he described as "just like the desert." So we trudged out of the wash and walked the concrete trail the master planners have placed here. Jim climbed the border wall and ran along its four-inch top with the unconscious facility of a mountain goat. We looked at his yard, which had not yet been landscaped, a rectangle of cracked desert caliche. Next door three children dressed fashionably in sporting attire shot baskets on a Michael Jordan Air Attack hoop. "We don't get along," Jim said. He didn't want me to go away in the end, and as I left he was still chattering hopefully. "My favorite store is Wild Kingdom of Pets," he called. "If you go there you can see Tasha the wildcat."

Some might call Green Valley a simulacrum[1] of a real place, Disneyland's Main Street done in Mediterranean hues, a city of haciendas with cardboard souls, a valley of the polished, packaged, and perfected, an empyrean of emptiness, a sanitized wasteland. They will note the Southwest's pastel palette coloring a community devoid of improvisation, of caprice, spontaneity, effusiveness, or the charm of error—a place where the process of commodification has at last leached life of the accidental and ecstatic, the divine, reckless, and enraged.

Still, many now reside in this corporate domain, driven here by insatiable fears. No class warfare here, no burning city. Green Valley beckons the American middle class like a fabulous and eternal dream. In the wake of our contemporary trembling and discontent, its pilgrims have sought out a corporate castle where in exchange for false security they pay with personal freedoms; where the corporation that does the job of walling others out also walls residents in. The principle, once political, is now economic. Just call your real estate agent.

---

1. simulacrum: An insubstantial image of something real. [Eds.]

David Guterson

In both his fiction and his essays, David Guterson's craft reminds us of an ornate tapestry: Intense focus on detail builds toward a complex and compelling portrait. He engages his readers on multiple levels – philosophical, psychological, and ethical – because, in his words, "I feel responsible to tell stories that inspire readers to consider more deeply who they are." In "No Place Like Home," which appeared in *Harper's* in November 1991, Guterson asks us to consider the kind of society we are producing as planned and gated communities proliferate and to reflect on our apparently contradictory needs for freedom and security.

Guterson (b. 1956) lives near Seattle on Bainbridge Island, where he spent twelve years teaching high school English. His publications include a collection of short stories, *The Country ahead of Us, the Country behind Us* (1989); a nonfiction argument in favor of homeschooling, *Family Matters* (1993); and the novels *Snow Falling on Cedars* (1994), *East of the Mountains* (1999), *Our Lady of the Forest* (2003), and *The Other* (2008). Guterson is currently a contributing editor to *Harper's* magazine.

SEEING

1. "To the casual eye," writes David Guterson, "Green Valley, Nevada . . . would appear to be a pleasant place to live" (para. 1). How does Guterson suggest the *critical* eye would see Green Valley? Find specific examples of the language Guterson uses and the details he focuses on to support your answer. What does he mean when he says that "Green Valley is as much a verb as a noun" (para. 2) or that Green Valley "is designed to embody a corporate ideal not only of streets and houses but of image and feeling" (para. 11)?

2. What principle of organization does Guterson employ in his analysis of planned communities? Do you think the organization is effective? What specific examples does he provide to illustrate his point that Green Valley is "a place where the process of commodification has at last leached life of the accidental and ecstatic, the divine, reckless, and enraged" (para. 37)? What sources and perspectives does he draw on to help paint a picture of suburban life in general? What opinions and perspectives does he omit? How would you characterize the tone of this piece? What words, phrases, and passages lead you to this characterization?

WRITING

1. "Walls are everywhere in Green Valley too," Guterson writes; "they're the first thing a visitor notices. Their message is subliminal and at the same time explicit; controlled access is as much metaphor as reality" (para. 21). Choose a wall, fence, or some other physical divider in your neighborhood or on campus. What purpose does it serve? What does it keep in or out? Write the first draft of an essay in which you characterize the literal and metaphorical functions of the wall you have chosen.

2. In paragraph 10, Guterson recounts Robert Fishman's explanation for the development of America's suburbs: "In the middle of the nineteenth century," suburbia offered an "escape from the squalor and stench of the new industrial cities." Write an analytical essay in which you identify and discuss the middle-class ideal of the suburban community. Why do middle-class Americans continue to cling to that ideal – why do the sales of homes in planned communities continue to rise – when the suburbs have become just "a new form of city"?

Mark Peterson
Image of Homelessness, 1994

Mark Peterson

Born in 1955 and raised in Minneapolis, Mark Peterson began his career as a photographer while doing odd jobs for a photojournalist. "I was failing miserably as a writer," he said in a recent interview, "and thought photography would be easy. That was my first mistake in photography." After working in both Minneapolis and New York, Peterson moved to New Jersey to pursue freelance photography. His photographs, which he describes as "day in the life" reportage, have appeared in *Life*, *Newsweek*, *Fortune*, and the *New York Times Magazine*.

Peterson's recent projects include photographing teenagers in recovery from drug and alcohol addiction and exhibiting his photographs of New York's hip-hop scene in a retrospective series entitled No Sleep 'till Brooklyn. In 2004 Peterson published a book of photographs, *Acts of Charity*, which examines the "culture of philanthropy" in upper-class New York.

The photograph here is from Peterson's series Across the Street, in which the photographer captures the divide between rich and poor living on and along Fifth Avenue in New York City.

SEEING

1. What exactly is the place captured by this photograph – the box? the park? the urban scene? How does the fact that someone sleeps inside the box create a sense of place? What other elements in the image mark the box as a place? How can you tell whether there is – or was – someone inside?

2. What does the photographer gain by positioning the homeless person's "place" clearly in the foreground of the image? What does he lose? Given what is visible in the picture, what changes – say, in perspective or focus – might you suggest to highlight the dramatic impact of this redefinition of *place*? What effect(s) does the photographer accentuate in the image by including the phrase "HANDLE WITH CARE"? by including the out-of-focus background of Burger King?

WRITING

1. Imagine the following scenario: The Olympic Games of 2012 are going to take place in your state. The opening ceremony is a few weeks away, and the city council is debating a resolution: that all homeless people in the city should be removed to shelters for the duration of the Games. You have been charged with advocating or challenging passage of the resolution. Write a draft of the speech you would make to the city council.

Working with Sources

2. In a 1998 essay entitled "Distancing the Homeless," the writer and social critic Jonathan Kozol argues that the homeless are subject to many misconceptions. "A misconception . . . is not easy to uproot, particularly when it serves a useful social role. The notion that the homeless are largely psychotics who belong in institutions, rather than victims of displacements at the hands of enterprising realtors, spares us from the need to offer realistic solutions to the . . . extremes of wealth and poverty in the United States." Review the professional literature on the causes of homelessness published over the past eighteen months. Choose a still-popular misconception about homelessness – one that involves coming to terms with a sense of place – and write an argumentative essay in which you correct the mistaken or unexamined assumptions evident in this misconception.

I've had the pleasure of thinking about what a sense of place means, and it occurs to me that it is as large as one's birthplace or the country one adopts. And it can be as small as a mood that has a ground, or as small as a thought that takes place in a room. In fact when thoughts do take place in a room they have a wonderful sense of place. At any rate, what I love about it is that, when you're writing, there's nothing more difficult than to come up with a good description of place. Writers often feel that sometimes they do what they do through their work, and once in a while they get a gift from the various powers either up there or coming up from below, and we've never asked where the gift comes from, whether on high or below; we're just happy enough to get the gift, 'cause writing can be a dreary activity. Anyway, when we get that good sense of place we're happy with it. And it doesn't happen that often.

— Norman Mailer, from *Three Minutes or Less* (2000)

HOMEPLACE
Scott Russell Sanders

As a boy in Ohio, I knew a farm family, the Millers, who suffered from three tornadoes. The father, mother, and two sons were pulling into their driveway after church when the first tornado hoisted up their mobile home, spun it around, and carried it off. With the insurance money, they built a small frame house on the same spot.

Several years later, a second tornado peeled off the roof, splintered the garage, and rustled two cows. The Millers rebuilt again, raising a new garage on the old foundation and adding another story to the house. That upper floor was reduced to kindling by a third tornado, which also pulled out half the apple trees and slurped water from the stock pond. Soon after that I left Ohio, snatched away by college as forcefully as by any cyclone. Last thing I heard, the family was preparing to rebuild yet again.

Why did the Millers refuse to move? I knew them well enough to say they were neither stupid nor crazy. Plain stubbornness was a factor. These were people who, once settled, might have remained at the foot of a volcano or on the bank of a flood-prone river or beside an earthquake fault. They had relatives nearby, helpful neighbors, jobs and stores and schools within a short drive, and those were all good reasons to stay. But the main reason, I believe, was that the Millers had invested so much of their lives in the land, planting orchards and gardens, spreading manure on the fields, digging ponds, building sheds, seeding pastures. Out back of the house were groves of walnuts, hickories, and oaks, all started by hand from acorns and nuts. April through October, perennial flowers in the yard pumped out a fountain of blossoms. This farm was not just so many acres of dirt, easily exchanged for an equal amount elsewhere; it was a particular place, intimately known, worked on, dreamed over, cherished.

Psychologists tell us that we answer trouble with one of two impulses, either fight or flight. I believe that the Millers exhibited a third instinct, that of staying put. They knew better than to fight a tornado, and they chose not to flee. Their commitment to the place may have been foolhardy, but it was also grand. I suspect that most human achievements worth admiring are the result of such devotion.

5   The Millers dramatize a choice we are faced with constantly: whether to go or stay, whether to move to a situation that is safer, richer, easier, more attractive, or to stick where we are and make what we can of it. If the shine goes off our marriage, our house, our car, do we trade it for a

new one? If the fertility leaches out of our soil, the creativity out of our job, the money out of our pocket, do we start over somewhere else? There are voices enough, both inner and outer, urging us to deal with difficulties by pulling up stakes and heading for new territory. I know them well, for they have been calling to me all my days. I wish to raise here a contrary voice, to say a few words on behalf of staying put, learning the ground, going deeper.

Claims for the virtues of moving on are familiar and seductive to Americans, this nation founded by immigrants and shaped by restless seekers. From the beginning, our heroes have been sailors, explorers, cowboys, prospectors, speculators, backwoods ramblers, rainbow chasers, vagabonds of every stripe. Our Promised Land has always been over the next ridge or at the end of the trail, never under our feet. In our national mythology, the worst fate is to be trapped on a farm, in a village, in the sticks, in some dead-end job or unglamorous marriage or played-out game.

Stand still, we are warned, and you die. Americans have dug the most canals, laid the most rails, built the most roads and airports of any nation. In a newspaper I read that, even though our sprawling system of interstate highways is crumbling, politicians think we should triple its size. Only a populace drunk on driving, a populace infatuated with the myth of the open road, could hear such a proposal without hooting.

Novelist Salman Rushdie chose to leave his native India for England, where he has written a series of brilliant books from the perspective of a cultural immigrant. In his book of essays *Imaginary Homelands* he celebrates the migrant sensibility: "The effect of mass migrations has been the creation of radically new types of human being: people who root themselves in ideas rather than places, in memories as much as in material things." He goes on to say that "to be a migrant is, perhaps, to be the only species of human being free of the shackles of nationalism (to say nothing of its ugly sister, patriotism)." Lord knows we could do with less nationalism (to say nothing of its ugly siblings, racism, religious sectarianism, and class snobbery). But who would pretend that a history of migration has immunized the United States against bigotry? And even if, by uprooting ourselves, we shed our chauvinism, is that all we lose?

In this hemisphere, many of the worst abuses—of land, forests, animals, and communities—have been carried out by "people who root themselves in ideas rather than places." Migrants often pack up their visions and values with the rest of their baggage and carry them along. The Spaniards devastated Central and South America by imposing on this New World the religion, economics, and politics of the Old. Colonists brought slavery with them to North America, along with smallpox and Norway rats. The Dust Bowl of the 1930s was caused not by drought but by the transfer onto the Great Plains of farming methods that were suitable to wetter regions. The habit of our industry and commerce has been to force identical schemes onto differing locales, as though the mind were a cookie cutter and the land were dough.

10   I quarrel with Rushdie because he articulates as eloquently as anyone the orthodoxy that I wish to counter: the belief that movement is inherently good, staying put is bad; that uprooting brings tolerance, while rootedness breeds intolerance; that to be modern, enlightened, fully of our time is to be displaced. Wholesale displacement may be inevitable in today's world; but we should not suppose that it occurs without disastrous consequences for the Earth and for ourselves. People who root themselves in places are likelier to know and care for those places than are people who root themselves in ideas. When we cease to be migrants and become inhabitants, we might begin to pay enough heed and respect to where we are. By settling in, we have a chance of making a durable home for ourselves, our fellow creatures, and our descendants.

The poet Gary Snyder writes frequently about our need to "inhabit" a place. One of the key problems in American society now, he points out, is people's lack of commitment to any given place:

> Neighborhoods are allowed to deteriorate, landscapes are allowed to be strip-mined, because there is nobody who will live there and take responsibility; they'll just move on. The reconstruction of a people and of a life in the United States depends in part on people, neighborhood by neighborhood, county by county, deciding to stick it out and make it work where they are, rather than flee.

But if you stick in one place, won't you become a stick-in-the-mud? If you stay put, won't you be narrow, backward, dull? You might. I have met ignorant people who never moved; and I have also met ignorant people who never stood still. Committing yourself to a place does not guarantee that you will become wise, but neither does it guarantee that you will become parochial.

To become intimate with your home region, to know the territory as well as you can, to understand your life as woven into the local life does not prevent you from recognizing and honoring the diversity of other places, cultures, ways. On the contrary, how can you value other places if you do not have one of your own? If you are not yourself *placed*, then you wander the world like a sightseer, a collector of sensations, with no gauge for measuring what you see. Local knowledge is the grounding for global knowledge. Those who care about nothing beyond the confines of their parish are in truth parochial, and are at least mildly dangerous to their parish; on the other hand, those who *have* no parish, those who navigate ceaselessly among postal zones and area codes, those for whom the world is only a smear of highways and bank accounts and stores, are a danger not just to their parish but to the planet.

Since birth, my children have regularly seen images of the Earth as viewed from space, images that I first encountered when I was in my twenties. Those photographs show vividly what in our sanest moments we have always known—that the Earth is a closed circle, lovely and rare. On the wall beside me as I write there is a poster of the big blue marble encased in its white swirl of clouds. That is one pole of my awareness; but the other pole is what I see through my window. I try to keep both in sight at once.

For all my convictions, I still have to wrestle with the fear—in myself, in my children, and even in some of my neighbors—that our place is too remote from the action. This fear drives many people to pack their bags and move to some resort or burg they have seen on television, leaving behind what they learn to think of as the boondocks. I deal with my own unease by asking just what action I am remote *from*—a stock market? a debating chamber? a drive-in mortuary? The action that matters, the work of nature and community, goes on everywhere.

15   Since Copernicus, we have known better than to see the Earth as the center of the universe. Since Einstein, we have learned that there is no center; or alternatively, that any point is as good as any other for observing the world. I find a kindred lesson in the words of the Zen master Thich Nhat Hanh: "This spot where you sit is your own spot. It is on this very spot and in this very moment that you can become enlightened. You don't have to sit beneath a special tree in a distant land." If you stay put, your place may become a holy center, not because it gives you special access to the divine, but because in your stillness you hear what might be heard anywhere.

I think of my home ground as a series of nested rings, with house and family and marriage at the center, surrounded by the wider and wider hoops of neighborhood and community, the bioregion within walking distance of my door, the wooded and rocky hills of southern Indiana, the watershed of the Ohio Valley, and so on outward—and inward —to the ultimate source.

The longing to become an inhabitant rather than a drifter sets me against the current of my culture, which nudges everyone into motion. Newton taught us that a body at rest tends to stay at rest, unless it is acted on by an outside force. We are acted on ceaselessly by outside forces—advertising, movies, magazines, speeches—and also by the inner force of biology. I am not immune to their pressure. Before settling in my present home, I lived in seven states and two countries, tugged from place to place in childhood by my father's work and in early adulthood by my own. This itinerant life is so common among the people I know that I have been slow to conceive of an alternative. Only by knocking against the golden calf of mobility, which looms so large and shines so brightly, have I come to realize that it is hollow. Like all idols, it distracts us from what is truly divine.

I am encouraged by the words of a Crow elder, quoted by Gary Snyder in *The Practice of the Wild*: "You know, I think if people stay somewhere long enough—even white people—the spirits will begin to speak to them. It's the power of the spirits coming up from the land. The spirits and the old powers aren't lost, they just need people to be around long enough and the spirits will begin to influence them."

As I write this, I hear the snarl of earth movers and chain saws a mile away destroying a farm to make way for another shopping strip. I would rather hear a tornado, whose damage can be undone. The elderly woman who owned the farm had it listed in the National Register, then willed it to her daughters on condition they preserve it. After her death, the daughters, who live out of state, had the will broken, so the land could be turned over to the chain saws and earth movers. The machines work around the clock. Their noise wakes me at midnight, at three in the morning, at dawn. The roaring abrades my dreams. The sound is a reminder that we are living in the midst of a holocaust. I do not use the word lightly. The Earth is being pillaged, and every one of us, willingly or grudgingly, is taking part. We ask how sensible, educated, supposedly moral people could have tolerated slavery or the slaughter of Jews. Similar questions will be asked about us by our descendants, to whom we bequeath an impoverished planet. They will demand to know how we could have been party to such waste and ruin.

20   What does it mean to be alive in an era when the Earth is being devoured, and in a country that has set the pattern for that devouring? What are we called to do? I think we are called to the work of healing, both inner and outer: healing of the mind through a change in conscious-

ness, healing of the Earth through a change in our lives. We can begin that work by learning how to inhabit a place.

"The man who is often thinking that it is better to be somewhere else than where he is excommunicates himself," we are cautioned by Thoreau, that notorious stay-at-home. The metaphor is religious: To withhold yourself from where you are is to be cut off from communion with the source. It has taken me half a lifetime of searching to realize that the likeliest path to the ultimate ground leads through my local ground. I mean the land itself, with its creeks and rivers, its weather, seasons, stone outcroppings, and all the plants and animals that share it. I cannot have a spiritual center without having a geographical one; I cannot live a grounded life without being grounded in a *place*.

In belonging to a landscape, one feels a rightness, an at-homeness, a knitting of self and world. This condition of clarity and focus, this being fully present, is akin to what the Buddhists call mindfulness, what Christian contemplatives refer to as recollection, what Quakers call centering down. I am suspicious of any philosophy that would separate this-worldly from other-worldly commitment. There is only one world, and we participate in it here and now, in our flesh and our place.

Scott Russell Sanders

The value of staying put is a recurring theme in Scott Russell Sanders's essays, which are featured in numerous collections including *In Limestone Country* (1991) and *A Private History of Awe* (2006). Sanders interweaves explorations of place with reflections on nature and the importance of the natural environment for healthful living. He has also written novels, short story collections, and numerous books for children.

Born in Memphis in 1945, Sanders has lived since 1971 in Bloomington, where he is a professor of English at Indiana University. Frequently compared with Henry David Thoreau and Wendell Berry, Sanders is devoted to exploring the unique aspects of nature and social life in the Midwest. "Because there is no true human existence apart from family and community," says Sanders, "I feel a deep commitment to my region, to the land, to the people and all other living things with which I share this place." This commitment, he adds, is strengthened by "a regard compounded of grief and curiosity and love." The essay "Homeplace" appeared in *Orion* magazine in 1992.

SEEING

1. Arguing against "the belief that movement is inherently good," Scott Russell Sanders asserts that "people who root themselves in places are likelier to know and care for those places than are people who root themselves in ideas" (para. 10). What strategies does Sanders use to build his argument on behalf of staying put? How, for example, does he define being *settled*, being *placed*, and being *an inhabitant*? What factors does Sanders identify that prompt people to refuse to move? Comment on the nature and effectiveness of the examples he uses to illustrate each point. What additional sources and examples would strengthen his argument?

2. Characterize the tone of Sanders's essay, citing specific words and phrases as examples. Imagine yourself directing someone to read this essay aloud. What tone of voice would you instruct the reader to use? Compare Sanders's tone of voice with that of Richard Ford in his essay "At Home. For Now" (pp. 182–85). Which voice do you find more engaging? more convincing? Explain why.

Page 182

WRITING

1. Sanders recounts the story of the Millers, a family that refused to yield to the ravages of several tornadoes. He notes, "The Millers dramatize a choice we are faced with constantly: whether to go or stay, whether to move to a situation that is safer, richer, easier, more attractive, or to stick where we are and make what we can of it" (para. 5). Consider a difficult set of circumstances or a conflict that you, your family, or someone you know faced. Draft a personal essay in which you recount both the nature of the problem and its resolution. Did you or someone else yield, as Sanders notes, to voices "both inner and outer, urging us to deal with difficulties by pulling up stakes and heading for new territory" (para. 5)?

Working with Sources

2. Sanders claims that "many of the worst abuses" in this hemisphere have come about through "the habit of our industry and commerce . . . to force identical schemes onto differing locales" (para. 9). Select an example of this habit in contemporary American experience, and write an argumentative essay in which you consider equally whether it's better to move, as Salman Rushdie argues, or to stay, as Sanders contends (paras. 8–10). Provide sufficient evidence to validate each point in your argument and to account for opposing points of view.

The Road to Success. Artist and date unknown.
From Katharine Harmon, *You Are Here: Personal Geographies and Other Maps of the Imagination* (2004)

Katharine Harmon

A lifelong collector and enthusiast of imaginative maps, Katharine Harmon explains that *You Are Here: Personal Geographies and Other Maps of the Imagination* (2004) contains over 150 maps that "mostly ignore mapping conventions" and "find their essence in some other goal than just taking us from point A to point B." The maps, similar to the one shown here as "The Road to Success," use word and image in combination to explore psychological and social landscapes. Some are humorous, like "A New Yorker's Idea of the United States of America," which depicts Manhattan and Brooklyn as larger than California. Some are dated, like the heart-shaped 1960s map from *McCall's* magazine entitled "Geographical Guide to a Man's Heart with Obstacles and Entrances Clearly Marked." And some are serious, like "Body Map of My Life," which labels physical and emotional scars on an image of the artist's body and explains the meaning of each.

Harmon is passionate about the written word as well. She is the founder of the Northwest Bookfest, an annual literary festival for the Seattle area, and is also the founder of Tributary Books, a book development company that produces original books and helps design other publishers' books. Harmon currently lives in Seattle with her husband.

SEEING

1. Examine the illustration carefully. How does each of the stops along the road to success help create an overall context for defining and experiencing success? Please be as specific as possible.

2. How would you approximate a date for the image's creation? Based on what evidence? What evidence can you identify to support that this map was created by a man or by a woman?

WRITING

1. Write the first draft of an essay in which you analyze the specific ways in which the image can be viewed as a commentary on success. What features, for example, does the artist accentuate? What does the artist omit?

2. Write a first-person narrative describing a moment in your life when you felt successful. Try including a metaphor that helps to describe what success felt like to you.

Responding Visually

Draw a map of your own personal road to success. Swap maps with a classmate. Write a brief essay in which you compare and contrast the differences between your map and your classmate's.

"The Road to Success" is taken from the book *You Are Here: Personal Geographies and Other Maps of the Imagination*, edited by Katharine Harmon. Neither the artist nor the date of this map is known. In an excerpt from the book's introduction, Harmon explains the continuous fascination individuals have with creating maps to help locate themselves and to understand their relation to other people and places.

As a youngster . . . I came to know intimately the ceiling of the room where I was supposed to be napping. I stared upward for hours, making out forms of imagined countries in the water-stained plaster. Why was I seeing international borders even before I knew the meaning of the concept? It was a natural way to pass the time and kept my restless imagination engaged far beyond that bedroom. . . .

Maps intrigue us, perhaps none more than those that ignore mapping conventions. These are maps that find their essence in some other goal than just taking us from point A to point B. They are a vehicle for the imagination, fueled up and ready to go. . . .

Of course, part of what fascinates us when looking at a map is inhabiting the mind of its maker. . . . If I had mapped that landscape, we ask ourselves, what would I have chosen to show, and how would I have shown it? The coded visual language of maps is one we all know, but in making maps of our worlds we each have our own dialect.

I map, therefore I am: This could be the motto for the contributors to this book. *You Are Here* is my own personal proof of the mapping instinct: an idiosyncratic collection of maps that transcend the norm, either because of the mapmaker's personal viewpoint, or sense of humor, or ingenuity, or all of the above. These are maps of the imagination, as all maps are, only more so.

Harmon believes that the "mapping instinct" is one that all humans share, and is in fact "part of what makes us human." Do you share Harmon's urge to create maps? Do you agree that this is an instinct all humans share? Why or why not?

AT HOME. FOR NOW
Richard Ford

I don't think about home very much. I mean, the concept of home — the direction finder we're all supposedly equipped with, that leads us onward (or back) to the place we belong, where we'll be . . . what? Happy? At peace? At rest? Permanent? I'm not really sure. Which is one underlying reason I don't think about home much. I don't know what it means.

Oh, I know some of what home means — to other people. That direction-finder idea is somebody else's. Home means, simply enough, where you come from, where you're born and where they always have to take you in (though we all know they don't). Home can also partake of "final matters" — where you want to be, in the last analysis of things. Or home can be where you choose to live, because that's where you like it best. In this last version, home would be a designation you make, not so different from your "weekend home," or from "my hunting cabin on Lake Winnipegosis." Nothing necessarily lasting. When my wife and I visit some faraway city and fetch up in a gloomy Ramada or Crowne Plaza, she will often, at the end of a long evening, gaze across the dinner table at me and smile and say, "Why don't we go home now?" By that she doesn't mean, why don't we go back to the place where you were born, or let's go visit our grave site. She just means let's go back to the room and get in bed. Home, in my wife's parlance, and in all of ours, is a variable concept.

Because I'm the kind of person who does this sort of thing, I looked "home" up in the *Oxford English Dictionary*. And I'm sorry to say that this venerable old word coffin doesn't have any firmer purchase on home than I do. In fact, it has a much less firm one than I do, by virtue of having many different purchases: from the predictable "abode, fixed residence, seat of one's interests, resting place" — all the way out to "the grave," or a future state, or one's country, or a place free from attack (no longer true of the United States), then onward to "state of unrestraint," prepared to receive visitors, full in from the sea, and extending all the way to "to move intimately," that is, to "home" in on something, which has nothing to do with where we live. I could go on, because the OED does — four and a half pages of "homes," in the big-print edition (which you have to keep at home). Anyone would close the big blue book with a confirmed sense that home is, indeed, a subject worthy of serious speculation, but for which a tidy definition (like the one, say, for "homarine," the generic name for the lobster) isn't going to be good enough.

Over the years I've lived in a lot of American places—California, Vermont, Chicago, New Jersey, New Orleans, Flint, Michigan. And plenty more. I can't really explain why I've done that, but I never thought any of these places were home when I lived there. Sometimes all this barging around will baffle someone, so I'll feel compelled to offer up one or another entirely made-up rationale for all this hectic moving: that my father was a traveling salesman, so I caught the moving bug early; that my grandparents ran a big hotel, so transience seemed normal to me; that when you're born and raised in Jackson, Mississippi (as I was), you either think you live at the center of the universe, or else you think you live on Pluto—which is what I thought. Or the quasi-intellectual rationale: that much drama in all things American draws upon the rub between an inherited European or African village past (where you have to stay home) and the magnetism of a vast new continent (where you hit the road). But they all come down to mean roughly the same thing: that moving's not unusual, but still home's a notion we routinely put in play, and that I myself am just an ordinary fish aswim in a confluence of swirling currents.

5   Though in the course of all these many moves, and in the many residences that have resulted, I've almost always had my feelers out for some certifiable sense of home-ness. You could say, in spite of all, that I've been "home-hungry" all my life—nosing around, sampling the genie spirit or the townscape of some new burg or county where I've somehow landed, determining where this or that road leads, musing about what family lives in this or that house, or used to live there, and for how long and how all that worked out for them. I've pictured my history or my future in whatever place it was—Missoula, Montana; Greenwood, Mississippi; Ann Arbor—always hoping, expecting to feel something *enfolding*, something protectively familiar, some sensation of belonging. (You can't tell from this that I've settled on the idea of home as a place I choose, rather than a place where I was simply, will-lessly born.)

And, truthfully, once in a while that homey-enfolding feeling has actually welled up in me, its richer ethers filling my nose, my heart surging, my brain spangling with all the lavish yet humble possibilities of belonging: of being automatically served "the usual" at my favorite diner, of being fast-tracked into the dentist's chair when my molar's cracked; of being on a first-name basis with the service guy at the Chevy dealership so my truck gets out by 10; of having free entry to our one-screen movie theater when I've forgotten my billfold but everybody trusts me; of neighbors who've all read all of my books and understood and enjoyed them because they talk about them when I'm not around. I've savored all these symptoms of home. Though admittedly I've experienced them the way I used to dream of playing fullback for the Packers, or of kicking the bejesus out of some tough guy who'd stolen my girlfriend; or of being able to play "Sentimental Journey" to an astonished crowd of those same neighbors at the opera house when the scheduled act doesn't show up, even though I'd never played the saxophone before. Which is to say they were, these ethers and heart-swellings, as fleeting as a dream. But a good dream. (Generally they last only long enough for me to grow skittish about all the less appealing attributes of home—permanence setting in like an acrid fog, the flavorless absence of the new, the raw bestilled boredom of imprisoning familiarity—the same life worries that propel desperate men off to the Foreign Legion, or that once sent wide-eyed and fearful homesteaders out across the oceanic prairie to nowhere, yet to whatever's next.)

Have we always had a sense of home, I wonder? Did it come to us straight from the cave men and cave women? Or, possibly, from the resourceful Dutch—ever focused and grounded—who're said to have perfected the home concept along the way to inventing bourgeois existence? But more important, is it so bad if we don't have a rock-solid sense of home? Or only have a weak one? Or maybe just don't have one yet? Home-less-ness is always imagined, in our security-obsessed era, as a bottomed-out and desperate state, akin to being a man without a country or to a life like a character in a Beckett play or that figure in the Munch painting—gaping, yawing, moaning, at-risk pointlessness. Only I wonder if *all* the residents of that state think it's so bad? I bet not.

Where I live, here on the coast of Maine, I frankly don't have much of a daily, practicing sense of home. I've been here nearly eight years, and so far the people seem friendly. (There *are* a few "originals," old and young farts who sneer at the likes of me for being from "away"; though many of these originals turn out to be from New Hampshire.) There's a small but detectable racial "mix." And there's a good feeling of authenticity to things, which I'm sure I benefit from. (Authenticity is the corroborating sensation that all Americans crave but are also perfectly happy to fabricate wherever it's lacking.) Here in East Boothbay (estimated permanent population 491), authenticity rests principally on the presence of history in everyday affairs—on the way citizens find a living (fishing and boat building); on the old-timey layout of our relatively few streets (School Street, Church Street), which persists unviolated by developers' schemes; on the placement of long-established residences; on the resilience of our few business concerns; and on the fact that many families have stayed in one place a long, long time. In other words memory—that great certifier—is still relatively seamless and reliable in East Boothbay. And, of course, much confidence is owed to our town's face being turned everlastingly to the sea.

How I traffic around here is, I would say, respectfully, though not reverentially, toward all these solid evidences of the unspurious. The waitresses at the Ebb Tide can't remember what I usually order (I don't come in often enough), but they seem silently to concede that I'm me. The men at Grover's Hardware (all jolly amateur comedians) are happy to share their yuks with me, though they don't seem to know my name or care what I do for a living. I've discovered places to hunt only minutes from my house—a good reason to stay on. I know my neighbors and the postmistress and her two sons. I have a pal who takes me striper fishing. And I like it here in the winter, Maine's signature season, the true test for the outsider.

10   Yet, here's the ocean, but I'm not a seafarer (the Atlantic, frankly, scares me). I don't have much taste for lobster. I don't assemble mornings at the general store, and I don't wear the high-school sweat shirt (I did buy a cap at the fire department open house but have never had it on). When I first arrived, and in the privacy of my house, I liked imitating the Mainers' thick-tongued, Down East accent. But over time I've quit doing that since it finally dawned on me I wasn't very good at it.

But taken all together, isn't that good enough? I'll never be a native here—which seems OK. I'm already a native someplace else, but I like it here better. Plus, we're all Americans. (It's not as if I was French.) Isn't that a persuasive profession of faith? Can authenticity only be a matter of accidents—of fate and temperament? I've always imagined my authenticity (which may be as close as I get to a real sense of home) depended on something else—something less, well, official. "To find my home in one sentence," the poet Czeslaw Milosz wrote, "concise, as if hammered in metal." Something along those lines seems right and makes anything else just a matter of real estate.

Home doesn't get any clearer than this for me. Most of the ageless essences I've sought and ultimately failed to inhabit in the pure and purifying way I thought I should and was sure everyone else did (I'm talking about home, love, victory, vocation, spirituality, loss, grief— all the big-ticket items), I finally had to conclude weren't perfectly inhabitable anyway. One size doesn't fit all, if it ever fits any of us. All the ageless essences demand not to be squeezed into like an ill-fitting suit, but rather to be incantations to flights of fruitful imagination, like a jollier version of the emperor's new clothes, which put on display—favorably, in my version—merely who the wearer is. Home, then, is whatever I say it is, even if it's just for today and I change my mind tomorrow. It's enough for me that, after all these years, I still can even think about home, still imagine it as a sweet notion—ever offshore, ever out of my reach, a place locked in a dream.

Richard Ford

Novelist and short story writer Richard Ford
has lived all over the United States and regularly writes about place. His protagonists are
typically drifters, in either a physical or psychological sense, and he often examines the concept of identifying oneself with a particular
landscape. Although originally from the South,
Ford eschews the label "Southern writer," and
he once said in an interview, "the really central
thing is that, no matter where I move, I always
write and I'm married to the same girl. All that
other stuff is just filigree."

Born in Jackson, Mississippi, in 1944, Ford
began his lifelong tendency toward relocation
when he attended Michigan State University, where he majored in literature. Although
married at an early age to Kristina Hensley
(the couple remain married to this day), Ford
spent a number of years moving from job to
job, place to place, eventually determining to
become a fiction writer. After obtaining his
MFA degree from the University of California –
Irvine, he began to write, publishing his first
novel, *A Piece of My Heart*, in 1976. Both
it and his second novel, *The Ultimate Good
Luck* (1981), were critically acclaimed; but
frustrated by poor book sales, Ford turned
his attention to sports writing. Ironically his
third novel, *The Sportswriter* (1986), based
on his new job experiences and written in his
spare time, was the one that established Ford
as an important novelist. The novel's sequel,
Independence Day (1995), won him both the
Pulitzer Prize and the PEN/Faulkner Award.
Ford has since published several collections of
short fiction and further novels, including *Lay
of the Land* (2006).

SEEING

1. Richard Ford's essay explores Americans'
yearning for a place they can call "home." What
does he find satisfying – and lacking – in the
"four and a half pages" (para. 3) of entries on
"home" in the *Oxford English Dictionary*? In
paragraph 6, Ford discusses various "symptoms of home." To what features of a place is
Ford especially drawn before he will consider
it a candidate worthy to be called *home*? What
does he point to as specifically "American" in
a definition of *home*?

2. Ford realizes his clearest sense of home in
a line by the poet Czeslaw Milosz: "To find my
home in one sentence, concise, as if hammered
in metal" (para. 11). In what ways do sentences
make homes for authors? After reviewing the
essay, which sentences do you think Ford
found a home in? What aspects of these sentences are "concise, as if hammered in metal"?

3. Ford does not let his reader settle into being
comfortable in his essay; his style is restless.
For example, he switches topics frequently
and moves swiftly between formal and everyday language. He also moves rapidly from one
metaphor to another. What are the effects of
Ford's decision to choose such an unsettling
strategy for his writing? Using three examples,
show how Ford's shifting styles and subjects
reinforce his main theme that home is hard to
find and difficult to define.

WRITING

1. In paragraph 6, Ford identifies what he calls "the less appealing attributes of home." What are these attributes for you? Do these attributes describe a residence? an area in a city? your hometown? Keep a journal over the course of several days. Make as many notes as you can about "the less appealing attributes" of your hometown or about the specific place in which you live. Instead of describing people and events, focus on general qualities, as Ford does – see, for example, such phrases as "the flavorless absence of the new" and "the raw bestilled boredom of imprisoning familiarity" (para. 6). Then write the first draft of an essay in which you explain why you agree – or disagree – with Ford's observation that the negative attributes you see display more about yourself than your hometown.

2. According to Ford, the *Oxford English Dictionary* lists four and a half pages of definitions for the word *home*. Without consulting this source, how many definitions can you think of immediately? (Consider, for example, such phrases as *home court*, *homework*, *home girl/boy*, etc.). In what ways are such phrases dependent on a consistent definition of home? What are the distinguishing features of that definition? As you develop your list, explain similarities and differences between and among these definitions. For example, in what specific ways is being safe after running "home" in baseball similar to – or different from – being safe after running "home" from a bully? Choose one of these expressions, and write an essay in which you define and illustrate how this phrase exemplifies the meaning of home.

VISUALIZING COMPOSITION:
TONE

In its simplest sense, *tone* refers to the quality or character of communication.

We talk about the tone of someone's voice: *She sounds mad* or *He had a resigned tone when he said he couldn't go.* The poet Robert Frost calls our ability to read tone "the hearing imagination."

We can read tone of voice even when we can't make out the exact words someone is saying.

In a MUSICAL COMPOSITION, *tone* refers to a distinct note, pitch or character of sound.

In ART, *tone* indicates the quality of color or the general effect of light in a painting or photograph.

When we're talking about our BODIES, *tone* refers to how visible our muscles are to the people who see us.

In WRITING, *tone* indicates the character of the text; it reflects the FEELINGS of the writer. A letter, an essay or a poem might be described as angry or skeptical in tone, formal or informal. When you are writing, no matter what the subject, remember that it is important to maintain a consistent **tone** and that the words you choose determine the tone your readers will hear.

Go to a couple of your favorite websites. As you read the content pay attention to the words and phrases that characterize the writer's different tones of voice. As you read the texts in this book—and compose your own—practice your ability to hear and to strike a distinctive tone.

THE STREETS CHANGE,
BUT MEMORIES ENDURE
Kenji Jasper

I grew up in the 1980s and '90s in a Washington, D.C., housing development called Fairfax Village. Back then, it was a neighborhood where
class lines blurred. Walking down the street, you were just as likely to
see a BMW as a broken-down van with a fender missing. The local playground where my friends and I hung out was well maintained and had
brand-new equipment. But it was also where kids from a rival housing
development once beat my friend with bats just because he happened to
be standing there.

There were plenty of trees and grass and sun in "the Village," but
when I called the police after our apartment had been robbed for the
third time, they brought an entire van full of officers to investigate.

Though it's been eleven years since my mother moved out of the
Village, I still drive through it whenever I'm in town, and I've seen a lot
of changes.

From the mid-1990s until the last few years, the violence and crime
deterred middle-class Washingtonians from planting stakes in the area.
But as real-estate prices soared, more and more prospective home buyers
began making their way to parts of the city they wouldn't have dared
even drive through in the days of my youth.

5   So as I tour the ten square blocks of my old stomping grounds, I'm
not surprised to see fresh paint on the buildings that were once peeling.
It doesn't shock me that the old tennis and basketball courts have been
leveled to make way for town houses, or that the gully filled with earth,
trees and trash next to the basement apartment where I was raised has
given way to new homes.

Still, I remember how we used to explore that great wide ditch as if it
were a real jungle. Runoff from sewage pipes had created a tiny stream at
its bottom, and we tried to navigate the water on an old wooden door that
had been tossed into the gully long before we were born.

I remember nearly running over my father when I turned the handlebars too far left as he was trying to teach me how to ride a bike, and sled-
ding down 38th Street with him when the street was covered with solid
ice during one of the city's harshest winters.

I remember the small forest of bamboo shoots behind one of the
buildings that my best friend, Butchie, and I broke off to use as swords

in imaginary duels. I remember when we discovered a syringe on the ground next to a Dumpster, having no idea what it had most likely been used for.

One friend went to jail around the same time that I went to college. Two others went to funeral homes: One was stabbed because of a neighborhood rivalry, and the other was shot during a dispute over a girl. My memories are very mixed.

10   The other day I saw a music video by a D.C. recording artist whom I recognized as the kid with a locker near mine in high school. One of the scenes in the video showed a man pointing at a T shirt that read KEEP D.C. BLACK. For a moment I wondered what this meant, until I remembered the way years of low interest rates and a nationwide home-renovation trend had begun to change the racial makeup of my hometown.

Now what used to be an undesirable neighborhood has become unaffordable for many of the people who grew up with me. Most of my friends who still live in the area have been forced into Prince George's County (just across the Maryland border), as rent and mortgage prices are now far beyond what they can afford.

I know that many African-Americans view these events as proof that racism is alive and well. But I believe that in the end, the shifting demographics of the Village are all about money.

The bottom line for me is that there is nothing left of myself in the blocks and buildings where I went from embryo to young man. The faces I pass on the streets of my childhood are unfamiliar. Friends who got in trouble with the law are back on the streets now, but they live elsewhere. My old girlfriends live far away from the playgrounds where we once walked hand in hand.

The neighborhood I remember is long gone, except in my mind, where it will live as long as I can remember it.

15   I will pass on this memory to my own children when that time comes. I hope they will do the same for their own offspring, keeping it alive without the need for deeds, permits or appraisals.

I left my 'hood more than a decade ago. But I'm making sure that it will never leave me.

Kenji Jasper

Born in the mid-1970s and raised in a tough neighborhood of Washington, D.C., Kenji Jasper draws heavily on his life in his work. As he said in an interview on National Public Radio, "Your neighborhood, growing up in the city, is pretty much the boundaries by which you define your life, and that's your frame of reference."

The son of a schoolteacher and administrator (his mother) and a graphic artist and entrepreneur (his father), Jasper began writing short stories at the age of nine. As a teenager he was one of the regulars on Black Entertainment Television's program *Teen Summit*. Jasper graduated from Morehouse College in 1997, whereupon he began to write freelance articles for *Essence*, *The Village Voice*, *The Source*, *Vibe*, and many other magazines. In 2001, his first novel, *Dark*, won him acclaim and led to a guest commentator spot on NPR. Since then he has proved himself to be a prolific writer and speaker, continuing not only to pen articles and make regular public appearances but also to write novels, including *Dakota Grand* (2002), *Seeking Salamanca Mitchell* (2004), and *Snow* (2007). His memoir, *House on Childress Street: A Memoir of My Grandfather*, was published in 2006.

SEEING

1. Through a series of trenchant observations, Kenji Jasper demonstrates that although gentrification has made his neighborhood unrecognizable, it nonetheless still serves as home for him. Which features of Fairfax Village does Jasper accentuate? with what effect(s)? What words and phrases does he use to characterize his neighborhood? Which are most effective? Explain why. Comment on Jasper's use of figurative language and irony in his essay.

2. Jasper does not mention his racial background, but what do you infer it to be from reading his essay? Point to evidence to support your response. Identify specific passages, and describe how their meaning would change if Jasper were of a different race. For example, explain the differences if a Chinese American, an African American, and a Latin American had written, "I know that many African-Americans view these events as proof that racism is alive and well. But I believe that in the end, the

shifting demographics of the Village are all about money" (para. 12). This essay appeared in the popular column "My Turn" in *Newsweek* magazine. Identify – and comment on the effectiveness of – the specific compositional strategies Jasper uses to speak compellingly to as many readers with different racial backgrounds as possible.

3. Without returning to Jasper's essay, prepare notes about how you envision Fairfax Village. Note what you remember about the "Village" in which Jasper grew up as well as what his neighborhood looked like when he returned as an adult. Then review your notes carefully for details such as "old tennis and basketball courts" to see how accurate your memory is. Why did certain passages strike you as more memorable than others?

WRITING

1. Write the first draft of a "biography" of your room, your house, or the street on which you live. Ask your parents or grandparents what things looked like before you were born. Ask them to describe in detail the furniture in your room or house, or the shops and people in your neighborhood that have since gone. Then write about what you remember once you came on the scene. What everyday, familiar objects that you loved as a child are now absent? Where have they gone, and what has replaced them? Finally, look around carefully and imagine what will disappear as you grow older. Finish your biography as if you were writing thirty years from now. What will change around you while your (future) memories endure?

Working with Sources
2. Research the history of gentrification. When did the practice begin, and why? In what ways are current gentrification projects different from past ones? Also focus on the word itself. How was *gentrification* defined when the word was introduced? What does *gentrification* have to do with *gentry* or *gentle*? Based on your research, write an expository essay in which you explain why you think Jasper is accurate – or inaccurate – in describing what happened to his "Village" as gentrification occurred.

PORTFOLIO–Flickr Student Spaces

Julie Mierwa
At University, Take Two, 2007

Patrick Moberg
MC's Dorm Room, 2005

Adrienne X. Shon
Clutter, 2006

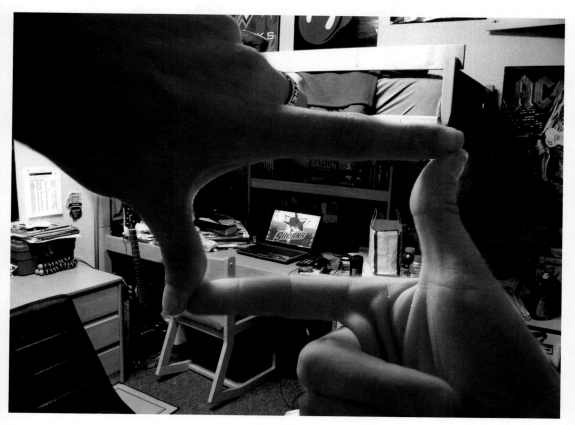

Matt Weir
My Space, 2007

Flickr

Advertised as an "online photo management and sharing application," Flickr is also a social networking web site where users discuss their own and other photographers' images and photographic style. Founded in 2004 by Stewart Butterfield and Caterina Fake, who managed the site until 2008, Flickr now houses over 2 billion photographs, making it the largest photo-sharing site of its kind, which like YouTube is also a repository of videos. Users can create personal profiles, upload and share their images, post and reply to comments, search photos and videos by keywords or tags, and even search by the camera brands used to take the photographs posted. On Flickr, multiple tags within the photograph describe the objects caught on film and reveal a great deal about the photographer's interests and preoccupations.

Julie Mierwa

This picture of Julie Mierwa's desk was taken when she was a hard-working graduate student. The photograph, with its dramatic lighting, limited color, and pileup of books and papers, conveys a serious mood at odds with the playfulness of some of the other Flickr images. Julie Mierwa is originally from Los Angeles. Her Flickr username is feministjulie.

Patrick Moberg

Currently a resident of New York City, Patrick Moberg (b. 1986) studied New Media at Rochester Institute of Technology. While traveling around the United States and visiting friends, Moberg took the photograph *MC's Dorm Room*. A composite of ten digitally captured images, the photograph depicts his friend Chris sitting in their mutual friend Mary Claire's dorm room in Charleston, South Carolina. In addition to working in the field of web design, Moberg sells his artwork and photography online. His Flickr username is patrickmoberg.

Adrienne X. Shon

Originally from San Diego, California, Adrienne (Flickr username: ohsnap) is currently a journalism student at Northwestern University. She loves to create, whether it is a piece of writing or a web design. Photography is one of Adrienne's favorite mediums because she values how a photograph can capture one moment in time. *Clutter* was made originally for an online layout. All of the items have specific meaning in Adrienne's life and so she kept them all in the frame, even the tissues (an indicator of bad seasonal allergies) to make the image an intimate portrait of her life.

Matt Weir

Originally from the Bay Area of California, Matt Weir (b. 1989) has been intensely involved in taking pictures since he was eight years old. Currently a student at California State University – Fresno, Weir is a photography major with much experience already behind him. He has done graphic design work for over five years (for his first assignment, he was paid a guitar), has had many photographs published in local newspapers, and has won a regional photography award. Weir's photography interests "span from taking artistic/informative photos to enhancing and manipulating digitally," the latter interest demonstrated in his inventive *My Space* dorm room photo, in which the area boxed off with his fingers is in color and focuses in on his computer monitor, while the area outside of the "box" is in black and white. μΛ††'s is Weir's Flickr username.

SEEING

1. This portfolio of images of students' personal spaces was posted on Flickr, the enormously popular web site that serves as an image and video "warehouse" and online community platform. As you study each image, please make notes about where your eye is first drawn. Where does your attention move: from left to right? top to bottom? vice versa? What observations can you make about each representation of a student's personal space? What reasonable inferences can you draw from your observations of each photo?

2. After having worked closely with each of the images, shift your perspective to a larger, more comparative frame. What points of similarity and difference do you notice between and among the four images of student space reprinted here? Please be specific in your response. Which aspects of each photo do you find most – and least – engaging? Explain why. Overall, which photo, if any, would you seek to emulate if you were to post an image of your personal space? Explain why. If you have already posted such an image, compare and contrast your presentation with one of those reprinted here.

WRITING

1. If you have not yet viewed the Flickr web site, please do so. Consider for a few moments the nature and extent of the ways in which you use Flickr as a site and a service. Make as many observations as possible about what you post on the site as well as how you interact with material posted by others. What reasonable inferences can you draw from these observations? Based on your observations and inferences, write an expository essay in which you document the ways in which you work with Flickr. Then consider how representative your experience is when compared to that of other users among your classmates and friends. Based on this information, what reasonable conclusion(s) can you draw about what accounts for Flickr's extraordinary success?

Working with Sources

2. The language of the Internet is full of spatial metaphors. We spend time in *cyberspace*, create *web sites*, and frequent *chat rooms* and *multi-user domains* (MUDs). In what ways are cyber spaces like physical spaces? Why is this comparison useful? Where does the analogy break down? Some call the Internet a global village. Do you agree? Or can you point to evidence of national or regional community on the Internet? How does the Internet affect your own view of place?

Choose a web site, chat room, or MUD as your focus for exploring the use of spatial metaphors to describe Internet experience. Prepare the first draft of an expository essay in which you analyze the use of spatial metaphors – and their aptness – to describe the nature and workings of the Internet.

Pobilio Diaz
Camino a Manabao, 1993

NEIGHBORS
Julia Alvarez

On the road up the mountain to their place near Manabao, they always see these little girls standing in doorways with their hands clapped over their mouths.

"What is it with them?" her husband asked the last time. "Why are they so surprised?"

"Maybe they've never seen a white person," she said. "Maybe they think of us as invading their territory."

"Little girls don't have territory," he retorted. "Especially little black girls who are part Haitian on the road to Manabao."

5 He had a point. But she was bothered that he, the American, should be explaining her native land to her.

This time, when they see a little girl standing in a doorway in her green shift, still wet from doing the wash, she says, "Stop! I'm going to ask her what's up."

"Oh, come on," he says, but he pulls the pickup onto the narrow shoulder in front of the plywood shack. She opens the door and steps out.

The girl watches with big, wary eyes. She's pretty, with skin a rich cacao brown that makes the woman feel that white is not a good color for human beings. The girl's hand is at her mouth.

"*Buenas!*" she calls out, and then she doesn't know what to say. How can she talk to someone who is covering her mouth?

10 There is a strong smell coming from inside the shack, a smell of too many people living in too tight a space. Maybe that's why the girl's hand is on her face. Maybe she is inhaling the smell of lye soap to offset the stench of the house behind her.

From inside, a man calls out in Creole. She waits, hoping the little girl will answer. She is invested now in having the girl say something. She wants to see the girl's full face, her little white teeth, her pink tongue curled inside her mouth as if it were a vital organ. But the girl says nothing. In a minute someone is going to open the door to see what is going on—fearing, perhaps that *la guardia* has come to pack them off to the border now that the harvest is over.

It happens every year. In late October truckloads of Haitians are hauled east to cut cane or pick coffee, crowded in *bateys*[1] no better than

---

1. *bateys:* Barracks established by sugarcane growers for workers. [Eds.]

the holds of slave ships, their pay withheld until the last cane has been squeezed for its last drop of sugar, the last red berry plucked from the last coffee tree. Then the raids begin, workers gathered up before they can demand payment. In 1937, instead of going through the bother of deportation, the army mowed down the Haitians, using machetes and knives to make the massacre look like a popular uprising. Twenty thousand perished. But it was not an important holocaust. Sometimes when she talks about it to her husband, he thinks she is exaggerating.

Last year, on the highway, they saw a truck headed for Dajabón, a tarp thrown over the top as if the cargo were *plátanos* or *tayotas*. Between the slats of the truck bed a hand reached out, opened, the palm pink and innocent. The other side of the girl's hand must be that color, she thinks now.

"We're neighbors," she tells the girl. "We live up the road on that hill, see?" She points toward the crest of the hill opposite the girl's house, where she and her husband bought their property a year ago. Each time they come, they sit in a circle with workers and ask them how they feel about the work they have done. But the workers won't wager an opinion. "You're the ones to say," they always reply.

15   Her husband calls from the truck, "Don't you see you're scaring her?"

"Come and see us," she says finally, backing away from the girl, whose hand has not moved from her mouth. Behind her, the door opens a crack wider and then closes — someone, checking to see who it is, has decided the white woman cannot be trusted.

Back in the truck, all the way up to their place, she looks out the window, not saying a word. Her husband accuses her of pouting for no good reason at all.

"What do you expect?" he keeps asking her. "What on earth do you expect?"

Julia Alvarez

Although she was born in New York City, Julia Alvarez spent most of the first ten years of her life in the Dominican Republic. In 1960 her family hurriedly returned to the United States because of her father's association with the Mirabal sisters, leaders of an underground movement to overthrow dictator Rafael Leónidas Trujillo. Alvarez attended Middlebury College and received her MFA degree from Syracuse University in 1975. She taught English and writing for a number of years until 1998, when she resigned her tenured position to write fulltime.

Her widely acclaimed works include her now-famous first novel, *How the Garcia Girls Lost Their Accents* (1991), her 1994 novel *In the Time of the Butterflies* (which fictionalizes the murder of the Mirabal sisters), and a nonfiction book about growing up Latina in America, *Once upon a Quinceañera* (2007).

Many aspects of Alvarez's novels, short stories, essays, and poems are informed by the question of what happens when people of two different places meet. As Alvarez has said, "I am a Dominican, hyphen, American. As a fiction writer, I find that the most exciting things happen in the realm of that hyphen—the place where two worlds collide or blend together." In "Neighbors," Alvarez uses just a few short paragraphs and minimal dialogue to bring an entire community to life—and two cultures into contact.

SEEING

1. In how many ways do people fail to communicate in "Neighbors"? What is Alvarez's point about attempting to learn about other people and cultures? Please be as specific as possible in supplying evidence from the story to support your response.

2. In an interview, Alvarez praised fiction for providing "a way to emotionally integrate and make sense of this mysterious world through story and character." In what ways does "Neighbors" meet this standard? Identify the different emotions Alvarez brings together in this story. Comment on the effectiveness of the ways in which she does so. After reading the story, what makes sense to you that was previously mysterious? If you feel and understand no differently after reading than before, where specifically do the characters and story fall short of making sense of this mysterious world?

WRITING

1. Pobilio Diaz's photograph *Camino a Manabao* stirred the storyteller in Julia Alvarez. Choose a photograph, not from your own life, and write a short story about the people and the landscape captured on the film.

Working with Sources

2. Plan a trip to Manabao. How much will it cost? When is the best time of year to visit? Where will you stay, and for how long? Whom do you want to meet when you go there, and why? Make your itinerary as realistic as possible by consulting friends, travel agents, airlines, maps, encyclopedias, and other sources. Will you ever go? Why or why not?

Responding Visually

The final word in "Neighbors," *expect*, is loaded with meaning in a story inspired by a photograph. *Expect* comes from a word that meant "looking" (*spect*ator, *spect*acle) "outward" (*ex-*). In what ways does the story preserve and extend this meaning? What role does visual expectation play in the story? Keeping in mind the connection between seeing and expecting, create a postcard that answers the husband's last question with both words and a picture: "What on earth do you expect?"

The ideal environment
for me as a writer
is a quiet room
with few distractions.

Adrian Varner, student at
Southern Polytechnic State University

What one writer can make
in the solitude of one room
is something no power
can easily destroy.

Salman Rushdie, winner of the Booker Prize

LOOKING CLOSER – Envisioning America

The earliest representations of America in English were essentially promotional material written and illustrated to solicit support for subsequent voyages. Lured by such tempting accounts of the new world, generation after generation of immigrants has envisioned America as a land of limitless possibility.

First- and second-generation American immigrant writers and artists have recounted in compelling verbal and visual terms the struggle to reconcile the realities of their daily experience with the widely circulated and wondrous images of America that helped lure them. In "Imagining Homelands," Bharati Mukherjee explores assimilation as a process that transforms both immigrant and mainstream culture. In "Fish Cheeks," Amy Tan has written a powerfully insightful narrative about the social mishaps that surface during a Christmas Eve dinner with her Chinese family, a minister, and his "blond-haired" son. Tan's essay also records the powerful, sometimes inhibiting influence of her mother and many aspects of Chinese culture on her life. Jesse Gordon's photoessay "What Is America?" underscores how central and inspirational the image of the Stars and Stripes is to both immigrants and native-born Americans. And Pat Mora's poem "Immigrants" artfully examines the theme of borders – political, cultural, social, and emotional.

IMAGINING HOMELANDS
Bharati Mukherjee

This essay is about four narratives, those of expatriation, exile, immigration, and repatriation. From those subnarratives, I hope to weave a revisionist theory for contemporary residency and citizenship, or at least to suggest new terms in the unresolved debate that threatens to grow louder and more rancorous in years to come.

The question, as always, is, What is America? Is it a place or an idea, is it a patchwork of diverse communities, or a nuanced, accented, multicolored myth of shared values? Are we heading, in these final years of the millennium, toward the ancient dream of unity through diversity— *e pluribus unum*—or have we already taken the first steps down the long slope to chaos? Far from unity, we can't seem to find consensus on anything these days, not on affirmative action, on national educational standards, on needle exchanges, on family values, a drug policy, a trade policy, Most-Favored-Nation status for China, environmental protection, medical care, bilingual education, or even the designated hitter rule.

Both tendencies, chaos and unity, have attended our history. We are both a liberal experiment and a bulwark of reaction. De Tocqueville saw both tendencies, as did Lincoln, Faulkner, Melville and Emerson, and W. E. B. Du Bois, Frederick Douglass, and Martin Luther King Jr.

I'm not a historian, only a fiction writer born and raised on a different continent who did not even become an American citizen until a dozen years ago. My work is set almost entirely within "immigrant communities," as they are so designated, although seen from the inside there is little that is communal about them, and only a minority of their inhabitants are even immigrants. Nevertheless, it is the reality of transplantation and psychological metamorphosis that is my material, not the world I left behind. I call myself an American writer, not an Indian one. I do not do this for material advantage (as Indian critics often assume), for there is far more commercial interest in the West in the India of tropical languor, dowry-death, and caste-strife than in scraped-knuckled, bruised-elbow immigration. I do it because I see in the process of immigration (in its widest sense, including at least three stages that have very little to do with changing citizenship) the stage, and the battleground, for the most exciting dramas of our time. A neighborhood like Jackson Heights, Queens, is on a par with Renaissance Venice for its richness of character and depth of intrigue. The same is true of my current home of San

Francisco, my teaching campus of Berkeley, of Miami and Brooklyn, San Antonio and Detroit.

5   The national myth of immigration, the heart-warming saga of babushka-clad refugees climbing to the deck of the tramp steamer for a glimpse of the Statue of Liberty ("Look, Mama, just like the pictures we saw in Minsk, or Abruzzi, or Crete"), is just that, an image out of aging newspapers or our collective pop-memory banks. Today's arrivals are more likely to be discharged on a beach and told to swim ashore, or dropped in a desert and told to run, if they survive at all. Immigration, as I experience it, is made up of several conflicting parts. For my purposes here, *immigration* refers to the act of adopting new citizenship, of going the full nine yards of transformation. As such, it is but one option to be exercised by noncitizens living in this country.

Definitions seem to be in order. *Expatriation* is an act of sustained self-removal from one's native culture, balanced by a conscious resistance to total inclusion in the new host society. The motives for expatriation are as numerous as the expatriates themselves: aesthetic and intellectual affinity, a better job, a more interesting or less hassled life, greater freedom or simple tax relief, just as the motives for nonintegration may range from principle, to nostalgia, to laziness or fear. The roster of notable expatriates in the realm of literature alone is immensely long, rich in honors and deep in respect: Henry James, T. S. Eliot, Joseph Conrad, V. S. Naipaul (before their formal acceptance of British citizenship), Vladimir Nabokov, James Joyce, Samuel Beckett, Paul Bowles, Mavis Gallant, Gabriel García Márquez, Witold Gombrowicz, Anthony Burgess, Graham Greene, Derek Walcott, Malcolm Lowry, Wilson Harris—names, even with a few glaring omissions that any literate audience can fill in, that we'd all agree rise to the top of any listing of the twentieth century's most notable literary achievements.

They are, in fact, our great voices of modernism as well as a few of postmodernism; their works are encyclopedic, their visions ironic and penetrating, their analyses detached and scrupulous, their styles experimental yet crystalline. If the ultimate goal of literature is to achieve universality and a kind of god-like omniscience, expatriation—the escape from small-mindedness, from niggling irritations—might well be a contributing factor.

The expatriate is the ultimate self-made artist, even the chooser of a language in which to operate, as Conrad, Beckett, Kundera, and Nabokov testify, an almost literal exponent of Joyce's dream of self-forging in the smithy of his soul. It is possible, in expatriation, to step out of the constraints into which one has been born and to exercise to the fullest the dual vision of the detached outsider. The expatriate Hungarian, Czech, or Pole of an earlier era, or today's Yugoslav or Bangladeshi, Algerian or Palestinian expatriate, asks only that the host culture permit him or her to retain an alien core that will not be compromised or surrendered. The bargain is thus struck: I will be a model resident. In return for your tolerance and noninterference, I will not attack the fundamental flaws of your society with anything like the zeal I bring to the dissection of my own people. I will imagine a new homeland built on reclaimed land.

I confess, it is an attractive bargain, one which I entertained myself, many years ago.

10   In the case of *exile*, the comparative luxury of self-removal is replaced by harsh compulsion. The spectrum of choice is gravely narrowed; the alternatives may be no more subtle than death, imprisonment, or a one-way ticket to oblivion. We all cheered the arrival of Aleksandr Solzhenitsyn in America, thinking we would gain a new voice in our literature as we did with Auden and Isherwood, or a new superstar as we have with so many singers and actors, or sensational tennis players. The list of twentieth-century exiles is an alternate Who's Who of Nobel listings in the sciences and literature, as well as an honor roll of world-class painters, dancers, performers, and composers. In some cases, the urgency of exile may, in time, blend into the serendipity of expatriation—Milan Kundera in Paris, Picasso in Arles, Chaplin in Switzerland—but for the most part, the exile does not achieve the same Olympian detachment enjoyed by the expatriate. The exile is still tied to a mother country and a major cause that are the source of his wounding, and he may or may not choose, or have the option of choosing, to translate his passions or his words. The United States at present is home to dozens of exiles writing in their native Spanish and Russian and Arabic, in Chinese and Burmese, in Tamil and Aramaic, publishing in their own form of *samizdat* or exile presses, interviewed on ethnic radio and reviewed in the ethnic press, and few of us will ever have the good fortune to read their work or know of their existence. Similar, if not larger, populations cluster in Paris, Toronto, and London, in Berlin and Mexico City, in Amsterdam and Barcelona.[1]

---

1. Exile may become the subject of great literature, but it does not encourage the conditions for its production. For every Solzhenitsyn or Thomas Mann, every Freud, Kundera, or Skvorecky, every Ngugi wa Thiong'o or Wole Soyinka, every Liu Binyan, there are still today's Isaac Babels trapped behind the lines of their own despotisms. Read the heartbreaking reports of Amnesty International or of PEN's Freedom to Write committee and you will learn that the free world is still comparatively blind and deaf to the fate of Algerian, Turkish, Iranian, Malaysian, Indonesian, Cuban, Chinese, Burmese, Sierra Leonean, Nigerian, Egyptian, Cambodian, Tamil, and Sinhalese dissidents. Their names are not known, their causes are not sexy, their languages are not in wide distribution in the West, and for these reasons,

Exile lacks the grandeur, the majesty, of expatriation. The expatriate, at least, is validated by a host culture which extends the hospitality, and he often returns it in civic dutifulness. But the exile is a petitioner. He brings with him the guilty reminders of suffering, his stay is provisional and easily revoked, and he is often consigned to the underworld of ethnic intrigue, outside the purview of the law or of the press. If expatriation is the route of cool detachment, exile is for some that of furious engagement.

I must confess my own years of furious engagement, not in this country, but in my husband's Canada. When we lived in the Greek neighborhoods of Montreal, we were brought into daily contact with the passions of pro- and anti-"Colonels" Greek immigrants, the threats of arson by pro-junta Greeks on anti-junta businesses. In Toronto and Vancouver, the early years of the Punjab civil war were playing themselves out on the streets of various Little Indias. In all cases, police response, despite appeals for protection by what are called in Canada "visible minorities," and by simple Canadian citizens such as myself, harassed on the streets and in public transportation by white youths, was a variant of "It's not our [meaning white, Canadian] problem. You guys" — or more likely, *you little people* — "settle it among yourselves."[2]

In November 1996, the *New York Times* asked me to contribute an op-ed piece inspired by the so-called immigration debate that was then raging on both sides during the election battle. Are we "all immigrants," as the pietistic national myth would have it, therefore duty-bound to support immigration as an apple pie or motherhood issue, or are most new immigrants cheats and rip-off artists, as many nativists seem to believe?

I chose to write of my older sister and myself, two Calcutta-born women from identical backgrounds with the same Cambridge-tested accent, the same convent education, who have been in the United States

---

along with those of trade and political influence, their lives, their bravery, and their work go unvalidated.

It makes you wonder, sometimes, if anyone stays at home. Is some sort of major disruption essential for great writing? Of course that's not the truth, as even a moment's reflection can show, but the list of expatriate and exiled writers is nevertheless a daunting one to contemplate. It might be truer to say that all writers are expatriates to one degree or another, or they are internal exiles; certainly William Faulkner or Flannery O'Connor, Bernard Malamud or Cynthia Ozick, hail from a country without a passport. [All notes are Mukherjee's.]

2. I should add that it very much was a "white, Canadian" problem. The eventual outcome of such racist smugness was the bloodiest terrorist act of modern times, the blowing up, by a small group of Sikh extremists, of an Air-India 747 over the coast of Ireland, with the loss of 329 Canadian lives. If you can find a copy of the book, *The Sorrow and the Terror*, which my husband and I co-authored in 1987, you'll understand some of the urgency that has motivated both of our writings since that tragic event.

for over thirty-five years. My sister married an Indian student in Detroit and has remained in the same job and the same house, wearing saris, cooking familiar food, guarding the accent, for the past thirty years. She holds the much-valued U.S. green card but feels her home is still India, where she intends to retire in the next few years. I, too, married a fellow student in the Writers' Workshop at the University of Iowa, an American of Canadian parentage, and we have lived in Canada and in several parts of the United States, moving at least twenty times, and have often been obliged by professional circumstances to live many years apart. I am a U.S. citizen and could not imagine returning to India for other than family visits and relaxed vacations. My accent is an amalgam of the places I've lived, my wardrobe is a similar hodgepodge, and so is our daily menu.

15   The question I meant to raise was simply this: Which one of us is the freak? Someone who retains the food, the clothes, the accent of expatriation, or her T-shirted, blue-jeaned sister? The answer is by no means clear.

That little article, anecdotal in nature, aroused more passions than many of my novels. When I give readings or interviews in India, it becomes a lead-question (the article was reprinted in several Indian newspapers), and the questioners are often anything but cordial. Conversely, the article has been celebrated by the liberal mainstream in this country as a bold statement of faith in the American experiment, warts and all. Neither reaction is entirely satisfactory.

Among some Indian intellectuals it is read as a polarizing document, an implicit rejection of the worth of hundreds of thousands of law-abiding, tax-paying, communally and religiously conservative, contributing Indian nationals, like my sister, working and residing overseas. At its fringes, that interpretation tends to bracket my pro-immigration, let-it-go stance with those of some unsavory company, English-only, "American First"-ers of a stripe with Enoch Powell or the current crop of French and Austrian race-baiters who even propose cleansing the various European motherlands of Turks, Gypsies, North Africans, Kurds, and Bosnian/Kosovo refugees. We all know the end-point of such appeals to purity, especially in Europe.

Given my presumed respectability in the United States as a member of a prominent minority community, and my access to mainstream media, I try at every opportunity to distinguish my position from those of ill-disposed, anti-immigrant Americans as well as of instinctive Americaphobes, a large number of whom, unfortunately, can be found among India-born academics in American universities. I know I'm not the only person from a minority community who weighs American promise against American history on a daily basis and who still finds a positive balance, but it still seems necessary to emphasize my basic position. I am an integrationist and, to use a deliberately ugly word, a mongrelizer. My sister, like most expatriates or exiles, is not. Mongrels lose a lot of prestige and pedigree in their travels, they're not as classically proportioned or predictably behaved as purebreds, and, more to the point, their presence creates a third, unpredictable, sometimes undesirable, and often untrainable mutt. Because I am here, I am changed totally by you and by my commitment to this country and its problems, but so are you. You are now implicated in my life; you probably entrust your health, or aspects of it, to Indian doctors or dentists, you can now eat my food in nearly any town, run India-designed software on your India-designed computer. I'm just as mainstream as anyone else. I am also a proud India-born, Bengali-speaking Hindu. These positions need not be antithetical.

Like my academic colleagues with whom I have conducted many public quarrels, I too grew up in a British-centered universe in India. As a college student I too would have snickered at the pretense of an American culture, of an American literature. To declare my Americanness, and not to retain the genteel expatriation of an upper-class Bengali Brahmin, is, in their minds, to be linked with and to share the historical guilt of slavery, segregation, extermination of Native Americans, the CIA, Vietnam, and to be linked with the hypocrisy of supporting both freedom and dictatorships, and with a generally vulgar "Coca-Cola" and "McDonald's" culture.

20   That is a far less comforting heritage than that of my forebears, at least as it was communicated to me. My city, my religion, my caste, were always the innocent victims of foreign invaders. We were the colonized, the humiliated, the despised. History had cleansed us of all ancestral sins. Many of my colleagues apparently still believe in the myth of national innocence, and will do anything to maintain it.

The tale of two sisters of course suggests larger narratives, those of expatriation and those of immigration. The narrative of expatriation calls to mind villas in the south of France, on the shores of Lake Geneva, apartments in Paris, but it is no stranger to Detroit as well. The narrative of expatriation fairly drips with respectability, or at least with privilege, but the narrative of immigration calls to mind crowded tenements, Ellis Island, sweatshops, accents, strange foods, taxicab drivers, bizarre holidays, strange religions, unseemly ethnic passions.

And it must be admitted, especially in New York City, that the narrative of immigration is a scripted cliché. Little Italy, the Lower East Side, Chinatown, Brighton Beach, Yorkville, Harlem, the South Bronx, and the Upper East Side, the Upper West Side—we can almost populate those neighborhoods from central casting, from war movies, B-movies, TV dramas, sitcoms, and musicals. It is a cliché because it is the story of the parents and grandparents of second- and third-generation Americans and it's been handed over to *me* and to millions like me, unchanged. The narrative turned out happily, in general; the poor became middle class, the foreign became more American than Americans, traditional national values were not deeply challenged, but were even upheld and strengthened. (For those who didn't fit in, and there were many, things turned out differently. Sacco and Vanzetti were executed, so was Bruno Hauptmann, so were the Rosenbergs.) It's a cliché because the language has not been updated.

Central-casting immigration is European, white, Christian and Jewish. The distance between America and Europe a hundred years ago seemed vast, unimaginable; the linguistic, cultural, and religious differences tested the very limits of contemporary assimilation. Of course, more alien populations were simply barred from any thought of immigration, Asians were "sojourners" whose wives were not admitted; African Americans were denied the vote; Latinos and French-Canadians (who were called "blue-eyed Chinese") clustered in enclaves near their borders; they were considered unassimilable.

The immigration narrative changed with the end of colonialism. Vast populations were no longer hemmed in by colonial legislation. The old European-favored quota system was challenged; talent, merit, and family unification became an aim of immigration policy. The new arrivals were no longer populating an empty landscape or providing muscle for labor-intensive heavy industry.

25 We Americans fought bitter wars in alien areas, we disrupted civilizations and admitted some of the survivors. The cold war sent its refugees to Florida, to Brooklyn, to Minneapolis. We wanted professionals, we needed doctors, engineers, researchers, and entrepreneurs. We educated the Third World's brightest in our schools and then we kept them. They brought in their parents, their cousins, they sponsored others. Immigrant communities grew from a dozen epicenters, from Queens to Glendale, Miami to Minnesota, and each community became self-sustaining. Dithering and cynical politics allowed uncountable millions of undocumented workers to enter, and while their net value to the economy is not really in dispute, their likely contribution to a broadening of American democracy certainly is, especially if they are kept underground, not permitted to educate their children or to enjoy some semblance of public acceptance. In California, we can already see how we've permitted the situation to coarsen the public dialogue.

There are now Little Indias, Koreas, Jamaicas, Colombias, Saigons, Moscows, Mexicos, Vientianes, Manilas, Chinas, in cities that had never experienced immigration communities in earlier waves. My concern is definitely not with their presence here, it is with our ability *to adjust to* their presence and to make it a productive, that is, a mongrelizing encounter. If five million undocumented aliens are now in the country, living in slums and barrios, working at odd jobs, hiding from authorities, sending money home, neglecting their children, engaging in criminal activity (my New York apartment was ransacked by that most innocent icon of Manhattan life, the Chinese take-out delivery man, whose hotbox contained an acetylene torch for cutting through my firedoor), we may never encounter one another except in figurative dark alleys—and that is an immigration tragedy.

Immigration may be an uplifting narrative, but it's not pretty and certainly not elegant, like expatriation. It's low-tech. I am an immigrant, and to achieve that honor, I gave up status that I'll never be able to achieve in the New World. I became this thing new to U.S. history, someone who had never existed before me and hundreds of thousands like me: an Indo-American. As a writer, I had to decide how to describe myself— Asian-American, Indo-American, unhyphenated American? I claim myself as an American in the immigrant tradition of writers I most admire, Henry Roth and Bernard Malamud; yet it is still, after fifteen years of aggressive correction, a rare literary notice that does not identify me as "Indian." It's apparently easier for Monica Seles to be accepted as American than me, and I wonder why that might be.

We are still fighting the tradition of nineteenth-century exclusivism, the branding of the "visibly foreign" or the non-Judeo/Christian as unsuited for naturalization. It was the price paid by native-born Japanese-Americans in World War II, by the Latino-appearing in Los Angeles, by Asians just about anywhere: accepted as "sojourners" doing dirty and underpaid work, but not as Americans altering the appearance, eventually, of us all.

There is a fourth narrative, not often mentioned, but one which complicates even the murkier aspects of immigration. I think of it as *repatriation*, a repopulation of formerly Spanish lands, formerly French lands, formerly Native American lands, which involves the undocumented movement of millions over borders that we may think of as unviolable but which others have long considered mere extensions of their homeland. When my husband, Clark Blaise, was researching a book about his French-Canadian father, he was struck by the fact that Léo Blais's native village in Quebec was part of the same parish that reached into Maine, that family members were buried on both sides of the border, that my father-in-law could emigrate from Canada in 1912 and arrive in Manchester, New Hampshire, work in the mills and go to school and never learn a word of English. What was true in New England ninety years ago has always been true in the Rio Grande Valley and East Los Angeles; it has become the rule in South Florida, in East Harlem and the South Bronx. If we speak seriously of the Pacific Rim, and of profiting from its markets and asserting our influence upon it, we are implicitly inviting all Asia to our shores—particularly if our history also includes a significant amount of historical "collateral damage," as in the case of the Philippines and Vietnam. It's America's own version of Israel's Law of Return. Immigrant groups are reclaiming their lands and feel no need to make apologies or accommodations to the latest landlords. Geography is once again dictating destiny. (Anyone who doubts it should take a look at Vancouver, British Columbia, now a virtual extension of Hong Kong.) We English-speakers are a minority in the New World; we are integrating our economies, and the implication is that we must adjust to the free movement of workers in much the way Europe does today.

30   Expatriation, exile, immigration, and repatriation, four ways of accommodating the modern restlessness, the modern dislocations, the abuses of history, the hopes of affluence. It seems to me we have entered a supra-national age, in which traditional citizenship is likely to be a murky identification and where technical proficiency is the true passport to acceptance. Somehow, we must find a way of integrating all four modes of entry into our narrative of Americanism, for the cruelties of history itself have imposed too heavy a burden on the normal channels of transformation.

With the pietistic formula "we are all immigrants," I have to disagree. We are not, and never were. We have reinvented the myths of our founding so many times, and for so many audiences, that we've probably lost all trace of a unifying narrative. Many never had the chance to immigrate; many never wanted to. Did we come seeking religious freedom? I didn't. Did we come to escape oppression, the shackles of dictatorship? I didn't. Did we rejoin the remnants of our scattered family? I didn't. Have we come seeking happiness and fortune?—for both, I should have stayed where I was. We are expatriates, exiles, slaves, and dispossessed, we are conquerers, plunderers, refugees, and amnesty-seekers, we are temporary workers, undocumented workers, visitors, students, tourists, we are joy-seekers, claim-jumpers, parole-violaters.

While it would not work for me, and I do feel the process of classic immigration has liberated me in ways that expatriation never could, I must be prepared to accept the validity of my sister Mira's narrative of expatriation and those of others like her. Their voices are hidden inside me, I have written some of their stories, and I grieve for them far more than I resent them—it's a reaction curiously similar to that of most Third World writers toward the work of V. S. Naipaul. "Damn him," I want to shout, damn his superior airs, damn his cold detachment, damn his vast talent, damn his crystalline sentences. I want him to manifest love, for just a paragraph or two, to cut loose. This does not affect my respect for his work. I want my sister to feel love for this country that she, in the depths of her heart, cannot. This does not affect the contribution she makes to schoolchildren in Detroit.

I have met the undocumented and I have written about them; I too want them to know some of our freedoms, I want them to know relief from poverty, from fear of deportation, from exploitation, but I realize America will never be more for them than a chance to work, to pocket a little money and snatch a little fun. It was their country and we were the interlopers, and in their hearts and in their history it is still their land. For us to call them aliens in those strings of mission-named California cities, we must surrender a bit of our own sanity.

We must be prepared to accept the bitter, exiled discourse, whether it comes from the Cuban Americans of Miami, the Vietnamese of California, or the Russian Jews of Brighton Beach and Los Angeles, their tight defensiveness, their aggressiveness, their blinkered vision. And what of the vast minority discourse in this country, the African American expressions with their anti-Semitic and anti-Asian notes, their own internal dispute with the world that brought them here, that refused to integrate them but then stole every degree of their self-expression?

35   And beyond that, we must understand, and truly accept, that the United States for all its power is only a minority state. It must accommodate itself to the preponderance of Latin Americans in this hemisphere, and it must understand that part of its core is the acceptance of the cruel fact of its minority status.

Samantha Appleton
A Mexican American Family Celebrates a Quinciniera, 2007

Monica Almeida
A Mother Walks Home with Her Children after School in Dearborn, Michigan, 2002

Jon Lowenstein
Protest in Humboldt Park against Bomb Testing on the Island of Vieques, Puerto Rico, 2000

Alex Webb
Little India, 2005

FISH CHEEKS
Amy Tan

I fell in love with the minister's son the winter I turned fourteen. He was not Chinese, but as white as Mary in the manger. For Christmas I prayed for this blond-haired boy, Robert, and a slim new American nose.

When I found out that my parents had invited the minister's family over for Christmas Eve dinner, I cried. What would Robert think of our shabby Chinese Christmas? What would he think of our noisy Chinese relatives who lacked proper American manners? What terrible disappointment would he feel upon seeing not a roasted turkey and sweet potatoes but Chinese food?

On Christmas Eve, I saw that my mother had outdone herself in creating a strange menu. She was pulling black veins out of the backs of fleshy prawns. The kitchen was littered with appalling mounds of raw food: A slimy rock cod with bulging fish eyes that pleaded not to be thrown into a pan of hot oil. Tofu, which looked like stacked wedges of rubbery white sponges. A bowl soaking dried fungus back to life. A plate of squid, crisscrossed with knife markings so they resembled bicycle tires.

And then they arrived—the minister's family and all my relatives in a clamor of doorbells and rumpled Christmas packages. Robert grunted hello, and I pretended he was not worthy of existence.

5   Dinner threw me deeper into despair. My relatives licked the ends of their chopsticks and reached across the table, dipping into the dozen or so plates of food. Robert and his family waited patiently for platters to be passed to them. My relatives murmured with pleasure when my mother brought out the whole steamed fish. Robert grimaced. Then my father poked his chopsticks just below the fish eye and plucked out the soft meat. "Amy, your favorite," he said, offering me the tender fish cheek. I wanted to disappear.

At the end of the meal my father leaned back and belched loudly, thanking my mother for her fine cooking. "It's a polite Chinese custom, to show you are satisfied," he explained to our astonished guests. Robert was looking down at his plate with a reddened face. The minister managed to muster a quiet burp. I was stunned into silence for the rest of the night.

After all the guests had gone, my mother said to me, "You want be same like American girls on the outside." She handed me an early gift. It was a miniskirt in beige tweed. "But inside, you must always be Chinese. You must be proud you different. You only shame is be ashame."

And even though I didn't agree with her then, I knew that she understood how much I had suffered during the evening's dinner. It wasn't until many years later—long after I had gotten over my crush on Robert—that I was able to appreciate fully her lesson and the true purpose behind our particular menu. For Christmas Eve that year, she had chosen all my favorite foods.

The Tan family—(left to right) Peter, John, me, and Daisy—in Oakland, California, the day after I was born, 1952

"freedom"
Yen, Vietnam

"money"
Frankie, Queens

"imperialism"
Aaron, New York City

"diversity"
Karine, New York City

"religious freedom"
Dhananjay, India

"plastics"
Ian, Canada

"possibility"
Raymond, St. Kitts

"choice"
Melissa, New York City

"ignorance"
Devo, Kansas City

"my adopted country"
Sister Mary, England

"needs healing"
Elijah, South Carolina

"hope"
Pat, Staten Island

Coming to Terms with Place / 220

"open-minded"
Isaac, Brooklyn

"jazz"
Valerie, Connecticut

"ketchup"
Constantino, Greece

"original ideas"
Charles, New York City

"business"
Adaib, Yemen

"consumerism"
Silvia, Barcelona

"fun"
Nobuhisa, Japan

"lost opportunities"
Dan, Seattle

"excess"
Katherine, Boston

"*sundar* (beautiful)"
Sharada, India

"everything"
Larry, Puerto Rico

"ahhhh!"
Jadah and Joziah,
New York City

Jesse Gordon
What Is America? 2000

THE AMERICANO DREAM
Angela M. Balcita

You start by dreaming: You dream of green lawns, big cars, and a house with many rooms. You don't tell your father of your dreams. He would tell you you're being immodest. "Why always so big and fancy?" he would ask. You don't listen to those who doubt you. They talk about how you'll be back in a year, how America is a tough place to cut it. You take your wife and you hop the next twenty-two-hour flight from the Philippines to the States. From the plane, you watch your island country grow smaller and smaller.

You arrive in America in a suit and tie. You find an apartment in a big city. The walls are thin, and you don't like the way it smells. You notice how the city is tight, with barely room to breathe. You thought there would be more trees. You have an apartment on the fifth floor, and when you look out the window to the cement sidewalk below, you think how nice it would be if you were closer to the ground.

Even though you were a doctor back home, you work at a blood bank here until you fulfill all of the U.S. tests and qualifications. They give you the crazy shifts, the ones that everyone else passes on. You learn to ignore the woman who requests to see an "American" doctor. You give her care, but you don't tell her to come back.

The grocery clerks snap at you. "It's ham, sir, not hum," they say. "If you want Tang, don't say tongue!" You write this down and you remember this. At a meeting at the hospital, the director turns to you and asks, "What's the matter? Cat got your tongue?" You buy a book of American idioms and you find out what he means. When he asks a question during the next meeting, you are compelled to say, "The proof is in the pudding!" Everyone looks at you, puzzled.

5 **You learn that Americans are so tall.** You don't seem to fit. The pants are too long and your shoulders are tiny in their tailored shirts. You buy your clothes from the boys' department, and you don't tell anybody. They are cheaper anyway.

You learn to love baseball, a game they don't play where you're from. You dedicate yourself to your local team. The Boston Red Sox. What do you love? How the game can change in the matter of an inning. How you can be down 8–0 in the eighth inning and have a nine-run rally at the top of the ninth with two outs to spare. Just like that. You yell at the TV when the ump calls a ball a strike. You swear at him in Tagalog. From the kitchen, your wife throws things at you.

You have a son. He looks like you. Small thin bones, thick black hair. You look at him and worry. "My son," you say. You talk to him in Tagalog; his first word is in English. He turns down his mother's noodle dishes and opts to eat American food. Cheese. Hot dogs cut up in tiny pieces. "My son?" you ask.

You take your son to the Big Apple. The glowing lights and the tall buildings amaze him. You watch as he points up, up, up into the skyline. By now, you think you know your way. You're abrupt with the cashier when you ask for subway tokens; you move quickly through the streets so you don't get pickpocketed. You go to a deli for a sandwich. The serious man behind the counter looks you and your son up and down and says, "We can't serve you here. We don't serve your kind." At first, you are offended. But then you realize that it's not because of the color of your skin, or because of your accent, since the clerk, too, has an accent and dark skin and dark hair that pokes out from under his shirt. He won't serve you because your son is wearing a Boston Red Sox cap in a deli in Queens, New York. You fight to keep a smile from appearing on your face as you walk out the door.

You naturalize. You memorize the U.S. presidents in order. You put your hand over your heart. You look at that flag and you wonder: How can I still be Filipino if I am American?

10 **Your father dies.** He is thousands of miles away, and there are aunts to deal with, and cousins, and you wonder how they'll get along and, while you send what money you can, you wish you could send more. You wish you could send more.

You get robbed by a man wearing pantyhose on his head in the garage of your apartment building. His gun is big and silver, and he is angry that there is no money in your wallet. You are so scared you offer to bring him upstairs. You have more money up there. He throws the wallet back at you and you run like hell.

You move away from the big city to a small town where there are those expansive green lawns. You have neighbors who smile at you; you have parties to go to. You don't forget about baseball, though. You play catch with your son in the backyard, and now you're watching different games on TV. St. Louis versus Chicago. Pittsburgh versus Cincinnati.

You start to think: Where do my allegiances lie? Do I cheer for the place I'm from or the place I'm going? Can I be split?

You find yourself accidentally becoming a gardener. You know what a hosta is. You kneel in the grass and feel the soil in your hands. You trim the oak tree in the front yard and you notice its roots, thick and gnarly, how deeply embedded they are in the dirt, how securely anchored into the ground. Yet you notice how they extend out, far beyond your view, almost reaching the end of the lawn. They don't seem to stop growing.

Things start to move slower now, and you don't mind. You take your son to a baseball game; you buy cheap tickets from scalpers. You listen to the calls of the vendors; you feel the hot summer air on your face. You watch the new player come to bat, the Dominican with a killer swing. You remember reading in the paper that he grew up poor, that he used to play ball with a stick and a rock. You hold your son close as he falls asleep in his seat and you whisper to him, "Always, always root for the underdog."

IMMIGRANTS
Pat Mora

wrap their babies in the American flag,
feed them mashed hot dogs and apple pie,
name them Bill and Daisy,
buy them blonde dolls that blink blue
5 eyes or a football and tiny cleats
before the baby can even walk,
speak to them in thick English,
hallo, babee, hallo,
whisper in Spanish or Polish
10 when the babies sleep, whisper
in a dark parent bed, that dark
parent fear, "Will they like
our boy, our girl, our fine american
boy, our fine american girl?"

Bharati Mukherjee

Born in Calcutta in 1940, Bharati Mukherjee describes herself as an "American writer of Indian origin." Although she has lived in Europe and resided in Canada for over ten years with her husband (and fellow author), Clark Blaise, she has lived most of her adult life in the United States. Her novels include *The Tiger's Daughter* (1971), *Wife* (1975), *Jasmine* (1989), *The Holder of the World* (1993), *Leave It to Me* (1997), *Desirable Daughters* (2002), and *Tree Bride* (2004). She has also written several works of nonfiction, two collections of short stories, and a memoir. The essay presented here was first published in 1997. Like all of her work, it explores assimilation as a process that transforms both immigrant and mainstream culture.

In another essay, "American Dreamer" (1997), Mukherjee describes her sense of place this way: "I am an American, not an Asian-American. My rejection of hyphenation has been called race treachery, but it is really a demand that America deliver the promises of its dream to all its citizens equally. As a writer, my literary agenda begins by acknowledging that America has transformed me. . . . I want to talk of arrival as gain." Among other awards and distinctions, Mukherjee has received the National Book Critics Circle Award and a National Endowment for the Arts grant. She teaches at the University of California – Berkeley, where she is a professor of English.

You can find an interview with Bharati Mukherjee online at *www.seeingandwriting.com.*

Samantha Appleton

Raised in Camden, Maine, documentary photographer Samantha Appleton (b. 1975) began her career as a writer but switched to photojournalism after a year assisting renowned photographer James Nachtwey. Since that career change in 2000, Appleton has traveled the world to capture images of people and places as varied as the inhabitants of the slums of Lagos, Nigeria, rescue workers in lower Manhattan immediately after 9/11/2001, recent immigrants in the United States, and – most famously – the soldiers and citizens of war-torn Iraq, where she has worked on numerous occasions.

Speaking on behalf of Noor photography agency, a collective whose mission is to tell the truth through photography no matter how painful the images, and where she is one of nine documentary photographers on the roster, Appleton says, "We don't apologize for ruining your day and making you think hard about things. Some people probably will have a problem with that, and those are the people we're trying to reach the most." Yet Appleton's photographs can also be gentle, like the image of the formally dressed young people reproduced here.

Currently Appleton splits her time between New York and Portland, Maine. She is the recipient of numerous photography awards, has had her work published in high-profile magazines such as *National Geographic*, *The Atlantic*, and the *New York Times Magazine*, and frequently works on assignment for *Time* and *The New Yorker.*

Monica Almeida

Thanks to her position as a national photographer for the *New York Times,* Monica Almeida's (b. 1960) photographs and articles frequently grace the pages of the paper. Raised in La Puenta, California, Almeida earned her undergraduate degree from the University of California – Long Beach, where she first developed an interest in documentary photography, and her MFA degree from Otis Art Institute. She began her career as an intern for the *Los Angeles Times* and by 1986 had relocated to New York to work as a staff photographer for the *Daily News.* In 1992 she became a staff photographer at the *New York Times*, covering such events as the Clinton presidential campaign, the Oklahoma City bombing, the Los Angeles riots, and the Northridge, California, earthquake. Eventually she relocated to the newspaper's Los Angeles bureau, where she remains today.

Having lived on both coasts, Almeida is well aware that stereotypes about place and the people who live in a given place are not valid. In a recent interview she stated, "After spending so many years on both coasts I am well aware of the clichés and stereotypes that are tossed back and forth." Her photographs often convey this perspective.

Jon Lowenstein

Joining Samantha Appleton and others as part of the Noor collective in 2008, Massachusetts-born Jon Lowenstein (b. 1970) shares a similar interest in hard-hitting documentary photography. After attending the University of Iowa, where he graduated in 1993, and relocating to Chicago, Lowenstein began work on a long-range portrait of undocumented Latino immigrants. Eventually called Shadow Lives, of which this photo is a part, the project has not only focused on the immigrants living in his adopted home's South Side but has also led to photographic tours of Central and South America to track the origins of the people Lowenstein has come to know intimately through his work.

More than many of his Noor colleagues, Lowenstein has a particularly strong interest in the idea of place. While Shadow Lives is about the places we adopt as our homes and the places from which we originate, Lowenstein's other preoccupation is documenting – in beautiful black and white images – the city of Chicago, where he is himself a transplant from another place.

The winner of numerous awards and grants, including a World Press Photo Award, Lowenstein teaches photography and has published his work in such periodicals as the New York Times, Mother Jones, Time, U.S. News and World Report, and Nature Conservancy.

Alex Webb

In many ways, the work of celebrated American photographer Alex Webb (b. 1952) has always been about exploring places that represent the opposite of his place of origin. His first collections of photographs explored life in the American South, on the U.S.-Mexico border, and in Haiti, all far from the New England of his childhood and youth. As Webb has said, "I come from New England . . . where things really happen very much behind closed doors. You do not have the sense of life out on the street. Going to the U.S.-Mexico border or to Haiti was a sense of energy and immediacy on the street. I found it very exciting." To this day, Webb continues to be fascinated with the vibrant street life of southern places, a fascination that shows thorough in his richly colorful and kinetic images.

Webb's interest in photography began at an early age and continued through college, when he simultaneously studied history and literature at Harvard University and photography at the Carpenter Center for the Visual Arts. In addition to winning numerous awards and fellowships, Webb has exhibited his work throughout the world, is part of numerous permanent museum collections, and has been published in seven collections, from Hot Light/ Half-Made Worlds (1986) to Istanbul: City of a Hundred Names (2007).

Amy Tan

Although best known for The Joy Luck Club (1989), the best-selling novel – later made into a motion picture – in which she explores four mother-daughter relationships, Amy Tan (b. 1952) has published several other novels, including The Kitchen God's Wife (1991), The Hundred Secret Senses (1995), The Bonesetter's Daughter (2001), and Saving Fish from Drowning (2005). She has also written a number of children's books and a nonfiction book, The Opposite of Fate: A Book of Musings (2003), where "Fish Cheeks" first appeared. This essay explores one of the themes common to almost all of Tan's work: the powerful, sometimes inhibiting influence of her mother and certain elements of Chinese culture on her life.

When asked in an interview in 1995 about being expected to serve as a role model for other Chinese Americans, Tan replied, "Placing on writers the responsibility to represent a culture is an onerous burden. Someone who writes fiction is not necessarily writing a depiction of any generalized group, they're writing a very specific story. There's also a danger in balkanizing literature, as if it should be read as sociology, or politics, or that it should answer questions like, 'What does *The Hundred Secret Senses* have to teach us about Chinese culture?' As opposed to treating it as literature — as a story, language, memory."

Jesse Gordon

A writer and filmmaker, Jesse Gordon lives in New York City. The twenty-four photographs shown here were among thirty-five that appeared in an Op-Ed piece in the *New York Times* on July 3, 2000. The question posed to those in the photographs was "What is America?"

Angela M. Balcita

Born in 1974 of recently emigrated Filipino American parents in Springfield, Massachusetts, Balcita began writing after being inspired by other minority women writers, especially Sandra Cisneros, Gloria Naylor, and Zora Neale Hurston. She received her MFA degree in nonfiction writing from the University of Iowa writing program. Her essays and stories have appeared in the *UTNE Reader*,

The Iowa Review, the *New York Times*, *The Florida Review*, and the anthology *Waking Up American: Coming of Age Biculturally* (edited by Angela Jane Fountas, 2005).

Balcita says of her work as a whole, and about "The Americano Dream" in particular, "I'm always interested in characters who straddle two worlds, who live in one culture but remain connected to another. This essay in particular is about my father. I've always admired his courage to leave a place he knew so well and move to a strange, new land." First published in the *UTNE Reader*, "The Americano Dream" has much to say about both of the places that form Balcita's cultural identity.

Pat Mora

One of the most respected and prolific American poets and children's book authors working today, Pat Mora is also an essayist and memoirist who writes about the Mexican American experience. Born in El Paso, Texas, in 1942, she received her bachelor's degree from Texas Western College and her master's degree from the University of Texas – El Paso. Early in her career she taught at both the high school and college levels, but it wasn't until the early 1980s that she began to write. She quickly established herself as a poet and children's book author with a clear cultural perspective. Among her collections of poetry are *Chants* (1984), *Borders* (1986), *Communion* (1991), *Agua Santa* (1995), *Aunt Carmen's Book of Practical Saints* (1997), and *Adobe Odes* (2006). She has also written a memoir, *House of Houses* (1997), and two collections of essays.

Mora frequently writes about "borders," not only the borders between Mexico and the United States, but also the internal borders that separate – and connect – people. According to Mora, she writes about this topic "because I am a border woman. I grew up moving back and forth between these two countries with ease. . . . I've always had that sense that I could have been born on the other side. So borders interest me."

SEEING

1. Bharati Mukherjee begins her essay by observing that "this essay is about four narratives, those of expatriation, exile, immigration, and repatriation" (para. 1). How does she define each of these terms? Summarize the spirit and substance of the points she makes about each narrative. Which of these narratives does she seem to prefer? Explain why. To what extent do the words *homeland* and *land* condition her response to the different narratives?

2. In the second sentence, Mukherjee tells her readers that she hopes "to weave a revisionist theory for contemporary residency and citizenship, or at least to suggest new terms in the unresolved debate that threatens to grow louder and more rancorous in years to come." Identify the characteristics of that revisionist theory. What distinctive perspective does she adopt in developing the theory? Given your reading of the essays by Amy Tan and Angela M. Balcita as well as the poem by Pat Mora, comment on the extent to which each would agree – or disagree – with the nature of Mukherjee's observations and the implications for envisioning America as home.

3. To what extent is your understanding of immigration dependent on images from popular culture? Cite specific examples to support your response. What countervailing views do Mukherjee, Tan, Balcita, Gordon, and Mora point to in order to balance their readers' views of the immigrant experience?

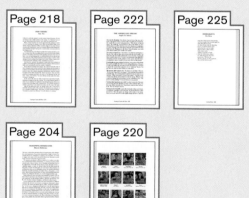

| Page 218 | Page 222 | Page 225 |

| Page 204 | Page 220 |

WRITING

1. In paragraph 2 Mukherjee asks, "What is America? Is it a place or an idea, is it a patchwork of diverse communities, or a nuanced, accented, multicolored myth of shared values?" As you reread "Imagining Homelands,"

keep Mukherjee's question in mind. "Are we heading . . . toward the ancient dream of unity through diversity – *e pluribus unum* – or have we already taken the first steps down the long slope to chaos?" (para. 2). Write the first draft of an essay in which you argue on behalf of either the unity or the chaos perspective.

2. Reread Jesse Gordon's photoessay "What Is America?" (p. 220) and Angela M. Balcita's essay "The Americano Dream" (p. 222). Write an essay comparing and contrasting the two pieces. Whom do you imagine as the audience for each one? What associations does each essay create between America and specific values and beliefs? How does each essay emphasize America as a place that inspires specific virtues and beliefs, and what are the effects of this emphasis?

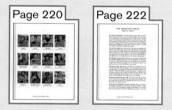

| Page 220 | Page 222 |

Responding Visually

Imagine that you have been asked to create an advertisement to sell America. Please keep in mind that the ad should seek to capitalize on the traditional American values and ideals associated with place. What type of language would you use? What visuals would you use? What would the layout look like? Prepare a draft and a rough sketch of your advertisement and pay special attention to the interrelation between the language and the visual imagery.

Responding Visually

Create your own version of Jesse Gordon's Op-Ed piece. Photograph at least ten people holding the American flag and responding to the question, "What is America?" Arrange your photographs and captions on a page, as Gordon does, or in another format of your choice – a portfolio, for example, a series of web pages, or a PowerPoint presentation.

3

CAPTURING

MEMORABLE

MOMENTS

Each generation of Americans shares memorable moments. Most Americans over age fifty, for example, remember precisely where they were and what they were doing when they heard the news that President John F. Kennedy had been assassinated. At one time or another, nearly all Americans have seen the film footage of JFK and Jackie waving from their car in Dallas the second before the fatal shots were fired.

Identifying a single memorable moment for younger generations of Americans has been more difficult. Yet there has been no shortage of natural and political catastrophes and milestones. On August 28, 2005, Hurricane Katrina hit the southern coast of the United States with devastating force, killing scores of people and leaving millions homeless. On April 16, 2007, a mentally ill student left a murderous trail on the campus of Virginia Tech University: Twenty-seven students and five professors were killed before the gunman turned his weapon on himself. On November 4, 2008, Barack Obama was elected the forty-fourth president of the United States, the first African American to hold the highest office in the nation. Celebrities and sports figures also captured our attention: On August 7, 2007, Barry Bonds broke Henry Aaron's record for the most home runs in baseball history and was indicted three months later for perjury during his testimony before a grand jury investigating the use of performance-enhancing drugs in sports. In July 2008, actress Angelina Jolie gave birth to twins Knox Léon and Vivienne Marcheline at a hospital in France. In August, *People* magazine published the first photos of the twins for a reported $14 million. But none of those moments seems to define today's generation.

Brian Gnatt, a student editor at the University of Michigan's *Daily* in the mid-1990s, put it aptly when he suggested that the defining moments of his generation could be found in Hollywood rather than in the political realm:

> I . . . remember when, where, and who I was with when I saw the *Star Wars* films. To my generation, nothing we have experienced together has been as huge a phenomenon as *Star Wars.* Luke Skywalker and Han Solo are more than household names – they will be ingrained in all of our memories until the day we die.

"While my parents' generation vividly remembers where they were when JFK was shot," Gnatt explained, "my generation [has] no single event of the same caliber."

That changed on September 11, 2001, when terrorists attacked the World Trade Center and the Pentagon. Young and old will never forget the horrible image of the second plane hitting the South Tower, a scene played over and over again as television commentators, like the rest of us, tried to make sense of what they had witnessed.

The events of September 11 have altered the American political and cultural landscape in profound ways. The images of that day have been etched on our national consciousness. And our perspectives on who we are – as individuals and

as a nation – have been seared by our aware-
ness of what took place that morning in New
York City, in Washington, D.C., and in a field in
Pennsylvania.

We can point with certainty to the moments
that define us as a nation, that shape our national
consciousness: a president assassinated, a
plane flying into a skyscraper – events so widely
reported and commented on then and now.

It is far more difficult to sift through diverse
and idiosyncratic personal experiences to find a
single event or image that defines smaller groups
of people, such as college students. After all,
every college student has experienced different
rites of passage and customs: a confirmation,
a bat mitzvah, becoming an Eagle Scout, a first
date, a first day at a first job, wining a championship game. The moments we expect – or are
expected – to remember, the events and cere-
monies we feel obliged to record in our photo
albums or on our Facebook pages, are not
always those that affect the largest number of
people. Often the most memorable experiences
occur when we least expect them or are difficult to capture in a picture frame on a mantel:
becoming blood sisters with a childhood friend;
nervously finding a seat in your first college
lecture class, only to find that you're in the wrong
room; struggling through a complex mathematical equation and finally getting it; receiving
the news that a loved one has died.

Telling stories about the most memorable
moments in our lives often includes explaining
how they have become etched in our minds. In

fact, private moments, like public ones, are inextricably linked to the technologies with which we record them. Most of our special occasions involve cameras; in fact, it is often the camera at a wedding, rather than the bride and groom, that commands everyone's attention and cooperation. It almost seems as though an event has not taken place if it hasn't been photographed or videotaped. Instant replay and stop-action photography allow us to relive, slow down, and freeze our most cherished or embarrassing moments. The proliferation of reality television shows as well as the popularity of YouTube video diaries testify to the increasing importance of the video camera in Americans' private lives.

Whether we take photographs, create scrapbooks, use home-video cameras, keep journals, describe our experiences in letters or e-mails to friends, share family stories during the holidays, or simply replay memories in our minds, we are framing our experiences – for ourselves and often for others. As those memorable events drift into the past, we often revise and embellish our stories about them. Indeed, we continually reshape the nature and tone of our stories each time we recall them.

The selections that follow provide an opportunity for you to practice and develop your skills of narration and revision by noticing how other writers and artists capture memorable moments. From Joe Rosenthal's dramatic photograph of marines raising the American flag at Iwo Jima to James Nachtwey's insightful reflections on the terror and loss in the wake of September 11, each selection in this chapter conveys a public or personal moment of revelation. Pay attention to the techniques and methods each artist and writer employs to tell his or her story. As you read, observe, and write about these selections, consider the range of ways in which you capture the memorable moments in your own life. How does the process of transcribing (writing, photo-graphing, painting, videotaping, etc.) shape or change your understanding of those moments? How can you as a writer enable readers to "get inside" your own experience, to understand the details and nuances that make each particular experience memorable?

Martin Parr
Paris, 18th District, 2000

Martin Parr
Greece, Athens, Acropolis, 1991

Martin Parr
Latvia Beaches, 1999

Martin Parr
Italy, Pisa, Leaning Tower, 1990

Martin Parr

Born in England in 1952, Martin Parr became interested in photography at a young age, encouraged by his grandfather, George Parr. Parr spent three years studying photography at Manchester Polytechnic and then worked on several freelance projects. His fresh eye for imagery and his satirical approach to social documentary won him three awards from the Arts Council of Great Britain before he turned thirty. "The best way to describe my work," says Parr, "is subjective documentary." He is known for his interest in such subjects as consumerism, modern society, and tourism.

In 1994 Parr became a member of Magnum Photos, a cooperative of internationally renowned photographers. In addition, his interest in filmmaking led to several documentaries, including *It's Nice up North* (2006). He also applies his talents to the fashion advertising industry: His work has been featured in campaigns for Hewlett-Packard, Absolut Vodka, and Sony.

In 2002 the Barbican Art Gallery and the National Museum in England exhibited a retrospective of Parr's work that included some of the images shown here. The retrospective continues to travel to museums across the world. Parr is currently professor of photography at the University of Wales – Newport.

SEEING

1. Martin Parr is an unusually skillful contemporary photographer who is especially adept at capturing the subtleties and ironies of ordinary people in search of memorable moments to photograph. Which of the photographs here most effectively captures your attention? Why? Point to specific aspects of the photograph to support each point you make. Which photograph strikes you as most humorous? most ironic? most subtle?

2. Comment on Parr's use of background in each of these photographs. In what specific ways – and with what specific effects – does he draw on the scenes that serve as a backdrop for his subjects? How do his angle of vision and his attitude toward the people and scenes he photographs contribute to the overall effect of each image?

WRITING

1. In several of the pictures here, Parr is photographing a subject who is also taking a picture. Have you ever taken a photograph of someone taking a photograph? What prompted you to take the picture? What effect were you hoping to create? How successful were you? Why? Write the first draft of a personal essay in which you describe the moment, your motivation, and what you hoped to achieve in taking the photograph. Then offer a judgment, supported by specific evidence, about whether you succeeded in achieving your goal, artistic or otherwise. If you have never taken a photograph of someone else taking a picture, then use Parr's photographs as your source and write an analytical essay about them.

2. After reviewing Parr's photographs carefully, select one that strikes you as a particularly effective statement of irony. Write the first draft of an essay in which you analyze the nature and the artistic impact of Parr's use of irony.

VIVIAN, FORT BARNWELL
Ethan Canin

I tell my wife, I'll always remember this photograph of my mother. She's out in back, hanging the blankets to dry on our backyard lines after one of our picnics, and she looks so young, the way I remember her before we moved to California. I was ten, I think. We used to have picnics out there under the water tower when my father got home from work, out in back on the grass on a set of big gray movers' blankets. My father and the man next door had built a pool from a truck tire set in concrete, and they filled it with water for my brother and me to splash in. I remember the day this picture was taken, because my mother had to hang the blankets to dry after we'd soaked them from the pool. My father was mad but she wasn't. She was never mad at us. I haven't seen that picture in years, I tell my wife. But I remember it.

And then one day, for no reason I can fathom, my wife is looking through the old cardboard-sided valise where my mother had kept her pictures, and she says, Here? Is this the one you're always talking about? And I say, Yes, I can't believe you found it. And she says, Those aren't movers' blankets, those are some kind of leaves up in the foreground.

They look like something tropical, maybe rubber leaves. She's not hanging laundry at all. I say, Wait a minute—let me see. And I laugh and say, You're right. How can that be? My whole life I've remembered that picture of her hanging those blankets after we'd soaked them. I can even remember the picnic. She says, That's funny, isn't it? I say, My mother was so beautiful.

Our own children are out back in our own yard. It's too cool here for a pool, but I've built them a swing set from redwood, and I take a look out the window at them climbing it the way I've told them not to.

5 And then a few minutes later my wife says, Look at this, and she hands me the picture again, turned over. On the back it says, Vivian, Fort Barnwell, 1931. That's not your mother at all, she says. That's your grandmother. I say, Let me see that. I say, My God, you're right. How could that have happened?

Ethan Canin
Vivian, Fort Barnwell, 1931

Ethan Canin

Born in 1960 in Ann Arbor, Michigan, Ethan Canin grew up in California. He studied engineering at Stanford University and then earned an MFA from the University of Iowa in 1984. Not expecting that he could earn a living from writing, he got a medical degree at Harvard in 1991. Canin's career plans changed when his first collection of short stories, *Emperor of the Air* (1988), became a critically acclaimed best seller. Since then he has published another collection of short stories and four novels, most recently *Carry Me across the Water* (2001) and *America America* (2008).

The very short story "Vivian, Fort Barnwell" appeared in the fall 1998 issue of *DoubleTake* magazine, accompanied by this editorial note: "A photograph may be seen as a window to a story, but how that story takes shape depends upon the viewer. We were curious as to how the story of this photograph would unfold in the hands of a fiction writer. Here, then, is one moment from an imagined life."

SEEING

1. How would you describe the punch line of Canin's story? How does it recall your own experiences with personal and family photographs? Interview a classmate about an experience from his or her own life that resonates with Canin's. Using Canin's narratives as well as the experiences you've gathered from your own life and those of your classmate, what inferences might you draw about the relationships between photographs and memory?

2. "A photograph may be seen as a window to a story, but how that story takes shape depends upon the viewer," wrote the editors of *DoubleTake* magazine when they printed Canin's short story. What connections do you notice between the photograph and Canin's story? What details does Canin draw on? What additional details do you notice about the photograph? How might they inspire you to craft different versions of the photograph's narrative?

WRITING

1. Imagine that the editors of *DoubleTake* magazine have asked you to write a short story based on this photograph. Your guidelines are simple: The story must not exceed one page in length, and its connection to the photograph must be evident to your readers. You might begin by brainstorming a list of different captions for the photograph. Write as many as you can think of, choose your favorite, and then write the first draft of a story that elaborates on it.

2. "Through photographs," writes Susan Sontag in "On Photography" (p. 304), "each family constructs a portrait-chronicle of itself — a portable kit of images that bears witness to its connectedness" (para. 3). Reread Canin's short story with Sontag's statement in mind. In what ways does it support or refute her assertion? Write the first draft of an essay in which you examine the assumptions that Canin's short story reveals regarding the role of photography and personal and collective memory.

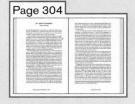

Page 304

THE FIRST THANKSGIVING
Sarah Vowell

When I invited my mom and dad to come to New York City to have Thanksgiving at my house, I never expected them to say yes. Not only had they never been to New York, they had never been east of the Mississippi. Nor had they ever visited me. I've always had these fantasies about being in a normal family in which the parents come to town and their adult daughter spends their entire visit daydreaming of suicide. I'm here to tell you that dreams really do come true.

I was terrified we wouldn't have enough to talk about. In the interest of harmony, there's a tacit agreement in my family; the following subjects are best avoided in any conversation longer than a minute and a half: national politics, state and local politics, any music by any person who never headlined at the Grand Ole Opry, my personal life, and their so-called god. Five whole days. When I visit them back home in Montana, conversation isn't a problem because we go to the movies every afternoon. That way, we can be together but without the burden of actually talking to each other. Tommy Lee Jones, bless his heart, does the talking for us.

But my sister, Amy, is coming and bringing her lively seven-month-old son, Owen, along, so the cinema's not an option. Which means five days together—just us—no movies. We are heading into uncharted and possibly hostile waters, pioneers in a New World. It is Thanksgiving. The pilgrims had the *Mayflower*. I buy a gravy boat.

It's lucky that Amy's coming with Mom and Dad. Amy still lives six blocks away from them in Bozeman. She would act as interpreter and go-between among my parents and me. Like Squanto.

5 Amy's husband, Jay, has decided to stay home in Montana to go deer hunting with his brother. Everyone else arrives at my apartment in Chelsea. Amy and Owen are bunking with me, so I walk my parents around the corner to check them into their hotel on Twenty-third.

"Here we are," says Mom, stopping under the awning of the Chelsea Hotel. There she stands, a woman whose favorite book is called, simply, Matthew, right on the spot where the cops hauled Sid Vicious out in handcuffs after his girlfriend was found stabbed to death on their hotel room floor.

"No, Mother," I say, taking her arm and directing her down the block to the Chelsea Savoy, a hotel where they go to the trouble to clean the rooms each day.

It is around this time, oh, twenty minutes into their trip, that my dad starts making wisecracks like "Boy, kid, bet you can't wait until we're out of here." My father, a man who moved us sixteen hundred miles away from our Oklahoma relatives so he wouldn't have to see them anymore, makes a joke on average every two hours he is here about how much I'm anticipating the second they'll say good-bye. I find this charming but so disturbingly true I don't know what to say.

By halfway through the first day, I discover I needn't have worried what we would talk about, with the baby preventing us from seeing movies. When you have a baby around, the baby is the movie. We occupy an entire entertaining hour just on drool, nonnarrative drool. At this stage, baby Owen is laughing, sitting up, and able to roll over. He is the cutest, the funniest, sweetest, smartest, best-behaved baby in the world.

10   Then there's the sightseeing. First stop, Ellis Island. The thing about going to Ellis Island is that it's a lot like going to Ellis Island. Perhaps to help you better understand the immigrant experience, they make you stand in line for the crammed ferry for an hour and a half in the windy cold. By the time we step onto the island, we are huddled masses yearning to breathe free.

Our great-grandmother Ellen passed through here on her way from Sweden. We watch a video on the health inspections given to immigrants, walk past oodles of photos of men in hats and women in shawls. Though no one says anything, I know my father and mother and sister are thinking what I'm thinking. They're thinking about when we moved away from Oklahoma to Montana, how unknown that was, how strange and lonesome. I read a letter in a display case that says, "And I never saw my mother again," and I think of my grandfather, how we just drove off, leaving him behind, waving to us in the rearview mirror. And here we are in New York, because here I am in New York, because ever since Ellen's father brought her here, every generation moves away from the one before.

It is curious that we Americans have a holiday—Thanksgiving—that's all about people who left their homes for a life of their own choosing, a life that was different from their parents' lives. And how do we celebrate it? By hanging out with our parents! It's as if on the Fourth of July we honored our independence from the British by barbecuing crumpets.

Just as Amy and I grew up and left our parents, someday Owen will necessarily grow up and ditch my sister. And, appropriately enough, it is on this weekend that Owen spends the very first night of his life away from his mother. My parents babysit while Amy and I go to a rock show.

Owen lives through it, as does she, though she talks about him all night, which I guess is how it goes.

Thanksgiving morning, my parents take Owen to see the Macy's parade while Amy and I start making dinner. Let me repeat that—my mother leaves while I cook. Specifically, cornbread dressing, a dish my mother has made every Thanksgiving since before I was born. To her credit, she has not inquired about my process since she phoned to ask me if she should bring cornmeal in her suitcase. As an Okie, my mom only uses white cornmeal processed by the Shawnee Company in Muskogee. She does not even consider my cornbread to be cornbread at all because I make it with yellow cornmeal and, heresy, sugar. "You don't make cornbread," she told me, in the same deflated voice she uses to describe my hair. "You make johnnycake."

15 I'm standing at the cutting board chopping sage and it hits me what it means that she is letting me be in charge of the dressing: I am going to die. Being in charge of the dressing means you are a grown-up for real, and being a grown-up for real means you're getting old, and getting old means you are definitely, finally, totally going to die. My mother is a grandmother and my sister is a mother and I have decided the dressing will be yellow this year, therefore, we'll all be dead someday.

"Is that enough celery?" Amy asks, pointing to a green mound on the counter. Is there ever enough celery? Do my parents have more celery in their past than they do in their future? Do I?

I have invited my friends John and David to join us for dinner, and I was a little nervous about how everyone would get along. To my delight, the meal is smooth and congenial. My friends and I talk about the West Nile virus killing birds on Long Island. My father counters with a lovely anecdote about an open copper pit in Butte that filled up with contaminated rainwater and killed 250 geese in one day. There is nothing like eating one dead bird and talking about a bunch of other dead birds to really bring people together.

The next morning, right about the time Owen starts to cry while—simultaneously—my mother jams the bathroom door and my father's on his hands and knees prying it open with a penknife, a cloud passes over me. Once or twice a day, I am enveloped inside what I like to call the Impenetrable Shield of Melancholy. This shield, it is impenetrable. Hence the name. I cannot speak. And while I can feel myself freeze up, I can't do anything about it. As my family fusses, I spend an inordinate amount of time pretending to dry my hair, the bedroom door closed, the hair dryer on full blast, pointed at nothing.

Everybody in the family goes through these little spells. I just happen to be the spooky one at this particular moment. When people ask me if I'm the black sheep of the family I always say that, no, we're all black sheep. Every few hours they're here, I look over at my dad, nervously crunching his fingers together. If he were at home for Thanksgiving, he'd be ignoring us and spending all his time in his shop. I watch him move his fingers in the air and realize he's turning some hunk of metal on an imaginary lathe.

20   The thing that unites us is that all four of us are homebody claustrophobes who prefer to be alone and are suspicious of other people. So the trait that binds us together as a family—preferring to keep to ourselves—makes it difficult to *be* together as a family. Paradoxically, it's at these times that I feel closest to them, that I understand them best, that I love them most. It's just surprising we ever breed.

The next day, we do the most typical thing we could possibly do as a family. We split up. I stay home cleaning, Mom goes to Macy's, Amy and Owen visit the Museum of Modern Art, and Dad tours Teddy Roosevelt's birthplace. By the time we all reconvene on Saturday evening, my ragged mother becomes so ambitious with her sightseeing that I can tell she's decided that she's never coming back. "Do you guys want to see Rockefeller Center?" I ask, and she says, "Yeah, because who knows when I'll be back again." Ditto the Empire State Building, "because who knows when I'll be back again."

If you are visiting the Empire State Building, may I offer some advice? If you are waiting in the very long line for the very last elevator and an attendant says that anyone who wants to walk up the last six flights may do so now, right away, and you are with your aging parents and a sister who is carrying a child the size of a fax machine, stay in the line for the elevator. But if you must take the stairs, go first, and do not look back; otherwise your parents will look like one of those Renaissance frescoes of Adam and Eve being expelled from the Garden of Eden, all hunched over and afraid.

So we make it to the observation deck, Brooklyn to the south of us, New Jersey to the west, places that people fled to from far away, places that people now run away from, to make another life. It's dark and cold and windy, and we're sweaty from climbing the stairs. It's really pretty though. And there we stand, side by side, sharing a thought like the family we are. My sister wishes she were home. My mom and dad wish they were home. I wish they were home too.

Sarah Vowell

Best known for her humorous social commentaries on NPR's *This American Life*, Sarah Vowell (b. 1969) also writes several columns, and her articles have appeared in *Esquire*, *Artforum*, *The Village Voice*, and other publications. This essay, "The First Thanksgiving," was published in her third book, *The Partly Cloudy Patriot* (2002), a best seller. Her most recent book is *The Wordy Shipmates* (2008), a humorous blend of insights about the Puritans and the religious, social, and historical contexts of their settlement, with wry observations about her own family, education, travels, hopes, and fears.

In an interview with *The Onion*, Vowell described both her introversion and her willingness to share personal stories in her readings and essays: "I have no . . . nervousness or fear addressing two thousand people. But when that's over, and I'm sitting at the book-signing table having to make small talk with people one-on-one, then I can get kind of uncomfortable. The radio feels so abstract. You're basically telling a secret to a microphone. . . . Last week, I was on vacation with my sister . . . and she's telling the coffee-shop person about how I live in New York. . . . I was like, 'Can you please not broadcast my personal business to the whole coffee shop?' Then, later, I realized how hypocritical that was, because I will tell 1 million people about our Thanksgiving dinner."

Vowell was raised in Oklahoma and Montana; she currently lives in New York City.

SEEING

1. "The First Thanksgiving" offers Vowell's perspective on the patterns her family has fallen into over the years. In what ways is the Thanksgiving she describes in the essay the "first"? Is the title serious? sardonic? How does your response to the title affect your understanding of the essay? Did you finish the text with a sense that this particular Thanksgiving marks the beginning of something new? If so, why?

2. In paragraph 12, Vowell writes that Thanksgiving is "all about people who left their homes for a life of their own choosing, a life that was different from their parents' lives." To what extent do you agree with her description of the holiday? Why or why not? In the same paragraph she notes that we celebrate the decision to live a different life from our parents by spending the holiday with them. Why do you think Vowell asked her family to have Thanksgiving at her home? How would you describe her relationship with her father? her mother? her sister? Use examples from the essay to support your answers.

sardonic: Disdainfully or skeptically humorous; derisively mocking.

WRITING

1. Vowell begins her piece saying that her parents had "never been east of the Mississippi." She continues to use place names and locales throughout the essay, both to describe the places her family visits in New York City and to function as a kind of shorthand for the differences she sees between herself and her parents. Think about your own holiday geography. Are certain places significant to your holidays, past and present? What local places, in addition to your home, figure in your celebrations? Draft an essay about a place, other than your home, that has played or continues to play an important role in your celebration of Thanksgiving or another holiday.

2. Reread Vowell's essay. What specific writing strategies does she use to elicit a humorous response from her audience? What roles do memory and tradition play in achieving that humorous effect? Write the first draft of a humorous essay in which you draw on memory and tradition in your own family's Thanksgiving customs—or those of another holiday.

RETROSPECT–Yearbook Photos

1920s   1930s

1960s   1970s

2000s

1940s   1950s

1980s   1990s

THE PHOTOGRAPH
N. Scott Momaday

When I first lived on the Navajo reservation there were no cars, except those that were government property or that belonged to the Indian Service employees. The Navajos went about in wagons and on horseback, everywhere. My father worked for the Roads Department on the Navajo reservation. I lived for those trips, for he would often take me with him. I got a sense of the country then; it was wild and unending. In rainy weather the roads became channels of running water, and sometimes a flash flood would simply wash them away altogether, and we would have to dig ourselves out of the mud or wait for the ground to freeze. And then the wagons would pass us by or, if we were lucky, some old man would unhitch his team and pull us out to firm ground.

"*Ya'at'eeh*," the old man would say.

"*Ya'at'eeh, shicheii*," my father would reply.

"*Hagosha' diniya?*"

5   "Nowhere," my father would say, "we are going nowhere."

"*Aoo', atiin ayoo hastlish.*" Yes, the road is very muddy, the old man would answer, laughing, and we knew then that we were at his mercy, held fast in the groove of his humor and goodwill. My father learned to speak the Navajo language in connection with his work, and I learned something of it, too—a little. Later, after I had been away from the Navajo country for many years, I returned and studied the language formally in order to understand not only the meaning but the formation of it as well. It is a beautiful language, intricate and full of subtlety, and very difficult to learn.

There were sheep camps in the remote canyons and mountains. When we ventured out into those areas, we saw a lot of people, but they were always off by themselves, it seemed, living a life of their own, each one having an individual existence in that huge landscape. Later, when I was learning to fly an airplane, I saw the land as a hawk or an eagle sees it, immense and wild and all of a piece. Once I flew with a friend to the trading post at Low Mountain where we landed on a dirt road in the very middle of the reservation. It was like going backward in time, for Low Mountain has remained virtually undiscovered in the course of years, and there you can still see the old people coming in their wagons to get water and to trade. It is like Kayenta was in my earliest time on the reservation, so remote as to be almost legendary in the mind.

My father had a little box camera with which he liked to take photographs now and then. One day an old Navajo crone came to our house and asked to have her picture taken. She was a gnarled old woman with gray hair and fine pronounced features. She made a wonderful subject, and I have always thought very well of the photograph that my father made of her. Every day thereafter she would come to the house and ask to see the print, and every day my father had to tell her that it had not yet come back in the mail. Having photographs processed was a slow business then in that part of the world. At last the day came when the print arrived. And when the old woman came, my father presented it to her proudly. But when she took a look at it, she was deeply disturbed, and she would have nothing to do with it. She set up such a jabber, indeed, that no one could understand her, and she left in a great huff. I have often wondered that she objected so to her likeness, for it was a true likeness, as far as I could tell. It is quite possible, I think, that she had never seen her likeness before, not even in a mirror, and that the photograph was a far cry from what she imagined herself to be. Or perhaps she saw, in a way that we could not, that the photograph misrepresented her in some crucial respect, that in its dim, mechanical eye it had failed to see into her real being.

N. Scott Momaday

Born on a Kiowa reservation in Oklahoma in 1934, N. Scott Momaday had a Kiowa father and a mother who was Cherokee, French, and English. He has spent his life and his career reconstructing the story of the Kiowa tribe – its myths, its history, and most important, its oral tradition. His first novel, *House Made of Dawn* (1968), focuses on the clash between the Native American world and the white world. The book not only won a Pulitzer Prize but also paved the way for a renaissance in Native American literature.

Momaday has since written essays, poetry, autobiography, and fiction, almost all of which draws on and explores the story of his people and their land. Among his many published works are *Apples of Geese and Other Poems* (1974), *The Names* (1976), *The Gourd Dancer* (1976), *The Ancient Child* (1989), *In the Presence of the Sun* (1991), and *Three Plays* (2007). From 1982 until he retired, he was a professor of English at the University of Arizona – Tucson. He is presently a Senior Scholar at the School of American Research in Santa Fe, New Mexico.

SEEING

1. Momaday describes several different literal and figurative vantage points from which he has viewed Navajo culture. How many can you identify? Which ones do you find most memorable? Why?

2. How would you describe the structure of Momaday's brief essay? What relationship do the parts have to one another? How would you describe the essay's central message, and how does the essay's structure help convey its message?

WRITING

1. Ask one of your classmates to take your portrait and e-mail it to you. Leave the compositional choices up to your classmate for this exercise. When you receive your portrait in your inbox, write nonstop for ten minutes about what you see. What aspects of yourself do think the photograph captures well? What aspects of your personality does it leave out?

Working with Sources

2. The camera's "dim mechanical eye . . . had failed to see into her real being," writes Momaday about his father's portrait of a Navajo crone (para. 8). Do you think that a photographic portrait can capture someone's essence? Why or why not? Choose two photographic portraits – from your own, or a public, collection. Write the first draft of an essay in which you take a stand on this question, using your photographs to support your point.

crone: A withered old woman.

The most difficult aspect
of writing is putting all of my
jumbled thoughts and ideas
down. I'll start writing something
and know exactly how I want it
to end when I start writing,
but by the time I am finished, the
whole thing is entirely different
than originally planned.

Anne Trent, student at Las Positas College

I write ideas, tropes, images,
observations, snippets of dialogue,
themes, factoids, descriptions
on these Post-it notes and put them
in relevant zones on the wall.
Then I organize them into scrapbooks, then I turn them into
books. Then I write more ideas,
etc., on Post-it notes. And so it
goes on: the auto-cannibalization
of the fictive world.

Will Self, novelist and journalist

Steve McCurry
Sharbat Gula, Pakistan, 1985

Steve McCurry
Sharbat Gula, Pakistan, 2002

Steve McCurry

In his career as a photojournalist, Steve McCurry (b. 1950) has covered many international conflicts and has even been reported dead twice. His primary interest is in the effects of war on individuals – people such as Sharbat Gula.

A member of the prestigious Magnum Photos group since 1986, McCurry has won almost every major photography award and has published numerous books, including *The Imperial Way* (1985), *Monsoon* (1988), *Portraits* (1999), *South Southeast* (2000), *Sanctuary* (2002), *The Path to Buddha* (2003), *Steve McCurry* (2005), and *Looking East* (2006).

SEEING

1. *National Geographic* hired several experts to confirm that the woman Steve McCurry photographed in 2002 was the same person pictured in the earlier photograph. What makes you think that the two pictures are both of Sharbat Gula? What details do you notice in these photographs that suggest that they capture younger and older versions of the same person? What details might lead you to doubt that they are of the same person?

2. Read "Context – Sharbat Gula" on page 259 and consider the role of purpose in these photographs. What was the photographer's purpose? the subject's? Why do you think the magazine underwrote the project and published the photographs?

WRITING

1. Ask an older family member for two pictures: one taken when he or she was a young adult; the other a current snapshot. Lay the photographs side by side. What has changed? What has stayed the same? Suppose young and old could meet. What would they talk about? What would they feel? For example, what would your grandfather have to say to the young man he was in the earlier photograph? What would the young man think of the choices his future self has made? Write the conversation you imagine them having.

2. *National Geographic* told the story of McCurry's two photographs in April 2002, in an article titled "A Life Revealed." What does it mean to reveal someone's life? The article describes Sharbat Gula as a "private woman, uncomfortable with the attention of strangers." Why do you think it might have been inappropriate to reveal this woman's life to the world? or why not? Why would or wouldn't you want your own life revealed in a photograph? Look up the word *reveal* in the dictionary, paying special attention to its etymology. What do the roots of *reveal* tell us about McCurry's purpose in photographing Gula? Write an essay in which you examine the meaning of "a life revealed" in the context of McCurry's photographs. Who is doing the revealing? How? Why? And to what effect?

Steve McCurry first photographed Sharbat Gula in 1985, in a refugee camp in Pakistan. "I remember the noise and confusion. . . . I asked permission from the teacher to enter the girls' school tent to photograph her. . . . The Soviets had been in Afghanistan for five years, and Sharbat's parents had both been killed during airstrikes on her village." The photograph, printed on the cover of *National Geographic* in June 1985, became one of the most famous ever printed in the magazine. McCurry says that not a day goes by when he doesn't receive a letter requesting more information about the girl in the photo. So, almost two decades later, McCurry traveled to Pakistan with *National Geographic* staff to find the girl who had captivated audiences around the world with her stunning green eyes.

McCurry went to the refugee camp near Peshawar where he had first met Sharbat Gula, and he spoke to the inhabitants to see if anyone remembered her and knew of her whereabouts. Word of the journalists' hunt reached a man who claimed to know Sharbat Gula. He offered to bring her back to Pakistan.

When Sharbat Gula walked into the room three days later, McCurry knew it was her. A team of experts, including ophthalmologists and FBI agents, proved what McCurry already knew: This was the girl from the photograph. He called that meeting one of the most memorable moments in his life.

Sharbat Gula had moved back to Afghanistan and now lived in the mountains near Tora Bora with her husband and three daughters. Although their life is difficult, it is a wonder that Sharbat survived at all. Initially she did not want to be photographed again. "But . . . when we explained how Steve's original photograph had inspired people to go to work in refugee camps," recalls producer Carrie Regan, "she knew that this story could once again help bring attention to the plight of Afghan people and mobilize people to help. She was willing to do it, I think, because she saw it as a sacrifice she was doing for her people."

How does learning more about Sharbat Gula's life change your reading of her photograph?

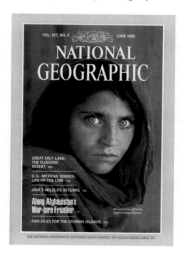

THIS IS OUR WORLD
Dorothy Allison

The first painting I ever saw up close was at a Baptist church when I was seven years old. It was a few weeks before my mama was to be baptized. From it, I took the notion that art should surprise and astonish, and hopefully make you think something you had not thought until you saw it. The painting was a mural of Jesus at the Jordan River done on the wall behind the baptismal font. The font itself was a remarkable creation — a swimming pool with one glass side set into the wall above and behind the pulpit so that ordinarily you could not tell the font was there, seeing only the painting of Jesus. When the tank was flooded with water, little lights along the bottom came on, and anyone who stepped down the steps seemed to be walking past Jesus himself and descending into the Jordan River. Watching baptisms in that tank was like watching movies at the drive-in, my cousins had told me. From the moment the deacon walked us around the church, I knew what my cousin had meant. I could not take my eyes off the painting or the glass-fronted tank. It looked every moment as if Jesus were about to come alive, as if he were about to step out onto the water of the river. I think the way I stared at the painting made the deacon nervous.

The deacon boasted to my mama that there was nothing like that baptismal font in the whole state of South Carolina. It had been designed, he told her, by a nephew of the minister — a boy who had gone on to build a shopping center out in New Mexico. My mama was not sure that someone who built shopping centers was the kind of person who should have been designing baptismal fonts, and she was even more uncertain about the steep steps by Jesus' left hip. She asked the man to let her practice going up and down, but he warned her it would be different once the water poured in.

"It's quite safe though," he told her. "The water will hold you up. You won't fall."

I kept my attention on the painting of Jesus. He was much larger than I was, a little bit more than life-size, but the thick layer of shellac applied to protect the image acted like a magnifying glass, making him seem larger still. It was Jesus himself that fascinated me, though. He was all rouged and pale and pouty as Elvis Presley. This was not my idea of the Son of God, but I liked it. I liked it a lot.

5   "Jesus looks like a girl," I told my mama.

She looked up at the painted face. A little blush appeared on her cheek-bones, and she looked as if she would have smiled if the deacon were not frowning so determinedly. "It's just the eyelashes," she said. The deacon nodded. They climbed back up the stairs. I stepped over close to Jesus and put my hand on the painted robe. The painting was sweaty and cool, slightly oily under my fingers.

"I liked that Jesus," I told my mama as we walked out of the church. "I wish we had something like that." To her credit, Mama did not laugh.

"If you want a picture of Jesus," she said, "we'll get you one. They have them in nice frames at Sears." I sighed. That was not what I had in mind. What I wanted was a life-size, sweaty painting, one in which Jesus looked as hopeful as a young girl—something other-worldly and pecu-liar, but kind of wonderful at the same time. After that, every time we went to church I asked to go up to see the painting, but the baptismal font was locked tight when not in use.

The Sunday Mama was to be baptized, I watched the minister step down into that pool past the Son of God. The preacher's gown was tailored with little weights carefully sewn into the hem to keep it from rising up in the water. The water pushed up at the fabric while the weights tugged it down. Once the minister was all the way down into the tank, the robe floated up a bit so that it seemed to have a shirred ruffle all along the bottom. That was almost enough to pull my eyes away from the face of Jesus, but not quite. With the lights on in the bottom of the tank, the eyes of the painting seemed to move and shine. I tried to point it out to my sisters, but they were uninterested. All they wanted to see was Mama.

10   Mama was to be baptized last, after three little boys, and their gowns had not had any weights attached. The white robes floated up around their necks so that their skinny boy bodies and white cotton underwear were perfectly visible to the congregation. The water that came up above the hips of the minister lapped their shoulders, and the shortest of the boys seemed panicky at the prospect of gulping water, no matter how holy. He paddled furiously to keep above the water's surface. The water started to rock violently at his struggles, sweeping the other boys off their feet. All of them pumped their knees to stay upright, and the minister, realizing how the scene must appear to the congregation below, speeded up the baptismal process, praying over and dunking the boys at high speed.

Around me the congregation shifted in their seats. My little sister slid forward off the pew, and I quickly grabbed her around the waist and barely stopped myself from laughing out loud. A titter from the back of the church indicated that other people were having the same difficulty keeping from laughing. Other people shifted irritably and glared at the noisemakers. It was clear that no matter the provocation, we were to pretend nothing funny was happening. The minister frowned more fiercely and prayed louder. My mama's friend Louise, sitting at our left, whispered a soft "Look at that," and we all looked up in awe. One of the hastily blessed boys had dog-paddled over to the glass and was staring out at us, eyes wide and his hands pressed flat to the glass. He looked as if he hoped someone would rescue him. It was too much for me. I began to giggle helplessly, and not a few of the people around me joined in. Impatiently the minister hooked the boy's robe, pulled him back, and pushed him toward the stairs.

My mama, just visible on the staircase, hesitated briefly as the sodden boy climbed up past her. Then she set her lips tightly together, and reached down and pressed her robe to her thighs. She came down the steps slowly, holding down the skirt as she did so, giving one stern glance to the two boys climbing past her up the steps, and then turning her face deliberately up to the painting of Jesus. Every move she made communicated resolution and faith, and the congregation stilled in respect. She was baptized looking up stubbornly, both hands holding down that cotton robe, while below, I fought so hard not to giggle, tears spilled down my face.

Over the pool, the face of Jesus watched solemnly with his pink, painted cheeks and thick, dark lashes. For all the absurdity of the event, his face seemed to me startlingly compassionate and wise. That face understood fidgety boys and stubborn women. It made me want the painting even more, and to this day I remember it with longing. It had the weight of art, that face. It had what I am sure art is supposed to have—the power to provoke, the authority of a heartfelt vision.

I imagine the artist who painted the baptismal font in that Baptist church so long ago was a man who did not think himself much of an artist. I have seen paintings like his many times since, so perhaps he worked from a model. Maybe he traced that face off another he had seen in some other church. For a while, I tried to imagine him a character out of a Flannery O'Connor short story, a man who traveled around the South in the fifties painting Jesus wherever he was needed, giving the Son of God the long lashes and pink cheeks of a young girl. He would be the kind of man who would see nothing blasphemous in painting eyes that followed the congregation as they moved up to the pulpit to receive a blessing and back to the pews to sit chastened and still for the benediction. Perhaps he had no sense of humor, or perhaps he had one too refined for intimidation. In my version of the story, he would have a case of whiskey in his van, right behind the gallon containers of shellac and buried notebooks of his own sketches. Sometimes, he would read thick journals of art criticism while sitting up late in cheap hotel rooms and then get roaring drunk and curse his fate.

15   "What I do is wallpaper," he would complain. "Just wallpaper." But the work he so despised would grow more and more famous as time passed. After his death, one of those journals would publish a careful consideration of his murals, calling him a gifted primitive. Dealers would offer little churches large sums to take down his walls and sell them as installations to collectors. Maybe some of the churches would refuse to sell, but grow uncomfortable with the secular popularity of the paintings. Still, somewhere there would be a little girl like the girl I had been, a girl who would dream of putting her hand on the cool, sweaty painting while the Son of God blinked down at her in genuine sympathy. Is it a sin, she would wonder, to put together the sacred and the absurd? I would not answer her question, of course. I would leave it, like the art, to make everyone a little nervous and unsure.

I love black-and-white photographs, and I always have. I have cut photographs out of magazines to paste in books of my own, bought albums at yard sales, and kept collections that had one or two images I wanted near me always. Those pictures tell me stories—my own and others, scary stories sometimes, but more often simply everyday stories, what happened in that place at that time to those people. The pictures I collect leave me to puzzle out what I think about it later. Sometimes, I imagine my own life as a series of snapshots taken by some omniscient artist who is just keeping track—not interfering or saying anything, just capturing the moment for me to look back at it again later. The eye of God, as expressed in a Dorothea Lange or Wright Morris. This is the way it is, the photograph says, and I nod my head in appreciation. The power of art is in that nod of appreciation, though sometimes I puzzle nothing out, and the nod is more a shrug. No, I do not understand this one, but I see it. I take it in. I will think about it. If I sit with this image long enough, this story, I have the hope of understanding something I did not understand before. And that, too, is art, the best art.

My friend Jackie used to call my photographs sentimental. I had pinned them up all over the walls of my apartment, and Jackie liked a few of them but thought on the whole they were better suited to being tucked away in a book. On her walls, she had half a dozen bright prints in bottle-cap metal frames, most of them bought from Puerto Rican artists at street sales when she was working as a taxi driver and always had cash in her pockets. I thought her prints garish and told her so when she made fun of my photographs.

"They remind me of my mama," she told me. I had only seen one photograph of Jackie's mother, a wide-faced Italian matron from Queens with thick, black eyebrows and a perpetual squint.

"She liked bright colors?" I asked.

20   Jackie nodded. "And stuff you could buy on the street. She was always buying stuff off tables on the street, saying that was the best stuff. Best prices. Cheap skirts that lost their dye after a couple of washes, shoes with cardboard insoles, those funky little icons, weeping saints and long-faced Madonnas. She liked stuff to be really colorful. She painted all the ceilings in our apartment red and white. Red-red and white-white. Like blood on bone."

I looked up at my ceiling. The high tin ceiling was uniformly bloody when I moved in, with paint put on so thick, I could chip it off in lumps. I had climbed on stacks of boxes to paint it all cream white and pale blue.

"The Virgin's colors," Jackie told me. "You should put gold roses on the door posts."

"I'm no artist," I told her.

"I am," Jackie laughed. She took out a pencil and sketched a leafy vine above two of my framed photographs. She was good. It looked as if the frames were pinned to the vine. "I'll do it all," she said, looking at me to see if I was upset.

25   "Do it," I told her.

Jackie drew lilies and potato vines up the hall while I made tea and admired the details. Around the front door she put the Virgin's roses and curious little circles with crosses entwined in the middle. "It's beautiful," I told her.

"A blessing," she told me. "Like a bit of magic. My mama magic." Her face was so serious, I brought back a dish of salt and water, and we blessed the entrance. "Now the devil will pass you by," she promised me.

I laughed, but almost believed.

For a few months last spring I kept seeing an ad in all the magazines that showed a small child high in the air dropping toward the upraised arms of a waiting figure below. The image was grainy and distant. I could not tell if the child was laughing or crying. The copy at the bottom of the page read: "Your father always caught you."

30   "Look at this," I insisted the first time I saw the ad. "Will you look at this?"

A friend of mine took the magazine, looked at the ad, and then up into my shocked and horrified face.

"They don't mean it that way," she said.

I looked at the ad again. They didn't mean it that way? They meant it innocently? I shuddered. It was supposed to make you feel safe, maybe make you buy insurance or something. It did not make me feel safe. I dreamed about the picture, and it was not a good dream.

I wonder how many other people see that ad the way I do. I wonder how many other people look at the constant images of happy families and make wry faces at most of them. It's as if all the illustrators have television sitcom imaginations. I do not believe in those families. I believe in the exhausted mothers, frightened children, numb and stubborn men. I believe in hard-pressed families, the child huddled in fear with his face hidden, the father and mother confronting each other with their emotions hidden, dispassionate passionate faces, and the unsettling sense of risk in the baby held close to that man's chest. These images make sense to me. They are about the world I know, the stories I tell. When they are accompanied by wry titles or copy that is slightly absurd or unexpected, I grin and know that I will puzzle it out later, sometimes a lot later.

35 I think that using art to provoke uncertainty is what great writing and inspired images do most brilliantly. Art should provoke more questions than answers and, most of all, should make us think about what we rarely want to think about at all. Sitting down to write a novel, I refuse to consider if my work is seen as difficult or inappropriate or provocative. I choose my subjects to force the congregation to look at what they try so stubbornly to pretend is not happening at all, deliberately combining the horribly serious with the absurd or funny, because I know that if I am to reach my audience I must first seduce their attention and draw them into the world of my imagination. I know that I have to lay out my stories, my difficult people, each story layering on top of the one before it with care and craft, until my audience sees something they had not expected. Frailty—stubborn, human frailty—that is what I work to showcase. The wonder and astonishment of the despised and ignored, that is what I hope to find in art and in the books I write—my secret self, my vulnerable and embattled heart, the child I was and the woman I have become, not Jesus at the Jordan but a woman with only her stubborn memories and passionate convictions to redeem her.

"You write such mean stories," a friend once told me. "Raped girls, brutal fathers, faithless mothers, and untrustworthy lovers—meaner than the world really is, don't you think?"

I just looked at her. Meaner than the world really is? No. I thought about showing her the box under my desk where I keep my clippings. Newspaper stories and black-and-white images—the woman who drowned her children, the man who shot first the babies in her arms and then his wife, the teenage boys who led the three-year-old away along the train track, the homeless family recovering from frostbite with their eyes glazed and indifferent while the doctor scowled over their shoulders. The world is meaner than we admit, larger and more astonishing. Strength appears in the most desperate figures, tragedy when we have no reason to expect it. Yes, some of my stories are fearful, but not as cruel as what I see in the world. I believe in redemption, just as I believe in the nobility of the despised, the dignity of the outcast, the intrinsic honor among misfits, pariahs, and queers. Artists—those of us who stand outside the city gates and look back at a society that tries to ignore us—we have an angle of vision denied to whole sectors of the sheltered and indifferent population within. It is our curse and our prize, and for everyone who will tell us our work is mean or fearful or unreal, there is another who will embrace us and say with tears in their eyes how wonderful it is to finally feel as if someone else has seen their truth and shown it in some part as it should be known.

"My story," they say. "You told my story. That is me, mine, us." And it is.

We are not the same. We are a nation of nations. Regions, social classes, economic circumstances, ethical systems, and political convictions—all separate us even as we pretend they do not. Art makes that plain. Those of us who have read the same books, eaten the same kinds of food as children, watched the same television shows, and listened to the same music, we believe ourselves part of the same nation—and we are continually startled to discover that our versions of reality do not match. If we were more the same, would we not see the same thing when we look at a painting? But what is it we see when we look at a work of art? What is it we fear will be revealed? The artist waits for us to say. It does not matter that each of us sees something slightly different. Most of us, confronted with the artist's creation, hesitate, stammer, or politely deflect the question of what it means to us. Even those of us from the same background, same region, same general economic and social class, come to "art" uncertain, suspicious, not wanting to embarrass ourselves by revealing what the work provokes in us. In fact, sometimes we are not sure. If we were to reveal what we see in each painting, sculpture, installation, or little book, we would run the risk of exposing our secret selves, what we know and what we fear we do not know, and of course incidentally what it is we truly fear. Art is the Rorschach test for all of us, the projective hologram of our secret lives. Our emotional and intellectual lives are laid bare. Do you like hologram roses? Big, bold, brightly painted canvases? Representational art? Little boxes with tiny figures posed precisely? Do you dare say what it is you like?

40   For those of us born into poor and working-class families, these are not simple questions. For those of us who grew up hiding what our home life was like, the fear is omnipresent—particularly when that home life was scarred by physical and emotional violence. We know if we say anything about what we see in a work of art we will reveal more about ourselves than the artist. What do you see in this painting, in that one? I see a little girl, terrified, holding together the torn remnants of her clothing. I see a child, looking back at the mother for help and finding none. I see a mother, bruised and exhausted, unable to look up for help, unable to believe anyone in the world will help her. I see a man with his fists raised, hating himself but making those fists tighter all the time. I see a little girl, uncertain and angry, looking down at her own body with hatred and contempt. I see that all the time, even when no one else sees what I see. I know I am not supposed to mention what it is I see. Perhaps no one else is seeing what I see. If they are, I am pretty sure there is some cryptic covenant that requires that we will not say what we see. Even when looking at an image of a terrified child, we know that to mention why that child might be so frightened would be a breach of social etiquette. The world requires that such children not be mentioned, even when so many of us are looking directly at her.

There seems to be a tacit agreement about what it is not polite to mention, what it is not appropriate to portray. For some of us, that polite behavior is set so deeply we truly do not see what seems outside that tacit agreement. We have lost the imagination for what our real lives have been or continue to be, what happens when we go home and close the door on the outside world. Since so many would like us to never mention anything unsettling anyway, the impulse to be quiet, the impulse to deny and pretend, becomes very strong. But the artist knows all about that impulse. The artist knows that it must be resisted. Art is not meant to be polite, secret, coded, or timid. Art is the sphere in which that impulse to hide and lie is the most dangerous. In art, transgression is holy, revelation a sacrament, and pursuing one's personal truth the only sure validation.

Does it matter if our art is canonized, if we become rich and successful, lauded and admired? Does it make any difference if our pictures become popular, our books made into movies, our creations win awards?

What if we are the ones who wind up going from town to town with our notebooks, our dusty boxes of prints or Xeroxed sheets of music, never acknowledged, never paid for our work? As artists, we know how easily we could become a Flannery O'Connor character, reading those journals of criticism and burying our faces in our hands, staggering under the weight of what we see that the world does not. As artists, we also know that neither worldly praise nor critical disdain will ultimately prove the worth of our work.

Some nights I think of that sweating, girlish Jesus above my mother's determined features, those hands outspread to cast benediction on those giggling uncertain boys, me in the congregation struck full of wonder and love and helpless laughter. If no one else ever wept at that image, I did. I wished the artist who painted that image knew how powerfully it touched me, that after all these years his art still lives inside me. If I can wish for anything for my art, that is what I want—to live in some child forever—and if I can demand anything of other artists, it is that they attempt as much.

Dorothy Allison

"I know in my bones that to write well you must inhabit your creations: male, female, whatever," says Dorothy Allison, a self-described "lesbian, feminist, Southern femme partnered to a self-defined butch musician, incest survivor, . . . mother . . . working-class escapee."

Born in Greenville, South Carolina, in 1949, Allison grew up in a poor, working-class family. She says that she knew from her earliest years that she was an outsider, that she didn't fit in, but that not fitting in is one of her strengths as a writer. "Some days I think I have a unique advantage, an outsider's perspective that lets me see what others ignore." Her writing gives voice to her experience of the working-poor South, where her stepfather raped her when she was five years old. Her first novel, *Bastard Out of Carolina* (1992), which was a finalist for the National Book Award, is about escaping from that world. Her second novel, *Cavedweller* (1998), is about returning to it. A third novel *She Who*, is forthcoming.

"As a teacher I invariably require that my students write across their own barriers," she says, "forcing young lesbians to write as middle-aged men (straight or gay) and the most fervently macho men to speak as tender girls. Climbing into a stranger's skin is the core of the writer's experience, stretching the imagination to incorporate the unimagined." "This Is Our World" first appeared in the summer 1998 issue of *DoubleTake* magazine.

SEEING

1. At one point in "This Is Our World," Dorothy Allison describes a magazine ad "that showed a small child high in the air dropping toward the upraised arms of a waiting figure below" (para. 29). What varying "versions of reality" (para. 39) does Allison see in this image? How does her description of each version exemplify her point that "if we were to reveal what we see in each painting, sculpture, installation, or little book, we would run the risk of exposing our secret selves" (para. 39)?

2. Allison begins her essay with memories of the first painting she "ever saw up close." At what points – and with what effects – does she refer to those memories later in the essay? When does Allison shift from personal anecdotes to more general commentary? To what extent do you think that movement is successful?

WRITING

1. "The world is meaner than we admit," Allison writes, referring to the stash of newspaper clippings she keeps under her desk (para. 37). Use a newspaper clipping of your choice to agree or disagree with Allison's assertion. Use details from your text and your knowledge of violence to support your points.

Working with Sources

2. From the painting of Jesus she marveled at as a child, Allison writes, she "took the notion that art should surprise and astonish, and hopefully make you think something you had not thought until you saw it" (para. 1). Choose a piece of art – a visual image, an essay, or some other work – that surprised and astonished you, and use it to support or refute Allison's claim about what art should do. If you disagree with Allison, make sure you start with your own definition of the purpose of art.

THIS JUST IN: I'M TWITTERING
How a Social Networking App Turns
Trivial Updates into Your Posse's Sixth Sense
Clive Thompson

Twitter is the app that everyone loves to hate. Odds are you've noticed people—probably much younger than you—manically using Twitter, a tool that lets you post brief updates about your everyday thoughts and activities to the Web via browser, cell phone, or IM. The messages are limited to 140 characters, so they lean toward pithy, haiku-like utterances. When I dropped by the main Twitter page, people had posted notes like "Doing lunch and picking up father-in-law from senior center." Or "Checking out *Ghost Whisperer*" or simply "Thinking I'm old." (Most users are between eighteen and twenty-seven.)

It might seem like blogging taken to a supremely banal extreme. Productivity guru Tim Ferriss calls Twitter "pointless email on steroids." One Silicon Valley businessman I met complained that his staff had become Twitter-obsessed. "You can't say anything in such a short message," he said, baffled. "So why do it at all?"

They're precisely right: Individually, most Twitter messages are stupefyingly trivial. But the true value of Twitter—and the similarly mundane Dodgeball, a tool for reporting your real-time location to friends—is cumulative. The power is in the surprising effects that come from receiving thousands of pings from your posse. And this, as it turns out, suggests where the Web is heading.

When I see that my friend Misha is "waiting at Genius Bar to send my MacBook to the shop," that's not much information. But when I get such granular updates every day for a month, I know a lot more about her. And when my four closest friends and worldmates send me dozens of updates a week for five months, I begin to develop an almost telepathic awareness of the people most important to me.

5   It's like proprioception, your body's ability to know where your limbs are. That subliminal sense of orientation is crucial for coordination: It keeps you from accidentally bumping into objects, and it makes possible amazing feats of balance and dexterity.

Twitter and other constant-contact media create *social* proprioception. They give a group of people a sense of itself, making possible weird, fascinating feats of coordination.

For example, when I meet Misha for lunch after not having seen her for a month, I already know the wireframe outline of her life: She was nervous about last week's big presentation, got stuck in a rare spring snowstorm, and became addicted to salt bagels. With Dodgeball, I never actually race out to meet a friend when they report their nearby location; I just note it as something to talk about the next time we meet.

It's almost like ESP, which can be incredibly useful when applied to your work life. You know who's overloaded—*better not bug Amanda today*—and who's on a roll. A buddy list isn't just a vehicle to chat with friends but a way to sense their presence. Are they available to talk? Have they been away? This awareness is crucial when colleagues are spread around the office, the country, or the world. Twitter substitutes for the glances and conversations we had before we became a nation of satellite employees.

So why has Twitter been so misunderstood? Because it's experiential. Scrolling through random Twitter messages can't explain the appeal. You have to *do* it—and, more important, do it with friends. (Monitoring the lives of total strangers is fun but doesn't have the same addictive effect.) Critics sneer at Twitter and Dodgeball as hipster narcissism, but the real appeal of Twitter is almost the inverse of narcissism. It's practically collectivist—you're creating a shared understanding larger than yourself.

10   Mind you, quick-ping media can be a massive time-suck. You also may not want more information pecking at your frayed attention span. And who knows? Twitter's rabid fans (their numbers are doubling every three weeks) may well abandon it for a shinier new toy. It happened to Friendster.

But here's my bet: The animating genius behind Twitter will live on in future apps. That factile sense of your community is simply too much fun, too useful—and it makes the group more than the sum of its parts.

Clive Thompson

Contributing frequently to major publications such as the *New York Times*, *New York* magazine, and *Wired* magazine, Clive Thompson is a science writer who explores the ways that technology affects our culture. He has been anthologized in the 2003 edition of *Best American Science Writing* and is a former Knight Science Journalism Fellow at MIT. Apart from his more formal media outlets, he can be read at his blog, *www.collisiondetection.net*, which also includes a link to his Twitter page.

SEEING

1. "You can't say anything in such a short message, so why do it at all?" wonders a Silicon Valley businessman, according to Clive Thompson (para. 2). How does Thompson's essay answer this question? Why do you think Twitter is popular? If you're not already familiar with Twitter, take a few moments to explore the site (*www.twitter.com*). Why do people bother to constantly update their activities? What does Thompson mean when he says that "the true value of Twitter . . . is cumulative" (para. 3)? Do you agree with Thompson? Why or why not?

2. Thompson says in paragraph 3 that "the power is in the surprising effects that come from receiving thousands of pings from your posse. And this, as it turns out, suggests where the Web is heading." What future does Thompson envision for the web? How will the future of news reporting change? What examples or images does he use to illustrate his vision? What examples of online or offline tools and technology would you use to support or refute his vision?

WRITING

1. Go to *www.twitter.com* and, as Thompson says (para. 9), monitor the life of a total stranger. Then write a short story about that person and his or her life based on some of the daily activities that you read about.

2. Traditionally, journalists who write for newspapers and talk on radio and television news shows report on moments that are significant and will one day still be collectively remembered, like political campaigns, natural disasters, and changes in the economy. How does a source like Twitter change the definition of a memorable moment? Write an expository essay in which you define what makes a moment memorable and explain how Twitter does or does not change that definition.

(opposite page and following) Seeing and writing the major news stories on any one day can vary greatly. Consider, for example, November 5, 2008. Compare and contrast the front pages of the newspapers shown here. Each reports on the historic election of Barack Obama. How would you describe the choices in content, focus, scope, tone, and overall presentation in each? Based on your observations, what inferences can you draw about the principles that drive each publication's editorial decisions? For additional examples of such differences, explore the web site *www.newseum.org,* where you can compare and contrast the presentation of front pages on the same day from across the country.

www.usatoday.com
FINAL SCORES
THE NATION'S NEWSPAPER
75 CENTS

Your guide to the election

Results '08
528 races across USA
■ Also, interactive map at politics.usatoday.com has latest on 3,100 counties

USA TODAY

NO. 1 IN THE USA

Wednesday, November 5, 2008

Congressional races

Hagan knocks off Dole in N.C.
■ GOP senator loses seat; Warner wins in Virginia, 11-13A

By Ellen Ozier, Reuters
Kay Hagan: Five-term state senator.

America makes history
Obama wins

'Change has come to America,' he says after election to presidency erases a racial barrier; Democrats make gains

Where the race was won

Florida
McCain 49%
✔Obama 51%
98% of the vote

Colorado
McCain 45%
✔Obama 53%
66% of the vote

Ohio
McCain 48%
✔Obama 51%
83% of the vote

Pennsylvania
McCain 44%
✔Obama 55%
99% of the vote

Virginia
McCain 48%
✔Obama 52%
98% of the vote

The new first family: Barack Obama and his wife, Michelle, and daughters, Sasha, 7, and Malia, 10, greet supporters in Chicago on Tuesday.
By Jack Gruber, USA TODAY

How the states voted
As of 1:15 a.m. ET today

■ McCain   ■ Obama   Undecided

More detailed map, 15A
Source: The Associated Press   *By Julie Snider, USA TODAY*

Newsline

■ News ■ Money ■ Sports ■ Life

Chicago celebrates Obama victory
'Is this real?' reveler asks; others pray, weep. 3A.
► Michelle Obama's focus on family. 3A.

Gay-marriage ban gains in California
Constitutional amendments also leading in Arizona, Florida; two states legalize marijuana. 18A.
► Democrats win statehouse in Missouri. 13A.

Money: Winner faces economic mess
President-elect will need plan of action to deal with urgent marketplace issues. 1B.
► GOP presidents not better for stocks. 1B.

Crossword, Sudoku 10B
Editorial/Forum 22-23A
Lotteries 9C
Marketplace Today 10B
Market scoreboard 4B
Weather 24A

Taps into the public's anger over economy and war

By William M. Welch
USA TODAY

Democrat Barack Obama secured a historic presidential victory Tuesday, shattering a racial barrier that once seemed unbreakable by tapping voter anger over the sinking economy and a long-running war.

Obama swept at least seven states that President Bush carried in 2004, including Florida, Virginia and Ohio, as he reshaped the political map. Republican John McCain saw his candidacy crushed under the weight of an unpopular GOP president and his own vigorous support for the Iraq war.

Obama, 47, will be the first African-American president and one of the youngest. Just four years ago, the son of a Kenyan father and a white woman from Kansas was elected to the Senate from Illinois.

"It's been a long time coming," Obama told more than 200,000 supporters jammed around Chicago's Grant Park. "Because of what we did on this day, in this election, in this defining moment, change has come to America."

The crowd chanted "Yes, we can" as emotions flowed. Obama recalled the grandmother who raised him and died two days before the triumph that will make him the nation's 44th president.

"I'm almost past words," said Clara Jones, 58, a retired store manager in Chicago. "This is something I hoped I'd see but never expected to see in my lifetime . . . We can't stop smiling."

McCain congratulated Obama and conceded before a tearful crowd of supporters in Phoenix. "The American people have spoken, and they have spoken clearly," the Arizona senator said.

"This is a historic election, and I recognize the special significance it has for African Americans and for the special pride that must be theirs tonight."

That a person of Obama's background won the White House is remarkable in a nation where race relations are still sometimes tense. Only four decades ago, when Obama was 4 years old, Congress passed the Voting Rights Act to ensure blacks can vote.

He far exceeded the 270 electoral votes needed for victory and became the first Democrat since 1976 to capture a popular-vote majority.

Obama swept Democrats to victory across the country: His party gained at least five Senate seats in Colorado, Virginia, North Carolina, New Hampshire and New Mexico and picked up at least 11 House seats. Among the ousted GOP senators was North Carolina's Elizabeth Dole, a White House hopeful in 2000. Democrat Jay Nixon was elected Missouri's governor.

For McCain, 72, a former Navy pilot and prisoner of war in Vietnam, the loss likely ended his White House dreams. He fell short of the GOP nomination in 2000 and was among the oldest nominees ever.

Surveys of voters as they left polling places showed broad support for Obama, especially among young voters, women and minorities.

Strong voter interest was visible in lines at polls in many states — evidence of a likely record turnout. A much-feared meltdown at the polls failed to materialize. Scattered problems included hours-long delays caused by faulty malfunctioning machines.

Contributing: Martha T. Moore in Chicago

In Congress, a Democratic wave

Economic concerns fuel a 'turning point' in politics

By Susan Page
USA TODAY

WASHINGTON — America's election of an African American as president wasn't the only breakthrough Tuesday night.

By defeating John McCain in such reliably Republican states as Colorado and Virginia — capital of the Confederacy and a state that hasn't backed a Democrat for president in four decades — Barack Obama reshaped the electoral map that has defined American politics for a generation.

Surveys of voters as they left polling places nationwide also showed shifts in allegiances among young people, Hispanics, upscale voters and others that could reverberate through future elections.

Obama's victory and Democratic gains in the House and Senate led Democrats to their strongest governing position since the post-Watergate election in 1976. Among the Republicans who lost re-election bids were North Carolina Sen. Elizabeth Dole and New Hampshire Sen. John Sununu, members of two of the GOP's signature families.

Some analysts see a turning point in American politics like what occurred in 1980, when Republican Ronald Reagan's victory over President Carter set the nation on a more conserva-

Cover story

Please see COVER STORY next page ►

By M. Spencer Green, USA TODAY
John McCain: At outdoor rally in Phoenix.

McCain: 'People have spoken'
■ Republican candidate concedes and pledges his support to Obama, 7A

Front page, USA Today, Wednesday, November 5, 2008

Front page, Anchorage Daily News, *Wednesday, November 5, 2008*

THE
COMMERCIAL
APPEAL

108TH YEAR
50¢
★★★★
WEDNESDAY
NOVEMBER 5, 2008
COMMERCIALAPPEAL.COM

ON THE WEB
Up to the minute
election news
COMMERCIALAPPEAL.COM

INSIDE
12 pages of news
and analysis

YES HE DID

HISTORY | Democrat Barack Obama becomes first black man to be elected president
NEXT STEP | Tells thousands gathered to celebrate in Chicago that 'change has come'

The son of a black father from Kenya and a white mother from Kansas, Barack Obama waves to thousands who gathered to celebrate his election victory Tuesday night in Chicago.

Pablo Martinez Monsivais/Associated Press

Electoral votes

State-by-state snapshot of the presidential race: 270 needed to win

■ McCain **145**   ■ Obama **338**   ■ Too close to call

Washington
D.C. ■

Unofficial
results as of
11:30 CST

Source: Associated Press

ALL THE LATEST INFORMATION

Get updated results of all the big political contests
at **commercialappeal.com**

At 10:01 p.m. CST Tuesday, after a number of swing states including Pennsylvania, Ohio, Virginia and Florida were declared for him, Democrat Barack Obama of Illinois became the first black man elected president of the United States.

Obama sealed his victory by defeating Republican John McCain in a number of hard-fought battleground states.

As groups across the country erupted in jubilation at the news of Obama's victory, he told a huge crowd gathered in Chicago's Grant Park that his win proved the power of democracy. "They believed this time must be different, that their voices could be that difference."

After calling Obama to concede defeat, McCain spoke to his supporters in Arizona, telling them, "The American people have spoken, and spoken clearly." | STORY, A9

MORE INSIDE

Obama wins Shelby; GOP takes Tenn.

Still a red state: Despite Shelby County's high turnout and strong support, Obama can't turn Tennessee blue as McCain holds strong. | **A10**

Republicans hold on
Republicans hold Tenn. and Miss. seats as Democrats gain more Senate posts nationally. | **A6**

Cohen, Blackburn win
Democrat Steve Cohen and Republican Marsha Blackburn re-elected to U.S. House. | **A7**

Abundant sun
Warmth stays with us.
High 77. Low 58.

Forecast by News Channel 3
DETAILS, C4

ELECTION NEWS: AROUND THE REGION

Referendums in spotlight | B1
Ballot issues: Voters take a close look at 10 issues on the city and county ballots, including term limits, staggered terms and the sale of MLGW.

It's all about possibilities | B1
Wendi C. Thomas: While the election was a national litmus test on race, it was also about what America can be, and is already becoming.

Waiting for a new councilman | B1
Adding up the votes: Scanner malfunction slows counting to see which of four candidates will replace Scott McCormick on the Memphis City Council.

© Copyright 2008
The Commercial Appeal
A B C D

7 49377 10040 0

For a list of top stories from
commercialappeal.com
go to page A2

Interactive Weather

Weekdays with Jim Syoen on commercialappeal.com
Travel outlook • Weather headlines • 5-day local forecast • Local events

ALL METAL ROOFING SYSTEMS
The Tin Man
Sponsored by

Front page, The Commercial Appeal, *Wednesday, November 5, 2008*

Front page, The Oregonian, *Wednesday, November 5, 2008*

VISUALIZING COMPOSITION: STRUCTURE

Understanding the relationship between the parts and the whole is fundamental to intellectual analysis.

WHOLE

PART PART PART PART

STRUCTURE is a term that arises when we talk about writing, but it also comes up when we talk about many disciplines such as science, art, nature, the social sciences and literature. For example, in the social sciences, STRUCTURE points to something that is made up of parts, like a **hierarchical structure.**

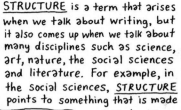

MEDIEVAL EUROPEAN FEUDAL STRUCTURE

KING
NOBLES
KNIGHTS
PEASANTS

Student

In biology, **STRUCTURE** refers to the arrangement or formation of the tissues, organs, or other parts of an organism —a cartoon professor, for example.

STRUCTURE OF CARTOON PROFESSOR:

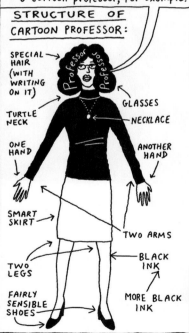

SPECIAL HAIR (WITH WRITING ON IT)

Professor Jossofor

GLASSES

TURTLE NECK

NECKLACE

ONE HAND

ANOTHER HAND

SMART SKIRT

TWO ARMS

BLACK INK

TWO LEGS

FAIRLY SENSIBLE SHOES

MORE BLACK INK

In writing in general, and literature in particular, **STRUCTURE** can be defined as the framework of a story, poem, play or essay.

In an essay, you can determine **STRUCTURE** by following the pattern of topics that the writer presents.

ESSAY:

MAIN TOPIC

SUB-TOPIC ONE

SUB-TOPIC TWO

SUB-SUB TOPIC ONE

SUB-SUB-SUB TOPIC ONE

SUB-SUB-SUB-SUB TOPIC ONE

THE VENDOR

MADE IN CHINA

THE DESIGNER

THE SIZE: MEDIUM

SAY THIS FIRST OR LAST???

WHY I BOUGHT IT

ON DAY BEFORE 9/11 NEAR WORLD TRADE CENTER

HOW I DIDN'T EVEN LIKE IT—AT FIRST

BOUGHT ON VACATION

WHY I ♡ IT

MY "I♡LOVE NY" T-SHIRT

ON 9/10/01

NEW YORK? I ♡ NY

student

Choose a photograph or painting reproduced in a recent magazine.

Examine the image carefully, paying special attention to the way in which the scene or circumstances are presented and framed.

Write an essay in which you use the photograph or painting to illustrate your working definition of structure.

PORTFOLIO–Savulich

PEOPLE WATCHING JUMPER ON HOTEL ROOF.

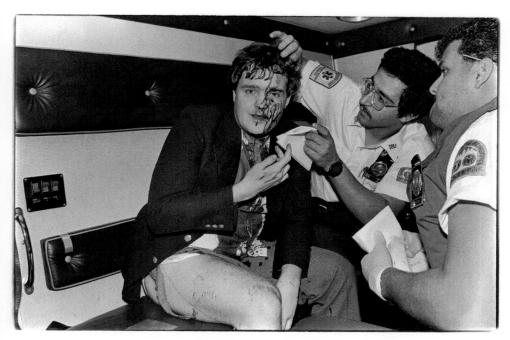

MAN COMPLAINING THAT HE WAS ATTACKED AFTER HE GAVE HIS MONEY TO ROBBERS.

TAXI DRIVER EXPLAINING HOW AN ARGUMENT WITH HIS PASSENGER CAUSED HIM TO DRIVE INTO THE RESTAURANT.

WOMAN laughing AFTER CAR WRECK.

Andrew Savulich

Before turning to freelance photography, Andrew Savulich worked as a landscape architect. After fifteen years of freelance work, he became a staff photographer for the *New York Daily News*. His work has been exhibited in the United States and abroad, and he has received numerous awards, including a grant from the National Endowment for the Arts.

Savulich is a master of spot news — spontaneous photographs of the violence and accidents, the humorous and odd events of everyday life, especially in urban areas. He explains his motivation: "We're at a point in our society where very weird things are happening in the streets, and I like taking pictures because I feel I'm recording something that's really *happening*." He thrives on the hunt: "There's a kind of adrenaline rush when you're doing this work. . . . It's all spontaneous: You have to figure things out, and you never really know what you have. That uncertainty is attractive, I think."

Savulich adds a handwritten caption below each photograph he takes, many of which are collected in *City of Chance* (2002). "I felt that the pictures needed something to describe what was happening. And I thought the easiest way would be just to write a little description on the prints themselves. And I liked the way it looked."

SEEING

1. What story does each of these photographs tell? What is especially striking and memorable about each one? What similarities or differences do you find in these four images?

2. Look carefully at each of the photographs for Andrew Savulich's artistic presence. Comment, for example, on the camera angle, the precise moment at which he chooses to take each photograph, as well as what he includes. What makes his style distinct from that of the other photographers whose work is presented in this chapter?

Responding Visually

Choose a photograph from this book, from your own collection, or from a magazine or newspaper. Write at least three different captions for it. Experiment with a range of styles — descriptive, sensational, or humorous, for example. How does each caption help shift the overall impact of the image? Or, to use John Berger's phrase (p. 705), how does the image "illustrate the sentence"?

WRITING

1. Much of the story in each of Savulich's photographs is conveyed by its caption. Think of alternate captions for each image. Would a different caption significantly change the way you read the photograph? Write a brief essay explaining why or why not.

2. Choose one of Savulich's photographs, and write a two-page journalistic account to accompany it in a newspaper. Include the sequence of events that led up to the moment depicted in the photograph, conveying the emotional aspects of the event as you do so. Base as much of your report as possible on details you see in the image, and then embellish your article with quotations, names, background information, or any other "facts" that would make your news story more compelling.

James Nachtwey
Crushed Car, 2001

GROUND ZERO
James Nachtwey

When the attack first started, I was in my own apartment near the South Street Seaport, directly across lower Manhattan. I heard a sound that was out of the ordinary. I was far enough away so that the sound wasn't alarming, but it was definitely out of the ordinary.

When I saw the towers burning, my first reaction was to take a camera, to load it with film, go up on my roof, where I had a clear view, and photograph the first tower burning. Then I wanted to go directly to the site. I went back down and loaded my gear and went over. It was a ten-minute walk.

When I got there, people were being evacuated from both towers. In the interim, the plane had hit the second tower. Medical treatment centers were being set up on the sidewalks. It wasn't as chaotic as you might think. On the street, the people coming out initially were not seriously wounded. They were frightened, some were hurt in a minor way. I think that the real chaos was happening up inside the towers with the people who were trapped.

When the first tower fell, people ran in panic. They ran from the falling debris, girders that were falling down in an avalanche in the thick smoke and dust. Documenting a crisis situation that's clearly out of control is always very instinctual. There's no road map. No ground rules. It's all improvisations. My instinct initially, in this case, was to photograph the human situation. But once the tower fell, the people really all disappeared. They either ran away or were trapped. So my instinct then was to go to where the tower had fallen. It seemed to me absolutely unbelievable that the World Trade Center could be lying in the street, and I felt compelled to make an image of this. I made my way there through the smoke. The area was virtually deserted. It seemed like a movie set from a science-fiction film. Very apocalyptic—sunlight filtering through the dust and the destroyed wreckage of the buildings lying in the street.

5   As I was photographing the destruction of the first tower, the second tower fell, and I was standing right under it, literally right under it. Fortunately for me, and unfortunately for people on the west side of the building, it listed to the west. But I was still underneath this avalanche of falling debris—structural steel and aluminum siding, glass, just tons of material falling directly down onto me. I realized that I had a few seconds to find cover or else I'd be killed. I dashed into the lobby of the Millenium Hilton

hotel, directly across the street from the North Tower, and I realized instantly that this hotel lobby was going to be taken out, that the debris would come flying through the plate glass and there would be no protection at all. There was no other place to turn, certainly no more time.

I saw an open elevator and dashed inside. I put my back against the wall, and about a second later the lobby was taken out. There was a construction worker who dashed inside there with me just as the debris swept through the lobby. It instantly became pitch black, just as if you were in a closet with the light out and a blindfold on. You could not see anything. It was very difficult to breathe. My nose, my mouth, my eyes were filled with ash. I had a hat on, so I put it over my face and began to breathe through it. And together, this other man and I crawled, groping, trying to find our way out. I initially thought that the building had fallen on us and that we were in a pocket, because it was so dark. We just continued to crawl, and I began to see small blinking lights, and I realized that these were the turn signals of cars that had been destroyed and the signals were still on. At that point I realized that we were in the street, although it was just as black in the street as it was in the hotel lobby, and that we would be able to find our way out.

My experiences photographing combat and being in life-threatening situations played a very important part in my being able to survive this and continue to work. It was, as I said, all instinct. I was making fast decisions with very little time to spare. And I guess that I made the right decisions, because I'm still here. I was lucky, too. I don't fold up in these situations. I've been in them enough times to somehow have developed the capacity to continue to do my job. On my way out of the smoke and ash, I was actually photographing searchers coming in. Once I got clear, I tried to clear my eyes as best I could and catch my breath. I realized I had to make my way toward what has now become known as Ground Zero. It took a while to make my way there. I spent the day there, photographing the firemen searching for people who had been trapped.

If I had been needed to help someone, I certainly would have done it, as I have many times in the past. I would have put down my camera to lend a hand, as I think anyone would have. The place was filled with firemen and rescue workers and police, and I was not needed to play that role. I realized that very clearly and therefore went about doing my job.

When I'm photographing I don't censor myself, or second-guess myself. I try to be aware of my own inner voice, my own instincts, as much as I can, and I try to follow them.

10   The level of dust and ash in the air was so intense that it was impossible to protect myself or my camera or my film. I've never had negatives

that were so scratched and filled with marks as these. It looks like there are railroad tracks across my negatives. Every time you opened your camera back, there was no time even to dust it off, because more ash would fall in.

I worked all day until night, at which point I felt that it was time to leave. I was exhausted; I felt rather sick from all the smoke and ash that I had inhaled—not only initially, but all day long. The scene was burning and filled with acrid smoke; my lungs had burned all day long. The next day I was quite sick, almost incapacitated. Feeling dizzy, exhausted. Quite out of it.

After the buildings fell, there wasn't really any more danger, as long as you watched your footing. It wasn't as if people were shooting at us or we were being shelled or there were land mines there.

The frontline troops in this particular battle were firemen, and they put themselves in jeopardy. A lot of them lost their lives. They were frontline troops [who] didn't kill anyone; they were there to save people. That made this story very different from the wars I've covered.

The rescue workers were generally too busy to pay us [photographers] much mind. And because we weren't in the way they didn't have to pay us much mind, unless they felt like it, for whatever personal reason they might have had. The police were another matter. They instinctively try to keep us away from anything. I think that it's just the nature of the relationship, unfortunately. But there was so much chaos at the beginning that it was easy to elude the police, and once you were with the rescue workers, they didn't seem to mind at all.

15   I didn't see the dead. They were underneath, and it wasn't clear how many were under there at that moment. I didn't witness people suffering, because they were invisible. I didn't feel it as strongly as when I witnessed people starving to death or when I've seen innocent people cut down by sniper fire. I haven't completely processed this event.

For me personally, the worst moment was when I was underneath the second tower as it fell and this tidal wave of deadly debris was about to fall on me. When I saw Ground Zero I was in a state of disbelief. It was disturbing to see this massive destruction in my own city, in my own country. I was in Grozny when it was being pulverized by Russian artillery and aircraft. I spent a couple of years in Beirut during various sieges and bombardments. But now it was literally in my own backyard, and I think one thing Americans are learning from this is that now we are a part of the world in a way we never have been before.

The first day that *Time.com* had my essay on their web site, at least 600,000 people had a look at it. To me, as a communicator, that's very gratifying. I hope publishers and editors are paying attention to this. There is power in the still image that doesn't exist in other forms. I think that there even is a necessity for it, because that many people wouldn't be looking at still pictures unless they needed to do that. I know that 600,000 people looking at a web site is small compared to a typical TV audience, but it is [nonetheless] a sizable number of people, and the fact that people are turning to the Internet instead of television is significant. This is sort of a test case of mass appeal.

To me it's quite obvious that a tremendous crime against humanity — a barbaric act — has been perpetrated on innocent civilians. There's nothing that can justify that act.

Many years ago, I felt that I had seen too much [violence], that I didn't want to see any more tragedies in this world. But unfortunately history continues to produce tragedies, and it is very important that they be documented with compassion and in a compelling way. I feel a responsibility to continue. But believe me when I say that I would much rather these things never happen [so that] I could either photograph something entirely different or not be a photographer at all. But that's not the way the world is.

James Nachtwey

"The primary function of my photographs," explained James Nachtwey recently, "is to be in mass-circulation publications – during the time that the events are happening. I want them to become part of people's daily dialogue and create public awareness, public opinion, that can help bring pressure for change. That's the first and most important use of my work. A secondary use is to become an archive entered into our collective memory, so that these events are never forgotten."

Born in Syracuse, New York, in 1948, Nachtwey has photographed violence and human suffering around the world – from Kosovo to Rwanda, from Afghanistan to Iraq. He has published several collections of photographs and received numerous awards, including a Heinz Foundation Achievement Award in 2006 for his body of work. *War Photographer*, a documentary on his life, was nominated for an Oscar in 2001.

Despite an impressive list of photojournalism accolades, Nachtwey would like his viewers to focus on the subjects of his images rather than the photographer behind them. "I don't want people to be concerned about me. I want them to be concerned about the people in the pictures. . . . I want the first impact, and by far the most powerful impact, to be about an emotional, intellectual, and moral reaction to what is happening to these people. I want my presence to be transparent." This eyewitness photograph and essay appeared in *American Photo* 13.1.

SEEING

1. James Nachtwey is a veteran photographer who has documented wars in several parts of the world. What similarities and differences does he establish between his wartime experiences and his photographing of the collapse of the World Trade Center? In paragraph 8 Nachtwey explains that "the place was filled with firemen and rescue workers and police, and I was not needed to play that role. I realized that very clearly and therefore went about doing my job." What do you think the role of a photographer should be during a time of war or in a crisis situation?

2. In paragraph 17 Nachtwey tells us that "there is power in the still image that doesn't exist in other forms. I think that there even is a necessity for it, because that many people wouldn't be looking at still pictures unless they needed to do that." Compare the power of Nachtwey's prose narrative of the events of September 11 to *Crushed Car*, one of the photographs he took that day (p. 284). This image is part of a photoessay (you can see that essay at *www.time.com/photoessays/shattered*). Which do you find more articulate – Nachtwey's prose or his visual essay? Why? To what extent is the power of each a reflection of its medium?

WRITING

1. In paragraph 17, Nachtwey announces that he found it "very gratifying" to know that there were 600,000 visits to his photoessay on the *Time* web site. "The fact that people are turning to the Internet instead of television is significant. This is sort of a test case of mass appeal." Write an argumentative essay in which you support – or challenge – the assertion that the events of September 11 caused a shift in the ways we receive information and the sources of that information.

Working with Sources

2. The code of ethics of the National Press Photographers Association notes that "many publications and stations have conduct codes or ethics codes requiring photojournalists to report truthfully, honestly and objectively. Their codes might include statements such as 'photojournalists should at all times maintain the highest standards of ethical conduct in serving the public interest' or 'a member shall present himself, his work, his services, and his premises in such a manner as will uphold and dignify his professional status and the reputation of the station.'" Using samples from Nachtwey's photojournalism, write an expository essay in which you apply these standards to combat photography.

Chris Jordan
Lakeview Sign among Debris, 2005

Chris Jordan
Remains of a Home, Ninth Ward, New Orleans, 2005

YEAR ONE
OF THE NEXT EARTH
Bill McKibben

*Look at these pictures. First question: is this a crime scene? It's clearly
a shame. But is it a crime too?*

Let's think for a moment about a hurricane. By the time it reaches shore
it has a name. We've been watching it circle for days, peering over the
shoulders of forecasters as they narrow the cone of possible landfalls,
predict the potential tidal surge, and calibrate the category to which this
whirlwind belongs. The storm seems malevolent, aberrant, sinister.

But of course, if you think about it, a hurricane is just heat made
manifest. The sun's rays beam down, and the portion of them absorbed
into the top layers of the sea's surface warm the water. When conditions
are right—when some ripple heads west off of Africa, when high-level
winds don't shear off the top of the storm, when the guiding air currents
are in place—that heat powers the rotating breeze that becomes a tropical depression and then a storm and then a hurricane and then an oh-my-
God destroyer of whole huge swaths of what we've taken for granted. But
at heart it's an expression of something purely normal; it's an equation.
And living, as we do, in its potential path is an equation too, a probabil-
ity. This is how the planet is supposed to work.

Or, how the planet *was* supposed to work. Until sometime in the last
twenty or thirty years. Sometime in the lifetime of most of the people reading these words. That's when we—meaning human beings generally and
Western human beings in particular—got big. Big enough to change the
equations. Change them profoundly.

5   By now most people know the story. When we burn coal and gas and
oil, that is, when we do almost any task in modern life, we release carbon
dioxide (CO_2) into the air. Lots of it. When you burn a gallon of gas,
which weighs about eight pounds, you send five-and-a-half pounds of carbon into the atmosphere. That carbon dioxide is not pollution the way
you're used to thinking of it; it's not brown or smelly or even particularly
dangerous in any direct way. But the molecular structure of that carbon
dioxide traps heat near the planet that would otherwise radiate back out
to space. It changes the equation. It makes your car and your air condi-
tioner and your always-on cable modem and your air travel (mine too)
part of the physical processes of the planet. A crucial part, it turns out.

When climate scientists really started worrying in the 1980s about the notion that humans were heating the planet, the consensus was that the process would be relatively slow—a problem for our children and grand-children more than for us. (Of course, you could argue that our children's problems are ours as well, but that's not an argument we've usually paid much attention to.) The climate scientists had underestimated how finely balanced the world was. So far, we've raised the temperature of the earth about one degree Fahrenheit, from fifty-nine degrees to sixty degrees. That's not much—you can't tell the difference between a fifty-nine degree after-noon and a sixty degree one. But it turns out that the globe can tell, and in a big way. This is what we now understand it to mean:

- Everything frozen on earth is melting, and fast. As the ice of the Green-land ice shelf thaws, some of the water sinks down to the base of the glaciers, lubricating their slide into the sea. That slide is happening much more quickly than was thought likely even a few years ago.
- In dry areas, the warmer sun evaporates water more quickly than before; warm air holds more water vapor than cold air. When the air eventually releases all that water, the downpours are harder and longer than we're used to. The number of gullywashers—storms that drop, say, more than two inches of rain in a twenty-four-hour period—has spiked dramatically across temperate latitudes.
- These shifts, in turn, start changing huge ecosystems. Across a vast area of Alaska, Canada, and the Pacific Northwest, trees are dying in record numbers as a parasitic insect takes advantage of warmer weather to spread its range dramatically. In warm areas, malarial mosquitoes break into new zones that once were too cold for their survival. On and on.

And hurricanes. Here's the trend on hurricanes. In August of 2005, a few weeks before Katrina hit, an MIT scientist named Kerry Emanuel pub-lished a fascinating paper analyzing the last half-century of the big storms. He'd managed to get all the available data—the windspeeds and wave heights measured by thousands of buoys and satellites—and feed it into a powerful computer. And what he found was wildly more dramatic than he'd expected. It turned out our small change in the variables of this particular equation seemed to be having an outsized effect. The average hurricane in our time was fifty percent stronger at its peak, and it lasted sixty percent longer than the hurricanes of our parents' and grandparents' time. The old extreme was the new norm.

Earth science is usually messy and vague; it's not often that a re-searcher gets to watch as the planet peer reviews his paper. But that's what happened as the fall of 2005 stretched on. Katrina, yes. And then Rita. And then Wilma, registering the lowest barometric pressure ever recorded in this hemisphere. And then we ran through the names set aside for 2005 and had to start dipping into the Greek alphabet: Alpha, Beta. Tropical Storm Zeta was spinning in the Atlantic on December 31, so it had the honor of marking the season's official end. And it was still spinning there on January 6, marking the start of 2006's onslaught. We had twenty-seven named storms in our basin in 2005, which broke the old record of twenty-one, a record that had stood for seventy-two years.

The equation had changed decisively. Hurricanes were now longer and stronger, all around the world. (In spring of 2006 a Katrina-sized storm named Larry slammed into Australia.) And they were going places hurricanes weren't supposed to go, further south down the coast of the Americas than ever before. As the 2006 season approached, forecasters started warning about the peril to the Northeast coast. The world was a different place, fundamentally physically different.

10   And the chaos we've unleashed so far is the merest beginning. The computer models, more robust with each passing iteration, can now give us a reasonably good weather forecast for the century to come. They express the possibilities as a range of predictions. At the top end of the range, if (as unfortunately has happened so far) all the feedback from natural systems is amplifying the warming instead of slowing it down, the earth might be ten degrees Fahrenheit warmer by the end of the century. Or maybe eleven or twelve, depending on which model you're looking at. That's a science fiction world; no one has written a convincing account of what it might be like or how we might inhabit it. Chances are, most of us couldn't.

So let's hope for something else. Let's hope for the best-estimate outcome, the consensus middle-of-the-road prediction from most of the computer modelers about what the future holds. They say: a four or five degrees Fahrenheit increase in warming by the year 2100. Enough to take the planet to sixty-five degrees. Enough to make it warmer than it's been for millions of years, warmer than it was before primate evolution got underway. Nasty warm.

Look at these pictures. Let's talk for a moment about the question of blame. If there's a crime, is there a criminal?

When the Industrial Revolution began, the atmospheric concentration of carbon dioxide was 275 parts per million. When the first scientist decided we ought to begin measuring its accumulation in our atmosphere in the late 1950s, that number had grown to 315 parts per million. Three decades later, when a young NASA scientist named Jim Hansen told the United States Congress that global warming was underway, that number was up to 350 parts per million. By 1995, when the world's climatologists, assembled by the United Nations in the Intergovernmental Panel on Climate Change (ITCC), essentially confirmed Hansen's declaration, the number was 360 parts per million. By the time Katrina struck, it was nearing 380 parts per million. Unless we do something very dramatic, the best guess is that it will be 550 parts per million—double its pre–Industrial Revolution concentrations—by mid-twenty-first century. These, by the way, are very high numbers. There's already more carbon in the atmosphere than there's been for twenty million years.

But we're talking blame here. We're clearly not morally culpable before 1988, when Hansen sounded his warning. Back then we didn't know that CO_2 was trouble. Scientists had always defined a clean-burning engine as one that gave off water vapor and carbon dioxide; no one ever told us that the carbon dioxide was dangerous. (Well, there were a few scientists, such as the Swedish chemist Svante Arrhenius, who did tell us at the end of the nineteenth century, but no one listened.) If you don't know you're doing something wrong, you're not to blame. Ignorance of the law is no excuse, but ignorance that a physical law even exists seems an airtight alibi.

15   You could argue that from 1988 to 1995 we were not entirely to blame either. Plenty of scientists were making plenty of noise doubting global warming. We probably should have taken some simple precautionary steps, say, raised gas mileage requirements for our cars—as soon as we had an inkling. But that may be too much to expect; it's human to resist change until you're sure you have to shift.

After 1995, though, it's pretty much on us. The remaining skeptical scientists bore an alarming resemblance to those Tobacco Council lobbyists still claiming that you couldn't prove that smoking killed you. Anyone with a reasonably healthy sense of how the world worked could have noted that most of their funding came from Exxon or the coal industry. Certainly the rest of the developing world was sufficiently convinced to start taking some action. They developed the Kyoto Protocol in an attempt to regulate carbon emissions from the industrialized world, set about the almost impossible process of ratifying it without our participation, and managed to pull it off. Sweden, Britain, Spain, Japan—industrial lands like these have created master plans to cut half the carbon from their economies over the next few decades. They've put up windmills on every ridgetop. Japan and Germany now utilize the most solar panels on earth. Is it because they're the sunniest places? Not exactly.

It's because they deal in reason, long-term thinking, and some kind of commitment to the common good.

Whereas we have—what is a polite way of saying it?—not engaged. The Clinton-Gore Administration knew all about global warming, but they spent their political capital elsewhere (NAFTA, GATT) and watched as America launched its love affair with the "sport utility" vehicle. Clinton was the most sensitive machine ever designed for gauging public opinion, and he figured it would be too tough to take on the issue. Bottom line: by the time he left office, America was emitting fifteen percent more carbon dioxide than when he entered.

And his successors, of course, are worse. Tools of the fossil fuel industry, they have put forth a national energy plan that foresees an endless future of drilling and refining and burning—Japan and Germany in reverse. They've redacted[1] every official document on climate change to make it seem less urgent, and they've done their best to sabotage ongoing international negotiations. They've even tried to gag scientists like Hansen.

So yes, there's some blame.

20   And then came Katrina, which put a face on global warming. Look at the pictures [. . .]. This is what global warming looks like: wrecked houses, wrecked lives, wrecked communities. Now, deep down, just about everybody knows. The polling shows it: eighty-five percent of Americans say climate change is real. And it's part of the zeitgeist[2] now—people just understand on a different level, we've finally begun to figure out what's at stake. We've begun to understand that this is a civilization-scale challenge, like the threat of all-out thermonuclear war. We've done pretty well on that one so far. This one, not so good.

But now we really know, so maybe that will change. We know what a million domestic refugees looks like. A few weeks later, when Rita headed our way, we saw what it looked like when a major city tried to evacuate. (Darkly funny is what it looked like, with hundreds of Expeditions and Navigators and Explorers running out of gas in hundred-mile traffic jams and coasting uselessly to the shoulder.) Now, when computer modelers like the ones at Oxford University say that by mid-century we can expect 150 million environmental refugees at any one time globally (people fleeing storms, rising waters, forest fires, droughts), we should be able to at least begin picturing it. Now, with imaginations engaged, is when it is really, finally, inescapably our responsibility to do something. The next 150 parts per million are on us. The next two or three degrees.

---

1. redacted: Edited or revised; made ready for publication. [Eds.]

2. zeitgeist: The intellectual, cultural, moral, ethical, and political climate of an era. [Eds.]

Look at these pictures.

Imagine, as President Bush insisted in his 2006 State of the Union Address, that we're addicted to oil. Imagine that this addiction has something to do with what happened in New Orleans, and even more to do with what will happen—entirely predictable—in the decades to come in Dhaka and the Maldives and Fort Lauderdale and the Yucatán and Jamaica and Ocracoke and Long Island and the Pearl River Delta and . . .

What are you supposed to do when you admit your addiction? Make amends as best as you can for the damage you've done under the influence. That is, help out. And people are helping out. The Red Cross collected lots of cash. Thousands of college kids are passing up Daytona Beach and descending on New Orleans during spring break to help pull down ceilings and clean up mold. But this qualifies as, at best, a small start, as do the FEMA trailers and all the rest.

25   Katrina exposed not only the new physics of global warming, but also the new chemistry of politics in our country. For a quarter century, beginning with Ronald Reagan, we've been relentlessly privatizing and cutting taxes and using government as a tool to enable the richest in our society to grow richer; and it turned out that, what do you know, we weren't prepared to deal with a crisis. And we won't be, until we decide once again that we owe each other something as citizens, as neighbors.

What exactly do we owe? That's the tough part. It's easy to say, as one politician after another said brightly in the wake of Hurricane Katrina, that we will rebuild the Gulf Coast and its communities. And as Susan Zakin shows with her incisive reportage, that is possible. But it's also possible, in this new world we've inadvertently created, that there are plenty of places now so squarely in harm's way that we will be unable to keep ahead of the damage. A way of saying this is: we'll probably rebuild something in New Orleans once. But twice?

No, what needs rebuilding is the infrastructure of the nation. Not because it's broken but because it's doing damage every day. That coal-fired power plant? It's pushing the sea level steadily higher. That Ford factory? It's churning out extravagant new vehicles that guarantee a few more parts per million of carbon dioxide. That big new subdivision, the one with the 4,500-sq. ft. houses with the absurd little turrets? It's contributing to the next hurricane. So a real commitment to the people of the Gulf—and to the rest of us—means windmills, even if you don't want to look at them out the windows of your beach house on Cape Cod or your ski house in Vermont. It means a law requiring fifty miles per gallon of gasoline for all cars (and yes, that includes SUVs). It means a building code that meets hurricane survival standards in Florida, but also hurricane *prevention* standards in Atlanta: smaller square footage, lots of insulation, energy-sipping appliances. It means treating fossil fuel as something dangerous that we need to use with care, because if we keep mishandling it, the result is—well, look at the pictures.

And what needs rebuilding even more is the psyche of our nation. First and foremost, we need to reconsider the hyperindividualism that is our culture's greatest legacy. We need to look at those habits that have gotten us to our current place and start changing them. If we can't imagine ever taking the bus or the train, then we can't imagine a world without Katrinas. If we can't imagine spending the money to make our cities pleasant enough to stop spinning off suburbs and prevent sprawl, then it's useless to try and defend New Orleans.

Does this sound like some grim sentence? Not necessarily. Think about something as simple as food. On average, every bite of it travels fifteen hundred miles before it reaches our lips. Our food is essentially marinated in oil—crude oil. It takes ten calories of fossil energy to raise and ship every calorie we eat. What better tribute to New Orleans, capital of fine eating, than to rebuild local food networks that can cut energy use by half or more. And give us food that tastes like food again. And that forces us once more to really know our neighbors and to depend on them, to build the kind of strong community that we've let dissolve.

30   There's a word for this kind of post-addiction world: "Europe." Swedes and Brits and the Dutch use half the energy that Americans do. They're half as addicted as we are, and working much harder to cut that addiction. And yet they're not living in caves; their world is dignified and elegant. In fact, apart from its love of revelry, one of the things we liked most about the pre-Katrina New Orleans was, in certain respects, how European it was, as European as any city in North America.

In the early days of talking about global warming, enlightened policymakers would sometimes propose what they called a "no-regrets strategy." That is, they would endorse a suite of ideas that would make sense even if global warming turned out not to be the problem our scientists have been predicting. Higher mileage cars, for instance, is one such strategy, and it would save drivers money.

As it happens, we didn't do any of that. Now we have regrets. And we'll have many more regrets. We aren't going to stop global warming, though we may still be able to keep the problem from getting entirely out of hand.

But the no-regrets strategy of this moment is different. It involves building the kinds of communities that not only don't contribute as much to global warming, but that also can survive more easily in a fraught world. It's entirely possible that scenes like the ones in this book may become the new normal, or at least one aspect of it. And if they do, then we need economies that make a different and more basic kind of sense, ones that can reliably supply us with food, shelter, and comfort.

That would be a new, different world from the one we know now. But the point is, we live in a new world already. Look at the pictures. This is year one of the next earth. This is where we start.

Chris Jordan
Remains of a Home with Canal and Levee in Background, Chalmette, 2005

Chris Jordan
Refrigerator in a Tree near Port Sulphur, 2005

Bill McKibben

Via his best-selling 1989 book *The End of Nature*, environmentalist and author Bill McKibben was one of the first people to bring an understanding of the threat of global warming to the general public. Born in 1960 and raised in Massachusetts, McKibben attended Harvard University, where he was president of the university's *Harvard Crimson* newspaper. Following graduation he worked as a staff writer for *The New Yorker*. Since publication of *The End of Nature*, McKibben has worked tirelessly as a freelance writer, focusing primarily on nature and the environment – often, as a devout Methodist, from a spiritual point of view. In addition to publishing magazine and newspaper articles, writing over ten books (including a collection of essays, *The Bill McKibben Reader*, published in 2008), and winning many awards and fellowships, McKibben has become a key figure in the movement to fight global warming. In 2006 he organized a five-day walk across Vermont to demand action on global warming, the largest demonstration of its kind up to that point; since then he has formed Step It Up and *350.org* to organize nationwide rallies and to apply pressure on the government to act on global warming.

"Year One of the Next Earth," an essay McKibben contributed to Chris Jordan's photographic collection, *In Katrina's Wake: Portraits of Loss from an Unnatural Disaster* (2006), is less an attempt to capture the devastation of Hurricane Katrina in words than an opportunity to educate the general public about the history of global warming and get people to rethink their views about how we as humans live on this planet. As McKibben said in an interview with *Common Ground* magazine, "The organizing principle for the last one hundred years was: what will make the economy grow larger? And anything that met that test, we did. For the next one hundred years, the organizing principle has got to be: what makes the planet more durable? That has got to be the new lens through which we look at the world."

Chris Jordan

After practicing law for over ten years, Chris Jordan (b. 1963) decided in the early 2000s to concentrate fulltime on his art, and his artistic career has grown remarkably quickly since then. All three of his major series, Running the Numbers (2003), In Katrina's Wake (2005), and Intolerable Beauty (2006), have received international attention and acclaim.

Jordan's most recognized series to date, In Katrina's Wake (from which the four photographs included here are taken), is the result of his visit to New Orleans in November and December 2005, just a few months after Hurricane Katrina devastated the city. Although the subject of the photographs is the aftermath of a seemingly unpreventable natural disaster, Jordan subtitles the series (and the book in which it was published) *Portraits of Loss from an Unnatural Disaster*. According to Jordan, mass consumerism had as much to do with the catastrophe as the hurricane itself: Not only has Katrina's intensity been linked to human-generated global warming, but a focus on consumerism at the expense of everything else, including preserving the protective barriers to the city, both manmade (the levees) and natural (the surrounding wetlands), led directly to its flooding. Says Jordan about the series, whose proceeds have all gone directly to Katrina relief: "My hope is that these images might encourage some reflection on the part that we each play, and the loss that we all suffer, when a preventable catastrophe of this magnitude happens to the people of our own country. Katrina has illuminated our interconnectedness, and it makes our personal accountability as members of a conscious society ever more difficult to deny."

SEEING

1. Why does Bill McKibben claim that "we're clearly not morally <u>culpable</u> before 1988" (para. 14)? culpable for what? If 1988 marked a clear moral line, why did global warming continue to escalate? If you were born after this year, do you feel responsible, at least in part, for global warming? Why or why not? McKibben compares those who deny any responsibility for what happened in New Orleans to the tobacco executives who denied that cigarettes were harmful or addictive. In what ways is this comparison unfair? What does the metaphor of oil addiction add to your understanding of global warming? What does the metaphor overlook?

2. After Hurricane Katrina, entire square miles of New Orleans were found churned into rubble. In what ways do Chris Jordan's images memorialize the devastation? Which of the pictures best shows the hurricane's effect? Why? What aspects of the devastation do these photographs accentuate? What is missing from them? As McKibben suggests, think of yourself as a police photographer at a crime scene. For whom are you taking pictures? What are your responsibilities? With these thoughts in mind, evaluate the pictures as though you were a professional photographer — by considering factors such as field and focus, light, angle, frame, purpose, subject matter, and the like. What aspects of Jordan's photographs do you think were especially well captured? What aspects of the photographs were less successful? Explain why. To what extent do these photographs help you determine whether a crime was committed?

<u>culpable: Meriting condemnation or blame, especially for having done something wrong or harmful.</u>

WRITING

1. Imagine a trial focused on global warming. It is convened to answer two of McKibben's questions: "Is it a crime?" and "Is there a criminal?" Take the role of either the defense attorney (no crime and no criminal) or the prosecutor (crime and criminal), and draft an opening speech to the jury that lays out your case. Courtroom drama and emotional appeals are encouraged, but your opening presentation to the jury should feature all of the evidence that is available to you. Scrutinize

Jordan's images for factual support and visceral persuasion. Pay attention to both what is there and what is not. Look carefully at the images for points of focus for your jury. For example, how might you turn the image of the refrigerator in the tree to your argumentative advantage? What story do the bathroom fixtures tell in relation to the surrounding chaos depicted on page 299?

Working with Sources

2. Use McKibben's information to calculate the amount of carbon dioxide that has been released in the atmosphere by you, or because of you. If you own a car or ride the bus, estimate the gallons of gas used to transport yourself through the course of a day, and then multiply by 5½ (see para. 5). Consider the total number of calories that you have consumed since you were a baby, including infant formula, baby food, hot dogs, soda, and the like, and multiply by 10 (see para. 29); then find out how many calories a gallon of gas generates. Think of the carbon dioxide involved in producing all the clothes you've worn and the books you've read as well as every breath you've exhaled. To help you refine your lifetime atmospheric responsibility, the Internet offers several sites where you can closely calculate your contribution to global warming. Visit a few to get a sense of your personal contribution: See, for example, *www.istl.org/01-fall/internet.html*. Then write the first draft of an expository essay comparing and contrasting your numbers to your friends' and families'. Determine how and to what extent they differ.

LOOKING CLOSER – Shaping Memory

Joe Rosenthal said of his famous photograph, *Marines Raising the Flag on Mount Suribachi, Iwo Jima*, "It has been, it is said, the most widely reproduced photograph of all time." Throughout the years, the World War II image has graced the cover of stamps and postcards and has inspired paintings and sculptures. In the week after September 11, 2001, Thomas E. Franklin snapped a shot of three firemen raising a flag in the wreckage of the World Trade Center. Franklin's image struck a chord with many Americans because it is reminiscent of the original Rosenthal image that came to represent American victory in World War II. In his essay, Rosenthal describes his experience capturing the image that has become so widely reproduced and referenced. In an excerpt from her now-classic essay "On Photography," Susan Sontag offers a theoretical framework for unpacking our personal and collective relationship to the ubiquitous art form.

ON PHOTOGRAPHY
Susan Sontag

Recently, photography has become almost as widely practiced an amusement as sex and dancing—which means that, like every mass art form, photography is not practiced by most people as an art. It is mainly a social rite, a defense against anxiety, and a tool of power.

Memorializing the achievements of individuals considered as members of families (as well as of other groups) is the earliest popular use of photography. For at least a century, the wedding photograph has been as much a part of the ceremony as the prescribed verbal formulas. Cameras go with family life. According to a sociological study done in France, most households have a camera, but a household with children is twice as likely to have at least one camera as a household in which there are no children. Not to take pictures of one's children, particularly when they are small, is a sign of parental indifference, just as not turning up for one's graduation picture is a gesture of adolescent rebellion.

Through photographs, each family constructs a portrait-chronicle of itself—a portable kit of images that bears witness to its connectedness. It hardly matters what activities are photographed so long as photographs get taken and are cherished. Photography becomes a rite of family life just when, in the industrializing countries of Europe and America, the very institution of the family starts undergoing radical surgery. As that claustrophobic unit, the nuclear family, was being carved out of a much larger family aggregate, photography came along to memorialize, to restate symbolically, the imperiled continuity and vanishing extendedness of family life. Those ghostly traces, photographs, supply the token presence of the dispersed relatives. A family's photograph album is generally about the extended family—and, often, is all that remains of it.

As photographs give people an imaginary possession of a past that is unreal, they also help people to take possession of space in which they are insecure. Thus, photography develops in tandem with one of the most characteristic of modern activities: tourism. For the first time in history, large numbers of people regularly travel out of their habitual environments for short periods of time. It seems positively unnatural to travel for pleasure without taking a camera along. Photographs will offer indisputable evidence that the trip was made, that the program was carried out, that fun was had. Photographs document sequences of consumption carried on outside the view of family, friends, neighbors. But dependence on the camera, as the device that makes real what one is experiencing, doesn't fade when people travel more. Taking photographs fills the same need for the cosmopolitans accumulating photograph-trophies of their boat trip up the Albert Nile or their fourteen days in China as it does for lower-middle-class vacationers taking snapshots of the Eiffel Tower or Niagara Falls.

5   A way of certifying experience, taking photographs is also a way of refusing it—by limiting experience to a search for the photogenic, by converting experience into an image, a souvenir. Travel becomes a strategy for accumulating photographs. The very activity of taking pictures is soothing, and assuages general feelings of disorientation that are likely to be exacerbated by travel. Most tourists feel compelled to put the camera between themselves and whatever is remarkable that they encounter. Unsure of other responses, they take a picture. This gives shape to experience: Stop, take a photograph, and move on. The method especially appeals to people handicapped by a ruthless work ethic—Germans, Japanese, and Americans. Using a camera appeases the anxiety which the work-driven feel about not working when they are on vacation and supposed to be having fun. They have something to do that is like a friendly imitation of work: They can take pictures.

People robbed of their past seem to make the most fervent picture-takers, at home and abroad. Everyone who lives in an industrialized society is obliged gradually to give up the past, but in certain countries, such as the United States and Japan, the break with the past has been particularly traumatic. In the early 1970s, the fable of the brash American tourist of the 1950s and 1960s, rich with dollars and Babbittry,[1] was replaced by the mystery of the group-minded Japanese tourist, newly released from his island prison by the miracle of overvalued yen, who is generally armed with two cameras, one on each hip.

Photography has become one of the principal devices for experiencing something, for giving an appearance of participation. One full-page ad shows a small group of people standing pressed together, peering out of the photograph, all but one looking stunned, excited, upset. The one who wears a different expression holds a camera to his eye; he seems self-possessed, is almost smiling. While the others are passive, clearly alarmed spectators, having a camera has transformed one person into something active, a voyeur: Only he has mastered the situation. What do these people see? We don't know. And it doesn't matter. It is an Event: something worth seeing—and therefore worth photographing. The ad copy, white letters across the dark lower third of the photograph

---

1. *Babbittry* is a crassness, a grasping for things material. The term came into use following publication of Sinclair Lewis's novel *Babbitt* (1922). [Eds.]

like news coming over a teletype machine, consists of just six words: ".．．Prague．．．Woodstock．．．Vietnam．．．Sapporo．．．Londonderry．．． LEICA." Crushed hopes, youth antics, colonial wars, and winter sports are alike—are equalized by the camera. Taking photographs has set up a chronic voyeuristic relation to the world which levels the meaning of all events.

A photograph is not just the result of an encounter between an event and a photographer; picture-taking is an event in itself, and one with ever more peremptory rights—to interfere with, to invade, or to ignore whatever is going on. Our very sense of situation is now articulated by the camera's interventions. The omnipresence of cameras persuasively suggests that time consists of interesting events, events worth photo-graphing. This, in turn, makes it easy to feel that any event, once under way, and whatever its moral character, should be allowed to complete itself—so that something else can be brought into the world, the pho-tograph. After the event has ended, the picture will still exist, conferring on the event a kind of immortality (and importance) it would never otherwise have enjoyed. While real people are out there killing them-selves or other real people, the photographer stays behind his or her camera, creating a tiny element of another world: the image-world that bids to outlast us all.

Photographing is essentially an act of nonintervention. Part of the horror of such memorable coups of contemporary photojournalism as the pictures of a Vietnamese bonze[2] reaching for the gasoline can, of a Bengali guerrilla in the act of bayoneting a trussed-up collaborator, comes from the awareness of how plausible it has become, in situations where the photographer has the choice between a photograph and a life, to choose the photograph. The person who intervenes cannot record; the person who is recording cannot intervene. Dziga Vertov's great film, *Man with a Movie Camera* (1929), gives the ideal image of the photographer as someone in perpetual movement, someone moving through a pano-rama of disparate events with such agility and speed that any interven-tion is out of the question. Hitchcock's *Rear Window* (1954) gives the complementary image: The photographer played by James Stewart has an intensified relation to one event, through his camera, precisely because he has a broken leg and is confined to a wheelchair; being temporarily immobilized prevents him from acting on what he sees, and makes it even more important to take pictures. Even if incompatible with intervention in a physical sense, using a camera is still a form of participation. Although the camera is an observation station, the act of photographing is more

---

2. A *bonze* is a Buddhist monk. [Eds.]

than passive observing. Like sexual voyeurism, it is a way of at least tacitly, often explicitly, encouraging whatever is going on to keep on happening. To take a picture is to have an interest in things as they are, in the status quo remaining unchanged (at least for as long as it takes to get a "good" picture), to be in complicity with whatever makes a subject interesting, worth photographing—including, when that is the interest, another person's pain or misfortune.

Joe Rosenthal
Marines Raising the Flag on Mount Suribachi, Iwo Jima, 1945

FLAG RAISING ON IWO JIMA, FEBRUARY 23, 1945
Joe Rosenthal

On the fourth day of the battle I had gone out to the command ship to send a package of film back to Guam to be processed at headquarters. The next morning, I was informed that General Holland Smith and the secretary of the navy were on a smaller ship and were going in one mile offshore with binoculars to scan the battlefield. So I transferred to this boat. I took a photo of General Smith and Secretary of the Navy Forrestal at the railing with Mount Suribachi in the background. This was still in the morning, so I transferred to another boat so I could get closer to shore and then on to another that could take me in. I heard from a radioman that there was a patrol going up the mountain to plant our flag. I was surprised, you know, that by the morning of the fifth day they could do this. I said, "I gotta get a picture of that." About halfway up we ran into four marines, including Staff Sergeant Louis Lowery, who was a photographer for the marines' magazine, *Leatherneck*. Lowery and the others said that the patrol had raised a flag at the summit and that he had photographed the flag raising, but I made up my mind that I wanted to get a shot of the flag anyway. There continued isolated fire, but mortar was not reaching us. At the northern end of the island a mile and a half away there was still heavy fighting. When I came to an area where I could see over a rise, I could see our flag fluttering. I clutched my throat. It was our flag. As I got closer I observed there were three marines kneeling beside a long pole, and one of them had a flag folded in the triangled, traditional manner. "What's doing, fellas?" "We're going to raise this larger flag so it can be seen by the troops all over the island," and they added they were going to keep the first one as a souvenir. I moved around to where I could await what these fellas had told me they were going to do. I selected a position, and then I had to estimate how far back to get in order to get the full length of this pole swinging up. Because there were some chewed-up bushes in the foreground that might cut off the bottom half of these marines that were going to raise the flag, I grabbed a couple of rocks and a couple of old sandbags left from a Japanese outpost that had been blasted there, to stand on. This got me up a foot or two. Just about the time that I stood on top, Bill Genaust, a marine movie cameraman, came across and went to my right at arm's length and asked, "I'm not in your way, am I, Joe?" And I turned and said, "No, Bill, that's fine — oh, there it goes, Bill!" Bill had just time to swing his camera around to capture that wonderful, beautiful, extraordinary movie that shows the flag raising from the ground up. You notice it doesn't start with any preliminary footage. We had no signal beforehand. [Genaust was killed in action nine days after the flag raising.] The pole was a heavy iron or lead pipe probably twenty feet long. It came from either a heating system or water system for the Japanese outpost that was up there. It was originally the three marines I had met, but a couple of others saw what they were doing and could observe that it required more heft to lift it. One man kneeled down to hold it in position. When they got it into a little indentation in the ground—not very deep—three of the men held it there while one got a rope and tied it down three ways. Then they shoved a lot of rocks to keep it in position. Later, down below, I was told that it had raised a great cheer. I was more or less reporting an incident in the turn of the battle. Up until this point the news going back home from Iwo Jima was very sad. On Iwo Jima it was touch and go. Some of the advances were measured in a couple of feet. So this was a great boost to the people back home.

U.S. Postal Service
Three-cent Stamp, 1945

Mark Zingarelli
Memorial Day, 1994

Thomas E. Franklin
Flag Raising, World Trade Center, 2001

David J. Phillip
Superbowl XXXVI, 2002

Susan Sontag

Born in New York City, Susan Sontag (1933–2004) was one of America's foremost intellectuals, social commentators, and provocateurs. Her essays brilliantly explained the country and its culture, especially the avant-garde. In "Notes on Camp" (1964) she accurately described the absurdity of attributes of taste; in "Against Interpretation" (1966) she limned Anglo-American fiction; in "Illness as Metaphor" (1978), which grew out of her own battle with breast cancer, she cast a fresh eye on disease, a subject that she revisited in "AIDS and Its Metaphors" (1988). Her novel *The Volcano Lover* (1992) was a best seller: "No book I ever wrote came near to selling as many copies or as reaching as many readers," she said.

The essay offered here is an excerpt from "On Photography" (2001), winner of the National Book Critics Circle Award for Criticism at the time of its initial publication in 1977. Sontag's final book, *Regarding the Pain of Others* (2003), is about the photography of war. An excerpt from this book appears on page 650.

Joe Rosenthal

Born in Washington state, Joe Rosenthal (1911–2006) became a staff photographer with the *San Francisco Examiner* soon after graduating from college. His poor eyesight made him ineligible to be a U.S. military photographer at the outbreak of World War II, but he was later sent to cover the Pacific War by the Associated Press.

On February 23, 1945, he took what would become the most celebrated photograph of his career. The shot of the flag raising at Iwo Jima has been characterized as one of the most famous images of war in the twentieth century, and it was recently the subject of Clint Eastwood's film *Flags of Our Fathers.* The photograph won Rosenthal the Pulitzer Prize, inspired the U.S. Marine Corps Memorial in Washington, D.C., appeared on a commemorative postage stamp, and has been reproduced in countless personal and public monuments and works of art.

After the war, Rosenthal became chief photographer and manager of Times Wide World Photos and a photographer for the *San Francisco Chronicle* until he retired in 1981. He frequently downplayed his role as a photographer: "I can best sum up what I feel by saying that of all the elements that went into the making of this picture, the part I played was the least important. To get that flag up there, America's fighting men had to die on that island and on other islands and off the shores and in the air. What difference does it make who took the picture? I took it, but the marines took Iwo Jima."

United States Postal Service

Issued by the U.S. Postal Service in July 1945, the three-cent Iwo Jima commemorative postage stamp almost never saw the light of day. Initially the Postal Service rejected the idea for the design depicting Joe Rosenthal's famous photograph, arguing that no living person should

appear on a stamp. The public demand was so strong, however, that the U.S. Congress intervened to facilitate the commemorative stamp's production. More than 137 million of the widely popular stamps were purchased.

Mark Zingarelli

A cartoon parody of the iconic *Marines Raising the Flag* photograph, Mark Zingarelli's *Memorial Day* appeared on the cover of *The New Yorker* on June 6, 1994. The artist was born in 1952 and grew up in a suburban neighborhood outside of Pittsburgh, Pennsylvania. A professional illustrator since 1975, Zingarelli has seen his work appear in *Newsweek*, *Entertainment Weekly*, *Esquire*, the *New York Daily News*, and numerous other publications. His portfolio is available on his web site at *www.houseofzing.com.*

Thomas E. Franklin

A New Jersey–based photographer for the *Bergen Record*, Thomas E. Franklin (b. 1966) took his most famous photograph shortly after the attacks of 9/11. Standing by the West Side Highway in New York City, Franklin caught this image of firefighters raising the American flag over the rubble of the fallen World Trade Center. Franklin was a Pulitzer Prize finalist in 2002 for his images. Currently he produces a weekly column for the *Bergen Record* called "Picture This," which explores life in New Jersey.

David J. Phillip

The halftime show during Superbowl XXXVI in 2002 featured a tribute to the victims of the 9/11 attacks. The photograph by David J. Phillip catches a moment wherein the pose of Joe Rosenthal's photograph is re-created in the stadium. The ceremony also included a performance by U2 and the unveiling of a large banner bearing the names of 9/11 victims. Phillip is a sports photographer whose work appears in a number of print and Internet publications, including *ESPN.com*, the *Washington Post*, and the *Boston Globe*.

SEEING

1. Susan Sontag observes that "photography is not practiced by most people as an art. It is mainly a social rite, a defense against anxiety, and a tool of power" (para. 1). Given your own experience taking pictures, would you agree or disagree with her assertion? Now examine each of the images in this section. To what extent do you think each visual artist represented here would agree or disagree with Sontag? In what ways are the photographs like the ones by Joe Rosenthal and Thomas E. Franklin a "defense against anxiety"? If so, anxiety about what? In what ways might the U.S. Postal Service's three-cent stamp, David J. Phillip's *Superbowl XXXVI*, and Mark Zingarelli's cover from *The New Yorker* be viewed as a "tool of power"?

2. Sontag declares that "a photograph is not just the result of an encounter between an event and a photographer; picture-taking is an event in itself, and one with ever more peremptory rights – to interfere with, to invade, or to ignore whatever is going on. Our very sense of situation is now articulated by the camera's interventions" (para. 8). Sontag seems to be saying that the camera or the act of taking pictures is more important than either the photographer or the event. Do you agree? Use any of the selections in this section to support your argument.

WRITING

1. Sontag writes, "For at least a century, the wedding photograph has been as much a part of the ceremony as the prescribed verbal formulas" (para. 2). Write an expository essay in which you compare and contrast the differences between (1) the function – and the visibility – of photography in your parents' wedding, and (2) its presence and role in a wedding you attended in the past year or two. Draw inferences about the extent to which the role of photography in the more recent wedding has become analogous to what Sontag calls "prescribed verbal formulas."

2. Sontag observes that "a family's photograph album is generally about the extended family – and, often, is all that remains of it" (para. 3). How important are photographs to your sense of family? Write an expository essay in which you describe your extended family – grandparents, aunts, uncles, cousins – using family photographs to frame your argument.

Responding Visually

Choose a recent event that was well covered in the print and broadcast media and that involved a great deal of heroism – heroism that lends itself to visual reenactment. Based on the images that you have seen here, create a visual adaptation of Joe Rosenthal's famous photograph to represent this more recent act of heroism.

4

PROJECTING

GENDER

From a very early age we are taught to identify with one of the two most universally recognized icons: 🕴 and 🕴. Created in the early 1970s, these simple symbols for male and female have become so pervasive we take them for granted. Yet a more careful look raises important questions: How exactly do these icons communicate gender difference? What cultural assumptions are embedded in them? Why are differences in clothing such a clear indicator of gender identity and sex? How do different cultures train children to identify with — and project — gender from an early age? How do these representations of difference relate to larger issues of the equality of the sexes and the social construction of gender?

One hundred years ago the terms *sex* and *gender* were used interchangeably, but they mean different things today. *Sex* refers to biological structure and function, to being born with male or female genitalia. The chromosomes we inherit determine our sex. *Gender* refers to a cultural category, to the behavioral or psychological standards a society sets for masculine or feminine behavior. By definition, then, gender expectations can change with place and time. Consider, for example, the vastly different expectations that shape the lives of a twenty-one-year-old woman living in San Francisco and a woman of the same age living in Beijing or Baghdad. Or think about a boy growing up in Ames, Iowa, today with a concept of masculinity that is quite different from the one that shaped his counterpart fifty years ago.

We are all born with a biological sex, and we all soon learn about — and develop attitudes toward — gender roles: how men and women should act in private and public life, what we should wear, how we should talk, how we should interact with others, even what life choices we should make. What codes for gender behavior can you identify in your own life? on campus? in your family? among friends?

Magazine and advertising headlines insistently proclaim that men and women are different. Indeed, representations of these differences can be seen everywhere in popular culture. Advertisers, for example, make money by invoking categories of essential difference. Smoking Virginia Slims is "a woman thing"; drinking Jim Beam helps you "get in touch with your masculine side." Men love beer; women love jewelry. Men love watching sports; women love watching soaps. We "know" these things to be true because we read them and see them everywhere — and clearly many people believe that anatomy is destiny.

Yet despite these messages about the essential differences between men and women, gender lines are breaking down. More women are working, for more money and at better jobs than thirty years ago; more men are choosing to stay home. More women are graduating from medical school, and more men are becoming nurses. Certainly in theory men and women can wear the same clothes, get the same education, work the same jobs, and behave the same way — and many do in practice. Today the public discourse is focused both on the black-and-white question of the similarities and differences between men and women, and on the gray area in between.

How do you read current signs of gender difference? Is the recent trend in super-spiky high heels a throwback to the traditional feminine code that feminists fought against, or does it reveal a more nuanced and ironic expression of femininity? Is it a myth that men are afraid of intimacy? How do *you* respond to public and private constructions of gender identity? The men and women whose work appears in this chapter explore this question from distinct points of view, from sociocultural (for example, Art Spiegelman in *Nature vs. Nurture*) to economic (Susan Bordo in "Never Just Pictures") to personal (Judith Ortiz Cofer in "The Story of My Body").

Robert Mapplethorpe
Self-Portrait, 1980

Robert Mapplethorpe
Self-Portrait, 1980

Robert Mapplethorpe

Born in 1946 in New York, Robert Mapplethorpe achieved celebrity status as a photographer in the years before his death in 1989. At the age of sixteen he began to study art at Pratt Institute in Brooklyn. Trained as a painter and sculptor, he approached photographic subjects with an acute sense of symmetrical composition. He was encouraged to pursue photography by Sam Wagstaff, a former museum curator. Mapplethorpe had his first solo exhibition in New York City in 1976, and the first major museum retrospective of his work was presented by the Whitney Museum of American Art in 1988. He remains one of the most important figures in contemporary photography.

Whether photographing flowers, erotic scenes, individuals, or presenting photographic self-portraits (pp. 320–21), Mapplethorpe manipulated light, shadow, and setting in ways that often provoked tension between his subject matter and his formalist aesthetic. He summed up the effect when he said, "My work is about seeing things like they haven't been seen before."

SEEING

1. As you examine these two self-portraits carefully, what strikes you as masculine or feminine? Comment, for example, on Mapplethorpe's choice of hairstyle, facial expression, clothing, and accessories. What gender conventions and stereotypes does Mapplethorpe invoke in these images? Can you find any visual references to certain eras in American history?

2. Museum curator and writer Jennifer Blessing observes that Mapplethorpe's portraits "are more frequently consciously contrived studio portraits. His images demonstrate the high value he placed on formal aesthetics. His portraits suggest the conventions of celebrity advertisements. Their flat backgrounds, tight cropping, iconic centrality, and minimal distracting detail focus all attention on the subject." What cropping choices has Mapplethorpe made in the images here? With what effect(s)? How might the tone and effect of the photographs change if Mapplethorpe had shot them in a nonstudio context?

cropping: Trimming a photograph either when composing it (e.g., moving closer to or farther away from the subject to include less or more of the background) or when developing it, by printing part of the negative rather than the whole image (e.g., cutting away some of the background to obtain a new perspective on the subject).

WRITING

1. What do you like about being female? about being male? As a college student, what do you see as the major differences between being female or male? Write an essay in which you imagine changing your sex for a day. How do you think your day would be different?

Working with Sources

2. The dangling cigarette is a prominent part of Mapplethorpe's masculine self-portraits. Choose a cigarette advertisement that draws explicitly on gender conventions—Virginia Slims or Camel, for example. How can smoking make you more of a woman or more of a man? Write an essay in which you answer that question, arguing for or against the claims made by the copy and image in the ad you've chosen.

PAIR–Cardona & Martínez

BATO CON KHAKIS
Jacinto Jesús Cardona

Too bold for my mother's blood,
bato was not a household word.
Oh, but to be a bato con khakis
waiting to catch the city bus,

5 my thin belt exuding attitude,
looking limber in a blue vest,
laid-back in my dark shades.

Alas! I'm the bifocals kid;
cool bato I am not,
10 but I could spell gelato.
Could I be the bookish bato?

Oh, but to be a bato con khakis
deep in the Hub of South Texas,
blooming among bluebonnets.

César A. Martínez
Bato con Khakis, 1982

Jacinto Jesús Cardona

Jacinto Jesús (Jesse) Cardona was born in Palacios, a town along the coast of Texas, but he grew up in Alice, a small town in the heartland of South Texas. His poetry reflects his upbringing: The images in poems like "Bato con Khakis" are strongly reminiscent of life in a small South Texas town.

Cardona received his BS degree in English from what is now Texas A&M University–Kingsville, and he often returns to college and high school campuses to read his poetry. Cardona received the Imagineer Award for teaching creative writing and has published his poetry in various literary journals. He is the author of a chapbook, "At the Wheel of a Blue Chevrolet," and *Pan Dulce* (1998), a book of poems. He has read from this collection on National Public Radio and PBS stations, and he is featured in the documentary *Voices from Texas* (2003).

Cardona has taught English at high schools in San Antonio. He currently is a job coach for special needs students at a high school in El Paso, and he is also a faculty member of Upward Bound, a program that helps low-income and first-generation college students pursue postsecondary education through academic, cultural, interpersonal, and personal development. "Bato con Khakis" was first published in *Heart to Heart: New Poems Inspired by Twentieth-Century American Art* (2001).

César A. Martínez

Born in Laredo, Texas, in 1944, César A. Martínez has become well known for his depictions of South Texans. His Mexican-influenced portraits provided a visual dimension to the Chicano movement of the 1970s and 1980s and have helped define Latin American culture as a whole. In 1999 Martínez was named the San Antonio Art League Museum's Artist of the Year for his "significant contribution to the arts in South Texas as well as to the history of Chicano art." The museum also mounted an exhibition of thirty-one of his works coinciding with the publication of *César Martínez: A Retrospective* (1999).

Martínez has participated in the creation of many short films and books on Latin American art. He also has participated in the Visual Arts Visiting Artist Program at the University of Texas – San Antonio, and he was an artist-in-residence at Artpace San Antonio. Most recently his work has been a part of two major traveling exhibitions, ¡Arte Caliente! and Chicano Visions, and has been featured in the books *Chicano Art for Our Millennium* (2004) and *Triumph of Our Communities: Four Decades of Mexican American Art* (2005). A part of the Joe A. Diaz collection in San Antonio, Texas, *Bato con Khakis* is a work of mixed media on paper.

SEEING

1. When you first read Cardona's poem, what did you think the word *bato* meant? What associations did the word summon? "Bato," reports Jacinto Jesús Cardona, is "a Spanglish greeting equivalent to 'Hey, man!' but it's also associated with <u>pachucos</u>, the alienated youth associated with the <u>zoot suiters</u>." What does the term *Spanglish* mean? What other words can you identify as examples of Spanglish? To what extent does the word *bato* work effectively in this poem? Why? How successfully does César Martínez's painting represent your image of a zoot suiter? Point to specific features of the image to support your response. How do these details embody the character's identity?

2. Why is *bato* "too bold" a word for the speaker's "mother's blood" (l. 1)? What do you make of the third stanza of the poem (ll. 8–11)? What does it add to the meaning and success of the poem? What do the last two lines contribute to the poem?

3. In the poem, Cardona writes "my thin belt exuding attitude" (l. 5). How would you describe that attitude? Point to other details in the painting that reinforce the *bato* image.

<u>pachucos:</u> A southwestern Chicano subculture, prevalent in the 1940s, distinguished by clothing – oversized zoot suits – and versions of Spanish dialect. Because of their distrust of mainstream assimilation, *pachucos* were sometimes seen as gangsters.

<u>zoot (also spelled zuit) suit:</u> A suit with high-waisted, wide-legged, tight-cuffed, pegged trousers and a long coat with wide lapels and wide padded shoulders. The word *zoot* was probably first coined by Mexican American pachucos as part of their slang, "Calo," evolving from the Mexican Spanish pronunciation of the English word *suit* with "s" taking on the sound of "z." The zoot suit first gained popularity in the Harlem jazz culture in the late 1930s and was widely adopted by young Mexican Americans.

WRITING

1. Imagine that César Martínez is a friend who approaches you with the original of the mixed-media work of art reproduced here, and that he invites you to write a poem or prose piece based on this illustration. Which would you prefer to write – a poem, a piece of fiction, or an autobiographical or expository essay? Why? Choose a form, and write a first draft of a work inspired by careful observation of Martínez's mixed-media work. Which elements in the image would you emphasize? Why? What criteria would you apply to measure your success in establishing connections between the art and your writing?

2. Examine both the poem and the painting. Do you think the poem is made more effective by Martínez's visual rendition of it? Write an essay in which you defend – or challenge – the claim that the painting gives the poem its impact.

William H. Johnson
Li'L Sis, 1944

GIRL
Jamaica Kincaid

Wash the white clothes on Monday and put them on the stone heap; wash the color clothes on Tuesday and put them on the clothesline to dry; don't walk barehead in the hot sun; cook pumpkin fritters in very hot sweet oil; soak your little cloths right after you take them off; when buying cotton to make yourself a nice blouse, be sure that it doesn't have gum on it, because that way it won't hold up well after a wash; soak salt fish overnight before you cook it; is it true that you sing benna[1] in Sunday school?; always eat your food in such a way that it won't turn someone else's stomach; on Sundays try to walk like a lady and not like the slut you are so bent on becoming; don't sing benna in Sunday School; you mustn't speak to wharf-rat boys, not even to give directions; don't eat fruits on the street—flies will follow you; *but I don't sing benna on Sundays at all and never in Sunday school*; this is how to sew on a button; this is how to make a buttonhole for the button you have just sewed on; this is how to hem a dress when you see the hem coming down and so to prevent yourself from looking like the slut I know you are so bent on becoming; this is how you iron your father's khaki shirt so that it doesn't have a crease; this is how you iron your father's khaki pants so that they don't have a crease; this is how you grow okra—far from the house, because okra tree harbors red ants; when you are growing dasheen,[2] make sure it gets plenty of water or else it makes your throat itch when you are eating it; this is how you sweep a corner; this is how you sweep a whole house; this is how you sweep a yard; this is how you smile to someone you don't like too much; this is how you smile to someone you don't like at all; this is how you smile to someone you like completely; this is how you set a table for tea; this is how you set a table for dinner; this is how you set a table for dinner with an important guest; this is how you set a table for lunch; this is how you set a table for breakfast; this is how to behave in the presence of men who don't know you very well, and this way they won't recognize immediately the slut I have warned you against becoming; be sure to wash every day, even if it is with your own spit; don't squat down to play marbles—you are not a boy, you know; don't pick people's flowers—you might catch something; don't throw stones at

---

1. benna: Calypso music. [All notes are the editors'.]

2. dasheen: The edible rootstock of taro, a tropical plant.

blackbirds, because it might not be a blackbird at all; this is how to make a bread pudding; this is how to make doukona;[3] this is how to make pepper pot;[4] this is how to make a good medicine for a cold; this is how to make a good medicine to throw away a child before it even becomes a child; this is how to catch a fish; this is how to throw back a fish you don't like, and that way something bad won't fall on you; this is how to bully a man; this is how a man bullies you; this is how to love a man, and if this doesn't work there are other ways, and if they don't work don't feel too bad about giving up; this is how to spit up in the air if you feel like it, and this is how to move quick so that it doesn't fall on you; this is how to make ends meet; always squeeze bread to make sure it's fresh; *but what if the baker won't let me feel the bread?*; you mean to say that after all you are really going to be the kind of woman who the baker won't let near the bread?

---

3. doukona: A spicy plantain pudding.

4. pepper pot: A stew.

Jamaica Kincaid

Born in Antigua in 1949, Jamaica Kincaid immigrated to the United States at age seventeen as an au pair. Her novel *Lucy* (1990) is loosely based on her experience of coming into adulthood in a foreign country. Kincaid has transformed other personal experiences into richly textured fiction and nonfiction in *At the Bottom of the River* (1983), *Annie John* (1985), *A Small Place* (1988), *The Autobiography of My Mother* (1996), *My Brother* (1997), and *Mr. Potter* (2002). She lives in Bennington, Vermont, and teaches at Harvard University. In her recent book *Among Flowers: A Walk in the Himalaya* (2005), Kincaid chronicles her journey to the Himalayas in search of rare plants for her Vermont garden.

Kincaid discovered her talent and passion for writing when, in her twenties, she was asked to contribute sketches on Caribbean and African American culture to *The New Yorker*'s "Talk of the Town" column. Before long she was invited to become a staff writer, and in 1978 "Girl," her first piece of published fiction, appeared in the magazine. "I'm someone who writes to save her life," Kincaid says. "I can't imagine what else I would do if I didn't write. I would be dead or I would be in jail because what else could I do? . . . All the things that were available to someone in my position involved being a subject person. And I'm very bad at being a subject person."

SEEING

1. Who is the speaker in Jamaica Kincaid's story, and how would you describe that person? Who is the speaker addressing? What, according to the narrator, are the prescriptions for being a "girl"? If this is a portrait, who is being portrayed?

2. "Girl" is filled with detailed descriptions of a daily routine. What kind of life do you see by the end of the essay? Where do you think the people invoked by the description live, and what specific details suggest a certain place to you?

WRITING

1. Kincaid describes a girl whose growing up involves lessons of gender, obedience, and domesticity. Do you think girls today are taught the same kinds of lessons? If so, how? Write the first draft of an essay in which you describe the lessons you think young girls are learning today, and explain the cultural importance of each lesson.

2. Compare the tone of "Girl" and of William Johnson's *Li'L Sis*, a portrait of the artist's younger sister who grew up in the rural South in the early 1900s. What mood does each of these portraits evoke? What details can you identify in the painting that reveal what was expected from this girl?

Page 328

Responding Visually
How would you "translate" Kincaid's "Girl" into a drawing? You can either sketch it out or describe that drawing in writing, but you should try to be as detailed as possible. After completing your visual portrait, write a paragraph in which you sum up what you've learned about seeing and writing.

THE STORY OF MY BODY
Judith Ortiz Cofer

Migration is the story of my body.
—Victor Hernández Cruz

Skin

I was born a white girl in Puerto Rico but became a brown girl when I
came to live in the United States. My Puerto Rican relatives called me tall;
at the American school, some of my rougher classmates called me Skinny
Bones, and the Shrimp because I was the smallest member of my classes
all through grammar school until high school, when the midget Gladys
was given the honorary post of front row center for class pictures and
scorekeeper, bench warmer, in P.E. I reached my full stature of five feet
in sixth grade.

I started out life as a pretty baby and learned to be a pretty girl from
a pretty mother. Then at ten years of age I suffered one of the worst cases
of chicken pox I have ever heard of. My entire body, including the inside of my ears and in between my toes, was covered with pustules which
in a fit of panic at my appearance I scratched off my face, leaving permanent scars. A cruel school nurse told me I would always have them—
tiny cuts that looked as if a mad cat had plunged its claws deep into my
skin. I grew my hair long and hid behind it for the first years of my adolescence. This was when I learned to be invisible.

Color

In the animal world it indicates danger: The most colorful creatures are
often the most poisonous. Color is also a way to attract and seduce a
mate. In the human world color triggers many more complex and often
deadly reactions. As a Puerto Rican girl born of "white" parents, I spent
the first years of my life hearing people refer to me as *blanca*, white. My
mother insisted that I protect myself from the intense island sun because
I was more prone to sunburn than some of my darker, *trigueño* play-
mates. People were always commenting within my hearing about how
my black hair contrasted so nicely with my "pale" skin. I did not think
of the color of my skin consciously except when I heard the adults talking
about complexion. It seems to me that the subject is much more common

in the conversation of mixed-race peoples than in mainstream United States society, where it is a touchy and sometimes even embarrassing topic to discuss, except in a political context. In Puerto Rico I heard many conversations about skin color. A pregnant woman could say, "I hope my baby doesn't turn out *prieto*" (slang for "dark" or "black") "like my husband's grandmother, although she was a good-looking *negra* in her time." I am a combination of both, being olive-skinned—lighter than my mother yet darker than my fair-skinned father. In America, I am a person of color, obviously a Latina. On the Island I have been called everything from a *paloma blanca*, after the song (by a black suitor), to *la gringa*.

My first experience of color prejudice occurred in a supermarket in Paterson, New Jersey. It was Christmastime, and I was eight or nine years old. There was a display of toys in the store where I went two or three times a day to buy things for my mother, who never made lists but sent for milk, cigarettes, a can of this or that, as she remembered from hour to hour. I enjoyed being trusted with money and walking half a city block to the new, modern grocery store. It was owned by three good-looking Italian brothers. I liked the younger one with the crew-cut blond hair. The two older ones watched me and the other Puerto Rican kids as if they thought we were going to steal something. The oldest one would sometimes even try to hurry me with my purchases, although part of my pleasure in these expeditions came from looking at everything in the well-stocked aisles. I was also teaching myself to read English by sounding out the labels on packages: L&M cigarettes, Borden's homogenized milk, Red Devil potted ham, Nestle's chocolate mix, Quaker oats, Bustelo coffee, Wonder bread, Colgate toothpaste, Ivory soap, and Goya (makers of products used in Puerto Rican dishes) everything—these are some of the brand names that taught me nouns. Several times this man had come up to me, wearing his blood-stained butcher's apron, and towering over me had asked in a harsh voice whether there was something he could help me find. On the way out I would glance at the younger brother who ran one of the registers and he would often smile and wink at me.

5   It was the mean brother who first referred to me as "colored." It was a few days before Christmas, and my parents had already told my brother and me that since we were in Los Estados now, we would get our presents on December 25 instead of Los Reyes, Three Kings Day, when gifts are exchanged in Puerto Rico. We were to give them a wish list that they would take to Santa Claus, who apparently lived in the Macy's store downtown—at least that's where we had caught a glimpse of him when we went shopping. Since my parents were timid about entering the fancy

store, we did not approach the huge man in the red suit. I was not interested in sitting on a stranger's lap anyway. But I did covet Susie, the talking schoolteacher doll that was displayed in the center aisle of the Italian brothers' supermarket. She talked when you pulled a string on her back. Susie had a limited repertoire of three sentences: I think she could say: "Hello, I'm Susie Schoolteacher," "Two plus two is four," and one other thing I cannot remember. The day the older brother chased me away, I was reaching to touch Susie's blonde curls. I had been told many times, as most children have, not to touch anything in a store that I was not buying. But I had been looking at Susie for weeks. In my mind, she was my doll. After all, I had put her on my Christmas wish list. The moment is frozen in my mind as if there were a photograph of it on file. It was not a turning point, a disaster, or an earth-shaking revelation. It was simply the first time I considered—if naively—the meaning of skin color in human relations.

I reached to touch Susie's hair. It seems to me that I had to get on tiptoe, since the toys were stacked on a table and she sat like a princess on top of the fancy box she came in. Then I heard the booming "Hey, kid, what do you think you're doing!" spoken very loudly from the meat counter. I felt caught, although I knew I was not doing anything criminal. I remember not looking at the man, but standing there, feeling humiliated because I knew everyone in the store must have heard him yell at me. I felt him approach, and when I knew he was behind me, I turned around to face the bloody butcher's apron. His large chest was at my eye level. He blocked my way. I started to run out of the place, but even as I reached the door I heard him shout after me: "Don't come in here unless you gonna buy something. You PR kids put your dirty hands on stuff. You always look dirty. But maybe dirty brown is your natural color." I heard him laugh and someone else too in the back. Outside in the sunlight I looked at my hands. My nails needed a little cleaning as they always did, since I liked to paint with watercolors, but I took a bath every night. I thought the man was dirtier than I was in his stained apron. He was also always sweaty—it showed in big yellow circles under his shirtsleeves. I sat on the front steps of the apartment building where we lived and looked closely at my hands, which showed the only skin I could see, since it was bitter cold and I was wearing my quilted play coat, dungarees, and a knitted navy cap of my father's. I was not pink like my friend Charlene and her sister Kathy, who had blue eyes and light brown hair. My skin is the color of the coffee my grandmother made, which was half milk, *leche con café* rather than *café con leche*. My mother is the opposite mix. She has a lot of *café* in her color. I could not understand how my skin looked like dirt to the supermarket man.

I went in and washed my hands thoroughly with soap and hot water, and borrowing my mother's nail file, I cleaned the crusted watercolors from underneath my nails. I was pleased with the results. My skin was the same color as before, but I knew I was clean. Clean enough to run my fingers through Susie's fine gold hair when she came home to me.

Size

My mother is barely four feet eleven inches in height, which is average for women in her family. When I grew to five feet by age twelve, she was amazed and began to use the word tall to describe me, as in "Since you are tall, this dress will look good on you." As with the color of my skin, I didn't consciously think about my height or size until other people made an issue of it. It is around the preadolescent years that in America the games children play for fun become fierce competitions where everyone is out to "prove" they are better than others. It was in the playground and sports fields that my size-related problems began. No matter how familiar the story is, every child who is the last chosen for a team knows the torment of waiting to be called up. At the Paterson, New Jersey, public schools that I attended, the volleyball or softball game was the metaphor for the battlefield of life to the inner-city kids—the black kids versus the Puerto Rican kids, the whites versus the blacks versus the Puerto Rican kids; and I was 4-F, skinny, short, bespectacled, and apparently impervious to the blood thirst that drove many of my classmates to play ball as if their lives depended on it. Perhaps they did. I would rather be reading a book than sweating, grunting, and running the risk of pain and injury. I simply did not see the point in competitive sports. My main form of exercise then was walking to the library, many city blocks away from my barrio.

Still, I wanted to be wanted. I wanted to be chosen for the teams. Physical education was compulsory, a class where you were actually given a grade. On my mainly all A report card, the C for compassion I always received from the P.E. teachers shamed me the same as a bad grade in a real class. Invariably, my father would say: "How can you make a low grade for *playing games*?" He did not understand. Even if I had managed to make a hit (it never happened) or get the ball over that ridiculously high net, I already had a reputation as a "shrimp," a hopeless nonathlete. It was an area where the girls who didn't like me for one reason or another—

mainly because I did better than they in academic subjects—could lord it over me; the playing field was the place where even the smallest girl could make me feel powerless and inferior. I instinctively understood the politics even then; how the *not* choosing me until the teacher forced one of the team captains to call my name was a coup of sorts—there, you little show-off, tomorrow you can beat us in spelling and geography, but this afternoon you are the loser. Or perhaps those were only my own bitter thoughts as I sat or stood in the sidelines while the big girls were grabbed like fish and I, the little brown tadpole, was ignored until Teacher looked over in my general direction and shouted, "Call Ortiz," or, worse, "Somebody's *got* to take her."

10 No wonder I read Wonder Woman comics and had Legion of Super Heroes daydreams. Although I wanted to think of myself as "intellectual," my body was demanding that I notice it. I saw the little swelling around my once-flat nipples, the fine hairs growing in secret places; but my knees were still bigger than my thighs, and I always wore long- or half-sleeve blouses to hide my bony upper arms. I wanted flesh on my bones—a thick layer of it. I saw a new product advertised on TV. Wate-On. They showed skinny men and women before and after taking the stuff, and it was a transformation like the ninety-seven-pound-weakling-turned-into-Charles-Atlas ads that I saw on the back covers of my comic books. The Wate-On was very expensive. I tried to explain my need for it in Spanish to my mother, but it didn't translate very well, even to my ears—and she said with a tone of finality, eat more of my good food and you'll get fat—anybody can get fat. Right. Except me. I was going to have to join a circus someday as Skinny Bones, the woman without flesh.

Wonder Woman was stacked. She had a cleavage framed by the spread wings of a golden eagle and a muscular body that has become fashionable with women only recently. But since I wanted a body that would serve me in P.E., hers was my ideal. The breasts were an indulgence I allowed myself. Perhaps the daydreams of bigger girls were more glamorous, since our ambitions are filtered through our needs, but I wanted first a powerful body. I daydreamed of leaping up above the gray landscape of the city to where the sky was clear and blue, and in anger and self-pity, I fantasized about scooping my enemies up by their hair from the playing fields and dumping them on a barren asteroid. I would put the P.E. teachers each on their own rock in space too, where they would be the loneliest people in the universe, since I knew they had no "inner resources," no imagination, and in outer space, there would be no air for them to fill their deflated volleyballs with. In my mind all P.E. teachers have blended into one large spiky-haired woman with a whistle on a string around her neck and a volleyball under one arm. My Wonder Woman fantasies of revenge were a source of comfort to me in my early career as a shrimp.

I was saved from more years of P.E. torment by the fact that in my sophomore year of high school I transferred to a school where the midget, Gladys, was the focal point of interest for the people who must rank according to size. Because her height was considered a handicap, there was an unspoken rule about mentioning size around Gladys, but of course, there was no need to say anything. Gladys knew her place: front row center in class photographs. I gladly moved to the left or to the right of her, as far as I could without leaving the picture completely.

Looks

Many photographs were taken of me as a baby by my mother to send to my father, who was stationed overseas during the first two years of my life. With the army in Panama when I was born, he later traveled often on tours of duty with the navy. I was a healthy, pretty baby. Recently, I read that people are drawn to big-eyed round-faced creatures, like puppies, kittens, and certain other mammals and marsupials, koalas, for example, and, of course, infants. I was all eyes, since my head and body, even as I grew older, remained thin and small-boned. As a young child I got a lot of attention from my relatives and many other people we met in our barrio. My mother's beauty may have had something to do with how much attention we got from strangers in stores and on the street. I can imagine it. In the pictures I have seen of us together, she is a stunning young woman by Latino standards: long, curly black hair, and round curves in a compact frame. From her I learned how to move, smile, and talk like an attractive woman. I remember going into a bodega for our groceries and being given candy by the proprietor as a reward for being *bonita*, pretty.

I can see in the photographs, and I also remember, that I was dressed in the pretty clothes, the stiff, frilly dresses, with layers of crinolines underneath, the glossy patent leather shoes, and, on special occasions, the skull-hugging little hats and the white gloves that were popular in the late fifties and early sixties. My mother was proud of my looks, although I was a bit too thin. She could dress me up like a doll and take me by the hand to visit relatives, or go to the Spanish mass at the Catholic church, and show me off. How was I to know that she and the others who called me "pretty" were representatives of an aesthetic that would not apply when I went out into the mainstream world of school?

15   In my Paterson, New Jersey, public schools there were still quite a few white children, although the demographics of the city were changing rapidly. The original waves of Italian and Irish immigrants, silk-mill workers, and laborers in the cloth industries had been "assimilated." Their children were now the middle-class parents of my peers. Many of them moved their children to the Catholic schools that proliferated enough to have leagues of basketball teams. The names I recall hearing still ring in my ears: Don Bosco High versus St. Mary's High, St. Joseph's versus St. John's. Later I too would be transferred to the safer environment of a Catholic school. But I started school at Public School Number 11. I came there from Puerto Rico, thinking myself a pretty girl, and found that the hierarchy for popularity was as follows: pretty white girl, pretty Jewish girl, pretty Puerto Rican girl, pretty black girl. Drop the last two categories; teachers were too busy to have more than one favorite per class, and it was simply understood that if there was a big part in the school play, or any competition where the main qualification was "presentability" (such as escorting a school visitor to or from the principal's office), the classroom's public address speaker would be requesting the pretty and/ or nice-looking white boy or girl. By the time I was in the sixth grade, I was sometimes called by the principal to represent my class because I dressed neatly (I knew this from a progress report sent to my mother, which I translated for her) and because all the "presentable" white girls had moved to the Catholic schools (I later surmised this part). But I was still not one of the popular girls with the boys. I remember one incident where I stepped out into the playground in my baggy gym shorts and one Puerto Rican boy said to the other: "What do you think?" The other one answered: "Her face is OK, but look at the toothpick legs." The next best thing to a compliment I got was when my favorite male teacher, while handing out the class pictures, commented that with my long neck and delicate features I resembled the movie star Audrey Hepburn. But the Puerto Rican boys had learned to respond to a fuller figure: Long necks and a perfect little nose were not what they looked for in a girl. That is when I decided I was a "brain." I did not settle into the role easily. I was nearly devastated by what the chicken pox episode had done to my self-image. But I looked into the mirror less often after I was told that I would always have scars on my face, and I hid behind my long black hair and my books.

After the problems at the public school got to the point where even nonconfrontational little me got beaten up several times, my parents enrolled me at St. Joseph's High School. I was then a minority of one among the Italian and Irish kids. But I found several good friends there—other girls who took their studies seriously. We did our homework together and talked about the Jackies. The Jackies were two popular girls, one blonde and the other red-haired, who had women's bodies. Their curves showed even in the blue jumper uniforms with straps that we all wore. The blonde Jackie would often let one of the straps fall off her shoulder, and although she, like all of us, wore a white blouse underneath, all the boys stared at her arm. My friends and I talked about this and practiced letting our straps fall off our shoulders. But it wasn't the same without breasts or hips.

My final two and a half years of high school were spent in Augusta, Georgia, where my parents moved our family in search of a more peaceful environment. There we became part of a little community of our army-connected relatives and friends. School was yet another matter. I was enrolled in a huge school of nearly two thousand students that had just that year been forced to integrate. There were two black girls and there was me. I did extremely well academically. As to my social life, it was, for the most part, uneventful—yet it is in my memory blighted by one incident. In my junior year, I became wildly infatuated with a pretty white boy. I'll call him Ted. Oh, he was pretty: yellow hair that fell over his forehead, a smile to die for—and he was a great dancer. I watched him at Teen Town, the youth center at the base where all the military brats gathered on Saturday nights. My father had retired from the navy, and we had all our base privileges—one other reason we had moved to Augusta. Ted looked like an angel to me. I worked on him for a year before he asked me out. This meant maneuvering to be within the periphery of his vision at every possible occasion. I took the long way to my classes in school just to pass by his locker, I went to football games, which I detested, and I danced (I too was a good dancer) in front of him at Teen Town—this took some fancy footwork, since it involved subtly moving my partner toward the right spot on the dance floor. When Ted finally approached me, "A Million to One" was playing on the jukebox, and when he took me into his arms, the odds suddenly turned in my favor. He asked me to go to a school dance the following Saturday. I said yes, breathlessly. I said yes, but there were obstacles to surmount at home. My father did not allow me to date casually. I was allowed to go to major events like a prom or a concert with a boy who had been properly screened. There was such a boy in my life, a neighbor who wanted to be a Baptist missionary and was practicing his anthropological skills on my family. If I was desperate to go somewhere and needed a date, I'd resort to Gary. This is the type of religious nut that Gary was: When the school bus did not show up one day, he put his hands over his face and prayed to Christ to get us a way to get to school. Within ten minutes a mother in a station wagon, on her way to town, stopped to ask why we weren't in school. Gary informed her that the Lord had sent her just in time to find us a way to get there in time for roll call. He assumed that I was impressed. Gary was even good-looking in a bland sort of way, but he kissed me with his lips tightly pressed together. I think Gary probably ended up marrying a native woman from wherever he may have gone to preach the Gospel according to Paul. She probably believes that all white men pray to God for transportation and kiss with their mouths closed. But it was Ted's mouth, his whole beautiful self, that concerned me in those days. I knew my father would say no to our date, but I planned to run away from home if necessary. I told my mother how important this date was. I cajoled and pleaded with her from Sunday to Wednesday. She listened to my arguments and must have heard the note of desperation in my voice. She said very gently to me: "You better be ready for disappointment." I did not ask what she meant. I did not want her fears for me to taint my happiness. I asked her to tell my father about my date. Thursday at breakfast my father looked at me across the table with his eyebrows together. My mother looked at him with her mouth set in a straight line. I looked down at my bowl of cereal. Nobody said anything. Friday I tried on every dress in my closet. Ted would be picking me up at six on Saturday: dinner and then the sock hop at school. Friday night I was in my room doing my nails or something else in preparation for Saturday (I know I groomed myself nonstop all week) when the telephone rang. I ran to get it. It was Ted. His voice sounded funny when he said my name, so funny that I felt compelled to ask: "Is something wrong?" Ted blurted it all out without a preamble. His father had asked who he was going out with. Ted had told him my name. "Ortiz? That's Spanish, isn't it?" the father had asked. Ted had told him yes, then shown him my picture in the yearbook. Ted's father had shaken his head. No. Ted would not be taking me out. Ted's father had known Puerto Ricans in the army. He had lived in New York City while studying architecture and had seen how the spics lived. Like rats. Ted repeated his father's words to me as if I should understand *his* predicament when I heard why he was breaking our date. I don't remember what I said before hanging up. I do recall the darkness of my room that sleepless night and the heaviness of my blanket in which I wrapped myself like a shroud. And I remember my parents' respect for my pain and their gentleness toward me that weekend. My mother did not say "I warned you," and I was grateful for her understanding silence.

In college, I suddenly became an "exotic" woman to the men who had survived the popularity wars in high school, who were now practicing to be worldly: They had to act liberal in their politics, in their life-styles, and in the women they went out with. I dated heavily for a while, then married young. I had discovered that I needed stability more than social life. I had brains for sure and some talent in writing. These facts were a constant in my life. My skin color, my size, and my appearance were variables — things that were judged according to my current self-image, the aesthetic values of the times, the places I was in, and the people I met. My studies, later my writing, the respect of people who saw me as an individual person they cared about, these were the criteria for my sense of self-worth that I would concentrate on in my adult life.

Judith Ortiz Cofer

In an essay entitled "The Myth of the Latin Woman: I Just Met a Girl Named Maria," Judith Ortiz Cofer (b. 1952) talks of the prejudice she encountered as a youth: "As a Puerto Rican girl growing up in the United States and wanting like most children to 'belong,' I resented the stereotype that my Hispanic appearance called forth from many people I met."

Cofer speaks with insight and eloquence about the costs of cultural transplantation and has established a reputation for writing finely crafted and deeply moving expressions of contemporary Puerto Rican experience. She first earned recognition for her literary talents through several collections of poetry. Her first novel, *The Line of the Sun* (1989), was nominated for a Pulitzer Prize. The selection here is taken from *The Latin Deli* (1993), a collection of prose and poetry. Cofer has also written numerous short stories, essays, and young adult novels. Her most recent work, *A Love Story Beginning in Spanish* (2005), is a collection of poems.

Cofer explains that "my personal goal in my public life is to replace the old pervasive stereotypes and myths about Latinas with a much more interesting set of realities. . . . I hope the stories I tell, the dreams and fears I examine in my work, can achieve some universal truth which will get my audience past the particulars of my skin color, my accent, or my clothes."

SEEING

1. What are the features of the ideal body that Judith Ortiz Cofer imagines for herself? What kind of language does she use to describe her real body? Who does she look up to during her childhood? Why? From what aspects of the culture were these figures drawn? In what specific ways does Cofer's memory of going to the local grocery store remind you of Eudora Welty's account of a similar experience? (See "The Little Store," p. 147.)

2. What principle of organization governs Cofer's essay? What logical thread links one paragraph to another? Comment on the effectiveness of her use of metaphor and irony, supporting your response with specific examples. What does Cofer identify as constants and variables in her life? What conclusions do you draw from the ending? To what extent, for

example, does our identity vary according to the context in which we find ourselves? Having reread the essay and thought about it carefully, what cultural implications can you identify in the title "The Story of My Body"?

Page 147

irony: An often-humorous aspect of writing that calls attention to the difference between the actual result of a sequence of events and the expected result.

WRITING

1. Cofer describes reaching to touch the doll despite having "been told many times, as most children have, not to touch anything in a store that I was not buying" (para. 5). What admonitions can you recall hearing "many times" as a child? Which one do you associate with an especially memorable experience? Write the first draft of a narrative essay in which you recount how that maxim was invoked as a means of regulating your behavior.

2. At several points in her essay Cofer speaks of herself as "the Shrimp" and as "Skinny Bones." When you were a child, what nicknames were you called at home? in school? Did you have a name you called yourself when you said or did something silly? Write the first draft of an expository essay in which you account for the origins—and the personal consequences—of your nicknames.

THE VEIL

THIS IS ME WHEN I WAS 10 YEARS OLD. THIS WAS IN 1980.

AND THIS IS A CLASS PHOTO. I'M SITTING ON THE FAR LEFT SO YOU DON'T SEE ME. FROM LEFT TO RIGHT: GOLNAZ, MAHSHID, NARINE, MINNA.

IN 1979 A REVOLUTION TOOK PLACE. IT WAS LATER CALLED "THE ISLAMIC REVOLUTION".

THEN CAME 1980: THE YEAR IT BECAME OBLIGATORY TO WEAR THE VEIL AT SCHOOL.

WEAR THIS!

WE DIDN'T REALLY LIKE TO WEAR THE VEIL, ESPECIALLY SINCE WE DIDN'T UNDERSTAND WHY WE HAD TO.

IT'S TOO HOT OUT!

EXECUTION IN THE NAME OF FREEDOM.

GIVE ME MY VEIL BACK!

YOU'LL HAVE TO LICK MY FEET!

OOH! I'M THE MONSTER OF DARKNESS.

GIDDYAP!

By Marjane Satrapi

AND ALSO BECAUSE THE YEAR BEFORE, IN 1979, WE WERE IN A FRENCH NON-RELIGIOUS SCHOOL.

WHERE BOYS AND GIRLS WERE TOGETHER.

AND THEN SUDDENLY IN 1980...

ALL BILINGUAL SCHOOLS MUST BE CLOSED DOWN.

THEY ARE SYMBOLS OF CAPITALISM.

BRAVO!

WHAT WISDOM!

OF DECADENCE.

THIS IS CALLED A "CULTURAL REVOLUTION."

WE FOUND OURSELVES VEILED AND SEPARATED FROM OUR FRIENDS.

AND THAT WAS THAT...

EVERYWHERE IN THE STREETS THERE WERE DEMONSTRATIONS FOR AND AGAINST THE VEIL.

AT ONE OF THE DEMONSTRATIONS, A GERMAN JOURNALIST TOOK A PHOTO OF MY MOTHER.

I WAS REALLY PROUD OF HER. HER PHOTO WAS PUBLISHED IN ALL THE EUROPEAN NEWSPAPERS.

AND EVEN IN ONE MAGAZINE IN IRAN. MY MOTHER WAS REALLY SCARED.

HAVE YOU SEEN THIS?

DON'T WORRY, DARLING.

SHE DYED HER HAIR,

AND WORE DARK GLASSES FOR A LONG TIME.

I REALLY DIDN'T KNOW WHAT TO THINK ABOUT THE VEIL. DEEP DOWN I WAS VERY RELIGIOUS BUT AS A FAMILY WE WERE VERY MODERN AND AVANT-GARDE.

I WAS BORN WITH RELIGION.

AT THE AGE OF SIX I WAS ALREADY SURE I WAS THE LAST PROPHET. THIS WAS A FEW YEARS BEFORE THE REVOLUTION.

O' Celestial light!

BEFORE ME THERE HAD BEEN A FEW OTHERS.

A WOMAN?

I AM THE LAST PROPHET.

I WANTED TO BE A PROPHET...

BECAUSE OUR MAID DID NOT EAT WITH US.

BECAUSE MY FATHER HAD A CADILLAC.

AND, ABOVE ALL, BECAUSE MY GRANDMOTHER'S KNEES ALWAYS ACHED.

COME HERE MARJI! HELP ME TO STAND UP.

DON'T WORRY. SOON YOU WON'T HAVE ANY MORE PAIN. YOU'LL SEE.

LIKE ALL MY PREDECESSORS I HAD MY HOLY BOOK.

THE FIRST THREE RULES CAME FROM ZARATHUSTRA. HE WAS THE FIRST PROPHET IN MY COUNTRY BEFORE THE ARAB INVASION.

YOU MUST BASE EVERYTHING ON THESE THREE RULES: BEHAVE WELL, SPEAK WELL, ACT WELL.

I ALSO WANTED US TO CELEBRATE THE TRADITIONAL ZARATHUSTRIAN HOLIDAYS, LIKE THE FIRE CEREMONY,

BEFORE THE PERSIAN NEW YEAR, NOROUZ, ON MARCH 21ST, THE FIRST DAY OF SPRING.

ONLY MY GRANDMOTHER KNEW ABOUT MY BOOK.

RULE NUMBER SIX: EVERY-BODY SHOULD HAVE A CAR.

RULE NUMBER SEVEN: ALL MAIDS SHOULD EAT AT THE TABLE WITH THE OTHERS.

RULE NUMBER EIGHT: NO OLD PER-SON SHOULD HAVE TO SUFFER.

IN THAT CASE, I'LL BE YOUR FIRST DISCIPLE.

REALLY?

BUT TELL ME HOW YOU'LL ARRANGE FOR OLD PEOPLE NOT TO SUFFER?

IT WILL SIMPLY BE FORBIDDEN.

Marjane Satrapi

When Marjane Satrapi's series of comic strips entitled *Persepolis: The Story of a Childhood*, depicting the impact of Iran's cultural revolution on her life there, was published in France in 2001, it was an immediate success. In 2007, the comic strips were made into a critically acclaimed film. Satrapi works from a unique perspective: She was born in Iran in 1969, the daughter of Marxists and the great-granddaughter of an emperor. She began her education at a French school in Tehran, but by 1980 Islamic fundamentalists had outlawed bilingual education. They also forced even young girls to wear the veil. In 1984 Satrapi left Iran to study in Austria and then in France.

In a recent interview Satrapi described how her cultural identity has shifted over time. When she arrived in France, she wanted only to assimilate; later she began to reclaim an Iranian identity. Satrapi comments that whereas most people have a one-word answer when asked where they come from, "for an Iranian, it's a one-hour explanation: 'I am Iranian but . . .' Today I just say 'I am Iranian.'"

Satrapi, who now lives and writes in Paris, has written a sequel to *Persepolis* entitled *Persepolis 2: The Story of a Return* (2004) as well as *Embroideries* (2005), *Chicken with Plums* (2006), and several children's books.

SEEING

1. Representations of both public and private moments recur throughout "The Veil." What visual cues help signal a public moment? a private moment? How do men and women figure in both? What do her drawings suggest about Satrapi's attitudes toward gender in public spaces in Iran? How did her attitudes change over time?

2. In "The Veil" Satrapi depicts several groupings of people—a class photograph, an angry mob, small groups of children at play—all framed and arranged in distinctive ways. Which of these arrangements seems most realistic to you? Which seems most impressionistic? How do you think Satrapi made her framing decisions? To what extent are they effective? How does she use labeled images at the beginning of the piece to add resonance to later images that she does not explain fully?

WRITING

1. Consider the point where Satrapi chooses to end "The Veil." In what ways does this seem an appropriate ending to you? In what ways do you find it surprising? At what other points in the story might Satrapi have stopped? Write a short essay in which you take the story Satrapi tells to a point in the future – a day later, a week later, or years later. How does this exercise change your understanding of the arc Satrapi has established?

2. In "The Veil" Satrapi describes both a moment of great social change and a series of private events or emotions that help her frame that change and understand its meaning. Think of a moment from your childhood that you thought of as personal but later understood to be part of a wider event or social movement, and then write the first draft of an essay about it.

Visit *seeingandwriting.com* for an interactive exercise based on "The Veil."

Responding Visually

Use images and text to compose the first draft of a recollection of a significant change or event from your childhood. Your images can be personal photographs or drawings, or photographs or drawings cut out from magazines. Write short (one or two sentences) captions to accompany them. Borrowing from Satrapi's first frame in "The Veil," begin your piece with a single image and the text "This is me when I was ____ years old. This was in _____." Limit your first draft to three pages.

"The Veil" is the first chapter of Marjane Satrapi's book *Persepolis*. In the book's introduction, which follows, the author offers an overview of the political and historical context for the experiences she describes as a child growing up in Iran.

She also discusses her purpose in writing *Persepolis*. How would you characterize that purpose? Reread "The Veil" with Satrapi's purpose in mind. To what extent do you think she has achieved her compositional purpose?

Introduction

In the second millennium B.C., while the Elam nation was developing a civilization alongside Babylon, Indo-European invaders gave their name to the immense Iranian plateau where they settled. The word "Iran" was derived from "Ayryana Vaejo," which means "the origin of the Aryans." These people were semi-nomads whose descendants were the Medes and the Persians. The Medes founded the first Iranian nation in the seventh century B.C.; it was later destroyed by Cyrus the Great. He established what became one of the largest empires of the ancient world, the Persian Empire, in the sixth century B.C. Iran was referred to as Persia—its Greek name—until 1935 when Reza Shah, the father of the last Shah of Iran, asked everyone to call the country Iran.

Iran was rich. Because of its wealth and its geographic location, it invited attacks: From Alexander the Great, from its Arab neighbors to the west, from Turkish and Mongolian conquerors, Iran was often subject to foreign domination. Yet the Persian language and culture withstood these invasions. The invaders assimilated into this strong culture, and in some ways they became Iranians themselves.

In the twentieth century, Iran entered a new phase. Reza Shah decided to modernize and westernize the country, but meanwhile a fresh source of wealth was discovered: oil. And with the oil came another invasion. The West, particularly Great Britain, wielded a strong influence on the Iranian economy. During the Second World War, the British, Soviets, and Americans asked Reza Shah to ally himself with them against Germany. But Reza Shah, who sympathized with the Germans, declared Iran a neutral zone. So the Allies invaded and occupied Iran. Reza Shah was sent into exile and was succeeded by his son, Mohammad Reza Pahlavi, who was known simply as the Shah.

In 1951, Mohammed Mossadeq, then prime minister of Iran, nationalized the oil industry. In retaliation, Great Britain organized an embargo on all exports of oil from Iran. In 1953, the CIA, with the help of British intelligence, organized a coup against him. Mossadeq was overthrown and the Shah, who had earlier escaped from the country, returned to power. The Shah stayed on the throne until 1979, when he fled Iran to escape the Islamic revolution.

Since then, this old and great civilization has been discussed mostly in connection with fundamentalism, fanaticism, and terrorism. As an Iranian who has lived more than half of my life in Iran, I know that this image is far from the truth. This is why writing *Persepolis* was so important to me. I believe that an entire nation should not be judged by the wrongdoings of a few extremists. I also don't want those Iranians who lost their lives in prisons defending freedom, who died in the war against Iraq, who suffered under various repressive regimes, or who were forced to leave their families and flee their homeland to be forgotten.

One can forgive but one should never forget.

Marjane Satrapi
Paris, September 2002

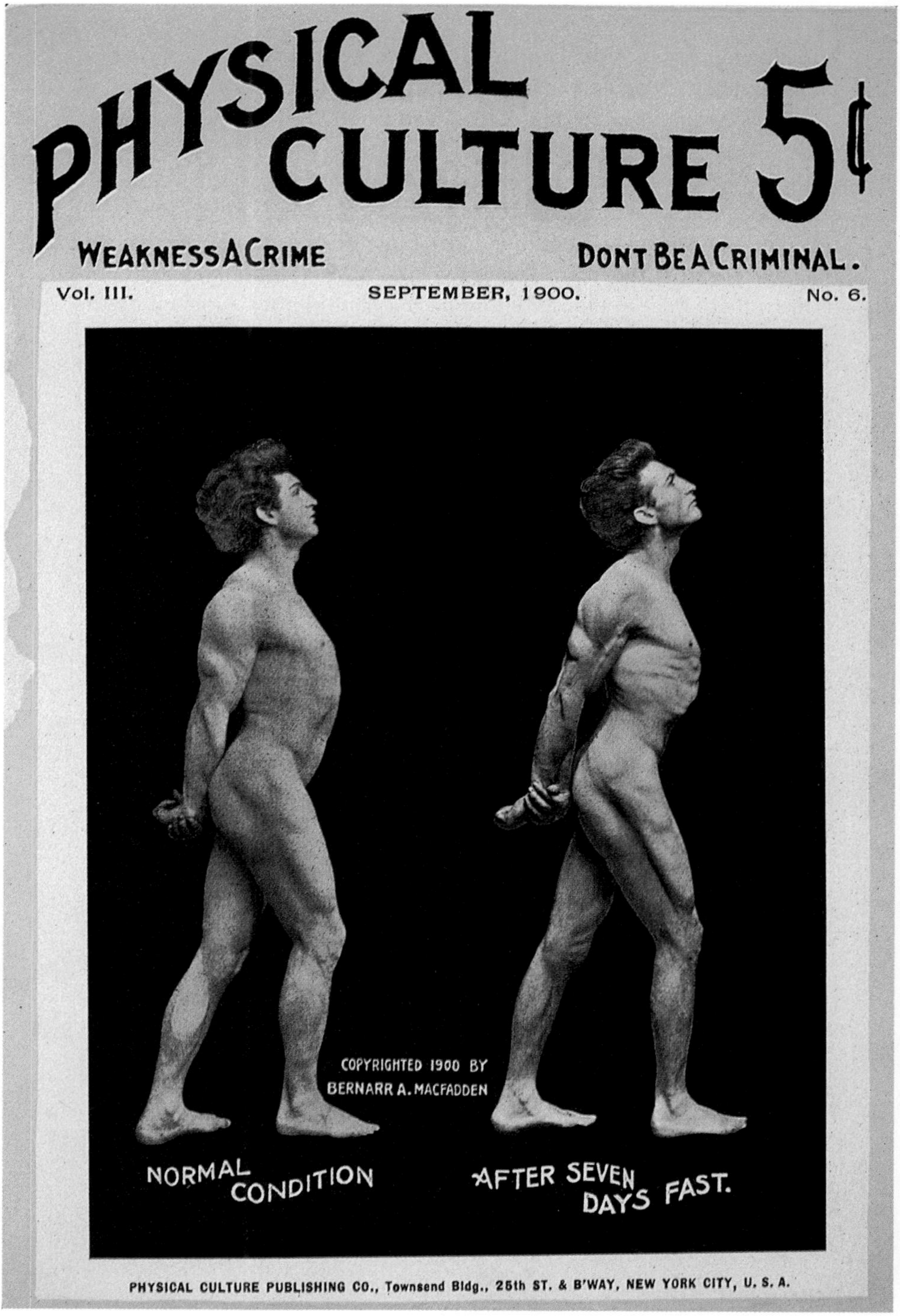
PHYSICAL CULTURE 5¢
WEAKNESS A CRIME
DONT BE A CRIMINAL.
Vol. III.
SEPTEMBER, 1900.
No. 6.
COPYRIGHTED 1900 BY
BERNARR A. MACFADDEN
NORMAL CONDITION
AFTER SEVEN DAYS FAST.
PHYSICAL CULTURE PUBLISHING CO., Townsend Bldg., 25th ST. & B'WAY, NEW YORK CITY, U. S. A.

1900

I Can Make YOU a New Man, Too, in Only 15 Minutes a Day!

If YOU, like Joe, have a body that others can "push around"— if you're ashamed to strip for sports or a swim—then give me just 15 minutes a day! I'll PROVE you can have a body you'll be proud of, packed with red-blooded vitality! "*Dynamic Tension*." That's the secret! That's how I changed myself from a spindle-shanked, scrawny weakling to winner of the title, "World's Most Perfectly Developed Man."

"Dynamic Tension" Does It!

Using "*Dynamic Tension*" only 15 minutes a day, in the privacy of your own room, you quickly begin to put on muscle, increase your chest measurements, broaden your back, fill out your arms and legs. Before you know it, this easy,

NATURAL method will make you a finer specimen of REAL MAN-HOOD than you ever dreamed you could be! You'll be a New Man!

FREE Info Kit

Thousands of fellows have used my marvelous system. Read what **my Amazing Info Kit talks about!**

Send NOW for this **Info Kit** It tells all about "*Dynamic Tension*," shows you actual photos of men I've turned from puny weaklings into Atlas Champions. It tells how I can do the same for YOU. Don't put it off! Address me personally: Charles Atlas.

Charles Atlas

—*actual photo of the man who holds the title, "The World's Most Perfectly Developed Man."*

1944

Charles Atlas®, "How Joe's Body Brought Him Fame Instead of Shame" copyright 2008, under license from Charles Atlas, Ltd. PO Box "D" Madison Square Station NY, NY 10159 (www.CharlesAtlas.com)

How Relax-A-cizor Reduces the Size of your Waistline...

Effortless exercise does it while you REST!

What happened to your waistline? Have those belly muscles "stretched-out-of-shape"? And — you KNOW you need exercise but don't want to take the time.

NOW — there's a way! Now you can reduce the size of your abdomen and waistline . . . firm-up and tone those muscles with real exercise . . . while you REST at home! Or, do it at the office while you do your desk-work. About ½ hour a day is all the time it takes! Relax-A-cizor gives exercise WHILE YOU TAKE IT EASY!

■ **NOT A VIBRATOR ■ NOT MASSAGE ■ NOT A BICYCLE ■ NOT A COUCH ■ No weight loss!** Relax-A-cizor does not cause or depend upon weight loss. Instead, it reduces SIZE by exercising and firming selected areas of muscles — and does this without effort. Doesn't make you tired; you REST while you use it. Read a book. Watch TV. Take it easy — that's the Relax-A-cizor way.

■ This is Relax-A-cizor being used with the abdominal belt. Slip it on and, in minutes, you're ready for your exercises while you REST!

Easy to use! Compact. All you do is put a pair of Relax-A-cizor pads on the body area you want reduced in size . . . twist a dial and, presto, you're exercising — *really* exercising — those muscles. Those abdominal muscles move 40 times a minute! 1200 times in a ½ hour! This concentrated, active exercise gives those waistline and abdominal muscles that "hold-you-in" a real workout!

Why Relax-A-cizor works. Many men lack good muscle tone because they don't get enough exercise. Relax-A-cizor exercises — but, without effort — such body areas as the waistline and abdomen 40 times a minute. This exercise firms and tones these muscles. Regular use causes these areas to reduce in size measurably to the extent these muscles lack tone because of insufficient exercise. And the less the muscle tone, the greater the degree of size reduction.

FOR WOMEN, TOO! Relax-A-cizor is the luxuriously effortless way to reduce the size of hips, waistline, abdomen and thighs. Relax-A-cizor beauty exercises tone and firm these muscles without a whit of work. Send coupon for free illustrated information.

OTHER USES, TOO: You'll use your Relax-A-cizor for restful, invigorating exercise of tense, tired muscles of shoulders, back, neck, arms and legs. Feels great!

FREE! Find out all about it. Send coupon TODAY and we'll mail your complete information and the free men's booklet "HOW TO REDUCE THE SIZE OF YOUR WAISTLINE." No cost. No obligation.

PRINCIPAL OFFICES: NEW YORK, NEW YORK, 575 Madison Ave., MU 8-4690/CHICAGO, ILL., 29 East Madison St., ST 2-5680/LOS ANGELES, CAL., 980 N. La Cienega Bl., OL 5-8000. Available in Canada, Mexico City, Hong Kong, Manila, Milan *(foreign franchises available)*

RelaxAcizor®

Free!

Relax-A-cizor, Dept. 20-603
980 No. La Cienega Blvd.
Los Angeles, California 90054
Please mail me free information about how to reduce the size of waistline and abdomen. No cost. No obligation.

☐ MR.   ☐ MRS.   ☐ MISS

NAME _____

ADDRESS _____

CITY _____   STATE _____

ZIP _____   PHONE _____

☐ I am under 18.   ☐ I am over 18.   20-603 707

© Relax-A-cizor 1967

1967

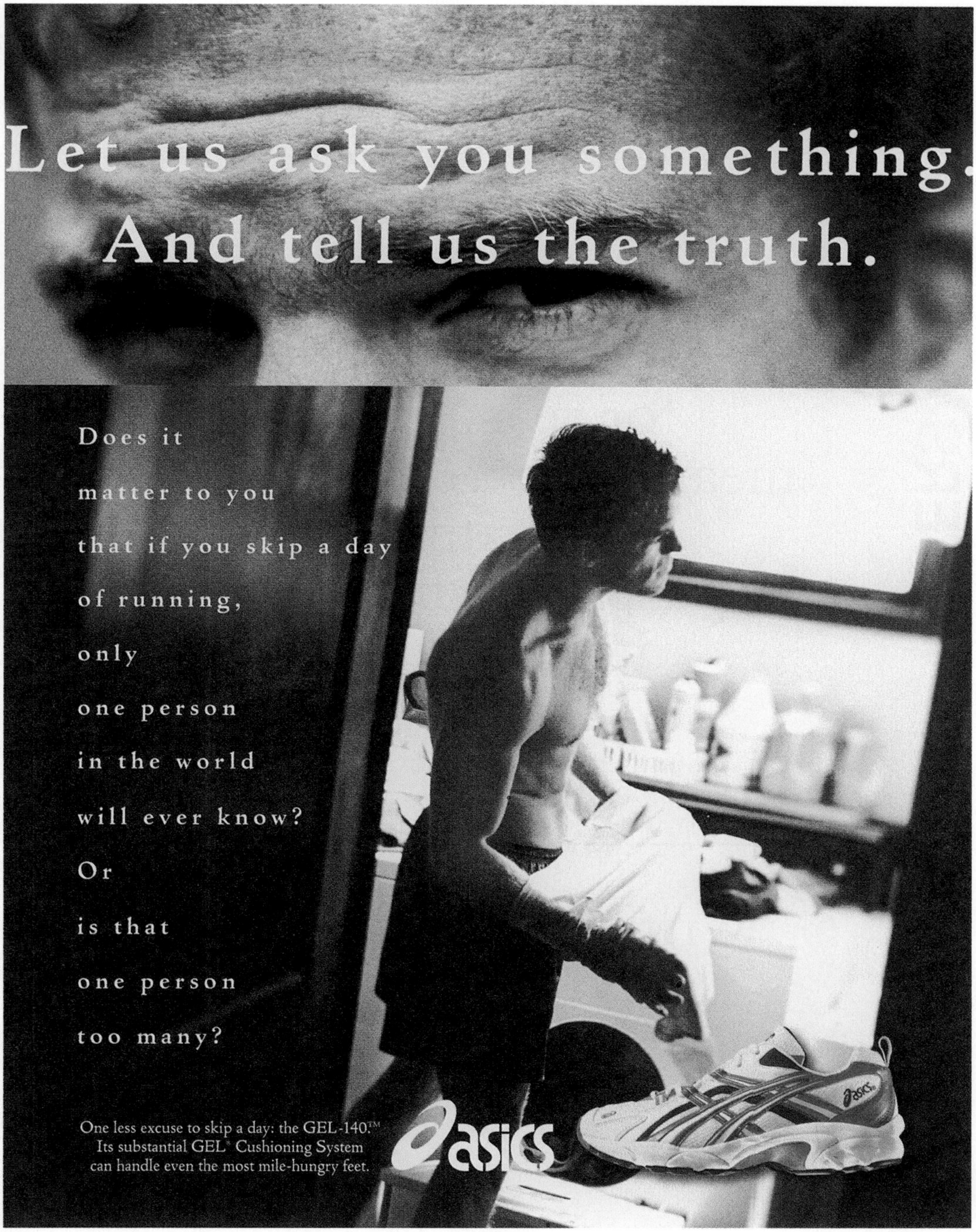

Let us ask you something.
And tell us the truth.

Does it
matter to you
that if you skip a day
of running,
only
one person
in the world
will ever know?
Or
is that
one person
too many?

One less excuse to skip a day: the GEL-140.™
Its substantial GEL® Cushioning System
can handle even the most mile-hungry feet.

asics

1999

I end up writing so much for reasons which mean little to me.... When my writing has a purpose, I find myself most productive.

Andy Coen, student at
Southern Polytechnic State University

Writing is making sense out of life.

Nadine Gordimer, political activist
and recipient of the Nobel Prize in Literature

VISUALIZING COMPOSITION:
PURPOSE

Your PURPOSE is your reason for writing. You write with a goal in mind and your PURPOSE provides the direction for your writing. Think of PURPOSE like a lighthouse that guides you along a path toward a specific compositional destination.

Before you write ask yourself some questions:

IS YOUR ESSAY MEANT TO DESCRIBE, NARRATE, EXPLAIN, CONVINCE OR PERSUADE? WHAT RESPONSES DO YOU WANT YOUR WRITING TO EVOKE IN READERS? WHAT CONSEQUENCES DO YOU WANT YOUR WRITING TO PRODUCE?

Some of the most common purposes of writing are to DEFINE, to CLASSIFY, to ILLUSTRATE, to COMPARE, to CONTRAST, to DRAW ANALOGY, to ANALYZE, and to ESTABLISH CAUSE—AND—EFFECT RELATIONSHIPS.

My purpose then is to... Convince people that solar power could replace fossil fuels as an energy source in the future. And I need to include evidence that proves this.

Right, so your purpose is to write an ARGUMENT that PERSUADES your reader that solar power can replace fossil fuels.

Advertisements offer the most common examples of persuasion in American culture.

Wow, NEW BRIGHTO really does make my clothes cleaner than my old laundry detergent!!!

SPECIFIC CLAIM

WASHED WITH OLD LAUNDRY DETERGENT

SUPPORTING EVIDENCE

WASHED WITH NEW BRIGHTO

When the purpose of an essay is stated directly, it is often called the...

THESIS STATEMENT

Although the thesis statement expresses what you are trying to achieve in writing, it doesn't explain your purpose. Your writing will be stronger if you have a clear purpose and a thesis statement in mind before you begin writing.

NOTES:
THESIS STATEMENT:
Solar power can replace fossil fuels.
PURPOSE:
Persuade readers of the student newspaper that fossil fuels are bad for the environment, and the US should invest in solar power.

Hooray!

EVIDENCE:

PORTFOLIO—Burson

Nancy Burson

Born in St. Louis in 1948, Nancy Burson was trained as a painter, but soon after moving to New York in 1968 became interested in combining computer technology (then in its infancy) with photography. A project proposal "to simulate the aging process" led to a collaboration with MIT engineers and the development of computer programs to predict facial changes through aging, such as those now used to find long-missing children, identify criminal suspects, and plan reconstructive surgery. In fact, Burson received a patent for the technology in 1981. Her further work also involved manipulating the human face through computer technology. She became most well known in the 1980s for her composites of human faces; for instance, she created a composite of all of the world's races based on population proportions and a composite of world leaders as a means of showing what "the face of power" looks like.

Shifting her focus in the 1990s, Burson continued to use the human face as her subject, but in a more direct way. For example, in her *Faces* series (1993) she presented realistic and nonexploitative photographs of children and adults with startling facial deformities. Burson explains that the androgynous images here, from the He/She series (1997–98), are "more about the commonality of people rather than about their differences or separateness. They're meant to challenge the individual's notions of self-perception and self-acceptance by allowing viewers to see beyond superficial sexual differences to our common humanity."

More recently Burson's work has been featured in a traveling retrospective entitled Seeing Is Believing, and she has devised a "human race machine" that scans a person's face and alters it to show what that person would look like if he or she were of a different race.

SEEING

1. Carefully examine each of Nancy Burson's photographs. In your judgment, which are portraits of a man? of a woman? What evidence can you point to in each image to verify your reading? Do you find it easier to determine the subject's gender in some of these photographs than in others? Why? How do your choices compare with those of your classmates?

2. In these photographs Burson set out to mask her subjects' gender. To that end, what artistic choices did she make? What aspects of each subject has she chosen to highlight? What does she conceal? What might these choices reveal about the ways in which we all subconsciously differentiate between men and women?

WRITING

1. The He/She series attempts, in Burson's words, "to see beyond superficial sexual differences." Yet the images tease viewers with an implicit question: He or she? In an essay, explain why you think many people find it so important to be able to identify an individual's gender. What cultural assumptions does androgyny challenge?

2. Write an essay in which you compare and contrast Burson's portraits with Mapplethorpe's two self-portraits (pp. 320–21). Setting aside the differences between a portrait and a self-portrait, what statements about gender is each of these artists making? How would you compare their artistic techniques and styles? How do these images illustrate the social construction of masculinity and femininity?

Page 320

NEVER JUST PICTURES
Susan Bordo

When Alicia Silverstone, the svelte nineteen-year-old star of *Clueless*, appeared at the Academy Awards just a smidge more substantial than she had been in the movie, the tabloids ribbed her cruelly, calling her "fat-girl" and "buttgirl" (her next movie role is Batgirl) and "more *Babe* than babe."[1] Our idolatry of the trim, tight body shows no signs of relinquishing its grip on our conceptions of beauty and normality. Since I began exploring this obsession it seems to have gathered momentum, like a spreading mass hysteria. Fat is the devil, and we are continually beating him—"eliminating" our stomachs, "busting" our thighs, "taming" our tummies—pummeling and purging our bodies, attempting to make them into something other than flesh. On television, infomercials hawking miracle diet pills and videos promising to turn our body parts into steel have become as commonplace as aspirin ads. There hasn't been a tabloid cover in the past few years that didn't boast of an inside scoop on some star's diet regime, a "fabulous" success story of weight loss, or a tragic relapse. (When they can't come up with a current one, they scrounge up an old one; a few weeks ago the *National Enquirer* ran a story on Joan Lunden's fifty-pound weight loss fifteen years ago!) Children in this culture grow up knowing that you can never be thin enough and that being fat is one of the worst things one can be. One study asked ten- and eleven-year-old boys and girls to rank drawings of children with various physical handicaps; drawings of fat children elicited the greatest disapproval and discomfort, over pictures of kids with facial disfigurements and missing hands.

Psychologists commonly believe that girls with eating disorders suffer from "body image disturbance syndrome": They are unable to see themselves as anything but fat, no matter how thin they become. If this is a disorder, it is one that has become a norm of cultural perception. Our ideas about what constitutes a body in need of a diet have become more and more pathologically trained on the slightest hint of excess. This ideal of the body beautiful has largely come from fashion designers and models.

---

1. I give great credit to Alicia Silverstone for her response to these taunts. In *Vanity Fair* she says, "I do my best. But it's much more important to me that my brain be working in the morning than getting up early and doing exercise. . . . The most important thing for me is that I eat and that I sleep and that I get the work done, but unfortunately . . . it's the perception that women in film should look a certain way" ("Hollywood Princess," September 1996, pp. 292–294). One wonders how long she will manage to retain such a sane attitude! [All notes are Bordo's unless otherwise specified.]

(Movie stars, who often used to embody a more voluptuous ideal, are now modeling themselves after the models.) They have taught us "to love a woman's pelvis, her hipbones jutting out through a bias-cut gown . . . the clavicle in its role as a coat hanger from which clothes are suspended."[2] (An old fashion industry justification for skinniness in models was that clothes just don't "hang right" on heftier types.) The fashion industry has taught us to regard a perfectly healthy, nonobese body such as the one depicted in figure 1 [p. 373] as an unsightly "before" ("Before CitraLean, no wonder they wore swimsuits like that"). In fact, those in the business have admitted that models have been getting thinner since 1993, when Kate Moss first repopularized the waif look. British models Trish Goff and Annie Morton make Moss look well fed by comparison,[3] and recent ad campaigns for Jil Sander go way beyond the thin-body-as-coat-hanger paradigm to a blatant glamorization of the cadaverous, starved look itself.* More and more ads featuring anorexic-looking young men are appearing too.

The main challenge to such images is a muscular aesthetic that *looks* more life-affirming but is no less punishing and compulsion-inducing in its demands on ordinary bodies. During the 1996 Summer Olympics—which were reported with unprecedented focus and hype on the fat-free beauty of muscular bodies—commentators celebrated the "health" of this aesthetic over anorexic glamour. But there is growing evidence of rampant eating disorders among female athletes, and it's hard to imagine that those taut and tiny Olympic gymnasts—the idols of preadolescents across the country—are having regular menstrual cycles. Their skimpy level of body fat just won't support it. During the Olympics I heard a commentator gushing about how great it was that the 1996 team was composed predominantly of eighteen- and nineteen-year-old women rather than little girls. To me it is far more disturbing that these nineteen-year-olds still *look* (and talk) like little girls! As I watched them vault and leap, my admiration for their tremendous skill and spirit was shadowed by thoughts

---

2. Holly Brubach, "The Athletic Esthetic," the *New York Times Magazine*, June 23, 1996, p. 51.

3. In early 1996 the Swiss watch manufacturer Omega threatened to stop advertising in British *Vogue* because of *Vogue*'s use of such hyperthin models, but it later reversed this decision. The furor was reminiscent of boycotts that were threatened in 1994 when Calvin Klein and Coca-Cola first began to use photos of Kate Moss in their ads. In neither case has the fashion industry acknowledged any validity to the charge that their imagery encourages eating disorders. Instead, they have responded with defensive "rebuttals."

* For reasons of copyright, we are unable to reproduce the Jil Sander advertisement shown in Bordo's essay [eds.].

of what was going on *inside* their bodies—the hormones unreleased because of insufficient body fat, the organ development delayed, perhaps halted.

Is it any wonder that despite media attention to the dangers of starvation dieting and habitual vomiting, eating disorders have spread throughout the culture?[4] In 1993 in *Unbearable Weight* I argued that the old clinical generalizations positing distinctive class, race, family, and "personality" profiles for the women most likely to develop an eating disorder were being blasted apart by the normalizing power of mass imagery. Some feminists complained that I had not sufficiently attended to racial and ethnic "difference" and was assuming the white, middle-class experience as the norm. Since then it has been widely acknowledged among medical professionals that the incidence of eating and body-image problems among African American, Hispanic, and Native American women has been grossly underestimated and is on the increase.[5] Even the gender gap is being narrowed, as more and more men are developing eating disorders and exercise compulsions too. (In the mid-eighties the men in my classes used to yawn and pass notes when we discussed the pressure to diet; in 1996 they are more apt to protest if the women in the class talk as though it's their problem alone.)

5   The spread of eating disorders, of course, is not just about images. The emergence of eating disorders is a complex, multilayered cultural "symptom," reflecting problems that are historical as well as contemporary, arising in our time because of the confluence of a number of factors.[6] Eating disorders are overdetermined in this culture. They have to do not only with new social expectations of women and ambivalence toward their bodies but also with more general anxieties about the body as the source of hungers, needs, and physical vulnerabilities not within our control. These anxieties are deep and long-standing in Western philosophy and religion, and they are especially acute in our own time. Eating disorders are also

---

4. Despite media attention to eating disorders, an air of scornful impatience with "victim feminism" has infected attitudes toward women's body issues. Christina Hoff-Sommers charges Naomi Wolf (*The Beauty Myth*) with grossly inflating statistics on eating disorders and she pooh-poohs the notion that women are dying from dieting. Even if some particular set of statistics is inaccurate, why would Sommers want to deny the reality of the problem, which as a teacher she can surely see right before her eyes?

5. For the spread of eating disorders in minority groups, see, for example, "The Art of Integrating Diversity: Addressing Treatment Issues of Minority Women in the 90's," in *The Renfrew Perspective*, Winter 1994; see also Becky Thompson, *A Hunger So Wide and So Deep* (Minneapolis: University of Minnesota Press, 1994).

6. See my *Unbearable Weight* (Berkeley: University of California Press, 1993).

linked to the contradictions of consumer culture, which is continually encouraging us to binge on our desires at the same time as it glamorizes self-discipline and scorns fat as a symbol of laziness and lack of will-power. And these disorders reflect, too, our increasing fascination with the possibilities of reshaping our bodies and selves in radical ways, creating new bodies according to our mind's design.

The relationship between problems such as these and cultural images is complex. On the one hand, the idealization of certain kinds of bodies foments and perpetuates our anxieties and insecurities, that's clear. Glamorous images of hyperthin models certainly don't encourage a more relaxed or accepting attitude toward the body, particularly among those whose own bodies are far from that ideal. But, on the other hand, such images carry fantasized solutions to our anxieties and insecurities, and that's part of the reason why they are powerful. They speak to us not just about how to be beautiful or desirable but about how to get control of our lives, get safe, be cool, avoid hurt. When I look at the picture of a skeletal and seemingly barely breathing young woman in figure 2 [p. 373], for example, I do not see a vacuous fashion ideal. I see a visual embodiment of what novelist and ex-anorexic Stephanie Grant means when she says in her autobiographical novel, *The Passion of Alice*, "If I had to say my anorexia was about any single thing, I would have said it was about living without desire. Without longing of any kind."[7]

Now, this may not seem like a particularly attractive philosophy of life (or a particularly attractive body, for that matter). Why would anyone want to look like death, you might be asking. Why would anyone want to live without desire? But recent articles in both *The New Yorker* and the *New York Times* have noted a new aesthetic in contemporary ads, in which the models appear dislocated and withdrawn, with chipped black nail polish and greasy hair, staring out at the viewer in a deathlike trance, seeming to be "barely a person." Some have called this wasted look "heroin chic": Ex-model Zoe Fleischauer recalls that "they wanted models that looked like junkies. The more skinny and fucked-up you look, the more everybody thinks you're fabulous."[8]

Hilton Als, in *The New Yorker*, interprets this trend as making the statement that fashion is dead and beauty is "trivial in relation to depression."[9] I read these ads very differently. Although the photographers may see

---

7. Stephanie Grant, *The Passion of Alice* (New York: Houghton Mifflin, 1995), 58.

8. Zoe Fleischauer quoted in "Rockers, Models, and the New Allure of Heroin," *Newsweek*, August 26, 1996.

9. Hilton Als, "Buying the Fantasy," *The New Yorker*, October 10, 1996, p. 70.

themselves as ironically "deconstructing" fashion, the reality is that no fashion advertisement can declare fashion to be dead—it's virtually a grammatical impossibility. Put that frame around the image, whatever the content, and we are instructed to find it glamorous. These ads are not telling us that beauty is trivial in relation to depression, they are telling us that depression is beautiful, that being wasted is *cool*. The question then becomes not "Is fashion dead?" but "Why has death become glamorous?"

Freud tells us that in the psyche death represents not the destruction of the self but its return to a state prior to need, thus freedom from unfulfilled longing, from anxiety over not having one's needs met. Following Freud, I would argue that ghostly pallor and bodily disrepair, in "heroin chic" images, are about the allure, the safety, of being beyond needing, beyond caring, beyond desire. Should we be surprised at the appeal of being without desire in a culture that has invested our needs with anxiety, stress, and danger, that has made us craving and hungering machines, creatures of desire, and then repaid us with addictions, AIDS, shallow and unstable relationships, and cutthroat competition for jobs and mates? To have given up the quest for fulfillment, to be unconcerned with the body or its needs—or its vulnerability—is much wiser than to care.

10 So, yes, the causes of eating disorders are "deeper" than just obedience to images. But cultural images themselves *are* deep. And the way they become imbued and animated with such power is hardly mysterious. Far from being the purely aesthetic inventions that designers and photographers would like to have us believe they are—"It's just fashion, darling, nothing to get all politically steamed up about"—they reflect the designers' cultural savvy, their ability to sense and give form to flutters and quakes in the cultural psyche. These folks have a strong and simple motivation to hone their skills as cultural Geiger counters. It's called the profit motive. They want their images and the products associated with them to sell.

The profit motive can sometimes produce seemingly "transgressive" wrinkles in current norms. Recently designers such as Calvin Klein and Jil Sander have begun to use rather plain, ordinary-looking, un-madeup faces in their ad campaigns. Unlike the models in "heroin chic" ads, these men and women do not appear wasted so much as unadorned, unpolished, stripped of the glamorous veneer we have come to expect of fashion spreads. While many of them have interesting faces, few of them qualify as beautiful by any prevailing standards. They have rampant freckles, moles in unbeautiful places, oddly proportioned heads. Noticing these ads, I at first wondered whether we really were shifting into a new gear, more genuinely accepting of diversity and "flaws" in appearance. Then it suddenly hit me that these imperfect faces were showing up in clothing and perfume ads only and the *bodies* in these ads were as relentlessly normalizing as ever—not one plump body to complement the facial "diversity."

I now believe that what we are witnessing here is a commercial war. Clothing manufacturers, realizing that many people—particularly young people, at whom most of these ads are aimed—have limited resources and that encouraging them to spend all their money fixing up their faces rather than buying clothes is not in their best interests, are reasserting the importance of body over face as the "site" of our fantasies. In the new codes of these ads a too madeup look signifies a lack of cool, too much investment in how one looks. "Just Be," Calvin Klein tells us in a recent CK One ad. But looks—a lean body—still matter enormously in these ads, and we are still being told *how* to be—in the mode which best serves Calvin Klein. And all the while, of course, makeup and hair products continue to promote their own self-serving aesthetics of facial perfection.

Before.

CitraLean™ is an all-natural maximum strength appetite suppressant that contains the revolutionary new ingredient CitriMax,™ plus a combination of Chromium, Vanadyl Sulfate and Gymnema Sylvestre. This unique combination when taken in conjunction with a balanced diet and exercise, will help curb appetite, speed up calorie burning, help lower cholesterol, inhibit fat production from carbohydrates, reduce food intake and balance sugar metabolism.

Now you can lose weight safely, effectively and naturally without the use of caffeine or chemical stimulants.

Available at General Nutrition Centers and other fine health food stores, or call 1-800-241-9111, ext. 359.

Figure 1
All our mothers needed to diet.

Figure 2
Advertising anorexia?

Susan Bordo

An archeologist of the culture of the body, Susan Bordo (b. 1947) has helped bring body studies to the forefront of feminist intellectual debate. She writes, "The body is a powerful symbolic form, a surface on which the central rules, hierarchies, and even metaphysical commitments of a culture are inscribed, and thus reinforced."

Bordo's best-known book, *Unbearable Weight: Feminism, Western Culture and the Body* (1993), was nominated for a Pulitzer Prize in 1993. In it she explores women's relationships to food, desire, and power. She is also the author of *The Fight to Objectivity: Essays on Cartesianism and Culture* (1987) and the co-editor of a collection of essays entitled *Gender/Body/Knowledge* (1989). The subjects of her numerous articles range from anorexia and cosmetic surgery to the impact of contemporary media. Her work on cultural analysis is exemplified by *Twilight Zones: The Hidden Life of Cultural Images from Plato to O. J.* (1997), from which the essay presented here is drawn. Bordo turned her attention to the male body in *The Male Body: A New Look at Men in Public and in Private* (1999).

Bordo is a professor of English and women's studies at the University of Kentucky, where she holds the Otis A. Singletary Chair in the Humanities. A new book, *My Father's Body and Other Unexplored Regions of Masculinity*, is forthcoming.

SEEING

1. Susan Bordo writes that "the spread of eating disorders . . . is not just about images. The emergence of eating disorders is a complex, multilayered cultural 'symptom,' reflecting problems that are historical as well as contemporary" (para. 5). Identify the problems that may have caused the spread of eating disorders. In what ways has the power of mass imagery exacerbated those problems?

In paragraph 7, Bordo introduces the topic of "heroin chic" ads. Along with her own interpretation, she provides several different readings of the messages in and the cultural significance of the ads. Which analysis do you find most convincing? Why? What is your reading of these ads? Where would you position your analysis in relation to the others?

What aspects of the ads does your reading attend to that the others do not?

2. Consider Lauren Greenfield's photograph <u>Ashleigh, 13</u>. Do you think the photograph is an apt illustration of Bordo's point that "children in this culture grow up knowing that you can never be thin enough and that being fat is one of the worst things one can be" (para. 1)? What dimensions to the issues of eating disorders and body-consciousness does Greenfield's photograph add to Bordo's discussion?

Page 378

WRITING

1. In the opening paragraph, Bordo reminds us that "on television, infomercials hawking miracle diet pills and videos promising to turn our body parts into steel have become as commonplace as aspirin ads." Choose an infomercial and examine it carefully. What appeals and promises does it trade on? What strategies do its producers use to induce viewers to buy the product? Write an expository essay in which you analyze the effectiveness of this infomercial. What recommendations, if any, would you offer to support – or resist – an effort to regulate more carefully the claims made by the promoters of goods and services?

Working with Sources

2. In the final paragraph, Bordo claims that clothing manufacturers "are reasserting the importance of body over face as the 'site' of our fantasies." Locate two or three advertisements aimed at young people, especially those with limited financial resources, and study them. Then write an essay in which you assess the "new codes" of values projected in the ads. What conclusions, however tentative, can you draw about the cultural implications of shifting the "site" of beauty from the face to the body?

Pirelli
Power Is Nothing without Control, 1994

Pirelli

A multinational corporation and a leading manufacturer of tires used by luxury car companies such as Alfa Romeo, Maserati, and Lamborghini, Pirelli often projects in its advertising the fast and sexy qualities associated with these high-end cars. The company began formal advertising in Italy in the late 1880s, and by World War II it was a leader in advertising design, with the distinctive "long P" logo. In 1963 Pirelli published the first *Calendario Pirelli*—the sultry Pirelli calendar that has become an annual tradition. Pirelli views the calendar as a reflection of "the evolution of culture and taste in our society."

The print advertisement included here debuted in 1994 as one of a handful featuring Olympic sprinter and long jumper Carl Lewis. The campaign, which showed Lewis running on water, sprinting up the Statue of Liberty, and long jumping between skyscrapers, represented a shift toward digital imaging and effects in advertising. Today Pirelli's television commercials are popular throughout Europe, and in January 2005 the company premiered a new campaign on the Internet.

SEEING

1. What would you identify as masculine or feminine about the representation of Carl Lewis's body in this advertisement? How would you characterize his body language? Comment, for example, on his facial expression, stance, and posture as well as on his choice of dress and accessories. What message(s) does each help to communicate? On what notions of masculinity and femininity does this advertisement capitalize?

2. Consider the use of the words *power* and *control* in this ad. How do you read their meaning in the phrase "Power is nothing without control"? What is your interpretation of the phrase? How do you interpret the phrase in the context of the Carl Lewis image used in this billboard? What specific aspects of the image support or contradict the phrase?

WRITING

1. How important to the overall effect of the ad is the audience's knowledge that Carl Lewis is an Olympic athlete? Choose two alternate models—a celebrity and an ordinary person—and imagine them in exactly the same dress and stance as Carl Lewis. Write a few paragraphs for each that explore how using the different models would change the impact and meaning of the ad.

Working with Sources

2. Choose a recent advertisement that either explicitly or implicitly invokes notions of masculinity to sell a product. You might, for example, look at an ad featuring a classic American male—a Ralph Lauren ad, for example. Write the first draft of an essay in which you compare and contrast that representation of masculinity with the ad here.

LOOKING CLOSER – Engendering Identity

We Americans – inspired by infomercials, make-overs on talk shows, ads for the hottest lines of clothing – are continually reinventing ourselves. Each of us creates and expresses identities through our physical appearance and by asso- ciating ourselves with particular objects, roles, and fashion images and statements. How do you create an identity for yourself? How do you choose to present your personal style?

A crucial component of personal style is gender. Art Spiegelman, a puzzled parent in *Nature vs. Nurture*, suggests that genetics plays the larger role in defining gender. Katha Pollitt acknowledges that "most boys don't play with dolls," but she attributes that to the pervasive influence of the fashion industry and to other cultural pressures. The impact of those pres- sures on adolescents and older teens is clearly visible in Lauren Greenfield's *Ashleigh, 13*, and in Brian Finke's *Untitled (Cheerleading #81)* and *Untitled (Football #75).* And by both reinforcing and subverting traditional male and female roles, the U.S. Military's ad tells us those pressures continue to be felt into adulthood.

Lauren Greenfield
Ashleigh, 13, with Her Friend and Parents, Santa Monica, 1997

WHY BOYS DON'T PLAY WITH DOLLS
Katha Pollitt

It's twenty-eight years since the founding of NOW,[1] and boys still like trucks and girls still like dolls. Increasingly, we are told that the source of these robust preferences must lie outside society—in prenatal hormonal influences, brain chemistry, genes—and that feminism has reached its natural limits. What else could possibly explain the love of preschool girls for party dresses or the desire of toddler boys to own more guns than Mark from Michigan?

True, recent studies claim to show small cognitive differences between the sexes: He gets around by orienting himself in space; she does it by remembering landmarks. Time will tell if any deserve the hoopla with which each is invariably greeted, over the protests of the researchers themselves. But even if the results hold up (and the history of such research is not encouraging), we don't need studies of sex-differentiated brain activity in reading, say, to understand why boys and girls still seem so unalike.

The feminist movement has done much for some women, and something for every woman, but it has hardly turned America into a playground free of sex roles. It hasn't even got women to stop dieting or men to stop interrupting them.

Instead of looking at kids to "prove" that differences in behavior by sex are innate, we can look at the ways we raise kids as an index to how unfinished the feminist revolution really is, and how tentatively it is embraced even by adults who fully expect their daughters to enter previously male-dominated professions and their sons to change diapers.

5   I'm at a children's birthday party. "I'm sorry," one mom silently mouths to the mother of the birthday girl, who has just torn open her present— Tropical Splash Barbie. Now, you can love Barbie or you can hate Barbie, and there are feminists in both camps. But apologize for Barbie? Inflict Barbie, against your own convictions, on the child of a friend you know will be none too pleased?

Every mother in that room had spent years becoming a person who had to be taken seriously, not least by herself. Even the most attractive, I'm willing to bet, had suffered over her body's failure to fit the impossible American ideal. Given all that, it seems crazy to transmit Barbie to the

---

1. *NOW*: National Organization for Women. [Eds.]

next generation. Yet to reject her is to say that what Barbie represents—being sexy, thin, stylish—is unimportant, which is obviously not true, and children know it's not true.

Women's looks matter terribly in this society, and so Barbie, however ambivalently, must be passed along. After all, there are worse toys. The Cut and Style Barbie styling head, for example, a grotesque object intended to encourage "hair play." The grown-ups who give that probably apologize, too.

How happy would most parents be to have a child who flouted sex conventions? I know a lot of women, feminists, who complain in a comical, eyeball-rolling way about their sons' passion for sports: the ruined weekends, obnoxious coaches, macho values. But they would not think of discouraging their sons from participating in this activity they find so foolish. Or do they? Their husbands are sports fans, too, and they like their husbands a lot.

Could it be that even sports-resistant moms see athletics as part of manliness? That if their sons wanted to spend the weekend writing up their diaries, or reading, or baking, they'd find it disturbing? Too antisocial? Too lonely? Too gay?

10 Theories of innate differences in behavior are appealing. They let parents off the hook—no small recommendation in a culture that holds moms, and sometimes even dads, responsible for their children's every misstep on the road to bliss and success.

They allow grown-ups to take the path of least resistance to the dominant culture, which always requires less psychic effort, even if it means more actual work: Just ask the working mother who comes home exhausted and nonetheless finds it easier to pick up her son's socks than make him do it himself. They let families buy for their children, without *too* much guilt, the unbelievably sexist junk that the kids, who have been watching commercials since birth, understandably crave.

But the thing the theories do most of all is tell adults that the *adult* world—in which moms and dads still play by many of the old rules even as they question and fidget and chafe against them—is the way it's supposed to be. A girl with a doll and a boy with a truck "explain" why men are from Mars and women are from Venus, why wives do housework and husbands just don't understand.

The paradox is that the world of rigid and hierarchical sex roles evoked by determinist theories is already passing away. Three-year-olds may indeed insist that doctors are male and nurses female, even if their own mother is a physician. Six-year-olds know better. These days, something like half of all medical students are female, and male applications to nursing school are inching upward. When tomorrow's three-year-olds play doctor, who's to say how they'll assign the roles?

With sex roles, as in every area of life, people aspire to what is possible, and conform to what is necessary. But these are not fixed, especially today. Biological determinism may reassure some adults about their present, but it is feminism, the ideology of flexible and converging sex roles, that fits our children's future. And the kids, somehow, know this.

15   That's why, if you look carefully, you'll find that for every kid who fits a stereotype, there's another who's breaking one down. Sometimes it's the same kid—the boy who skateboards *and* takes cooking in his afterschool program; the girl who collects stuffed animals *and* A-pluses in science.

Feminists are often accused of imposing their "agenda" on children. Isn't that what adults always do, consciously and unconsciously? Kids aren't born religious, or polite, or kind, or able to remember where they put their sneakers. Inculcating these behaviors, and the values behind them, is a tremendous amount of work, involving many adults. We don't have a choice, really, about *whether* we should give our children messages about what it means to be male and female—they're bombarded with them from morning till night.

Brian Finke
Untitled (Cheerleading #81), 2003

Brian Finke
Untitled (Football #75), 2003

When Valerie Vigoda's band GrooveLily tours the United States, they encounter new reasons to turn around and go home every day – long hours, bad food, bad weather, homesickness – things that try to convince them that they'd be better off in some 9-to-5 job or just chillin' on the couch.

PERSEVERANCE

– VALERIE VIGODA
U.S. ARMY ROTC/NATIONAL GUARD 1984-1995

What keeps Valerie going? A deep love of music, an addiction to applause and a few qualities that weren't exactly listed in the course guide at Princeton. Stamina. Follow-through. And what she calls "the ability to play the hand you're dealt."

U.S. Military
Today's Military, 2003

Lauren Greenfield

After graduating from Harvard University in 1987, Lauren Greenfield launched her career with the photographic documentary *Fast Forward: Growing Up in the Shadow of Hollywood* (1997). Her disquieting images capture a wide range of young people, from Beverly Hills debutantes to Los Angeles gang members, all buying into what writer and cultural critic Richard Rodriguez calls "a dream of adolescence." From her own experience growing up in Los Angeles, Greenfield understands how that dream can become a nightmare for those who live it. She offers unremitting criticism of a culture that measures success by how closely one conforms to stereotypical images of power, wealth, and beauty.

Fast Forward, in which *Ashleigh, 13*, appears, received numerous awards. Greenfield's photographs have appeared in *Time*, *Newsweek*, *Vanity Fair*, *Life*, and the *New York Times Magazine*. Recently Greenfield has published two photographic collections, *Girl Culture* (2002) and *Thin* (2006), in which she documents women at a facility for eating disorders.

Art Spiegelman

Born in Sweden in 1948 and raised in New York City, Art Spiegelman won a special Pulitzer Prize for his graphic novel *Maus* (1991), a memoir about the Holocaust. Spiegelman sees nothing odd about addressing weighty subjects in what traditionally has been considered a light medium. Comics are his form of communication – the only way, he says, that he knows how to tell a story. They are also his medium for "trying to understand myself and trying to understand other things." Through his work he has expanded the scope of comics, almost single-handedly showing that cartoon images can hold the interest of serious readers.

Among Spiegelman's numerous books are *The Complete Maus* (1996) and *In the Shadow of No Towers* (2004). In 2005 *Time*

magazine named him one of the top 100 most influential people. His most recent book of comics is *Breakdowns: Portrait of the Artist as a Young %@?*!*

Katha Pollitt

Born in New York City in 1949, Katha Pollitt earned a BA degree from Radcliffe College in 1972. She is a widely published poet and essayist whose writing began appearing in the 1970s in such magazines as *The New Yorker* and *The Atlantic. Antarctic Traveller* (1982), a collection of Pollitt's poems, won a National Book Critics Circle Award. Her book *Reasonable Creatures: Essays on Women and Feminism* appeared in 1994. Pollitt has received numerous honors, including a grant from the National Endowment for the Arts and a Guggenheim Fellowship. Her essays and criticism reach a wide audience through such publications as *Mother Jones*, the *New York Times*, *The New Yorker*, and *The Nation,* where as an associate editor she writes a regularly featured column.

Pollitt's recent books include *Virginity or Death! And Other Social and Political Issues of Our Time* (2006) and *Learning to Drive: And Other Life Stories* (2007). A new collection of poems, *The Mind-Body Problem*, is forthcoming.

Brian Finke

Photographer Brian Finke received a BFA degree from the School of Visual Arts in New York City in 1998. His work has appeared in *The New Yorker*, *Esquire*, the *New York Times Magazine*, *Time*, *Newsweek*, and other publications. His subject matter ranges from child labor in India (a Tides Center project) to the photographs shown here of American college cheerleaders and young football players.

For *2-4-6-8: American Cheerleaders and Football Players* (2003), his first book, Finke was interested in finding the individual sensibilities behind the group image of cheerleaders and football players – in revealing how individuals differed from the group. "These teens struggle between being a part of a group and defining themselves," Finke says. "I am very fortunate to be granted the kind of access to these subjects that allows me to create extremely private and personal images."

His latest book, *Flight Attendants* (2008), depicts the daily working lives of flight attendants around the world.

U.S. Military

In June 2003, only a few months after the United States entered the war in Iraq, the Department of Defense issued a series of print advertisements entitled "Today's Military." The advertisements were designed to attract young people who might be interested in volunteering for the armed services, and their adult parents, teachers, and other mentors. It was hoped that these advertisements would generate a new view of the military among this audience and persuade them not to discourage young people from enlisting.

The eight advertisements presented a variety of Americans who had done military service and highlighted the life skills they had learned from that experience. Although five of the eight ads profiled men, the one featuring Vigoda stood out because it is one of the few military ads to target women as potential military volunteers, and it persuades adults to see women in the role of military personnel.

SEEING

1. How would you summarize Katha Pollitt's analysis of "why boys don't play with dolls"? What are the most compelling aspects of her

argument? the least convincing? Why? Pollitt notes that "the thing the theories do most of all is tell adults that the *adult* world – in which moms and dads still play by many of the old rules even as they question and fidget and chafe against them – is the way it's supposed to be" (para. 12). What exactly is "the way it's supposed to be"?

2. How does the notion of gender training apply to Lauren Greenfield's thirteen-year-old? to Brian Finke's cheerleaders and football players? to the military ad? How does it apply to Art Spiegelman's comic strip? What sort of childhood play is the father encouraging? Imagine the comic strip with no text. What would make you assume that the child is a girl?

WRITING

1. How did toys contribute to your childhood understanding of gender difference? What were your favorite toys or play activities? Would you describe them as typically male or female? Write a two-page recollection of a childhood toy or play activity that somehow informed your notions of masculinity and femininity.

2. Several authors in this book recall childhood experiences with superheroes. See, for example, Judith Ortiz Cofer's "The Story of My Body" (p. 332). What superhero were you fond of as a child? How did this superhero contribute to your childhood notions of what it means to be a man or a woman? How representative is your experience of others your age? Write the first draft of an analytic essay in which you explain the nature of the appeal of superheroes.

Page 332

5

EXAMINING

DIFFERENCE

"The problem of the twentieth century," wrote W. E. B. Du Bois in 1903, "is the problem of the color-line." As we come to the close of the first decade of the twenty-first century, racial and ethnic identity still remain at—or near—the center of many national issues. More than 140 years after the abolition of slavery, and despite civil rights legislation, the election of Barack Obama as president of the United States, and the increasingly prominent presence of people of color in American public life, racial and ethnic inequalities persist in nearly every dimension of American life and culture. In an essay in the *New York Times*, Harvard sociologist Orlando Patterson has called for the abolition of race as a category in the U.S. Census. "Getting rid of racial characterization," he argues, "helps rid America of our biggest myth: that race is a meaningful, valid classification."

Americans have talked about racial and ethnic categories for a long time, and racial issues have been—and continue to be—serious problems in our nation. Yet statistical evidence suggests that most white Americans do not consider themselves to be prejudiced, a function perhaps of a tendency among whites to measure all other identities by a notion of "whiteness." Here's how one white undergraduate describes that phenomenon:

> When Europeans, or Asians or Africans for that matter, think of America, they think of white people, because white people are mainstream, white people are general. . . .

So, if you're a black person trying to assert yourself, and express your culture, there's something wrong with you, because to do that is to be diametrically opposed to everything this country stands for. And everything this country stands for is white. African Americans, Asian Americans, brown Hispanics, and Native Americans have compellingly argued that they cannot mask their color; Irish, Jewish, Italian, and other ethnic groups can. As a result, members of minority groups must learn to educate themselves about the still-dominant white population. As the playwright Angus Wilson has explained, "Blacks know more about whites in white culture and white life than whites know about blacks. We have to know because our survival depends on it. White people's survival does not depend on knowing blacks."

This student's assumptions reflect conceptions about race and ethnicity embedded deep within contemporary American culture. The word *black*, for example, continues to be used in a negative sense: *Black sheep, black magic, blacklist, blackballed, blackmailed*, and *black hole* are but a few of many examples of linguistic prejudice. If prejudice is about ideas—unreasonable judgments or convictions—then discrimination is about behavior—unreasonable treatment based on class or category. Racism is a structural problem, a form of discrimination based on group identity that is grounded in institutional processes of exclusion. As such, racism is a social construct, more a cause than a product of race.

The concept of race has ancient origins that emphasized the physical, linguistic, and cultural differences among groups of people. By the mid-nineteenth century, Western science and culture used the word *race* to classify people on the basis of physical features as well as on the basis of mental and moral behavior. These conceptions of race depended on then-prevailing notions of heredity and superiority. In the nineteenth century, the word *Negro* suggested skin color, hair texture, and other genetic characteristics, *and* inferior social status, especially in cultures where "Negroes" were marked as slaves.

Color has long provided the simplest and most convenient explanation of racial differences among people. By 1805, French comparative anatomist Georges Cuvier had divided the world into three races: white, yellow, and black. Cuvier's theory circulated for generations, not only because it told a seemingly easy-to-verify story about classifying humankind but also because his color categories implied a gradation from superior to inferior.

The publication of Charles Darwin's *On the Origin of Species* (1859) added the notion of natural selection to prevailing racial theory. This principle preserved the hierarchical relationship among the races and added—under the rubric *eugenics*—the possibility of controlling racial development. This way of thinking, called social Darwinism, provided an elaborate explanation for either dominating or marginalizing races labeled inferior as well as a moral impetus for colonizing and "civilizing" them.

By the last decades of the nineteenth century, the widely circulated phrase "white man's burden" conveyed the responsibility of whites to lift the spirits and boost the fortunes of those races designated as inferior. The efforts of anthropologists, sociologists, linguists, and other researchers to validate claims about differences among people continued well into the twentieth century, curtailed only by World War II and the extermination of millions of people during the Holocaust.

Responding to the horrors of World War II, the United Nations endorsed the 1951 UNESCO "Statement on the Nature of Race and Racial Difference." This document declared that race, when considered in biological terms, could refer to nothing more than a group with particular genetic concentrations. The document also rejected efforts to define race in terms of intellectual and biological categories and underscored the importance of environment rather than genetics in shaping individual behavior and culture.

A resurgence of popular interest in the relationship between biology and theories of race in the 1960s repositioned race at the center of debates about human differences and led to the emergence of sociobiology in the 1970s. Its fundamental theory advocated the belief that social behavior can be transmitted genetically and is subject to evolutionary processes. These debates were fueled by oversimplifications of biological speculation rather than by attention to the cultural complexities of *ethnicity*, a word used to describe human difference in terms of shared values, beliefs, culture, tradition, language, and social behavior. *Ethnicity*, like *race*, is a social construct rather than a biological attribute, and both terms are the product of historical processes.

Given that race has become one of the primary ways by which people identify themselves, notes scholar Kwame Anthony Appiah, it may well come as "a shock to many to learn that there is a fairly widespread consensus in the sciences of biology and anthropology that the word 'race,' at least as it is used in most unscientific discussions, refers to nothing that science should recognize as real." Appiah has also observed that scientists have rejected not only the assertions that someone's racial "essence" can explain, say, his or her intellectual and moral behavior but also such standard nineteenth-century classifications as Negroid, Caucasian, and Mongoloid. "There are simply too many people who do not fit into any such category," Appiah explains, and "even when you succeed in assigning someone to one of these categories . . . that implies very little about most of their other biological characteristics." Like a belief in ghosts, a belief in race, however inaccurate, can have serious consequences for social and cultural life.

Despite the discrediting of so-called objective criteria for defining race, scientific explanations—

and their representations in popular culture—linger in both behavior and institutional practice. Racism remains in effect a product of attitudes.

Although racial categories and divisions among the races may never have been clearly defined, even a cursory glance at popular culture and music today reveals an unprecedented mixing of cultures and ethnic groups. Signs of hip-hop, for example, once a street culture and musical style of African Americans and Latinos in the South Bronx, can now be found everywhere, from MTV videos to the baggy pants of young white suburbanites across the country. "Not since pre-Civil War blackface minstrelsy has popular culture been such a racial free-for-all," writes Charles Aaron, music editor of *Spin* magazine. The stories, essays, and images in this chapter provide an opportunity to examine difference—to read, think, and write about wide-ranging expressions of and reactions to the continued existence and blurring of these racial and ethnic categories.

Nikki S. Lee
The Ohio Project (7), 1999

Nikki S. Lee
The Punk Project (6), 1997

Nikki S. Lee
The Hispanic Project (27), 1998

Nikki S. Lee
The Yuppie Project (19), 1998

Nikki S. Lee
The Seniors Project (12), 1999

Nikki S. Lee

Born in Kye-Chang, Korea, in 1970, Nikki S. Lee studied at the Fashion Institute of Technology in New York City and then received an MA in photography from New York University. Her work has been featured in solo exhibitions in the United States, Europe, and Japan, and she has participated in several international group shows.

The photographs here are from *Nikki S. Lee: Projects* (2001), a book that is more than a collection of photographs. It is a piece of performance art: Lee appears in every image. Each project was the result of weeks spent infiltrating a subculture – punks, Latinos/Latinas, seniors – drastically altering her hair, makeup, clothing, body language, and even weight to "fit in." The photographs were taken with a point-and-shoot camera by friends or strangers. Says Lee of her art form, "I want to control it, but I know I can't."

Lee's photographs are currently in the collections of the Metropolitan Museum of Art, the Solomon R. Guggenheim Museum, and the International Center of Photography. Her latest published collection is *Nikki S. Lee: Parts* (2005); her film *A.K.A. Nikki S. Lee*, premiered at the Museum of Modern Art in New York in 2006. Lee lives and works in New York City.

SEEING

1. What did you notice when you first examined this portfolio of photographs by Nikki S. Lee? Which image held your attention longest? Why? How are the photographs alike? How are they different? What is Lee saying about "difference" in her work? Using details from each image, describe how the image underscores Lee's notion of difference.

2. Lee positions the people in her photographs in very specific ways. How does that shape the perspective and attitude of each photograph? At what point in the process of studying Lee's images did you begin to draw inferences from them? What were those inferences? How would you characterize your overall impressions of Lee's work?

WRITING

1. Choose one of Lee's photographs and write an expository essay in which you discuss the specific elements in the photograph that draw you to it. What is there about the photograph that holds your attention? Why?

2. Write the first draft of an essay in which you compare one of Lee's photographs with one by <u>Carlton Davis</u> (pp. 440–44). What statement about difference is each photographer making? How would you compare their artistic techniques and styles? How do these images illustrate difference as a social construct?

Page 440

Stefano Giovannoni
The Chin Family

THE SQUINT AND THE WAIL
Michael Hsu

When I first saw the Chin family, Stefano Giovannoni's 2007 tabletop collection for Alessi, I had just one question: Why not call it the Ching Chong Family? The line of salt and pepper shakers, spice grinders, kitchen timers, and egg cups have Oriental features so exaggerated I wondered how they escaped censure by an anti-defamation league.

I showed pictures of the gadgets to my left-leaning New York acquaintances of European descent. One friend gasped. "They couldn't have made this more offensive if they tried!" she said. Others erupted into cringing, nervous laughter.

Then I approached my left-leaning, first generation Chinese-American friends, expecting the same indignation.

"I feel like punching them," Kathy said.

5   "Because they're derogatory?" I asked. "No, because they look like those inflatable toys that bounce back up when you hit them."

I pointed out the slant in Mr. Chin's eyes and asked if it bothered her.

"The eyes?" Kathy said. "I didn't even notice them."

Flummoxed, I turned to my parents, both of whom emigrated from Taiwan in the '60s. My father told me that the Manchus of the Qing Dynasty (from which the Chin Family gets its name) would often apply makeup so that their eyes appeared more elongated, a feature that conveyed heroism.

When the Chin Family debuted in Taiwan this summer, it was a resounding success. Commissioned by the National Palace Museum in Taipei, home of the world's most famous collection of Chinese art, the pieces sold out at the museum's gift store within two weeks. They are available through Alessi dealers worldwide, and sales have reportedly been brisk.

10   How can an object that makes so many Americans squirm be so palatable to the rest of the world?

"You can say it's a stereotype, but it's an accurate representation," said Houng Wanyu, who, as editor of the National Palace Museum's publication department, oversaw the Chin Family's development. "It would be weird for them to have Hello Kitty's little round eyes."

Houng added that museum curators who collaborated with Giovannoni raised the question of stereotyping, but it was "a very small matter." The curators were much more concerned about the pieces' historical accuracy—ensuring, for example, that motifs from the Song and Qing dynasties didn't get mixed up.

I spoke to Giovannoni himself: "This is a Chinese icon, so of course the eyes are one of the most recognizable elements," he told me over the phone from Milan. He clearly had no intention to offend, and I had a hard time holding the features against him.

I came to realize that my unease with the Chin Family's orbs resembled any other position of intolerance. It was a refusal to see an apparent act of indecency as simply a cultural viewpoint. Slanted eyes appear throughout Asia in advertisements, cartoons, and product packaging. What I saw as a mockery of Asian features—by an Italian designer, no less—was, to my peers and parents, a non-issue.

15   Humbled, I took the pepper and salt shakers home and set them on my dining table. After a few days, they had morphed in my view from outrageous tchotchkes to authentic East-West mash-ups. Almost every decorative element of the Chin Family is rooted in Chinese history. Even the vibrant colors, which feel so contemporary, were inspired by Chinese porcelain fired centuries ago. Yet these motifs are expressed in Western salt shakers and egg cups.

For Giovannoni, the Chin Family is part of a much larger project to uncouple household objects from status. "People don't need their objects to say, 'I am rich,' or 'I have culture.' We have to think of them not as abstract designs but as individual characters with a personal identity—characters who can communicate with us in a more direct way."

In the cultural mosh pit of America, with our heightened sensitivity toward otherness, a slant-eyed pepper grinder isn't just cute; it can also be appalling—which means we're in an excellent position to realize Giovannoni's intentions. How better to strip away the feelings of superiority derived from highfalutin design preferences than by embracing a culturally questionable object? The more honestly I confronted my discomfort with the Chin Family, the less abstract the products became, and my relationship to them grew that much more personal.

I've even given the shakers names: Mr. Ching and Mrs. Chong. That's not racist, is it?

Stefano Giovannoni

Born in 1954 in La Spezia, Italy, internationally renowned designer Stefano Giovannoni graduated with a degree in architecture from Florence University in 1978. Since then he has had a multifaceted career as an architect, industrial designer, interior designer, and professor of architecture and design (at Florence University, Domus Academy in Milan, Università del Progetto in Reggio Emilia, and University of Architecture in Genoa). The winner of numerous awards, Giovannoni first gained notoriety via his collaborative work with Guido Venturini, with whom he founded the King Kong design studio in the 1980s. The two designers created the successful Girotondo line of household products for the Italian firm Alessi and have continued to work collaboratively. Giovannoni favors plastic in many of his designs, but he also works with a variety of other media – as in the watches he designs for Seiko.

The Chin Family line came about when Alessi approached Giovannoni to design a series of household products in a traditional Taiwanese style, as commissioned by the National Palace Museum in Taipei, Taiwan. As these products have enjoyed enormous success both in Taiwan and abroad, Alessi continues to add to the Chin Family line with Giovannoni's full involvement. When asked about his philosophy as a designer, Giovannoni has said, "Design must . . . on one side . . . be up-to-date, while on the other side it must have a strong emotional and sensorial appeal so that it can easily be an object of desire for the public. From my point of view an object that doesn't satisfy these aspects is not a good product."

Michael Hsu

In "The Squint and the Wail," which originally appeared in the industrial design magazine *I.D.*, Michael Hsu, a second-generation Taiwanese American, explores his reaction to the slanted eyes of an anthropomorphic line of tabletop products. According to Hsu, the article was "extremely difficult to write initially. But I spent a lot of time with the objects, which allowed me to confront them and think deeply about them. Forcing myself to move beyond my original position of outrage was the key to writing this. Once I had a shift in perspective, the essay pretty much wrote itself."

Hsu (b. 1975 in Ann Arbor, Michigan) has written for *GQ*, the *New York Times*, *Slate*, *Wired*, and other publications. He was formerly an editor at *Harper's* and *Transition* and is currently a *GQ* contributing editor. Hsu has also worked with the Fire Department of New York's Fire Zone (a fire-safety learning center), StoryCorps (a public radio oral-history project), and the New York City Ballet Education Department. He lives in Brooklyn, NY.

SEEING

1. At the beginning of Michael Hsu's essay, his caustic phrase "Ching Chong Family" stands for racist Asian stereotypes, but at the end he affectionately names his salt and pepper shakers "Mr. Ching and Mrs. Chong." What made him change his mind about the shakers' conveying a racist stereotype? Revisit his conversations with his friends, his family, and the designer to find out how they persuaded him not to see the shakers as "another mockery of Asian features" but to understand their design as "a non-issue" (para. 14). Were you similarly persuaded by his essay? Why or why not?

2. Michael Hsu's essay appears in the section entitled "Rant" in *I.D.* magazine. In what specific ways does this information have a bearing on your reading of his essay? Where specifically is he ranting, and what is he ranting about? What features of his essay mark it as a <u>rant</u>? How would your reaction change if the magazine section had instead been called "Meditation"? "A Modest Proposal"? Similarly, what are the implications of Hsu's choice of title "The Squint and the Wail"? In what specific ways does the essay "squint" and when does it "wail"? How effectively does the title prepare you for Hsu's essay?

<u>rant (n): A violent, loud, or extravagant speech.</u>

WRITING

1. Design your own "East-West mash-up" that is "rooted in Chinese history" (para. 15). For example, you might create a casserole recipe based on food enjoyed during the Qing dynasty. Or you might design baseball uniforms that use patterns and colors from Ming ceramics. Or write a sonnet inspired by a poem from the ancient poetry collection *Shu Jing* (*Classic of Poetry*). Why might someone describe your creation as a "culturally questionable object" (para. 17)? How would you respond?

Working with Sources

2. In an advertisement for the 2008 Olympics in China, the members of Spain's basketball team pulled their eyes at the corners to make them narrow and slanted. The advertisement sparked a good deal of controversy, with some sports writers deploring the gesture and others waving it off as a non-issue. Check recent newspaper archives (in the campus library or online) to read the contrasting views on this controversy. If you speak other languages, such as Spanish or Mandarin, check carefully about how people in other countries responded to the controversy. What were the players' reactions? the advertising company's? Based on your research, write the first draft of an expository essay in which you answer Hsu's question, "Is it racist?"

BE DIFFERENT!
(LIKE EVERYONE ELSE!)
Luc Sante

Are you a unique individual? What a stupid question! How could you not
be? You are the only person ever to have been born at 12:08:32 a.m. on
June 17, 1973, in the maternity ward of Enos T. Throop Memorial Hospital in Picpus, N.Y. You are easily distinguishable from the infants born
in the same location on the same day at 12:07 and 12:09, respectively —
their parents were different from yours, for one thing, unless, of course,
you are one of a set of twins or triplets. Even then, your fingerprints will
be unique, and the graph of your voiceprint equally singular, identifiably
yours alone, even when you talk in a growl or a falsetto. Anyway, the important thing is that you know that you are you, an inimitable human being, with a collection of tastes, tendencies, tropisms, penchants, and small
perversities that have never been gathered together in exactly the same
way in the history of the world.

So how do you express this uniqueness of yours? Maybe you always
and unfailingly wear red socks. Or you wear your watch on the pulse side
of your wrist. Or you have a hummingbird tattooed just above your ankle.
Or you carry special imported tea bags with you everywhere and will
drink nothing else. Or you are never seen without your tiny, trembling dog.
Or you have a cabochon emerald implanted in one of your front teeth.
Or you drive a converted army ambulance. Or you write with a fountain
pen the size of a celery stalk. Or you wear shorts even in winter. Or you
wear a baseball cap even to church. Or you wear the same outfit every
day. Or you rig your car with vanity plates that encode your nickname.
Or you have everything monogrammed, down to your unmentionables.

These are hard times for individuality. If you practice any of the above
small eccentricities, you've got to know that at least a zillion people do
the same (and that includes the implanted stone in your tooth, which will
forever appear to the casual eye like a forgotten piece of spinach). Even
if you engage in some kind of radical piercing, like encasing both eyebrows in tight rows of small rings, and by this means emphatically announce to the world that you are not employed in middle management
at a Fortune 500 company, you are hardly doing something unprecedented. The fact that you have carried out such a thing virtually insures
that you've taken notice of all other humans in your town or on your
travels who have done the same. Perhaps, then, you are not proclaiming

your individuality so much as establishing your kinship with others of the same micropersuasion.

The compulsion to express one's individuality by means of eccentric style was for centuries restricted to members of the aristocracy, the only people who had the means or the time to pay attention to style, much less to feel constrained by prevalent fashions. Things changed in the nineteenth century, with the rise of the bourgeoisie, which imposed a set of instant standards and latter-day traditions upon the general population. The first people to set themselves apart from these dictates were the earliest bohemians, specifically the *Jeune France* crowd in Paris circa 1830, which included Gérard de Nerval, today much better known to English speakers for having walked a lobster on a leash through the gardens of the Palais Royal than for his visionary poems. His friends drank wine from human skulls, assumed bizarre names, dyed or perfumed or sculptured their beards in strange shapes, slept in tents pitched on the floors of their garrets, and so on. The connection between art and eccentricity was thus forged. Although when monolithic rules were in place it wasn't hard to announce one's uniqueness and, as a bonus, get a rise from the enforcers of those rules. When all men wore black suits, and those suits necessarily had to be cut by tailors, it wasn't much more expensive to procure a bolt of broadcloth in, say, purple, and have a suit made that would cause passersby to stop in their tracks, in horror, admiration, or a hybrid of the two.

5   The United States, meanwhile, has always had an equivocal attitude toward individualism. It has given the idea quite a bit of lip service over the years, in part as a wedge against collectivism and in part with respect to the prevalent notion that success stories are the hard-won results of solo efforts. The "rugged individual" who at least used to figure so often in political rhetoric was generally someone who had built an empire with his bare hands, unless he was a mythic embodiment: the lone prospector, for example. Otherwise, people who looked, talked, or acted funny were not often encouraged in their pursuits or invited to move in next door. They might serve as entertainment, but only at a distance. In the waning days of the universal dress code, the Beats were tabloid fixtures for more than a decade, a fascination based on their beards, leotards, berets, and perceived reluctance to bathe. You might take a tour bus to go stare at the beatniks in their own habitat, but if they showed up in your town they would be swiftly escorted out again. Their appearance alone would have raised eyebrows, but their homosexuality, race mixing, marijuana, and poverty definitely did not fit community standards.

In the following decade the hippies appeared, and quite apart from their even longer hair, sometimes wilder mores and more active politics, they were frightening because of their broad success. The Beats were, after all, intellectuals, and so automatically limited in their reach, but the hippies made only vague and easily consumable feints in that direction. The package of lifestyle accessories they promoted actually sold, big time. Less than a decade separated the time when having long hair could get one beaten up from the time when many of those who did the beating grew their own hair over their collars. Yet the allure of being part of a counterculture persisted, an outlaw thrill despite mounting evidence that the outlaws were mainstream. I think it was in the late winter of 1971 that I cut high school to go buy tickets to see the Allman Brothers in Passaic, N.J. As I stood shivering in the endless line for the box office it struck me that every single human being on the line was wearing blue jeans. Somehow I had previously failed to appreciate the inescapability of the phenomenon. As the sociologist Ned Polsky has pointed out, blue jeans, which had formerly been worn only by farmers and miners and cowboys, and then seldom off the job, were one of the beatniks' few lasting contributions to middle-class culture. Well before the end of Richard Nixon's first term they had become a uniform.

Blue jeans had thus crossed several lines: from utility to style, from emblem of rebellion to mark of adherence, and from in-group insignia to mass-culture requisite. As the tide of human affairs turned yet again during the 1970s, the alleged hipness of blue jeans (along with, to be sure, their comfort, ease, and versatility) continued to work its charms upon those formerly young people who had perhaps smoked a little reefer in their school days but were now coming up in the world. Something more, however, was needed, something that would distinguish *their* blue jeans from those of the panhandler, the yurt dweller, the Black Sabbath fan, and of course, the plumber. Thus was born the designer jean: the same product, perhaps a trifle more flatteringly cut, at many times the price and with a fancy label visible on the rear. This in turn set a pattern that has been repeated with various permutations many times over the past quarter century and that shows no signs of abating.

Youth styles are now assimilated so rapidly that there is no longer any lag time between their appearance on the street and the confection of upmarket versions. Ever since hip-hop, the last decisive style wave, initially clocked in twenty years ago, everything has pretty much been present all at once. If you are young and run with a set you will be aware of the shifting meanings of a shoe brand or a leg width—and woe betide you if you miss a ripple—but everybody else can blink twice, and the significance will have gone all the way around the cycle and come back to its starting point. The ferocious appetite of the market has met the constraints of gang signs, which have been forced to abandon the simple color patterns or arrangements of shoelaces of yore and instead become so fleeting and subtle as to escape the notice of hostile outsiders.

Of course, everyone everywhere speaks in some sort of code—speaks, that is, a language that will be understood by a particular crowd that can include friends, colleagues, co-religionists, fellow hobbyists, members of one's club, cabal, social class, income bracket, sexual persuasion, political tendency, age cluster, or any other sort of affinity group. The message being communicated is simple: "I am one of you." Your shoes say, "I am an architect"; your bumper sticker says, "I am a Dead-head"; your tie pin says, "I am a Royal Arch Mason"; your handbag says, "I make a great deal of money but don't flaunt it"; your eyeglasses say, "I am pretending to be European"; your earring says, "I still remember my misspent youth": your sports utility vehicle says, "I believe everything I see on television." In other words, all your appurtenances are gang signs.

10   Such coded messages have long existed, particularly the ones relating to class, but they have lately been proliferating to the point where there are simply no alternatives, nothing that cannot be read in a minute by a large number of people. A degree of invisibility can be conferred by adopting the lowest common denominator, but singularity is something else. I thought that the theatricality of large public events had always been good for bringing the weirdos down from the hills, so I checked in at Woodstock '99. Although I hadn't made it to the original, I remembered how large outdoor concerts of that era and even a decade or more later had encouraged people to dress themselves up as Merlin or Little Bo Peep, to put together bizarre collages of stuff they found in the dump or the garage—in short, to make a spectacle of themselves if only for one day. Instead what I saw were baseball caps worn frontward or backward, golf hats in various degrees of floppiness, T-shirts, shorts, sneakers. Oh, and skin, the commonest of denominators. The only novelty of much significance came in the form of garish airbrush body paintings—not unlike the things you see on the sides of vans driven by dudes—that were administered in a midway tent that also provided tattoos and piercings. The paintings were striking, although it wasn't exactly as if the wearers had worked them out themselves. Almost everybody else, assuming they had packed shirts without slogans or illustrations, could have shown up at the pep rally or the church barbecue with just a few minor tweakings.

We seem to be living in an age of conformity, the chief difference from other such ages being that conformity has been decentralized. You can call it niche conformity. This is because of the Argus-like omnipresence of marketing in all aspects of life, also the generalized exhaustion and the sense that everything has already been done twice over, also the age-old factors of fear and loneliness. These days individuals no longer have recourse to outsider camps that can cosset and protect them while they behave as oddly as they wish. (Nor can they abandon bohemia and go home again—in the past, there was always the fallback position. The dandy could probably go back to his midwestern town, the beatnik to graduate school.)

Every group has become a focus group, which promotes adherence to a norm and aggressively markets any viable stylistic innovations so that they move from the street to the nation in about a minute. Most important, the margins of society are no longer an option but a sentence. The trade-off used to mean exchanging mainstream comforts like new-model cars and steaks and color televisions for a cold-water flat and meals of rice and beans and cheap Chianti. Now it is economically impossible to sacrifice comfort for freedom, not unless you can savor freedom while sleeping in doorways and shelters and holding tanks. Right now, everything is for sale, including you, and if you are not saleable, you will starve. So you tailor and trim and adapt yourself, sand down your edges, maximize your appeal. There is still a you there, but it has gone underground, meaning somewhere deep within.

Luc Sante

Although essayist and cultural critic Luc Sante argues in the 1999 *New York Times* article included here that true difference, or individuality, no longer exists, he is nonetheless one of the most individualistic writers working today, and in his work he often views the world from the lone outsider's perspective. Sante, who was born in Belgium in 1954 and grew up in New Jersey after his parents emigrated in the early 1960s, says about his interest in outsiders, "I grew up thinking of myself as an outsider, being both an immigrant and having no ethnic community to belong to as a Belgian – there aren't many of us Belgians running around."

In his over twenty-year writing career, Sante has produced an impressively diverse and unpredictable body of work. In addition to writing about photography, he has published *Low Life: Lures and Snares of Old New York* (1991), a history of late nineteenth- and early twentieth-century downtown New York focused on the extremely poor and criminal classes (which led to a job as Martin Scorsese's historical consultant on the movie *Gangs of New York*); *The Factory of Facts* (1998), a personal memoir; a translation of eccentric early nineteenth century French writer Félix Fénéon's *Novels in Three Lines* (2007); and numerous articles on all manner of subjects, collected in *Kill All Your Darlings: Pieces 1990–2005* (2007).

Sante also contributes articles to a variety of periodicals, has received numerous literary awards, edits a series of reissued classic crime novels, was the recipient of a Guggenheim Fellowship, and even won a Grammy Award for his liner notes for the 1997 reissue of *Anthology of American Folk Music*. Sante lives in upstate New York with his family and teaches creative writing and photography at Bard College.

SEEING

1. What leads Sante to the conclusion that "all your appurtenances are gang signs" (para. 9)? Why is it jarring and unnerving to compare fashion choices to gang signs? Which of his examples support his claim, and which do not? What does he mean when he writes that "the ferocious appetite of the market has met the constraints of gang signs" (para. 8)? How does he show the market's appetite? And how do gang signs constrain it?

2. Using Sante's idea that individual characteristics are at best "micropersuasions" (para. 3), what trends do his own words follow? Compare the specific features of Sante's style to that of other authors in this book. Choose one writer on whom to focus your attention. In what specific ways are their respective styles similar? different? Please support your responses with evidence from the texts of each writer. For example, what resemblance is there between the use of personal stories in each? What roles do lists play? Which author(s) structure their essays in the same way as Sante? Beyond these similarities, unearth what makes Sante's writing unique to him, "underground, meaning somewhere deep within" (para. 12).

appurtenance: Something subordinate to another, more important thing; an adjunct; an accessory.

WRITING

1. If "everyone everywhere speaks in some sort of code" (para. 9), then in what kind of code do your personal tastes speak? To whom are they speaking? How do people go about deciphering your code, and how do you decipher theirs? Which parts of your personality cannot be decoded through what people see? The word *personality* comes from a word that meant "mask." How do the clothes you wear resemble masks? When do you put on one type of mask rather than another? What are your criteria for doing so? What are you disguising? for whom? and why? To answer these questions, write an expository essay – or a short film script – exploring and explaining the relation among codes, masks, personality, and individualism.

Working with Sources

2. Trace the history of three fashions. For example, you might find out where earrings came from. Or you might explore the evolution of tennis shoes (sneakers, kicks, etc.) – from shoes used when playing a sport to everyday (and expensive) accessories. Compare the histories to find similarities and differences in how the fashions come to be widespread. Based on your research, write an expository essay in which you explain how initially unique fashions become widespread cultural norms.

COOL LIKE ME
Donnell Alexander

I'm cool like this:

I read fashion magazines like they're warning labels telling me what not to do.

When I was a kid, Arthur Fonzarelli seemed a garden-variety dork.

I got my own speed limit.

5 I come when I want to.

I maintain like an ice cube in the remote part of the freezer.

Cooler than a polar bear's toenails.

Cooler than the other side of the pillow.

Cool like me.

10 Know this while understanding that I am in essence a humble guy.

I'm the kinda nigga who's so cool that my neighbor bursts into hysterical tears whenever I ring her doorbell after dark. She is a new immigrant who has chosen to live with her two roommates in our majority-black Los Angeles neighborhood so that, I'm told, she can "learn about all American cultures." But her real experience of us is limited to the space between her Honda and her front gate; thus, much of what she has to go on is the vibe of the surroundings and the images emanating from the television set that gives her living room a minty cathode glow. As such, I'm a cop-show menace and a shoe commercial demi-god—one of the rough boys from our 'hood and the living, breathing embodiment of hip-hop flava. And if I can't fulfill the prevailing stereotype, the kids en route to the nearby high school can. The woman is scared in a cool world. She smiles as I pass her way in the light of day, unloading my groceries or shlepping my infant son up the stairs. But at night, when my face is visible through the window of her door lit only by the bulb that brightens the vestibule, I, at once familiar and threatening, am just too much.

Thus being cool has its drawbacks. With cool come assumptions and fears, expectations and intrigue. My neighbor wants to live near cool, but she's not sure about cool walking past her door after dark. During the day, she sees a black man; at night what she sees in the shadow gliding across her patio is a nigga.

Once upon a time, little need existed for making the distinction between a nigga and a black—at least not in this country, the place where niggas were invented. We were just about all slaves, so we were all niggas. Then we became free on paper yet oppressed still. Today, with as many as a third of us a generation or two removed from living poor (depending on who's counting), niggadom isn't innate to every black child born. But with the poverty rate still hovering at around 30 percent, black people still got niggas in the family, even when they themselves aren't niggas. Folks who don't know niggas can watch them on TV, existing in worlds almost always removed from blacks. Grant Hill is black, Allen Iverson is a nigga. Oprah interviewing the celebrity du jour is a black woman; the woman being handcuffed on that reality TV show is a nigga.

The question of whether black people are cooler than white people is a dumb one, and one that I imagine a lot of people will find offensive. But we know what we're talking about, right? We're talking about style and spirit and the innovations that those things spawn. It's on TV; it's in the movies, sports and clothes and language and gestures and music.

15   See, black cool is cool as we know it. I could name names—Michael Jordan and Chris Rock and Me'shell Ndegeocello and Will Smith and bell hooks and Lil' Kim—but cool goes way back, much further than today's superstars. Their antecedents go back past blaxploitation cinema, past Ike Turner to Muddy Waters, beyond even the old jazz players and blues singers whose names you'll never know. Cool has a history and cool has a meaning. We all know cool when we see it, and now, more than at any other time in this country's history, when mainstream America looks for cool we look to black culture. Countless new developments can be called great, nifty, even keen. But, cool? That's a black thang, baby.

And I should know. My being cool is not a matter of subjectivity or season. Having lived as a nigga has made me cool. Let me explain. Cool was born when the first plantation nigga figured out how to make animal innards—massa's garbage, hog maws, and chitlins—taste good enough to eat. That inclination to make something out of nothing and then to make that something special articulated itself first in the work chants that slaves sang in the field and then in the hymns that rose out of their churches. It would later reveal itself in the music made from cast-off Civil War marching-band instruments (jazz); physical exercise turned to public spectacle (sports); and street life styling, from pimps' silky handshakes to the corner crack dealer's baggy pants.

Cool is all about trying to make a dollar out of 15 cents. It's about living on the cusp, on the periphery, diving for scraps. Essential to cool is being outside looking in. Others—Indians, immigrants, women, gays— have been "othered," but until the past 15 percent of America's history, niggas in real terms have been treated by the country's majority as, at best, subhuman and, at worst, an abomination. So in the days when they were still literally on the plantation they devised a coping strategy called cool, an elusive mellowing strategy designed to master time and space. Cool, the basic reason blacks remain in the American cultural mix, is an industry of style that everyone in the world can use. It's finding the essential soul while being essentially lost. It's the nigga metaphor. And the nigga metaphor is the genius of America.

Gradually over the course of this century, as there came to be a growing chasm of privilege between black people and niggas, the nature of cool began to shift. The romantic and now-popular image of the pasty Caucasian who hung out in a jazz club was one small subplot. Cool became a promise—the reward to any soul hardy enough to pierce the inner sanctum of black life and not only live to tell about it but also live to live for it. Slowly, watered-down versions of this very specific strain of cool became the primary means of defining American cool. But it wasn't until Elvis that cool was brought down from Olympus (or Memphis) to majority-white culture. Mass media did the rest. Next stop: high fives, chest bumps, and "Go girl!"; Air Jordans, Tupac, and low-riding pants.

White folks began to try to make the primary point of cool—recognition of the need to go with the flow—a part of their lives. But cool was only an avocational interest for them. It could never be the necessity it was for their colored co-occupants. Some worked harder at it than others. And as they came to understand coolness as being of almost elemental importance, they began obsessing on it, asking themselves, in a variety of clumsy, indirect ways: Are black people cooler than white people and, if so, why?

20   The answer is, of course, yes. And if you, the reader, had to ask some stupid shit like that, you're probably white. It's hard to imagine a black person even asking the question, and a nigga might not even know what you mean. Any nigga who'd ask that question certainly isn't much of one; niggas invented the shit.

Humans put cool on a pedestal because life at large is a challenge, and in that challenge we're trying to cram in as much as we can—as much fine loving, fat eating, dope sleeping, mellow walking, and substantive working as possible. We need spiritual assistance in the matter. That's where cool comes in. At its core, cool is useful. Cool gave bass to twentieth-century American culture, but I think that if the culture had needed more on the high end, cool would have given that, because cool closely resembles the human spirit. It's about completing the task of living with enough spontaneity to splurge some of it on bystanders, to share with others working through their own travails a little of your bonus life. Cool is about turning desire into deed with a surplus of ease.

Some white people are cool in their own varied ways. I married a white girl who was cooler than she ever knew. And you can't tell me Jim Jarmusch and Ron Athey and Delbert McClinton ain't smooth.

There's a gang of cool white folks, all of whom exist that way because they've found their essential selves amid the abundant and ultimately numbing media replications of the coolness vibe and the richness of real life. And there's a whole slew more of them ready to sign up if you tell 'em where. But your average wigger in the rap section of Sam Goody ain't gone nowhere; she or he hasn't necessarily learned shit about the depth and breadth of cool, about making a dollar out of 15 cents. The problem with mainstream American culture, the reason why irony's been elevated to raison d'être status and neurosis increasingly gets fetishized, is its twisted approach to cool. Most think cool is something you can put on and take off at will (like a strap-on goatee). They think it's some shit you go shopping for. And that taints cool, giving the mutant thing it becomes a deservedly bad name. Such strains aren't even cool anymore, but an evil ersatz-cool, one that fights real cool at every turn. Advertising agencies, record-company artist-development departments, and over-art-directed bars are where ersatz-cool dwells. What passes for cool to the white-guy passerby might be—is probably—just rote duplication without an ounce of inspiration.

The acceptance of clone cool by so many is what makes hip-hop necessary. It's what negates the hopelessness of the postmodern sensibility at its most cynical. The hard road of getting by on metaphorical chitlins kept the sons and daughters of Africa in touch with life's essential physicality, more in touch with the world and what it takes to get over in it: People are moved, not convinced; things get done, they don't just happen. Real life doesn't allow for much fronting, as it were. And neither does hip-hop. Hip-hop allows for little deviation between who one is and what one can ultimately represent.

25   Rap—the most familiar, and therefore the most emblematic, example of hip-hop expression—is about the power of conveying through speech the world beyond words. Language is placed on a par with sound and, ultimately, vibes. Huston Smith, a dope white guy, wrote: "Speech is alive—literally alive because speaking is the speaker. It's not the whole of the speaker, but it is the speaker in one of his or her living modes. This shows speech to be alive by definition. . . . It possesses in principle life's qualities, for its very nature is to change, adapt, and invent. Indissolubly contextual, speaking adapts itself to speaker, listener, and situation alike. This gives it an immediacy, range, and versatility that is, well, miraculous."

Which is why hip-hop has become the most insidiously influential music of our time. Like rock, hip-hop in its later years will have a legacy of renegade youth to look back upon fondly. But hip-hop will insist that its early marginalization be recognized as an integral part of what it comes to be. When the day comes that grandmothers are rapping and beatboxing as they might aerobicize now, and samplers and turntables are as much an accepted part of leisure time as channel surfing, niggas will be glad. Their expression will have proven ascendant.

But that day's not here yet. If white people were really cool with black cool, they'd put their stuff with our stuff more often to work shit out. I don't mean shooting hoops together in the schoolyard as much as white cultural institutions like college radio, indie film, and must-see TV. Black cool is banished to music videos, sports channels, and UPN so whites can visit us whenever they want without having us live right next door in the media mix. Most of the time, white folks really don't want to be part of black cool. They just like to see the boys do a jig every once in a while.

At the same time, everyday life in black America is not all Duke Ellington and Rakim Allah. Only a few black folks are responsible for cool. The rest copy and recycle. At the historical core of black lives in this country is a clear understanding that deviation from society's assigned limitations results in punitive sanctions: lynching, hunger, homelessness. The fear of departing from the familiar is where the inclination to make chitlins becomes a downside. It's where the shoeshine-boy reflex to grin and bear it was born. Black rebellion in America from slave days onward was never based on abstract, existentialist grounds. A bird in the hand, no matter how small, was damn near everything.

Today, when deviation from normalcy not only goes unpunished but is also damn near demanded to guarantee visibility in our fast-moving world, blacks remain woefully wedded to the bowed head and blinders. Instead of bowing to massa, they slavishly bow to trend and marketplace. And this creates a hemming-in of cool, an inability to control the cool one makes. By virtue of their status as undereducated bottom feeders, many niggas will never overcome this way of being. But, paradoxically, black people—who exist at a greater distance from cool than niggas—can and will. That's the perplexity of the cool impulse. As long as some black people have to live like niggas, cool, as contemporarily defined, will live on. As long as white people know what niggas are up to, cool will continue to exist, with all of its baggage passed on like, uh, luggage. The question "Are black people cooler than white people?" is not the important one. "How do I gain proximity to cool, and do I want it?" is much better. The real secret weapon of cool is that it's about synthesis. Just about every important black cultural invention of this century has been about synthesizing elements previously considered antithetical. MLK merged Eastern thought and cotton-field religious faith into the civil rights movement. Chuck Berry merged blues and country music into rock 'n' roll. Michael Jordan incorporated the old school ball of Jerry West into his black game. Talk about making a dollar out of 15 cents.

30   Out in the netherworld of advertising, they tell us we're all Tiger Woods. He plays the emblematic white man's game as good as anyone. Well, only one nigga on this planet gets to be that motherfucker, but we all swing the same cool, to whatever distant ends. The coolness construct might tell us otherwise, but we're all handed the same basic tools at birth; it's up to us as individuals to work on our game. Some of us have sweet strokes, and some of us press too hard, but everybody who drops outta their mama has the same capacity to take a shot.

Donnell Alexander

Born in 1967 in Sandusky, Ohio, Donnell Alexander attended junior college in Fresno, California, and began writing for local college papers and the alternative press. Soon he was writing about hip-hop culture, sports, and entertainment for *LA Weekly* and *ESPN The Magazine.*

Throughout his career, Alexander has examined topics ranging from what suit to wear on NBA draft day to the life of security guards. As a former staff writer for *LA Weekly*, he covered that city's booming hip-hop music scene as well as the O. J. Simpson trial.

Alexander's work confronts head-on the preconceptions white Americans have of African American men. Speaking with an insider's ease, Alexander has developed a style that is at once articulate, rigorous, and highly metaphorical.

Alexander left *ESPN The Magazine* to work on his memoir, *Ghetto Celebrity: Searching for My Father in Me* (2003), about his development as a writer and the challenges he faced growing up without a father. His latest book (with Bruce Williams) is *Rollin' with Dre: An Insider's Tale of the Rise, Fall, and Rebirth of West Coast Hip Hop* (2008).

SEEING

1. Donnell Alexander states that "Cool has a history and cool has a meaning" (para. 15). Sketch out the history that Alexander presents for "cool." How does he define the term? According to Alexander, what is the difference between "nigga" and "black"? What does he mean when he talks of the "nigga metaphor" (para. 17)? Outline the logical steps Alexander takes in constructing his argument about making "hip-hop necessary" (para. 24).

2. Consider the list with which Alexander begins this piece. What does he gain – and lose – by opening the essay in this manner? How would you characterize his tone at the beginning of the essay? Does it remain consistent throughout the piece? If not, when does it change, and with what effects? Comment on his <u>diction</u> as well.

<u>diction: Style of speaking or writing as reflected in one's choice of words; also, manner of pronunciation and enunciation.</u>

WRITING

1. Alexander claims that evidence of "cool" is everywhere in American popular culture. "We all know cool when we see it, and now, more than at any other time in this country's history, when mainstream America looks for cool we look to black culture" (para. 15). Choose an example of cool – a musician, a celebrity, an athlete, or a style of dress, to name a few possibilities – or something that passes for cool (what Alexander calls "cool clone") in mainstream American culture. Write an essay in which you use his explanation of the relationship between black culture and cool. Explain why you think your subject is "authentic" cool or a "wanna-be."

2. Early in the essay Alexander claims he is "a cop-show menace and a shoe commercial demi-god" (para. 11). This observation underscores the impression that African Americans are usually regarded as falling within one of these two categories. Consider your own experience with media representations of African Americans. Do you agree with Alexander's claim? Can you identify well-known African Americans who transcend these categories? Where, for example, would you place someone such as Bill Cosby? In what ways does someone like Cosby satisfy Alexander's definition of cool? Write an essay in which you assess the media representations of African Americans. Who among contemporary public figures can be said to be cool, and why? You might focus your attention on deciding whether President Barack Obama can be called "cool," and if so, then explain why.

Roger Shimomura
24 People for Whom I Have Been Mistaken, 1999

Roger Shimomura

The child of Japanese American parents, Roger Shimomura was born in Seattle in 1939. After the bombing of Pearl Harbor, he and his family were forced into Minidoka internment camp. Shimomura graduated from the University of Washington with a degree in commercial design and earned an MFA from Syracuse University. Since 1968, he has been very successful at incorporating American pop art with traditional Japanese woodblock printing (*ukiyo-e*). Following his retirement as a professor at the School of Fine Arts, University of Kansas, in 2004, Shimomura's body of work was collected in two books: *Minidoka Revisited: The Paintings of Roger Shimomura* (2005) and *The Prints of Roger Shimomura* (2007).

Shimomura's work often touches on his internment experiences and on the xenophobia and racism he still encounters in America. Of being both Japanese and American he says: "My culture is not Japanese culture, it's this culture. . . . I don't live in Japan; I live in Kansas, but I don't live in midwestern culture either; there are very few Asian Americans there. . . . Anyone who isn't like everyone else is seen as invasive; you live and die with that sense as a person of color in this country."

Shimomura addresses racial insensitivity directly in his 2003 exhibition, Stereotypes and Admonition. The piece presented here, *24 People for Whom I Have Been Mistaken*, is composed of found photographs; it too reflects the challenges Shimomura has faced as a Japanese American.

SEEING

1. What do you notice about these images individually and as a group? What similarities and differences do you see? What would you describe as the characteristic shared most by those pictured? What does being mistaken for someone else mean? What social or cultural dynamics are involved?

2. Shimomura has said that "to most non-Asians in this country, the differences between the Japanese, Chinese, and other Asian people are either indistinguishable or immaterial." At first glance, which of the faces would you be most likely to mistake for another? What particular features make them seem so alike? Which people would you be unlikely to mistake? What clues does your eye use to distinguish among the faces? Compare your answers with those of a classmate from a different race. How much does what you notice in the faces depend on your race? If your answer is "nothing," think about what led Shimomura to claim that differences among Asian people are indistinguishable to most non-Asians.

WRITING

1. Take a moment to look at each of the twenty-four images. Write one or two sentences describing the unique appearance of each of the people pictured. Then write a paragraph summarizing their common characteristics. Which task do you find more challenging? Why?

2. Whom have you been mistaken for? What aspects of the experience made an impression on you? What has the experience revealed to you about other people's assumptions about you? Write an essay in which you describe the experience of mistaken identity and its significance to you.

Responding Visually

Compose your own version of *24 People for Whom I Have Been Mistaken*. Choose photographs, clippings, or other found objects to create your own grid of images. Write a one-page artist's statement to accompany your work.

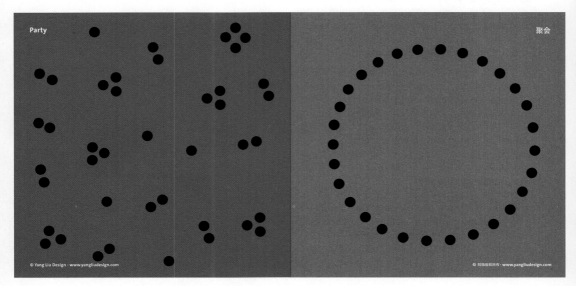

Yang Liu
Party, 2003–2004

Yang Liu
Ich, 2003–2004

Yang Liu

Born in Beijing, China, in 1976, Yang Liu has lived in Berlin, Germany, since 1990. She received her undergraduate degree from the University of the West of England – Bristol and her master's degree in design from the Berlin University of the Arts in 2000. Upon graduation she embarked on a successful design career, culminating in the formation of her own design firm, Yang Liu Design, in 2004.

Although her graphic work has garnered attention and has won awards since 1998, perhaps her greatest success has been East Meets West, a series of striking poster designs through which Liu explores her dual cultural identity as both Chinese (Eastern) and German (Western). These sharply contrasting images, wherein the blue panels on the left represent her German identity and the red panels on the right represent her Chinese identity, have attracted international attention and have been shown in numerous galleries and museums. This sucess may be due not only to the images' provocative exploration of cultural identity, but also to their being based on internationally recognized signage illustrations like those found on highway signs, in national parks, and in other public spaces across the world. Interestingly, Liu began the series while visiting New York: Her time there "helped me . . . to identify myself. I'm feeling myself more of a person, who belongs to all the places I have been to."

SEEING

1. Liu's East Meets West series has been exhibited throughout the world. Explain how her choice of simple colors, shapes, and arrangements communicates complex ideas and emotions. Pay particular attention to symbolism. What do blue and red stand for? Why are the boxes the same size? Why are these seemingly simple pictures so successful?

2. In an interview, Yang Liu (Chinese born, German raised) credited her time visiting a foreign city (New York) as a major influence for East Meets West: "The distance gave me a better view on my personal history." Why would spending time away from home – where identity is formed – help an artist know herself better? How could being far away from where one's history happened make that history clearer? Consider the images reprinted here as chapters in Liu's autobiography. What stories do you see in them that tell about her identity and her history?

For a full account of the interview with Liu, please see: www.notcot.com/ archives/2007/11/_jean_posted_ab.php

WRITING

1. Use Liu's artistic style to compose similar images for other opposed pairs of words and concepts beyond East and West. For example, you might diagram the view of life by love and hate, birth and death, or justice and injustice. Now focus on drawing subtler distinctions: happiness and joy at a party, for example. Push Liu's techniques to their limits. What categories cannot be represented well by using her methods? Why not?

Working with Sources

2. How accurately do Liu's graphics illustrate what happens when East meets West? Select one well-documented meeting from history, and show how the participants' actions could be explained – or not – using Liu's techniques. For example, could her type of graphics illuminate the Mongolian Kublai Khan's encounter with the Venetian Marco Polo? diplomatic relations between the Tokugawa shogunate in Japan and the United States's Commodore Matthew Perry? early Arab interactions with the Vikings? Mark Twain's adventures on the West Coast? Which meetings do you think are unfair tests for the explanatory power of Liu's graphics? Explain why.

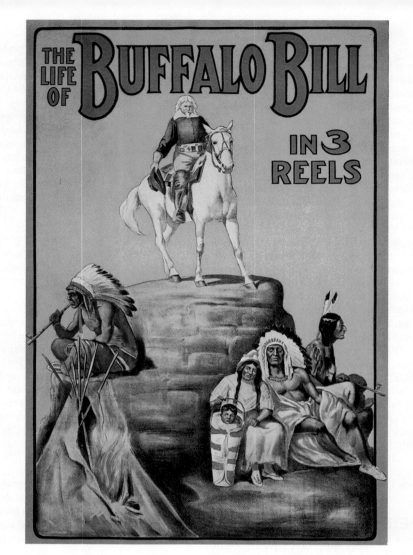

1910

1929

1933–1954

1938

1953

1967

1998

I try to use as many
specific examples as I can
when writing for
an audience. I never
assume anything.

Brittany Mann, student at Las Positas College

Every successful creative
person creates with an
audience of one in mind.

Kurt Vonnegut, novelist

Tibor Kalman
"Arnold Schwarzenegger," 1993

Tibor Kalman
"Queen Elizabeth II," 1993

Kalman / "Queen Elizabeth II" / 437

Tibor Kalman

Born in Budapest, Tibor Kalman (1949–1999) and his family left Hungary in 1956 and settled in Poughkeepsie, New York. Kalman studied journalism at New York University, where he also found an outlet for his social activism. He then worked for a number of years creating signs, advertisements, and displays for the bookstore that would become Barnes & Noble.

In 1979 Kalman and his wife, Maira, founded M&Co, a design firm whose irreverence attracted clients ranging from Talking Heads (for whom he designed their *Remain in Light* album cover) to New York's Museum of Modern Art. To counteract both the dishonesty and the superficiality of corporate advertising, Kalman created an offbeat, often humorous design vocabulary. It was that vocabulary that brought him to the attention of Benetton. The company wanted to launch a magazine, and it wanted Kalman to come to Rome and be its editor. In *Colors* Kalman found a platform for both his design aesthetic and his politics. Witness the images here, for a feature titled "What If . . ." in a 1993 issue of *Colors* devoted to race.

In 1995 artistic differences and the first symptoms of the lymphoma that would take his life four years later brought Kalman back to New York City. He began working on several projects, including *Chairman* (1998), a book about chair designer Rolf Fehlbaum, and *(un)Fashion* (2000), a study of "how real people dress," which his wife completed after Kalman died. He also worked closely with Michael Beirut and Peter Hall on *Tibor Kalman: Perverse Optimist* (1998).

SEEING

1. How did you respond to Kalman's altered images? What response does each photograph elicit from you? How does each photograph challenge your assumptions about these public figures? Which image do you find more plausible? Explain why.

2. Comment on Kalman's choices in manipulating the skin color, hair style, and eyes of both public figures. In what ways does each of these images seem more striking, more contrived, or more realistic than others you've seen of public figures? Do you find Kalman's images humorous? satiric? ironic? some combination of the three? Explain your answer. What do you think Kalman was trying to accomplish? Do you think he was successful? Why or why not?

WRITING

1. Kalman employed computer technology to manipulate the racial identity of these public figures. Imagine that you were able to assume a different racial identity. Which would you choose? Why? What would be the consequences of doing so? How might your daily life be different as a result? Write the first draft of an essay in which you imagine the impact that change would have on the spirit and substance of your daily life.

2. Choose one of the photographs, and write an essay in which you explain what Kalman's manipulation of the image suggests about the role of race in that person's public life. How much does the public identity of each person portrayed here depend on his or her racial identity?

VISUALIZING COMPOSITION:
AUDIENCE

Carlton Davis
Gevonni Davis, Witchita, 2004

Carlton Davis
Andrew "Twin" Jones, New York, 2003

Carlton Davis
Imam Taalib Mahdee, Boston, 2003

Carlton Davis
Stanley Nelson, New York, 2003

Carlton Davis
James Anthony, Natchez, 2004

Carlton Davis

Photographer Carlton Davis explains the inspiration for Hue Man, his series of portraits of African American men: "The portrayal of black men has affected me since I was a young man, even before I became aware of myself as black. In the media, black men were either super heroes or super villains." As a result, Davis set out in 2002 to dispense with the hero/villain dialectic and photograph black men in a realistic way, as a means of capturing their full humanity. To do so he traveled across America, booking various venues, announcing his project through the local media, and photographing (in the most naturalistic way possible) anyone who decided to participate. For each photograph, Davis's aim was to "approach everyone with the same level of respect through a singular visual treatment." Using the same camera, similar backgrounds (either red, white, or blue), and unobtrusive lighting, Davis created a series designed to "minimize the viewer's awareness of the photograph as a photograph, and allow viewers to really see the person and look into his eyes."

Davis's interest in photography developed when he was sixteen years old. Since 1990 he has been a commercial and artistic photographer, with an interest not only in "observing everyday people in everyday situations" but also in exploring the connection between photography and music. He lives in New York with his wife and daughter.

SEEING

1. What specific details do you notice about the individuals in each of these photographs? What differences and similarities do you notice in their expressions, body language, and gazes into – or away from – the camera? What can you reasonably infer about each subject's reactions – if any – to being photographed? Be as specific as possible in supporting your response.

2. "My aim was to approach everyone with the same level of respect through a singular visual treatment," writes Davis in his Artist Statement (p. 446). What are the defining characteristics of his visual treatment? To what extent do you think these compositional choices are successful? Point to specific evidence to support your response.

WRITING

1. Experiment with the interrelations between images and text by drafting several different types of captions for these photographs. For each image, please draft one descriptive caption, one in which you create a fictional quotation from the subject, and one to accompany an imaginary ad for a product or nonprofit organization. After drafting your captions, write a one-page account of your observations about how each line of text changes the meaning and impact of the photograph.

2. Writing about his portraits, Davis explains that "I wanted an approach that would minimize the viewer's awareness of the photograph as a photograph, and allow viewers to really see the person and look into his eyes." Select another photograph, illustration, advertisement, or painting – in or beyond this book – that makes its subject noticeably accessible to viewers. Write the first draft of an expository essay in which you describe and then compare and contrast the specific compositional choices that enable you to "really see" the subject. Comment on the extent to which each image minimizes the viewer's awareness of its medium.

Responding Visually
Choose a group of people that interests you – family members, members of your sports team, or members of your class, to name a few examples. Create your own portfolio of five photographic portraits. While you need not follow Davis's specific compositional choices, please choose a consistent visual treatment to capture your subjects.

The portrayal of black men has affected me since I was a young man, even before I became aware of myself as black. In the media, black men were either super heroes or super villains. I found positive role models in my immediate family; but in other ways, the family also fulfilled negative stereotypes of black men. As an adult, I began to want to explore these tensions, and my view of black men, through the lens of my camera.

In 2002, I set out to create a series of portraits of black men of all different ages, from all different walks of life. I traveled across the country visiting fifteen states for more than two years with a photo/production assistant. From Anchorage to Atlanta, our process was the same: I made announcements about the project in local churches, community centers, and malls inviting black men to participate. We set a time and place, and I photographed everyone who showed up.

My aim was to approach everyone with the same level of respect through a singular visual treatment. My portable studio consisted of an 8 × 10 camera, three different backgrounds – red, white, or blue – and consistent lighting. I created a calm space so that subjects weren't distracted. I am interested in creating beautiful images, but more importantly for this project, I wanted an approach that would minimize the viewer's awareness of the photograph as a photograph, and allow viewers to really see the person and look into his eyes.

I can look at myself in the mirror and study my face, and myself. But I rarely have a chance to take time and behold other men who are black. After hundreds of encounters, I see that we are much more than black men. We are human beings. This project gave me that opportunity. I hope it will allow others to question their own preconceptions and expand the way they experience humanity.

"THIS IS HOW WE LOST
TO THE WHITE MAN"
Ta-Nehisi Coates

Last summer, in Detroit's St. Paul Church of God in Christ, I watched Bill
Cosby summon his inner Malcolm X. It was a hot July evening. Cosby was
speaking to an audience of black men dressed in everything from Enyce
T-shirts or polos to blazers and ties. Some were there with their sons.
Some were there in wheelchairs. The audience was packed tight, rows of
folding chairs extended beyond the wooden pews to capture the overflow.
But the chairs were not enough, and late arrivals stood against the long
shotgun walls, or out in the small lobby, where they hoped to catch a
snatch of Cosby's oratory. Clutching a cordless mic, Cosby paced in the
front of the church, shifting between prepared remarks and comic ad-libs.
A row of old black men, community elders, sat behind him, nodding and
grunting throaty affirmations. The rest of the church was in full call-and-
response mode, punctuating Cosby's punch lines with laughter, applause,
or cries of "Teach, black man! Teach!"

He began with the story of a black girl who'd risen to become vale-
dictorian of his old high school, despite having been abandoned by her
father. "She spoke to the graduating class and her speech started like
this," Cosby said. "'I was five years old. It was Saturday and I stood looking out the window, waiting for him.' She never said what helped turn
her around. She never mentioned her mother, grandmother, or great-
grandmother."

"Understand me," Cosby said, his face contorted and clenched like a
fist. "Men? Men? Men! Where are you men?"

Audience: "Right here!"

5   Cosby had come to Detroit aiming to grab the city's black men by
their collars and shake them out of the torpor that has left so many of
them—like so many of their peers across the country—undereducated,
over-incarcerated, and underrepresented in the ranks of active fathers.
No women were in the audience. No reporters were allowed, for fear that
their presence might frighten off fathers behind on their child-support
payments. But I was there, trading on race, gender, and a promise not to
interview any of the allegedly skittish participants.

"Men, if you want to win, we can win," Cosby said. "We are not a
pitiful race of people. We are a bright race, who can move with the best.
But we are in a new time, where people are behaving in abnormal ways

and calling it normal. . . . When they used to come into our neighborhoods, we put the kids in the basement, grabbed a rifle, and said, 'By any means necessary.'

"I don't want to talk about hatred of these people," he continued. "I'm talking about a time when we protected our women and protected our children. Now I got people in wheelchairs, paralyzed. A little girl in Camden, jumping rope, shot through the mouth. Grandmother saw it out the window. And people are waiting around for Jesus to come, when Jesus is already within you."

Cosby was wearing his standard uniform — dark sunglasses, loafers, a sweat suit emblazoned with the seal of an institution of higher learning. That night it was the University of Massachusetts, where he'd gotten his doctorate in education thirty years ago. He was preaching from the book of black self-reliance, a gospel that he has spent the past four years carrying across the country in a series of events that he bills as "call-outs." "My problem," Cosby told the audience, "is I'm tired of losing to white people. When I say I don't care about white people, I mean let them say what they want to say. What can they say to me that's worse than what their grandfather said?"

From Birmingham to Cleveland and Baltimore, at churches and colleges, Cosby has been telling thousands of black Americans that racism in America is omnipresent but that it can't be an excuse to stop striving. As Cosby sees it, the antidote to racism is not rallies, protests, or pleas, but strong families and communities. Instead of focusing on some abstract notion of equality, he argues, blacks need to cleanse their culture, embrace personal responsibility, and reclaim the traditions that fortified them in the past. Driving Cosby's tough talk about values and responsibility is a vision starkly different from Martin Luther King's gauzy, all-inclusive dream: It's an America of competing powers, and a black America that is no longer content to be the weakest of the lot.

10   It's heady stuff, especially coming from the man white America remembers as a sitcom star and affable pitchman for E. F. Hutton, Kodak, and Jell-O Pudding Pops. And Cosby's race-based crusade is particularly jarring now. Across the country, as black politics has become more professionalized, the rhetoric of race is giving way to the rhetoric of standards and results. Newark's young Ivy League–educated mayor, Cory Booker, ran for office promising competence and crime reduction, as did Washington's mayor, Adrian Fenty. Indeed, we are now enjoying a moment of national self-congratulation over racial progress, with a black man running for president as the very realization of King's dream. Barack Obama defied efforts by the Clinton campaign to pigeonhole him as a "black"

candidate, casting himself instead as the symbol of a society that has moved beyond lazy categories of race.

Black America does not entirely share the euphoria, though. The civil-rights generation is exiting the American stage—not in a haze of nostalgia but in a cloud of gloom, troubled by the persistence of racism, the apparent weaknesses of the generation following in its wake, and the seeming indifference of much of the country to black America's fate. In that climate, Cosby's gospel of discipline, moral reform, and self-reliance offers a way out—a promise that one need not cure America of its original sin in order to succeed. Racism may not be extinguished, but it can be beaten.

Has Dr. Huxtable, the head of one of America's most beloved television households, seen the truth: that the dream of integration should never supplant the pursuit of self-respect; that blacks should worry more about judging themselves and less about whether whites are judging them on the content of their character? Or has he lost his mind?

From the moment he registered in the American popular consciousness, as the Oxford-educated Alexander Scott in the NBC adventure series *I Spy*, Cosby proffered the idea of an America that transcended race. The series, which started in 1965, was the first weekly show to feature an African American in a lead role, but it rarely factored race into dialogue or plots. Race was also most inconspicuous in Cosby's performances as a hugely popular stand-up comedian. "I don't spend my hours worrying how to slip a social message into my act," Cosby told *Playboy* in 1969. He also said that he didn't "have time to sit around and worry whether all the black people of the world make it because of me. I have my own gig to worry about." His crowning artistic and commercial achievement—*The Cosby Show*, which ran from 1984 to 1992—was seemingly a monument to that understated sensibility.

In fact, blackness was never absent from the show or from Bill Cosby. Plots involved black artists like Stevie Wonder or Dizzy Gillespie. The Huxtables' home was decorated with the works of black artists like Annie Lee, and the show featured black theater veterans such as Roscoe Lee Brown and Moses Gunn. Behind the scenes, Cosby hired the Harvard psychiatrist Alvin Poussaint to make sure that the show never trafficked in stereotypes and that it depicted blacks in a dignified light. Picking up Cosby's fixation on education, Poussaint had writers insert references to black schools. "If the script mentioned Oberlin, Texas Tech, or Yale, we'd circle it and tell them to mention a black college," Poussaint told me in a phone interview last year. "I remember going to work the next day and white people saying, "What's the school called Morehouse?" In 1985,

Cosby riled NBC by placing an anti-apartheid sign in his Huxtable son's bedroom. The network wanted no part of the debate. "There may be two sides to apartheid in Archie Bunker's house," the *Toronto Star* quoted Cosby as saying. "But it's impossible that the Huxtables would be on any side but one. That sign will stay on that door. And I've told NBC that if they still want it down, or if they try to edit it out, there will be no show." The sign stayed.

15   Offstage, Cosby's philanthropy won him support among the civil-rights crowd. He made his biggest splash in 1988, when he and his wife gave $20 million to Spelman College, the largest individual donation ever given to a black college. "Two million would have been fantastic; twenty million, to use the language of the hip-hop generation, was off the chain," says Johnetta Cole, who was then president of Spelman. Race again came to the fore in 1997, when Cosby's son was randomly shot and killed while fixing a flat on a Los Angeles freeway. His wife wrote an op-ed in *USA Today* arguing that white racism lay behind her son's death. "All African-Americans, regardless of their educational and economic accomplishments, have been and are at risk in America simply because of their skin colors," she wrote. "Most people know that facing the truth brings about healing and growth. When is America going to face its historical and current racial realities so it can be what it says it is?"

The column cased a minor row, but most of white America took little notice. To them, Cosby was still America's Dad. But those close to Cosby were not surprised. Cosby was an avowed race man, who, like much of his generation, had come to feel that black America had lost its way. The crisis of absentee fathers, the rise of black-on-black crime, and the spread of hip-hop all led Cosby to believe that, after the achievements of the 1960s, the black community was committing cultural suicide.

His anger and frustration erupted into public view during an NAACP awards ceremony in Washington in 2004 commemorating the fiftieth anniversary of *Brown v. Board of Education*. At that moment, the shades of mortality and irrelevance seemed to be drawing over the civil-rights generation. Its matriarchs, Rosa Parks and Coretta Scott King, would be dead within two years. The NAACP's membership rolls had been shrinking; within months, its president, Kweisi Mfume, would resign (it was later revealed that he was under investigation by the NAACP for sexual harassment and nepotism—allegations that he denied). Other movement leaders were drifting into self-parody: Al Sharpton would soon be hosting a reality show and, a year later, would be doing ads for a predatory loan company; Sharpton and Jesse Jackson had recently asked MGM to issue an apology for the hit movie *Barbershop*.

That night, Cosby was one of the last honorees to take the podium. He began by noting that although civil-rights activists had opened the door for black America, young people today, instead of stepping through, were stepping backward. "No longer is a person embarrassed because they're pregnant without a husband," he told the crowd. "No longer is a boy considered an embarrassment if he tries to run away from being the father of the unmarried child."

There was cheering as Cosby went on. Perhaps sensing that he had the crowd, he grew looser. "The lower-economic and lower-middle-economic people are not holding their end in this deal," he told audience.

20   Cosby disparaged activists who charge the criminal-justice system with racism. "These are people going around stealing Coca-Cola. People getting shot in the back of the head over a piece of pound cake," Cosby said. "Then we all run out and are outraged: 'The cops shouldn't have shot him.' What the hell was he doing with the pound cake in his hand? I wanted a piece of pound cake just as bad as anybody else. And I looked at it and I had no money. And something called parenting said, 'If you get caught with it, you're going to embarrass your mother.'"

Then he attacked African American naming traditions, and the style of dress among young blacks: "Ladies and gentlemen, listen to these people. They are showing you what's wrong. . . . What part of Africa did this come from? We are not Africans. Those people are not Africans. They don't know a damned thing about Africa—with names like Shaniqua, Shaligua, Mohammed, and all that crap, and all of them are in jail." About then, people began to walk out of the auditorium and cluster in the lobby. There was still cheering, but some guests milled around and wondered what had happened. Some thought old age had gotten the best of Cosby. The mood was one of shock.

After what has come to be known as "the Pound Cake speech"—it has its own Wikipedia entry—Cosby came under attack from various quarters of the black establishment. The playwright August Wilson commented, "A billionaire attacking poor people for being poor. Bill Cosby is a clown. What do you expect?" One of the gala's hosts, Ted Shaw, the director-counsel of the NAACP Legal Defense and Education Fund, called his comments "a harsh attack on poor black people in particular." Dubbing Cosby an "Afristocrat in Winter," the Georgetown University professor Michael Eric Dyson came out with a book, *Is Bill Cosby Right? Or Has the Black Middle Class Lost Its Mind?*, that took issue with Cosby's bleak assessment of black progress and belittled his transformation from vanilla humorist to social critic and moral arbiter. "While Cosby took full advantage of the civil rights struggle," argued Dyson, "he resolutely denied it a seat at his artistic table."

But Cosby's rhetoric played well in black barbershops, churches, and backyard barbecues, where a unique brand of conservatism still runs strong. Outsiders may have heard haranguing in Cosby's language and tone. But much of black America heard instead the possibility of changing their communities without having to wait on the consciences and attention spans of policy makers who might not have their interests at heart. Shortly after Cosby took his Pound Cake message on the road, I wrote an article denouncing him as an elitist. When my father, a former Black Panther, read it, he upbraided me for attacking what he saw as a message of black enpowerment. Cosby's argument has resonated with the black mainstream for just that reason.

The split between Cosby and critics such as Dyson mirrors not only America's broader conservative/liberal split but black America's own historic intellectual divide. Cosby's most obvious antecedent is Booker T. Washington. At the turn of the twentieth century, Washington married a defense of the white South with a call for black self-reliance and became the most prominent black leader of his day. He argued that southern whites should be given time to adjust to emancipation; in the meantime, blacks should advance themselves not by voting and running for office but by working, and ultimately owning, the land.

25   W. E. B. Du Bois, the integrationist model for the Dysons of our day, saw Washington as an apologist for white racism and thought that his willingness to sacrifice the black vote was heretical. History ultimately rendered half of Washington's argument moot. His famous Atlanta Compromise — in which he endorsed segregation as a temporary means of making peace with southerners — was answered by lynchings, land theft, and general racial terrorism. But Washington's appeal to black self-sufficiency endured.

After Washington's death, in 1915, the black conservative tradition he had fathered found a permanent and natural home in the emerging ideology of Black Nationalism. Marcus Garvey, its patron saint, turned the Atlanta Compromise on its head, implicitly endorsing segregation not as an olive branch to whites but as a statement of black supremacy. Black Nationalists scorned the Du Boisian integrationists as stooges or traitors, content to beg for help from people who hated them.

Garvey argued that blacks had rendered themselves unworthy of the white man's respect. "The greatest stumbling block in the way of progress in the race has invariably come from within the race itself," wrote Garvey.

"The monkey wrench of destruction as thrown into the cog of Negro Progress, is not thrown so much by the outsider as by the very fellow who is in our fold, and who should be the first to grease the wheel of progress rather than seeking to impede." Decades later, Malcolm X echoed that sentiment, faulting blacks for failing to take charge of their destinies. "The white man is too intelligent to let someone else come and gain control of the economy of his community," Malcolm said. "But you will let anybody come in and take control of the economy of your community, control the housing, control the education, control the jobs, control the businesses, under the pretext that you want to integrate. No, you're out of your mind."

Black conservatives like Malcolm X and Louis Farrakhan, the leader of the Nation of Islam, have at times allied themselves with black liberals. But in general, they have upheld a core of beliefs laid out by Garvey almost a century ago: a skepticism of (white) government as a mediating force in the "Negro problem," a strong belief in the singular will of black people, and a fixation on a supposedly glorious black past.

Those beliefs also animate *Come On People*, the manifesto that Cosby and Poussaint published last fall. Although it does not totally dismiss government programs, the book mostly advocates solutions from within as a cure for black America's dismal vital statistics. "Once we find our bearings," they write, "we can move forward, as we have always done, on the path from victims to victors." *Come On People* is heavy on black pride ("no group of people has had the impact on the culture of the whole world that African Americans have had, and much of that impact has been for the good"), and heavier on the idea of the Great Fall—the theory, in this case, that post–Jim Crow blacks have lost touch with the cultural traditions that enabled them to persevere through centuries of oppression.

30   "For all the woes of segregation, there were some good things to come out of it," Cosby and Poussaint write. "One was that it forced us to take care of ourselves. When restaurants, laundries, hotels, theaters, groceries, and clothing stores were segregated, black people opened and ran their own. Black life insurance companies and banks thrived, as well as black funeral homes. . . . Such successes provided jobs and strength to black economic well-being. They also gave black people that gratifying sense of an interdependent community." Although the authors take pains to put some distance between themselves and the Nation of Islam, they approvingly quote one of its ministers who spoke at a call-out in Compton, California: "I went to Koreatown today and I met with the Korean merchants," the minister told the crowd. "I love them. You know why? They

got a place called what? Koreatown. When I left them, I went to China-town. They got a place called what? Chinatown. Where is your town?"

The notion of the Great Fall, and the attendant theory that segre-gation gave rise to some "good things," are the stock-in-trade of what Christopher Alan Bracey, a law professor at Washington University, calls (in his book, *Saviors or Sellouts*) the "organic" black conservative tra-dition: conservatives who favor hard work and moral reform over pro-tests and government intervention, but whose black-nationalist leanings make them anathema to the Heritage Foundation and Rush Limbaugh. When political strategists argue that the Republican Party is missing a huge chance to court the black community, they are thinking of this mostly male bloc—the old guy in the barbershop, the grizzled Pop Warner coach, the retired Vietnam vet, the drunk uncle at the family reunion. He votes Democratic, not out of any love for abortion rights or progressive taxation, but because he feels—in fact, he knows—that the modern-day GOP draws on the support of people who hate him. This is the audience that flocks to Cosby: culturally conservative black Americans who are convinced that integration, and to some extent the entire liberal dream, robbed them of their natural defenses.

"There are things that we did not see coming," Cosby told me over lunch in Manhattan last year. "Like, you could see the Klan, but because these things were not on a horse, because there was no white sheet, and the people doing the deed were not white, we saw things in the light of family and forgiveness. . . . We didn't pay attention to the dropout rate. We didn't pay attention to the fathers, to the self-esteem of our boys."

Given the state of black America, it is hard to quarrel with that analy-sis. Blacks are 13 percent of the population, yet black men account for 49 percent of America's murder victims and 41 percent of the prison pop-ulation. The teen birth rate for blacks is 63 per 1,000, more than double the rate for whites. In 2005, black families had the lowest median income of any ethnic group measured by the Census, making only 61 percent of the median income of white families.

Most troubling is a recent study released by the Pew Charitable Trusts, which concluded that the rate at which blacks born into the middle class in the 1960s backslid into poverty or near-poverty (45 percent) was three times that of whites—suggesting that the advances of even some of the most successful cohorts of black America remain tenuous at best. Another Pew survey, released last November, found that blacks were "less upbeat about the state of black progress now than at any time since 1983."

35   The rise of the organic black conservative tradition is also a response to America's retreat from its second attempt at Reconstruction. Blacks

have watched as the courts have weakened affirmative action, arguably the country's greatest symbol of state-sponsored inclusion. They've seen a fraudulent war on drugs that, judging by the casualties, looks like a war on black people. They've seen themselves bandied about as playthings in the presidential campaigns of Ronald Reagan (with his 1980 invocation of "states' rights" in Mississippi), George Bush (Willie Horton), Bill Clinton (Sister Souljah), and George W. Bush (McCain's fabled black love-child). They've seen the utter failures of school busing and housing desegregation, as well as the horrors of Katrina. The result is a broad distrust of government as the primary tool for black progress.

In May 2004, just one day before Cosby's Pound Cake speech, the *New York Times* visited Louisville, Kentucky, once ground zero in the fight to integrate schools. But the *Times* found that sides had switched, and that black parents were more interested in educational progress than in racial parity. "Integration? What was it good for?" one parent asked. "They were just setting up our babies to fail."

In response to these perceived failures, many black activists have turned their efforts inward. Geoffrey Canada's ambitious Harlem Children's Zone project pushes black students to change their study habits and improve their home life. In cities like Baltimore and New York, community groups are focusing on turning black men into active fathers. In Philadelphia last October, thousands of black men packed the Liacouras Center, pledging to patrol their neighborhoods and help combat the rising murder rate. When Cosby came to St. Paul Church in Detroit, one local judge got up and urged Cosby and other black celebrities to donate more money to advance the cause. "I didn't fly out here to write a check," Cosby retorted. "I'm not writing a check in Houston, Detroit, or Philadelphia. Leave these athletes alone. All you know is Oprah Winfrey and Michael Jackson. Forget about a check. . . . This is how we lost to the white man. 'Judge said Bill Cosby is gonna write a check, but until then . . .'"

Instead of waiting for handouts or outside help, Cosby argues, disadvantaged blacks should start by purging their own culture of noxious elements like gangsta rap, a favorite target. "What do record producers think when they churn out that gangsta rap with antisocial, women-hating messages?," Cosby and Poussaint ask in their book. "Do they think that black male youth won't act out what they have repeated since they were old enough to listen?" Cosby's rhetoric on culture echoes—and amplifies—a swelling strain of black opinion: Last November's Pew study reported that 71 percent of blacks feel that rap is a bad influence.

The strain of black conservatism that Cosby evokes has also surfaced in the presidential campaign of Barack Obama. Early on, some commentators speculated that Obama's Cosby-esque appeals to personal responsibility would cost him black votes. But if his admonishments for black kids to turn off the PlayStation and for black fathers to do their jobs did him any damage, it was not reflected at the polls. In fact, this sort of rhetoric amounts to something of a racial double play, allowing Obama and Cosby to cater both to culturally conservative blacks and to whites who are convinced that black America is a bastion of decadence. (Curiously, Cosby is noncommittal verging on prickly when it comes to Obama. When Larry King asked him whether he supported Obama, he bristled: "Do you ask white people this question? . . . I want to know why this fellow especially is brought up in such a special way. How many Americans in the media really take him seriously, or do they look at him like some prize brown baby?" The exchange ended with Cosby professing admiration for Dennis Kucinich. Months later, he rebuffed my request for his views on Obama's candidacy.)

40 The shift in focus from white racism to black culture is not as new as some social commentators make it out to be. Standing in St. Paul Church on that July evening listening to Cosby, I remembered the last time The Street felt like this: in the summer of 1994, after Louis Farrakhan announced the Million Man March. Farrakhan barnstormed the country holding "men only" meetings (but much larger). I saw him in my native Baltimore, while home from Howard University on vacation. The march itself was cathartic. I walked with four of five other black men, and all along the way black women stood on porches or out on the street, shouting, clapping, cheering. For us, Farrakhan's opinions on the Jews mostly seemed beside the point; what stuck was the chance to assert our humanity and our manhood by marching on the Mall, and not acting like we were all fresh out of San Quentin. We lived in the shadow of the '80s crack era. So many of us had been jailed or were on our way. So many of us were fathers in biology only. We believed ourselves disgraced and clung to the march as a public statement: the time had come to grow up.

Black conservatives have been dipping into this well of lost black honor since the turn of the twentieth century. On the one hand, vintage black nationalists have harked back to a golden age of black Africa, where mighty empires sprawled and everyone was a king. Meanwhile, populist black conservatives like Cosby point to pre-1968 black America as an era when blacks were united in the struggle: Men were men, and a girl who got pregnant without getting married would find herself bundled off to Grandpa's farm.

What both visions share is a sense that black culture in its present form is bastardized and pathological. What they also share is a foundation in myth. Black people are not the descendants of kings. We are—and I say this with big pride—the progeny of slaves. If there's any majesty in our struggle, it lies not in fairy tales but in those humble origins and the great distance we've traveled since. Ditto for the dreams of a separate but noble past. Cosby's, and much of black America's, conservative analysis flattens history and smoothes over the wrinkles that have characterized black America since its inception.

Indeed, a century ago, the black brain trust was pushing the same rhetoric that Cosby is pushing today. It was concerned that slavery had essentially destroyed the black family and was obsessed with seemingly the same issues—crime, wanton sexuality, and general moral turpitude—that Cosby claims are recent developments. "The early effort of middle-class blacks to respond to segregation was, aside from a political agenda, focused on a social-reform agenda," says Khalil G. Muhammad, a professor of American history at Indiana University. "The National Association of Colored Women, Du Bois in *The Philadelphia Negro*, all shared a sense of anxiety that African Americans were not presenting their best selves to the world. There was the sense that they were committing crimes and needed to keep their sexuality in check." Adds William Jelani Cobb, a professor of American history at Spelman College: "The same kind of people who were advocating for social reform were denigrating people because they didn't play piano. They often saw themselves as reluctant caretakers of the less enlightened."

In particular, Cosby's argument—that much of what haunts young black men originates in post-segregation black culture—doesn't square with history. As early as the 1930s, sociologists were concerned that black men were falling behind black women. In his classic study, *The Negro Family in the United States*, published in 1939, E. Franklin Frazier argued that urbanization was undermining the ability of men to provide for their families. In 1965—at the height of the civil-rights movement—Daniel Patrick Moynihan's milestone report, "The Negro Family: The Case for National Action," picked up the same theme.

45 At times, Cosby seems willfully blind to the parallels between his arguments and those made in the presumably glorious past. Consider his problems with rap. How could an avowed jazz fanatic be oblivious to the similar plaints once sparked by the music of his youth? "The tired longshoreman, the porter, the housemaid and the poor elevator boy in search

of recreation, seeking in jazz the tonic for weary nerves and muscles," wrote the lay historian J. A. Rodgers, "are only too apt to find the boot-legger, the gambler and the demi-monde who have come there for victims and to escape the eyes of the police."

Beyond the apocryphal notion that black culture was once a fount of virtue, there's still the charge that culture is indeed the problem. But to reach that conclusion, you'd have to stand on some rickety legs. The hip-hop argument, again, is particularly creaky. Ronald Ferguson, a Harvard social scientist, has highlighted that an increase in hip-hop's popularity during the early 1990s corresponded with a declining amount of time spent reading among black kids. But gangsta rap can be correlated with other phenomena, too — many of them positive. During the 1990s, as gangsta rap exploded, teen pregnancy and the murder rate among black men declined. Should we give the blue ribbon in citizenship to Dr. Dre?

"I don't know how to measure culture. I don't know how to test its effects, and I'm not sure anyone else does," says the Georgetown economist Harry Holzer. "There's a liberal story that limited opportunities, and barriers, lead to employment problems and criminal records, but then there's another story that has to do with norms, behaviors, and opposi-tional culture. You can't prove the latter statistically, but it still might be true." Holzer thinks that both arguments contain truth and that one doesn't preclude the other. Fair enough. Suffice it to say, though, that the evidence supporting structural inequality is compelling. In 2001, a researcher sent out black and white job applicants in Milwaukee, ran-domly assigning them a criminal record. The researcher concluded that a white man with a criminal record had about the same chance of getting a job as a black man without one. Three years later, researchers pro-duced the same results in New York under more rigorous conditions.

The accepted wisdom is that such studies are a comfort to black people, allowing them to wallow in their misery. In fact, the opposite is true — the liberal notion that blacks are still, after a century of struggle, victims of pervasive discrimination is the ultimate collective buzz-kill. It effectively means that African Americans must, on some level, accept that their children will be "less than" until some point in the future when white racism miraculously abates. That's not the sort of future that any black person eagerly awaits, nor does it make for particularly motivating talk-ing points.

Last summer, I watched Cosby give a moving commencement speech to a group of Connecticut inmates who'd just received their GEDs. Before the speech, at eight in the morning, Cosby quizzed correctional officials on the conditions and characteristics of their inmate population. I wished, then, that my seven-year-old son could have seen Cosby there, to take in the same basic message that I endeavor to serve him every day — that manhood means more than virility and strut, that it calls for discipline and dutiful stewardship. That the ultimate fate of black people lies in their own hands, not in the hands of their antagonists. That as an African American, he has a duty to his family, his community, and his ancestors.

50   If Cosby's call-outs simply ended at that — a personal and communal creed — there'd be little to oppose. But Cosby often pits the rhetoric of personal responsibility against the legitimate claims of American citizens for their rights. He chides activists for pushing to reform the criminal-justice system, despite solid evidence that the criminal-justice system needs reform. His historical amnesia — his assertion that many of the problems that pervade black America are of a recent vintage — is simply wrong, as is his contention that today's young African Americans are somehow weaker, that they've dropped the ball. And for all its positive energy, his language of uplift has its limitations. After the Million Man March, black men embraced a sense of hope and promise. We were supposed to return to our communities and families inspired by a new feeling of responsibility. Yet here we are again, almost fifteen years later, with seemingly little tangible change. I'd take my son to see Bill Cosby, to hear his message, to revel in its promise and optimism. But afterward, he and I would have a very long talk.

On the day last summer when Cosby met me for lunch in the West Village, it was raining, as it had been all week, and New York was experiencing a record-cold August. Cosby had just come from Max Roach's funeral and was dressed in a natty three-piece suit. Despite the weather, the occasion, and the oddly empty dining room, Cosby was energized. He had spent the previous day in Philadelphia, where he spoke to a group in a housing project, met with state health officials, and participated in a community march against crime. Grassroots black activists in his hometown were embracing his call. He planned, over the coming year, to continue his call-outs and release a hip-hop album. (He has also noted, however, that there won't be any profanity on it.)

Cosby was feeling warm and nostalgic. He asked why I had not brought my son, and I instantly regretted dropping him off at my partner's workplace for a couple of hours. He talked about breaking his shoulder playing school football, after his grandfather had tried to get him to quit. "Granddad Cosby got on the trolley and came over to the apartment," he recalled. "I was so embarrassed. I was laid out on the sofa. He was talking to my parents, and I was waiting for the moment when he would say, 'See, I told you, Junior.' He came back and reached in his pocket and gave me a quarter. He said, 'Go to the corner and get some ice cream. It has calcium in it.'"

Much pop psychology has been devoted to Cosby's transformation into such a high-octane, high-profile activist. His nemesis Dyson says that Cosby, in his later years, is following in the dishonorable tradition of upper-class African Americans who denounce their less fortunate brethren. Others have suggested more sinister motivations—that Cosby is covering for his own alleged transgressions. (In 2006, Cosby settled a civil lawsuit filed by a woman who claimed that he had sexually assaulted her; other women have come forward with similar allegations that have not gone to court.) But the depth of his commitment would seem to belie such suspicions, and in any case, they do not seem to have affected his hold on his audience: In the November Pew survey, 85 percent of all African American respondents considered him a "good influence" on the black community, above Obama (76 percent) and second only to Oprah Winfrey (87 percent).

Part of what drives Cosby's activism, and reinforces his message, is the rage that lives in all African Americans, a collective feeling of disgrace that borders on self-hatred. As the comedian Chris Rock put it in one of his infamous routines, "Everything white people don't like about black people, black people really don't like about black people. . . . It's like a civil war going on with black people, and it's two sides—there's black people and there's niggas, and niggas have got to go. . . . Boy, I wish they'd let me join the Ku Klux Klan. Shit, I'd do a drive-by from here to Brooklyn." (Rock stopped performing the routine when he noticed that his white fans were laughing a little too hard.) Liberalism, with its pat logic and focus on structural inequities, offers no balm for this sort of raw pain. Like the people he preaches to, Cosby has grown tired of hanging his head.

55   This disquiet spans generations, but it is most acute among those of the civil-rights era. "I don't know a better term than *angst*," says Johnnetta Cole. "I refuse to categorize every young African American with the same language, but there are some 'young'uns'—and some of us who are not 'young'uns'—who must turn around and look at where we are, because where we're headed isn't pretty." Like many of the stars of the civil-rights movement, Cole has gifts that go beyond social activism. She rose out of the segregated South and went to college at age fifteen, eventually earning a bachelor's from Oberlin and a doctorate in anthropology from Northwestern. That same sort of dynamism exists today among many younger blacks, but what troubles the older generation is that their energy seems directed at other pursuits besides social uplift.

Cosby is fond of saying that sacrifices of the '60s weren't made so that rappers and young people could repeatedly use the word *nigger*. But that's exactly why they were made. After all, chief among all individual rights awarded Americans is the right to be mediocre, crass, and juvenile—in other words, the right to be human. But Cosby is aiming for something superhuman—twice as good, as the elders used to say—and his homily to a hazy black past seems like an effort to redeem something more than the present.

When people hear Bill Cosby's message, many assume that he is the product of the sort of family he's promoting—two caring parents, a stable home life, a working father. In fact, like many of the men he admonishes, Cosby was born into a troubled home. He was raised by his mother because his father, who joined the navy, abandoned the family when Cosby was a child. Speaking to me of his youth, Cosby said, "People told me I was bright, but nobody stayed on me. My mother was too busy trying to feed and clothe us." He was smart enough to be admitted to Central High School, a magnet school in Philadelphia, but transferred and then dropped out in the 10th grade and followed his father into the service.

But the twists and turns of that reality seem secondary to the tidier, more appealing world that Cosby is trying to create. Toward the end of our lunch, in a long, rambling monologue, Cosby told me, "If you looked at me and said, 'Why is he doing this? Why right now?,' you could probably say, 'He's having a resurgence of his childhood.' What do I need if I am a child today? I need people to guide me. I need the possibility of change. I need people to stop saying I can't pull myself up by my own bootstraps. They say that's a myth. But these other people have their mythical stories—why can't we have our own?"

Ta-Nehisi Coates

In many ways, the writings of Ta-Nehisi Coates (b. 1975) have been informed by a desire to bridge the gap between the two seemingly contradictory sides of the inner-city African American experience he witnessed growing up in 1980s Baltimore. While on one hand the community in which he was raised was in chaos, with gang violence and crack cocaine use at an all-time high, another side of the same community was deeply committed to creating strong families, a solid community, and a better future for its children. The title and subject matter of Coates's critically acclaimed memoir, *The Beautiful Struggle: A Father, Two Sons, and an Unlikely Road to Manhood* (2008), illuminate his interest in exploring how these two halves of the same world work in tandem. It is largely the story of his father, Paul Coates, a former Black Panther and political idealist in the 1960s and 1970s, who with his wife, Cheryl Waters, struggled to raise two sons in the 1980s.

Originally published in *The Atlantic*, Coates's article "This Is How We Lost to the White Man," which takes its title from a Bill Cosby quotation, is a thorough and eloquent dissection of Cosby's campaign to lift up black America through self-reliance. In Coates's view, Cosby's campaign is a deeply conservative one that, in its open disdain for cultural movements such as rap and reverence for an idealized African American past, represents self-hatred and an unrealistic view of the past rather than progress.

Coates, whose articles have appeared in *Time*, the *New York Times Magazine*, *The Village Voice*, and *The Atlantic*, among other publications, is now a regular blog columnist for *The Atlantic*'s web site, where he writes about American culture and politics from an African American perspective. He currently lives in Harlem, New York.

SEEING

1. Look back over Coates's essay, and summarize the specific ways in which Bill Cosby thinks blacks have lost to the white man. What has been lost, and what happened to black identity after the white man won? How do Coates and Cosby think blacks can recover what has been lost? Identify the points on which Coates and Cosby disagree. Whom do you find more convincing on each of these points? Please be as specific as possible in explaining your response. Coates's essay offers a model of effective writing. To what extent is his essay weakened by his decision not to include notes identifying the sources of his quotations?

2. Bill Cosby seems to have several different identities in the essay: Cosby the speaker, Cosby the wealthy man, the television star, father, son, and so on. What do these shifting perspectives contribute to Coates's essay? How does he use them to make his points? For example, why does he choose to tell the story of Cosby as grandson at the end of the essay? Why do the themes Coates explores require these multiple identities?

WRITING

1. What reasons might have prompted Coates largely to exclude black women from his essay? What are the implications—and the consequences—of this decision? Write the first draft of your own "pound cake speech" (paras. 20–22) from the perspective of a black woman responding to both Coates and Cosby. For example, describe how you feel about the implication that black women rarely raise successful children without the help of men. Why would you accept not being permitted to attend Cosby's self-empowerment speech in St. Paul's Church of God? Which black women's opinions would you add to the males' that Coates cites on black history and culture?

2. What is "structural inequality" (paras. 47, 54)? Review Coates's essay to come up with a working definition, and then look for examples in your own life. For example, are children structurally unequal to adults? students to teachers? poor people to rich people? Are the structures and inequalities morally reasonable or necessary? Why or why not? In what ways are these other sorts of structural inequality similar to—and different from—those for which Coates has the most concern? When you have answered these questions, write the first draft of an expository essay in which you explain how one group lost to the other, such as "This Is How Children Lost to Adults."

LOOKING CLOSER – Doubling Consciousness

The United States Census predicts that in the year 2050 the number of multiracial Americans will have more than tripled what it is today. In fact, it is becoming more and more difficult for a large portion of our country's population to identify themselves by one race. The following selections examine the difficulties and advantages associated with having a racial makeup that cannot easily be explained by one simple word.

Writing almost a century ago, W. E. B. Du Bois provides a compelling account of the consequences of the segregated identity in "Double Consciousness," an excerpt from his famous publication *The Souls of Black Folk.* James McBride presents a contemporary example of how a feeling of two-ness continues to surface in his memoir, *What Color Is Jesus?* Kip Fulbeck's portraits give a firsthand account of what it feels like to be multiracial, and Naomi Schaefer Riley examines the problems associated with racial labels.

DOUBLE CONSCIOUSNESS
W. E. B. Du Bois

... The problem of the twentieth century is the problem of the colorline. ...

After the Egyptian and Indian, the Greek and Roman, the Teuton and Mongolian, the Negro is a sort of seventh son, born with a veil, and gifted with second-sight in this American world—a world which yields him no true self-consciousness, but only lets him see himself through the revelation of the other world. It is a peculiar sensation, this double-consciousness, this sense of always looking at one's self through the eyes of others, of measuring one's soul by the tape of a world that looks on in amused contempt and pity. One ever feels his two-ness—an American, a Negro; two souls, two thoughts, two unreconciled strivings; two warring ideals in one dark body, whose dogged strength alone keeps it from being torn asunder.

The history of the American Negro is the history of this strife,—this longing to attain self-conscious manhood, to merge his double self into a better and truer self. In this merging he wishes neither of the older selves to be lost. He would not Africanize America, for America has too much to teach the world and Africa. He would not bleach his Negro soul in a flood of white Americanism, for he knows that Negro blood has a message for the world. He simply wishes to make it possible for a man to be both a Negro and an American, without being cursed and spit upon by his fellows, without having the doors of Opportunity closed roughly in his face.

Work, culture, liberty,—all these we need, not singly but together, not successively but together, each growing and aiding each, and all striving toward that vaster ideal that swims before the Negro people, the ideal human brotherhood, gained through the unifying ideal of Race; the ideal of fostering and developing the traits and talents of the Negro, not in opposition to or contempt for other races, but rather in large conformity to the greater ideals of the American Republic, in order that some day on American soil two world-races may give each to each those characteristics both so sadly lack. We the darker ones come even now not altogether empty-handed: there are to-day no truer exponents of the pure human spirit of the Declaration of Independence than the American Negroes; there is no true American music but the wild sweet melodies of the Negro slave; the American fairy tales and folk-lore are Indian and African; and, all in all, we black men seem the sole oasis of simple faith and reverence in a dusty desert of dollars and smartness.

Guillermo Gómez-Peña
Authentic Cuban Santera, 1993

WHAT COLOR IS JESUS?
James McBride

Just before I quit my last job in Washington, I drove down into Virginia to see my stepfather's grave for the first time. He was buried in a little country graveyard in Henrico County, near Richmond, about a hundred yards from the schoolhouse where he learned to read. It's one of those old "colored" graveyards, a lonely, remote backwoods place where the wind blows through the trees and the graves are marked by lopsided tombstones. It was so remote I couldn't find it by myself. I had to get my aunt Maggie to show me where it was. We drove down a dirt road and then parked and walked down a little dusty path the rest of the way. Once we found his grave, I stood over it for a long time.

I was fourteen when my stepfather died. One minute he was there, the next—boom—gone. A stroke. Back then I thought a stroke was something you got from the sun. I didn't know it could kill you. His funeral was the first I had ever attended. When the funeral director, a woman with white gloves, unlatched the coffin, I was horrified. I couldn't believe she was going to open it up. I begged her in my mind not to open it up—please—but she did, and there he was. The whole place broke up. Even the funeral director cried. I thought I would lose my mind.

Afterward, they took him out of the church, put him in a car, and flew him down to Virginia. My mother and older brother and little sister went, but I'd seen enough. I didn't want to see him anymore. As a kid growing up in New York, I'd been embarrassed by him because he wasn't like the other guys' fathers, who drove hot rods, flew model airplanes with their sons, and talked about the Mets and civil rights. My father was solitary, gruff, busy. He worked as a furnace fireman for the New York City Housing Authority for thirty-six years, fixing oil burners and shoveling coal into big furnaces that heated the housing projects where my family lived. He drove a Pontiac, a solid, clean, quiet car. He liked to dress dapper and drink Rheingold beer and play pool with his brother Walter and their old-timey friends who wore fedoras and smoked filterless Pall Malls and called liquor "likka" and called me "boy." They were weathered Southern black men, quiet and humorous and never bitter about white people, which was out of my line completely. I was a modern-day black man who didn't like the white man too much, even if the white man was my mother.

My mother was born Jewish in Poland, the eldest daughter of an Orthodox rabbi. She married my natural father, a black man, in 1941. He died in 1957, at forty-eight, while she was pregnant with me. She married my stepfather, Hunter L. Jordan, Sr., when I was about a year old. He raised me and my seven brothers and sisters as his own—we considered him to be our father—and he and my mother added four more kids to the bunch to make it an even twelve.

5   My parents were unique. As unique as any parents I have known, which I suppose makes their children unique. However, being unique can spin you off in strange directions. For years I searched for a kind of peace. I vacillated between being the black part of me that I accept and the white part of me that I could not accept. Part writer, part musician, part black man, part white man. Running, running, always running. Even professionally I sprinted, from jazz musician to reporter and back again. Bounding from one life to the other—the safety and prestige of a journalism job to the poverty and fulfillment of the musician's life.

Standing over my stepfather's grave, thinking about quitting my gig to move back to New York to be a musician and freelance writer, I was nervous. He would never approve of this jive. He would say: "You got a good job and you quit that? For what? To play jazz? To write? Write what? You need a job." Those were almost the exact words my mother always used.

My aunt Maggie, who's about seventy-two, was standing there as I waged this war in my mind. She came up behind me and said, "He was a good man. I know y'all miss him so much."

"Yep," I said, but as we walked up the dusty little path to my car to go to the florist to get flowers, I was thinking, "Man, I'm sure glad he's not here to see me now."

I'm a black man and I've been running all my life. Sometimes I feel like my soul just wants to jump out of my skin and run off, things get that mixed up. But it doesn't matter, because what's inside is there to stay no matter how fast you sprint. Being mixed feels like that tingly feeling you have in your nose when you have to sneeze—you're hanging on there waiting for it to happen, but it never does. You feel completely misunderstood by the rest of the world, which is probably how any sixteen-year-old feels, except that if you're brown-skinned like me, the feeling lasts for the rest of your life. "Don't you sometimes feel like just beating up the white man?" a white guy at work once asked me. I hate it when people see my brown skin and assume that all I care about is gospel music and fried chicken and beating up the white man. I could care less. I'm too busy trying to live.

10   Once a mulatto, always a mulatto, is what I say, and you have to be happy with what you have, though in this world some places are more conducive to the survival of a black man like me than others. Europe is okay, Philly works, and in New York you can at least run and hide and

get lost in the sauce; but Washington is a town split straight down the middle—between white and black, haves and have-nots, light-skinned and dark-skinned—and full of jive-talkers of both colors. The blacks are embittered and expect you to love Marion Barry unconditionally. The whites expect you to be either grateful for their liberal sensibilities or a raging militant. There's no middle ground. No place for a guy like me to stand. Your politics is in the color of your face, and nothing else counts in Washington, which is why I had to get out of there.

All of my brothers and sisters—six boys, five girls, wildly successful by conventional standards (doctors, teachers, professors, musicians)— have had to learn to plow the middle ground. Music is my escape, because when I pick up the saxophone and play, the horn doesn't care what color I am. Whatever's inside comes out, and I feel free.

My family was big, private, close, poor, fun, and always slightly con- fused. We were fueled by the race question and also befuddled by it. Everyone sought their own private means of escape. When he was little, my older brother Richie, a better sax player than I and the guy from whom I took all my cues, decided he was neither black nor white, but green, like the comic book character the Hulk. His imagination went wild with it, and he would sometimes lie on our bed facedown and make me bounce on him until he turned green.

"Do I look green yet?" he'd ask.

"Naw . . ."

15   "Jump some more."

I'd bounce some more.

"How about now?"

"Well, a little bit."

"RRRrrrrr . . . I'm the Hulk!" And he'd rise to attack me like a zombie.

20   Richard had a lot of heart. One morning in Sunday school, he raised his hand and asked our Sunday school teacher, Reverend Owens, "Is Jesus white?"

Reverend Owens said no.

"Then why is he white in this picture?" and he held up our Sunday school Bible.

Reverend Owens said, "Well, Jesus is all colors."

"Then why is he white? This looks like a white man to me." Richie held up the picture high so everyone in the class could see it. "Don't he look white to you?" he asked. Nobody said anything.

25   Reverend Owens was a nice man and also a barber who tore my head up about once a month. But he wasn't that sharp. I could read better than he could, and I was only twelve.

So he kind of stood there, wiping his face with his handkerchief and making the same noise he made when he preached. "Well . . . ahhh . . . well . . . ahhh . . . ."

I was embarrassed. The rest of the kids stared at Richie like he was crazy. "Richie, forget it," I mumbled.

"Naw. If they put Jesus in this picture here, and he ain't white, and he ain't black, they should make him gray. Jesus should be gray."

Richie stopped going to Sunday School after that, although he never stopped believing in God. My mother tried to make him go back, but he wouldn't.

30   When we were little, we used to make fun of our mother singing in church. My mother can't sing a lick. She makes a shrill kind of sound, a cross between a fire engine and Curly of the Three Stooges. Every Sunday morning, she'd stand in church, as she does today, the only white person there, and the whole congregation going, "Leaannnnnning, ohhh, leaning on the crossss, ohhhhh Laaawwwd!" and her going, "Leeeeeaaannnning, ohhhh, clank! bang! @*%$@*!," rattling happily along like an old Maytag washer. She wasn't born with the gift for gospel music, I suppose.

My mother, Ruth McBride Jordan, who today lives near Trenton, is the best movie I've ever seen. She's seventy-six, pretty, about five three, bowlegged, with curly dark hair and pretty dark eyes. She and my father and stepfather raised twelve children and sent them to college and graduate school, and at age sixty-five she obtained her own college degree in social welfare from Temple University. She's a whirlwind, so it's better to test the wind before you fly the kite. When I began writing my book about her, she said, "Ask me anything. I'll help you as much as I can." Then I asked her a few questions and she snapped: "Don't be so nosy. Don't tell all your business. If you work too much, your mind will be like a brick. My pot's burning on the stove. I gotta go."

When we were growing up, she never discussed race. When we asked whether we were black or white, she'd say, "You're a human being. Educate your mind!" She insisted on excellent grades and privacy. She didn't encourage us to mingle with others of any color too much. We were taught to mind our own business, and the less people knew about us, the better.

When we'd ask if she was white, she'd say, "I'm light-skinned," and change the subject. But we knew she was white, and I was embarrassed by her. I was ten years old when Martin Luther King, Jr., was killed, and I feared for her life because it seemed like all of New York was going to burn. She worked as a night clerk-typist at a Manhattan bank and got home every night about 2 a.m. My father would often be unavailable, and one of the older kids would meet her at the bus stop while the rest of us lay awake, waiting for the sound of the door to open. Black militants scared me. So did the Ku Klux Klan. I thought either group might try to kill her.

I always knew my mother was different, knew my siblings and I were different. My mother hid the truth from her children as long as she could. I was a grown man before I knew where she was born.

35   She was born Ruchele Dwajra Sylska in a town called Dobryn, near Gdansk, Poland. Her father was an Orthodox rabbi who lived in Russia. He escaped the Red Army by sneaking over the border into Poland. He married my grandmother, Hudis, in what my mother says was an arranged marriage, emigrated to America in the early 1920s, changed his name, and sent for his family. My mother landed on Ellis Island like thousands of other European immigrants.

The family settled in Suffolk, Virginia, and operated a grocery store on the black side of town. Her father also ran a local synagogue. Theirs was the only store in town open on Sundays.

He was feared within the family, my mother says. His wife, who suffered from polio, was close to her three children—a son and two daughters—but could not keep the tyranny of the father from driving them off. The oldest child, my mother's brother, left home early, joined the army, and was killed in World War II. The remaining two girls worked from sunup to sundown in the store. "My only freedom was to go out and buy little romance novels," my mother recalls. "They cost a dime." In school, they called her "Jew-baby."

When she was seventeen, she went to New York to visit relatives for the summer and worked in a Bronx factory owned by her aunt. At the factory, there was a young black employee named Andrew McBride, from High Point, North Carolina. They struck up a friendship and a romance. "He was the first man who was ever kind to me," my mother says. "I didn't care what color he was."

Her father did, though. When she returned home to finish her senior year of high school, her father arranged for her to marry a Jewish man after graduation. She had other plans. The day after she graduated, she packed her bags and left. After floating between New York and Suffolk for a while, she finally decided to marry my father in New York City. Her father caught up to her at the bus station the last time she left home. He knew that she was in love with a black man. The year was 1941.

40   "If you leave now, don't ever come back," he said.

"I won't," she said.

She gave up Judaism, married Andrew McBride, and moved to a one-room flat in Harlem where she proceeded to have baby after baby. Her husband later became a minister, and together they started New Brown Memorial Baptist Church in Red Hook, Brooklyn, which still exists. The mixed marriage caused them a lot of trouble—they got chased up Eighth Avenue by a group of whites and endured blacks murmuring under their breath, and she was pushed around in the hallway of the Harlem building by a black woman one day. But she never went home. She tried to see her mother after she married, when she found out her mother was ill and dying. When she called, she was told the family had sat shiva for her, as if she had died. "You've been out; stay out," she was told. She always carried that guilt in her heart, that she left her mother with her cruel father and never saw her again.

In 1957, Andrew McBride, Sr., died of cancer. My mother was thirty-six at the time, distraught after visiting him in the hospital, where doctors stared and the nurses snickered. At the time, she was living in the Red Hook project in Brooklyn with seven small kids. She was pregnant with me. In desperation, she searched out her aunt, who was living in Manhattan. She went to her aunt's house and knocked on the door. Her aunt opened the door, then slammed it in her face.

She told me that story only once, a few years ago. It made me sick to hear it, and I said so.

45   "Leave them alone," she said, waving her hand. "You don't understand Orthodox Jews. I'm happy. I'm a Christian. I'm free. Listen to me: When I got home from your daddy's funeral, I opened our mailbox, and it was full of checks. People dropped off boxes of food—oranges, meat, chickens. Our friends, Daddy's relatives, the people from the church, the people you never go see, they gave us so much money. I'll never forget that for as long as I live. And don't you forget it, either."

A number of years ago, after I had bugged her for months about details of her early life, my mother sat down and drew me a map of where she had lived in Suffolk. She talked as she drew: "The highway goes here, and the jailhouse is down this road, and the slaughterhouse is over here. . . ."

I drove several hours straight, and was tired and hungry once I hit Suffolk, so I parked myself in a local McDonald's and unfolded the little map. I checked it, looked out the window, then checked it again, looked out the window again. I was sitting right where the store used to be.

I went outside and looked around. There was an old house behind the McDonald's. I knocked on the door, and an old black man answered.

"Excuse me . . ." and I told him my story: Mother used to live here. Her father was a rabbi. Jews. A little store. He fingered his glasses and looked at me for a long time. Then he said, "C'mon in here."

50　　He sat me down and brought me a soda. Then he asked me to tell my story one more time. So I did.

He nodded and listened closely. Then his face broke into a smile. "That means you the ol' rabbi's grandson?"

"Yep."

First he chuckled, then he laughed. Then he laughed some more. He tried to control his laughing, but he couldn't, so he stopped, took off his glasses, and wiped his eyes. I started to get angry, so he apologized. His name was Eddie Thompson. He was sixty-six. He had lived in that house all of his life. It took him a minute to get himself together.

"I knew your mother," he said. "We used to call her Rachel."

55　　I had never heard that name before. Her name was Ruth, but he knew her as Rachel, which was close to Ruchele, the Yiddish name her family called her.

"I knew the whole family," Thompson said. "The ol' rabbi, boy, he was something. Rachel was the nice one. She was kindhearted. Everybody liked her. She used to walk right up and down the road here with her mother. The mother used to limp. They would say hello to the people, y'know? Old man, though . . ." and he shrugged. "Well, personally, I never had no problem with him."

He talked for a long time, chuckling, disbelieving. "Rachel just left one day. I'm telling you she left, and we thought she was dead. That whole family is long gone. We didn't think we'd ever see none of them again till we got to the other side. And now you pop up. Lord knows it's a great day."

He asked if we could call her. I picked up the phone and dialed Philadelphia, got my mother on the line, and told her I had somebody who wanted to talk to her. I handed the phone to him.

"Rachel? Yeah. Rachel. This is Eddie Thompson. From down in Suffolk. Remember me? We used to live right be—yeaaaah, that's right." Pause. "No, I was one of the little ones. Well, I'll be! The Lord touched me today.

60　　"Rachel? That ain't you crying now, is it? This is old Eddie Thompson. You remember me? Don't cry now."

I went and got some flowers for my stepfather's grave and laid them across it. My mother wanted me to make sure the new tombstone she got him was in place and it was. It said OUR BELOVED DADDY, HUNTER L. JORDAN, AUGUST 11, 1900, TO MAY 14, 1972.

He was old when he died and a relatively old fifty-eight when he married my mother. They met in a courtyard of the Red Hook housing project where we lived, while she was selling church dinners on a Saturday to help make ends meet. He strolled by and bought some ribs, came back the next Saturday and bought some more. He ended up buying the whole nine yards—eight kids and a wife. He used to joke that he had enough for a baseball team.

I never heard him complain about it, and it never even occurred to me to ask him how he felt about white and black. He was quiet and busy. He dealt with solid things. Cars. Plumbing. Tricycles. Work. He used to joke about how he had run away from Richmond when he was a young man because Jim Crow was tough, but racism to him was a detail that you stepped over, like you'd step over a crack in the sidewalk. He worked in the stockyards in Chicago for a while, then in a barbershop in Detroit, where, among other things, he shined Henry Ford's shoes. He went to New York in the 1920s. He never told me those things; his brother Walter did. He didn't find those kinds of facts interesting. All he wanted to talk about was my grades.

He was strong for his age, full and robust, with brown eyes and handsome American Indian features. One night, he had a headache, and the next day he was in the hospital with a stroke. After a couple of weeks, he came home. Then two days later, he asked me to come out to the garage with him. I was one of the older kids living at home; most were away at college or already living on their own. He could barely walk and had difficulty speaking, but we went out there, and we got inside his Pontiac. "I was thinking of maybe driving home one more time," he said. He was talking about Henrico County, where we spent summer vacations.

65 He started the engine, then shut it off. He was too weak to drive. So he sat there, staring out the windshield, looking at the garage wall, his hand on the steering wheel. He was wearing his old-timey cap and his peacoat, though it was May and warm outside. Sitting there, staring straight ahead, he started talking, and I listened closely because he never gave speeches.

He said he had some money saved up and a little land in Virginia, but it wasn't enough. He was worried about my mother and his children. He said I should always mind her and look out for my younger brothers and sisters, because we were special. "Special people," he said, "And just so special to me." It was the only time I ever heard him refer to race, however vaguely, but it didn't matter because right then I knew he was going to die, and I had to blink back my tears. Two days later, he was gone.

Standing over his grave—it seemed so lonely and cold, with the wind blowing through the trees—part of me wanted to throw myself on the ground to cover and warm him. We arranged the flowers. Plastic ones, because, as Aunt Maggie said, they lasted longer. I took one last look and thought, Maybe he would understand me now. Maybe not. I turned and left.

I suppose I didn't look too happy, because as I started up the little road toward my car, Aunt Maggie put her arm in mine. I'd known her since I was a boy, just like I'd known these woods as a boy when he took us down here, but I'd blanked her and these woods out of my mind over the years, just like you'd blank out the words of a book by covering them with a piece of paper. She didn't judge me, which is what I always appreciated most about our friends and relatives over the years, the white and the black. They never judged, just accepted us as we were. Maybe that's what a black white man has to do. Maybe a black white man will never be content. Maybe a black white man will never fit. But a black white man can't judge anybody.

I remember when I was ten years old, when I pondered my own race and asked my mother, as she was attempting to fix our dinner table that had deteriorated to three-legged status, whether I was white or black. She paused a moment, then responded thoughtfully: "Pliers."

70 "Huh?"

"Hand me the pliers out of the kitchen drawer."

I handed her the pliers and she promptly went to work on the kitchen table, hammering the legs and tops until dents and gouges appeared on all sides. When the table finally stood shakily on all fours, she set the pliers down, stood up and said, "Pliers can fix anything."

"What about me being black?" I asked.

"What about it?" she said. "Forget about black. You are a human being."

75 "But what do I check on the form at the school that says White, Black, Other?"

"Don't check nothing. Get a hundred on your school tests and they won't care what color you are."

"But they do care."

"I don't," she said, and off she went.

Perturbed, I picked up the pliers and sought out my father, hammering at the fuel pump of his 1969 Pontiac. "Am I black or white?" I asked.

80 "Where'd you get my pliers?" he asked.

"I got 'em from Ma."

"I been looking for 'em all day." He took them and immediately put them to work.

"Am I black or white, Daddy?"

He grabbed a hose in his hand and said, "Hold this." I held it. He went inside the car and cranked the engine. Fuel shot out of the line and spilled all over me. "You all right?" he asked. I shook my head. He took me inside, cleaned me up, put the hose in the car, and took me out for ice cream. I forgot about my color for a while.

85   But the question plagued me for many years, even after my father's death, and I never did find out the answer because neither he nor my mother ever gave any. I was effectively on my own. I searched for years to find the truth, to find myself as a black white man. I went to Africa, got VD, came home with no answers. I went to Europe, sipped café and smoked in Paris for months, came home empty. Last year, while working on my '53 Chevy at my home in Nyack, while my four-year-old son rolled around in the leaves and ate mud, it hit me. I asked him to hand me the pliers, and as he did so, he asked me, "What color is Grandma?"

"She's white," I said.

"Why isn't she like me?"

"She is like you, she's just whiter."

"Why is she whiter?"

90   "I don't know. God made her that way."

"Why?"

"I don't know. Would you like her better if she looked more like you?"

"No. I like her the way she is."

It occurred to me then that I was not put on this earth to become a leader of mixed-race people, wielding my race like a baseball bat, determined to force white people to accept me as I am. I realized then that I did not want to be known as Mr. Mulatto, whose children try to be every race in the world, proudly proclaiming Indian blood, African blood, Jewish blood, singing Peter, Paul, and Mary songs at phony private schools where yuppie parents arrive each morning hopping out of Chevy Suburban tanks with bumper stickers that read "Question Authority." I want the same thing every parent wants—a good home for my wife and children, good schools, peace and quiet, a good set of wrenches, and a son big enough to hand them to me. And when he gets big enough to have his own tools and work on his own car, maybe he will understand that you can't change someone's opinion about you no matter how many boxes you check, no matter how many focus groups you join, no matter how much legislation you pass, no matter how much consciousness raising you do. It's a real simple answer. Give 'em God. Give 'em pliers. Give 'em math. Give 'em discipline. Give 'em love, and let the chips fall where they may. Pontificating about it is okay. Passing laws is important, but I never once in my life woke up not knowing whether I should eat matzo ball or fried chicken. I never once felt I'd be able to play the sax better if my mom had been black, or that I'd have been better at math if my father were Jewish. I like me, and I like me because my parents liked me.

I am a person of color.
I am not half-"white".
I am not half-"Asian".
I am a whole "other".

☑ Other

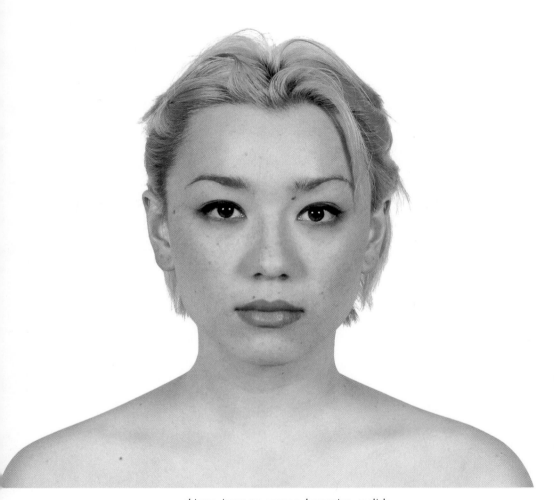

chinese, japanese, german, hungarian, english

I AM A DAILY CONTEST TO GUESS WHAT I AM.

japanese, german

My last boyfriend told me
he liked me because of my race.
So I dumped him.

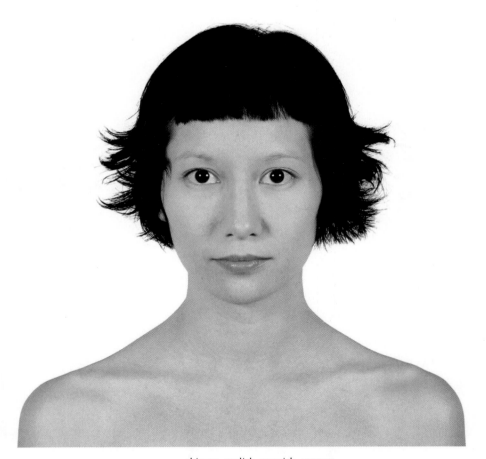

chinese, english, scottish, german

I AM CHARLES BARKLEY TO MY FAMILY, MONTEL WILLIAMS TO MY FRIENDS, AFRICAN AMERICAN TO THE POLICE, AND BALDY TO MY WIFE.

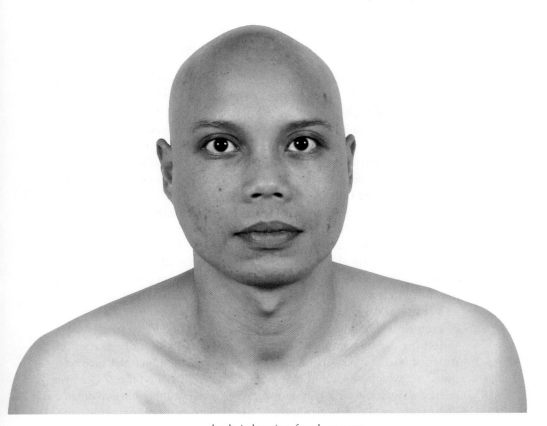

dutch, indonesian, french, german

THE RISKS OF
MULTIRACIAL IDENTIFICATION
Naomi Schaefer Riley

The comment period has closed on proposed new guidelines from the U.S. Department of Education on how colleges should ask students about race. No longer, the guidelines say, should applicants simply be given the choice of black, white, Asian, American Indian (or Alaska Native), or native Hawaiian (or other Pacific Islander). Now they should be allowed to check off more than one box, as well as note whether they identify as Hispanic. Eugene L. Anderson, an associate director of the American Council on Education, told *Diverse*, a higher-education magazine, that he expected colleges would be pleased with the new guidelines: "They make sense; they respect peoples' individual notion of racial identity, which is important."

No doubt colleges also appreciate the department's instructions for practical reasons. The proliferation of multiracial options on a variety of forms, including college applications, reflects the new demographic reality in America. On the 2000 census, nearly seven million Americans checked off two or more racial boxes. And a study last year by researchers at Cornell University found that the number of interracial marriages involving white people, black people, or Hispanics each year in the United States has jumped tenfold since the 1960s.

In a sense, these developments represent the realization of the dream of a melting pot. In 1963 Norman Podhoretz, the editor of *Commentary*, penned a controversial essay called "My Negro Problem—and Ours," expressing despair about the chances for real racial integration in this country. That could not occur, he wrote, "unless color does *in fact* disappear: and that means not integration, it means assimilation, it means— let the brutal word come out—miscegenation."

I remember reading the essay for the first time and being struck by the simple logic. After centuries of enslavement and decades of segregation, America had made startling progress in ending the rancor of race relations. But what to do about the bitterness remaining? Podhoretz's answer seemed to guarantee that ultimately racism would simply have to die out.

5   At the time, he sensed that there would be resistance to assimilation. He worried intensely about whether white people like himself would come around to accepting interracial marriages. And he was prescient about another obstacle; that some black people would oppose them.

In the forty-three years since the essay appeared, both Podhoretz's highest hopes and his greatest fears have been realized. Interracial marriage is on the rise, but the products of those marriages seem more focused than ever on figuring out and defining themselves by each individual part of their racial identity. Rather than becoming comfortable moving in a variety of racial and ethnic environments, they are expressing discomfort in every one. At the same time that color is beginning to "disappear," as Podhoretz would say, it seems more relevant than ever in some circles.

An article last semester in *The Harvard Crimson* detailed the complaints of a number of mixed-race students who said they felt uneasy attending the meetings of groups that were meant for only one of their multiple ethnicities. Paloma A. Zepeda, half Mexican and half Russian, said that when she came to meetings for the Mexican American student group Raza, people would say, "Look, white people come to Raza." Ms. Zepeda protested, "I am a member of the Hispanic community, but I don't think that's the sum total of everything."

Then there was Yalun H. Tu. He told the *Crimson* reporter he felt uncomfortable at the Chinese-student gatherings: "They would talk about how Chinese mothers are overbearing and strict. But my mother is Caucasian and relaxed, so I couldn't empathize." He lamented, "I just didn't feel that communal bond that I think often binds these groups."

Some of these "outcasts" have started forming new groups. Harvard now has ReMixed, a new multiracial organization on the campus. The University of California at Berkeley has a Mixed Student Union, then there is Brown University's Organization of Multiracial and Biracial Students and Bryn Mawr College's Half and Half. Several campuses have "Hapa" organizations for "half-Asian" students.

10   But even those mixed-race groups cannot satisfy some students. One told the *Crimson* that her acquaintances at Harvard's Hapa group focused too much on East Asian identities, instead of South Asian ones. They went out, she complained, for dim sum, "which I enjoy, but don't identify with culturally." But she didn't feel welcome in the regular South Asian group, either, because in a theatrical performance the group's leaders cast her in the role of a white person.

The level of specificity that seems to be required for many young men and women to feel comfortable today is bordering on the absurd. Ultimately it's sad. Advocates of diversity on college campuses insist that they are not just assembling faces of different colors for aesthetic purposes; they are trying to offer students a model of how to live in a multiracial, multiethnic society. But students do not seem to be learning to be more tolerant of people unlike them. They are demanding that they be surrounded and sheltered by people who are *exactly* like them.

Colleges have long experienced what sociologists refer to as the "lunch-table problem." That tendency toward racial self-segregation may find its origins in students' upbringings, but it is surely furthered by campus multiculturalists. Over the years, I have had many students I've interviewed tell me that they were never encouraged to identify themselves by their race so much as when they set foot on a college campus. Both administrators and student-run organizations often pressured them to engage in activities that put them in a particular racial box. So it's not surprising that students now want activities that conform to every contour of their ancestry.

And today that multiracial pride is extending beyond college campuses. Witness the interest in tracing one's identity through DNA. Last winter Henry Louis Gates Jr., chairman of the department of African and African-American studies at Harvard, announced in a *Wall Street Journal* article, "My Yiddishe Mama," that blood tests revealed that his great-grandmother was an Ashkenazi Jew. Most people probably find that kind of information interesting, but not vital to their sense of identity. Presumably Mr. Gates has not since decided he feels comfortable only around people who have a mix of Jewish and African blood.

But there are plenty of people who attach a great deal of importance to this sort of thing. Last spring the *New York Times* reported on a white couple who had the DNA of their adopted twins tested to see if something in the boys' ancestry might help with their college-admissions prospects. Their sons turned out to be 9 percent Native American and 11 percent Northern African. Another man found through DNA testing that he was Jewish and demanded Israeli citizenship. A woman, a descendant of Jamaican slaves, claimed a Scottish slave owner was her mother's great-great-grandfather. So she demanded (she said it was mostly playful) property from the man's family in Scotland. One can only imagine the complex mathematical formulas that would be employed if reparations for slave descendants were ever instituted. Perhaps a new kind of "one-drop rule" would be needed.

15   Of course some people identify as mixed race not just because of a strand of DNA, but because they are simply not easily identifiable, or they want to celebrate their identity. Earlier this year, the artist Kip Fulbeck brought out *Part Asian, 100% Hapa* (Chronicle Books), a photo album in which he asked more than one hundred Hapas, "What are you?" The

project, he said, was intended to help turn a derogatory word into a term of pride.

It seems inevitable that one day no one will bother asking Fulbeck's question because no one will find multiracial faces worthy of notice. Indeed, the other day I found myself a little startled when I boarded a commuter train out of New York City and found nine blond-haired, blue-eyed college students sitting together. What a rare sight. My first thought was that they must be Swedish tourists.

Though I am confident that racial mixing will become increasingly common thanks to greater tolerance in our society and the effects of globalization, I am not at all confident that it will have the kind of harmonious effect Podhoretz once predicted. Perhaps human beings just have too great a desire to identify with people who look like them, or to find out what their ancestors looked like. Perhaps no matter how many boxes they have to check off, no matter how complicated the system of racial classification becomes, people will hang on to racial identity for dear life because that's what their fathers and grandfathers did before them.

But we are exacerbating an already problematic tendency with faddish ideology. When a "multicultural" sensibility doesn't seek to overcome race but makes it central to one's identity, and when one can be truly at home only with people who share that identity, the result is a ludicrous situation in which people can empathize only with a smaller and smaller group of their peers. That sort of isolation is my problem—and ours.

W. E. B. Du Bois

Double consciousness is a term developed by William Edward Burghardt Du Bois, the guiding intellectual light behind the establishment of the modern movement for the rights of African Americans. Du Bois first used the term in an article entitled "Strivings of the Negro People," which originally appeared in *The Atlantic Monthly* in 1897 and which he revised (under the title "Of Our Spiritual Strivings") for inclusion in his groundbreaking book *The Souls of Black Folk* (1903). The portion reprinted here, an excerpt from that revised essay, represents one of the first published examinations of racial difference in America.

Du Bois was born in Massachusetts in 1868, and in 1895 he was the first African American to earn a doctorate from Harvard University. In his long career he simultaneously distinguished himself not only as a writer but also as a historian, sociologist, criminologist, poet, political activist, and more. Among his many accomplishments he co-founded in 1909 the National Association for the Advancement of Colored People (NAACP), an organization that thrives to this day; he published many books, including *The Philadelphia Negro* (1899), *Black Reconstruction* (1935), and *Black Folk: Then and Now* (1939); and he pioneered the civil rights movement. In later life he moved to Ghana, where he became a naturalized citizen; he died in 1963 at the age of ninety-five.

Guillermo Gómez-Peña

Among the most popular performance artists of his generation, Guillermo Gómez-Peña has taken as his primary subject of exploration the "borders" between Mexico and the United States. Raised in Mexico City, where he was born in 1955, Gómez-Peña emigrated to the United States in 1978 and lived for many years in the San Diego area, a short ride from the Mexican border. It was here that he first fused performance, audio, video, radio, poetry, and art, pioneering mixed media as an art form.

Exploring the many "borders" (physical, cultural, language, etc.) between Mexico and the United States, Gómez-Peña's performances have had a major influence on contemporary performance art and have been seen all over the world. His words often fuse English, Spanish, and Spanglish, encourage audience participation, and incorporate elaborate costumes;

they tackle subjects such as immigration, cultural identity, race, and technology. Among his most well known works are *Border Brujo* (performed 1988–1989), *The Mexterminator Project* (performed 1997–1999), and, most recently, the *Mapa/Corpo* series (performed 2004–2008). Gómez-Peña is also a prolific writer, directs the San Franciso–based drama troupe La Pocha Nostra, contributes regularly to National Public Radio, is a contributing editor to *The Drama Revue*, is the recipient of a MacArthur Foundation "genius award," and is the winner of an American Book Award for *The New World Border* (1996).

James McBride

First published in the *Washington Post* in 1988, "What Color Is Jesus?" was one of James McBride's first explorations of being a biracial American in a society that often insists people be of one race or another. It is a subject he has continued to explore throughout his writing career. In a recent interview McBride said, "My goal is to be able to fill out one of those forms that asks *Who are you?* and be able to just put 'Human being,' you know? None of this stuff really matters."

Born in 1957 to an African American minister and a Jewish American Polish immigrant, McBride is not only a writer of nonfiction but also a novelist, composer, and jazz saxophonist. Raised in various parts of New York City (Harlem, Brooklyn, and Queens), he received his undergraduate degree from Oberlin College and his master's degree in journalism from Columbia University. Since then he has found success in two distinct careers. As a writer he has been on the staff of the *Boston Globe* and the *Washington Post* and has contributed to such magazines as *Essence,* the *New York Times*, and *Rolling Stone*; he has also published several books, including his 1996 memoir *The Color of Water: A Black Man's Tribute to His White Mother* and the novels *The Miracle of St. Anna*

(2003) and *Song Yet Sung* (2008). As a musician he has written songs for Anita Baker, Grover Washington Jr., and many others as well as performing with his own group, the Rock Bottom Remainders. He currently is a writer-in-residence at New York University.

Kip Fulbeck

The book *part asian, 100% hapa* was born from Kip Fulbeck's Hapa Project, a forum for Hapa people to answer the question "What are you?" *Hapa* is a slang term, Hawaiian in origin, describing mixed-race individuals of Asian or Pacific Islander ancestry. For the project, Fulbeck, an internationally recognized filmmaker, poet, and artist, traveled across the country taking photographic portraits of individuals who could identify themselves as Hapa. Over the course of the project, Fulbeck photographed over 1,200 subjects, 100 of which are featured in the book.

Currently a professor of art at the University of California–Santa Barbara, Fulbeck has been named Outstanding Faculty Member four times. He is also the author of *Paper Bullets: A Fictional Autobiography* (2001) and *Permanence: Tattoo Portraits* (2008) and is the director of a dozen short films including *Banana Split* (1991) and *Lilo & Me* (2003).

Virtues; as adjunct fellow at the Ethics and Public Policy Center, a conservative interest group "dedicated to applying the Judeo-Christian moral tradition to critical issues of public policy"; as contributing editor to *The American Enterprise*; and as assistant editor at the conservative Jewish political/cultural magazine *Commentary*. These experiences have contributed to her unique, often controversial perspectives on today's political issues, and she shows a particular interest in how religion and education meet – and clash. Despite this often uncomfortable coexistence, Riley states, "I think religion will eventually regain a place of respect in the classroom. People will be more willing to study the interaction between religion and literature, religion and philosophy, and even . . . religion and science."

Riley's dual interest in religion and education culminated in the publication of *God on the Quad: How Religious Colleges and the Missionary Generation Are Changing America* (2005). In this book she explores the growing popularity of religious colleges and universities in America, and she probes how students at these institutions view topics such as feminism, political activism, homosexuality, and race. Her interest in the racial-identity politics of undergraduates also led to the publication (in the *Chronicle of Higher Education*) of the article reprinted here. Riley is currently deputy taste editor at the *Wall Street Journal*.

Naomi Schaefer Riley

A self-described Conservative Jew, Naomi Schaefer Riley graduated from Harvard University in 1998 and immediately began writing for national publications such as the *New York Times*, *The New Republic*, and the *Weekly Standard*. Riley has also served as editor of the journal *In Character: A Journal of Everyday*

6

CONFRONTING

CLASS

Class is the great unspoken word on most campuses in the United States. There are many reasons to account for the reluctance of many people – within and far beyond the classroom – to discuss this concept vigorously and directly. As Paul Fussell, the author of *Class: A Painfully Accurate Guide through the American Status System*, wryly observes, "If you find an American who feels entirely class secure, stuff and exhibit him. He's a rare specimen." Questions about someone's class rarely surface in polite company. Perhaps that's because what you say and how you say it, what you eat and how and where you eat, where you work and what you do and earn there as well as what you watch on TV and even whether you watch TV at all are significant expressions of your class standing. Class is, as Fussell notes in the essay included in the readings that follow, "a touchy subject."

In its simplest sense *class* can refer to any grouping, such as plants or animals. But *class* is also a complex word – in both the range and depth of its meanings, and especially when it implies social distinctions. The Latin origin of the word, *classis*, underscored the separation of the people of Rome according to the property they held; by the time the word was introduced into English in the sixteenth century, social significance was attached to it, a notion that was reinforced by its association with education. Raymond Williams notes in his study *Keywords* that the "development of class in its modern social sense, with relatively fixed names for particular classes (lower class, middle class, upper class, working class and so on) belongs essentially to the period between 1770 and 1840, which is also the period of the Industrial Revolution and its decisive reorganization of society." From that point forward, the association of class with social and economic position became increasingly pronounced, and metaphors of mobility — the ability to move from one class to another — surfaced more frequently in American public discourse. Soon studying the features and the cultures of the lower, working, middle, and upper classes became the focal points for academic inquiry in several disciplines.

The essays and images that follow offer provocative perspectives on a subject that each of us has learned how to read and reflect on — often without any formal instruction in it. As Paul Fussell notes,

> You reveal a great deal about your social class by the amount of annoyance or fury you feel when the subject is brought up. A tendency to get very anxious suggests that you are middle class and nervous about slipping down a rung or two. On the other hand, upper-class people love the topic to come up: The more attention paid to the matter the better off they seem to be. Proletarians generally don't mind discussions of the subject because they know they can do little to alter their class identity.

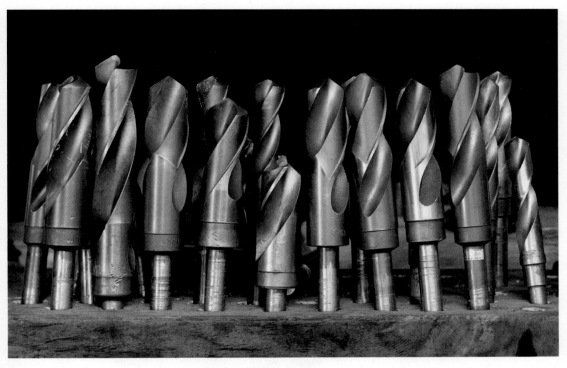

Brooks Jensen
Standing Drill Bits, Ellensburg, Washington, 1986

Two weeks after I photographed this metal shop, it burned to the ground.
Welding sparks splattered on the wooden floor, they said.

Brooks Jensen
Three Drills, Hockinson, Washington, 1987

He advised that a good drill would last me a lifetime. I suspect he was right.

Brooks Jensen
Felix Muñoz, Cuero, Texas, 1988

He drank a Dr. Pepper and rubbed bacon on a rusty, black bean pot as we talked.

Brooks Jensen
Vernon Barrow and Grandson, Denison, Kansas, 1989

As we talked, Paul Harvey spoke on the radio.
Every commercial, he'd say to his grandson how much he liked "Mr. Harvey."
I called him Mr. Barrow and he seemed to like that.

Brooks Jensen
Joe Sasak, Leroy, Wisconsin, 1989

"Don't ever ya t'row nutin' out. Ya never know when it might come in handy.
I made dis here door handle out a ole beer tap."

Brooks Jensen

Photographer Brooks Jensen was born in Laramie, Wyoming, in 1954 and developed an interest in photography at an early age. The editor since 1993 of the highly respected photographic arts magazine *LensWork* (which he edits in collaboration with his wife and fellow photographer, Maureen Gallagher), Jensen also teaches photography, has served as director of the Portland Photographer's Forum, has written two collections of essays about photography and the creative process (*Letting Go of the Camera: Essays on Photography and the Creative Life* and *Single Exposures: Random Observations on Photography, Art & Creativity*, both 2008), and has published *Made of Steel* (1993), a collection of his photographic work. He currently lives in Washington State.

According to Jensen, photography is not only about the subject's outer surface but also about what lies underneath. He has said, "If photography is truly an art, then what it expresses is human emotion. Not what the world looks like. . . . It's not about what's in front of you, it's about what's inside of you. . . . Expression, that's what it's all about. Artistic expression, not objective duplication." Jensen's words raise provocative questions about his artistic intentions and about the statements implicit in his powerfully engaging portraits of working-class life and of the men and the tools that keep America working.

SEEING

1. Brooks Jensen describes himself as "a maker of things, an observer, a commentator." His phrasing suggests that there may be an appreciable difference between being an "observer" and a "commentator." Is there? If so, what are the differences? As you review these photographs, what evidence can you identify to demonstrate that Jensen is much more than an observer of what he photographs? Choose two of the images to examine carefully. In what specific ways do they demonstrate that Jensen is a commentator and/or an observer? Consider as well the title of Jensen's series of photographs: Made of Steel. To what extent does the title support or subvert your response?

2. Examine carefully the photographs of the standing drill bits and the three drills. From what point of view does Jensen present these objects? To what extent does the way they are positioned influence your reaction to them? What specific aspects of these objects does Jensen focus on? How does this new angle of vision change your experience of seeing these seemingly commonplace objects? What adjectives would you use to characterize the photographs? Explain your choices. Now apply the same process – and standards – to the people depicted in Jensen's photographs. In what specific ways might the title *Made of Steel* also apply to these men? to the young man as well?

WRITING

1. One of Jensen's achievements is that his photographs enable us to perceive new aspects of seemingly simple objects and of the "ordinary" people who work with them. Compare and contrast Jensen's presentation of his subjects to the portfolio of images by Peter Menzel and Faith D'Aluisio (pp. 30–39). Which images do you find more engaging? more surprising? Explain why. Which images hold your attention longer? What angle(s) of vision are emphasized in these two portfolios of photographs? with what effect(s)? Which do you prefer? Why? Write the first draft of an expository essay in which you explain why you find one of these portfolios more artistically engaging and memorable than the other.

2. Outstanding works of art draw our eye to detail. We admire, for example, the care and sensitivity with which the artist calls our attention to the surface of the forms presented. Choose one of Jensen's photographs, and write notes about which details Jensen draws your attention to—and with what effects. One of the most important aspects of appreciating photography is the artist's use of light. The amount of light—and the direction from which it falls on the objects depicted—accentuates the dramatic effects of details. After you have studied Jensen's attentiveness to details and his use of light, write the first draft of an expository essay in which you explain how his use of detail and light contributes to the artistic success of the photograph.

Page 30

Pierre-Auguste Renoir
A Waitress at Duval's Restaurant, 1875

THE WAITRESS
Billy Collins

She brings a drink to the table,
sets it down
in front of me and smiles,

and after a little while she brings
5 another one with a menu
and takes the empty glass away.

She places before me a plate
of veal and a few thin wheels of lemon,
and when I asked for more bread

10 she smiles, brings it to me in a basket.
She keeps smiling and walking away,
then coming back to the table

to see if everything is OK
and to fill my glass with wine,
15 turning and walking away and returning

until she is every waitress
who has ever served me,
and every waiter, too.

I hold my fork in the air
20 and watch the blades of the fans
slowly turning on the ceiling,

and I begin to picture them all,
living and dead, gathered together
for one night in a vast ballroom

25 where they have removed their jackets,
their aprons and bowties,
and now they are having a cigarette

or they are dancing with one another,
turning slowly in each other's arms
30 to a five-piece syncopated band.

Which is all I can think about
after I leave some money for the bill
and a large, sentimental tip

and walk into the fluorescent streets,
35 my collar up against the October chill—
all the waitresses and waiters of my life

dancing slowly under what seem
to be colored lights
until I realize that the ballroom

40 is made of nothing but autumn leaves—
red, yellow, and gold—
just waiting for a sudden gust of wind

to scatter it all
into the dark spaces
45 beyond these late-night, nearly empty streets.

Pierre-Auguste Renoir

One of the most celebrated painters of the nineteenth-century Impressionist movement, which also included such artists as Édouard Manet, Claude Monet, Paul Cézanne, and Edgar Degas, Pierre-Auguste Renoir (1841–1919) specialized in candid portraits of people, usually Parisian women, from all walks of life. In *A Waitress at Duval's Restaurant*, included here, he sets his sights on a typical member of the Parisian working class, circa 1875. One of the basic ideas of Impressionism was the importance of capturing the essence of the landscape, object, or person being painted by using quick brush strokes and unique blends of colors, rather than by rendering precise, realistic details using traditional colors and techniques.

Born into the working class himself (he was the son of a tailor), Renoir originally apprenticed as a porcelain painter, but after the firm where he worked went bankrupt, he became increasingly attracted to making his living as a painter of canvases. He was lucky to be allowed to practice his skills by copying paintings at the Louvre after hours and to meet many other young painters through his studies with teacher Marc Gabriel Charles Gleyer and later at the École des Beaux Arts. It was in this environment that he and a small group of fellow students began formulating a new approach to painting. Initially controversial, Impressionism eventually took hold throughout the world – with Renoir considered one of its masters. During the last decades of his life, Renoir continued to paint despite developing rheumatoid arthritis, which severely limited mobility in his hands and shoulder. In 1919, shortly before his death, Renoir visited the Louvre and saw his paintings hanging with the old masters.

Billy Collins

In a recent interview, the poet Billy Collins said that he is not interested in writing difficult poetry that only a few people can understand, but instead poetry that communicates clearly and directly, almost like narrative fiction, to anyone: "I'm not writing for the podium. I'm just writing, trying to write in a fairly quiet tone to one other reader who is by herself, or himself, and I'm trying to interrupt some silence in their life." Perhaps because of his ability to connect with readers from all walks of life, he has become one of America's most widely read poets, one of the few to see his collections appear on best-seller lists. Collins's style and subject matter offer a subtle commentary about class, communicating indirectly that poetry is for everyone, not only for an elite few. One would not be surprised to see the waitress who is the subject of the poem reprinted here reading one of Collins's books on her break – and he would not have it any other way.

Born in 1941, Collins received his PhD in English from the University of California – Riverside. He has taught at City University of New York, Lehman College, since 1968 and has also taught at Columbia University and Sarah Lawrence College. Collins first found widespread success when a CD recording of his selected poems became a best seller in 1997. From 2001 to 2003 he held the position of Poet Laureate of the United States, during which time he read his poem "The Names" to the U.S. Congress on the first anniversary of the terrorist attacks of 9/11. His many collections of poetry include *Pokerface* (1977), *Questions about Angels* (1991), *The Art of Drowning* (1995), *Nine Horses* (2002), and *Ballistics* (2008). The recipient of numerous awards and fellowships, Collins currently lives in upstate New York.

SEEING

1. Examine Collins's poem and Renoir's painting carefully. As soon as you are prepared to talk in detailed terms about each text, explain how they convey the difference between cultural attitudes toward the waitressing profession in nineteenth-century France and in contemporary American society. Point to specific evidence in each work to support your assertions. After paying close attention to details, which representation do you think honors the waitress's craft more effectively? Which text reveals more interest in the woman than in the work? Explain why.

2. What are the effects of Renoir's decision to highlight certain parts of his painting and to shade others? For example, what does he achieve by painting the waitress's face, scarf, and apron with increasingly lighter shades of white? How do other colors relate to each other in the painting, such as the differently shaded walls? In what specific ways do light and color focus our attention in poetry as they do in painting? Using Collins's poem as an example, explain how they do or do not achieve the same effect in poetry as in painting.

WRITING

1. When you first looked at Renoir's painting of the waitress, how did you read her expression? Did she appear happy? relaxed? tired? stressed? Did your reading of her expression change after you read Collins's poem? If your reading of the waitress's expression changed, explain how she appears to you now. If your reading did not change, explain why.

Working with Sources

2. Let's assume that Collins and Renoir were well paid for their work, which would certainly be rare for most poets and painters. In what specific ways, if any, would their financial success change your judgment of their artistry? Would it be morally objectionable for a relatively wealthy artist to profit from depicting a relatively poor subject such as a waitress? Explain why or why not. Should an artist be expected – or required – to pay the people they paint or write about in the same way that filmmakers must pay actors? Why or why not? What specific provisions, if any, can you find in state or federal law that govern artists' and their subjects' rights? Write the first draft of an essay in which you argue for – or against – requiring artists to pay the people who serve as the subjects of their art.

Responding Visually

Imagine that you are the waitress in either Collins's poem or Renoir's painting. Adopting her imagined point of view, create a visual text called "The Customer." Would the waitress depict the customer as an artist sitting in front of a canvas or as a patron sitting at a table? What clothes would the customer wear, and in which direction – and at whom – would he or she look? Which colors would the waitress use? What might the customer do when he or she leaves the restaurant? If you prefer to write a description rather than create a visual text, please be sure to describe the setting and the colors you would use.

A TOUCHY SUBJECT
Paul Fussell

Although most Americans sense that they live within an extremely complicated system of social classes and suspect that much of what is thought
and done here is prompted by considerations of status, the subject has
remained murky. And always touchy. You can outrage people today simply by mentioning social class, very much the way, sipping tea among the
aspidistras a century ago, you could silence a party by adverting too openly
to sex. When, recently, asked what I am writing, I have answered, "A
book about social class in America," people tend first to straighten their
ties and sneak a glance at their cuffs to see how far fraying has advanced
there. Then, a few minutes later, they silently get up and walk away. It is
not just that I am feared as a class spy. It is as if I had said, "I am working on a book urging the beating to death of baby whales using the dead
bodies of baby seals." Since I have been writing this book I have experienced many times the awful truth of R. H. Tawney's perception, in his
book *Equality* (1931): "The word 'class' is fraught with unpleasing associations, so that to linger upon it is apt to be interpreted as the symptom of a perverted mind and a jaundiced spirit."

Especially in America, where the idea of class is notably embarrassing.
In his book *Inequality in an Age of Decline* (1980), the sociologist Paul
Blumberg goes so far as to call it "America's forbidden thought." Indeed,
people often blow their tops if the subject is even broached. One woman,
asked by a couple of interviewers if she thought there were social classes
in this country, answered: "It's the dirtiest thing I've ever head of!" And
a man, asked the same question, got so angry that he blurted out, "Social
class should be exterminated."

Actually, you reveal a great deal about your social class by the amount
of annoyance or fury you feel when the subject is brought up. A tendency
to get very anxious suggests that you are middle class and nervous about
slipping down a rung or two. On the other hand, upper-class people love
the topic to come up: The more attention paid to the matter the better off
they seem to be. Proletarians generally don't mind discussions of the subject because they know they can do little to alter their class identity. Thus
the whole class matter is likely to seem like a joke to them—the upper
classes fatuous in their empty aristocratic pretentiousness, the middles
loathsome in their anxious gentility. It is the middle class that is highly
class-sensitive, and sometimes class-scared to death. A representative of

that class left his mark on a library copy of Russell Lynes's *The Taste-makers* (1954). Next to a passage patronizing the insecure decorating taste of the middle class and satirically contrasting its artistic behavior to that of some more sophisticated classes, this offended reader scrawled, in large capitals, "BULL SHIT!" A hopelessly middle-class man (not a woman, surely?) if I ever saw one.

If you reveal your class by your outrage at the very topic, you reveal it also by the way that you define the thing that's outraging you. At the bottom, people tend to believe that class is defined by the amount of money you have. In the middle, people grant that money has something to do with it, but think education and the kind of work you do almost equally important. Nearer the top, people perceive that taste, values, ideas, style, and behavior are indispensable criteria of class, regardless of money or occupation or education. One woman interviewed by Studs Terkel for *Division Street: America* (1967) clearly revealed her class as middle both by her uneasiness about the subject's being introduced and by her instinctive recourse to occupation as the essential class criterion. "We have right on this street almost every class," she said. "But I shouldn't say class," she went on, "because we don't live in a nation of classes." Then, the occupational criterion: "But we have janitors living on the street, we have doctors, we have businessmen, CPAs."

5   Being told that there are no social classes in the place where the interviewee lives is an old experience for sociologists. "'We don't have classes in our town' almost invariably is the first remark recorded by the investigator," reports Leonard Reissman, author of *Class in American Life* (1959). "Once that has been uttered and is out of the way, the class divisions in the town can be recorded with what seems to be an amazing degree of agreement among the good citizens of the community." The novelist John O'Hara made a whole career out of probing into this touchy subject, to which he was astonishingly sensitive. While still a boy, he was noticing that in the Pennsylvania town where he grew up, "older people do not treat others as equals."

Class distinctions in America are so complicated and subtle that foreign visitors often miss the nuances and sometimes even the existence of a class structure. So powerful is "the fable of equality," as Frances Trollope called it when she toured America in 1832, so embarrassed is the government to confront the subject—in the thousands of measurements pouring from its bureaus, social class is not officially recognized—that it's easy for visitors not to notice the way the class system works. A case in point is the experience of Walter Allen, the British novelist and literary critic. Before he came over here to teach at a college in the 1950s, he imagined that "class scarcely existed in America, except, perhaps, as divisions between ethnic groups or successive waves of immigrants." But living a while in Grand Rapids opened his eyes: There he learned of the snob power of New England and the pliability of the locals to the long-wielded moral and cultural authority of the old families.

Some Americans viewed with satisfaction the failure of the 1970s TV series *Beacon Hill*, a drama of high society modeled on the British *Upstairs, Downstairs*, comforting themselves with the belief that this venture came to grief because there is no class system here to sustain interest in it. But they were mistaken. *Beacon Hill* failed to engage American viewers because it focused on perhaps the least interesting place in the indigenous class structure, the quasi-aristocratic upper class. Such a dramatization might have done better if it had dealt with places where everyone recognizes interesting class collisions occur—the place where the upper-middle class meets the middle and resists its attempted incursions upward, or where the middle class does the same to the classes just below it.

If foreigners often fall for the official propaganda of social equality, the locals tend to know what's what, even if they feel some uneasiness talking about it. When the acute black from the South asserts of an ambitious friend that "Joe can't class with the big folks," we feel in the presence of someone who's attended to actuality. Like the carpenter who says: "I hate to say there are classes, but it's just that people are more comfortable with people of like backgrounds." His grouping of people by "like backgrounds," scientifically uncertain as it may be, is nearly as good a way as any to specify what it is that distinguishes one class from another. If you feel no need to explicate your allusions or in any way explain what you mean, you are probably talking with someone in your class. And that's true whether you're discussing the Rams and the Forty-Niners, RVs, the House (i.e., Christ Church, Oxford), Mama Leone's, the Big Board, "the Vineyard," "Baja," or the Porcellian.

In *Class: A Guide through the American Status System*, I am going to deal with some of the visible and audible signs of social class, but I stick largely with those that reflect choice. That means that I do not consider matters of race, or, except now and then, religion or politics. Race is visible, but it is not chosen. Religion and politics, while usually chosen, don't show, except for the occasional front-yard shrine or car bumper sticker. When you look at a person you don't see "Roman Catholic" or "liberal": You see "hand-painted necktie" or "crappy polyester shirt"; you hear *parameters* or *in regards to*. In attempting to make sense of indicators like these, I have been guided by perception and feel rather than by any method that could be deemed "scientific," believing with Arthur Marwick, author of *Class: Image and Reality* (1980), that "class . . . is too serious a subject to leave to the social scientists."

10 It should be a serious subject in America especially, because here we lack a convenient system of inherited titles, ranks, and honors, and each generation has to define the hierarchies all over again. The society changes faster than any other on Earth, and the American, almost uniquely, can be puzzled about where, in the society, he stands. The things that conferred class in the 1930s—white linen golf knickers, chrome cocktail shakers, vests with white piping—are, to put it mildly, unlikely to do so today. Belonging to a rapidly changing rather than a traditional society, Americans find Knowing Where You Stand harder than do most Europeans. And a yet more pressing matter, Making It, assumes crucial importance here. "How'm I doin?" Mayor Koch of New York used to bellow, and most of his audience sensed that he was, appropriately, asking the representative American question.

It seems no accident that, as the British philosopher Anthony Quinton says, "The book of etiquette in its modern form . . . is largely an American product, the great names being Emily Post . . . and Amy Vanderbilt." The reason is that the United States is preeminently the venue of newcomers, with a special need to place themselves advantageously and to get on briskly. "Some newcomers," says Quinton, "are geographical, that is, immigrants; others are economic, the newly rich; others again chronological, the young." All are faced with the problem inseparable from the operations of a mass society, earning respect. The comic Rodney Dangerfield, complaining that he don't get none, belongs to the same national species as that studied by John Adams, who says, as early as 1805: "The rewards . . . in this life are *esteem* and *admiration* of others—the punishments are *neglect* and *contempt*. . . . The desire of the esteem of others is as real a want of nature as hunger— and the neglect and contempt of the world as severe a pain as the gout or stone. . . ." About the same time the Irish poet Thomas Moore, sensing the special predicament Americans were inviting with the egalitarian Constitution, described the citizens of Washington, D.C., as creatures "born to be slaves, and struggling to be lords."

Thirty years later, in *Democracy in America*, Alexis de Tocqueville put his finger precisely on the special problem of class aspiration here. "Nowhere," he wrote, "do citizens appear so insignificant as in a democratic nation." Nowhere, consequently, is there more strenuous effort to achieve— earn would probably not be the right word—significance. And still later in the nineteenth century, Walt Whitman, in *Democratic Vistas* (1871), perceived that in the United States, where the form of government promotes a condition (or at least an illusion) of uniformity among the citizens, one of the unique anxieties is going to be the constant struggle for individual self-respect based upon social approval. That is, where everybody is somebody, nobody is anybody. In a recent Louis Harris poll, "respect from others" is what 76 percent of respondents said they wanted most. Addressing prospective purchasers of a coffee table, an ad writer recently spread before them this most enticing American vision: "Create a rich, warm, sensual allusion to your own good taste that will demand respect and consideration in every setting you care to imagine."

The special hazards attending the class situation in America, where movement appears so fluid and where the prizes seem available to anyone who's lucky, are disappointment, and, following close on that, envy. Because the myth conveys the impression that you can readily earn your way upward, disillusion and bitterness are particularly strong when you find yourself trapped in a class system you've been half persuaded isn't important. When in early middle life some people discover that certain limits have been placed on their capacity to ascend socially by such apparent irrelevancies as heredity, early environment, and the social class of their immediate forebears, they go into something like despair, which, if generally secret, is no less destructive.

De Tocqueville perceived the psychic dangers. "In democratic times," he granted, "enjoyments are more intense than in the ages of aristocracy, and the number of those who partake in them is vastly larger." But, he added, in egalitarian atmospheres "man's hopes and desires are oftener blasted, the soul is more stricken and perturbed, and care itself more keen."

15   And after blasted hopes, envy. The force of sheer class envy behind vile and even criminal behavior in this country, the result in part of disillusion over the official myth of classlessness, should never be underestimated. The person who, parking his attractive car in a large city, has returned to find his windows smashed and his radio aerial snapped off will understand what I mean. Speaking in West Virginia in 1950, Senator Joseph R. McCarthy used language that leaves little doubt about what he was really getting at—not so much "Communism" as the envied upper-middle and upper classes. "It has not been the less fortunate or members of minority groups who have been selling this nation out," he said, "but rather those who have had all the benefits, the finest homes, the finest college education. . . ." Pushed far enough, class envy issues in revenge egalitarianism, which the humorist Roger Price, in *The Great Roob Revolution*

(1970), distinguishes from "democracy" thus: "Democracy demands that all of its citizens begin the race even. Egalitarianism insists that they all *finish* even." Then we get the situation satirized in L. P. Hartley's novel *Facial Justice* (1960), about "the prejudice against good looks" in a future society somewhat like ours. There, inequalities of appearance are redressed by government plastic surgeons, but the scalpel isn't used to make everyone beautiful—it's used to make everyone plain.

Despite our public embrace of political and judicial equality, in individual perception and understanding—much of which we refrain from publicizing—we arrange things vertically and insist on crucial differences in value. Regardless of what we say about equality, I think everyone at some point comes to feel like the Oscar Wilde who said, "The brotherhood of man is not a mere poet's dream: it is a most depressing and humiliating reality." It's as if in our heart of hearts we don't want agglomerations but distinctions. Analysis and separation we find interesting, synthesis boring.

Although it is disinclined to designate a hierarchy of social classes, the federal government seems to admit that if in law we are all equal, in virtually all other ways we are not. Thus the eighteen grades into which it divides its civil-servant employees, from grade 1 at the bottom (messenger, etc.) up through 2 (mail clerk), 5 (secretary), 9 (chemist), to 14 (legal administrator), and finally 16, 17, and 18 (high-level administrators). In the construction business there's a social hierarchy of jobs, with "dirt work," or mere excavation, at the bottom; the making of sewers, roads, and tunnels in the middle; and work on buildings (the taller, the higher) at the top. Those who sell "executive desks" and related office furniture know that they and their clients agree on a rigid "class" hierarchy. Desks made of oak are at the bottom, and those of walnut are next. Then, moving up, mahogany is, if you like, "upper middle class," until we arrive, finally, at the apex: teak. In the army, at ladies' social functions, pouring the coffee is the prerogative of the senior officer's wife because, as the ladies all know, coffee outranks tea.

There seems no place where hierarchical status-orderings aren't discoverable. Take musical instruments. In a symphony orchestra the customary ranking of sections recognizes the difficulty and degree of subtlety of various kinds of instruments: Strings are on top, woodwinds just below, then brass, and, at the bottom, percussion. On the difficulty scale, the accordion is near the bottom, violin near the top. Another way of assigning something like "social class" to instruments is to consider the prestige of the group in which the instrument is customarily played. As the composer Edward T. Cone says, "If you play a violin, you can play in a string quartet or symphony orchestra, but not in a jazz band and certainly not in a marching band. Among woodwinds, therefore, flute, and oboe, which are primarily symphonic instruments, are 'better' than the clarinet, which can be symphonic, jazz, or band. Among brasses, the French horn ranks highest because it hasn't customarily been used in jazz. Among percussionists, tympani is high for the same reason." And (except for the bassoon) the lower the notes an instrument is designed to produce, in general the lower its class, bass instruments being generally easier to play. Thus a sousaphone is lower than a trumpet, a bass viol lower than a viola, etc. If you hear "My boy's taking lessons on the trombone," your smile will be a little harder to control than if you hear "My boy's taking lessons on the flute." On the other hand, to hear "My boy's taking lessons on the viola da gamba" is to receive a powerful signal of class, the kind attaching to antiquarianism and museum, gallery, or "educational" work. Guitars (except when played in "classical"— that is, archaic—style) are low by nature, and that is why they were so often employed as tools of intentional class degradation by young people in the 1960s and '70s. The guitar was the perfect instrument for the purpose of signaling these young people's flight from the upper-middle and middle classes, associated as it is with Gypsies, cowhands, and other personnel without inherited or often even earned money and without fixed residence.

The former Socialist and editor of the *Partisan Review* William Barrett, looking back thirty years, concludes that "the Classless Society looks more and more like a Utopian illusion. The socialist countries develop a class structure of their own," although there, he points out, the classes are very largely based on bureaucratic toadying. "Since we are bound . . . to have classes in any case, why not have them in the more organic, heterogeneous and variegated fashion" indigenous to the West? And since we have them, why not know as much as we can about them? The subject may be touchy, but it need not be murky forever.

Paul Fussell

In 1924 Paul Fussell was born into an upper-middle-class family in Pasadena, California. The selection presented here is taken from his book *Class: A Guide through the American Status System* (1983). Fussell is the author of more than fifteen books, including *The Great War and Modern Memory* (1975), which won the National Book Critics Circle Award and the National Book Award, and his most recent, *The Boys' Crusade: The American Infantry in Northwestern Europe, 1944–1945* (2003). In 2007 he was one of the veterans interviewed for Ken Burns's PBS documentary *The War*.

Fussell believes that his life has been shaped by his experience in World War II. He was wounded in France and narrowly escaped with his life. In a 1998 interview he described his writing career as his attempt at "stripping off the wrappings from things which make them look pleasant or acceptable and showing how complicated real life is." He recently retired from teaching at the University of Pennsylvania; he currently lives in Philadelphia.

SEEING

1. Paul Fussell's essay offers a wide range of perspectives on how the question of class is projected in contemporary American culture. What definitions does he offer for the word *class*? What similarities and differences do you notice between Fussell's definitions of *class* and those of <u>William Deresiewicz in "The Dispossessed"</u> (p. 529)? Based on your analysis of these sources, how would you define *class*?

2. Make a list of Fussell's <u>assertions</u> in this essay. What specific examples and sources does he use to support each of his assertions? Which of his arguments do you find most compelling? Explain why. Which arguments fall short? In what specific ways? What additional references or examples would you invoke to support or refute his points?

Page 529

<u>assertion: Declaration; affirmation.</u>

WRITING

1. Fussell claims that evidence of class exists everywhere in contemporary American life. In paragraph 3 he notes, "Actually, you reveal a great deal about your social class by the amount of annoyance or fury you feel when the subject is brought up." Write the first draft of a narrative essay in which you recount the events leading up to and then culminating in someone's expressed annoyance or fury when the subject of class came up in conversation. What were the consequences of that reaction?

2. Keep a list of the instances on a typical day in which the people, places, events, and advertisements you encounter can be seen as expressions of an individual's—or a group's—anxiety about their status. Choose one of these instances, and write an expository essay in which you explain how class issues were revealed and then illustrated in that experience.

Margaret Bourke-White
The Louisville Flood, 1937

Margaret Bourke-White

One of the most famous and successful photographers of the 1930s, Margaret Bourke-White (1904–1971) was the first woman photographer to be hired by *Life* magazine. Her photograph *Fort Peck Dam* became the cover of *Life*'s first issue (November 23, 1936), and her photoessay in that issue is thought to be the first photoessay ever printed. She was also the first female war correspondent, admired for her sophisticated technique, classical composition, and masterful use of the flash.

As a *Life* correspondent, Bourke-White traveled the world, photographing political leaders from Joseph Stalin to Mohandas Gandhi. She documented the Dust Bowl, World War II combat (photographing under fire as she traveled with General Patton's troops), and Nazi death camps after the war.

The Louisville Flood is one of the iconic images of the Great Depression.

SEEING

1. What specific aspects of this photograph strike you as the most memorable? Explain why. How would you describe the interplay between text and image in the photograph? How would you characterize the range of facial expressions and gazes captured in it? How would you describe this photograph to someone who has never seen it? What specific attributes have made it such a memorable – and iconic – photograph?

2. Notice the compositional choices Bourke-White made in framing and cropping this photograph. You might consider, for example, the presence of contrast; the use of horizontal, vertical, and diagonal lines; the interplay between text and image. How, specifically, does each of these compositional choices contribute to the photograph's overall effect?

iconic: Widely accepted as a symbol.

WRITING

1. The top half of Bourke-White's photograph captures a billboard sponsored by the National Association of Manufacturers. (The full view of the billboard can be seen on the facing page in the photograph taken by Dorothea Lange. For more on Dorothea Lange, see page 578. For another example of her work, please see p. 577.) Consider the phrase used in the ad: "There's no way like *the American way*." Write a one-page exploration of the phrase's meaning. When you hear or invoke *the American way*, what images and words are called up? What specific associations and meanings does the phrase evoke in you? Please include two examples of recent events or texts that embody your understanding of the phrase *the American way*.

2. "I picked up a camera because it was my choice of weapons against what I hated most about the universe: racism, intolerance, poverty," said Gordon Parks in an interview in 2000. Like Bourke-White's *The Louisville Flood*, his photograph American Gothic (p. 525) has become an icon of social criticism. Write an essay in which you compare and contrast Bourke-White's photograph with Parks's, exploring how their compositional choices contribute to a clear and strong visual image – and social message – with appreciable impact.

Page 515

Page 525

Responding Visually

Choose one of the two statements captured in Bourke-White's iconic photograph: "World's Highest Standard of Living" or "There's no way like the American way," and create a one-page visual/verbal composition in which you combine the statement with an image of your choice. What comment does your new "mash-up" make about the meaning of the statement?

Dorothea Lange
Billboard on U.S. Highway 99, 1937

Grant Wood
American Gothic, 1930

Grant Wood

For many Americans, Grant Wood's *American Gothic* is as familiar as Leonardo da Vinci's *Mona Lisa*. The problem: No one has ever known definitively what to make of it. Are the two people in the picture father and daughter? husband and wife? Are their dour faces meant to be a real representation of traditional midwestern working-class folks, or is Wood poking fun at them? Wood never helped resolve the controversy, but he did reveal that the house standing in the background of *American Gothic* was located in Eldon, Iowa. He was taken with the gothic-style windows and sketched the house on a piece of paper. Later he asked his sister Nan and his dentist, Dr. B. H. McKeeby, to pose as the couple in the picture.

We do know quite a bit about Wood himself. He was born in 1891 in Iowa and spent most of his life there, dying at age fifty in 1942. He started his career as an artist when he was fourteen years old, studied at the School of the Art Institute of Chicago, traveled several times to Europe to study art during the 1920s, founded the Stone City Art Colony in the 1930s to help support artists during the Great Depression, and taught painting at the University of Iowa's school of art. His style of painting (which was also represented by the work of another well-known artist, Thomas Hart Benton) was known as regionalism, which focused on scenes of rural life in the Midwest and was very popular during the 1930s.

SEEING

1. Whether or not you are familiar with Grant Wood's *American Gothic,* please take a few moments to examine the image carefully. What is your overall impression of the painting? of its use of detail, color, and tone? What responses does it evoke? Which aspects of the painting seem most prominent to you? In what ways might the painting be said to be a quintessential expression of American identity? What specific elements in the painting give it the status of a cultural icon?

2. How do you read the woman's and the man's expressions in Wood's painting? In what specific ways do you find their expressions to be similar? different? Please point to specific examples to support your points. How does your reading of their expressions change the impact the painting has on you?

WRITING

1. Compare and contrast the portraits of the man and woman in Wood's painting to any other portrait in the book. You may consider Carlton Davis's Hue Man series or Nancy Burson's He/She series, for example. Describe the similarities and differences in how photographic and paint media capture a portrait.

Page 440

Page 360

Working with Sources

2. *American Gothic* is widely recognized as an American cultural icon. What contemporary American images, if any, can you point to that you believe can claim this same iconic status? Write the first draft of an essay in which you argue for—or against—granting a specific contemporary image the status of a cultural icon.

THE GEOGRAPHY
OF THE IMAGINATION
Guy Davenport

A geography of the imagination would extend the shores of the Mediterranean all the way to Iowa.

Eldon, Iowa—where in 1929 Grant Wood sketched a farmhouse as the background for a double portrait of his sister Nan and his dentist, Dr. B. H. McKeeby, who donned overalls for the occasion and held a rake. Forces that arose three millennia ago in the Mediterranean changed the rake to a pitchfork, as we shall see.

Let us look at this painting to which we are blinded by familiarity and parody. In the remotest distance against this perfect blue of a fine harvest sky, there is the Gothic spire of a country church, as if to seal the Protestant sobriety and industry of the subjects. Next there are trees, seven of them, as along the porch of Solomon's temple, symbols of prudence and wisdom.

Next, still reading from background to foreground, is the house that gives the primary meaning of the title, *American Gothic*, a style of architecture. It is an example of a revolution in domestic building that made possible the rapid rise of American cities after the Civil War and dotted the prairies with decent, neat farmhouses. It is what was first called in derision a balloon-frame house, so easy to build that a father and his son could put it up. It is an elegant geometry of light timber posts and rafters requiring no deep foundation, and is nailed together. Technically, it is, like the clothes of the farmer and his wife, a mail-order house, as the design comes out of a pattern-book, this one from those of Alexander Davis and Andrew Downing, the architects who modified details of the Gothic Revival for American farmhouses. The balloon-frame house was invented in Chicago in 1833 by George Washington Snow, who was orchestrating in his invention a century of mechanization that provided the nails, wirescreen, sash-windows, tin roof, lathe-turned posts for the porch, doorknobs, locks, and hinges—all standard pieces from factories.

5   We can see a bamboo sunscreen—out of China by way of Sears Roebuck—that rolls up like a sail: nautical technology applied to the prairie. We can see that distinctly American feature, the screen door. The sash-windows are European in origin, their glass panes from Venetian technology as perfected by the English, a luxury that was a marvel of the eighteenth century, and now as common as the farmer's spectacles,

another revolution in technology that would have seemed a miracle to previous ages. Spectacles begin in the thirteenth century, the invention of either Salvino degl'Armati or Alessandro della Spina; the first portrait of a person wearing specs is of Cardinal Ugone di Provenza, in a fresco of 1352 by Tommaso Barisino di Modena. We might note, as we are trying to see the geographical focus that this painting gathers together, that the center for lens grinding from which eyeglasses diffused to the rest of civilization was the same part of Holland from which the style of the painting itself derives.

Another thirteenth-century invention prominent in our painting is the buttonhole. Buttons themselves are prehistoric, but they were shoulder-fasteners that engaged with loops. Modern clothing begins with the buttonhole. The farmer's wife secures her Dutch Calvinist collar with a cameo brooch, an heirloom passed down the generations, an eighteenth-century or Victorian copy of a design that goes back to the sixth century B.C.

She is a product of the ages, this modest Iowa farm wife: She has the hair-do of a mediaeval madonna, a Reformation collar, a Greek cameo, a nineteenth-century pinafore.

Martin Luther put her a step behind her husband; John Knox squared her shoulders; the stock-market crash of 1929 put that look in her eyes.

The train that brought her clothes — paper pattern, bolt cloth, needle, thread, scissors — also brought her husband's bib overalls, which were originally, in the 1870s, trainmen's workclothes designed in Europe, manufactured here for J. C. Penney, and disseminated across the United States as the railroads connected city with city. The cloth is denim, from Nîmes in France, introduced by Levi Strauss of blue-jean fame. The design can be traced to no less a person than Herbert Spencer, who thought he was creating a utilitarian one-piece suit for everybody to wear. His own example was of tweed, with buttons from crotch to neck, and his female relatives somehow survived the mortification of his sporting it one Sunday in St. James Park.

His jacket is the modification of that of a Scots shepherd which we all still wear.

Grant Wood's Iowans stand, as we might guess, in a pose dictated by the Brownie box camera, close together in front of their house, the farmer looking at the lens with solemn honesty, his wife with modestly averted eyes. But that will not account for the pitchfork held as assertively as a minuteman's rifle. The pose is rather that of the Egyptian prince Rahotep, holding the flail of Osiris, beside his wife Nufrit — strict with pious rectitude, poised in absolute dignity, mediators between heaven and earth, givers of grain, obedient to the gods.

This formal pose lasts out 3,000 years of Egyptian history, passes to some of the classical cultures—Etruscan couples in terra cotta, for instance—but does not attract Greece and Rome. It recommences in northern Europe, where (to the dismay of the Romans) Gaulish wives rode beside their husbands in the war chariot. Kings and eventually the merchants of the North repeated the Egyptian double portrait of husband and wife: van Eyck's Meester and Frouw Arnolfini; Rubens and his wife Helena. It was this Netherlandish tradition of painting middle-class folk with honor and precision that turned Grant Wood from Montparnasse, where he spent two years in the 1920s trying to be an American post-Impressionist, back to Iowa, to be our Hans Memling.

If Van Gogh could ask, "Where is my Japan?" and be told by Toulouse-Lautrec that it was Provence, Wood asked himself the whereabouts of his Holland, and found it in Iowa.

Just thirty years before Wood's painting, Edwin Markham's poem "The Man with the Hoe" had pictured the farmer as a peasant with a life scarcely different from that of an ox, and called on the working men of the world to unite, as they had nothing to lose but their chains. The painting that inspired Markham was one of a series of agricultural subjects by Jean François Millet, whose work also inspired Van Gogh. A digging fork appears in five of Van Gogh's pictures, three of them variations on themes by Millet, and all of them are studies of grinding labor and poverty.

15   And yet the Independent Farmer had edged out the idle aristocrat for the hand of the girl in Royal Tyler's "The Contrast," the first Native American comedy for the stage, and in Emerson's "Concord Hymn" it is a battle-line of farmers who fire the shot heard around the world. George III, indeed, referred to his American colonies as "the farms," and the two Georges of the Revolution, Hanover and Washington, were proudly farmers by etymology and in reality.

The window curtains and apron in this painting are both calico printed in a reticular design, the curtains of rhombuses, the apron of circles and dots, the configuration Sir Thomas Browne traced through nature and art in his *Garden of Cyrus*, the quincunxial arrangement of trees in orchards, perhaps the first human imitation of a phyllotaxis, acknowledging the symmetry, justice, and divine organization of nature.

Curtains and aprons are as old as civilization itself, but their presence here in Iowa implies a cotton mill, a dye works, a roller press that prints calico, and a wholesale–retail distribution system involving a post office, a train, its tracks, and, in short, the Industrial Revolution.

That revolution came to America in the astounding memory of one man, Samual Slater, who arrived in Philadelphia in 1789 with the plans of all Arkwright's, Crompton's, and Hargreaves's machinery in his head, put himself at the service of the rich Quaker Moses Brown, and built the first American factory at Pawtucket, Rhode Island.

The apron is trimmed with rickrack ribbon, a machine-made substitute for lace. The curtains are bordered in a variant of the egg-and-dart design that comes from Nabataea, the Biblical Edom, in Syria, a design which the architect Hiram incorporated into the entablatures of Solomon's temple — "and the chapiters upon the two pillars had pomegranates also above, over against the belly which was by the network: and the pomegranates were two hundred in rows round about" (1 Kings 7:20) — and which formed the border of the high priest's dress, a frieze of "pomegranates of blue, and of purple, and of scarlet, around about the hem thereof; and bells of gold between them round about" (Exodus 28:33).

20   The brass button that secures the farmer's collar is an unassertive, puritanical understatement of Matthew Boulton's eighteenth-century cut-steel button made in the factory of James Watt. His shirt button is mother-of-pearl, made by James Boepple from Mississippi fresh-water mussel shell, and his jacket button is of South American vegetable ivory passing for horn.

The farmer and his wife are attended by symbols, she by two plants on the porch, a potted geranium and sansevieria, both tropical and alien to Iowa; he by the three-tined American pitchfork whose triune shape is repeated throughout the painting, in the bib of the overalls, the windows, the faces, the siding of the house, to give it a formal organization of impeccable harmony.

If this painting is primarily a statement about Protestant diligence on the American frontier, carrying in its style and subject a wealth of information about imported technology, psychology, and aesthetics, it still does not turn away from a pervasive cultural theme of Mediterranean origin — a tension between the growing and the ungrowing, between vegetable and mineral, organic and inorganic, wheat and iron.

Transposed back into its native geography, this icon of the lord of metals with his iron sceptre, head wreathed with glass and silver, buckled in tin and brass, and a chaste bride who has already taken on the metallic thraldom of her plight in the gold ovals of her hair and brooch, are Dis and Persephone posed in a royal portrait among the attributes of the first Mediterranean trinity, Zeus in the blue sky and lightning rod, Poseidon in the trident of the pitchfork, Hades in the metals. It is a picture of a sheaf of golden grain, female and cyclical, perennial and the mother of civilization; and of metal shaped into scythe and hoe: nature and technology, earth and farmer, man and world, and their achievement together.

Guy Davenport

The extremely prolific poet, short story author, essayist, critic, translator, illustrator, painter, and educator Guy Davenport was born in Anderson, South Carolina, in 1927. His dual interest in writing and art can be traced to a neighborhood newspaper he both wrote and illustrated as an adolescent. In later life, as a way of connecting his interests, he said of his writing, "The prime use of words is for imagery: My writing is drawing." Educated in both art and English at Duke University, Davenport continued his studies as a Rhodes Scholar at Oxford University in the late 1940s. After two years in the army, he taught for several years and then earned his PhD from Harvard University, returning afterwards to teach at Haverford College and later at the University of Kentucky until his retirement in 1990, soon after he received a MacArthur Fellowship. He died in 2005.

The consummate intellectual, Davenport published more than thirty books, including five collections of poetry, ten translations of Greek classics, over a dozen collections of fiction, two collections of drawings and paintings, three books of collected letters, and hundreds of published essays and reviews. The piece presented here is from *The Geography of the Imagination* (1981), a collection of forty essays. An analysis of Grant Wood's *American Gothic*, the essay also makes numerous connections that relate the ordinary American couple to everything from ancient Egypt to medieval Holland.

SEEING

1. Describe how Guy Davenport's reading of *American Gothic* enhances or changes your understanding and appreciation of the painting by Grant Wood. In his essay, Davenport focuses on the cultural and historical aspects of each element in the painting. How could you supplement his analysis by focusing on the painting's compositional elements?

2. To what extent does Jane Yolen's poem about the painting supplement or change your reading of Davenport's essay? Cite specific examples to support your response.

Page 516 Page 523

WRITING

1. Jane Yolen's poem "Grant Wood: American Gothic" offers directions for responding to the iconic painting. How does her point of view differ from Davenport's? Summarize the structure of Yolen's poem. What relationship can you establish between the first three parts of the poem (ll.1–5, 6–9, and 10–11) and its last two lines? What do you notice about the structure of the final lines? How does the final line depend for its meaning on the penultimate line? Write the first draft of an expository essay in which you explain how the final two lines of the poem do–or do not–encapsulate its meaning.

Working with Sources

2. Choose a painting–one with which you are already familiar or one you find in this or another book, at a museum or gallery, or on the web. Write an essay in which you read the painting closely, using Davenport's essay as a model. Focus on several key elements of the painting, and provide your readers with the historical, cultural, or social meaning of each element.

GRANT WOOD:
AMERICAN GOTHIC
Jane Yolen

Do not dwell on the fork,
the brooch at the throat,
the gothic angel wing
of window pointing toward
5 a well-tended heaven.
Do not become
a farmer counting cows
as if the number of the herd
defines you.
10 Look behind the eyes,
to see who looks out at you.
We are not what we own
We own what we would be.

Americans have long been fascinated with copies, duplicates, and replicas of all sorts – counterfeits, mannequins, decoys, and, more recently, digital images, photocopies, even instant replays. Few works of American art are as celebrated – or as reproduced, imitated, and parodied – as Grant Wood's *American Gothic.* Viewing this painting might remind some of the immortal words of the legendary baseball star and hero of American folklore, Yogi Berra: "It's *déjà vu* all over again."

As Guy Davenport remarks in his analysis of Wood's *American Gothic,* this image has taken on an identity and status to which we have become "blinded by familiarity and parody" (para. 3). Like the *Mona Lisa, American Gothic* has been so often reproduced on T-shirts, postcards, and coffee mugs, as well as referenced – or alluded to – in the work of numerous painters, artists, and writers, that it has assumed the status of an American cultural icon. Few works of American art are as celebrated – and less understood.

Consider, for example, Gordon Parks's photograph. What specific elements of Wood's painting does Parks repeat? With what effect(s)? How does he play off the tone and overall qualities of the painting?

Using the library and the web for research, identify other artists who have tried to reproduce the central image and distinguishing features of Wood's *American Gothic.* Then write an expository essay in which you demonstrate the extent to which Wood's image changes in the specific cultural contexts in which it is reproduced. Show how the original cultural and historical significance of the painting changes to make room for the cultural associations and meanings expressed by new generations.

Gordon Parks
American Gothic, 1942

RETROSPECT—An American Classic Revisited

1960

2001

2003–2007

2008

Workers Leaving Pennsylvania Shipyard, Beaumont, Texas, June 1943

THE DISPOSSESSED
William Deresiewicz

Sometimes you don't realize that something's been missing—it doesn't matter how big it is—until, for a moment or two, it isn't. About ten years ago, I was listening to an interview with the choreographer Bill T. Jones, who had just published his memoirs. Jones is gay and black, and when the interviewer asked him what his father had thought about his becoming a dancer, Jones, somewhat testily, said something like, "You don't understand. This wasn't a middle-class family. The goal wasn't to become a professional: the goal was to better yourself." The first thing that hit me about this was that it had nothing to do with race or sexuality. The second thing that hit me was that it had everything to do with class, specifically the working class—which, I suddenly realized, I never heard anyone talk about. A little while later, I read a profile of Roseanne Barr in *The New Yorker*. Only middle-class women care about feminism, Barr claimed. Working-class women already have power, because they're the ones in charge at home.

Working-class career expectations, working-class family structures: two things I knew nothing about. Each revelation gratified me with the feeling of learning something interesting and important and new, but together they enraged me with the recognition that the reason they felt new, the reason I was so abysmally ignorant about this world that lay all around me—the American working class—was that such knowledge had been withheld from me by my culture. It's not just that I'm middle class myself. I'm white, too, but mainstream culture (popular entertainment, the news media) has exposed me to a steady stream of images and information about blacks. I suspect that American gentiles also know quite a lot about Jews. But the working class is American culture's great lost continent.

There are exceptions: Roseanne's show was one, Michael Moore's *Roger & Me* (as well as the whole persona he's constructed) is another, as was the recent HBO series *Family Bonds*. But much of what was seen as important and "edgy" in those productions was their working-class subject matter, which shows how rare any serious, extended, or sympathetic popular treatment of the working class now is. (Analogous things could be said about Bruce Springsteen, or novelists like Richard Russo and Russell Banks, or the *New York Times*'s recent multipart series on class in America. Imagine how superfluous it would have been for the

Times to do a series about race or sexuality, topics that permeate half the stories it publishes.) Among mainstream films of the last decade, *Mystic River* and *Good Will Hunting* come to mind, but far more typical is the kind of thing we got in *Million Dollar Baby*, where the heroine's family was presented as loutish, contemptible trailer trash, or on *The Simpsons*, where Homer's working-class characteristics (and he seems to be the working-class breadwinner of a middle-class family) are played strictly for laughs. There are working-class characters all over the place: cops on detective shows, nurses and orderlies on doctor shows, and so forth. But it's the nature of such dramas to present people only in terms of their jobs, asking few or no questions about the rest of their lives. Look at a show or a movie that takes you into its characters' homes, and you'll find that the homes you're being taken into are almost always middle or upper class, even when the characters belong to that vast, imaginary social group we might call the pseudo-working class, people with working-class jobs but middle-class lifestyles, like the Simpsons or the Gilmore girls or those lucky kids on *Friends*.

What we don't have in this country, in other words, is anyone like Mike Leigh, who makes art out of working-class lives by refusing to prettify them. We no longer have anyone, among our major novelists, like Steinbeck or Dos Passos. We don't even have any TV shows like *The Honeymooners* or *All in the Family*, whose frank depictions of the material conditions of working-class life (think of the Kramdens' kitchen, with its bridge table and two chairs) didn't prevent them from achieving a monumental universality. When we do get the rare serious mainstream treatment of working-class life, it comes from a middle-class observer like Barbara Ehrenreich.[1] So why is it that the only working-class person anyone will pay attention to these days is a middle-class journalist masquerading as one? More fundamentally, why is it that the working class is treated as an exotic species, while the middle class, which it heavily outnumbers, is regarded as normal and normative?

5   It's not hard to begin to answer these questions. First, the people who get paid to create mainstream culture—journalists, editors, writers, producers—are, ipso facto, members of the middle class. As social mobility shows, more and more of them originate in that class. The middle class is not only what they know and identify with, it often seems to be the only thing they're aware of. Today's army of cultural commentators, who speak so confidently about the way "we" live now—the crazy hours, the overscheduled kids, the elite colleges and nursery schools—mistake

---

1. An essay by Barbara Ehrenreich, "This Land Is Their Land," appears on page 549. [Eds.]

their tiny world of urban and university-town professionals for the whole of society. Second, as TV's creation of a pseudo-working class suggests, looking at the real one is kind of a bummer. Just as everyone on TV has to be beautiful, so does everyone have to have money, or at least live like they do. Nobody wants to watch a show about some fat guy struggling to make the rent. Finally and most important, we simply don't talk about class at all anymore. Why should we, when we're all supposedly part of a single one, the great middle? What we talk about is race and sexuality. (Or in the academy, race, gender, and sexuality, the great triumvirate. The humanities, despite their claim to transformative significance, have all but forgotten about class.) Instead of Steinbeck and Dos Passos, we have Toni Morrison, Maxine Hong Kingston, Oscar Hijuelos, Jhumpa Lahiri, and Michael Cunningham.

It was Morrison, in fact, who provided one of the most telling indications of our loss of the working class as an imaginative category, her famous anointment of Bill Clinton as our "first black president": "Clinton displays almost every trope of blackness: single-parent household, born poor, working-class, saxophone-playing, McDonald's-and-junk-food-loving boy from Arkansas." At least Morrison still employs the term *working class*, but it's still merely a secondary category for her. If it weren't, she would have seen that what those attributes really added up to wasn't that Clinton was black (or "black"), but that he was our first working-class president, if not ever, then in a while, and our most flamboyantly so in a long while. But of course working-class attributes are going to look like tropes of blackness. Just about the only images we have of the working class are images of black people, understood as black people. In fact, many of the things we think of as characteristically black are really true of the working class as a whole (and aren't true of middle-class blacks.) Consider the realm of family structure: having children at an early age, having them outside of marriage, raising them as a single parent, raising them with the help of an older relative—and not being stigmatized by your community for doing any of these things. It's an old American story: Race becomes a surrogate for class, which is to say, a way of not thinking about it at all.

On the rare occasions when we do think about class, our fixation on race makes us confuse the working class with the poor, as the response to the Katrina disaster demonstrated. For an interval that proved predictably brief, Americans started talking about class again, but we still missed the true picture. For one thing, our discussion of poverty was all too quickly subsumed, again, into a discussion about race. (It's funny how few images we saw of poor, dispossessed whites, though many such people must have existed.) More important is that most of the blacks we saw wandering the highways or abandoned at the Convention Center were surely not the truly indigent (the homeless, the unemployed); they were laborers and waitresses and hospital workers and maids, members of New Orleans's socially cohesive and culturally vibrant working-class black communities. These are the same communities that are now struggling for the right to rebuild themselves, struggling to get the rest of us to acknowledge that their neighborhoods were more than just slums. The people who lived in these communities may have looked dirty and disheveled on TV, and some of them may have acted desperately at times, but how would you have looked, and how would you have acted after four or five days in those circumstances? Yet so deeply has the notion of a working class been pushed to the recesses of our consciousness, and so powerful is the link in our minds between poverty and race, that when we're shown a working-class black, we see a poor person—and when we're shown a working-class white, we don't see anything at all.

What is the working class? As a first approximation, I'd suggest that a member of the working class is someone who receives an hourly wage. (There are exceptions both ways: airline pilots on the one hand, secretaries on the other.) The virtue of this definition is that it not only excludes the true middle class—professionals, managers, and small-business owners—it also reminds us that working-class people have a very different relationship to their work and their workplace than do those who earn a salary. By this criterion, the working class comprises about 80 percent of the American workforce. Even if one claims that the cop or the fireman or unionized factory worker, who might well live in the suburbs and drive a big car, actually belongs to the middle class, the working class still comprises a large majority of the country. (Besides, as Paul Krugman recently argued in a *New York Times* column on the wage-and-benefit squeeze in the auto industry, a lot of those factory workers—the "working middle class"—will find themselves squarely back in the working class soon anyway.) The poor may literally be "invisible in America," as the subtitle of David K. Shipler's recent book puts it, out of sight in the human garbage heaps of ghettos and trailer parks, but the great bulk of the working class—which is to say, most of America—is invisible only because "we" aren't seeing what's right in front of our faces: the people who serve our food, ring up our purchases, fix our cars, change our bedpans.

It's as if the vast space between the poor and the middle class didn't exist. The term *working class* has been erased from our political discourse, replaced by working poor and the insidious working families. *Working poor* is a valuable term, because it reminds us how meagerly many jobs pay these days and belies the notion of what used to be called the idle poor. But working poor is not at all the same as working class, though the trailer-trash stereotype would have us think so. Some working-class people are poor, but the great majority are not, they just aren't well-off enough to be middle class. *Working families* isn't the same as *working class*, either. Whether in the mouth of a Clinton or a Bush, the term is designed to treat the working and middle classes as a monolith. By conflating the two (the doctor struggling to pay for his kids to go to Harvard, the cashier struggling to pay for medicine), the term eliminates the working class as a political as well as a cultural category.

10   But class hasn't completely dropped out of our political discourse. In fact, it's made a comeback of late, only in a particularly devious new guise, our new ruling paradigm of red state vs. blue state—where ideology is rewritten as region (Republicans are from red states, Democrats from blue), region as culture (red-staters drink beer, blue-staters drink wine), and culture as class, though only implicitly (what do you think beer and wine really mean?). Fifty-seven million people voted for John Kerry in the last election; to speak as if all of them were Chardonnay-sipping professors, or even professionals, is ridiculous. Simple arithmetic tells us that millions of them were members of the working class. But according to the dominant syllogism, if Kerry voters are effete elitists while Bush voters are "ordinary Americans" (the closest anyone comes to actually saying working class anymore) than the working class looks like the stereotypical Bush voter: rural, Southern, conservative, nationalist, and fundamentalist—in other words, redneck. This is as gross an oversimplification as imagining that the middle class is composed exclusively of leftist academics. But absent any other or better images of the working class, the redneck myth not only means that Republicans get to present themselves as champions of the working class while ostensibly denying its existence (as Thomas Frank has argued in *What's the Matter with Kansas?*), it also means that the true character of the working class, in all its enormous breadth and diversity, remains hidden.

It remains hidden, in particular, from the working class itself, among whom the redneck myth does in fact seem to be taking hold. I lived in Portland, Oregon, last year, a heavily working-class town, and I was struck by the affinity the working class there seems to feel with Southern culture. (Country Music Television, for example, is part of the basic cable package.) The South is the one place where the white working class doesn't hide itself, as the essayist Richard Rodriguez recently noted, and its lead cultural expressions—country music and NASCAR—are becoming those of the white working class as a whole. This southernization of the working class surely owes a lot to the red-state/blue-state nonsense, to the ascendancy of southern Republicans, and to the scarcity of other kinds of working-class images.

But it also owes a lot to the decline of organized labor. I've suggested that working-class images haven't always been so hard to find in the mainstream, and it's no accident that their virtual disappearance over the past few decades has coincided with that decline. Fifty years ago, more than one in three American workers were unionized; today, one in eight is. Along with a huge loss in political power has come the loss of a confident, self-conscious, working-class culture. Not only were workers visible to the classes above them, they had their own voices, their own cultural institutions, their own sense of who they were and what they did; in short, they weren't dependent on the middle class to define them. People used to speak of the "dignity of labor," and the phrase meant that being a worker was something to be proud of, that the working class saw itself as something more than a collection of people who couldn't make it, that it had its own traditions and values, constituted its own community.

I've spent a lot of time thinking about the working class in the ten years since those inciting recognitions. I've kept my eyes open to whatever I could glean from the media and from my immediate surroundings. I've had long talks on the subject with my wife, who spent many years in a working-class environment, and with a former student, who grew up in one. I've come to believe not only that the working class constitutes a coherent culture very different from the middle-class one that's presented to us as natural and universal, but that that culture possesses a genuine set of virtues. *New York Times* columnist David Brooks has been singing the praises lately of bourgeois values like industry, temperance, prudence, and thrift. I have nothing against these things, especially since, as a member of the middle class, I practice them myself. But industry, temperance, prudence, and thrift are not the be-all and end-all of the good life. In fact, they are apt to be accompanied by a countervailing array of bourgeois vices, like narrowness, prudery, timidity, and meanness, not to mention hypocrisy and self-conceit.

As for the working class, I'll grant, for the sake of argument, that its vices tend to be the negative of bourgeois values, that working-class people are, compared to the middle class, less temperate, prudent, thrifty, and industrious (though that last seems a rather unfair description of people who do manual labor, work two jobs, or put up with forced overtime). But by the same token, working-class life breeds its own virtues: loyalty, community, stoicism, humility, and even tolerance. Not that every working-class person is a paragon of these virtues; like Brooks, I'm trying to articulate the general contours of a class culture as it arises from the facts of every-day existence. If only because of their limited possibilities in life, working-class people care more about their families and their friends and the places they're from than they do about their careers. Because they haven't been taught to believe that they're entitled to the best of everything, they take what life brings them without whining or self-pity. Because they don't preen themselves on where they went to school or what kind of job they have, they don't act like they're better than everyone else. And when it comes right down to it, they aren't any more prejudiced than the middle class, and may even be less so. Middle-class prejudices are just more respectable—in fact, they tend to be directed against the working class itself—as well as more carefully concealed. What's more, while the middle class espouses tolerance, working-class people, because they can't simply insulate themselves from those they don't like with wads of money, are much more likely, in practice, to live and let live. Maybe what this country needs are fewer bourgeois values and more proletarian ones.

Pike County, Kentucky, 1979

Hurricane Katrina Evacuees outside the Reliant Center in Houston

William Deresiewicz

As William Deresiewicz's essay "The Dispossessed" so eloquently points out, the fact that the American working class even exists has been almost completely erased from the American consciousness. He argues that most of us living in America believe that there are three distinct social classes: the wealthy, the middle class, and the poor. But what of the millions of Americans – the majority, in fact – who make up the working class: those who hold steady jobs and are not quite poor but are struggling to make ends meet on a daily basis, one paycheck away from home foreclosure? According to Deresiewicz, while television programs once celebrated such working-class icons as the Kramdens (from *The Honeymooners*), the Bunkers (from *All in the Family*), and the Connor family (from *Roseanne*), we rarely see the working class depicted in popular culture anymore, and if we do, their status as working-class Americans is barely acknowledged. What accounts for this great American denial? Deresiewicz provides few answers, preferring instead to open up the topic for discussion, because in his view a discussion of this invisible majority is exactly what is most needed.

Deresiewicz, formerly an associate professor of English at Yale University, is a well-published literary and cultural critic. Often controversial, his articles have appeared in magazines such as *The Nation* and the *New York Times Magazine*. A nominee for a National Magazine Award in 2008 and winner of numerous other awards and fellowships, he is also the author of *Jane Austen and the Romantic Poets* (2004).

SEEING

1. How does Deresiewicz define *working class*? Who portrays its members in mainstream American culture, and what does he think these representations lack? Which virtues and vices are specific to the working class, and how do these differ from those of the middle class? What reasons does he offer for insisting that we distinguish among *working class, working poor,* and *working families*?

2. Who is included in the audience that Deresiewicz addresses in his essay? Reread his essay carefully for evidence that supports your interpretation about his target audience.

For example, who might be expected to know Bill T. Jones, Roseanne Barr, and Barbara Ehrenreich? Who reads the *New York Times* and watches the Country Music Channel? Like Deresiewicz's, your goal is not to describe a particular individual but to "articulate the general contours of a class culture as it arises from the facts" (para. 14) of his writing. Choose a specific passage, and show how the essay would change if it were written for a different audience.

virtue: A commendable quality or trait.

vice: A moral fault or failing.

WRITING

1. If Deresiewicz identifies two classes as "upper" and "middle," why doesn't he refer to the third as "lower class"? What does the adjective *working* accomplish that *lower* cannot? Which term do you think more accurately represents this third group of Americans? What are some other ways to divide classes? If you are familiar with other societies and cultures, compare their divisions. For example, how does India's five-tiered caste system map onto the United States's three-class social structure? Write the first draft of an expository essay in which you analyze the specific advantages – and limitations – of such designations for Americans.

2. Prepare the first draft of a science fiction story entitled "The Invisible Working Class." Use this opportunity to imagine what would happen if you took Deresiewicz's claim literally: "the great bulk of the working class – which is to say, most of America – is invisible" (para. 8). What would happen if 80 percent of America really could not be seen? Think sensitively about the issue from both sides of visibility. How would you respond to having your hair cut by invisible hands? How would you feel if you were served food by someone you couldn't see? How, in effect, can – and do – you know about someone when you can't see him or her? If the invisible class were only sounds, smells, touches, and tastes, what would you know about the people in it?

Words for a writer are like colors for a painter.

Kyle Jones, student at Los Positos College

The pen is worse than the sword.

Robert Burton, author of
The Anatomy of Melancholy

PORTFOLIO–How Class Works

A Land of Opportunity

More than ever, Americans cherish the belief that it is possible to become rich. Three-quarters think the chances of moving up to a higher class are the same as or greater than thirty years ago. Still, more than half thought it unlikely that they would become wealthy. A large majority favors programs to help the poor get ahead.

Is it possible to start out poor, work hard, and become rich?

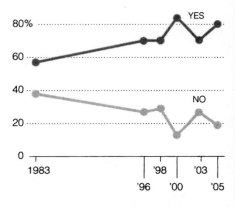

Compared with their social class when growing up, people said their current class was:

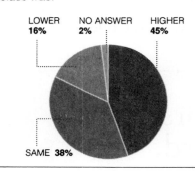

LOWER **16%** NO ANSWER **2%** HIGHER **45%**

SAME **38%**

How likely is it that you will ever become financially wealthy?

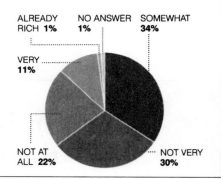

ALREADY RICH **1%** NO ANSWER **1%** SOMEWHAT **34%**

VERY **11%**

NOT AT ALL **22%**   NOT VERY **30%**

*Compared with thirty years ago,
is the likelihood of moving up from one
social class to another:*

LESS
23%

NO ANSWER
2%

GREATER
40%

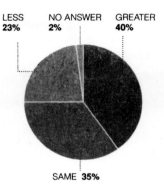

SAME **35%**

*Compared with European countries, is
moving up from one social class to
another:*

HARDER
13%

NO ANSWER
16%

EASIER
46%

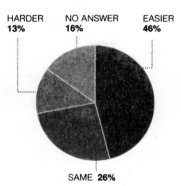

SAME **26%**

*The federal government should tax
estates worth:*

OVER $3.5
MILLION
20%

NO ANSWER
7%

NOT AT
ALL
50%

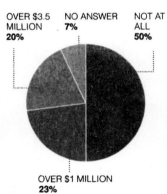

OVER $1 MILLION
23%

*Do you favor or oppose programs
that make special efforts to help
people get ahead who come from
low-income backgrounds, regardless
of gender or ethnicity?*

OPPOSE
10%

NO ANSWER
6%

FAVOR
84%

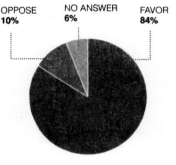

Note: Numbers
may not add up
to 100 because
of rounding.

The New York Times

Who Is Rich

How much does an American family need to make to be considered rich?

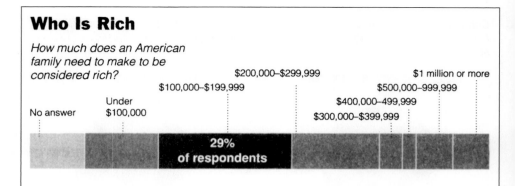

No answer | Under $100,000 | $100,000–$199,999 | $200,000–$299,999 | $300,000–$399,999 | $400,000–499,999 | $500,000–999,999 | $1 million or more

29% of respondents

And How Wealth Changes Things

On some subjects, there are strong differences among income groups. For example, lower–income respondents give greater weight to the importance of faith. More of them feel that the rich have too much power and that there is "a lot" of tension between rich and poor.

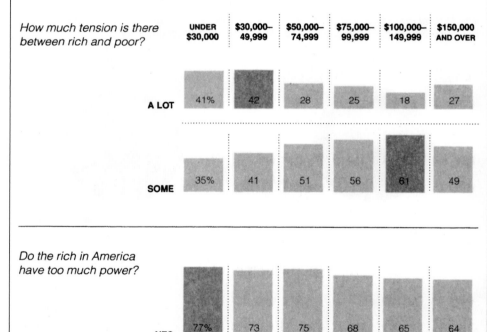

How much tension is there between rich and poor?

	UNDER $30,000	$30,000– 49,999	$50,000– 74,999	$75,000– 99,999	$100,000– 149,999	$150,000 AND OVER
A LOT	41%	42	28	25	18	27
SOME	35%	41	51	56	61	49

Do the rich in America have too much power?

	UNDER $30,000	$30,000– 49,999	$50,000– 74,999	$75,000– 99,999	$100,000– 149,999	$150,000 AND OVER
YES	77%	73	75	68	65	64

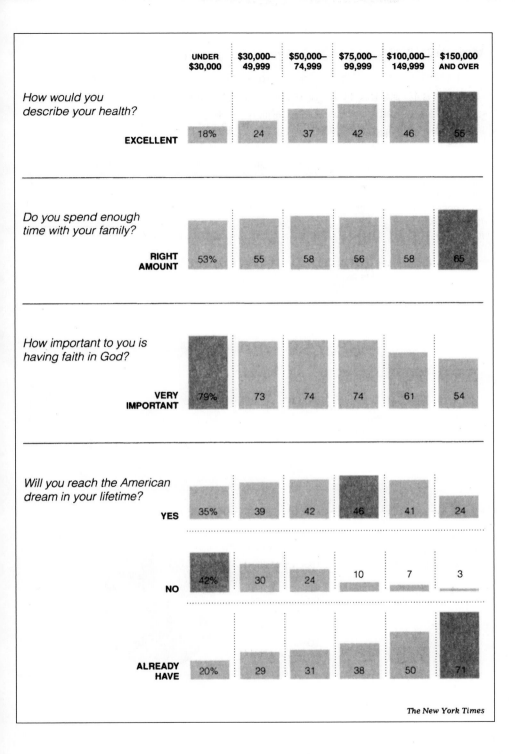

	UNDER $30,000	$30,000–49,999	$50,000–74,999	$75,000–99,999	$100,000–149,999	$150,000 AND OVER
How would you describe your health? EXCELLENT	18%	24	37	42	46	55
Do you spend enough time with your family? RIGHT AMOUNT	53%	55	58	56	58	65
How important to you is having faith in God? VERY IMPORTANT	79%	73	74	74	61	54
Will you reach the American dream in your lifetime? YES	35%	39	42	46	41	24
NO	42%	30	24	10	7	3
ALREADY HAVE	20%	29	31	38	50	71

The New York Times

What It Takes to Get Ahead . . .

Hard work—more than education, natural ability, or the right connections—is regarded as crucial for getting ahead in life. While other factors can help a person's advancement, most Americans, regardless of income level, regard the individual's efforts as critical.

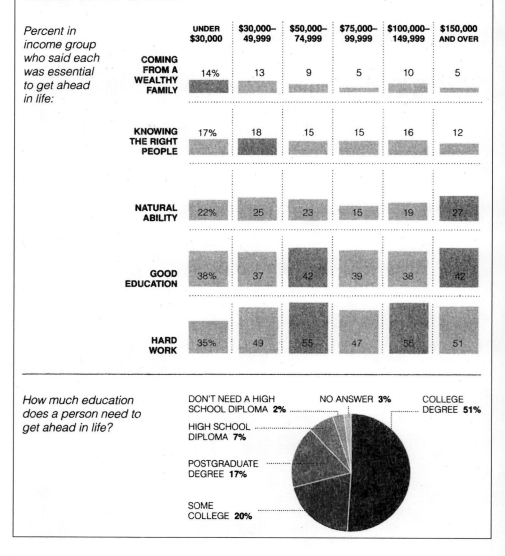

Percent in income group who said each was essential to get ahead in life:

	UNDER $30,000	$30,000– 49,999	$50,000– 74,999	$75,000– 99,999	$100,000– 149,999	$150,000 AND OVER
COMING FROM A WEALTHY FAMILY	14%	13	9	5	10	5
KNOWING THE RIGHT PEOPLE	17%	18	15	15	16	12
NATURAL ABILITY	22%	25	23	15	19	27
GOOD EDUCATION	38%	37	42	39	38	42
HARD WORK	35%	49	55	47	55	51

How much education does a person need to get ahead in life?

DON'T NEED A HIGH SCHOOL DIPLOMA **2%**

HIGH SCHOOL DIPLOMA **7%**

POSTGRADUATE DEGREE **17%**

SOME COLLEGE **20%**

NO ANSWER **3%**

COLLEGE DEGREE **51%**

. . . And Will You Get There

Compared with your parents when they were the age you are now, is your standard of living now . . .

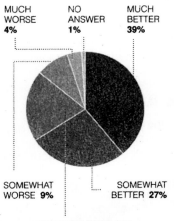

MUCH WORSE 4%

NO ANSWER 1%

MUCH BETTER 39%

SOMEWHAT WORSE 9%

SOMEWHAT BETTER 27%

ABOUT THE SAME 20%

If parent: When your children are the age you are now, will their standard of living be . . .

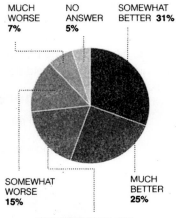

MUCH WORSE 7%

NO ANSWER 5%

SOMEWHAT BETTER 31%

SOMEWHAT WORSE 15%

MUCH BETTER 25%

ABOUT THE SAME 18%

The New York Times Poll, which is the source of this and the previous charts in this chapter, was based on telephone interviews conducted March 9–14, 2005, with 1,764 adults throughout the United States. People with low household incomes or high household incomes were oversampled and then weighted to their proper proportion of the overall sample. In theory, in 19 out of 20 cases, the overall results will differ by no more than 3 percentage points in either direction from what would have been obtained by seeking out all American adults. For smaller subgroups, the margin of sampling error is larger. In addition to sampling error, the practical difficulties of conducting any survey of public opinion may introduce other sources of error into the poll. Complete methods, poll questions, and results are available in the appendix and at www.nytimes.com/class.

The New York Times

Where Do You Fit In?

The box below is a way of visualizing how income and education, two key elements of class, match up in the American population. It shows who's on top, who's at the bottom, and who's in the middle. The box on the next page shows how poll respondents described their class versus where they actually fell on the same income-education spectrum. Given a choice of five classes, the better-off poll respondents shunned the top (upper class) and the poor shunned the bottom (lower class). Most everyone placed themselves in the middle three classes: working, middle, and upper middle.

Where People Are

The shaded rectangles show the proportion of Americans over twenty-five at each income and education level.

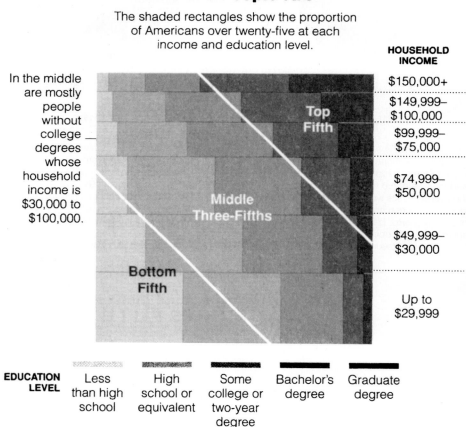

In the middle are mostly people without college degrees whose household income is $30,000 to $100,000.

Top Fifth

Middle Three-Fifths

Bottom Fifth

HOUSEHOLD INCOME

$150,000+

$149,999– $100,000

$99,999– $75,000

$74,999– $50,000

$49,999– $30,000

Up to $29,999

EDUCATION LEVEL

Less than high school

High school or equivalent

Some college or two-year degree

Bachelor's degree

Graduate degree

Where People Think They Are

How poll respondents across the income-education spectrum most commonly described their class.

HOUSEHOLD INCOME

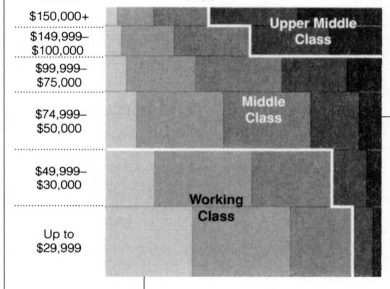

$150,000+

$149,999–$100,000

$99,999–$75,000

Upper Middle Class

$74,999–$50,000

Middle Class

$49,999–$30,000

Working Class

Up to $29,999

People with four-year college degrees tended to consider themselves middle class even if they earned little. So did people making over $50,000 but with no college degree.

Very few respondents called themselves lower class or upper class—7 percent and 1 percent.

Sources: Census Bureau and Susan Weber and Andrew Beveridge, Queens College Sociology Department; perception from New York Times *Poll of 1,764 adults in March 2005*

Bill Keller/*New York Times*

Bill Keller, who wrote the introduction for and oversaw the team of *New York Times* editors who assembled *Class Matters* (2005), is the executive editor for the *Times*. Born in 1949, Keller graduated from Pomona College in 1970 and received a degree in management from the Wharton School of the University of Pennsylvania in 2000. In between, he was a reporter for *The Oregonian,* the *Congressional Quarterly Weekly Report*, and the *Dallas Times Herald* before joining the *New York Times* in 1984. At the *Times* he held a variety of positions, including reporter, bureau chief (in both Moscow, USSR, and Johannesburg, South Africa), foreign editor, managing editor, senior writer and Op-Ed columnist, and finally executive editor. He won a Pulitzer Prize for his coverage of the Soviet Union in 1989. The *New York Times*, the newspaper through which Keller has built his career, was founded in 1851 and continues to be one of the world's most influential sources of news.

A fascinating and sobering book, *Class Matters* explores how relevant social class in America still is, despite the many commentators who argue that class is no longer an issue in this country. Through its fourteen essays, illustrated with the graphs and charts reprinted here, the book follows a cross-section of Americans – including three individuals who suffer heart attacks and have very different recovery experiences – and demonstrates how their problems and fortunes are directly linked to their class status.

SEEING

1. Which aspects of these survey results confirmed your assumptions about American attitudes toward – and experiences with – class? Which ones surprised you? Explain why. Review each of the graphs and illustrations closely. What reasonable inferences can you draw from each set of illustrations – about American attitudes toward mobility, about the relationships between rich and poor, and about opportunities for advancement?

2. Compare the conclusions drawn in the *New York Times* survey to the discussions of class in the other texts and images presented in this chapter. What do photographs convey that essays and poems do not? How do statistics and graphs inform your understanding of class

in ways that other visual and verbal texts cannot? Which selections in this chapter do you judge to be the most striking and memorable representations of class? Explain why.

WRITING

1. Create a list of the survey questions used in the *New York Times* polls that are reprinted in this portfolio, and use them as the basis for interviewing at least three people about how they experience questions and issues focused on class. Write the first draft of an expository essay in which you summarize your findings, and analyze the extent to which the responses of those you polled were consistent with – or different from – the responses reported in the *Times*'s 2005 survey.

2. "What It Takes to Get Ahead . . ." offers insight into American attitudes toward advancement. "While other factors can help a person's advancement," the *Times* editors explain, "most Americans, regardless of income level, regard the individual's efforts as critical." Consider each of the factors included in the *Times* survey questions: coming from a wealthy family, knowing the right people, natural ability, good education, hard work, and so on. Write the first draft of an essay in which you argue that two of these attributes are the most critical determinants of success. Please use specific examples from your own life, the lives of people you know, or public figures to support your assertion.

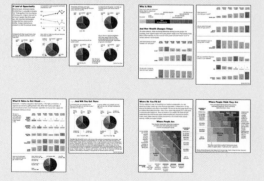

THIS LAND IS THEIR LAND
Barbara Ehrenreich

I took a little vacation recently—nine hours in Sun Valley, Idaho, before an evening speaking engagement. The sky was deep blue, the air crystalline, the hills green and not yet on fire. Strolling out of the Sun Valley Lodge, I found a tiny tourist village, complete with Swiss-style bakery, multistar restaurant, and "opera house." What luck—the boutiques were displaying outdoor racks of summer clothing on sale! Nature and commerce were conspiring to make this the perfect micro-vacation.

But as I approached the stores things started to get a little sinister— maybe I had wandered into a movie set or Paris Hilton's closet?—because even at 60 percent discount, I couldn't find a sleeveless cotton shirt for less than $100. These items shouldn't have been outdoors; they should have been in locked glass cases.

Then I remembered the general rule, which has been in effect since sometime in the 1990s: If a place is truly beautiful, you can't afford to be there. All right, I'm sure there are still exceptions—a few scenic spots not yet eaten up by mansions. But they're going fast.

About ten years ago, for example, a friend and I rented a snug, inexpensive one-bedroom house in Driggs, Idaho, just over the Teton Range from wealthy Jackson Hole, Wyoming. At that time, Driggs was where the workers lived, driving over the Teton Pass every day to wait tables and make beds on the stylish side of the mountains. The point is, we low-rent folks got to wake up to the same scenery the rich people enjoyed and hike along the same pine-shadowed trails.

5   But the money was already starting to pour into Driggs—Paul Allen of Microsoft, August Busch III of Anheuser-Busch, Harrison Ford— transforming family potato farms into vast dynastic estates. I haven't been back, but I understand Driggs has become another unaffordable Jackson Hole. Where the wait staff and bed-makers live today I do not know.

I witnessed this kind of deterioration up close in Key West, Florida, where I first went in 1986, attracted not only by the turquoise waters and frangipani-scented nights but by the fluid, egalitarian social scene. At a typical party you might find literary stars like Alison Lurie, Annie Dillard, and Robert Stone, along with commercial fishermen, waitresses, and men who risked their lives diving for treasure (once a major blue-collar occupation). Then, at some point in the '90s, the rich started pouring in. You'd see them on the small planes coming down from Miami—taut-skinned, linen-clad, and impatient. They drove house prices into the seven-figure range. They encouraged restaurants to charge upward of $30 for an entree. They tore down working-class tiki bars to make room for their waterfront "condotels."

Of all the crimes of the rich, the aesthetic deprivation of the rest of us may seem to be the merest misdemeanor. Many of them owe their wealth to the usual tricks: squeezing their employees, overcharging their customers, and polluting any land they're not going to need for their third or fourth homes. Once they've made (or inherited) their fortunes, the rich can bid up the price of goods that ordinary people also need—housing, for example. Gentrification is dispersing the urban poor into overcrowded suburban ranch houses, while billionaires' horse farms displace rural Americans into trailer homes. Similarly, the rich can easily fork over annual tuitions of $50,000 and up, which has helped make college education a privilege of the upper classes.

There are other ways, too, that the rich are robbing the rest of us of beauty and pleasure. As the bleachers in stadiums and arenas are cleared to make way for skybox "suites" costing more than $100,000 for a season, going out to a ballgame has become prohibitively expensive for the average family. At the other end of the cultural spectrum, superrich collectors have driven up the price of artworks, leading museums to charge ever rising prices for admission.

It shouldn't be a surprise that the Pew Research Center finds happiness to be unequally distributed, with 50 percent of people earning more than $150,000 a year describing themselves as "very happy," compared with only 23 percent of those earning less than $20,000. When nations are compared, inequality itself seems to reduce well-being, with some of the most equal nations—Iceland and Norway—ranking highest, according to the UN's Human Development Index. We are used to thinking that poverty is a "social problem" and wealth is only something to celebrate, but extreme wealth is also a social problem, and the superrich have become a burden on everyone else.

10   If Edward O. Wilson is right about "biophilia"—an innate human need to interact with nature—there may even be serious mental health consequences to letting the rich hog all the good scenery. I know that if I don't get to see vast expanses of water, 360-degree horizons, and mountains piercing the sky for at least a week or two of the year, chronic, cumulative claustrophobia sets in. According to evolutionary psychologist Nancy Etcoff, the need for scenery is hard-wired into us. "People like to be on a hill, where they can see a landscape. And they like somewhere to go where they can *not* be seen themselves," she told *Harvard Magazine*

last year. "That's a place desirable to a predator who wants to avoid becoming prey." We also like to be able to see water (for drinking), low-canopy trees (for shade), and animals (whose presence signals that a place is habitable).

Ultimately, the plutocratic takeover of rural America has a downside for the wealthy too. The more expensive a resort town gets, the farther its workers have to commute to keep it functioning. And if your heart doesn't bleed for the dishwasher or landscaper who commutes two to four hours a day, at least shed a tear for the wealthy vacationer who gets stuck in the ensuing traffic. It's bumper to bumper westbound out of Telluride, Colorado, every day at 5, or eastbound on Route 1 out of Key West, for the Lexuses as well as the beat-up old pickup trucks.

Or a place may simply run out of workers. Monroe County, which includes Key West, has seen more than 2,000 workers leave since the 2000 Census, a loss the *Los Angeles Times* calls "a body blow to the service-oriented economy of a county with only 75,000 residents and 2.25 million overnight visitors a year." Among those driven out by rents of more than $1,600 for a one-bedroom apartment are many of Key West's wait staff, hotel housekeepers, gardeners, plumbers, and handymen. No matter how much money you have, everything takes longer—from getting a toilet fixed to getting a fish sandwich at Pepe's.

Then there's the elusive element of charm, which quickly drains away in a uniform population of multimillionaires. The Hamptons had their fishermen. Key West still advertises its "characters"—sun-bleached, weather-beaten misfits who drifted down for the weather or to escape some difficult situation on the mainland. But the fishermen are long gone from the Hamptons and disappearing from Cape Cod. As for Key West's characters—with the traditional little conch houses once favored by shrimpers flipped into million-dollar second homes, these human sources of local color have to be prepared to sleep with the scorpions under the highway overpass.

In Telluride even a local developer is complaining about the lack of affordable housing. "To have a real town," he told the *Financial Times*, "Telluride needs some locals hanging out"—in old-fashioned diners, for example, where you don't have to speak Italian to order a cup of coffee.

15   When I was a child, I sang "America the Beautiful" and meant it. I was born in the Rocky Mountains and raised, at various times, on the coasts. The Big Sky, the rolling surf, the jagged, snowcapped mountains—all this seemed to be my birthright. But now I flinch when I hear Woody Guthrie's line "This land was made for you and me." Somehow, I don't think it was meant to be sung by a chorus of hedge-fund operators.

Barbara Ehrenreich

According to Barbara Ehrenreich, as Americans we don't just ignore the working class in America – we are afraid to talk about class at all: "We don't even hear the word 'class.' It's kind of a dirty word in America." As a result of this gap in American discussion, Ehrenreich has committed her career to speaking out about class through her many columns, articles, essays, books, and posts on her own blog. According to Ehrenreich, "As for the badge of class warfare – well, I'd say, yes, that's what I'm engaged in. . . . It's time somebody was fighting back."

Born in Montana in 1941, Ehrenreich is particularly suited to writing about class in America, having lived on various levels of the class spectrum. Her father, originally a poor coal miner, was able to secure an education and move the family up to middle-class status; through her writing Ehrenreich managed to move from middle-class to upper-class status, publishing several books about feminism throughout the 1970s, writing articles for numerous magazines, and contributing a regular column for *Time* magazine. Ehrenreich's biggest success, ironically, occurred through the publication of her book about the impossibility of living in America on a minimum-wage salary. The book, *Nickel and Dimed: On (Not) Getting By in America* (2001), was a best seller and led to several other books, essays, and articles about class, including *Bait and Switch: The (Futile) Pursuit of the American Dream* (2005) and *This Land Is Their Land: Reports from a Divided Nation* (2008). A committed social activist, Ehrenreich founded United Professionals, an organization for white-collar workers interested in reaching out to help "unemployed, underemployed, and anxiously employed" Americans, and she continues to write and speak passionately about this important subject.

SEEING

1. In what specific ways does Ehrenreich unpack the idea of home to make her point about extreme wealth being a social problem? When does she refer to homes (or houses), and with what effect(s)? Consider carefully the role of such related ideas as estate, condo, rent, and the like. For example, how does her initial choice to take a "vacation" – a time away from home – lead to the final impossibility of returning home, her "birthright" (para. 15)?

2. Point to specific instances where Ehrenreich effectively uses satire, sarcasm, irony, and ridicule in her essay. Analyze the particular effects she creates in each instance by employing these compositional techniques. For example, explain how irony or sarcasm energizes the saying "if a place is truly beautiful, you can't afford to be there" (para. 3). To what extent does ridicule or satire animate her description of rich people flying into Key West: "taut-skinned, linen-clad, and impatient" (para. 6)? How do these methods support – or undermine – the serious nature of her argument? Be as specific as possible in your response.

WRITING

1. Today the song <u>"This Land Is Your Land"</u> (p. 554) remains a patriotic staple, but Woody Guthrie wrote it in 1940 in response to "God Bless America," an anthem he considered unrealistic. Compare the two songs and decide which one paints a more realistic portrait of the America you experience daily. Which lyrics in each song resonate well with your experiences? Which melody is more in tune with the way you live your life? Which rhythm captures the tempo of your day? Why is one a better musical key for the United States than the other? Write the first draft of an expository essay in which you compare and contrast the lyrics of these two songs—as well as their implications for the way you experience everyday life in America.

2. As a group, wealthy people rarely respond openly to public criticism—partly because there are relatively few of them, and partly because criticizing poorer people will appear mean-spirited. Write a reasoned response to Ehrenreich's argument in which you take the side of the rich against the poor. Be sure to draft an essay that resists being elitist or unfair. What are the "crimes" of being poor? How do the poor "deny" the rich the experience of beauty and pleasure? Would the rich be psychologically better off without the poor? In what ways would society improve if everyone acted like the rich? As Ehrenreich does, support your position with personal observations, authoritative studies, and reliable statistics.

Page 554

THIS LAND IS YOUR LAND
Words and music by Woody Guthrie

Chorus:
This land is your land, this land is my land
From California, to the New York island;
From the redwood forest, to the Gulf Stream waters
This land was made for you and me

5 As I was walking that ribbon of highway,
I saw above me that endless skyway;
I saw below me that golden valley;
This land was made for you and me.

Chorus

I've roamed and rambled and I followed my footsteps
10 To the sparkling sands of her diamond deserts;
And all around me a voice was sounding:
This land was made for you and me.

Chorus

When the sun came shining, and I was strolling,
And the wheat fields waving and the dust clouds rolling,
15 As the fog was lifting a voice was chanting:
This land was made for you and me.

Chorus

As I went walking; I saw a sign there,
And on the sign it said "No Trasspassing"
But on the other side it didn't say nothing,
20 That side was made for you and me!

Chorus

In the shadow of the steeple I saw my people,
By the relief office I see my people;
As they stood there hungry, I stood there asking
Is this land made for you and me?

Chorus (2x)

Tina Barney
The Reunion, 1999

Tina Barney

Born in New York in 1945, Tina Barney collected photos long before she started to take her own. Inspired by Diane Arbus's family photographs, she began staging portraits of the people in her own world – family and friends of the upper class. Barney received a fellowship from the John Simon Guggenheim Memorial Foundation in 1991 and has had solo shows at numerous museums and galleries. Her work is also part of the permanent collection of the Museum of Modern Art in New York, the Museum of Fine Arts in Houston, and the Yale University Art Gallery. She has published three books of her own work: *Friends and Relations* (1991), *Theater of Manners* (1997), and *The Europeans* (2005). Barney currently lives in Watch Hill, Rhode Island, and New York.

SEEING

1. Much of Tina Barney's work focuses on capturing the friends and family she grew up with in New York's wealthiest neighborhoods. What specific details about this photograph signal upper-class culture? Discuss your observations with your classmates. To what extent do you agree on your answers? Could any of these objects, gestures, expressions, or postures "pass" for signs of working-class or middle-class culture? Why or why not?

2. Although Barney's photographs are full of candid expressions and gestures, they are the result of careful staging. She often plays a directorial role in setting up a scene, positioning her subjects, and carefully attending to lighting. What specific aspects of this photograph appear to be staged? What aspects seem candid or spontaneous? Explain your answers.

WRITING

1. "If you feel no need to explicate your allusions or in any way explain what you mean," writes Paul Fussell, "you are probably talking with someone in your class" (see p. 505, para. 8). In the photograph shown here, what do you imagine Barney's subjects are talking about? Write the first draft of a dialogue among the people in the photograph. You might consider the following questions: What occasion are they gathered for? What might some of their shared assumptions be about the experience? Are some of the "characters" speaking more, and with a more dominant presence, than others?

2. "When people say that there is a distance, a stiffness in my photographs, that the people look like they do not connect," said Tina Barney, "my answer is that this is the best that we can do. This inability to show physical affection is in our heritage." What evidence of this statement do you find in this photograph? In what specific ways are these people connecting? avoiding one another? showing or restraining physical affection? Write an expository essay in which you undertake a close analysis of the details and compositional choices in Barney's photograph as evidence of the upper-class cultural heritage she describes. How might Tina Barney stage a photograph to represent the spirit of Woody Guthrie's "This Land Is Your Land"?

Page 505

heritage: Tradition; inheritance; property that gets passed on to an heir.

As a reader, I am like a slug,
I am slow to get from
beginning to end,
and I leave a lot of drool
on the way there.

Matthew Eugene Groff, student at
Southern Polytechnic State University

Books must be read as
deliberately and reservedly
as they were written.

Henry David Thoreau, author and philosopher

VISUALIZING COMPOSITION:
METAPHOR

Metaphors surface frequently in everyday conversation, and many of us use them so often that we're not always conscious of doing so. Consider, for example, the metaphors undergraduates use to talk about attending school...

Their language and images are drawn from prison:

How long do you have to go?

Ugh! Four semesters!

And taking a course is described in terms of suffering from a disease:

What do you have this semester?

Ugh, math 2.0!

When writing, using metaphors can help add style and enliven the prose.
During the earliest phase of the writing process, metaphor can help generate ideas about a subject and create a structure for the prose.

DOG TIRED

You can't teach an old dog new tricks

dog eat dog

let sleeping dogs lie

the tail wags the dog

sick as a dog

dog-eared

top dog

it's a dog's life

gone to the dogs

dog day

doggy bag

hair of the dog

working like a dog

Top dog

Lap dog

dog end

By enabling us to clarify one subject in terms of another, metaphor can help us understand and appreciate the connections that can lead to new insights. In the language of advertising, metaphor is frequently used to establish a rhetorical relationship between people and products.

LAZINESS ILLUSTRATED

SIP!   BUZZZZ!

ZIP

BUZZY NRG DRINK

GO FROM COUCH POTATO TO BUZZY BEE IN **ONE** SIP

Carefully examine a recent issue of a magazine concentrating on the use of metaphor in the advertisements.
Write an essay in which you fully explain the various functions metaphor serves in one ad in the magazine.

LOOKING CLOSER – Rereading an Icon

"I saw and approached the hungry and desperate mother, as if drawn by a magnet," says Dorothea Lange of her experience photographing Florence Thompson and her children in a California pea-pickers' encampment in 1936, while on assignment documenting conditions for the New Deal's Farm Security Administration. "I do not remember how I explained my presence or my camera to her, but I do remember she asked me no questions. I made five exposures, working closer and closer from the same direction." Lange titled one of those exposures *Migrant Mother*, and it became one of the most widely viewed and discussed depictions of the Great Depression.

In "Passing Likeness: Dorothea Lange's *Migrant Mother* and the Paradox of Iconicity," Sally Stein traces the story of Lange's photograph as a contested symbol of American stereotypes of gender, race, and class. The interviews and images that Stein incorporates into her essay, as well as the images that follow, offer a broad context to deepen and extend your analysis. How do these multiple perspectives contribute to your analysis of Lange's famous photograph?

Gelatin silver print, 13½ x 10½ in. (34.8 x 26.7 cm), Oakland Museum of California, City of Oakland, the Dorothea Lange Collection, gift of Paul S. Taylor.

Dorothea Lange
Migrant Mother, Nipomo, California, 1936

PASSING LIKENESS
Dorothea Lange's *Migrant Mother*
and the Paradox of Iconicity
Sally Stein

Dorothea Lange's *Migrant Mother* is arguably the most familiar image from the Great Depression, haunting the nation and, in different ways, both the photographer and the picture's principal subject. Toward the end of her life, Lange was asked to write about her most famous photograph. She began that recollection by noting that some pictures take on a life of their own, overshadowing all the other pictures a photographer may consider to be equally, if not more important. Surely this image fits that description.[1]

Lange made the photograph at a migrant labor camp in Nipomo, California, in early March 1936, as part of her work documenting conditions of rural labor for the New Deal's Farm Security Administration (FSA). Within a few years, the FSA office used this photograph on an in-house poster to proclaim the multiple uses its growing file of government pictures served, for *Migrant Mother* had appeared in major newspapers and magazines, along with photography periodicals and museum exhibitions. In at least one installation photograph from the early 1940s, it already was being represented as worthy of special veneration and, for women, emulation. During and immediately following World War II, it seems to have been retired from active use. But it acquired new legs when its role was reprised for Edward Steichen's book and exhibition *The Family of Man* (1955), Beaumont and Nancy Newhall's book *Masters of Photography* (1958), and then Steichen's final MoMA exhibition and catalogue *The Bitter Years* (1962). As both social documentary and the populist politics of the Great Depression attracted the interest of the postwar generation coming of age in the 1960s, a wide variety of publications made frequent use of *Migrant Mother*. As a government picture in the public domain, it was readily available for minimal cost. Moreover, the picture's extensive prior usage only added to its serviceability as a shorthand emblem of both the depths of misery once widespread in this society and its heartfelt recognition by socially engaged New Dealers. Indeed, since the early 1960s, it has been reproduced so often that many

---

1. Dorothea Lange, "The Assignment I'll Never Forget." *Popular Photography* 46 (February 1960): 42. [All notes are Stein's.]

call it the most widely reproduced photograph in the entire history of photographic image-making.

Celebrity, we know, attracts critics along with acolytes. It is no surprise, then, that this national icon of maternal fortitude has provoked an unending series of challenges to its documentary authenticity. As much as anyone, the photographer helped lay the groundwork for subsequent skeptics. Two years after Lange made the series that already was gaining exceptional notice, she borrowed the negative from the Washington office in order to make a fine enlargement for a traveling museum exhibition. With art on her mind, she temporarily took leave of her New Deal political senses and decided to have a corner of the negative retouched. Since the picture had begun gaining special notice, Lange judged the intrusion of a thumb and index finger beside the tent pole to be an extraneous detail, detracting from an otherwise unified composition that was reminiscent of sacred Marian imagery. This embellishment of the picture may have led to her being fired, for one photographic historian has proposed that Lange's FSA boss, Roy Stryker, was so angered by her tampering with a government negative that he named Lange for termination when the FSA faced budget reductions at the end of the 1930s.[2]

Over time Stryker expunged this dispute from memory. In later years, he not only championed Lange's signal contribution to the file but also claimed that of all the thousands of FSA pictures *Migrant Mother* represented the apex of the documentary project.[3] But as the study of photography moved from an infancy of jubilant celebration to a more critical adolescence, others initiated their own investigations. Historian James C. Curtis questioned whether the presumed final picture was absolutely documentary; his reconstruction of the sequence of negatives she exposed in Nipomo demonstrates that Lange worked very selectively to achieve her portrait composition, in the process sacrificing any sense of location and even some family members.[4]

5   Feminists have brought other concerns to the reexamination of the picture. Cultural historian Wendy Kozol treated *Migrant Mother* as the

---

2. F. Jack Hurley, *Portrait of a Decade: Roy Stryker and the Development of Documentary Photography in the Thirties* (Baton Rouge: Louisiana State University Press, 1972), pp. 142–43.

3. "To me it was 'the' picture of Farm Security," Stryker declared toward the end of his life. Quoted in Nancy Wood's introductory essay, "Portrait of Stryker," in Roy Emerson Stryker and Nancy Wood, *In This Proud Land* (Greenwich, CT: New York Graphic Society, 1973), p. 19.

4. James Curtis, "'The Contemplation of Things as They Are': Dorothea Lange and *Migrant Mother*," in James Curtis, *Mind's Eye, Mind's Truth: FSA Photography Reconsidered* (Philadelphia: Temple University Press, 1989), pp. 45–67.

quintessential example of the FSA traffic in conservative stereotypes. This modern version of the longstanding pictorial genre of mother and child, Kozol argues, chiefly served to reassure the public in the Great Depression that the most fundamental social unit—the nuclear family— was beleaguered but still strong.[5] Subsequent scholarship has extended this critique of the way *Migrant Mother* both drew upon gender conventions and in turn helped keep them in circulation, thereby perpetuating pictorial and social clichés. "Whatever reality its subject first possessed," literary historian Paula Rabinowitz declared, "has been drained away and the image become icon."[6] Some scholars contend more bluntly that study of Depression culture would benefit from shifting attention to less-celebrated pictures, preferably those depicting women engaged in wage work instead of preoccupied with domestic responsibilities.[7]

Despite these critical admonitions, not all have heeded the call to shelve this familiar photograph but instead have explored new avenues for comprehending the picture's persistent power. One lacuna in earlier discussions of *Migrant Mother* was the lack of any detailed information about the woman. Lange spent so little time making the photograph that she did not even record the name of her subject. By the time Lange died in 1965, she had come to think of her model as having only the generic name *Migrant Mother*. But in the 1970s, a younger generation of photographers began to revisit places and people already rendered historic by earlier documentation. In that spirit of rephotography, Nebraska-based photojournalist Bill Ganzel spent years tracking down people and locations photographed by the FSA. With the aid of a story in the *Modesto* (California) *Bee*, Ganzel located Florence Thompson and persuaded her and the same children to pose for him in 1979. The book that resulted from his wide-ranging research was the first major publication to put a name to her face, yet in most other respects, the information supplied was sparse. Apparently wary of further national exposure,

---

5. Wendy Kozol, "Madonnas of the Fields: Photography, Gender, and 1930s Farm Relief," *Genders 2* (July 1988): 1–23.

6. Paula Rabinowitz, *They Must Be Represented: The Politics of Documentary* (London/New York: Verso, 1994), p. 87. Rabinowitz does not specify whether she means *icon* in the vernacular sense of shared cultural symbol, or in the more technical, semiotic sense of a sign that works by means of resonant likeness, or in the most traditional religious sense of an image meant for literal veneration, or some combination of these various meanings.

7. See the recent discussions of this image in Laura Hapke, *Daughters of the Great Depression: Women, Work and Fiction in the American 1930s* (Athens: University of Georgia Press, 1995), pp. 29–31; and Michael Denning, *The Cultural Front: The Laboring of American Culture in the Twentieth Century* (London/New York: Verso, 1996), pp. 137–38.

the family members offered only general remarks about the hard times they had survived.[8]

Bill Ganzel
Florence Thompson and her daughters Norma Rydlewski (in front), *Katherine McIntosh, and Ruby Sprague, at Norma's house, Modesto, California*

1979. Gelatin silver print, 11 x 14 in. (27.9 x 35.5 cm). Courtesy of the artist.

Ganzel's photograph offered a bit more information. For this unusual public portrait, Florence Thompson quietly displayed her own sense of style by donning white slacks and a white sleeveless top, adorned only by a Southwest-style squash blossom necklace. In itself, there is nothing conclusive about this detail; one response to the surge of Native American activism in the 1970s was the widespread fashion for silver-and-turquoise jewelry. But for Thompson it was a deliberate, if quiet, statement of identity. During the same period, this long-obscure celebrity made a point of acknowledging her Cherokee heritage in occasional interviews with news media. Thompson also volunteered that she always had resented the famed picture by Lange, and would never have allowed its being taken had she understood the way and the extent to which it would be used.[9]

---

8. Bill Ganzel, *Dust Bowl Descent* (Lincoln: University of Nebraska Press, 1984), pp. 10, 30–31.

9. One such news story circulated by Associated Press appeared in the *Los Angeles Times*, Saturday, II:1 (November 18, 1978), as cited and reproduced in Martha Rosler, *Three Works* (Halifax: Press of the Nova Scotia College of Art and Design, 1981), pp. 67, 75–76.

But for more than a decade after her widely reported death in September 1983 and the national circulation of Ganzel's book in 1984, public information about Florence Thompson consisted largely of a proper name. Then, in the early 1990s, Geoffrey Dunn, a freelance journalist and University of California doctoral student, resolved to reconstruct her life story. Extensive interviews with surviving members of the family left him shocked by the gulf between her actual situation and the minimal details Lange had recorded. The varied details of Thompson's life that Dunn pieced together for this first biographical essay were no less stunning than his overriding conclusion of the photograph's betrayal of its immediate subject.[10]

When her path crossed that of Lange's in March 1936, Florence Owens was thirty-two years old. Born Florence Leona Christie in September 1903, she grew up in the Indian Territory of the Cherokee Nation to which both her parents claimed blood rights. Her biological father left her mother before she was born, and her mother soon married a man who did not think of himself as Indian (though his children later came to think that he may have been of part-Choctaw descent). Throughout her youth, Florence believed her mother's second husband to be her biological father. Thus, although she grew up in Indian Territory, she did not identify herself as "pure" Cherokee. In 1921, at the age of seventeen, she married Cleo Owens, a farmer's son from Missouri, and over the next decade they proceeded to have five children.

10   Oklahoma in the first decades of the twentieth century bore little relation to the locale envisioned in the popular World War II–era musical. The long-running Broadway show simply eradicated the Indian presence and prior claim to the land, while suggesting unlimited opportunities for all newcomers. The historical record is more dramatic. Following the white land rush at the turn of the twentieth century that had been precipitated by the forced allotment system of the federally enacted Dawes Plan, opportunities to homestead turned cutthroat: "Of the thirty million allotted acres more than twenty-seven million passed from Indians to whites by fraudulent deeds, embezzlement, and murder."[11] Florence and Cleo Owens saw no chance of farming on their own, so by the mid-twenties they opted to move west, finding work and temporary

---

10. Geoffrey Dunn, "Photographic License," *Santa Clara Metro* 10:47 (January 19–25, 1995): 20–24.

11. Gerald Vizenor, "Manifest Manners," in *American Indian Persistence and Resurgence*, ed. Karl Kroeber (Durham: Duke University Press, 1994), p. 233: Vizenor quotes from the extensive research of lawyer and historian Rennard Strickland's meticulous demographic research in his book *The Indians in Oklahoma* (Norman: University of Oklahoma Press, 1980), particularly chapter 2, "The Dark Winter of Settlement and Statehood," pp. 31–54.

housing in the sawmill camps of California's Hill Country. By 1931, they were expecting a sixth child in northern California when Cleo Owens died of tuberculosis.

According to Dunn, Florence supported her family as a waitress and soon became involved with a local businessman. Florence's grandson Roger Sprague, who is currently preparing his own biography of the many generations of his grandmother's family, notes that the young widow was fiercely independent but made the mistake of obtaining county aid, which stipulated that any sexual relations with men would result in the removal of her children. When she became pregnant, she immediately left for her home state, determined to avoid any custody dispute.[12] But Oklahoma in the 1930s was devastated by drought and offered even fewer opportunities than it had in the previous decade. Florence quickly set out a second time for California.

Gelatin silver prints, dimensions vary.
Library of Congress.

Dorothea Lange
From *Migrant Mother* series, 1936

After returning to her adopted state, Florence became involved with Jim Hill, an unemployed local man who had turned to migrant work, and with whom she had a child in 1935 — the nursing infant in *Migrant Mother*. Hill had temporarily left the camp with one of Florence's sons when Lange happened upon the pea pickers' encampment and made her series of portraits. Though Hill was actually getting a radiator repaired, the photographer soon annotated the closest portrait with the detail that the family had been forced to sell the tires from their car. This factual embellishment offended the family's sense of logic as well as accuracy, since mobility was the key to even the poorest migrant's survival. Dunn's article makes no mention of when Florence married Thompson,

---

12. I am indebted to Roger Sprague who has allowed me to read his manuscript-in-progress, "Second Trail of Tears." Excerpts from his carefully researched text can be found on his website, www.migrantgrandson.com.

her last name at the time of her death. But from Roger Sprague's more extensive reconstruction of his family history, I learned that the marriage followed her separation from Hill in the 1940s, and again she outlived her husband.

As Dunn makes clear, Lange was quite careless with the facts. However, this was hardly the first time a scholar has noted the liberties Lange took in her documentary practice (as well as in the facts of her own biography). Accordingly, Dunn's wholesale condemnation of the famous photographer as manipulative, condescending, colonialistic, misleading, and disingenuous made less of an impression on me than the chronicle he had sketched of *Migrant Mother*'s Native American heritage.[13] On this count, I don't think we can condemn Lange for deliberately misrepresenting or burying the information.

From all available evidence, it does not seem that Lange ever realized she had cast a Native American for the European American role of New Deal madonna. She never questioned the stranger about her ethnic identity; in fact, making such an inquiry would have risked breaking whatever current of empathy she briefly sought to establish. But if there is anything recognizably "Indian" in this striking face, Lange's misperception is more than a little curious. She prided herself on being able to distill essential truths by looking closely.[14] Moreover, she had spent a fair amount of time studying Native Americans in the Southwest. Her first husband, Maynard Dixon, was a plein-air painter who had specialized in idyllic scenes of the pristine West inhabited solely by Native Americans. It was during an early sojourn with Dixon in the Southwest that Lange began to photograph seriously outside her studio, and those efforts led to one of her first distinctive portraits. Yet, in the resulting close-cropped print of a Hopi man's face, her framing excluded all conflicting cultural signs like modern, store-bought clothing. In this respect, she continued the quest to find or produce "authentic Indians,"

---

13. On Lange's radical misquotation in the case of her 1930s portrait of Nettie Featherston (*Woman of the High Plains*), long linked to the caption "If you die, you're dead — that's all," see Maren Stange, *Symbols of Ideal Life* (New York and Cambridge, England: Cambridge University Press, 1989), pp. 119–23; see also my interpretation of the photographer's logic for such counterfactual alteration in "Peculiar Grace: Dorothea Lange and the Testimony of the Body," in *Dorothea Lange: A Visual Life*, ed. Elizabeth Partridge (Washington, D.C.: Smithsonian Institution Press, 1984), pp. 81–84. On Lange's embellishment of her own educational background, see her first biography, Milton Meltzer's *Dorothea Lange: A Photographer's Life* (New York: Farrar, Straus and Giroux, 1978), p. 22.

14. Toward the end of her life she would express this idea in terms of "living the visual life," words that open the 1966 documentary film *The Closer for Me*, produced by Philip Greene and Robert Katz of KQED; transcript of the filmed interviews with the photographer in the Dorothea Lange Collection of the Oakland Museum of California.

Gelatin silver print, 7¼ x 7⁷⁄₁₆ in. (18.4 x 19.6 cm). Oakland Museum of California, City of Oakland, the Dorothea Lange Collection, gift of Paul S. Taylor.

Dorothea Lange
Left: *Hopi Indian Man* (full frame version), 1926. Gelatin silver print. Private Collection.
Right: *Hopi Indian Man*, 1926.

a tradition developed by a long line of artists including Dixon and photographers like Edward S. Curtis.[15] That these "authentic" stereotypes were manifestly superficial in spite of being deep-seated, proved especially true in Nipomo, California. The migrant woman who attracted Lange's attention displayed no obvious signs of "Indianness," so Lange proceeded to place her in a distinctly Euro-American scenario of hallowed Christian maternity. In turn, this iconographic context led all, including the photographer, to assume that the model was unarguably white.

15   Lange's mistaken assumption amplifies the generalizing tendencies in both New Deal culture and subsequent scholarship of the period. Photography and direct observation in that era came close to enjoying the powers of a fetish, magically replete without nominal recourse to factual or reasoned discourse. Though our eyes often deceive us, the objective character of photography encourages viewers to rely on sensory appearance as the incontrovertible bedrock of experience-based knowledge.

The photograph's history likewise exemplifies the way the New Deal was not only most concerned about "the forgotten man"—in Franklin Roosevelt's words—but equally, if less vocally, about the declining status of whites. The mass media were most inclined to focus on the plight of poor whites, and Lange's FSA boss was supremely media-oriented. On one occasion, Stryker rejected Lange's proposal to focus on the situation

15. On the deliberately selective practices of staging and framing by Curtis, see Christopher M. Lyman, *The Vanishing Race and Other Illusions: Photographs of Indians by Edward S. Curtis* (Washington, D.C.: Smithsonian Institution Press, 1982).

Photogravure, 6 x 8 in. (15 x 20.3 cm). National Anthropological Archives, Smithsonian Institution, Washington, D.C.

Edward S. Curtis
The Vanishing Race, 1907

of blacks and the urban poor, reminding her of the dearth of demand for such pictures.[16] Since there was even less public concern about Native Americans in this period, while traveling for the FSA in the Southwest Lange never proposed focusing on the living conditions of Native Americans. But Arthur Rothstein implicitly made such a proposal on one occasion, by sending the FSA a few preliminary studies of Native Americans he had photographed in Montana. Stryker's response was blatant:

> The Indian pictures are fine, but I doubt if we ought to get too far involved. There are so many other things to be done. You know I just don't get too excited about the Indians. I know it is their country and we took it away from them—to hell with it![17]

In this unguarded exchange, Stryker may have been expressing a personal and regional bias, for he came from western Colorado where his family had struggled as ranchers. But if his sentiments were at all representative of mainstream opinion in the New Deal, it is reasonable to

---

16. See the exchange of letters between Stryker and Lange, June 18–23, 1937, as well as their correspondence during October 1938; Stryker personal correspondence files, University of Louisville.

17. Stryker to Rothstein in Great Falls, Montana, May 26, 1939; from the Archives of American Art microfilm correspondence of Stryker's personal collection of FSA correspondence.

assume that had Lange recognized her subject as Native American, she might not have bothered to take any photographs. Or if she had discovered from extended conversation that the woman she had photographed was Native American and captioned the picture accordingly, the image's promotion and circulation would have been quite limited. It would have undermined conventional thinking in two ways: It directed attention away from Anglos, and it refused to support the image of Indians as a "vanishing race." Rather, Lange had depicted someone who seems determined to survive and who, as part of that process, had traveled out of the Dust Bowl region and into California—even the most skeletal caption is quick to inform us—thereby challenging the stereotypes of a defeated minority.

Once we recognize that what has been documented inadvertently is the migration not of a poor Anglo-Oklahoman but of an equally poor Native American Oklahoman with children, we may be led to question the basic concept that Lange and her second husband, University of California at Berkeley social scientist Paul S. Taylor, developed to frame their New Deal magnum opus, *An American Exodus*.[18] Together they wove pictures and text to trace the movement of whites and a smaller number of blacks suffering displacement and immiseration as recent (and frequently despised) newcomers to the industrialized agricultural fields of California. It was an ambitious cross-country chronicle, yet after gleaning just a bit about the background of *Migrant Mother*, it is hard to accept the contours of such a black-and-white story. Indeed, to think of exodus and migration with primary emphasis on the Great Depression fails to comprehend that whites were latecomers to the forced migration across a continent. Okie culture, in particular, was carried to the West not only by whites and blacks, but also by Native Americans who were banished from Georgia and other eastern states in the early nineteenth century. Those who managed to survive ordeals such as the infamous Trail of Tears were forced to resettle in Oklahoma,[19] and yet the records of so-called Okie migration rarely make reference to Native Americans.[20] Those migrations continue to be relegated to histories devoted

18. Dorothea Lange and Paul Schuster Taylor, *An American Exodus: A Record of Human Erosion* (New York: Reynal and Hitchcock, 1939).

19. Strickland, Indians in Oklahoma, pp. 1–7; see also Michael Paul Rogin, "Liberal Society and the Indian Question," in Rogin, *Ronald Regan, the Movie and Other Episodes in Political Demonology* (Berkeley: University of California Press, 1987), pp. 134–68.

20. For example, Indians and Native Americans do not even appear in the index to the book frequently cited as the definitive social history on Oklahomans in California; James N. Gregory, *American Exodus: The Dust Bowl Migration and Okie Culture in California* (New York: Oxford University Press, 1989).

exclusively to Native Americans, an example of our intellectual reservation system still in operation. The histories of Oklahoma settlement and resettlement need to be revisted and elaborated to portray the constant flux and mix in populations.

But the continuing gaps in our social histories should not prevent consideration of the symbolic implications in the long-standing assumptions about *Migrant Mother*'s whiteness. How to account for this error? On one hand are the viewers'—including Lange's—deeply ingrained stereotypes. On the other hand, it seems reasonable to assume that the migrant woman made no effort to publicize her identity as a person of color. When she was already living a life of bare-bones subsistence, what was the point of gratuitously announcing her minority status far away from her community of origin (which itself was increasingly dispersed)? The entrenched federal policy of sending Native American children to government boarding schools for training in assimilation provided more incentive to pass.[21]

20   The concept of passing implies unilateral deception for the sake of upward mobility and the avoidance of stigma. Deliberate misrepresentation is foisted upon another who seeks to police the boundaries of a racialized caste system and guard the gates of exclusivity. While making use of the term, I propose reloading its meanings so that we consider the role of whites, or any privileged group, more actively in the process. Misrecognition of conventional affinities may simply underscore the arbitrary character of such repressive systems of regulation. But misrecognition may also attest to the active desires that are being repressed, at least nominally. Since I find it surprising that it took virtually six decades before anyone began exploring Thompson's ethnic background, I propose that this lack of recognition of difference contains a wish toward generic inclusivity. Such inclusivity may not be motivated by disinterested liberality or the desire to dispense with all social barriers. Rather, for those in the mainstream, there may be other benefits that accrue from imagining oneself more closely connected to the other. At the most banal level, there may be a cosmetic motive (arguably masking an erotic impulse) to reimagine oneself and one's immediate relations with higher cheekbones and a more prominent, "noble" profile. Such a process of physiognomic affiliation may have helped European Americans justify their claims as rightful heirs to the continent. Likewise, the feeling of resemblance might convey the liberating promise of more intimate contact with nature and

---

21. Frederick E. Hoxie, *A Final Promise: The Campaign to Assimilate the Indians, 1880–1920* (Lincoln: University of Nebraska Press, 1984).

enhanced physical prowess.[22] What better figure with whom to create such a fantasy set of relations than a woman whose fair-haired child indicates that she has already entered the process of interracial union? Thus, the danger that Mary Douglas reminds us always accompanies thought of purity is conjured into a fantasy of pleasure, revitalization, and legitimation.[23]

Is it not fitting that a society struggling to weather a decade-long capitalist crisis would gravitate toward an image that faintly recalled the strong profiles it had already appropriated to legitimate its business? Gracing coins and government buildings, these figures embodied the natural powers that American capitalism both claimed and coerced so that the New World garden could be worked for profit.[24] That sentiment [had] already found expression in an early Depression report by literary critic and social journalist Edmund Wilson. On a quick visit to the Appalachian region, Wilson was astounded by the visual contrast between the "goggled eyes, thick lips, red, blunt-nosed, salmon-shaped visage" of the County Welfare agent and the "clear oval faces, pale and refined by starvation." These, he ruminates, represent "the pure type of that English race which, assimilated on the frontier to the Indians' hatchet profile and high cheekbones, inbred in Boston and Virginia, still haunts our American imagination as the norm from which our people have departed, the ideal towards which it ought to tend."[25] Wilson's idea allows for a bit of assimilation but mainly stresses the pale refining process in the production of prescriptive norms. By contrast, Lange's image is less concerned with paleness per se, but unwittingly she expresses a similar eugenic sensibility, and in the canonization of this image as mainstream Anglo icon, so too has the entire body politic.

News from the parochial world of photographic studies travels slowly, or perhaps stereotypical thinking proves remarkably tenacious. A recent book on the divisive role of race in twentieth-century America once again reproduces *Migrant Mother*, this time as a negative example of white

---

22. On the white desire to pass as Indian, at least for brief moments of recreation and resistance, see Philip J. Deloria, *Playing Indian* (New Haven: Yale University Press, 1998).

23. Mary Douglas, *Purity and Danger: An Analysis of the Concepts of Pollution and Taboo* (London: Routledge & Kegan Paul, 1966).

24. While she does not discuss the iconography of the nickel, Barbara Groseclose provides a good basis for such analysis in her genealogy of early official uses of Indian iconography; Groseclose, *Nineteenth-Century American Art* (New York: Oxford University Press, 2000), pp. 62–67. For a trenchant ideological analysis of the contradictory impulses in white paternalism, see Rogin, "Liberal Society and the Indian Question."

25. Edmund Wilson, "Red Cross and Country Agent" (written during Wilson's cross-country travels during 1930–31); reprinted in Wilson, *The American Earthquake* (Garden City, NY: Doubleday, 1958), p. 264.

supremacy. To encourage more critical readings of this familiar picture, the author adds his own interpretive caption:

> Part of the photograph's appeal lay in the sheer brilliance of its composition, but part depended, too, on its choice of a "Nordic" woman. Her suffering could be thought to represent the nation in ways the distress of a black, Hispanic, Italian, or Jewish woman never could.[26]

Even in a text that aims to challenge divisive ideologies, we encounter more evidence of the degree to which race and ethnicity elicits our categorizing impulses and simultaneously mocks them.

One could argue that "reclassifying" *Migrant Mother* as Native American only continues a caste-based tradition of racial labeling. There is something to be said for thinking that the ethnicity of the central subject in this revered picture should not matter, especially because in the past it never seemed to matter. Downplaying the belated revelation of *Migrant Mother*'s Native American identity may serve as proof that our society is moving close to a state of color blindness. Then again, can the eradication of racism ever be achieved if we ignore the racialized ground on which the nation established itself and continually expanded? An alternative goal might be that future generations will come to view *Migrant Mother* beside the highly contrived portrait studies of Edward S. Curtis, for example. Recontextualized thus, both depictions may appear as differing versions of Euro American misrecognitions of Native Americans: either as noble savages magically quite removed from encroaching European society, or conversely as fair-to-passing representative figures of that same civilization, with the Native American lending a fantasy of natural nobility to whites' wishful images of themselves and their supposedly resolute family values. If and when we finally become a society committed to problematizing the historic assumptions of normative whiteness, the notions of passing, and passing likeness, might finally admit thoroughgoing reconsideration of what has been missed with respect to difference and diversity.

---

26. Thanks to Tom Folland for directing me to this passage in Gary Gerstle, *American Crucible, Race and Nation in the Twentieth Century* (Princeton: Princeton University Press, 2001), pp. 180–81.

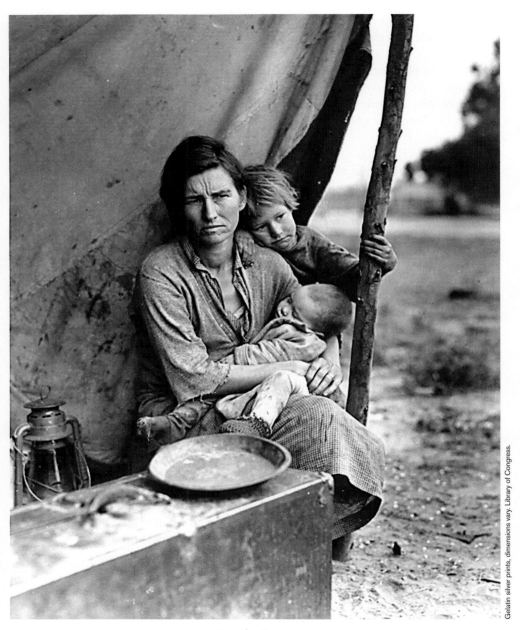

Dorothea Lange
From *Migrant Mother* series, 1936

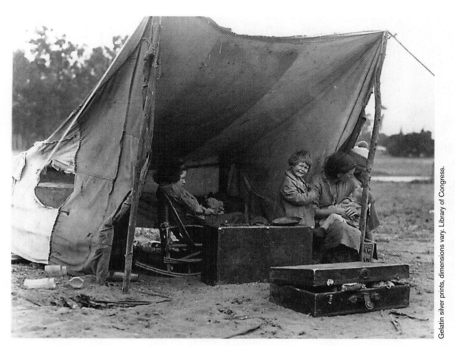

Dorothea Lange
From *Migrant Mother* series, 1936

Dorothea Lange
From *Migrant Mother* series, 1936

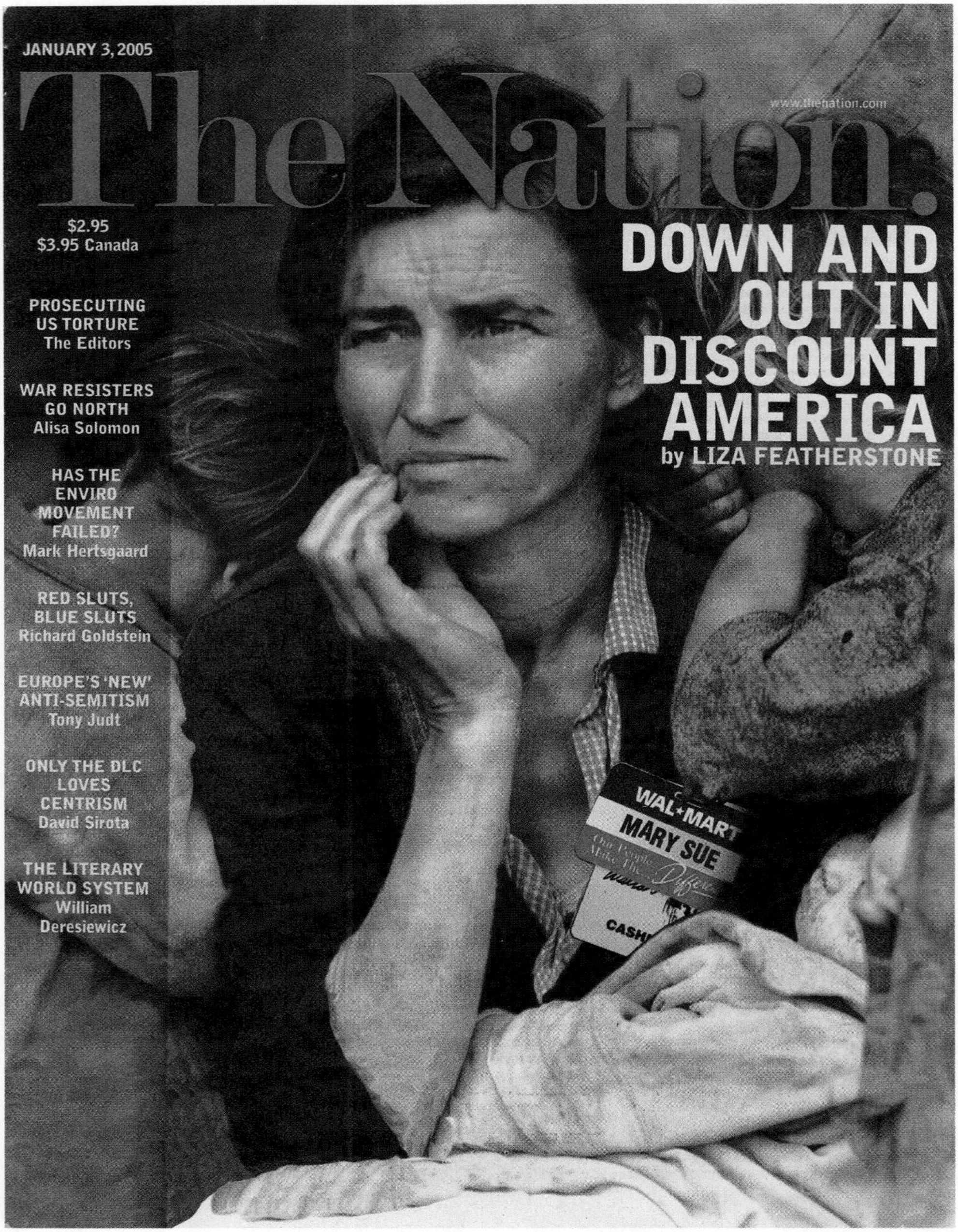

The Nation.

www.thenation.com

$2.95
$3.95 Canada

PROSECUTING
US TORTURE
The Editors

WAR RESISTERS
GO NORTH
Alisa Solomon

HAS THE
ENVIRO
MOVEMENT
FAILED?
Mark Hertsgaard

RED SLUTS,
BLUE SLUTS
Richard Goldstein

EUROPE'S 'NEW'
ANTI-SEMITISM
Tony Judt

ONLY THE DLC
LOVES
CENTRISM
David Sirota

THE LITERARY
WORLD SYSTEM
William
Deresiewicz

DOWN AND OUT IN DISCOUNT AMERICA
by LIZA FEATHERSTONE

WAL★MART
MARY SUE
CASH

Dorothea Lange
Eloy, Pinal County, Arizona, 1940

Sally Stein

Art historian Sally Stein specializes in the history of photography, in particular the photographic projects of Dorothea Lange, Walker Evans, and others who documented the Depression for the Farm Security Administration. Stein, an associate professor of art history and film and media studies at the University of California–Irvine, has authored many essays on twentieth-century documentary photography and material culture. The essay included here, "Passing Likeness," explores the racialized complexity of *Migrant Mother* as a Dust Bowl icon. It first appeared in *Only Skin Deep: Challenging Visions of the American Self* (2003). Another of her essays, "Peculiar Grace: Dorothea Lange and the Testimony of the Body," was published in *Dorothea Lange: A Visual Life* (1994).

Stein has co-curated several important shows. In 1979 she worked on the first survey exhibition of photographer Harry Callahan's color images. In 1988 she helped mount an exhibit of New Deal photography at the Smithsonian. In 1992 she worked on *Montage and Modern Life* for Boston's Institute of Contemporary Art and MIT. And in 2003 she helped curate a retrospective of the photography of Rohdal Partridge.

Visit seeingandwriting.com for an interactive exercise on Dorothea Lange's *Migrant Mother.*

Dorothea Lange

If any twentieth-century photographer could be described as having most heartbreakingly captured the plight of the American poor, Dorothea Lange (1895–1965) would be that photographer. Lange was born in Hoboken, New Jersey, studied at Columbia University, and began her photography career in New York, where she achieved a solid reputation as a portrait photographer–enough to enable her to move to San Francisco in 1919 and open her own studio. However, it was not until the Great Depression of the early 1930s that she found her "voice" as one of America's most recognizable photojournalists. Her photographs of the homeless in San Francisco resulted in a job as a documentary photographer with the Farm Security Administration, a federal program aimed at finding new homes for struggling migrant workers that President Franklin D. Roosevelt created as part of his New Deal economic relief programs. Lange reportedly took this opportunity to document the lives of the very poor with the hope that her images would move others to take action to help end poverty.

The two other Lange photographs included in this chapter represent some of her most indelible images: *Billboard on U.S. Highway 99 in California* (1937) depicts a shack in the middle of the desert, seemingly protected from the elements only by a billboard, while *Eloy, Pinal County, Arizona* (1940) portrays a crowd of people, all presumably without permanent homes, gathered in the back of a dilapidated truck. In 1939 many of Lange's photographs were published in *An American Exodus*, written in collaboration with her husband, Paul Schuster Taylor. Lange's success as one of America's premier photojournalists led to a Guggenheim Fellowship in 1942 (the first awarded to a woman) and many other influential photographic series.

The Nation

Founded in 1865 by abolitionists, *The Nation* is America's oldest weekly magazine and has long been an important voice in debates over social and political issues. According to its founding statement, *The Nation* approaches all questions with "a really critical spirit . . . to wage war upon the vices of violence, exaggeration, and misrepresentation by which so much of the political writing of the day is marred."

The Nation's January 3, 2005, cover makes use of Dorothea Lange's photograph *Migrant Mother* (1936). Lange was one of a number of photographers who traveled throughout the country during the Great Depression, documenting its effects. In the version shown here the mother has become a Wal-Mart employee, suggesting a continuum of both social injustice and the documentary tradition.

SEEING

1. In paragraph 5 Stein notes feminist criticisms of Lange's *Migrant Mother* for "perpetuating pictorial and social clichés." What pictorial and social clichés has the image projected over time, according to Stein? In what specific ways do you think the fact that the mother is Native American strengthens or weakens the feminist argument? To what extent are those stereotypes drawn on in *The Nation*'s use of the image for its cover article on labor conditions at Wal-Mart?

2. How do comments from Lange and Thompson change the way you view *Migrant Mother*? In what ways might Lange have intended to make a political statement in taking and promoting the photograph? Explain your answers. According to Stein, Florence Thompson "would never have allowed [the picture's] being taken had she understood the way and extent to which it would be used" (para. 7). Given what else we now know about Thompson, do you think she considered "the way" or "the extent" to be the bigger problem? Why? What besides frequency of replication makes an image iconic?

Page 576   Page 560

WRITING

1. According to Stein, literary historian Paula Rabinowitz believes that any reality *Migrant Mother* once possessed has vanished because of its iconic status. Does becoming an icon always reduce some dimension of an image's reality? Write an essay arguing your position on this question, using both Lange's photograph and another iconic image of your choice to support your argument.

2. Among the charges levied at Lange are that she altered the negative of the photograph in pursuit of a more coherent composition and that she willfully ignored her subject's ethnicity in pursuit of a more coherent narrative. Draft an essay comparing these two "offenses" and stating which of the two you would consider greater. Relate your position to the ethics required of a documentary photographer.

7

TAKING A

STAND

Each of the authors, artists, and designers presented in this chapter takes a stand on a current issue in American society. Some challenge traditional cultural assumptions; others investigate – and propose solutions for – complex social problems. All elicit strong personal responses from readers and viewers.

These texts and images address complex and challenging questions, and responding to them requires focus and sustained critical attention. For example, we present material that raises the question of whether there is a need for gun control, and we also provide occasions to discuss and write about both sides of the debate surrounding global warming. Such questions call upon all of us to articulate, and put into practice, our most deeply rooted convictions and beliefs. These issues require deliberate and purposeful intellectual work, and they highlight the contested nature of a great deal of thinking in writing.

Many of us learn about these controversial topics from the media – while watching TV, surfing the web, or reading newspapers and magazines – or noticing roadside billboard signs. In each of these contexts, words and images compete for our attention, and many media pundits would have us believe that images dominate. We invite you to take a stand on this issue as you examine the materials in this chapter. In the competition between words and images, which form is winning, and why? How do authors and artists use compositional choices to shape the power of their messages?

Images play an increasingly important role in what we know – and how we learn – about current events. In fact, more Americans receive their news from TV than from newspapers, and each televised story is accompanied by a stream of moving images on the screen: the devastation in New Orleans from Hurricane Katrina, the mass confusion in the wake of a terrorist attack in an urban area. Unfortunately the list of such indelible images grows longer each year. As media critic Neil Postman has observed, "We are now a culture whose information, ideas, and epistemology are given form by television, not by the printed word."

You have come of age at a time when images play an increasingly prominent role in determining American values, assumptions, and behavior. This is a time when questioning what you see – and taking a stand on the issues generated by images – is more important than ever before.

An unprecedented influx of information, data, news, and stories is saturating our lives at an incredible rate. Rapidly advancing computer and digital technologies are now making the copying, sending, and disseminating of images increasingly efficient and seemingly effortless. Just as the invention of the printing press facilitated the widespread distribution of print and required people to develop verbal literacy, today more and more people must demonstrate another kind of literacy, a visual literacy – the ability to read, understand, and act on the information conveyed in powerful contemporary images.

We often accept the image as our medium of choice. We channel surf, rapidly scanning dozens of images in a few seconds, or we click from icon to icon. How do these processes differ from that of reading a page of prose? Computers have given new meaning to the term *multitasking* for millions of us who shift back and forth among windows on our computer screen while simultaneously talking on the phone and chatting online. How does multitasking change the way in which we are expected to think? And how does it change the ways in which we read and write?

Writers today might well be expected to think like designers, and designers to think like writers. If you're writing text for a web page, how do the visual aspects of text design – space and design constraints – change the way you write as well as the content of your writing? How would you write an article or essay differently if you knew a photograph or illustration were going to accompany it? In more general terms, how – and to what extent – should college curricula adjust to the changing nature of reading and writing to help students become more confident and articulate readers and writers? We invite you to consider these issues carefully and to take a stand on them.

What consequence do you think the new "age of the image" has for thinking, reading, and writing? We invite you to explore this and related questions, and to form and rethink your own judgments, as you engage your analytical intelligence with the work of the authors and artists presented in this chapter.

IMAGINE by John Lennon © 1971, 1981 Lenono Music & Ono Music (BMI) admin. by EMI Blackwood Music Inc.

An 80-year-old woman, one of countless civilian war victims, living in the basement of her bombed-out Chechen home.
Magnum Photos

imagine

(all the people living life in peace)

Imagine a worldwide movement working to protect the dignity and rights of all people. And imagine it works.
For 40 years, Amnesty International members have saved countless lives - people persecuted, imprisoned,
or tortured simply for who they are or what they believe. Many more need your help. Take action. Log on. Join us.

www.amnestyusa.org

Collaborate/Amnesty International
Imagine All the People Living Life in Peace, 2002

Two refugee girls at risk of joining the
hundreds of thousands of child soldiers worldwide:
Photo: Peter Marlow/Magnum

imagine

(nothing to kill or die for)

Imagine a worldwide movement working to protect the dignify and rights of all people. And imagine it works.
For 40 years, Amnesty International members have saved countless lives - people persecuted, imprisoned,
or tortured simply for who they are or what they believe. Many more need your help. Take action. Log on. Join us.

www.amnestyusa.org

Collaborate/Amnesty International
Imagine Nothing to Kill or Die For, 2002

...UNTIL JUSTICE ROLLS DOWN LIKE WATERS AND RIGHTEOUSNESS LIKE A MIGHTY STREAM

MARTIN LUTHER KING JR

A young boy learns about the history of the
civil rights movement. Montgomery, Alabama.
Photo: Eli Reed/Magnum

imagine

(you may say i'm a dreamer, but i'm not the only one)

Imagine a worldwide movement working to protect the dignity and rights of all people. And imagine it works.
For 40 years, Amnesty International members have saved countless lives - people persecuted, imprisoned,
or tortured simply for who they are or what they believe. Many more need your help. Take action. Log on. Join us.

www.amnestyusa.org

Collaborate/Amnesty International
You May Say I'm a Dreamer, but I'm Not the Only One, 2002

Collaborate/Sierra Club & Amnesty International
Defend the Earth

Collaborate/Rock the Vote
Yes/No

Collaborate

Based in San Francisco, ad agency Collaborate works across media for a wide range of clients from the retail, consumer technology, entertainment, and nonprofit sectors. Its client roster includes Amnesty International, Gore-Tex, Logitech, Franklin Templeton Investments, Rock the Vote, Seagate, and the University of California–Berkeley.

Collaborate designed and produced the campaigns in this portfolio for Amnesty International, the Sierra Club, and Rock the Vote. Referred to in the advertising industry as "cause-related" work, each piece leverages the power of print, online, and broadcast media to help advocate a social or political issue to specific or mass audiences.

Amnesty International launched its *Imagine* campaign in 2002 after Yoko Ono gave the organization the rights to John Lennon's song in the wake of 9/11. The vision for the campaign, according to Amnesty International, is "to engage and inspire the next generation of human rights activists." The International Right to Know Initiative, a joint project for Amnesty International and the Sierra Club, promotes the intersection of environmental and human rights. Collaborate's award-winning *Yes/No* campaign for Rock the Vote utilized multiple media to feature graphic representations of social issues like gun control, same-sex marriage, the death penalty, and abortion.

SEEING

1. The posters and advertisements for Amnesty International, the Sierra Club, and Rock the Vote were created by Collaborate, a creative communications agency based in San Francisco. What do you understand to be the overarching message of each piece in this portfolio of challenging images? How would you characterize the relationship of words to illustration in each image? To what exent – and in what specific ways – does each visual text reinforce the verbal text?

2. What similarities – and differences – do you notice in the style, graphics, verbal strategy, and overall design of these images? How would you characterize Collaborate's style? Comment on the effects of the choices Collaborate has made in typeface and type size, the position of the language in relation to the illustration, and the use of color. What cultural references and allusions does Collaborate evoke in these pieces? Which do you judge to be the most effective? Why?

WRITING

1. Think carefully about the phrase "a picture is worth a thousand words." With what experiences do you associate this expression? What patterns can you identify between and among those experiences? Are they, for example, personal experiences? more public in nature? something else? Explain your answer. Write the first draft of an essay in which you argue for or against the applicability of this phrase to the circumstances of your life.

2. Turn to <u>Andrew Savulich's news photographs</u> (p. 278). Examine the role his descriptive titles play in establishing the impact of his photographs. How do even these brief descriptions affect your understanding of the photographs? How might you interpret Savulich's photographs if the titles were worded differently? Draft an essay in which you compare and contrast the manner and impact of combining words and images in Savulich's work and in Collaborate's.

Page 278

Frank Fournier
Omayra Sanchez, Colombia, 1985

OMAYRA SANCHEZ
Isabel Allende

When I saw this picture in 1985, I thought nothing like this could ever happen to my children, but I now have a daughter who's very ill and may die. Just as Omayra agonized trapped in the mud, so is my daughter trapped in a body that doesn't function anymore. For a year I have been at her bedside and often the memory of Omayra comes to me, she has never quite left me, really. She will always be with me. She brings the same message now as she did before: of endurance and the love of life, and, ironically, the acceptance of tragedy and death. When I first saw the picture I thought, "Maybe she's asking for help." Then I thought, "No, she has not died yet. She's still alive." It reminds me of how fragile life is. She demonstrates such passion, she never begged for help, never complained.

In all these years, I've become acquainted with her and I identify with her. In some ways I am her; she's inside me, there's something between us that's very strange. She's a ghost that haunts me. I often wonder about what she feels. I don't think she's thinking, she just *feels*. Later it was discovered that when her house had crumbled, she was stuck between two pieces of wood and the bodies of her brothers. Her body *feels* the cold, the fear, the stress. She looks so uncomfortable in the mud, so much in pain. And yet, look at her hands, they're so elegant.

The wonder of photography is that it does what no words can. I think in images. I remember my life in images. The earliest memory of my life, and the only memory I have of my father, is when I was two years old. My father and I are standing on the stairs of our house in Lima, where I was born. And I can see his legs and his shoes — back then, men wore shoes in two colors, black and white. And I remember my brother, who couldn't walk yet, wearing white pants and white shoes, and then, all of a sudden, he tumbled and fell, and there was blood. I have this image of my father's trousers stained with blood.

The lessons that Omayra has taught me are about life and about death. What I have learned, what she has taught me, is very complex. Every time I go back to this photograph, new things come up. This girl is alone. No one from her family is with her. I don't know if they were all dead at that time or if they had run away. The only people with her were cameramen, photographers, and people from the Red Cross who were strangers. She died alone, and I wish I had been there to hold her, the way I hold my daughter.

5   Western culture forces us to ignore anything that is inexplicable or uncontrollable, like poverty, death, sickness, or failure. But this is not so in the rest of the world, where people share pain more than they share happiness, because there is *more* pain than happiness most of the time. There's nothing surprising or horrifying about dying.

In this picture Omayra is not very afraid, maybe because she has seen so much death, and she has been poor all of her life. The life expectancy in Colombia isn't very high, so she walked around hand in hand with death, as most poor people do all over the world. Only people who live in very privileged bubbles think that they're going to live forever. This girl is dead, yet we're talking about her years later. We've never met her and are living at the other end of the world, but we've been brought together because of her. She never dies, this girl. She never dies. She's born every instant.

Frank Fournier

Born in France in 1948, Frank Fournier attended the School of Graphic Design in Vevey, Switzerland, and moved to New York City in 1972. During his career as a commercial photographer he has covered a range of international events. His work documenting the lives of Romanian babies with AIDS was on exhibit at the Musée de l'Élysée in Switzerland in the early 1990s. And his haunting photographs of a New York devastated by the attacks of September 11, 2001, have appeared in *Vanity Fair*, *Time* magazine, and *U.S. News & World Report*. Fournier also has contributed to Day in the Life projects in the United States, the former Soviet Union, Spain, and Canada. Most recently Fournier's work has been part of a Contact Press Images exhibition at the Australian Centre for Photography in Sydney.

The image here, of a young victim of a volcanic eruption in Colombia, was named World Press Photo of the Year in 1985. The slow death of Omayra Sanchez was broadcast on news programs around the world. "Some thirty thousand people died," Fournier recalls. "Very few survived, some fought very hard but never made it. Among them an incredible and heroic person, a small little girl of thirteen, Omayra. . . . Her courage and dignity in death contrasted the incredible cowardice of all the elected officials. . . . Anybody who saw her fight is older and a lot more humble."

Isabel Allende

Born in 1942 in Chile, Isabel Allende left her native country in 1975 after her uncle, President Salvador Allende, was assassinated. She worked as a journalist in Chile and then in Venezuela until 1984. Her first novel, *The House of Spirits* (published in the United States in 1985), began as a letter to her ninety-nine-year-old grandfather. It established Allende's reputation as one of the most important contemporary Latin American authors. She has subsequently received literary awards in Latin America, Europe, and the United States. Among her other works are *Of Love and Shadows* (1985), *The Stories of Eva Luna* (1988), *Daughter of Fortune* (1999), *My Invented Country: A Nostalgic Journey through Chile* (2003), *Kingdom of the Golden Dragon* (2004), *Zorro* (2005), *Inés of My Soul* (2006), and *La Suma de los Días* (2007; published in English as *The Sum of Our*

Days, 2008). *Paula* (1995) is a memoir she began as a gift for her daughter. She finished it as a memorial: Paula died in 1992.

Allende first encountered the image of Omayra Sanchez through television reports of the volcanic eruption in Colombia in 1985. Fournier's photograph of the thirteen-year-old left an indelible impression on her. She chose to write about it for Marvin Heiferman's book *Talking Pictures: People Speak about the Pictures That Speak to Them* (1994), in which seventy "people of our era – some famous, some not – speak out about the singular image that speaks to them."

SEEING

1. "The wonder of photography," Allende writes, "is that it does what no words can" (para. 3). In what ways has the image of a young girl whom Allende never met "spoken" to her since she first saw it?

2. What aspects of the photograph strike you the most? Consider how Fournier frames Omayra Sanchez in the photograph. What has he chosen to reveal about his subject? What has he left out? To what aspects of Fournier's photograph does Allende draw our attention? What details do you notice that Allende does not mention?

WRITING

1. The plight of Omayra Sanchez deeply affected both Frank Fournier and Isabel Allende. Which representation of Omayra moves you more – the photograph or the essay? Does reading one make the other more powerful? Write a page comparing the impact of the essay with that of the image.

Working with Sources

2. Twentieth-century technology has made it possible to broadcast the most personal and private moments to global audiences. Television, magazines, and the web allow us to visit a family's living room after they've successfully delivered sextuplets, or witness a stranger's turmoil in the wake of a disaster, without ever leaving home. Choose a published photograph or image of a memorable moment that made a profound impression on you. Write an essay that, like Allende's, describes both your first impression of the image and what it means to you today.

Can you tell the story of how you came to take this photograph?

Frank Fournier: It was on a Wednesday night that the Nevado del Ruiz volcano blew up. . . .

At 10:30 p.m., when villagers in and around Armero heard that there had been a small eruption, they all got scared and started to panic. There was a soccer game on television that night that everyone was watching. The electricity went out and everyone panicked. They knew that the volcano had done something and they went to church to pray. At around 11:15, about 45 minutes later, the first lava and water and stones started to reach Armero. In a very short amount of time, it wiped out the town and kept going. There was chaos, of course. I think the total was between 28 and 32,000 people killed.

These deaths could have been prevented. The church was involved, the military was involved, and the politicians were all involved. What was so frustrating was that none of them took the fundamental responsibility to protect the people. People were expecting some kind of leadership, but it never came. Knowing that there was going to be an eruption, an evacuation plan should have already been in place. . . .

When we arrived, Omayra was by herself because other villagers and rescue people were trying to take care of someone else a little further away. By then, the Colombian government had simply declared the entire area a "national cemetery." This was revolting to us, that in twenty-four hours the government would decide that this was a national cemetery, period. It cleared the government from further rescue attempts and allowed them to spray chalk over the entire area. (This is usually done to avoid the spread of disease and bacteria.)

. . . When I reached [Omayra], it was about 6:30 in the morning. I tried talking to her. She was confused about what had happened. She could remember that she had been in her house and that she had been to church, but after that, she could not remember a thing.

According to local people, Omayra was now about a mile away from her house. She had been pushed along with much debris against a hill on the edge of town. Among the debris was a lot of corrugated metal, along with sections of homes and parts belonging to coffee warehouses. Not only was she stuck, trapped from the waist down by a huge amount of weight that was putting pressure on her legs, but according to a villager who was at her side, she had also been perforated at the hips.

When I reached Omayra, she had already been trapped there for three days. Initially she had been stuck there with her aunt, who died attached to her. When the aunt died Omayra almost drowned with her. Many people tried to help Omayra. Phone calls were placed to rescue teams operating in the area. Medical equipment and personnel were badly needed, but none arrived.

My experience in these situations is that you need highly trained technicians and medical people to take care of a person in that kind of situation. When you have so much pressure on a leg, you have to run [an] IV with some kind of inflating device to maintain pressure on it, because if you release the pressure right away, toxic chemicals that form by a lack of circulation will spread through the body. You can kill a person this way. There had been big debates in Mexico a month before. People were pulled out of an earthquake very fast. They were alive and then two hours later they died from blood toxins. Other people were pulled out very slowly, and the survival rates were much higher.

So even if medical help had arrived in time, it would have been very challenging to save Omayra. I knew that at the time. When I saw her, I knew she was going to die, and I knew that there was no way out for her. I have a bit of a medical background. When I was younger, I studied medicine for four years, so I knew there was little chance.

I was devastated by what I was seeing, and by my inability to help her. You have to be pretty strong to face this kind of situation. To be so weak and unable to help is incredibly demanding and frustrating. I must say, I had been in difficult situations before, but my religious, ethical, and moral values were definitely going through an earthquake of their own. I was unable to help and save this person.

She was incredibly loving. She was twelve-and-a-half years old, very gentle and very sweet. She talked about where she came from. She saw that I was a foreigner and she even tried a couple of words in English with me. She even said: "Can you please help me get out of here? I don't want to be late for school; it starts at eight-thirty."

. . . Many people's first reaction to Omayra's photograph is to ask: Why didn't he help her? This reaction does not anger me. In a certain way, when people are mad at me or at the situation, I understand that reaction. I think it's healthy in some ways. Photography is not television; it's different. In a sense it can be more powerful. In general, people seem to remember photographs better than video. Nobody blames what the television shows. TV crews were interviewing Omayra like a sport person after an event . . . How was it? How do you feel? What's going on? Did you talk to your mother? Do you know that your father is dead? That kind of thing. And so when they saw the photograph, somehow they got mad at the photographer.

Why do you think that is?

I can't say why, I just know it's like that. People can take more time to look at a photograph. It's a more private kind of experience than television. With television, you have the sound; there is a distance between you and the screen. You may be watching the news as you prepare the evening meal. I think the photographic memory, and the connection to hold a magazine and look at it, makes it a little more physical and maybe helps people to connect better. One can take time – or not – to travel into the photograph and get details. You have time for emotions to develop; in television you have twenty seconds. . . .

The point is that Omayra reached many, many people. About a year after the eruption, the Colombian Ambassador to the Netherlands informed me that an enormous sum of money had reached Colombia to aid all of those who had survived and been displaced by the eruption. He also informed me that everybody in Colombia and in other parts of the world knew of Omayra. In a way, she and many other victims helped to create a real evacuation plan for the future. Local villagers were trained to flee to higher ground for safety. That is why I thought it was so important to report the death of Omayra. I wanted to be sure that survivors were helped and that people would never have to face a needless death.

This interview was conducted on April 21, 2005.

Visit *seeingandwriting.com* for the full text of the interview.

For biographical information about Frank Fournier, see page 593.

FARMER IN CHIEF
Michael Pollan

Dear Mr. President-Elect,

It may surprise you to learn that among the issues that will occupy much of your time in the coming years is one you barely mentioned during the campaign: food. Food policy is not something American presidents have had to give much thought to, at least since the Nixon administration—the last time high food prices presented a serious political peril. Since then, federal policies to promote maximum production of the commodity crops (corn, soybeans, wheat, and rice) from which most of our supermarket foods are derived have succeeded impressively in keeping prices low and food more or less off the national political agenda. But with a suddenness that has taken us all by surprise, the era of cheap and abundant food appears to be drawing to a close. What this means is that you, like so many other leaders through history, will find yourself confronting the fact—so easy to overlook these past few years—that the health of a nation's food system is a critical issue of national security. Food is about to demand your attention.

Complicating matters is the fact that the price and abundance of food are not the only problems we face; if they were, you could simply follow Nixon's example, appoint a latter-day Earl Butz as your secretary of agriculture and instruct him or her to do whatever it takes to boost production. But there are reasons to think that the old approach won't work this time around; for one thing, it depends on cheap energy that we can no longer count on. For another, expanding production of industrial agriculture today would require you to sacrifice important values on which you did campaign. Which brings me to the deeper reason you will need not simply to address food prices but to make the reform of the entire food system one of the highest priorities of your administration: Unless you do, you will not be able to make significant progress on the health care crisis, energy independence, or climate change. Unlike food, these are issues you did campaign on—but as you try to address them you will quickly discover that the way we currently grow, process, and eat food in America goes to the heart of all three problems and will have to change if we hope to solve them. Let me explain.

After cars, the food system uses more fossil fuel than any other sector of the economy—19 percent. And while the experts disagree about the exact amount, the way we feed ourselves contributes more greenhouse gases to the atmosphere than anything else we do—as much as 37 percent, according to one study. Whenever farmers clear land for crops and till the soil, large quantities of carbon are released into the air. But the twentieth-century industrialization of agriculture has increased the amount of greenhouse gases emitted by the food system by an order of magnitude; chemical fertilizers (made from natural gas), pesticides (made from petroleum), farm machinery, modern food processing and packaging, and transportation have together transformed a system that in 1940 produced 2.3 calories of food energy for every calorie of fossil-food energy it used into one that now takes 10 calories of fossil-fuel energy to produce a single calorie of modern supermarket food. Put another way, when we eat from the industrial-food system, we are eating oil and spewing greenhouse gases. This state of affairs appears all the more absurd when you recall that every calorie we eat is ultimately the product of photosynthesis—a process based on making food energy from sunshine. There is hope and possibility in that simple fact.

In addition to the problems of climate change and America's oil addiction, you have spoken at length on the campaign trail of the health care crisis. Spending on health care has risen from 5 percent of national income in 1960 to 16 percent today, putting a significant drag on the economy. The goal of ensuring the health of all Americans depends on getting those costs under control. There are several reasons health care has gotten so expensive, but one of the biggest, and perhaps most tractable, is the cost to the system of preventable chronic diseases. Four of the top 10 killers in America today are chronic diseases linked to diet: heart disease, stroke, Type 2 diabetes, and cancer. It is no coincidence that in the years national spending on health care went from 5 percent to 16 percent of national income, spending on food has fallen by a comparable amount—from 18 percent of household income to less than 10 percent. While the surfeit of cheap calories that the U.S. food system has produced since the late 1970s may have taken food prices off the political agenda, this has come at a steep cost to public health. You cannot expect to reform the health care system, much less expand coverage, without confronting the public-health catastrophe that is the modern American diet.

5   The impact of the American food system on the rest of the world will have implications for your foreign and trade policies as well. In the past several months more than 30 nations have experienced food riots, and so far one government has fallen. Should high grain prices persist and shortages develop, you can expect to see the pendulum shift decisively away from free trade, at least in food. Nations that opened their markets to the global flood of cheap grain (under pressure from previous administrations

as well as the World Bank and the I.M.F.) lost so many farmers that they now find their ability to feed their own populations hinges on decisions made in Washington (like your predecessor's precipitous embrace of bio-fuels) and on Wall Street. They will now rush to rebuild their own agri-cultural sectors and then seek to protect them by erecting trade barriers. Expect to hear the phrases "food sovereignty" and "food security" on the lips of every foreign leader you meet. Not only the Doha round, but the whole cause of free trade in agriculture is probably dead, the casualty of a cheap food policy that a scant two years ago seemed like a boon for every-one. It is one of the larger paradoxes of our time that the very same food policies that have contributed to overnutrition in the first world are now contributing to undernutrition in the third. But it turns out that too much food can be nearly as big a problem as too little—a lesson we should keep in mind as we set about designing a new approach to food policy.

Rich or poor, countries struggling with soaring food prices are being forcibly reminded that food is a national-security issue. When a nation loses the ability to substantially feed itself, it is not only at the mercy of global commodity markets but of other governments as well. At issue is not only the availability of food, which may be held hostage by a hostile state, but its safety: As recent scandals in China demonstrate, we have little control over the safety of imported foods. The deliberate contamina-tion of our food presents another national-security threat. At his valedic-tory press conference in 2004, Tommy Thompson, the secretary of health and human services, offered a chilling warning, saying, "I, for the life of me, cannot understand why the terrorists have not attacked our food sup-ply, because it is so easy to do."

This, in brief, is the bad news: The food and agriculture policies you've inherited—designed to maximize production at all costs and relying on cheap energy to do so—are in shambles, and the need to address the problems they have caused is acute. The good news is that the twinned crises in food and energy are creating a political environment in which real reform of the food system may actually be possible for the first time in a generation. The American people are paying more attention to food today than they have in decades, worrying not only about its price but about its safety, its provenance, and its healthfulness. There is a gathering sense among the public that the industrial-food system is broken. Markets for alternative kinds of food—organic, local, pasture-based, humane—are thriving as never before. All this suggests that a political constituency for change is building and not only on the left: Lately, conservative voices have also been raised in support of reform. Writing of the movement back to local food economies, traditional foods (and family meals), and more sustainable farming, *The American Conservative* magazine editorialized last summer that "this is a conservative cause if ever there was one."

There are many moving parts to the new food agenda I'm urging you to adopt, but the core idea could not be simpler: We need to wean the American food system off its heavy twentieth-century diet of fossil fuel and put it back on a diet of contemporary sunshine. True, this is easier said than done—fossil fuel is deeply implicated in everything about the way we currently grow food and feed ourselves. To put the food system back on sunlight will require policies to change how things work at every link in the food chain: in the farm field, in the way food is processed and sold, and even in the American kitchen and at the American dinner table. Yet the sun still shines down on our land every day, and photosynthesis can still work its wonders wherever it does. If any part of the modern economy can be freed from its dependence on oil and successfully resolarized, surely it is food.

How We Got Here

Before setting out an agenda for reforming the food system, it's important to understand how that system came to be—and also to appreciate what, for all its many problems, it has accomplished. What our food system does well is precisely what it was designed to do, which is to produce cheap calories in great abundance. It is no small thing for an American to be able to go into a fast-food restaurant and to buy a double cheeseburger, fries, and a large Coke for a price equal to less than an hour of labor at the minimum wage—indeed, in the long sweep of history, this represents a remarkable achievement.

10   It must be recognized that the current food system—characterized by monocultures of corn and soy in the field and cheap calories of fat, sugar, and feedlot meat on the table—is not simply the product of the free market. Rather, it is the product of a specific set of government policies that sponsored a shift from solar (and human) energy on the farm to fossil-fuel energy.

Did you notice when you flew over Iowa during the campaign how the land was completely bare—black—from October to April? What you were seeing is the agricultural landscape created by cheap oil. In years past, except in the dead of winter, you would have seen in those fields a checkerboard of different greens: pastures and hayfields for animals, cover crops, perhaps a block of fruit trees. Before the application of oil and natural gas to agriculture, farmers relied on crop diversity (and photosynthesis) both to replenish their soil and to combat pests, as well as to feed themselves and their neighbors. Cheap energy, however, enabled the creation of monocultures, and monocultures in turn vastly increased the productivity both of the American land and the American farmer; today the typical corn-belt farmer is single-handedly feeding 140 people.

This did not occur by happenstance. After World War II, the government encouraged the conversion of the munitions industry to fertilizer—ammonium nitrate being the main ingredient of both bombs and chemical fertilizer—and the conversion of nerve-gas research to pesticides. The government also began subsidizing commodity crops, paying farmers by the bushel for all the corn, soybeans, wheat, and rice they could produce. One secretary of agriculture after another implored them to plant "fence row to fence row" and to "get big or get out."

The chief result, especially after the Earl Butz years, was a flood of cheap grain that could be sold for substantially less than it cost farmers to grow because a government check helped make up the difference. As this artificially cheap grain worked its way up the food chain, it drove down the price of all the calories derived from that grain: the high-fructose corn syrup in the Coke, the soy oil in which the potatoes were fried, the meat and cheese in the burger.

Subsidized monocultures of grain also led directly to monocultures of animals: Since factory farms could buy grain for less than it cost farmers to grow it, they could now fatten animals more cheaply than farmers could. So America's meat and dairy animals migrated from farm to feedlot, driving down the price of animal protein to the point where an American can enjoy eating, on average, 190 pounds of meat a year—a half pound every day.

15   But if taking the animals off farms made a certain kind of economic sense, it made no ecological sense whatever: Their waste, formerly regarded as a precious source of fertility on the farm, became a pollutant—factory farms are now one of America's biggest sources of pollution. As Wendell Berry has tartly observed, to take animals off farms and put them on feedlots is to take an elegant solution—animals replenishing the fertility that crops deplete—and neatly divide it into two problems: a fertility problem on the farm and a pollution problem on the feedlot. The former problem is remedied with fossil-fuel fertilizer; the latter is remedied not at all.

What was once a regional food economy is now national and increasingly global in scope—thanks again to fossil fuel. Cheap energy—for trucking food as well as pumping water—is the reason New York City now gets its produce from California rather than from the "Garden State" next door, as it did before the advent of Interstate highways and national trucking networks. More recently, cheap energy has underwritten a globalized food economy in which it makes (or rather, made) economic sense to catch salmon in Alaska, ship it to China to be filleted, and then ship the fillets back to California to be eaten; or one in which California and Mexico can profitably swap tomatoes back and forth across the border; or Denmark and the United States can trade sugar cookies across the Atlantic. About that particular swap the economist Herman Daly once quipped, "Exchanging recipes would surely be more efficient."

Whatever we may have liked about the era of cheap, oil-based food, it is drawing to a close. Even if we were willing to continue paying the environmental or public-health price, we're not going to have the cheap energy (or the water) needed to keep the system going, much less expand production. But as is so often the case, a crisis provides opportunity for reform, and the current food crisis presents opportunities that must be seized.

In drafting these proposals, I've adhered to a few simple principles of what a twenty-first-century food system needs to do. First, your administration's food policy must strive to provide a healthful diet for all our people; this means focusing on the quality and diversity (and not merely the quantity) of the calories that American agriculture produces and American eaters consume. Second, your policies should aim to improve the resilience, safety, and security of our food supply. Among other things, this means promoting regional food economies both in America and around the world. And lastly, your policies need to reconceive agriculture as part of the solution to environmental problems like climate change.

These goals are admittedly ambitious, yet they will not be difficult to align or advance as long as we keep in mind this One Big Idea: Most of the problems our food system faces today are because of its reliance on fossil fuels, and to the extent that our policies wring the oil out of the system and replace it with the energy of the sun, those policies will simultaneously improve the state of our health, our environment, and our security.

I. Resolarizing the American Farm

20 What happens in the field influences every other link of the food chain on up to our meals—if we grow monocultures of corn and soy, we will find the products of processed corn and soy on our plates. Fortunately for your initiative, the federal government has enormous leverage in determining exactly what happens on the 830 million acres of American crop and pasture land.

Today most government farm and food programs are designed to prop up the old system of maximizing production from a handful of subsidized commodity crops grown in monocultures. Even food-assistance programs like WIC and school lunch focus on maximizing quantity rather than quality, typically specifying a minimum number of calories (rather than maximums) and seldom paying more than lip service to nutritional quality. This focus on quantity may have made sense in a time of food scarcity, but today it gives us a school-lunch program that feeds chicken nuggets and Tater Tots to overweight and diabetic children.

Your challenge is to take control of this vast federal machinery and use it to drive a transition to a new solar-food economy, starting on the farm. Right now, the government actively discourages the farmers it subsidizes from growing healthful, fresh food: Farmers receiving crop subsidies are prohibited from growing "specialty crops"—farm-bill speak for fruits and vegetables. (This rule was the price exacted by California and Florida produce growers in exchange for going along with subsidies for commodity crops.) Commodity farmers should instead be encouraged to grow as many different crops—including animals—as possible. Why? Because the greater the diversity of crops on a farm, the less the need for both fertilizers and pesticides.

The power of cleverly designed polycultures to produce large amounts of food from little more than soil, water, and sunlight has been proved, not only by small-scale "alternative" farmers in the United States but also by large rice-and-fish farmers in China and giant-scale operations (up to 15,000 acres) in places like Argentina. There, in a geography roughly comparable to that of the American farm belt, farmers have traditionally employed an ingenious eight-year rotation of perennial pasture and annual crops: After five years grazing cattle on pasture (and producing the world's best beef), farmers can then grow three years of grain without applying any fossil-fuel fertilizer. Or, for that matter, many pesticides: The weeds that afflict pasture can't survive the years of tillage, and the weeds of row crops don't survive the years of grazing, making herbicides all but unnecessary. There is no reason—save current policy and custom—that American farmers couldn't grow both high-quality grain and grass-fed beef under such a regime through much of the Midwest. (It should be noted that today's sky-high grain prices are causing many Argentine farmers to abandon their rotation to grow grain and soybeans exclusively, an environmental disaster in the making.)

Federal policies could do much to encourage this sort of diversified sun farming. Begin with the subsidies: Payment levels should reflect the number of different crops farmers grow or the number of days of the year their fields are green—that is, taking advantage of photosynthesis, whether to grow food, replenish the soil, or control erosion. If Midwestern farmers simply planted a cover crop after the fall harvest, they would significantly reduce their need for fertilizer, while cutting down on soil erosion. Why don't farmers do this routinely? Because in recent years fossil-fuel-based fertility has been so much cheaper and easier to use than sun-based fertility.

25   In addition to rewarding farmers for planting cover crops, we should make it easier for them to apply compost to their fields—a practice that improves not only the fertility of the soil but also its ability to hold water and therefore withstand drought. (There is mounting evidence that it also boosts the nutritional quality of the food grown in it.) The U.S.D.A. estimates that Americans throw out 14 percent of the food they buy; much more is wasted by retailers, wholesalers, and institutions. A program to make municipal composting of food and yard waste mandatory and then distributing the compost free to area farmers would shrink America's garbage heap, cut the need for irrigation and fossil-fuel fertilizers in agriculture, and improve the nutritional quality of the American diet.

Right now, most of the conservation programs run by the U.S.D.A. are designed on the zero-sum principle: Land is either locked up in "conservation" or it is farmed intensively. This either-or approach reflects an outdated belief that modern farming and ranching are inherently destructive, so that the best thing for the environment is to leave land untouched. But we now know how to grow crops and graze animals in systems that will support biodiversity, soil health, clean water, and carbon sequestration. The Conservation Stewardship Program, championed by Senator Tom Harkin and included in the 2008 Farm Bill, takes an important step toward rewarding these kinds of practices, but we need to move this approach from the periphery of our farm policy to the very center. Longer term, the government should back ambitious research now under way (at the Land Institute in Kansas and a handful of other places) to "perennialize" commodity agriculture: to breed varieties of wheat, rice, and other staple grains that can be grown like prairie grasses—without having to till the soil every year. These perennial grains hold the promise of slashing the fossil fuel now needed to fertilize and till the soil, while protecting farmland from erosion and sequestering significant amounts of carbon.

But that is probably a fifty-year project. For today's agriculture to wean itself from fossil fuel and make optimal use of sunlight, crop plants and animals must once again be married on the farm—as in Wendell Berry's elegant "solution." Sunlight nourishes the grasses and grains, the plants nourish the animals, the animals then nourish the soil, which in turn nourishes the next season's grasses and grains. Animals on pasture can also harvest their own feed and dispose of their own waste—all without our help or fossil fuel.

If this system is so sensible, you might ask, why did it succumb to Confined Animal Feeding Operations, or CAFOs? In fact there is nothing inherently efficient or economical about raising vast cities of animals in confinement. Three struts, each put into place by federal policy, support the modern CAFO, and the most important of these—the ability to buy grain for less than it costs to grow it—has just been kicked away. The second strut is F.D.A. approval for the routine use of antibiotics in feed, without which the animals in these places could not survive their crowded, filthy, and miserable existence. And the third is that the government does not require CAFOs to treat their wastes as it would require human cities of comparable size to do. The F.D.A. should ban the routine use of antibiotics in livestock feed on public-health grounds, now that we have evidence that the practice is leading to the evolution of drug-resistant bacterial diseases and to outbreaks of E. coli and salmonella poisoning. CAFOs should also be regulated like the factories they are, required to clean up their waste like any other industry or municipality.

It will be argued that moving animals off feedlots and back onto farms will raise the price of meat. It probably will—as it should. You will need to make the case that paying the real cost of meat, and therefore eating less of it, is a good thing for our health, for the environment, for our dwindling reserves of fresh water, and for the welfare of the animals. Meat and milk production represent the food industry's greatest burden on the environment; a recent U.N. study estimated that the world's livestock alone account for 18 percent of all greenhouse gases, more than all forms of transportation combined. (According to one study, a pound of feedlot beef also takes 5,000 gallons of water to produce.) And while animals living on farms will still emit their share of greenhouse gases, grazing them on grass and returning their waste to the soil will substantially offset their carbon hoof prints, as will getting ruminant animals off grain. A bushel of grain takes approximately a half gallon of oil to produce; grass can be grown with little more than sunshine.

30   It will be argued that sun-food agriculture will generally yield less food than fossil-fuel agriculture. This is debatable. The key question you must be prepared to answer is simply this: Can the sort of sustainable agriculture you're proposing feed the world?

There are a couple of ways to answer this question. The simplest and most honest answer is that we don't know, because we haven't tried. But in the same way we now need to learn how to run an industrial economy without cheap fossil fuel, we have no choice but to find out whether sustainable agriculture can produce enough food. The fact is, during the past century, our agricultural research has been directed toward the goal of maximizing production with the help of fossil fuel. There is no reason to think that bringing the same sort of resources to the development of more complex, sun-based agricultural systems wouldn't produce comparable yields. Today's organic farmers, operating for the most part without benefit of public investment in research, routinely achieve 80 to 100 percent of conventional yields in grain and, in drought years, frequently exceed conventional yields. (This is because organic soils better retain moisture.) Assuming no further improvement, could the world—with a population expected to peak at 10 billion—survive on these yields?

First, bear in mind that the average yield of world agriculture today is substantially lower than that of modern sustainable farming. According to a recent University of Michigan study, merely bringing international yields up to today's organic levels could increase the world's food supply by 50 percent.

The second point to bear in mind is that yield isn't everything—and growing high-yield commodities is not quite the same thing as growing food. Much of what we're growing today is not directly eaten as food but processed into low-quality calories of fat and sugar. As the world epidemic of diet-related chronic disease has demonstrated, the sheer quantity of calories that a food system produces improves health only up to a point, but after that, quality and diversity are probably more important. We can expect that a food system that produces somewhat less food but of a higher quality will produce healthier populations.

The final point to consider is that 40 percent of the world's grain output today is fed to animals; 11 percent of the world's corn and soybean crop is fed to cars and trucks, in the form of biofuels. Provided the developed world can cut its consumption of grain-based animal protein and ethanol, there should be plenty of food for everyone—however we choose to grow it.

35   In fact, well-designed polyculture systems, incorporating not just grains but vegetables and animals, can produce more food per acre than conventional monocultures, and food of a much higher nutritional value. But this kind of farming is complicated and needs many more hands on the land to make it work. Farming without fossil fuels—performing complex rotations of plants and animals and managing pests without petrochemicals—is labor intensive and takes more skill than merely "driving and spraying," which is how corn-belt farmers describe what they do for a living.

To grow sufficient amounts of food using sunlight will require more people growing food—millions more. This suggests that sustainable agriculture will be easier to implement in the developing world, where large rural populations remain, than in the West, where they don't. But what about here in America, where we have only about 2 million farmers left to feed a population of 300 million? And where farmland is being lost to development at the rate of 2,880 acres a day? Post-oil agriculture will need a lot more people engaged in food production—as farmers and probably also gardeners.

The sun-food agenda must include programs to train a new generation of farmers and then help put them on the land. The average American farmer today is fifty-five years old; we shouldn't expect these farmers to embrace the sort of complex ecological approach to agriculture that is called for. Our focus should be on teaching ecological farming systems to students entering land-grant colleges today. For decades now, it has been federal policy to shrink the number of farmers in America by promoting capital-intensive monoculture and consolidation. As a society, we devalued farming as an occupation and encouraged the best students to leave the farm for "better" jobs in the city. We emptied America's rural counties in order to supply workers to urban factories. To put it bluntly, we now need to reverse course. We need more highly skilled small farmers in more places all across America—not as a matter of nostalgia for the agrarian past but as a matter of national security. For nations that lose the ability to substantially feed themselves will find themselves as gravely compromised in their international dealings as nations that depend on foreign sources of oil presently do. But while there are alternatives to oil, there are no alternatives to food.

National security also argues for preserving every acre of farmland we can and then making it available to new farmers. We simply will not be able to depend on distant sources of food, and therefore need to preserve every acre of good farmland within a day's drive of our cities. In the same way that when we came to recognize the supreme ecological value of wetlands we erected high bars to their development, we need to recognize the value of farmland to our national security and require real-estate developers to do "food-system impact statements" before development begins. We should also create tax and zoning incentives for developers to incorporate farmland (as they now do "open space") in their subdivision plans; all those subdivisions now ringing golf courses could someday have diversified farms at their center.

The revival of farming in America, which of course draws on the abiding cultural power of our agrarian heritage, will pay many political and economic dividends. It will lead to robust economic renewal in the countryside. And it will generate tens of millions of new "green jobs," which is precisely how we need to begin thinking of skilled solar farming: as a vital sector of the twenty-first-century post-fossil-fuel economy.

II. Reregionalizing the Food System

40 For your sun-food agenda to succeed, it will have to do a lot more than alter what happens on the farm. The government could help seed a thousand new polyculture farmers in every county in Iowa, but they would promptly fail if the grain elevator remained the only buyer in town and corn and beans were the only crops it would take. Resolarizing the food system means building the infrastructure for a regional food economy— one that can support diversified farming and, by shortening the food chain, reduce the amount of fossil fuel in the American diet.

A decentralized food system offers a great many benefits as well. Food eaten closer to where it is grown will be fresher and require less processing, making it more nutritious. Whatever may be lost in efficiency by localizing food production is gained in resilience: Regional food systems can better withstand all kinds of shocks. When a single factory is grinding 20 million hamburger patties in a week or washing 25 million servings of salad, a single terrorist armed with a canister of toxins can, at a stroke, poison millions. Such a system is equally susceptible to accidental contamination: The bigger and more global the trade in food, the more vulnerable the system is to catastrophe. The best way to protect our food system against such threats is obvious: Decentralize it.

Today in America there is soaring demand for local and regional food; farmers' markets, of which the U.S.D.A. estimates there are now 4,700, have become one of the fastest-growing segments of the food market. Community-supported agriculture is booming as well: there are now nearly 1,500 community-supported farms, to which consumers pay an annual fee in exchange for a weekly box of produce through the season. The local-food movement will continue to grow with no help from the government, especially as high fuel prices make distant and out-of-season food, as well as feedlot meat, more expensive. Yet there are several steps the government can take to nurture this market and make local foods more affordable. Here are a few:

Four-Season Farmers' Markets. Provide grants to towns and cities to build year-round indoor farmers' markets, on the model of Pike Place in Seattle or the Reading Terminal Market in Philadelphia. To supply these markets, the U.S.D.A. should make grants to rebuild local distribution networks in order to minimize the amount of energy used to move produce within local food sheds.

Agricultural Enterprise Zones. Today the revival of local food economies is being hobbled by a tangle of regulations originally designed to check abuses by the very largest food producers. Farmers should be able to smoke a ham and sell it to their neighbors without making a huge investment in federally approved facilities. Food-safety regulations must be made sensitive to scale and marketplace, so that a small producer selling direct off the farm or at a farmers' market is not regulated as onerously as a multinational food manufacturer. This is not because local food won't ever have food-safety problems — it will — only that its problems will be less catastrophic and easier to manage because local food is inherently more traceable and accountable.

45 **Local Meat-Inspection Corps.** Perhaps the single greatest impediment to the return of livestock to the land and the revival of local, grass-based meat production is the disappearance of regional slaughter facilities. The big meat processors have been buying up local abattoirs only to close them down as they consolidate, and the U.S.D.A. does little to support the ones that remain. From the department's perspective, it is a better use of shrinking resources to dispatch its inspectors to a plant slaughtering four hundred head an hour than to a regional abattoir slaughtering a dozen. The U.S.D.A. should establish a Local Meat-Inspectors Corps to serve these processors. Expanding on its successful pilot program on Lopez Island in Puget Sound, the U.S.D.A. should also introduce a fleet of mobile abattoirs that would go from farm to farm, processing animals humanely and inexpensively. Nothing would do more to make regional, grass-fed meat fully competitive in the market with feedlot meat.

Establish a Strategic Grain Reserve. In the same way the shift to alternative energy depends on keeping oil prices relatively stable, the sun-food agenda — as well as the food security of billions of people around the world — will benefit from government action to prevent huge swings in commodity prices. A strategic grain reserve, modeled on the Strategic Petroleum Reserve, would help achieve this objective and at the same time provide some cushion for world food stocks, which today stand at perilously low levels. Governments should buy and store grain when it is cheap and sell when it is dear, thereby moderating price swings in both directions and discouraging speculation.

Regionalize Federal Food Procurement. In the same way that federal procurement is often used to advance important social goals (like promoting minority-owned businesses), we should require that some minimum percentage of government food purchases — whether for school-lunch programs, military bases, or federal prisons—go to producers located within one hundred miles of institutions buying the food. We should create incentives for hospitals and universities receiving federal funds to buy fresh local produce. To channel even a small portion of institutional food purchasing to local food would vastly expand regional agriculture and improve the diet of the millions of people these institutions feed.

Create a Federal Definition of "Food." It makes no sense for government food-assistance dollars, intended to improve the nutritional health of at-risk Americans, to support the consumption of products we know to be unhealthful. Yes, some people will object that for the government to specify what food stamps can and cannot buy smacks of paternalism. Yet we already prohibit the purchase of tobacco and alcohol with food stamps. So why not prohibit something like soda, which is arguably less nutritious than red wine? Because it is, nominally, a food, albeit a "junk food." We need to stop flattering nutritionally worthless foodlike substances by calling them "junk food"—and instead make clear that such products are not in fact food of any kind. Defining what constitutes real food worthy of federal support will no doubt be controversial (you'll recall President Reagan's ketchup imbroglio), but defining food upward may be more politically palatable than defining it down, as Reagan sought to do. One approach would be to rule that, in order to be regarded as food by the government, an edible substance must contain a certain minimum ratio of micronutrients per calorie of energy. At a stroke, such a definition would improve the quality of school lunch and discourage sales of unhealthful products, since typically only "food" is exempt from local sales tax.

A few other ideas: Food-stamp debit cards should double in value whenever swiped at a farmers' markets—all of which, by the way, need to be equipped with the Electronic Benefit Transfer card readers that supermarkets already have. We should expand the WIC program that gives farmers'-market vouchers to low-income women with children; such programs help attract farmers' markets to urban neighborhoods where access to fresh produce is often nonexistent. (We should also offer tax incentives to grocery chains willing to build supermarkets in underserved neighborhoods.) Federal food assistance for the elderly should build on a successful program pioneered by the state of Maine that buys low-income seniors a membership in a community-supported farm. All these initiatives have the virtue of advancing two objectives at once: supporting the health of at-risk Americans and the revival of local food economies.

III. Rebuilding America's Food Culture

50 In the end, shifting the American diet from a foundation of imported fossil fuel to local sunshine will require changes in our daily lives, which by now are deeply implicated in the economy and culture of fast, cheap, and easy food. Making available more healthful and more sustainable food does not guarantee it will be eaten, much less appreciated or enjoyed. We need to use all the tools at our disposal—not just federal policy and public education but the president's bully pulpit and the example of the first family's own dinner table—to promote a new culture of food that can undergird your sun-food agenda.

Changing the food culture must begin with our children, and it must begin in the schools. Nearly a half-century ago, President Kennedy announced a national initiative to improve the physical fitness of American children. He did it by elevating the importance of physical education, pressing states to make it a requirement in public schools. We need to bring the same commitment to "edible education"—in Alice Waters's phrase—by making lunch, in all its dimensions, a mandatory part of the curriculum. On the premise that eating well is a critically important life skill, we need to teach all primary-school students the basics of growing and cooking food and then enjoying it at shared meals.

To change our children's food culture, we'll need to plant gardens in every primary school, build fully equipped kitchens, train a new generation of lunchroom ladies (and gentlemen) who can once again cook and teach cooking to children. We should introduce a School Lunch Corps program that forgives federal student loans to culinary-school graduates in exchange for two years of service in the public-school lunch program. And we should immediately increase school-lunch spending per pupil by $1 a day—the minimum amount food-service experts believe it will take to underwrite a shift from fast food in the cafeteria to real food freshly prepared.

But it is not only our children who stand to benefit from public education about food. Today most federal messages about food, from nutrition labeling to the food pyramid, are negotiated with the food industry. The surgeon general should take over from the Department of Agriculture the job of communicating with Americans about their diet. That way we might begin to construct a less equivocal and more effective public-health message about nutrition. Indeed, there is no reason that public-health campaigns about the dangers of obesity and Type 2 diabetes shouldn't be as tough and as effective as public-health campaigns about the dangers of smoking. The Centers for Disease Control estimates that one in three

American children born in 2000 will develop Type 2 diabetes. The public needs to know and see precisely what that sentence means: blindness; amputation; early death. All of which can be avoided by a change in diet and lifestyle. A public-health crisis of this magnitude calls for a blunt public-health message, even at the expense of offending the food industry. Judging by the success of recent antismoking campaigns, the savings to the health care system could be substantial.

There are other kinds of information about food that the government can supply or demand. In general we should push for as much transparency in the food system as possible—the other sense in which "sunlight" should be the watchword of our agenda. The F.D.A. should require that every packaged-food product include a second calorie count, indicating how many calories of fossil fuel went into its production. Oil is one of the most important ingredients in our food, and people ought to know just how much of it they're eating. The government should also throw its support behind putting a second bar code on all food products that, when scanned either in the store or at home (or with a cellphone), brings up on a screen the whole story and pictures of how that product was produced: in the case of crops, images of the farm and lists of agrochemicals used in its production; in the case of meat and dairy, descriptions of the animals' diet and drug regimen, as well as live video feeds of the CAFO where they live and, yes, the slaughterhouse where they die. The very length and complexity of the modern food chain breeds a culture of ignorance and indifference among eaters. Shortening the food chain is one way to create more conscious consumers, but deploying technology to pierce the veil is another.

55   Finally, there is the power of the example you set in the White House. If what's needed is a change of culture in America's thinking about food, then how America's first household organizes its eating will set the national tone, focusing the light of public attention on the issue and communicating a simple set of values that can guide Americans toward sun-based foods and away from eating oil.

The choice of White House chef is always closely watched, and you would be wise to appoint a figure who is identified with the food movement and committed to cooking simply from fresh local ingredients. Besides feeding you and your family exceptionally well, such a chef would demonstrate how it is possible even in Washington to eat locally for much of the year, and that good food needn't be fussy or complicated but does depend on good farming. You should make a point of the fact that every night you're in town, you join your family for dinner in the Executive Residence—at a table. (Surely you remember the Reagan's TV trays.)

And you should also let it be known that the White House observes one meatless day a week—a step that, if all Americans followed suit, would be the equivalent, in carbon saved, of taking 20 million midsize sedans off the road for a year. Let the White House chef post daily menus on the Web, listing the farmers who supplied the food, as well as recipes.

Since enhancing the prestige of farming as an occupation is critical to developing the sun-based regional agriculture we need, the White House should appoint, in addition to a White House chef, a White House farmer. This new post would be charged with implementing what could turn out to be your most symbolically resonant step in building a new American food culture. And that is this: Tear out five prime south-facing acres of the White House lawn and plant in their place an organic fruit and vegetable garden.

When Eleanor Roosevelt did something similar in 1943, she helped start a Victory Garden movement that ended up making a substantial contribution to feeding the nation in wartime. (Less well known is the fact that Roosevelt planted this garden over the objections of the U.S.D.A., which feared home gardening would hurt the American food industry.) By the end of the war, more than 20 million home gardens were supplying 40 percent of the produce consumed in America. The president should throw his support behind a new Victory Garden movement, this one seeking "victory" over three critical challenges we face today: high food prices, poor diets, and a sedentary population. Eating from this, the shortest food chain of all, offers anyone with a patch of land a way to reduce their fossil-fuel consumption and help fight climate change. (We should offer grants to cities to build allotment gardens for people without access to land.) Just as important, Victory Gardens offer a way to enlist Americans, in body as well as mind, in the work of feeding themselves and changing the food system—something more ennobling, surely, than merely asking them to shop a little differently.

I don't need to tell you that ripping out even a section of the White House lawn will be controversial: Americans love their lawns, and the South Lawn is one of the most beautiful in the country. But imagine all the energy, water, and petrochemicals it takes to make it that way. (Even for the purposes of this memo, the White House would not disclose its lawn-care regimen.) Yet as deeply as Americans feel about their lawns, the agrarian ideal runs deeper still, and making this particular plot of American land productive, especially if the First Family gets out there and pulls weeds now and again, will provide an image even more stirring than that of a pretty lawn: the image of stewardship of the land, of self-reliance, and of making the most of local sunlight to feed one's family and community. The fact that surplus produce from the South Lawn Victory Garden (and there will be literally tons of it) will be offered to regional food banks will make its own eloquent statement.

60   You're probably thinking that growing and eating organic food in the White House carries a certain political risk. It is true you might want to plant iceberg lettuce rather than arugula, at least to start. (Or simply call arugula by its proper American name, as generations of Midwesterners have done: "rocket.") But it should not be difficult to deflect the charge of elitism sometimes leveled at the sustainable-food movement. Reforming the food system is not inherently a right-or-left issue: For every Whole Foods shopper with roots in the counterculture you can find a family of evangelicals intent on taking control of its family dinner and diet back from the fast-food industry—the culinary equivalent of home schooling. You should support hunting as a particularly sustainable way to eat meat—meat grown without any fossil fuels whatsoever. There is also a strong libertarian component to the sun-food agenda, which seeks to free small producers from the burden of government regulation in order to stoke rural innovation. And what is a higher "family value," after all, than making time to sit down every night to a shared meal?

Our agenda puts the interests of America's farmers, families, and communities ahead of the fast-food industry's. For that industry and its apologists to imply that it is somehow more "populist" or egalitarian to hand our food dollars to Burger King or General Mills than to support a struggling local farmer is absurd. Yes, sun food costs more, but the reasons why it does only undercut the charge of elitism: Cheap food is only cheap because of government handouts and regulatory indulgence (both of which we will end), not to mention the exploitation of workers, animals, and the environment on which its putative "economies" depend. Cheap food is food dishonestly priced—it is in fact unconscionably expensive.

Your sun-food agenda promises to win support across the aisle. It builds on America's agrarian past, but turns it toward a more sustainable, sophisticated future. It honors the work of American farmers and enlists them in three of the twenty-first century's most urgent errands: to move into the post-oil era, to improve the health of the American people, and to mitigate climate change. Indeed, it enlists all of us in this great cause by turning food consumers into part-time producers, reconnecting the American people with the American land, and demonstrating that we need not choose between the welfare of our families and the health of the environment—that eating less oil and more sunlight will redound to the benefit of both.

Michael Pollan

According to the American author and activist Michael Pollan (b. 1955), perhaps the most important issue of our time, one that our political leaders rarely discuss, is food. Although a grassroots movement to buy locally grown and organic foods may seem to be a minority effort to send out an anti-corporate message and/or to simply eat more healthily, the swift growth of this movement suggests that the reasons for its popularity run much deeper. In "Farmer in Chief," Pollan argues that our problematic food system directly impacts three of the most important social issues today that politicians *do* talk about: the health care crisis, energy independence, and climate change. The solution, Pollan argues, is to rethink where and how we get our food: "people are going to have to work a little harder to have a better food system, but . . . procuring your food, foraging for it, if you will . . . is one of the great pleasures of life. It is a lie that it's drudgery. And it's a lie perpetrated by marketers for very specific reasons. They make a lot of money selling convenience."

Writing about food from a wide variety of angles has always been Pollan's chief area of interest. After obtaining his master's degree from Columbia University in 1981 he embarked on a journalism career, quickly advancing to the position of executive editor at *Harper's* and later holding contributing editor positions at both *Harper's* and the *New York Times Magazine*, while focusing much of his attention on his books. Of his five published books to date, four deal with some aspect of food, from *Second Nature: A Gardener's Education* (1991) to *In Defense of Food: An Eater's Manifesto* (2008). In addition, he has written myriad articles and delivered numerous speeches on food-related subjects, and he is the recipient of many awards for his journalism and activism. Currently Pollan continues to write and lecture on this topic while serving as a graduate journalism professor at the University of California–Berkeley.

SEEING

1. According to Pollan, what is at stake in the choice between using sunlight or fossil fuel to farm? How did our current system of farming develop, and why has producing an abundance of cheap food become a far-less-than-admirable goal? What specific actions and measures can government take in order to change farming to ensure the health of the nation's food system? Comment on the extent to which you think the Farmer in Chief (the president) is likely to put Pollan's ideas into practice. Why or why not?

2. Comment on the length and structure of Pollan's essay. What arguments can you make to support – or challenge – the assertion that it is too long? If so, what should Pollan have done to attract and maintain his readers' interest? As you reread Pollan's essay, what section(s) can you identify as candidates to cut or to shorten – but without weakening the overall argument? Alternatively, if the essay held your attention, how does Pollan make seemingly bland facts about corn and cows and government policy more engaging and memorable? Choose one passage that you think would have been dull if written by someone less skilled than Pollan, and show how he succeeds at engaging our attention and sustaining our interest.

WRITING

1. Pollan aims his argument at politicians who have the power to make large-scale, sweeping changes. Write a complementary "memo" addressed to average people seeking to convince them of the "hope and possibility" in sunshine farming. Explain how individual choices can encourage polycultural practices. Describe what each person can do to wean his or her personal food consumption off of a diet based heavily on fossil fuel. Persuade ordinary readers that paying more and eating less are necessary for both personal health and national security.

Working with Sources

2. Millions of acres of U.S. farmland dried up and blew away during the Dust Bowl centered in Texas and Oklahoma during the 1930s. Write the first draft of an expository essay in which you compare and contrast the farming practices that devastated the nation in the Great Depression with those that Pollan argues are currently threatening the nation's food supply. Please be sure that your essay shows how Pollan's three-part plan would or would not have prevented the disaster of the Great Depression.

World Wildlife Fund

Produced by the international advertising agency EuroRSCG for the World Wildlife Fund, the three advertisements shown here make a strong case for the importance of addressing worldwide climate change by focusing on the plight of the animals most affected by it – polar bears, penguins, and seals – and placing those animals in a very human context. The metaphorical argument the images put forth is that *not* confronting climate change is like taking away the natural habitats of these animals and leaving them to fend for themselves on "skid row." Note how the ads' small print also calls for specific action by "choosing a low emission car," an action that not only reduces pollution and waste but also helps sustain wildlife.

Since its foundation in Switzerland in 1961, the World Wildlife Fund has taken a stand on the preservation and restoration of the environment. According to the WWF's vision statement, "Reconciling the needs of human beings and the needs of others that share the Earth, we seek to practice conservation that is humane in the broadest sense. We seek to instill in people everywhere a discriminating, yet unabashed, reverence for nature and to balance that reverence with a profound belief in human possibilities." The WWF, originally overseen by Julian Huxley and Max Nicholson, initially focused its attention exclusively on saving endangered species, but over the years its mission has expanded to include many other goals in support of a healthy planet.

SEEING

1. What are your initial impressions of these three ads – individually and as a set? Do you find them humorous? disturbing? <u>trite</u>? something else? Please explain. What core argument does each ad make? What is the call to action here? How effective are the ads in persuading viewers to take that action? Support your response with detailed references to each ad.

2. What argument do the visuals alone make in these ads? What argument does the text express? To what extent are the arguments the same, or do they differ? If so, in what specific ways? Do you find the images or the texts more effective in building the World Wildlife Fund's argument? Explain – and support – your response by pointing to detailed evidence in the three ads.

<u>trite: Boring from overuse; not fresh or original.</u>

WRITING

1. Imagine that the World Wildlife Fund has invited you to revise this advertising campaign to persuade audiences to help stop global warming. What recommendations would you offer? You might suggest specific revisions to the text and images of each ad. What suggestions would you offer to make each more effective? Would you instead recommend an entirely new concept for an ad campaign? If so, what would you propose as the distinguishing features of each ad? Choose one ad, and write a one-page summary of your suggestions explaining why you think these changes will help the World Wildlife Fund gain more support for its cause.

Working with Sources

2. Choose a social issue that you think is important, one about which you have strong views. Spend an appreciable amount of time researching – and summarizing – the most important arguments on each side of this issue. As soon as you are confident that you have a clear understanding of your stance on the issue, prepare the first draft of a proposal for an ad campaign that would convince local and/or national audiences of the validity of your point of view. Support your stance with concrete evidence. Your proposal should do all of the following: identify the purpose of your ad campaign; identify the importance of your cause; summarize your position on it; provide specific statistics, research, or other evidence to support your position; and describe in detail the proposal's visual and verbal components.

SERFS OF THE TURF
Michael Lewis

The three most lucrative college football teams in 2005 — Notre Dame, Ohio State, and the University of Texas — each generated more than $60 million for their institutions. That number, which comes from the Department of Education, fails to account for the millions of dollars alumni donated to their alma maters because they were so proud of their football teams. But it still helps to explain why so many strangers to football success have reinvented themselves as football powerhouses (Rutgers?), and also why universities are spending huge sums on new football practice facilities, new football stadium skyboxes, and new football coaches.

Back in 1958 the University of Alabama lured Bear Bryant with a promise of $18,000 a year, or the rough equivalent of $130,000 today; last year the university handed Nick Saban an eight-year deal worth roughly $32 million. Several dozen college football coaches now earn more than $1 million a year — and that's before the books, speeches, endorsement deals, and who knows what else. Earlier this season the head coach at Texas A&M, Dennis Franchione, was caught topping up his $2.09 million salary by selling to Aggie alums, for $1,200 a pop, his private football-gossip newsletter.

The sports media treated that particular scheme as scandalous. Texas A&M made its coach apologize and promise to stop writing for a living. But really Dennis Franchione's foray into high-priced journalism was just an ingenious extension of the entrepreneurial spirit that's turned college football into a gold mine. The scandal wasn't what he did but how it was made to seem — unusually greedy.

College football's best trick play is its pretense that it has nothing to do with money, that it's simply an extension of the university's mission to educate its students. Were the public to view college football as mainly a business, it might start asking questions. For instance: Why are these enterprises that have nothing to do with education and everything to do with profits exempt from paying taxes? Or why don't they pay their employees?

5   This is maybe the oddest aspect of the college football business. Everyone associated with it is getting rich except the people whose labor creates the value. At this moment there are thousands of big-time college football players, many of whom are black and poor. They perform for the intense pleasure of millions of rabid college football fans, many of whom

are rich and white. The world's most enthusiastic racially integrated marketplace is waiting to happen.

But between buyer and seller sits the National Collegiate Athletic Association, to ensure that the universities it polices keep all the money for themselves—to make sure that the rich white folk do not slip so much as a free chicken sandwich under the table to the poor black kids. The poor black kids put up with it because they find it all but impossible to pursue N.F.L. careers unless they play at least three years in college. Less than 1 percent actually sign professional football contracts and, of those, an infinitesimal fraction ever make serious money. But their hope is eternal, and their ignorance exploitable.

Put that way the arrangement sounds like simple theft; but up close, inside the university, it apparently feels like high principle. That principle, as stated by the N.C.A.A., is that college sports should never be commercialized. But it's too late for that. College football already is commercialized, for everyone except the people who play it. Were they businesses, several dozen of America's best-known universities would be snapped up by private equity tycoons, who would spin off just about everything but the football team. (The fraternities they might keep.)

If the N.C.A.A. genuinely wanted to take the money out of college football it'd make the tickets free and broadcast the games on public television and set limits on how much universities could pay head coaches. But the N.C.A.A. confines its anti-market strictures to the players—and God help the interior lineman who is caught breaking them. Each year some player who grew up with nothing is tempted by a booster's offer of a car, or some cash, and is never heard from again.

The lie at the bottom of the fantasy goes something like this: Serious college football players go to college for some reason other than to play football. These marvelous athletes who take the field on Saturdays and generate millions for their colleges are students first and football players second. They are like Franciscan monks set down in the gold mine. Yes, they play football, but they have no interest in the money. What they're really living for is that degree in criminology.

10   Of course, no honest person who has glimpsed the inside of a big-time college football program could actually believe this. Even from the outside the college end of things seems suspiciously secondary. If serious college football players are students first, why—even after a huge N.C.A.A. push to raise their graduation rates—do they so alarmingly fail to graduate? Why must the N.C.A.A. create incentives for football coaches to encourage their players even to attend classes? Why do we never hear of a great high school football player choosing a college for the quality of its professors?

Why, when college football coaches sell their programs to high school studs, do they stress the smoothness of the path they offer to the N.F.L.?

It's not that football players are too stupid to learn. It's that they're too busy. Unlike the other students on campus, they have full-time jobs: playing football for nothing. Neglect the task at hand, and they may never get a chance to play football for money.

Last year the average N.F.L. team had revenue of about $200 million and ran payrolls of roughly $130 million: 60 percent to 70 percent of a team's revenues, therefore, go directly to the players. There's no reason those numbers would be any lower on a college football team—and there's some reason to think they'd be higher. It's easy to imagine the Universities of Alabama ($44 million in revenue), Michigan ($50 million), Georgia ($59 million), and many others paying the players even more than they take in directly from their football operations, just to keep school spirit flowing. (Go Dawgs!)

But let's keep it conservative. In 2005, the 121 Division 1-A football teams generated $1.8 billion for their colleges. If the colleges paid out 65 percent of their revenues to the players, the annual college football payroll would come to $1.17 billion. A college football team has 85 scholarship players while an N.F.L. roster has only 53, and so the money might be distributed a bit differently.

"You'd pay up for the most critical positions," one N.F.L. front office executive told me on the condition that I not use his name. "You'd pay more for quarterbacks and left tackles and pass rushing defensive ends. You'd pay less for linebackers because you'd have so many of them. You could just rotate them in and out."

15   A star quarterback, he thought, might command as much as 8 percent of his college team's revenues. For instance, in 2005 the Texas Longhorns would have paid Vince Young roughly $5 million for the season. In quarterbacking the Longhorns free of charge, Young, in effect, was making a donation to the university of $5 million a year—and also, by putting his health on the line, taking a huge career risk.

Perhaps he would have made this great gift on his own. The point is that Vince Young, as the creator of the economic value, should have had the power to choose what to do with it. Once the market is up and running players who want to go to enjoy the pure amateur experience can continue to play for free.

And you never know. The N.C.A.A. might one day be able to run an honest advertisement for the football-playing student-athlete: a young man who valued so highly what the University of Florida had to teach him about hospitality management that he ignored the money being thrown at him by Florida State.

Michael Lewis

In a recent interview while speaking of his 2006 book, *Blind Side: Evolution of a Game*, Michael Lewis stated, "If there is one thing that sports does do with inner-city kids, it is that it finds the athletes and exploits them and makes use of them." This is the topic of "Serfs of the Turf," a *New York Times* Op-Ed article Lewis wrote a year after the publication of *Blind Side* that reflects his increasing anger with the economics of college football. As the article points out, college football is a contradictory business – while on one hand it is not a business at all (football players are presumably recruited to finance their educations and therefore don't get paid for their work), on the other hand it is also a multi-billion-dollar industry (in which colleges and coaches alone make huge profits). Along the way Lewis has plenty to say about the racial implications of this arrangement.

Born in New Orleans in 1960, Lewis attended college at Princeton University and obtained his master's degree from the London School of Economics in 1985. Although shortly thereafter he entered the world of high finance as a bond salesman for Solomon Brothers, he spent his free time honing his talents as a journalist. By 1989 he had published his first book, *Liar's Poker*, a memoir of his experiences in high finance as well as a critique of the culture of dishonesty on Wall Street. Since then Lewis has published numerous articles and books, many focusing on business and sports (or both). His other books include *The Money Culture* (1999), *The New New Thing: A Silicon Valley Story* (1999), *Moneyball: The Art of Winning an Unfair Game* (2003), and most recently, *Panic: The Story of Modern Financial Insanity* (2008). Lewis currently lives in Berkeley, California, writes regularly for the *New York Times*, is a columnist for *Slate* magazine, and is working on a book about Hurricane Katrina.

SEEING

1. Since colleges do not pay football players, what happens to the money that football generates? Choose a public college, and find out how it spends the revenue generated from football games. What is your opinion of how the money is spent? Does college football help pay for worthwhile services and programs? Are the problems Michael Lewis discusses worth the good that football money buys? Once you have formed your opinion, interview people involved in college football as players, coaches, administrators, and fans. Did your opinion change after speaking with them? Why or why not?

Working with Sources

2. Why does Lewis ask questions in an essay in which he presents his opinions? For example, if he knows why college football programs don't pay their players, then why doesn't he tell his readers? Analyze the questions asked in this essay (paras. 4, 10), and identify – and comment on – the rhetorical purpose(s) they serve. As a reader, is it more persuasive to be asked or told? Using examples from the essay, prove your case.

WRITING

1. Lewis offers two alternatives for the N.C.A.A. to avoid hypocrisy: either pay college football players, "whose labor creates the value" (para. 5), or "take the money out of college football" (para. 8). As you reread Lewis's essay and reflect on the nature of his argument, what other options can you propose that he does not consider? Write an essay in which you argue for the N.C.A.A. to conduct the "college football business" in ways that Lewis would not see as exploiting its student-athletes. Please make sure your solution answers specific charges, such as the failure of colleges to graduate players.

Working with Sources

2. What are the similarities and differences between the feudal laws that bound medieval serfs to their landlords and the N.C.A.A. regulations that govern college football players? What rules are common to both? Which freedoms did serfs have that college football players do not? What can players do that serfs could not? For each, how does control over small plots of land – the turf of colleges' football fields and of landlords' farms – result in control over large numbers of people? Based on your research, write an essay that supports – or challenges – Lewis's title linking college football players to feudal serfs.

Clay Bennett
Wiretaps and Privacy Rights, 2008

Clay Bennett

Pulitzer Prize–winning editorial cartoonist Clay Bennett has been drawing cartoons for as long as he can remember, but his interest in politically themed cartoons probably originated around age fourteen. According to Bennett, "That may sound very young to some folks, but it really wasn't unusual in my family. The Bennetts are a passionate and opinionated lot. With a family dynamic more like the McLaughlin Group than the Brady Bunch, debate and argument were commonplace in our house." With a conservative career army officer of a father on one side of family debates and two liberal older sisters on the other, Bennett learned "to express views more like those of my sisters, but to argue their virtues with the analytical skill of my dad." In *Phone Guy*, the cartoon reproduced here, Bennett takes a stance on the wiretapping of American phones by the National Security Administration.

Born in South Carolina in 1958, Bennett moved frequently as a child, a result of his father's nomadic profession, and graduated from high school in Huntsville, Alabama. He earned his undergraduate degrees in art and history from the University of North Alabama in 1980. From 1981 to 1994 he was a staff editorial cartoonist for the *Fayetteville Times*, and after his dismissal – which Bennett attributes to political differences with a new editor – he lived in "career oblivion" for several years before resuming work with the *Christian Science Monitor* in 1997. Up for the Pulitzer Prize on numerous occasions, Bennett received the award in 2002. He is married to artist Cindy Procious, has three children, and currently lives in Tennessee, where he draws for the *Chattanooga Times Free Press*.

SEEING

1. Comment on the specific ways in which this cartoon addresses issues of human rights. What argument does the artist make? How effective is it? Point to specific examples in the cartoon to validate your response.

2. Consider the relationship between seeing and writing in this cartoon. Do you think the image's argument would be strengthened if text had been added? Why or why not?

WRITING

Working with Sources

1. Download and read a copy of the Universal Declaration of Human Rights (UDHR) from the UN's web site. Which of the thirty articles does this cartoon address? Write the first draft of an expository essay in which you analyze the cartoon as an expression of one of the articles in the UDHR.

2. From web sites tracking online activity to video surveillance, workplace monitoring, wiretapping, and electronic communications, Americans are increasingly debating the definition and limits of the term *privacy*. Research the coverage of privacy issues in your local newspaper. What are the key issues surrounding privacy in your area? Choose one issue relevant to you at the local or national level, and write an argumentative essay in which you first explain the issue and then recommend a solution to the problem. Please support your argument with specific examples, and cite at least three different sources.

Responding Visually

Choose an aspect of human rights that you are most interested in, and create your own cartoon for an exhibit similar to the UN's cartoon exhibit, Sketching Human Rights (*www.un.org*). If you enjoy drawing or illustrating, please use your own skills and techniques. If not, consider creating a collage of image and text by cutting and pasting – digitally or by hand – images and text.

WATCHING TV
MAKES YOU SMARTER
Steven Johnson

The Sleeper Curve

Scientist A: Has he asked for anything special?
Scientist B: Yes, this morning for breakfast . . . he requested something called "wheat germ, organic honey and tiger's milk."
Scientist A: Oh, yes. Those were the charmed substances that some years ago were felt to contain life-preserving properties.
Scientist B: You mean there was no deep fat? No steak or cream pies or . . . hot fudge?
Scientist A: Those were thought to be unhealthy.

– From Woody Allen's *Sleeper*

On Jan. 24, the Fox network showed an episode of its hit drama *24*, the real-time thriller known for its cliffhanger tension and often-gruesome violence. Over the preceding weeks, a number of public controversies had erupted around *24*, mostly focused on its portrait of Muslim terrorists and its penchant for torture scenes. The episode that was shown on the 24th only fanned the flames higher: In one scene, a terrorist enlists a hit man to kill his child for not fully supporting the jihadist cause; in another scene, the secretary of defense authorizes the torture of his son to uncover evidence of a terrorist plot.

But the explicit violence and the post-9/11 terrorist anxiety are not the only elements of *24* that would have been unthinkable on prime-time network television twenty years ago. Alongside the notable change in content lies an equally notable change in form. During its forty-four minutes—a real-time hour, minus sixteen minutes for commercials—the episode connects the lives of twenty-one distinct characters, each with a clearly defined "story arc," as the Hollywood jargon has it: a defined personality with motivations and obstacles and specific relationships with other characters. Nine primary narrative threads wind their way through those forty-four minutes, each drawing extensively upon events and information revealed in earlier episodes. Draw a map of all those intersecting plots and personalities, and you get structure that—where formal complexity is concerned—more closely resembles *Middlemarch* than a hit TV drama of years past like *Bonanza*.

For decades, we've worked under the assumption that mass culture follows a path declining steadily toward lowest-common-denominator

standards, presumably because the "masses" want dumb, simple pleasures and big media companies try to give the masses what they want. But
as that *24* episode suggests, the exact opposite is happening: The culture
is getting more cognitively demanding, not less. To make sense of an
episode of *24*, you have to integrate far more information than you would
have a few decades ago watching a comparable show. Beneath the violence and the ethnic stereotypes, another trend appears: To keep up with
entertainment like *24*, you have to pay attention, make inferences, track
shifting social relationships. This is what I call the Sleeper Curve: The
most debased forms of mass diversion—video games and violent television dramas and juvenile sitcoms—turn out to be nutritional after all.

I believe that the Sleeper Curve is the single most important new force
altering the mental development of young people today, and I believe it
is largely a force for good: enhancing our cognitive faculties, not dumbing
them down. And yet you almost never hear this story in popular accounts
of today's media. Instead, you hear dire tales of addiction, violence, mindless escapism. It's assumed that shows that promote smoking or gratuitous
violence are bad for us, while those that thunder against teen pregnancy
or intolerance have a positive role in society. Judged by that morality-play
standard, the story of popular culture over the past fifty years—if not five
hundred—is a story of decline: The morals of the stories have grown
darker and more ambiguous, and the antiheroes have multiplied.

5   The usual counterargument here is that what media have lost in moral
clarity, they have gained in realism. The real world doesn't come in nicely
packaged public-service announcements, and we're better off with entertainment like *The Sopranos* that reflects our fallen state with all its ethical ambiguity. I happen to be sympathetic to that argument, but it's not
the one I want to make here. I think there is another way to assess the
social virtue of pop culture, one that looks at media as a kind of cognitive
workout, not as a series of life lessons. There may indeed be more "negative messages" in the mediasphere today. But that's not the only way to
evaluate whether our television shows or video games are having a positive impact. Just as important—if not more important—is the kind of
thinking you have to do to make sense of a cultural experience. That is
where the Sleeper Curve becomes visible.

Televised Intelligence

Consider the cognitive demands that televised narratives place on their
viewers. With many shows that we associate with "quality" entertainment—

The Mary Tyler Moore Show, Murphy Brown, Frasier—the intelligence arrives fully formed in the words and actions of the characters onscreen. They say witty things to one another and avoid lapsing into tired sitcom clichés, and we smile along in our living rooms, enjoying the company of these smart people. But assuming we're bright enough to understand the sentences they're saying, there's no intellectual labor involved in enjoying the show as a viewer. You no more challenge your mind by watching these intelligent shows than you challenge your body watching *Monday Night Football*. The intellectual work is happening onscreen, not off.

But another kind of televised intelligence is on the rise. Think of the cognitive benefits conventionally ascribed to reading: attention, patience, retention, the parsing of narrative threads. Over the last half-century, pro-gramming on TV has increased the demands it places on precisely these mental faculties. This growing complexity involves three primary elements: multiple threading, flashing arrows, and social networks.

According to television lore, the age of multiple threads began with the arrival in 1981 of *Hill Street Blues*, the Steven Bochco police drama in-variably praised for its "gritty realism." Watch an episode of *Hill Street Blues* side by side with any major drama from the preceding decades— *Starsky and Hutch*, for instance, or *Dragnet*—and the structural trans-formation will jump out at you. The earlier shows follow one or two lead characters, adhere to a single dominant plot, and reach a decisive conclu-sion at the end of the episode. Draw an outline of the narrative threads in almost every *Dragnet* episode, and it will be a single line: from the ini-tial crime scene, through the investigation, to the eventual cracking of the case. A typical *Starsky and Hutch* episode offers only the slightest varia-tion on this linear formula: the introduction of a comic subplot that usu-ally appears only at the tail ends of the episode, creating a structure that looks like the graph below. The vertical axis represents the number of individual threads, and the horizontal axis is time.

Starsky and Hutch (any episode)

A *Hill Street Blues* episode complicates the picture in a number of profound ways. The narrative weaves together a collection of distinct strands—sometimes as many as ten, though at least half of the threads involve only a few quick scenes scattered through the episode. The num-ber of primary characters—and not just bit parts—swells significantly. And the episode has fuzzy borders: picking up one or two threads from previous episodes at the outset and leaving one or two threads open at the end. Charted graphically, an average episode looks like this:

Hill Street Blues (episode 85)

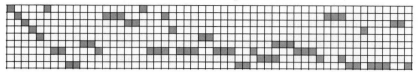

10   Critics generally cite *Hill Street Blues* as the beginning of "serious drama" narrative in the television medium—differentiating the series from the single-episode dramatic programs from the '50s, which were Broadway plays performed in front of a camera. But the *Hill Street* innovations weren't all that original; they'd long played a defining role in popular television, just not during the evening hours. The structure of a *Hill Street* episode—and indeed of all the critically acclaimed dramas that followed, from *thirtysomething* to *Six Feet Under*—is the structure of a soap opera. *Hill Street Blues* might have sparked a new golden age of television drama during its seven-year run, but it did so by using a few crucial tricks that *Guiding Light* and *General Hospital* mastered long before.

Bochco's genius with *Hill Street* was to marry complex narrative structure with complex subject matter. *Dallas* had already shown that the extended, interwoven threads of the soap-opera genre could survive the weeklong interruptions of a prime-time show, but the actual content of *Dallas* was fluff. (The most probing issue it addressed was the question, now folkloric, of who shot J. R.) *All in the Family* and *Rhoda* showed that you could tackle complex social issues, but they did their tackling in the comfort of the sitcom living room. *Hill Street* had richly drawn characters confronting difficult social issues and a narrative structure to match.

Since *Hill Street* appeared, the multi-threaded drama has become the most widespread fictional genre on prime time: *St. Elsewhere, L.A. Law, thirtysomething, Twin Peaks, N.Y.P.D. Blue, E.R., The West Wing, Alias, Lost.* (The only prominent holdouts in drama are shows like *Law and Order* that have essentially updated the venerable *Dragnet* format and thus remained anchored to a single narrative line.) Since the early '80s, however, there has been a noticeable increase in narrative complexity in these dramas. The most ambitious show on TV to date, *The Sopranos,* routinely follows up to a dozen distinct threads over the course of an episode, with more than twenty recurring characters. An episode from late in the first season looks like this:

The Sopranos (episode 8)

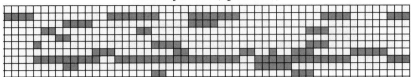

The total number of active threads equals the multiple plots of *Hill Street*, but here each thread is more substantial. The show doesn't offer a clear distinction between dominant and minor plots; each story line carries its weight in the mix. The episode also displays a chordal mode of storytelling entirely absent from *Hill Street*: A single scene in *The Sopranos* will often connect to three different threads at the same time, layering one plot atop another. And every single thread in this *Sopranos* episode builds on events from previous episodes and continues on through the rest of the season and beyond.

Put those charts together, and you have a portrait of the Sleeper Curve rising over the past thirty years of popular television. In a sense, this is as much a map of cognitive changes in the popular mind as it is a map of on-screen developments, as if the media titans decided to condition our brains to follow ever-larger numbers of simultaneous threads. Before *Hill Street*, the conventional wisdom among television execs was that audiences wouldn't be comfortable following more than three plots in a single episode, and indeed, the *Hill Street* pilot, which was shown in January 1981, brought complaints from viewers that the show was too complicated. Fast-forward two decades, and shows like *The Sopranos* engage their audiences with narratives that make *Hill Street* look like *Three's Company*. Audiences happily embrace that complexity because they've been trained by two decades of multi-threaded dramas.

15   Multi-threading is the most celebrated structural feature of the modern television drama, and it certainly deserves some of the honor that has been doled out to it. And yet multi-threading is only part of the story.

The Case for Confusion

Shortly after the arrival of the first-generation slasher movies—*Halloween, Friday the 13th*—Paramount released a mock-slasher flick called *Student Bodies*, parodying the genre just as the *Scream* series would do fifteen years later. In one scene, the obligatory nubile teenage baby sitter hears a noise outside a suburban house; she opens the door to investigate, finds nothing, and then goes back inside. As the door shuts behind her, the camera swoops in on the doorknob, and we see that she has left the door unlocked. The camera pulls back and then swoops down again for emphasis. And then a flashing arrow appears on the screen, with text that helpfully explains: "Unlocked!"

The flashing arrow is parody, of course, but it's merely an exaggerated version of a device popular stories use all the time. When a sci-fi script inserts into some advanced lab a nonscientist who keeps asking the science geeks to explain what they're doing with that particle accelerator, that's a flashing arrow that gives the audience precisely the information it needs in order to make sense of the ensuing plot. ("Whatever you do, don't spill water on it, or you'll set off a massive explosion!") These hints serve as a kind of narrative hand-holding. Implicitly, they say to the audience, "We realize you have no idea what a particle accelerator is, but here's the deal: All you need to know is that it's a fancy big thing that explodes when wet." They focus the mind on relevant details: "Don't worry about whether the baby sitter is going to break up with her boyfriend. Worry about that guy lurking in the bushes." They reduce the amount of analytic work you need to do to make sense of a story. All you have to do is follow the arrows.

By this standard, popular television has never been harder to follow. If narrative threads have experienced a population explosion over the past twenty years, flashing arrows have grown correspondingly scarce. Watching our pinnacle of early '80s TV drama, *Hill Street Blues*, we find there's an informational wholeness to each scene that differs markedly from what you see on shows like *The West Wing* or *The Sopranos* or *Alias* or *E.R.*

Hill Street has ambiguities about future events: Will a convicted killer be executed? Will Furillo marry Joyce Davenport? Will Renko find it in himself to bust a favorite singer for cocaine possession? But the present-tense of each scene explains itself to the viewer with little ambiguity. There's an open question or a mystery driving each of these stories — how will it all turn out? — but there's no mystery about the immediate activity on the screen. A contemporary drama like *The West Wing*, on the other hand, constantly embeds mysteries into the present-tense events: You see characters performing actions or discussing events about which crucial information has been deliberately withheld. Anyone who has watched more than a handful of *The West Wing* episodes closely will know the feeling: Scene after scene refers to some clearly crucial but unexplained piece of information, and after the sixth reference, you'll find yourself wishing you could rewind the tape to figure out what they're talking about, assuming you've missed something. And then you realize that you're supposed to be confused. The open question posed by these sequences is not "How will this turn out in the end?" The question is "What's happening right now?"

20   The deliberate lack of hand-holding extends down to the microlevel of dialogue as well. Popular entertainment that addresses technical issues— whether they are the intricacies of passing legislation, or of performing a heart bypass, or of operating a particle accelerator—conventionally switches between two modes of information in dialogue: texture and substance. Texture is all the arcane verbiage provided to convince the viewer that they're watching Actual Doctors at Work; substance is the material planted amid the background texture that the viewer needs to make sense of the plot.

Conventionally, narratives demarcate the line between texture and substance by inserting cues that flag or translate the important data. There's an unintentionally comical moment in the 2004 blockbuster *The Day After Tomorrow* in which the beleaguered climatologist (played by Dennis Quaid) announces his theory about the imminent arrival of a new ice age to a gathering of government officials. In his speech, he warns that "we have hit a critical desalinization point!" At this moment, the writer-director Roland Emmerich—a master of brazen arrow-flashing—has an official follow with the obliging remark: "It would explain what's driving this extreme weather." They might as well have had a flashing "Unlocked!" arrow on the screen.

The dialogue on shows like *The West Wing* and *E.R.*, on the other hand, doesn't talk down to its audiences. It rushes by, the words accelerating in sync with the high-speed tracking shots that glide through the corridors and operating rooms. The characters talk faster in these shows, but the truly remarkable thing about the dialogue is not purely a matter of speed; it's the willingness to immerse the audience in information that most viewers won't understand. Here's a typical scene from *E.R*:

[**Weaver** *and* **Wright** *push a gurney containing a 16-year-old girl. Her parents,* **Janna** *and* **Frank Mikami,** *follow close behind.* **Carter** *and* **Lucy** *fall in.*]
Weaver: 16-year-old, unconscious, history of biliary atresia.
Carter: Hepatic coma?
Weaver: Looks like it.
Mr. Mikami: She was doing fine until six months ago.
Carter: What medication is she on?

Mrs. Mikami: Ampicillin, tobramycin, vitamins A, D and K.

Lucy: Skin's jaundiced.

Weaver: Same with the scelera. Breath smells sweet.

Carter: Fetor hepaticus?

Weaver: Yep.

Lucy: What's that?

Weaver: Her liver's shut down. Let's dip a urine. [*To* **Carter**] Guys, it's getting a little crowded in here, why don't you deal with the parents? Start lactulose, 30 cc's per NG.

Carter: We're giving medicine to clean her blood.

Weaver: Blood in the urine, two-plus.

Carter: The liver failure is causing her blood not to clot.

Mrs. Mikami: Oh, God. . . .

Carter: Is she on the transplant list?

Mr. Mikami: She's been Status 2a for six months, but they haven't been able to find her a match.

Carter: Why? What's her blood type?

Mr. Mikami: AB

[*This hits* **Carter** *like a lightening bolt.* **Lucy** *gets it, too. They share a look.*]

There are flashing arrows here, of course—"The liver failure is causing her blood not to clot"—but the ratio of medical jargon to layperson translation is remarkably high. From a purely narrative point of view, the decisive line arrives at the very end: "AB." The sixteen-year-old's blood type connects her to an earlier plot line, involving a cerebral-hemorrhage victim who—after being dramatically revived in one of the opening scenes—ends up brain-dead. Far earlier, before the liver-failure scene above, Carter briefly discusses harvesting the hemorrhage victim's organs for transplants, and another doctor makes a passing reference to his blood type being rare AB (thus making him an unlikely donor). The twist here revolves around a statistically unlikely event happening at the E.R.—an otherwise perfect liver donor showing up just in time to donate his liver to a recipient with the same rare blood type. But the show reveals this twist with remarkable subtlety. To make sense of that last "AB" line— and the look of disbelief on Carter's and Lucy's faces—you have to recall a passing remark uttered earlier regarding a character who belongs to a completely different thread. Shows like *E.R.* may have more blood and guts than popular TV had a generation ago, but when it comes to story-telling, they possess a quality that can only be described as subtlety and discretion.

Even Bad TV Is Better

Skeptics might argue that I have stacked the deck here by focusing on relatively highbrow titles like *The Sopranos* or *The West Wing*, when in fact the most significant change in the last five years of narrative entertainment involves reality TV. Does the contemporary pop cultural landscape look quite as promising if the representative show is *Joe Millionaire* instead of *The West Wing*?

25   I think it does, but to answer that question properly, you have to avoid the tendency to sentimentalize the past. When people talk about the golden age of television in the early '70s—invoking shows like *The Mary Tyler Moore Show* and *All in the Family*—they forget to mention how awful most television programming was during much of that decade. If you're going to look at pop-culture trends, you have to compare apples to apples, or in this case, lemons to lemons. The relevant comparison is not between *Joe Millionaire* and *MASH*; it's between *Joe Millionaire* and *The Newlywed Game*, or between *Survivor* and *The Love Boat*.

What you see when you make these head-to-head comparisons is that a rising tide of complexity has been lifting programming at the bottom of the quality spectrum and at the top. *The Sopranos* is several times more demanding of its audiences than *Hill Street* was, and *Joe Millionaire* has made comparable advances over *Battle of the Network Stars*. This is the ultimate test of the Sleeper Curve theory: Even the junk has improved.

If early television took its cues from the stage, today's reality programming is reliably structured like a video game: a series of competitive tests, growing more challenging over time. Many reality shows borrow a subtler device from gaming culture as well: The rules aren't fully established at the outset. You learn as you play.

On a show like *Survivor* or *The Apprentice*, the participants—and the audience—know the general objective of the series, but each episode involves new challenges that haven't been ordained in advance. The final round of the first season of *The Apprentice*, for instance, threw a monkey wrench into the strategy that governed the play up to that point, when Trump announced that the two remaining apprentices would have to assemble and manage a team of subordinates who had already been fired in earlier episodes of the show. All of a sudden the overarching objective of the game—do anything to avoid being fired—presented a potential conflict to the remaining two contenders: The structure of the final round favored the survivor who had maintained the best relationships with his comrades. Suddenly, it wasn't enough just to have clawed your way to the top; you had to have made friends while clawing. The original

Joe Millionaire went so far as to undermine the most fundamental convention of all—that the show's creators don't openly lie to the contestants about the prizes—by inducing a construction worker to pose as man of means while twenty women competed for his attention.

Reality programming borrowed another key ingredient from games: the intellectual labor of probing the system's rules for weak spots and opportunities. As each show discloses its conventions, and each participant reveals his or her personality traits and background, the intrigue in watching comes from figuring out how the participants should best navigate the environment that has been created for them. The pleasure in these shows comes not from watching other people being humiliated on national television; it comes from depositing other people in a complex, high-pressure environment where no established strategies exist and watching them find their bearings. That's why the water-cooler conversation about these shows invariably tracks in on the strategy displayed on the previous night's episode: Why did Kwame pick Omarosa in that final round? What devious strategy is Richard Hatch concocting now?

30   When we watch these shows, the part of our brain that monitors the emotional lives of the people around us—the part that tracks subtle shifts in intonation and gesture and facial expression—scrutinizes the action on the screen, looking for clues. We trust certain characters implicitly and vote others off the island in a heartbeat. Traditional narrative shows also trigger emotional connections to the characters, but those connections don't have the same participatory effect, because traditional narratives aren't explicitly about strategy. The phrase "Monday-morning quarterbacking" describes the engaged feeling that spectators have in relation to games as opposed to stories. We absorb stories, but we second-guess games. Reality programming has brought that second-guessing to prime time, only the game in question revolves around social dexterity rather than the physical kind.

The Rewards of Smart Culture

The quickest way to appreciate the Sleeper Curve's cognitive training is to sit down and watch a few hours of hit programming from the late '70s on Nick at Nite or the SOAPnet channel or on DVD. The modern viewer who watches a show like *Dallas* today will be bored by the content—not just because the show is less salacious than today's soap operas (which it is by a small margin) but also because the show contains far less information in each scene, despite the fact that its soap-opera structure made it one of the most complicated narratives on television in its prime. With

Dallas, the modern viewer doesn't have to think to make sense of what's going on, and not having to think is boring. Many recent hit shows — *24, Survivor, The Sopranos, Alias, Lost, The Simpsons, E.R.* —take the opposite approach, layering each scene with a thick network of affiliations. You have to focus to follow the plot, and in focusing you're exercising the parts of your brain that map social networks, that fill in missing information, that connect multiple narrative threads.

Of course, the entertainment industry isn't increasing the cognitive complexity of its products for charitable reasons. The Sleeper Curve exists because there's money to be made by making culture smarter. The economics of television syndication and DVD sales mean that there's a tremendous financial pressure to make programs that can be watched multiple times, revealing new nuances and shadings on the third viewing. Meanwhile, the Web has created a forum for annotation and commentary that allows more complicated shows to prosper thanks to the fan sites where each episode of shows like *Lost* or *Alias* is dissected with an intensity usually reserved for Talmud scholars. Finally, interactive games have trained a new generation of media consumers to probe complex environments and to think on their feet, and that gamer audience has now come to expect the same challenges from their television shows. In the end, the Sleeper Curve tells us something about the human mind. It may be drawn toward the sensational where content is concerned—sex does sell, after all. But the mind also likes to be challenged; there's real pleasure to be found in solving puzzles, detecting patterns, or unpacking a complex narrative system.

In pointing out some of the ways that popular culture has improved our minds, I am not arguing that parents should stop paying attention to the way their children amuse themselves. What I am arguing for is a change in the criteria we use to determine what really is cognitive junk food and what is genuinely nourishing. Instead of a show's violent or tawdry content, instead of wardrobe malfunctions or the F-word, the true test should be whether a given show engages or sedates the mind. Is it a single thread strung together with predictable punch lines every thirty seconds? Or does it map a complex social network? Is your on-screen character running around shooting everything in sight, or is she trying to solve problems and manage resources? If your kids want to watch reality TV, encourage them to watch *Survivor* over *Fear Factor*. If they want to watch a mystery show, encourage *24* over *Law and Order*. If they want to play a violent game, encourage Grand Theft Auto over Quake. Indeed, it might be just as helpful to have a rating system that used mental labor and not obscenity and violence as its classification scheme for the world of mass culture.

Kids and grown-ups each can learn from their increasingly shared obsessions. Too often we imagine the blurring of kid and grown-up cultures as a series of violations: the nine-year-olds who have to have nipple broaches explained to them thanks to Janet Jackson; the middle-aged guy who can't wait to get home to his Xbox. But this demographic blur has a commendable side that we don't acknowledge enough. The kids are forced to think like grown-ups: analyzing complex social networks, managing resources, tracking subtle narrative intertwinings, recognizing long-term patterns. The grown-ups, in turn, get to learn from the kids: decoding each new technological wave, parsing the interfaces, and discovering the intellectual rewards of play. Parents should see this as an opportunity, not a crisis. Smart culture is no longer something you force your kids to ingest, like green vegetables. It's something you share.

Steven Johnson

Science writer Steven Johnson (b. 1968) has covered technology and culture since the beginning of the Internet age. Johnson is the author of *Emergence: The Connected Life of Ants, Brains, Cities and Software* (2001); *Mind Wide Open: Your Brain and the Neuroscience of Everyday Life* (2004); *Everything Bad Is Good for You: How Today's Popular Culture Is Actually Making Us Smarter* (2005), from which the essay here was reprinted; and *The Ghost Map* (2006). He has been a columnist for *Slate* and *Wired*, and in 1995 he founded the online magazine *Feed*. Johnson lives in Brooklyn, New York.

SEEING

1. What is the Sleeper Curve, and why does Steven Johnson argue that it is "the single most important new force altering the mental development of young people" (para. 4)? Based on his own standards ("multiple threading, flashing arrows, and social networks"; para. 7), how would you measure the nature and extent of the cognitive challenge presented in Johnson's essay? How many argumentative threads does Johnson introduce in his essay, and how successfully does he weave them together? Please point to specific examples to support your response. What kinds of shifting social relations exist between you as a reader and Johnson as an author? Graph the argumentative complexity of Johnson's essay, and make a case for its being higher or lower on the Sleeper Curve than *The Sopranos*.

2. Comment on the extent to which popular culture has become more or less cognitively "nutritional" since Johnson published his article in 2005. To make your case, compare the narrative complexity of current shows to that of past ones. How does the structure of MTV's *Laguna Beach*, for example, compare to that of *The Hills*? In what specific ways do shifting social relationships on web 2.0 applications such as Facebook require more complex thinking than less interactive web 1.0 applications such as personal blogs?

WRITING

1. Apply the Sleeper Curve to other socially devalued activities. For example, despite their enormous popularity, fashion magazines are often described as mindless reading. In what ways could you argue that their structure (if not their content) is much more complex than that of traditional books? How might the comic page in a newspaper give you a better cognitive workout than the business section? Also, consider the Sleeper Curve in relation to senses other than sight. Does tasting complex food (in terms of ingredients) traditionally viewed as unhealthy, such as donuts, make you smarter than tasting simple food thought to be healthy, such as carrots? Write the first draft of an essay in which you extend the nature of Johnson's argument about the Sleeper Curve to an example of American popular culture. As you prepare your draft, consider the extent to which Johnson would agree or disagree with your extensions of his Sleeper Curve argument.

2. If watching TV makes you smarter, then were people less intelligent before TV became widely available in the late 1940s? You might want to discuss (or debate) this question with your grandparents or even your great-grandparents. How do they respond to the idea that television's current multilayered complexity requires more cognitive work than the radio dramas that were popular entertainment before TV? To decide for yourself, listen carefully to several hours of old-time radio shows such as *The Shadow*, *The War of the Worlds*, and *Guiding Light*. Write the first draft of an expository essay in which you compare and contrast one of these radio programs with their recent television counterparts.

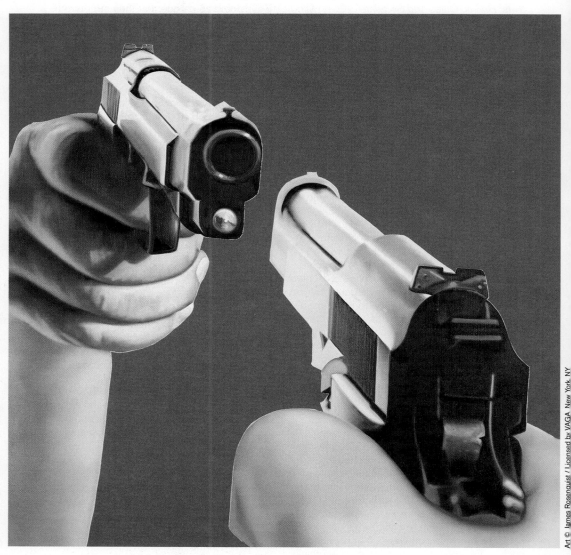

James Rosenquist
Professional Courtesy, 1996

James Rosenquist

The paintings of James Rosenquist often make political statements through their quotations from popular culture. For instance, of the image shown here, one of many in his gun-themed collection Target Practice, Rosenquist wrote, "I want to illustrate the stark look and confrontation of a handgun. . . . Young people are confused by the way guns are depicted in the movies and on television. It shows the hero being shot, getting up, brushing himself off, and then going on to act in another movie — becoming an even bigger star. The reality of being shot is really death forever and a big flame usually comes out of the real gun. These paintings are intended to be nondecorative and oblique. I hope they question the idea of who really is the target."

Born in North Dakota in 1933, Rosenquist moved to New York at age twenty-one to study at the Art Students League. During his early years in New York he was employed as a sign painter. He first gained notoriety in the early 1960s with *President Elect*, in which he took John F. Kennedy's face from a campaign poster and layered it with the images of "half a Chevrolet and a piece of stale cake," and *F-111*, which depicted a girl sitting under a hair dryer, spaghetti, and a nuclear bomb (among other images) on the side of a bomber plane. Together with other artists of the period such as Andy Warhol and Roy Lichtenstein, Rosenquist challenged standard notions of "fine art" in a movement that quickly became known as "pop art." Rosenquist remains one of the most important artists to emerge since the 1960s. Most recently he has been the subject of a retrospective at the Haunch of Venison Gallery in London.

SEEING

1. How would you characterize the overall effect of this painting? Where are your eyes drawn? Why? Rosenquist's painting measures 4 feet by 4 feet. What does this considerably reduced reproduction gain or lose by virtue of its size when compared with the original? What kinds of shapes, colors, and details become more or less important as the image becomes larger or smaller? Why? How does reducing the size of the painting change its impact on the viewer? Which aspects of the painting would you need to change to make the smaller image have the same impact as the original?

2. Rosenquist characterizes the series of paintings that includes *Professional Courtesy* in the following terms: "These paintings are intended to be nondecorative and oblique." What does he mean by these words, especially in this context? Under the headings "Nondecorative" and "Oblique," list specific elements in the painting that would justify the use of each adjective. Consider, for example, color, shape, style, and the relationships between and among these elements.

Visit *seeingandwriting.com* for an interactive exercise based on *Professional Courtesy*.

oblique: Neither perpendicular nor parallel; indirect.

WRITING

1. A commonplace saying is that "every picture tells a story." What story does Rosenquist's painting tell? Imagine that the painting is a photograph. Write the first draft of a narrative that tells the story of how the picture came to be. Make your story as realistic as possible, and account for such obvious elements as the two guns, the two hands, and the red background, as well as less obvious aspects of it: the shadows, the position of the photographer, and so on.

2. In everyday language *professional courtesy* is a service offered to someone who works in the same field. In what ways does the painting play with this meaning? How do the historical meanings of the words connect with the meaning of the painting? For example, the word *professional* comes from the word *profess*, which is made up of the Greek prefix *pro-* (which indicated motion from a source to a target) and *phatos* (which can be translated as "claim" or "statement"). A professional is like a gun: A gun shoots bullets, and a professional produces expert statements. Write an expository essay in which you explain how the two sets of meanings (historical and current) work together to enrich the painting's message and significance.

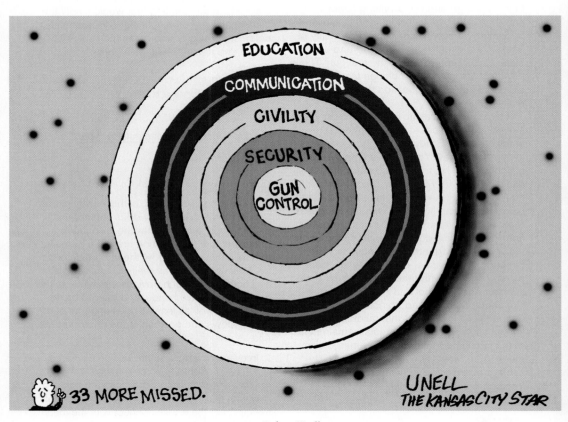

Robert Unell
The Kansas City Star, 2007

Wayne Stayskal
I'm Taking a Poll, Sir, 1999

THE TWENTIETH-CENTURY
UNIVERSITY IS OBSOLETE
Rev. John P. Minogue

Higher education, like the human species itself, is the product of evolutionary forces that produce structures—the DNA if you will—that enable one variant to thrive and cause another to falter.

The life form known as higher education was hatched in a monastic cocoon in the tenth century. From this beginning, higher education institutions took shape as an evolving species, changing form and mission in response to external forces. Familiar milestones on this evolutionary journey include secularization, development of academic disciplines, evolution of administrative structures, growth of the research university, and the concepts of academic freedom and tenure.

With the dawn of the Knowledge Age, the evolution of higher education has drastically accelerated so that the pace of change is now measured in years, not centuries. Higher education today is a global commodity with all the competition and product diversification that entails, including the splitting of the production from the distribution of knowledge. This is much like the movie industry, where a few companies make movies and many companies distribute them in theaters, on television, and on DVDs.

Research I universities[1] that produce new knowledge thrive in this new environment, but they are now dependent upon strong financial links with the economic agendas of companies and countries. They are no longer the sole citadels for the production of new knowledge, but rather just one node on a global network of corporate and national R&D sites.

5   The transformation of Higher Education Life Forms on the distribution side of knowledge is even more dramatic, evolving a new species that concentrates simply on distribution of currently available knowledge.

This new species features a small core of knowledge engineers who wrap courses into a degree to be distributed in cookie-cutter institutions and delivered by working professionals, not academics. There is no tenured faculty, no academic processes; the sole focus is on bottom-line economic results. These twenty-first-century institutions are not burdened with esoteric pursuits of knowledge; rather, they focus on professional degrees for adults that have a fairly clear market value for a given career path.

---

1. Research I university: A classification created by the Carnegie Classification of Institutions of Higher Education to identify universities with significant emphasis on research. [Eds.]

The exemplars of this new species are the for-profit universities, which are cutting their teeth on the weakness of the twentieth-century universities. Though new at the game, in a few years they will be capable of hunting with lethal success. This new species is market-driven. Its key survival mechanism is the ability to rapidly evolve to new environments and to position in the market. Since they do not carry tenured faculty, they can rapidly jettison disciplines of study that do not penetrate market. Since they do not have academic processes, they can rapidly bring to market programs that can capture market share.

Certainly, not all for-profit providers have the core capabilities to compete long term in the market. Some emerge quickly and as quickly become extinct, but others are proving quite adept at drawing strength from this globally competitive market.

As mass, longevity, and a voracious need for large quantities of prey (resources) proved lethal to the dinosaurs in the stark environments created by global darkening, so the universities of the early twentieth century may face serious thinning or perhaps even extinction in the new globally competitive environment of higher education. Universities rooted in the early twentieth century are intrinsically inefficient in today's environment of market valuation and brand identity. Given the current internal structure of tenure and faculty governance, these universities lack the capability to respond to market forces in a timely fashion—to close out product lines no longer playing in the market and rapidly bring new and more efficient product to market.

10   Still, these once elegant life forms persevere, but for reasons having nothing to do with innate capability to embrace change. Instead, at the undergraduate level it is the instinctual and perhaps irrational desire of many parents to see their children prosper in a traditional liberal arts environment, and so their willingness to spend inordinate amounts of money for education. At the graduate level, the "brand name" is the driver. The reputation of leading institutions, established in an era before global market competition, is based on a footing much different from that used today to obtain market position, but it still works to sustain the life form, at least among a few elite universities.

In addition, traditional universities have benefited from some serious slack in the evolutionary rope. The Industrial Age required a few knowledge workers and a lot of folks doing heavy lifting, whereas the Knowledge Age requires vast numbers of educated workers. Almost overnight, this has led to a massive spike in global demand for education, with motivated consumers increasing perhaps one hundred-fold. What was the privilege of a few has become the expectation of all.

But global supply falls far short of meeting demand. With a population of 295 million, the United States has only 15 million active seats in the higher education classroom; China, with a population of 1.2 billion, has 2 million seats available; Brazil, with a population 170 million, has 2.5 million seats available.

This imbalance between supply and demand has created a robust market for all providers. Suppliers of higher education simply have to dip their nets in the water to catch students. There is not yet the fight-to-the-death competition for market share, and inefficient institutions have received a short reprieve from their evolutionary fate. But at some point, as with all markets, a saturation point will be reached, with supply outstripping demand — perhaps in five, perhaps in fifteen years. When this inversion occurs, those life forms with the required flexibility to quickly adapt to a fiercely competitive environment will survive and the others will fade from memory.

As there is private health care for those who can afford to pay at any price point, so there will continue some form of higher education that will meet the need and the checkbook of those wealthy enough to afford it. But for most now driven to higher education to meet the requirements of the Knowledge Age, it is value (the ratio of perceived quality over price) that will be the key determinant of what institution they will choose for their tuition dollar. To further stress the current market, state funding is not keeping up with inflation or enrollment growth, forcing higher education institutions to rely more on tuition and donations. Thus higher education is being pushed to stand on its own financial bottom rather than be a subsidized commodity, once again forcing the value proposition.

15   So what will be demanded of twentieth-century universities to survive when market supply reaches or exceeds demand? As in every market, those producers that have driven efficiency into their production system and responsiveness into their market positioning have at least a chance at surviving. But the challenge is daunting because the twentieth-century university is trying to play serious catch-up in new markets — adults, women, diversities, the underprivileged — while using the same mentalities that allowed them to attract the eighteen-to-twenty-five-year-old male.

As with IBM, which played in the personal computer market, but really lived in the mainframe business market, there is no fire in the belly of twentieth-century universities for these new markets. These institutions have not changed the way they go about their business to serve these new markets; and if there has been some change, it has been accompanied by the widespread grumbling of the faculty: Why do we have to teach at night? Why do we have to teach at multiple campuses? Why do we have to provide support services in the evening? Why do we have to teach students who aren't educated the way we were? Why do we have to schedule classes so students can maximize their employment opportunities?

Meanwhile, twentieth-century universities are running average price increases twice the inflation rate and carrying multiple overheads of unproven value to the buying market. Walk into the library of any university today that has ubiquitous connections to the Internet, and you will find the stacks empty of both faculty and students. Is the traditional library a value add or a costly overhead? As with IBM, twentieth-century universities believe their brand will sustain price increases. "No frill, just degree" competitors are producing product without the high cost of minimalist full-time faculty workloads, large libraries, and multiple staff-intensive manual processes. As with the personal computer, will the buying market ultimately see any difference between the products except the name on the plastic and the price on the sticker?

What will be the destiny of the current life form we have called the twentieth-century university? It consumes far too many resources for what it returns to the environment, and though there are vast resources (markets) available, its structures do not let it tap these resources effectively. Its evolutionary tardiness has provided opportunity for a new species to take hold—the profit-driven university. As the evolution of the human race has picked up the pace with each passing millennium, a future life form that has little resemblance to current higher education life forms will emerge much sooner than the usual eons it takes for evolution to create the next iteration of life.

The twentieth-century university is indeed obsolete and faces extinction.

Rev. John P. Minogue

As the former president of DePaul University, Rev. John P. Minogue takes a surprisingly nontraditional stance regarding the future of higher education in his article "The Twentieth-Century University Is Obsolete." Originally published in *Inside Higher Education* magazine in 2006, the article argues that liberal arts education is out of touch with the changing needs of the marketplace, resulting in staggering tuitions that only the wealthy can afford and an inability to provide the resources students really need today to succeed in the rapidly changing world of work.

Minogue earned his undergraduate degree in philosophy from St. Mary of the Barrens College and Seminary, a master's degree in ministry from DePaul University, a second master's degree in theology from DeAndreis Institute of Theology, and an MD from the University of St. Mary of the Lake. He was a member of the Northwestern University faculty and then moved to his alma mater, where he served first as a member of the Board of Trustees and then as a professor of religious studies and president of the university from 1993 until 2004, at which time he accepted a seat on the Illinois Board of Education. In 2004 he was also awarded the Polish Cross of Merit from the Polish government for helping to establish a relationship between DePaul University and the Higher Business School in Nowy Sacz, Poland.

SEEING

1. According to Rev. John P. Minogue, who served as president of DePaul University, why are for-profit universities better adapted to survive in today's global market environment than research universities? How do twentieth-century universities continue to thrive despite being judged "obsolete"? What does the near future hold for higher education? What do you envision as its ultimate fate?

2. Minogue's argument relies on two metaphors. First, the university is a life form and therefore is affected by such evolutionary forces as competition and survival mechanisms. Second, higher education is a commodity and so is driven by market forces such as profit and supply and demand. Identify, track, and then evaluate several specific uses of each metaphor in his essay. Comment on what each metaphor contributes to Minogue's overall argument. For example, how does describing higher education as "hatched in a monastic cocoon" (para. 2) set up his later claim that research universities cannot survive in a global environment? Similarly, how does Minogue use the metaphor of value to prove that universities will ultimately become obsolete? To what extent is it reasonable to analyze education with the language of evolution and economics? Why or why not?

WRITING

1. Prepare to become rich: Write the first draft of a business plan for the new for-profit university you have founded. Your plan's goal is to persuade potential investors to fund your vision of education's profitable future. Explain how you will take advantage of the impending doom of research universities and how you will avoid their mistakes. Discuss how your university will respond quickly to global market forces and will promote new knowledge products. Also describe in detail how you will brand and value your commodity. Be specific and creative, including marketing campaigns, profit projections, celebrity endorsements, and the like.

Working with Sources

2. Minogue claims that for-profit universities are a "new species," but in ancient Greece both Plato and Aristotle criticized a school of philosophers called Sophists for taking money to teach students. Consult historical sources, such as Plato's dialogues and Aristotle's essays, to find out why they were against for-profit education. Using specific passages from your research, write a dialogue in which Plato and Aristotle persuade Minogue that education should not be conducted for cash.

VISUALIZING COMPOSITION: POINT OF VIEW

Whether we are responding to what someone else has written or are generating our own prose, it is important to pay attention to point of view.

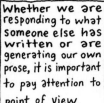

From whose "eye" do we see the story being told or the points being made in an argument?

What is the PERSPECTIVE from which a story is told or a line of reasoning is developed?

Is there a particular BIAS in that perspective?

In FICTION an author writes a story; someone else — a narrator — tells the story.

NARRATOR — I am Blorg from the planet Slorg. This is the story...

AUTHOR — His name is Blorg from the planet Slorg. This is the story...

Student

To determine a writer's point of view, pay attention to the writer's use of pronouns.

A writer uses...

...to tell a story or outline an opinion from a FIRST-PERSON point of view.

THIRD-PERSON narrative uses 'she said,' 'he did,' 'they decided,' and the like.

A more encompassing perspective is called OMNISCIENT POINT OF VIEW: The author creates a narrator who stands, almost godlike, outside the people and events being described, and "sees" all. This narrator not only can observe and...

...describe the action but also can see into the minds of the characters and account for what motivates them. For example, this human is fully aware that she's just a drawing...

...in a comic strip dedicated to a discussion about point of view. At this moment, she is feeling a bit hungry. But, before she dashes off for a doughnut she has one more assignment for you:

Carefully examine the cartoons about gun control in Chapter Seven. What points of view can you identify? What perspectives and bias are evident in each? Create a cartoon that displays your perspective on a current issue.

POKE!

REGARDING
THE PAIN OF OTHERS
Susan Sontag

Often something looks, or is felt to look, "better" in a photograph. Indeed, it is one of the functions of photography to improve the normal appearance of things. (Hence, one is always disappointed by a photograph that is not flattering.) Beautifying is one classic operation of the camera, and it tends to bleach out a moral response to what is shown. Uglifying, showing something at its worst, is a more modern function: didactic, it invites an active response. For photographs to accuse, and possibly to alter conduct, they must shock.

An example: A few years ago, the public health authorities in Canada, where it had been estimated that smoking kills 45,000 people a year, decided to supplement the warning printed on every pack of cigarettes with a shock photograph—of cancerous lungs, or a stroke-clotted brain, or a damaged heart, or a bloody mouth in acute periodontal distress. A pack with such a picture accompanying the warning about the deleterious effects of smoking would be 60 times more likely to inspire smokers to quit, a research study had somehow calculated, than a pack with only the verbal warning.

Let's assume this is true. Still one might wonder, for how long? Does shock have term limits? Right now the smokers of Canada are recoiling in disgust, if they do look at these pictures. Will those smoking five years from now still be upset? Shock can become familiar. Shock can wear off. Even if it doesn't, one can *not* look. People have means to defend themselves against what is upsetting—in this instance, unpleasant information for those wishing to continue to smoke. This seems normal, that is, adaptive. As one can become habituated to horror in real life, one can become habituated to the horror of certain images.

Yet there are cases where repeated exposure to what shocks, saddens, appalls does not use up a full-hearted response. Habituation is not automatic, for images (portable, insertable) obey different rules than real life. Representations of the Crucifixion do not become banal to believers, if they really are believers. This is even more true of staged representations. Performances of *Chushingura*, probably the best-known narrative in all of Japanese culture, can be counted on to make a Japanese audience sob when Lord Asano admires the beauty of the cherry blossoms on his way to where he must commit seppuku—sob each time, no matter how often they have followed the story (as a Kabuki or Bunraku play, as a film); the *ta'ziyah* drama of the betrayal and murder of Imam Hussayn does not cease to bring an Iranian audience to tears no matter how many times they have seen the martyrdom enacted. On the contrary. They weep, in part, because they have seen it many times. People want to weep. Pathos, in the form of a narrative, does not wear out.

5   But do people want to be horrified? Probably not. Still, there are pictures whose power does not abate, in part because one cannot look at them often. Pictures of the ruin of faces that will always testify to a great iniquity survived, at a cost: the faces of horribly disfigured First World War veterans who survived the inferno of the trenches; the faces melted and thickened with scar tissue of survivors of the American atomic bombs dropped on Hiroshima and Nagasaki; the faces cleft by machete blows of Tutsi survivors of the genocidal rampage launched by the Hutus in Rwanda—is it correct to say that people get *used* to these?

Indeed, the very notion of atrocity, of war crime, is associated with the expectation of photographic evidence. Such evidence is, usually, of something posthumous: the remains, as it were—the mounds of skulls in Pol Pot's Cambodia, the mass graves in Guatemala and El Salvador, Bosnia and Kosovo. And this posthumous reality is often the keenest of summations. As Hannah Arendt pointed out soon after the end of the Second World War, all the photographs and newsreels of the concentration camps are misleading because they show the camps at the moment the Allied troops marched in. What makes the images unbearable—the piles of corpses, the skeletal survivors—was not at all typical for the camps, which, when they were functioning, exterminated their inmates systematically (by gas, not starvation and illness), then immediately cremated them. And photographs echo photographs: It was inevitable that the photographs of emaciated Bosnian prisoners at Omarska, the Serb death camp created in northern Bosnia in 1992, would recall memories of the photographs taken in the Nazi death camps in 1945.

Photographs of atrocity illustrate as well as corroborate. Bypassing disputes about exactly how many were killed (numbers are often inflated at first), the photograph gives the indelible sample. The illustrative function of photographs leaves opinions, prejudices, fantasies, misinformation untouched. The information that many fewer Palestinians died in the assault on Jenin than had been claimed by Palestinian officials (as the Israelis had said all along) made much less impact than the pictures of the razed center of the refugee camp. And, of course, atrocities that are not secured in our minds by well-known photographic images, or of which we simply have had very few images—the total extermination of the

Herero people in Namibia decreed by the German colonial administration in 1904; the Japanese onslaught in China, notably the massacre of nearly 400,000 and the rape of 80,000 Chinese in December 1937, the so-called Rape of Nanking; the rape of some 130,000 women and girls (10,000 of whom committed suicide) by victorious Soviet soldiers unleashed by their commanding officers in Berlin in 1945—seem more remote. These are memories that few have cared to claim.

The familiarity of certain photographs builds our sense of the present and immediate past. Photographs lay down routes of reference, and serve as totems of causes: Sentiment is more likely to crystalize around a photograph than around a verbal slogan. And photographs help construct—and revise—our sense of a more distant past, with the posthumous shocks engineered by the circulation of hitherto unknown photographs. Photographs that everyone recognizes are now a constituent part of what a society chooses to think about, or declares that it has chosen to think about. It calls these ideas "memories," and that is, over the long run, a fiction. Strictly speaking, there is no such thing as collective memory—part of the same family of spurious notions as collective guilt. But there is collective instruction.

All memory is individual, unreproducible—it dies with each person. What is called collective memory is not a remembering but a stipulating: that *this* is important, and this is the story of how it happened, with the pictures that lock the story in our minds. Ideologies create substantiating archives of images, representative images, which encapsulate common ideas of significance and trigger predictable thoughts, feelings. Poster-ready photographs—the mushroom cloud of an A-bomb test, Martin Luther King Jr., speaking at the Lincoln Memorial in Washington, D.C., the astronaut on the moon—are the visual equivalent of sound bites. They commemorate, in no less blunt fashion than postage stamps, Important Historical Moments; indeed, the triumphalist ones (the picture of the A-bomb excepted) become postage stamps. Fortunately, there is no one signature picture of the Nazi death camps.

10   As art has been redefined during a century of modernism as whatever is destined to be enshrined in some kind of museum, so it is now the destiny of many photographic troves to be exhibited and preserved in museum-like institutions. Among such archives of horror, the photographs of genocide have undergone the greatest institutional development. The point of creating public repositories for these and other relics is to ensure that the crimes they depict will continue to figure in people's consciousness. This is called remembering, but in fact it is a good deal more than that.

The memory museum in its current proliferation is a product of a way of thinking about, and mourning, the destruction of European Jewry in the 1930s and 1940s, which came to institutional fruition in Yad Vashem in Jerusalem, the Holocaust Memorial Museum in Washington, D.C., and the Jewish Museum in Berlin. Photographs and other memorabilia of the Shoah have been committed to a perpetual recirculation, to ensure that what they show will be remembered. Photographs of the suffering and martyrdom of a people are more than reminders of death, of failure, of victimization. They invoke the miracle of survival. To aim at the perpetuation of memories means, inevitably, that one has undertaken the task of continually renewing, of creating, memories—aided, above all, by the impress of iconic photographs. People want to be able to visit—and refresh —their memories. Now many victim peoples want a memory museum, a temple that houses a comprehensive, chronologically organized, illustrated narrative of their sufferings. Armenians, for example, have long been clamoring for a museum in Washington to institutionalize the memory of the genocide of Armenian people by the Ottoman Turks. But why is there not already, in the nation's capital, which happens to be a city whose population is overwhelmingly African American, a Museum of the History of Slavery? Indeed, there is no Museum of the History of Slavery—the whole story, starting with the slave trade in Africa itself, not just selected parts, such as the Underground Railroad—anywhere in the United States. This, it seems, is a memory judged too dangerous to social stability to activate and to create. The Holocaust Memorial Museum and the future Armenian Genocide Museum and Memorial are about events that didn't happen in America, so the memory-work doesn't risk rousing an embittered domestic population against authority. To have a museum chronicling the great crime that was African slavery in the United States of America would be to acknowledge that the evil was *here*. Americans prefer to picture the evil that was *there*, and from which the United States—a unique nation, one without any certifiably wicked leaders throughout its entire history—is exempt. That this country, like every other country, has its tragic past does not sit well with the founding, and still all-powerful, belief in American exceptionalism. The national consensus on American history as a history of progress is a new setting for distressing photographs—one that focuses our attention on wrongs, both here and elsewhere, for which America sees itself as the solution or cure.

Susan Sontag

One of America's leading social commentators, Susan Sontag (1933–2004) was hailed as a brilliant critic and provocative thinker. Raised in Arizona and California, she studied at a number of universities, among them the University of Chicago, Harvard, and Oxford. Her formal schooling finished, she soon began writing essays for *The New Yorker*, *The New York Review of Books*, and other magazines.

Beginning in 1964 with "Notes on Camp," a penetrating essay on the avant-garde, Sontag's work was both widely discussed and well received. She published two groundbreaking collections of essays on culture and politics in the 1960s: *Against Interpretation* (1966) and *Styles of Radical Will* (1969). Over the next several decades she continued to explore a wide range of cultural phenomena, from illness to art. In later years she published work in other genres, including a best-selling historical novel, *The Volcano Lover* (1992).

The selection presented here is taken from *Regarding the Pain of Others* (2003), a book on war imagery in which the author decried the birth of a "culture of spectatorship," arguing that it "neutralized the moral force of photographs of atrocities."

Another selection by Sontag, an excerpt from "On Photography," appears on pages 304–07.

SEEING

1. Sontag's essay is dense with provocative statements and questions about the cultural functions and meanings of photography. Create an outline of her essay in which you title and then paraphrase each of her core arguments. List the examples she uses to support each assertion. To what extent do you agree with each of her points?

2. Review your outline, and imagine that you are going to elaborate on each of Sontag's points in an essay. Find at least one additional image – from this book or another source – that refutes or supports each argument. Cite the source of each image, and note how you would use it.

Responding Visually

"Photographs lay down routes of reference, and serve as totems of causes," writes Sontag; "Sentiment is more likely to crystalize around a photograph than around a verbal slogan" (para. 8). Choose a cause you believe in, and create an image to serve as its totem. You might take a photograph, draw a picture, or make a collage. Using an image, what is the minimum number of words you need to clearly communicate – and to generate sympathy for – your cause? Now create another version of your piece using only words. Did you find it necessary to add words? Which version do you and your classmates find more compelling? Why?

WRITING

1. Sontag writes that "the Holocaust Memorial Museum and the future Armenian Genocide Museum and Memorial are about events that didn't happen in America, so the memory-work doesn't risk rousing an embittered domestic population against authority. To have a museum chronicling the great crime that was African slavery in the United States of America would be to acknowledge that the evil was *here*" (para. 11). To what extent do you agree with Sontag's statement? Imagine that your town or city is considering a proposal for a museum of the history of slavery. Write an argumentative essay in which you argue for or against the proposal. Should the history of slavery be commemorated in a "memory museum"? Why or why not?

Working with Sources

2. What does Sontag mean when she writes in paragraph 6 that "photographs echo photographs: It was inevitable that the photographs of emaciated Bosnian prisoners at Omarska, the Serb death camp created in northern Bosnia in 1992, would recall memories of the photographs taken in the Nazi death camps in 1945"? Begin by conducting Internet searches for *Omarska* and *Nazi death camps*. Then look for examples of other photographs that "echo" each other. Write an expository essay in which you explain Sontag's statement by analyzing two additional sets of photographs that echo each other.

If someone walked into my room and observed me trying to get started writing, the person would see me sitting in a swivel chair in my bedroom. I would be wearing a pair of jeans and playing music. I would spend several minutes surfing the Internet and playing solitaire. Finally I would get started writing . . . that is, of course, if my nails were adequately clipped.

Andy Coen, student at
Southern Polytechnic State University

For me, the only way to write is to first spend a considerable amount of time not writing. And that, come to think of it, may be my form of inspiration: procrastination. Sure, it may look, from a distance, like I'm lazily cleaning out my navel, but beneath the surface my mind is getting ready to write. My navel isn't a cheap excuse for me to put off writing—rather, it's an integral partner in my writing process.

Tim Carvell, former writer for
The Daily Show with Jon Stewart

RETROSPECT—Picturing War

The Civil War

Alexander Gardner
Home of a Rebel Sharpshooter, Gettysburg, July, 1863

World War I

The Men of the 308th, the "Lost Battalion," April 28, 1919

World War II

Robert Capa
Omaha Beach, June 6, 1944

The Korean War

Greenhouse Dog, 1951

The Vietnam War

Nick Ut
Children Fleeing a Napalm Strike, Vietnam, June 8, 1972

The Iraq War

Jean-Marc Bouju
Iraqi Man at a Regroupment Center for POWs, Najaf, Iraq, March 31, 2003

My favorite kind of writing
is poetry because it is
the marriage of beauty
and rigorous thought.

Nii Martey Codjoe, student at
Southern Polytechnic State University

A poet is, before anything
else, a person who
is passionately in love
with language.

W. H. Auden, poet

LOOKING CLOSER—
Altering Images

Is seeing really believing? Photographs may never have been the documents of truth that they initially were assumed to be, and now the accessibility of digital technology has made it possible for even home-computer users to alter the look of a holiday portrait. Doctoring family snapshots may seem benign, but what are the ethics associated with altering images that appear in popular media? And what responsibility comes with fabricating an image of public figures? See, for example, the illustration of President Barack Obama and First Lady Michelle Obama that appeared on the cover of *The New Yorker* during the 2008 presidential campaign.

As Mitchell Stephens describes in "Expanding the Language of Photographs," magazines and advertisers have a history of enhancing and manipulating photographs. George Hunt's photograph is evidence that photo-doctoring has long been a staple of government propaganda, and the recent hoax photo created from Lance Cheung's and Charles Maxwell's images reminds us that the debate over tampering with images remains as heated as ever. In "Ethics in the Age of Digital Photography," John Long underscores how easily—and frequently—the manipulation of images can occur at a time when digital imagery is widely available to and understood by the general public.

EXPANDING THE LANGUAGE
OF PHOTOGRAPHS
Mitchell Stephens

A photo on the front page of *New York Newsday* on Feb. 16, 1994, showed two well-known Olympic ice skaters, Tonya Harding and Nancy Kerrigan, practicing together. By the standards of the tabloid war then raging in New York City (a war *New York Newsday* would not survive), this shot of Harding and the fellow skater she had been accused of plotting to assault did not seem particularly incendiary. But there was something extraordinary about this photograph: The scene it depicted had not yet taken place. Harding and Kerrigan, as the paper admitted in the caption, had not in fact practiced together. A computer had stitched together two separate images to make it appear as if they already had.

Newsday was certainly not the first publication to have taken advantage of techniques that allow for the digital manipulation of photographs. In 1982, for example, a *National Geographic* computer had nudged two pyramids closer together so that they might more comfortably fit the magazine's cover. In July 1992, *Texas Monthly* had used a computer to place the head of then-Gov. Ann Richards on top of the body of a model riding a Harley-Davidson motorcycle. But you had to be an expert on pyramids to figure out what *National Geographic* had done, and you had to miss a fairly broad joke to take umbrage with *Texas Monthly*. *New York Newsday*'s editors had fiddled with photos featuring two of the most talked-about individuals of the day, and they weren't joking. The results of their efforts were clearly visible on newsstands all over Manhattan.

Defenders of journalism's accuracy and reliability quickly grabbed their lances and mounted their steeds: "A composite photograph is not the truth," Stephen D. Isaacs, then acting dean of the Columbia Graduate School of Journalism, thundered. "It is a lie and, therefore, a great danger to the standards and integrity of what we do." The dean of the S. I. Newhouse School of Public Communication at Syracuse University, David M. Rubin, concluded that "*New York Newsday* has taken leave of its ethical moorings."

This front-page photo in a major daily seemed to announce that craven journalists had found a powerful new way to debase themselves: computer reworkings of photographs.

5   Others of us, however, heard a different announcement on that winter day in 1994: *Newsday*'s rather ordinary-looking attempt to further exploit

an unpleasant, mostly unimportant story, we believed, was an early indication that news images might finally be coming of age.

To understand the significance of *New York Newsday*'s digital manipulation of this photograph, it is first necessary to acknowledge all the other ways photographs are manipulated. Photographers choose angles, making sure, for example, that the crowd of reporters isn't in the shot. They use filters, adjust contrast, and vary depth of field. They frame and crop, and routinely transform reds, blues, and yellows into blacks, grays, and whites. Aren't these distortions of sorts?

It is also necessary to acknowledge the ways in which we manipulate language. Words are routinely arranged so that they describe events that are not currently occurring, as in the sentence: "Nancy Kerrigan and Tonya Harding will practice together." Words are even deployed in tenses that describe events that likely will not or definitely will not occur: "She might have won the gold medal." And words frequently speak of one thing as if it were another: Despite its proximity to New York harbor, *New York Newsday* did not literally possess "ethical moorings." Deans Isaacs and Rubin, for all their devotion to journalistic integrity, probably did not grab lances or mount steeds. In their efforts to approach the truth, words regularly depart from the literal truth.

In fact, words have gained much of their strength through speculation, negation, hypothesizing, and metaphor—through what, by Dean Isaacs's definition, might qualify as lies. In the first century and a half of their existence, photographic images, on the other hand, have been held back by their inability to speak of what will be, what might be, and what won't be; their inability to present something as if it were something else. "Pictures," the theorist Sol Worth wrote dismissively in 1975, "cannot depict conditionals, counter-factuals, negatives, or past future tenses." Well, now they can. Alert observers of journalism learned that on Feb. 16, 1994.

The above-board computer manipulation of photographs will give responsible journalists—those with their ethical moorings intact—a powerful new tool. Sometimes the results will be fanciful: an image of Bill Clinton and Newt Gingrich arm wrestling, perhaps. Sometimes such computer-altered photographs will be instructive: They might picture, for example, how that plane should have landed. Such reworked photos will allow us to peek, however hazily, into the future: showing not just how Harding and Kerrigan might look together on the ice but how that new building might change the neighborhood. They will also allow us to peek into the past: portraying, with photographic realism (not, as in TV reenactments, with clumsy actors), how a crime might have been committed. The idea should be to clarify, not to pretend.

10   For news photographs will not come of age by hoodwinking those who look at them. That must be emphasized. Before digital editing and digital photography, harried photographers occasionally rearranged backgrounds or restaged scenes; adept photo editors, armed with a thick black pencil, occasionally added hair where there was too little or subtracted a chin where there were too many. Computers make such attempts to deceive much easier but no more conscionable. There is no doubt that they have been used for such purposes already. *Time* magazine's surreptitious digital darkening of O. J. Simpson's face on its cover later in 1994 may qualify as an example. But *New York Newsday*'s Harding–Kerrigan photo was labeled as a "composite." "Tomorrow, they'll really take to the ice together" the paper explained on that front page, though not in as large type as we journalism professors would have liked.

Here is a standard journalism deans might more reasonably champion: Digitally manipulated photographs must not be used as a tool for deceiving. They must be labeled, clearly, as what they are. (Let's take a hard line on this, initially at least: no lightening of a shadow, no blurring of an inconvenient background without some sort of acknowledgment.) But the potential these photographs offer as a tool for communicating honestly must not be suppressed.

With the aid of computers, photographic images will be able to show us much more than just what might present itself at any one time to a well-situated lens, as words tell us about much more than just what is, at any one time, literally the case. And computers will be able to work this magic on moving as well as still photographic images, on television news video as well as newspaper and magazine photographs.

None of this should be that hard to imagine. The computer-produced graphics that increasingly illustrate print and television news stories have been perpetrating clever and effective reimaginings of reality for many years now: politicians' faces matched with piles of dollar bills, the affected states jumping out of maps, items flying in and out of shopping carts. And all this has been happening without attracting the ire of the defenders of journalism's integrity.

The notion that news photographs themselves—or just cartoon-like graphics—are subject to these new types of alteration will take some getting used to. The labels will have to be very clear, their type very large— particularly at the start. For we have been in the habit of accepting photography as what one of its inventors, William Henry Fox Talbot, called "the pencil of nature." That was always something of a misperception. Now, if we are to take advantage of the great promise of digital technology, we'll have to wise up.

15   For computers are going to expand our control over this pencil dramatically. Journalists will have unprecedented ability to shape the meanings their photographs, not just their sentences, can communicate. Their pictures will approach issues from many new directions. The language of photojournalism will grow. And that is good news for those who struggle to report with images.

George Hunt
Untitled, c. 1880s

ETHICS IN THE AGE
OF DIGITAL PHOTOGRAPHY
John Long

Two disclaimers need to be stated before we begin:

1. My purpose is not to give answers. My purpose is to provide you with a vocabulary so you can discuss the ethical issues that may arise when using computers to process photographs. I also want to present the principles I have found helpful when trying to make decisions of an ethical nature. I do not expect everyone to agree with me. I want you to think about the issues and arrive at your own conclusions in a logical and reasoned manner.
2. The advent of computers and digital photography has not created the need for a whole new set of ethical standards. We are not dealing with something brand new. We merely have a new way of processing images, and the same principles that have guided us in traditional photojournalism should be the principles that guide us in the use of the computers. This fact makes dealing with computer-related ethics far less daunting than if we had to begin from square one.

We have many problems in journalism today that threaten our profession and in fact threaten the Constitution of our country. Photo ops, lack of access to news events, rock show contracts, yellow tape, and bean counters are just a few. Everyone has a spin; everyone wants to control the news media. We are under attack from all sides.

One of the major problems we face as photojournalists is the fact that the public is losing faith in us. Our readers and viewers no longer believe everything they see. All images are called into question because the computer has proved that images are malleable, changeable, fluid. In movies, advertisements, TV shows, magazines, we are constantly exposed to images created or changed by computers. As William J. Mitchell points out in his book *The Reconfigured Eye, Visual Truth in the Post-Photographic Era* we are experiencing a paradigm shift in how we define the nature of a photograph. The photograph is no longer a fixed image; it has become a watery mix of moveable pixels, and this is changing how we perceive what a photograph is. The bottom line is that documentary photojournalism is the last vestige of the real photography.

Journalists have only one thing to offer the public and that is CREDIBILITY. This is the first vocabulary word I want you to remember, and the most important. Without credibility we have nothing. We might as well go sell widgets door to door since without the trust of the public we cannot exist as a profession.

5   Our credibility is damaged every time a reputable news organization is caught lying to the public, and one of the most blatant and widely recognized cases was the computer enhancement of the *Time* magazine cover photo of O. J. Simpson. *Time* took the mug shot of Simpson when he was arrested and changed it before using it on their cover. They would not have been caught if *Newsweek* had not used the same photo on their cover photo just as it had come from the police. The two covers showed up on the newsstands next to each other, and the public could see something was wrong.

Time darkened the handout photo, creating a five o'clock shadow and a more sinister look. They darkened the top of the photo and made the police lineup numbers smaller. They decided Simpson was guilty so they made him look guilty. (There are two issues here: One is a question of photographic ethics and the other is a question of racial insensitivity by *Time* in deciding that blacker means guiltier. The black community raised this issue when the story broke, and [it] needs to be the subject of another article. My concern is with the issue of photographic ethics.)

In an editorial the next week, *Time*'s managing editor wrote, "The harshness of the mug shot—the merciless bright light, the stubble on Simpson's face, the cold specificity of the picture—had been subtly smoothed and shaped into an icon of tragedy." In other words, they changed the photo from what it was (a document) into what they wanted it to be. *Time* was making an editorial statement, not reporting the news. They presented what looked like a real photograph and it turned out not to be real; the public felt deceived, and rightly so. By doing this, *Time* damaged their credibility and the credibility of all journalists.

In order to have a rational, logical discussion of ethics, a distinction needs to be drawn between ethics and taste. *Ethics* refers to issues of deception, or lying. *Taste* refers to issues involving blood, sex, violence, and other aspects of life we do not want to see in our morning paper as we eat breakfast. Not everyone defines *taste–ethics* this way, but I find it useful. Issues of taste can cause a few subscription cancellations and letters to the editor, but they tend to evaporate in a few days. Ethics violations damage credibility, and the effects can last for years. Once you damage your credibility, it is next to impossible to get it back.

The photo of the dead American soldier being dragged through the streets of Mogadishu raises issues of taste, not issues of ethics. This photo is a fair and accurate representation of what happened in Somalia that day. (I hesitate to use the word *truthful*. Truth is a loaded concept, open to personal interpretation. What is true for one person may not be true for another. I prefer to use the terms *fair* and *accurate*. These terms are more precise, though not completely without debate over their meaning.)

10   If we are to use this photo, a photo that is ethically correct but definitely of questionable taste (no one wants to see dead American soldiers in the newspaper), we need to have a compelling reason. Earlier I mentioned I would give you some principles that I find useful, and this is the first: If the public needs the information in the photo in order to make informed choices for society, then we must run the photo. We cannot make informed choices for our society unless we have access to fair and accurate information. A free society is based on this right. It is codified in our country as the First Amendment. We have to know what is happening in our towns, in our country, in our world, in order to make decisions that affect us as a society. The First Amendment does not belong to the press; it belongs to the American people. It guarantees all of us the right to the fair and accurate information we need to be responsible citizens.

We needed to see the dead soldier in the streets so we could make an informed choice as a country as to the correctness of our being in Somalia. Words can tell us the facts, but photos hit us in the gut. They give us the real meaning, the deep and emotional impact of what was happening, much better than words can. As a society we decided that we needed to leave that country.

I feel bad for the family of the soldier, but sometimes the needs of the many outweigh the needs of the few, or the one. In our country, we have the right to our privacy (usually the Sixth Amendment is cited) but we also have to live together and act collectively. This need is addressed by the First Amendment: "Congress shall make no law respecting an establishment of religion, or prohibiting the free exercise thereof; or abridging the freedom of speech or of the press; or the right of the people peaceably to assemble, and to petition the government for a redress of grievances."

Honest photographs can have an ethical dimension when it concerns the personal ethics of the photographer. Did the photographer violate some ethical standard in the process of making the picture?

For example, take the very famous photo of the young child dying in Sudan while a vulture stands behind her, waiting. It was taken by Kevin Carter, who won a Pulitzer Prize for the photo (a photo that raised a lot of money for the relief agencies). He was criticized for not helping the child; he replied there were relief workers there to do that. After receiving his Pulitzer, Kevin Carter returned to Africa and committed suicide. He had a lot of problems in his life but, with the timing of the sequence of events, I cannot help thinking there is a correlation between his photographing the child and his suicide.

15   This is the kind of choice all journalists will face sometime in [their] career; maybe not in the extreme situation that Carter faced, but in some way, we all will be faced with choices of helping or photographing. Someday we will be at a fire or a car accident and we will be called upon to put the camera down and help. It is a good idea to think about these issues in advance because when the hour comes, it will come suddenly and we will be asked to make a choice quickly.

Here is the principle that works for me. It is not a popular one and it is one that many journalists disagree with, but it allows me to sleep at night. If you have placed yourself in the position where you can help, you are morally obligated to help. I do not ask you to agree with me. I just want you to think about this and be prepared: At what point do you put the camera down and help? At what point does your humanity become more important than your journalism?

It is time to get back to the theme of this report—the ethics involved with the use of computers to process images.

I like the *Weekly World News*. It provides a constant source of photos for these discussions about ethics. One of the more famous front pages shows a space alien shaking hands with President Clinton. It is a wonderful photo, guaranteed to make the career of any photographer who manages to get an exclusive shot of this event.

We can laugh at this photo, and I have no real problem with the *Weekly World News* running such digitally created photos because of the context of where this photo is running. This is the second of the vocabulary words I want to give you: CONTEXT. Where the photo runs makes all the difference in the world. If this same photo ran on the front page of the *New York Times*, it would damage the credibility of the *Times*. In the context of *Weekly World News*, it cannot damage their credibility because that newspaper does not have any credibility to begin with (it seems we need to create a new set of terms when we can refer to the *Weekly World News* and the *New York Times* both as newspapers).

20   Context becomes a problem when we find digitally altered photos in reputable publications, and there have been many. For example, the cover of *Texas Monthly* once ran a photo of then Governor Ann Richards astride a Harley-Davidson motorcycle. It came out that the only part of the photo that was Ann Richards was her head. The body on the motorcycle belonged to a model, and the head of the governor was electronically attached to the model.

On the credit page in very small type, the editors claimed they explained what they had done and that this disclosure exonerated them. They wrote:

Cover photograph by Jim Myers

Styling by Karen Eubank

Accessories courtesy of Rancho Loco, Dallas; boots courtesy of Boot Town, Dallas; motorcycle and leather jacket courtesy of Harley-Davidson, Dallas; leather pants by Patricia Wolfe

Stock photograph (head shot) by Kevin Vandivier / Texastock

In the first place this was buried on the bottom of a page very few people look at, in a type size few over 40 can read, and was worded in a way as to be incomprehensible.

Secondly, my feeling is that no amount of captioning can forgive a visual lie. In the context of news, if a photo looks real, it better be real. This photo looked real, but it was a fake. We have an obligation to history to leave behind us a collection of real photographs. This photo of Ann Richards entered into the public domain, and on the day she lost her reelection bid, AP ran the photo on the wire for its clients. AP had to run a mandatory kill when they were informed it was not a real photo.

Janet Cooke was a reporter at the *Washington Post* who won a Pulitzer Prize in 1981 for a story she wrote about an 8-year-old heroin addict named Jimmy. The prize was taken back and she was fired when it was discovered that she made up the story. Can you imagine if the *Post* put a disclaimer in italics at the end of the story when it first ran, that said something along these lines: "We know this exact kid does not exist, but we also know this kind of thing does happen and so we created this one composite kid to personalize the story. Even though Jimmy does not exist, you can believe everything else we wrote." The *Post* would have been the laughing stock of the industry, and yet this is what *Texas Monthly* is doing by captioning away a visual lie. You have to have the same respect for the visual image as you have for the written word. You do not lie with words, nor should you lie with photographs.

In one of the early Digital Conferences, the Reverend Don Doll, S.J., pointed out that there are degrees of changes that can be done electronically to a photograph. There are technical changes that deal only with the aspects of photography that make the photo more readable, such as a little dodging and burning, global color correction, and contrast control. These are all part of the grammar of photography, just as there is a grammar associated with words (sentence structure, capital letters, paragraphs) that makes it possible to read a story, so there is a grammar of photography that allows us to read a photograph. These changes (like their darkroom counterparts) are neither ethical nor unethical—they are merely technical.

25   Changes to content can be Accidental or Essential (this is an old Aristotelian distinction)—Essential changes change the meaning of the photograph, and Accidental changes change useless details but do not change the real meaning. Some changes are obviously more important than others. Accidental changes are not as important as Essential changes, but both kinds are still changes.

If you had a photograph of a bride and groom and removed the groom, this would constitute an Essential change because it would change the meaning of the photograph. (In fact, there are companies that will provide this service if you get a divorce. I guess the wedding book would end up looking like the bride got all dressed up and married herself.)

In the two photos of the ladies on the parade float,[1] the photo on the left has a set of wires running behind the ladies. In the photo on the right, the lines have been removed. It takes only a few seconds with the cloning tool in Photoshop to remove these lines. Removing the lines is an Accidental change, a change of meaningless details. If we had changed the flag to a Confederate flag, or removed a couple of the ladies, this would have changed the meaning of the photo and it would have been an Essential change. But if we just remove the lines, what is the big deal? Who is harmed? As far as I am concerned, we are all harmed by any lie, big or small.

I do not think the public cares if it is a little lie or a big lie. As far as they are concerned, once the shutter has been tripped and the MOMENT has been captured on film, in the context of news, we no longer have the right to change the content of the photo in any way. Any change to a news photo—any violation of that MOMENT—is a lie. Big or small, any lie damages your credibility.

The reason I get so adamant when I discuss this issue is that the documentary photograph is a very powerful thing, and its power is based on the fact that it is real. The real photograph gives us a window on history; it allows us to be present at the great events of our times and the past. It gets its power from the fact that it represents exactly what the photographer saw through the medium of photography. The raw reality it depicts, the verisimilitude makes the documentary photo come alive. Look at the photo of Robert Kennedy dying on the floor of the hotel in California; look at the works of David Douglas Duncan or the

---

1. For reasons of space and copyright, we are unable to reproduce these two photos. [Eds.]

other great war photographers; look at the photo of Martin Luther King martyred on the balcony of a motel in Memphis. The power of these photographs comes from the fact they are real moments in time captured as they happened, unchanged. To change any detail in any of these photographs diminishes their power and turns them into lies. They would no longer be what the photographer saw but what someone else wanted the scene to be. The integrity of the Moment would be destroyed in favor of the editorial concept being foisted, as is the case in the O. J. Simpson *Time* cover.

30   There have been many cases of digital manipulation over the past twenty years or so, the first of note being the famous pyramids cover of *National Geographic* in 1982. *National Geographic* had a horizontal photo of the pyramids in Egypt and wanted to make a vertical cover from it. They put the photo in a computer and squeezed the pyramids together—a difficult task in real life but an easy task for the computer. They referred to it as the "retroactive repositioning of the photographer" (one of the great euphemisms of our age), saying that if the photographer had been a little to one side or the other, this is what he would have gotten. The photographer was not ten feet to the right and he did not get the photo they wanted, so they created a visual lie. They damaged their credibility, and (as I said before) taste issues have a short life span, ethics issues do not go away. Here we are almost twenty year later, and we are still talking about what *Geographic* did.

Sports Illustrated recently produced a special edition for Connecticut on the UConn national championship basketball season. In one photo, they showed a star player, Ricky Moore, going up for a layup with another player, Kevin Freeman, in the frame. They also used the same photo on the cover of the regular edition of the magazine, cropped tighter but with Kevin Freeman removed. I guess he cluttered up the cover, so he was expendable.

The point I want to make here is that if *Sports Illustrated* had not used the same photo twice, they would not have been caught. The computer allows for seamless changes that are impossible to see, and if you shoot with an electronic camera, you do not even have film to act as a referent. How many times has *Sports Illustrated* or *Time* or *Newsweek* or any of a long list of newspapers and magazines changed a photo and we the reading public not known about it? This is the Pandora's box of the computer age.

It is not just in the computer that photographers and editors can lie. We can lie by setting up photos or by being willing partners to photo ops. These things are as big, if not bigger, threats to our profession as the computers. The *L.A. Times* ran a photo of a fireman dousing his head with water from a swimming pool as a house burned in the background. In doing preparations for contest entries, they discovered that the photographer had said to the fireman something along the lines of, "You know what would make a good photo? If you went over by the pool and poured water on your head." The photo was a setup. It was withdrawn from competition, and the photographer was disciplined severely.

This is as much a lie as what can be done in Photoshop. Neither is acceptable.

35 "A Day in the Life" series of books has a long history of manipulated covers. In *A Day in the Life of California*, for example, the photo was shot on a gray day as a horizontal. The hand came from another frame; the surfboard was moved closer to the surfer's head, and the sky was made blue to match his eyes. They had about 30,000 images to pick from and could not find one that looked like California to them, so they had to create an image—an image of what they wanted California to look like.

The list can go on for pages: *Newsweek* straightened the teeth of Bobbi McCaughey, the mother of the septuplets; *Newsday* ran a photo supposedly showing Nancy Kerrigan and Tonya Harding skating together a day before the event really happened; *People* ran a photo of famous breast cancer survivors made from five separate negatives; the *St. Louis Post Dispatch* removed a Coke can from a photo of their Pulitzer Prize winner. This just scratches the surface. How many cases have not become known? The cumulative effect is the gradual erosion of the credibility of [the] entire profession, and I am not sure we can win this war. We are being bombarded from all sides, from movies, television, advertisements, the Internet, with images that are not real, that are created in computers, and documentary photojournalism is the victim.

We may be in a death struggle, but the end is worth fighting for. Real photos can change the hearts and minds of the people. Real photographs can change how we view war and how we view our society. Vietnam is a prime example. Two photos sum up that war: the Nick Ut photo of the girl burned by napalm running naked down the street and the Eddie Adams photo of the man being executed on the streets of Saigon. These photos changed how we perceived that war. They are powerful, and they get their power from the fact that they are real Moments captured for all time on film.

No one has the right to change these photos or the content of any documentary photo. It is our obligation to history to make sure this does not happen.

©Lance Cheung, U.S. Air Force

Lance Cheung
Members of the 129th Rescue Squadron,
Moffitt Federal Airfield, CA, 2001

Charles Maxwell
Breaching Great White Shark,
South Africa

"THE Photo of the Year," 2001 (hoax photograph)

"and you think your [sic] having a bad day at work!! Although this looks like a
picture taken from a Hollywood movie, it is in fact a real photo, taken near the South
African coast during a military exercise by the British Navy. It has been nominated
by National Geographic as 'THE photo of the year'."

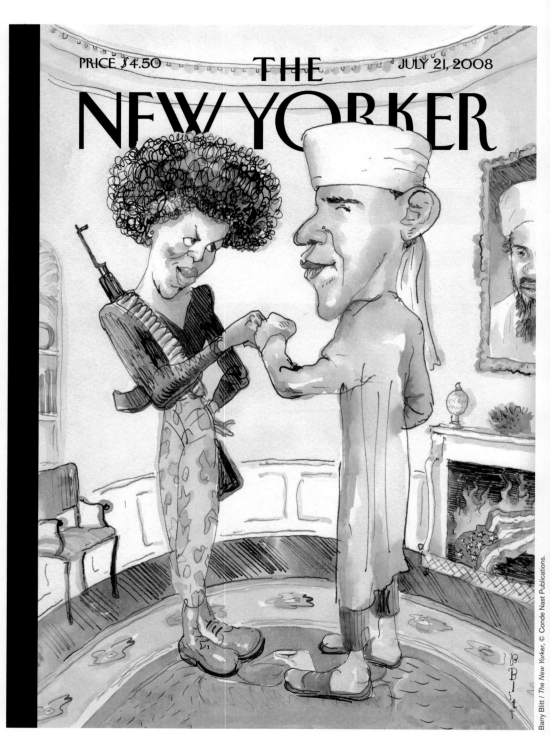

Barry Blitt
The Politics of Fear, 2008

Taking a Stand / 678

THE POLITICS OF THE
RETOUCHED HEADSHOT
Virginia Postrel

Last week, Fox News set off a short-lived controversy when it attacked *Newsweek* for not retouching the magazine's larger-than-life cover photo of Sarah Palin. Calling the headshot "ridiculously unfair to her," anchor Megyn Kelly declared that "any respectable magazine should be doing a little retouching."

Demanding that a news magazine manipulate photos in order to remain "respectable" may seem odd, all the more so since Governor Palin looks quite attractive in the photograph. But the criticism reveals more than ratings-plumping partisan grievance. In an image-savvy culture, we're increasingly forced to consider just what constitutes a valid portrait. The way most of us instinctively answer the question demonstrates the difference between objectivity and truth.

Consider the apolitical act of selecting a personal headshot: a bridal photo, a web site image, an author portrait. You don't just face the camera and accept the first photo that comes out. That's for driver's licenses, mug shots, and security badges—the ID photo most people find not only embarrassing but somehow untrue. At the very least, you want to choose a shot where your eyes are open, your smile looks genuine, and your cowlick is under control.

If strangers' snap judgments matter, you go for a bit more artifice. Take an attractive single friend of mine. When she moved to Los Angeles, she signed up with an online dating service, using a handy snapshot to illustrate her profile. She got no inquiries. Then she hired one of the many local photographers who specialize in actors' headshots. With exactly the same profile information but a more professional photo, my friend was suddenly inundated with emails from prospective dates. She didn't even use retouching or special makeup. The difference, she says, "was the lighting, the camera angles, plus the *sheer volume* of shots." She had hundreds to choose from.

5   Partisans demand that magazine portraits glamorize their heroes for the same reason my friend hired a professional photographer. Humans seem hard-wired to assume that good-looking means good and, conversely, to equate physical flaws with character flaws. We may preach that beauty is skin deep, but we're equally certain that portraits "reveal character." In a media culture, we not only judge strangers by how they look

but by the *images* of how they look. So we want attractive pictures of our heroes and repulsive images of our enemies.

Consider a recent political controversy involuntarily involving this magazine. After taking a series of shots for a conventional cover portrait of John McCain, Jill Greenberg tricked the candidate into having a picture taken in which she lit him from below, a classic technique to make the subject look evil. Neither the candidate nor his staff noticed that the photographer had literally cast McCain in a bad light. "I guess they're not very sophisticated," she told the online magazine *PDN*, boasting further that she hadn't retouched the neutral shot she sold *The Atlantic*. "I left his eyes red and his skin looking bad," she said.

As this story illustrates, having a portrait taken for publication demands a great deal of trust in the competence and good will of the photographer and photo editor. Greenberg deceived not only McCain but *The Atlantic*, which objected strenuously to the abuse of trust. But suppose the magazine had been in on the ruse. Does a portrait subject have a reasonable expectation of normal lighting?

Most people would say yes. In fact, except for professional models, photo subjects generally expect the wedding album standard to apply: Photos should look realistic, but as attractive as possible. Anything else, whatever artistic justification the photographer or editor may put forward, feels like an ambush. Nobody voluntarily agrees to an unappealing portrait.

After *The New York Times Magazine* used nonstandard film to shoot a 2006 cover picture of Virginia Governor Mark Warner, the publication apologized because the film altered the photo's colors, making Warner's gray suit appear maroon. But critics objected not only to the artificial colors but to what seemed like a deliberately unnatural and disturbing image of the governor, one that Gawker described as giving "off that smarmy politician vibe that made you turn over the magazine on your coffee table so you didn't have to keep looking at him."

10 Every portrait is inherently false: a static, two-dimensional representation of an ever-changing, three-dimensional face. And accuracy is not the same thing as truth. Even without deliberate distortions, a still photo captures distractions that the mind edits out. Some retouching is nothing more than recreating on paper the image held in memory—removing, for instance, a bit of red from McCain's eyes or a stray eyebrow hair from *Newsweek*'s Palin picture.

Like atypically good lighting, such manipulation is designed to create a "truer," more representative image by omitting quirks of the moment. "When I did my self-portrait," said Andy Warhol, "I left all the pimples out because you always should. Pimples are a temporary condition and they don't have anything to do with what you really look like. Always omit the blemishes—they're not a part of the good picture you want." An "objective" candid shot can be as biased as a heavily retouched photograph.

Candid shots are particularly perilous for people with animated faces, who illustrate their speech with bulging eyes or distorted mouths. In person, they look lively and entertaining. But, in between more flattering expressions, they produce a lot of strange shots. That's why Hillary Clinton's enemies have no trouble finding silly photos of her, while Barack Obama's foes must make do with shots in which the candidate isn't gazing glamorously upward. Obama's cool countenance makes weird candid shots less common.

As Hillary Clinton can attest, a good portrait is not a random selection of what the camera sees, with no subjective input from human observers. A good portrait offers not mechanical objectivity but what the historians of science Lorraine Daston and Peter Galison in their 2007 book *Objectivity* call "truth to nature," the standard Enlightenment naturalists used in their scientific atlases. "They conceived of fidelity," write Daston and Galison, "in terms of the exercise of informed judgment in the selection of 'typical,' 'characteristic,' 'ideal,' or 'average' images: all these were varieties of the reasoned image."

Like an eighteenth-century atlas maker illustrating a species of lily, portraiture chooses one image at one moment to stand for the complexities of a personality and a life. That's why partisans are vigilant about biased selection. They know that an editor can craft an impression just by picking the right—or wrong—picture. When we select our own photos, we choose the most attractive ones not only because we want others to think of us that way, but because we want to believe that others see us as we'd like to see ourselves. We like to think that even between takes we look our best.

15 A reasoned image is true, even if—in fact, *because*—it excludes the accidental details of the moment. Flattering portraits go further, transforming the characteristic into the ideal without losing sight of the truth. In the early seventeenth century, Ferdinando Gonzaga, the Duke of Mantua, praised a portrait of his wife Caterina de' Medici in words that might guide today's retouchers. "You have depicted her better than any other," he wrote to Alessandro Tiarini, "since you have improved and embellished her looks without diminishing her likeness."

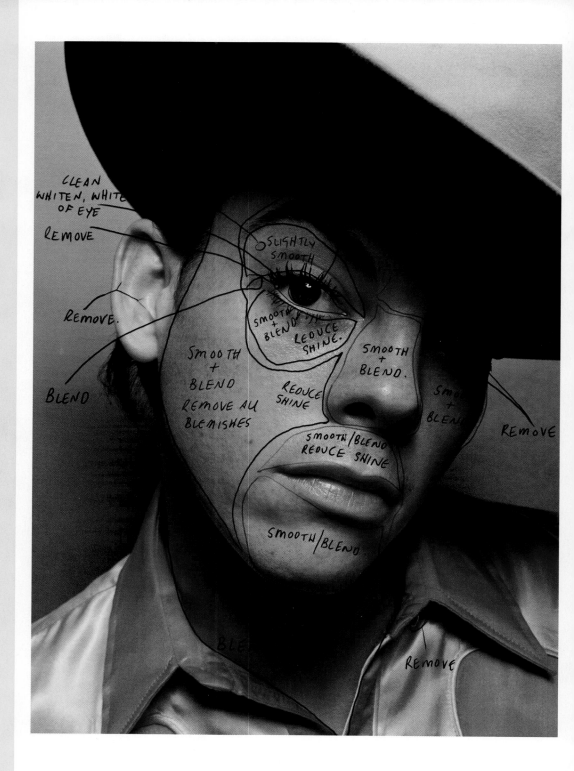

Rankin
Bootiful

Mitchell Stephens

An acclaimed commentator on the history and practice of journalism, Mitchell Stephens has written on the topic for newspapers and has also published several journalism textbooks. His general-interest publications include *A History of News* (3rd ed., 2006) and *The Rise of the Image, the Fall of the Word* (1998). In the latter work he challenges the belief that "visual" information is eroding the intelligence of the news audience, arguing instead that future viewers will become as adept at reading the subtleties of moving pictures and images as they now are at understanding the nuances of language.

Born in 1949, Stephens teaches journalism and mass communications at New York University. He recently spent a year traveling abroad, reporting on globalization for NPR's *On the Media*. He is currently writing a book on the history of atheism entitled *Without Gods*.

George Hunt

Anthropologist Franz Boas (1858–1942) and consultant/photographer George Hunt (1854–1933) were members of a late-nineteenth-century expedition to study and record the indigenous cultures of the Pacific Northwest, which were facing increasing Westernization. While cameras provided an ideal tool for capturing daily life and cultural practices, the still-cumbersome technology created ample opportunities for staging or manipulating "authentic" culture. This photograph, featured in an American Museum of Natural History exhibition, shows Boas (left) and Hunt (right) preparing a backdrop for a photo depicting a Kwakiutl woman making a cedar-bark weaving.

John Long

Former president of the National Press Photographers Association (1989–1990) and chair of its Ethics/Standards Committee, John Long recently left his position of editor and photographer at the *Hartford Courant* to teach photojournalism and ethics at Syracuse University.

The essay reprinted here was written in 1999. Long feels strongly that certain principles must guide photojournalists: "Each day when you step out onto the street, remember that you have been granted a sacred trust to be truthful. You have the responsibility to produce only honest images. You have no right to set up pictures; you have no right to stage the news; you have no right to distort the facts. Your fellow citizens trust you. If you destroy the credibility of your work, *even in small ways*, it destroys the credibility of your newspaper or TV station in the eyes of the people you are covering."

Hoax Photograph

This image, purportedly *National Geographic*'s "photo of the year," began circulating on the Internet in August 2001. By August 2002, its staff overwhelmed with inquiries, the magazine officially declared the image a hoax. It is actually a composite of a U.S. Air Force photograph of an HH-60G Pave Hawk helicopter taken by Lance Cheung near San Francisco's Golden Gate Bridge, and a photograph of a breaching great white shark taken by South African photographer Charles Maxwell. "I'd like to make contact with the person who did this," said Maxwell, "not to get him or her in trouble, but because it's a lot of fun and it is a good job. However, I must make clear that I would not like to see this happen to one of my photographs again. It is wrong to take images from a web site without permission."

Barry Blitt

The Politics of Fear, by illustrator Barry Blitt, appeared on the cover of *The New Yorker* on July 21, 2008, just months before the historic presidential election. The depiction of Barack and Michelle Obama as terrorists was highly controversial. Both Blitt and *The New Yorker* responded to criticism in the magazine. "I think the idea that the Obamas are branded as unpatriotic (let alone as terrorists) in certain sectors is preposterous," Blitt wrote. "It seemed to me that depicting the concept would show it as the fear-mongering ridiculousness that it is."

Blitt was born in Canada in 1959 and is best known for his cover illustrations for *The New Yorker*. After graduating from Ontario College of Art, he worked in advertising at the Toronto office of the Leo Burnett agency and then at the agency's London office. He moved to New York in 1989. His illustations have appeared in *Newsweek*, *Harper's*, *The Atlantic*, *Entertainment Weekly*, and other magazines. He has also illustrated two children's books. Blitt lives in Connecticut.

Virginia Postrel

In *The Future and Its Enemies: The Growing Conflict over Creativity, Enterprise, and Progress* (1998), Virginia Postrel (b. 1960) argues that people fall into two categories: "stasists," who are resistant to change and try to control the future; and "dynamists," who accept change and thrive on adapting to it. In her view, the notions of "conservative" and "liberal," "left wing" and "right wing" are no longer relevant, since those labeled "conservative" are actually amenable to change while the opposite holds true of those labeled "liberals."

Postrel formulated her theory as an undergraduate at Princeton University and went on to develop it as editor of the magazine *Reason* from 1989 to 2000. Postrel has been a contributing editor at *The Atlantic* and writes regularly for *Forbes* and other magazines. She is also the author of *The Substance of Style: How the Rise of Aesthetic Value Is Remaking Commerce, Culture, and Consciousness* (2003).

Rankin

British-born John Rankin Waddell (b. 1966) has earned an international reputation for his fashion and portrait photography. He began his career in Europe in the early 1990s and has since published many books of his work, including *CeleBritation* (2000), a collection of his celebrity portraits; *Visually Hungry* (2007), a retrospective of his work; and most recently *Beautyfull* (2007).

In 1991 he co-founded the British fashion magazine *Dazed & Confused* to capture what the magazine describes as the "unprecedented explosion of young creative talent in British fashion, music, art, and photography." From that venture sprang Dazed Books, which publishes hip, edgy fashion and photography titles. Rankin also has shot advertising campaigns for numerous products and directed the feature film *The Lives of the Saints* (2006).

"The world he portrays is a 'fake,'" wrote critic Von Jochen Siemens. "Rankin makes his pictures by drawing on the tensions and contradictions and glamour that lie between faked and authentic reality. For example, his photos of faces and heads painted with instructions of what is to be touched up and where. You could almost call it an act of piracy against the fake world of advertising photography—everybody can see how big a lie beauty really is."

SEEING

1. In "Expanding the Language of Photographs," Mitchell Stephens draws a distinction between *Time*'s manipulation of O. J. Simpson's image and *Newsday*'s composite image of Harding and Kerrigan. The former, Stephens argues, is unethical; the latter is not. To what extent do you agree with Stephens? What are the ethics involved in each case? What was manipulated in each instance, and how? Did the editors act ethically in each instance? Why or why not? In your view, is an image used as cover art subject to the same standards as a news photograph?

2. Here is what one critic said after the Kerrigan–Harding photo was printed: "Different standards applied to photographic and textual evidence [indicate] that photographs have a lower status in the editorial hierarchy. Whereas *Time*'s editors would presumably never consider rewriting a quotation from O. J. Simpson, attempting to say it better for him, they evidently felt fewer qualms about altering the police photograph in order to lift . . . 'a common police mug shot to the level of art, with no sacrifice to the truth.'" Do you agree with this distinction? with its implications?

WRITING

1. Stephens argues that manipulating photographs is not unlike choosing words in journalism, that words are shaped and edited. Compare and contrast a news photo and a written report of the same event. How is the event framed visually? verbally? What did the photographer and writer/editor choose to include? to omit? How would you compare the overall point of view and tone of the photograph with the same aspects of the verbal description? Draft an essay in which you argue for – or against – the assertion that visual and verbal material are held to the same standards of evidence in journalism.

2. Draft an argumentative essay in which you agree or disagree with Stephens's proposed standard for labeling manipulated news photos: "Digitally manipulated photographs must not be used as a tool for deceiving. They must be labeled, clearly, as what they are. (Let's take a hard line on this, initially at least: no lightening of a shadow, no blurring of an inconvenient background without some sort of acknowledgment.)" (para. 11).

Appendix A
On the Theory
and Practice
of Seeing

As visual images have become increasingly integrated into our lives, the call to define the term *visual literacy* has grown louder. What does it mean to be visually literate? How exactly do we see? How should we train ourselves to see clearly and read images analytically? How do images affect us? How are images different from or similar to words? How are visual images the products of their cultural contexts? Scholars and cultural commentators in the fields of art history, science, social history, design, and literary and cultural studies have responded to these questions in dozens of studies.

Appendix A presents two fundamental theoretical works: the first essay in John Berger's *Ways of Seeing* and the sixth chapter (entitled "Show and Tell") in Scott McCloud's *Understanding Comics: The Invisible Art*.

Of his book *Ways of Seeing*, John Berger writes in a note to the reader, "The form of the book has as much to do with our purpose as the arguments contained within it." The same might be said of Scott McCloud's illustrated "essay."

Each of these selections uses text and images to present theories on both *how we see* and *how visual images have been seen* throughout history. You are encouraged to use these texts to reexamine any of the visual and verbal selections presented in *Seeing & Writing 4*.

John Berger

John Berger was born in 1926 in London, where he attended Central School of Art and Chelsea School of Art. Known primarily as an art critic and social historian, Berger is also a distinguished novelist, artist, poet, essayist, Marxist critic, screenwriter, translator, and actor. He has published more than eight works of fiction and fifteen works of nonfiction, along with numerous articles and screenplays, during a remarkably prolific career. His novel *G: A Novel* won the Booker Prize in 1972.

Berger began his career as an artist and drawing teacher. While exhibiting his work at local galleries in London, he also wrote art criticism for British journals. Beginning with *Permanent Red: Essays in Seeing* (1960), Berger focused his criticism on the broad issues of seeing as a social and historical act. He introduced a mixed-media approach— combining poetry, photography, essays, and criticism—to the field of art criticism in books such as *Ways of Seeing* (1972), *About Looking* (1980), and *Another Way of Telling* (1982). His most recent work is *Here Is Where We Meet: A Fiction* (2005), a collection of semi-autobiographical vignettes. Berger currently lives and works in a small French village.

The selection printed here is the first essay in *Ways of Seeing*, which was based on a BBC television series.

WAYS OF SEEING
John Berger

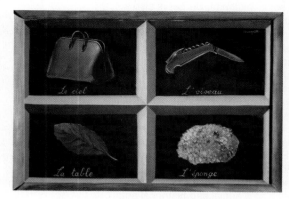

The Key of Dreams by Magritte (1898–1967)

Seeing comes before words. The child looks and recognizes before it can speak.

But there is also another sense in which seeing comes before words. It is seeing which establishes our place in the surrounding world; we explain that world with words, but words can never undo the fact that we are surrounded by it. The relation between what we see and what we know is never settled. Each evening we *see* the sun set. We *know* that the earth is turning away from it. Yet the knowledge, the explanation, never quite fits the sight. The Surrealist painter Magritte commented on this always-present gap between words and seeing in a painting called *The Key of Dreams*.

The way we see things is affected by what we know or what we believe. In the Middle Ages when men believed in the physical existence of Hell the sight of fire must have meant something different from what it means today. Nevertheless their idea of Hell owed a lot to the sight of fire consuming and the ashes remaining—as well as to their experience of the pain of burns.

When in love, the sight of the beloved has a completeness which no words and no embrace can match: a completeness which only the act of making love can temporarily accommodate.

5   Yet this seeing which comes before words, and can never be quite covered by them, is not a question of mechanically reacting to stimuli. (It can

only be thought of in this way if one isolates the small part of the process which concerns the eye's retina.) We only see what we look at. To look is an act of choice. As a result of this act, what we see is brought within our reach—though not necessarily within arm's reach. To touch something is to situate oneself in relation to it. (Close your eyes, move round the room and notice how the faculty of touch is like a static, limited form of sight.) We never look at just one thing; we are always looking at the relation between things and ourselves. Our vision is continually active, continually moving, continually holding things in a circle around itself, constituting what is present to us as we are.

Soon after we can see, we are aware that we can also be seen. The eye of the other combines with our own eye to make it fully credible that we are part of the visible world.

If we accept that we can see that hill over there, we propose that from that hill we can be seen. The reciprocal nature of vision is more fundamental than that of spoken dialogue. And often dialogue is an attempt to verbalize this—an attempt to explain how, either metaphorically or literally, "you see things," and an attempt to discover how "he sees things."

In the sense in which we use the word in this book, all images are manmade [see below]. An image is a sight which has been recreated or

reproduced. It is an appearance, or a set of appearances, which has been detached from the place and time in which it first made its appearance and preserved—for a few moments or a few centuries. Every image embodies a way of seeing. Even a photograph. For photographs are not, as is often assumed, a mechanical record. Every time we look at a photograph, we are aware, however slightly, of the photographer selecting that sight from an infinity of other possible sights. This is true even in the most casual family snapshot. The photographer's way of seeing is reflected in his choice of subject. The painter's way of seeing is reconstituted by the marks he makes on the canvas or paper. Yet, although every image embodies a way of seeing, our perception or appreciation of an image depends also upon our own way of seeing. (It may be, for example, that Sheila is one figure among twenty; but for our own reasons she is the one we have eyes for.)

Images were first made to conjure up the appearance of something that was absent. Gradually it became evident that an image could outlast what it represented; it then showed how something or somebody had once looked—and thus by implication how the subject had once been seen by other people. Later still the specific vision of the image-maker was also recognized as part of the record. An image became a record of how X had seen Y. This was the result of an increasing consciousness of individuality, accompanying an increasing awareness of history. It would be rash to try to date this last development precisely. But certainly in Europe such consciousness has existed since the beginning of the Renaissance.

10   No other kind of relic or text from the past can offer such a direct testimony about the world which surrounded other people at other times. In this respect images are more precise and richer than literature. To say this is not to deny the expressive or imaginative quality of art, treating it as mere documentary evidence; the more imaginative the work, the more profoundly it allows us to share the artist's experience of the visible.

Yet when an image is presented as a work of art, the way people look at it is affected by a whole series of learnt assumptions about art. Assumptions concerning:

Beauty
Truth
Genius
Civilization
Form
Status
Taste, etc.

Many of these assumptions no longer accord with the world as it is. (The world-as-it-is is more than pure objective fact, it includes consciousness.) Out of touch with the present, these assumptions obscure the past. They mystify rather than clarify. The past is never there waiting to be discovered, to be recognized for exactly what it is. History always constitutes the relation between a present and its past. Consequently fear of the present leads to mystification of the past. The past is not for living in; it is a well of conclusions from which we draw in order to act. Cultural mystification of the past entails a double loss. Works of art are made unnecessarily remote. And the past offers us fewer conclusions to complete in action.

When we "see" a landscape, we situate ourselves in it. If we "saw" the art of the past, we would situate ourselves in history. When we are prevented from seeing it, we are being deprived of the history which belongs to us. Who benefits from this deprivation? In the end, the art of the past is being mystified because a privileged minority is striving to invent a history which can retrospectively justify the role of the ruling classes, and such a justification can no longer make sense in modern terms. And so, inevitably, it mystifies.

Let us consider a typical example of such mystification. A two-volume study was recently published on Frans Hals.[1] It is the authoritative work to date on this painter. As a book of specialized art history it is no better and no worse than the average.

The last two great paintings by Frans Hals portray the Governors and the Governesses of an Alms House for old paupers in the Dutch seventeenth-century city of Haarlem. They were officially commissioned portraits. Hals, an old man of over eighty, was destitute. Most of his life he had been in debt. During the winter of 1664, the year he began painting these pictures, he obtained three loads of peat on public charity, otherwise he would have frozen to death. Those who now sat for him were administrators of such public charity.

Regents of the Old Men's Alms House
by Hals (1580–1666)

Regentesses of the Old Men's Alms House
by Hals (1580–1666)

1. Seymour Slive, *Frans Hals* (Phaidon, London). [Berger's note.]

15   The author records these facts and then explicitly says that it would be incorrect to read into the paintings any criticism of the sitters. There is no evidence, he says, that Hals painted them in a spirit of bitterness. The author considers them, however, remarkable works of art and explains why. Here he writes of the Regentesses:

> Each woman speaks to us of the human condition with equal importance. Each woman stands out with equal clarity against the *enormous* dark surface, yet they are linked by a firm rhythmical arrangement and the subdued diagonal pattern formed by their heads and hands. Subtle modulations of the *deep*, glowing blacks contribute to the *harmonious fusion* of the whole and form an *unforgettable contrast* with the *powerful* whites and vivid flesh tones where the detached strokes reach *a peak of breadth and strength*. [Berger's italics.]

The compositional unity of a painting contributes fundamentally to the power of its image. It is reasonable to consider a painting's composition. But here the composition is written about as though it were in itself the emotional charge of the painting. Terms like *harmonious fusion, unforgettable contrast, reaching a peak of breadth and strength* transfer the emotion provoked by the image from the plane of lived experience, to that of disinterested "art appreciation." All conflict disappears. One is left with the unchanging "human condition," and the painting considered as a marvellously made object.

Very little is known about Hals or the Regents who commissioned him. It is not possible to produce circumstantial evidence to establish what their relations were. But there is the evidence of the paintings themselves:

the evidence of a group of men and a group of women as seen by another man, the painter. Study this evidence and judge for yourself.

The art historian fears such direct judgement:

> As in so many other pictures by Hals, the penetrating characterizations almost seduce us into believing that we know the personality traits and even the habits of the men and women portrayed.

What is this "seduction" he writes of? It is nothing less than the paintings working upon us. They work upon us because we accept the way Hals saw his sitters. We do not accept this innocently. We accept it in so far as it corresponds to our own observation of people, gestures, faces, institutions. This is possible because we still live in a society of comparable social relations and moral values. And it is precisely this which gives the paintings their psychological and social urgency. It is this—not the painter's skill as a "seducer"—which convinces us that we *can* know the people portrayed.

The author continues:

> In the case of some critics the seduction has been a total success. It has, for example, been asserted that the Regent in the tipped slouch hat, which hardly covers any of his long, lank hair, and whose curiously set eyes do not focus, was shown in a drunken state. [below]

This, he suggests, is a libel. He argues that it was a fashion at that time to wear hats on the side of the head. He cites medical opinion to prove that the Regent's expression could well be the result of a facial paralysis. He insists that the painting would have been unacceptable to the Regents if one of them had been portrayed drunk. One might go on discussing each of these points for pages. (Men in seventeenth-century Holland wore their hats on the side of their heads in order to be thought of as adventurous and pleasure-loving. Heavy drinking was an approved practice. Etcetera.) But such a discussion would take us even farther away from the only confrontation which matters and which the author is determined to evade.

In this confrontation the Regents and Regentesses stare at Hals, a destitute old painter who has lost his reputation and lives off public charity; he examines them through the eyes of a pauper who must nevertheless try to be objective; i.e., must try to surmount the way he sees as a pauper. This is the drama of these paintings. A drama of an "unforgettable contrast."

20   Mystification has little to do with the vocabulary used. Mystification is the process of explaining away what might otherwise be evident. Hals was the first portraitist to paint the new characters and expressions created by capitalism. He did in pictorial terms what Balzac did two centuries later in literature. Yet the author of the authoritative work on these paintings sums up the artist's achievement by referring to

> Hals's unwavering commitment to his personal vision, which enriches our consciousness of our fellow men and heightens our awe for the ever-increasing power of the mighty impulses that enabled him to give us a close view of life's vital forces.

That is mystification.

In order to avoid mystifying the past (which can equally well suffer pseudo-Marxist mystification) let us now examine the particular relation which now exists, so far as pictorial images are concerned, between the present and the past. If we can see the present clearly enough, we shall ask the right questions of the past.

Today we see the art of the past as nobody saw it before. We actually perceive it in a different way.

This difference can be illustrated in terms of what was thought of as perspective. The convention of perspective, which is unique to European art and which was first established in the early Renaissance, centres everything on the eye of the beholder. It is like a beam from a lighthouse—only instead of light travelling outwards, appearances travel in. The conventions called those appearances *reality*. Perspective makes the single eye the centre of the visible world. Everything converges on to

the eye as to the vanishing point of infinity. The visible world is arranged for the spectator as the universe was once thought to be arranged for God.

According to the convention of perspective there is no visual reciprocity. There is no need for God to situate himself in relation to others: he is himself the situation. The inherent contradiction in perspective was that it structured all images of reality to address a single spectator who, unlike God, could only be in one place at a time.

25   After the invention of the camera this contradiction gradually became apparent.

> I'm an eye. A mechanical eye. I, the machine, show you a world the way only I can see it. I free myself for today and forever from human immobility. I'm in constant movement. I approach and pull away from objects. I creep under them. I move alongside a running horse's mouth. I fall and rise with the falling and rising bodies. This is I, the machine, manoeuvring in the chaotic movements, recording one movement after another in the most complex combinations.
>
> Freed from the boundaries of time and space, I coordinate any and all points of the universe, wherever I want them to be. My way leads towards the creation of a fresh perception of the world. Thus I explain in a new way the world unknown to you.[2]

The camera isolated momentary appearances and in so doing destroyed the idea that images were timeless. Or, to put it another way, the camera showed that the notion of time passing was inseparable from the experience of the visual (except in paintings). What you saw depended upon where you were when. What you saw was relative to your position in time and space. It was no longer possible to imagine everything converging on the human eye as on the vanishing point of infinity.

Still from *Man with a Movie Camera*
by Vertov (1895–1954)

---

2. This quotation is from an article written in 1923 by Dziga Vertov, the revolutionary Soviet film director. [Berger's note.]

This is not to say that before the invention of the camera men believed that everyone could see everything. But perspective organized the visual field as though that were indeed the ideal. Every drawing or painting that used perspective proposed to the spectator that he was the unique centre of the world. The camera—and more particularly the movie camera—demonstrated that there was no centre.

The invention of the camera changed the way men saw. The visible came to mean something different to them. This was immediately reflected in painting.

For the Impressionists the visible no longer presented itself to man in order to be seen. On the contrary, the visible, in continual flux, became fugitive. For the Cubists the visible was no longer what confronted the single eye, but the totality of possible views taken from points all round the object (or person) being depicted.

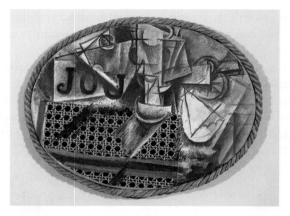

Still Life with Chair Caning by Picasso (1881–1973)

The invention of the camera also changed the way in which men saw paintings painted long before the camera was invented. Originally paintings were an integral part of the building for which they were designed. Sometimes in an early Renaissance church or chapel one has the feeling

Church of St. Francis of Assisi

that the images on the wall are records of the building's interior life, that together they make up the building's memory—so much are they part of the particularity of the building [see bottom, p. 698].

30

The uniqueness of every painting was once part of the uniqueness of the place where it resided. Sometimes the painting was transportable. But it could never be seen in two places at the same time. When the camera reproduces a painting, it destroys the uniqueness of its image. As a result its meaning changes. Or, more exactly, its meaning multiplies and fragments into many meanings.

This is vividly illustrated by what happens when a painting is shown on a television screen. The painting enters each viewer's house. There it is surrounded by his wallpaper, his furniture, his mementos. It enters the atmosphere of his family. It becomes their talking point. It lends its meaning to their meaning. At the same time it enters a million other houses and, in each of them, is seen in a different context. Because of the camera, the painting now travels to the spectator rather than the spectator to the painting. In its travels, its meaning is diversified.

One might argue that all reproductions more or less distort, and that therefore the original painting is still in a sense unique. Here is a reproduction of the *Virgin of the Rocks* by Leonardo da Vinci.

Having seen this reproduction, one can go to the National Gallery to look at the original and there discover what the reproduction lacks. Alternatively one can forget about the quality of the reproduction and simply be reminded, when one sees the original, that it is a famous painting of which somewhere one has already seen a reproduction. But in either case the uniqueness of the original now lies in it being *the original of a reproduction.* It is no longer what its image shows that strikes one as unique;

Virgin of the Rocks by Leonardo da Vinci (1452–1519). Reproduced by courtesy of the Trustees, The National Gallery, London.

its first meaning is no longer to be found in what it says, but in what it is.

This new status of the original work is the perfectly rational consequence of the new means of reproduction. But it is at this point that a process of mystification again enters. The meaning of the original work no longer lies in what it uniquely says but in what it uniquely is. How is its unique existence evaluated and defined in our present culture? It is defined as an object whose value depends upon its rarity. This market is affirmed and gauged by the price it fetches on the market. But because it is nevertheless "a work of art"—and art is thought to be greater than commerce—its market price is said to be a reflection of its spiritual value. Yet the spiritual value of an object, as distinct from a message or an example, can only be explained in terms of magic or religion. And since in modern society neither of these is a living force, the art object, the "work of art," is enveloped in an atmosphere of entirely bogus religiosity. Works of art are discussed and presented as though they were holy relics: relics which are first and foremost evidence of their own survival. The past in which they originated is studied in order to prove their survival genuine. They are declared art when their line of descent can be certified.

Virgin of the Rocks by Leonardo da Vinci (1452–1519), Louvre Museum.

35   Before the *Virgin of the Rocks* the visitor to the National Gallery would be encouraged by nearly everything he might have heard and read about the painting to feel something like this: "I am in front of it. I can see it. This painting by Leonardo is unlike any other in the world. The National Gallery has the real one. If I look at this painting hard enough, I should somehow be able to feel its authenticity. The *Virgin of the Rocks* by Leonardo da Vinci: it is authentic and therefore it is beautiful."

To dismiss such feelings as naive would be quite wrong. They accord perfectly with the sophisticated culture of art experts for whom the National Gallery catalogue is written. The entry on the *Virgin of the Rocks* is one of the longest entries. It consists of fourteen closely printed pages.

The Virgin and Child with St. Anne and St. John the Baptist by Leonardo da Vinci (1452–1519). Reproduced by courtesy of the Trustees, The Naitonal Gallery, London.

They do not deal with the meaning of the image. They deal with who commissioned the painting, legal squabbles, who owned it, its likely date, the families of its owners. Behind this information lie years of research. The aim of the research is to prove beyond any shadow of doubt that the painting is a genuine Leonardo. The secondary aim is to prove that an almost identical painting in the Louvre [see p. 700] is a replica of the National Gallery version.

French art historians try to prove the opposite.

The National Gallery sells more reproductions of Leonardo's cartoon of *The Virgin and Child with St. Anne and St. John the Baptist* [above] than any other picture in their collection. A few years ago it was known only to scholars. It became famous because an American wanted to buy it for two and a half million pounds.

Now it hangs in a room by itself. The room is like a chapel. The drawing is behind bullet-proof perspex. It has acquired a new kind of impressiveness. Not because of what it shows—not because of the meaning of its image. It has become impressive, mysterious, because of its market value.

* * *

40   The bogus religiosity which now surrounds original works of art, and which is ultimately dependent upon their market value, has become the substitute for what paintings lost when the camera made them reproducible. Its function is nostalgic. It is the final empty claim for the continuing values of an oligarchic, undemocratic culture. If the image is no longer unique and exclusive, the art object, the thing, must be made mysteriously so.

The majority of the population do not visit art museums. The following table [below] shows how closely an interest in art is related to privileged education.

The majority take it as axiomatic that the museums are full of holy relics which refer to a mystery which excludes them: the mystery of unaccountable wealth. Or, to put this another way, they believe that original masterpieces belong to the preserve (both materially and spiritually) of the rich. Another table [p. 703] indicates what the idea of an art gallery suggests to each social class.

In the age of pictorial reproduction the meaning of paintings is no longer attached to them; their meaning becomes transmittable: that is to say it becomes information of a sort, and, like all information, it is either put to use or ignored; information carries no special authority within itself. When a painting is put to use, its meaning is either modified or totally changed. One should be quite clear about what this involves. It is not a question of reproduction failing to reproduce certain aspects of an image faithfully; it is a question of reproduction making it possible, even inevitable, that an image will be used for many different purposes and that the reproduced image, unlike an original work, can lend itself to

National proportion of art museum visitors according to level of education: Percentage of each educational category who visit art museums

	Greece	Poland	France	Holland
With no educational qualification	0.02	0.12	0.15	—
Only primary education	0.30	1.50	0.45	0.50
Only secondary education	0.5	10.4	10	20
Further and higher education	11.5	11.7	12.5	17.3

Source: Pierre Bourdieu and Alain Darbel, *L'Amour de l'art*, Editions de Minuit, Paris 1969, Appendix 5, table 4.

Venus and Mars by Botticelli (1445–1510).
Reproduced by courtesy of the Trustees, The National Gallery, London.

them all. Let us examine some of the ways in which the reproduced image lends itself to such usage.

Reproduction isolates a detail of a painting from the whole. The detail is transformed. An allegorical figure becomes a portrait of a girl [see left].

45

When a painting is reproduced by a film camera it inevitably becomes material for the film-maker's argument.

A film which reproduces images of a painting leads the spectator, through the painting, to the film-maker's own conclusions. The painting lends authority to the film-maker. This is because a film unfolds in time and a painting does not. In a film the way one image follows another, their succession, constructs an argument which becomes irreversible. In

Of the places listed below which does a museum remind you of most?

	Manual workers	Skilled and white collar	Professional and upper managerial
	%	%	%
Church	66	45	30.5
Library	9	34	28
Lecture hall	—	4	4.5
Department store or entrance hall in public building	—	7	2
Church and library	9	2	4.5
Church and lecture hall	4	2	—
Library and lecture hall	—	—	2
None of these	4	2	19.5
No reply	8	4	9
	100 (n = 53)	100 (n = 98)	100 (n = 99)

Source: As left, Appendix 4, table 8.

Procession to Calvary by Breughel (1525–1569)

a painting all its elements are there to be seen simultaneously. The spectator may need time to examine each element of the painting but whenever he reaches a conclusion, the simultaneity of the whole painting is there to reverse or qualify his conclusion. The painting maintains its own authority.

Paintings are often reproduced with words around them.

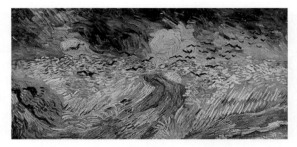

Wheatfield with Crows by Van Gogh (1853–1890)

This is a landscape of a cornfield with birds flying out of it. Look at it for a moment. Then see the painting below.

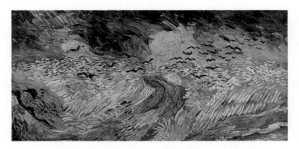

This is the last picture that Van Gogh painted before he killed himself.

It is hard to define exactly how the words have changed the image but undoubtedly they have. The image now illustrates the sentence.

50   In this essay each image reproduced has become part of an argument which has little or nothing to do with the painting's original independent meaning. The words have quoted the paintings to confirm their own verbal authority. . . .

Reproduced paintings, like all information, have to hold their own against all the other information being continually transmitted.

Consequently a reproduction, as well as making its own references to the image of its original, becomes itself the reference point for other images. The meaning of an image is changed according to what one sees immediately beside it or what comes immediately after it. Such authority as it retains, is distributed over the whole context in which it appears [left and below].

Because works of art are reproducible, they can, theoretically, be used by anybody. Yet mostly — in art books, magazines, films, or within gilt frames in living-rooms — reproductions are still used to bolster the illusion that nothing has changed, that art, with its unique undiminished authority, justifies most other forms of authority, that art makes inequality seem noble and hierarchies seem thrilling. For example, the whole concept of the National Cultural Heritage exploits the authority of art to glorify the present social system and its priorities.

The means of reproduction are used politically and commercially to disguise or deny what their existence makes possible. But sometimes individuals use them differently [see p. 707].

55   Adults and children sometimes have boards in their bedrooms or living-rooms on which they pin pieces of paper: letters, snapshots, reproductions of paintings, newspaper cuttings, original drawings, postcards. On each board all the images belong to the same language and all are more or

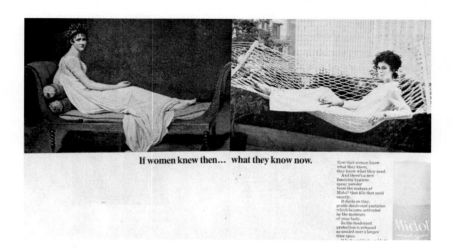

If women knew then... what they know now.

less equal within it, because they have been chosen in a highly personal way to match and express the experience of the room's inhabitant. Logically, these boards should replace museums.

What are we saying by that? Let us first be sure about what we are not saying.

We are not saying that there is nothing left to experience before original works of art except a sense of awe because they have survived. The way original works of art are usually approached—through museum catalogues, guides, hired cassettes, etc.—is not the only way they might be approached. When the art of the past ceases to be viewed nostalgically, the works will cease to be holy relics—although they will never re-become what they were before the age of reproduction. We are not saying original works of art are now useless.

Original paintings are silent and still in a sense that information never is. Even a reproduction hung on a wall is not comparable in this respect for in the original the silence and stillness permeate the actual material, the paint, in which one follows the traces of the painter's immediate gestures. This has the effect of closing the distance in time between the painting of the picture and one's own act of looking at it. In this special sense all paintings are contemporary. Hence the immediacy of their testimony. Their historical moment is literally there before our eyes. Cézanne made a similar observation from the painter's point of view. "A minute in the world's life passes! To paint it in its reality, and forget everything for that! To become that minute, to be the sensitive plate . . . give the image of what we see, forgetting everything that has appeared before our time . . ." What we make of that painted moment when it is before our eyes depends upon what we expect of art, and that in turn depends today upon how we have already experienced the meaning of paintings through reproductions.

Nor are we saying that all art can be understood spontaneously. We are not claiming that to cut out a magazine reproduction of an archaic Greek head, because it is reminiscent of some personal experience, and to pin it to a board beside other disparate images, is to come to terms with the full meaning of that head.

60 The idea of innocence faces two ways. By refusing to enter a conspiracy, one remains innocent of that conspiracy. But to remain innocent may also be to remain ignorant. The issue is not between innocence and knowledge (or between the natural and the cultural) but between a total approach to art which attempts to relate it to every aspect of experience and the esoteric approach of a few specialized experts who are the clerks of the nostalgia of a ruling class in decline. (In decline, not before the proletariat, but before the new power of the corporation and the state.) The real question is: to whom does the meaning of the art of the past properly belong? To those who can apply it to their own lives, or to a cultural hierarchy of relic specialists?

The visual arts have always existed within a certain preserve; originally this preserve was magical or sacred. But it was also physical: it was the place, the cave, the building, in which, or for which, the work was made. The experience of art, which at first was the experience of ritual, was set apart from the rest of life—precisely in order to be able to exercise power over it. Later the preserve of art became a social one. It entered the culture of the ruling class, whilst physically it was set apart and isolated in their palaces and houses. During all this history the authority of art was inseparable from the particular authority of the preserve.

What the modern means of reproduction have done is to destroy the authority of art and to remove it—or, rather, to remove its images which they reproduce—from any preserve. For the first time ever, images of art have become ephemeral, ubiquitous, insubstantial, available, valueless, free. They surround us in the same way as a language surrounds us. They have entered the mainstream of life over which they no longer, in themselves, have power.

Yet very few people are aware of what has happened because the means of reproduction are used nearly all the time to promote the illusion that nothing has changed except that the masses, thanks to reproductions, can now begin to appreciate art as the cultured minority once did. Understandably, the masses remain uninterested and sceptical.

Woman Pouring Milk by Vermeer (1632–1675)

If the new language of images were used differently, it would, through its use, confer a new kind of power. Within it we could begin to define our experiences more precisely in areas where words are inadequate. (Seeing comes before words.) Not only personal experience, but also the essential historical experience of our relation to the past: that is to say the experience of seeking to give meaning to our lives, of trying to understand the history of which we can become the active agents.

65   The art of the past no longer exists as it once did. Its authority is lost. In its place there is a language of images. What matters now is who uses that language for what purpose. This touches upon questions of copyright for reproduction, the ownership of art presses and publishers, the total policy of public art galleries and museums. As usually presented, these are narrow professional matters. One of the aims of this essay has been to show that what is really at stake is much larger. A people or a class which is cut off from its own past is far less free to choose and to act as a people or class than one that has been able to situate itself in history. This

is why—and this is the only reason why—the entire art of the past has now become a political issue.

Many of the ideas in the preceding essay have been taken from another, written over forty years ago* by the German critic and philosopher Walter Benjamin.

His essay was entitled The Work of Art in the Age of Mechanical Reproduction. *This essay is available in English in a collection called* Illuminations *(Cape, London, 1970).*

---

* Now over seventy years ago [eds].

Scott McCloud

"When I was a little kid I knew exactly what comics were," Scott McCloud writes in his book *Understanding Comics: The Invisible Art* (1993). "Comics were those bright, colorful magazines filled with bad art, stupid stories and guys in tights." But after looking at a friend's comic book collection, McCloud became "totally obsessed with comics" and in the tenth grade decided to become a comics artist.

In 1982, McCloud graduated with a degree in illustration from Syracuse University. "I wanted to have a good background in writing and art and also just liberal arts in general because I thought that just about anything can be brought to bear in making comics." Later McCloud worked in the production department of DC Comics until he began publishing his two comic series, "Zot!" (1984) and later "Destroy!!" (1986).

In *Understanding Comics*, a caricature of McCloud leads readers through an insightful study of the nature of sequential art by tracing the history of the relationship between words and images. "Most readers will find it difficult to look at comics in quite the same way ever again," wrote cartoonist Garry Trudeau of McCloud's work. In 2000, he published *Reinventing Comics*, which he describes as "the controversial 242-page follow-up" to *Understanding Comics*. His latest book is *Making Comics: Storytelling Secrets of Comics, Manga, and Graphic Novels* (2006). Recently McCloud has been working with comics in the digital environment. His web site is at *scottmccloud.com*. "Show and Tell" is the sixth chapter in *Understanding Comics*.

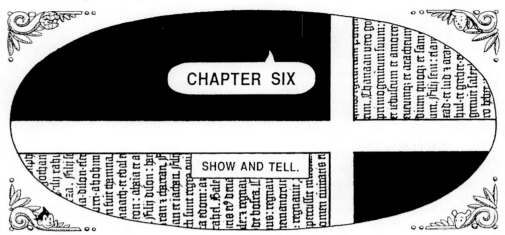

CHAPTER SIX

SHOW AND TELL.

THIS IS MY ROBOT.

WHAT CAN YOU *TELL* US ABOUT YOUR ROBOT, TOMMY?

WELL, UH...I LIKE IT 'CAUSE... 'CAUSE, UH...

IT'S GOT ONE OF *THESE* THINGS.

WHAT IS *THAT,* TOMMY?

138

On the Theory and Practice of Seeing / 712

140

MEANWHILE, WORDS AND *MOVING* PICTURES HAVE HALF THE WORLD IN THRALL TO THEIR CHARMS, BUT MUST STRUGGLE TO MAKE *THEIR* POTENTIAL UNDERSTOOD.

WORDS AND PICTURES ARE AS POPULAR AS EVER, BUT THIS WIDESPREAD FEELING THAT THE COMBINATION IS SOMEHOW *BASE* OR *SIMPLISTIC* HAS BECOME A *SELF-FULFILLING PROPHECY.*

THE ROOTS OF THIS ATTITUDE RUN PRETTY *DEEP.*

AS NEAR AS WE CAN TELL, PICTURES *PREDATE* THE WRITTEN WORD BY A *LARGE MARGIN.* HERE ARE SOME BIG HITS FROM THE GOLDEN AGE OF CAVE PAINTING, ABOUT 15,000 YEARS AGO.

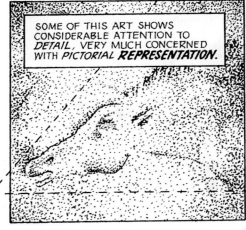

SOME OF THIS ART SHOWS CONSIDERABLE ATTENTION TO *DETAIL*, VERY MUCH CONCERNED WITH *PICTORIAL* **REPRESENTATION.**

BUT OTHERS WERE VERY *ICONIC*, ACTING AS *SYMBOLS* RATHER THAN *PICTURES* -- MORE LIKE A *PRIMITIVE LANGUAGE!*

141

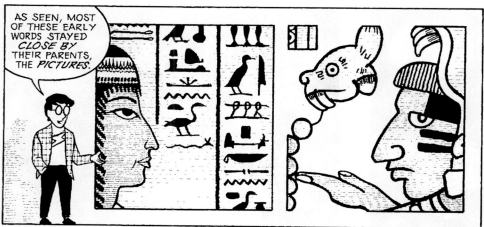

BUT, IN TIME, MOST MODERN WRITING WOULD COME TO REPRESENT *SOUND ONLY* AND LOSE ANY LINGERING RESEMBLANCE TO THE *VISIBLE WORLD.*

re's More! **Order Today and receive FREE G**

WITH THE INVENTION OF *PRINTING*, THE WRITTEN WORD TOOK A GREAT LEAP *FORWARD*--

--AND ALL OF HUMANITY WITH IT.

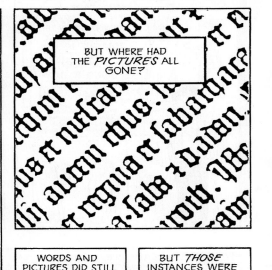

BUT WHERE HAD THE *PICTURES* ALL GONE?

WORDS AND PICTURES DID STILL *COEXIST* AT THIS STAGE IN WESTERN CIVILIZATION.*

BUT *THOSE* INSTANCES WERE BECOMING THE *EXCEPTION,* NOT THE *RULE.*

143

*IN ILLUMINATED MANUSCRIPTS, FOR EXAMPLE.

FACSIMILE DETAILS OF PORTRAITS BY DÜRER
(1519) REMBRANDT (1660) DAVID (1788) AND INGRES
(1810-15).

144

John Keats   1819
Ode on a Grecian Urn

1

Thou still unravish'd bride of quietness,
   Thou foster-child of silence and slow time,
Sylvan historian, who canst thus express
A flowery tale more sweetly than our rhyme:
What leaf fring'd legend haunts about thy shape
   Of deities or mortals, or of both,
      In Tempe or the dales of Arcady?
      What men or gods are these? What maidens loth?
What mad pursuit? What struggle to escape?
   What pipes and timbrels? What wild ecstasy?

BY THE EARLY 1800's, WESTERN ART AND WRITING HAD DRIFTED ABOUT AS FAR APART AS WAS *POSSIBLE.*

ONE WAS OBSESSED WITH *RESEMBLANCE, LIGHT* AND *COLOR,* ALL THINGS *VISIBLE...*

...THE *OTHER* RICH IN *INVISIBLE* TREASURES, SENSES, EMOTIONS, SPIRITUALITY, PHILOSOPHY...

PICTURES AND WORDS, ONCE *TOGETHER* IN THE CENTER OF OUR ICONIC ABSTRACTION CHART, HAVE AT *THIS* POINT DRIFTED TO *OPPOSITE CORNERS.*

145

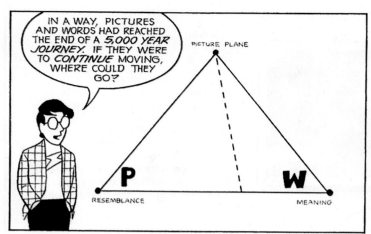

IN A WAY, PICTURES AND WORDS HAD REACHED THE END OF A *5,000 YEAR JOURNEY*. IF THEY WERE TO *CONTINUE* MOVING, WHERE COULD THEY GO?

PICTURE PLANE

P

W

RESEMBLANCE

MEANING

FOR *PICTURES*, THERE WAS ONLY *UP!*

IMPRESSIONISM SENT WESTERN ART TOWARD THE *ABSTRACT VERTEX*, BUT IN A WAY THAT *CLUNG* TO WHAT THE *EYE* SAW.

P

IMPRESSIONISM, WHILE IT COULD BE THOUGHT OF AS THE FIRST *MODERN* MOVEMENT, WAS MORE A *CULMINATION* OF THE *OLD*, THE *ULTIMATE STUDY* OF LIGHT AND COLOR.

FACSIMILE DETAIL OF 'A SUNDAY AFTERNOON ON THE ISLAND OF LA GRANDE JATTE' BY GEORGES SEURAT.

SOON AFTER CAME THE *EXPLOSION!* EXPRESSIONISM, FUTURISM, DADA, SURREALISM, FAUVISM, CUBISM, ABSTRACT EXPRESSIONISM, NEO-PLASTICISM, CONSTRUCTIVISM.

EVERY WHICH WAY BUT *BACKWARDS!*

P

STRICT REPRESENTATIONAL STYLES WERE OF LITTLE IMPORTANCE TO THE NEW SCHOOLS. *ABSTRACTION*, BOTH ICONIC AND *NON*-ICONIC MADE A SPECTACULAR *COMEBACK!*

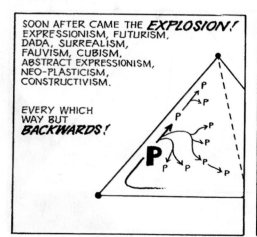

146

FACSIMILE DETAILS OF PORTRAITS BY PICASSO, LEGER AND KLEE.

SOME ARTISTS HEADED *UPWARD* TO THE *SUMMIT* OF THE PICTURE PLANE, WANTING NEITHER *RESEMBLANCE* NOR EXTERNAL "MEANING."

MONDRIAN A LA McCLOUD.

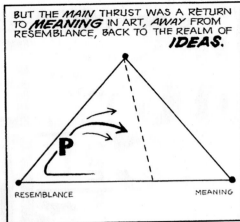

BUT THE *MAIN* THRUST WAS A RETURN TO *MEANING* IN ART, *AWAY* FROM RESEMBLANCE, BACK TO THE REALM OF *IDEAS.*

P

RESEMBLANCE   MEANING

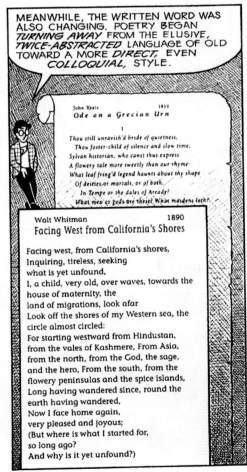

MEANWHILE, THE WRITTEN WORD WAS ALSO CHANGING. POETRY BEGAN *TURNING AWAY* FROM THE ELUSIVE, *TWICE-ABSTRACTED* LANGUAGE OF OLD TOWARD A MORE *DIRECT,* EVEN *COLLOQUIAL,* STYLE.

John Keats   1819
Ode on a Grecian Urn

I

Thou still unravish'd bride of quietness,
    Thou foster-child of silence and slow time,
Sylvan historian, who canst thus express
A flowery tale more sweetly than our rhyme:
What leaf-fring'd legend haunts about thy shape
    Of deities or mortals, or of both,
        In Tempe or the dales of Arcady?
What men or gods are these? What maidens loth?

Walt Whitman   1890
Facing West from California's Shores

Facing west, from California's shores,
Inquiring, tireless, seeking
what is yet unfound,
I, a child, very old, over waves, towards the
house of maternity, the
land of migrations, look afar
Look off the shores of my Western sea, the
circle almost circled:
For starting westward from Hindustan,
from the vales of Kashmere, From Asia,
from the north, from the God, the sage,
and the hero, From the south, from the
flowery peninsulas and the spice islands,
Long having wandered since, round the
earth having wandered,
Now I face home again,
very pleased and joyous;
(But where is what I started for,
so long ago?
And why is it yet unfound?)

IN PROSE, LANGUAGE WAS BECOMING EVEN MORE DIRECT, CONVEYING MEANING *SIMPLY* AND *QUICKLY,* MORE LIKE *PICTURES.*

"MEANING" WAS NOT *ABANDONED* BY *ANY MEANS,* BUT AUTHORS WERE DEFINITELY MOVING *LEFT*--

W

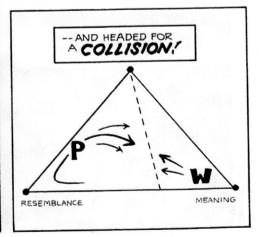

-- AND HEADED FOR A *COLLISION!*

P

W

RESEMBLANCE   MEANING

147

McCloud / Show and Tell / 721

DADA POSTER FOR THE PLAY
'THE BEARDED HEART'

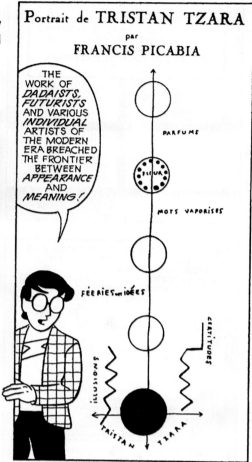

WHILE SOME ARTISTS ADDRESSED THE IRONIES OF WORDS AND PICTURES *HEAD-ON!*

148

AND IN *POPULAR* CULTURE THE TWO FORMS COLLIDED *AGAIN AND AGAIN* WITHOUT ANY PRETENSES OF *"HIGH"* ART.

NOWHERE IS THIS COLLISION MORE THOROUGHLY EXPLORED THAN THE MODERN COMIC. AND IT'S NOT A RECENT OBSESSION.

LET'S GO BACK TO THE EARLY 1800's BEFORE ANY OF THIS HAPPENED, WHEN WORDS AND PICTURES HAD DRIFTED AS FAR APART AS *POSSIBLE*.

UP TO THAT POINT, *EUROPEAN BROADSHEETS* HAD OFFERED *REMINDERS* OF WHAT WORDS AND PICTURES COULD DO WHEN COMBINED.

BUT AGAIN IT WAS *RODOLPHE TÖPFFER* WHO FORESAW THEIR *INTERDEPENDENCY* AND BROUGHT THE FAMILY *BACK TOGETHER* AT LAST.

M. CRÉPIN ADVERTISES FOR A TUTOR, AND MANY APPLY FOR THE JOB.

TRANSLATION BY E. WIESE.

I'M SURE THAT THESE IDEAS WERE THE *FURTHEST THING* FROM TÖPFFER'S MIND WHEN HE PUT *PEN TO PAPER*--

--BUT THE FACT THAT THE MODERN COMIC WAS BORN JUST AS ART AND WRITING WERE PREPARING TO CHANGE DIRECTION IS AT LEAST *INTRIGUING.*

AND PERHAPS THIS COMMON THREAD OF *UNIFICATION* DID GROW OUT OF A *SHARED INSTINCT* OF THE DAY...

...AN INSTINCT WHICH SAID THAT WE HAD REACHED THE END OF A *LONG JOURNEY* AND THAT IT WAS TIME AT LAST TO *HEAD FOR HOME.*

149

UNFORTUNATELY FOR *COMICS*, NO SOONER HAD THE FINE ARTS *REDISCOVERED* THE LINK BETWEEN WORDS AND PICTURES--

--THAN MODERN ART *ITSELF* BECAME VIRTUALLY *INCOMPREHENSIBLE* TO THE AVERAGE VIEWER!

WHAT THE HECK IS *THAT*?!

IT'S A *HOAX*, I TELL YA! MY TWO-YEAR-OLD *DAUGHTER* CAN PAINT BETTER THAN *THAT*!

DO PEOPLE REALLY PAY *MONEY* FOR THIS??

COOL

IN FACT, THE GENERAL PUBLIC'S PERCEPTIONS OF "GREAT" ART AND "GREAT" WRITING HASN'T CHANGED MUCH IN 150 YEARS.* ANY ARTIST WISHING TO DO GREAT WORK IN A MEDIUM *USING* WORDS AND PICTURES WILL HAVE TO *CONTEND* WITH THIS ATTITUDE.

Thou still unravish'd bride
 Thou foster-child of siler
Sylvan historian, who cans
A flowery tale more sweetl
What leaf fring'd legend h
Of deities or mortals, or
 In Tempe or the dales
What men or gods are th
What mad pursuit? What s
What pipes and timbrels

IN OTHERS *AND* IN *THEMSELVES*...

...BECAUSE, DEEP DOWN INSIDE, MANY COMICS CREATORS STILL MEASURE ART AND WRITING BY *DIFFERENT STANDARDS* AND ACT ON THE FAITH THAT "GREAT" ART AND "GREAT" WRITING WILL COMBINE HARMONIOUSLY BY VIRTUE OF *QUALITY ALONE*.

FACE → TWO EYES, ONE NOSE, ONE MOUTH.

Thy youth's proud livery so gaz'd on now...

* NOT AS MUCH AS WE LIKE TO *THINK* IT HAS, ANYWAY.

150

THE ART FORM OF COMICS IS MANY CENTURIES OLD, BUT IT'S *PERCEIVED* AS A RECENT INVENTION AND SUFFERS THE CURSE OF *ALL* NEW MEDIA.

THE CURSE OF BEING JUDGED BY THE STANDARDS OF THE OLD.

EVER SINCE THE INVENTION OF THE WRITTEN WORD, NEW MEDIA HAVE BEEN *MISUNDERSTOOD.*

CAREFUL, JACOB! IF YOU KEEP DOING THIS, YOU'LL STOP USING YOUR *MEMORY!*

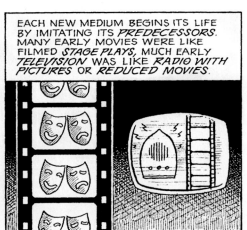

EACH NEW MEDIUM BEGINS ITS LIFE BY IMITATING ITS *PREDECESSORS.* MANY EARLY MOVIES WERE LIKE FILMED *STAGE PLAYS*, MUCH EARLY *TELEVISION* WAS LIKE *RADIO WITH PICTURES* OR *REDUCED MOVIES.*

FAR TOO MANY COMICS CREATORS HAVE NO HIGHER GOAL THAN TO MATCH THE ACHIEVEMENTS OF OTHER MEDIA, AND VIEW ANY CHANCE TO *WORK* IN OTHER MEDIA AS A *STEP UP.*

AND *AGAIN*, AS LONG AS WE VIEW COMICS AS A *GENRE* OF WRITING OR A *STYLE* OF GRAPHIC ART THIS ATTITUDE MAY *NEVER* DISAPPEAR.

151

152

153

ANOTHER TYPE IS THE **ADDITIVE** COMBINATION WHERE WORDS *AMPLIFY* OR *ELABORATE* ON AN IMAGE OR *VICE VERSA.*

MY HEAD FEELS LIKE A *SMASHED PUMPKIN!*

HOW D'YA LIKE MY *NEW THREADS,* BABE?

IS THIS THE SAME *JUPITER* OF MY YOUTH?

IN *PARALLEL* COMBINATIONS, WORDS AND PICTURES SEEM TO FOLLOW VERY DIFFERENT COURSES--WITHOUT *INTERSECTING.*

"TALKED TO *BILL* YET?"

"*SALLY* DID. *WHY?*"

"THE *TEST RESULTS* CAME BACK. ALL *NEGATIVE.*"

"*REALLY?* THAT'S *GREAT!*"

WELL...

PEPPER.

CEREAL.

MILK. BUTTER.

LIGHT BULBS.

STILL ANOTHER OPTION IS THE *MONTAGE* WHERE WORDS ARE TREATED AS INTEGRAL *PARTS* OF THE PICTURE.

CASH PUBL FLOW BOTTO LINE ANNUA REPORT

HAPPY!

154

PERHAPS THE MOST *COMMON* TYPE OF WORD/PICTURE COMBINATION IS THE *INTER-DEPENDENT*, WHERE WORDS AND PICTURES GO *HAND IN HAND* TO CONVEY AN IDEA THAT NEITHER COULD CONVEY *ALONE.*

MEANWHILE...

DID ANYONE *SEE* YOU?

THIS IS ALL I NEED TO *STOP* HIM!

I ASK YOU, DOES THIS GUY LOOK LIKE A C.E.O. TO *YOU*??

"AND JUST *GUESS* WHO DROVE UP IN BOB'S TRUCK AN HOUR LATER!"

HEY, MARGE!

OH, MY *GOD!*

"AFTER COLLEGE, I PURSUED A CAREER IN *HIGH FINANCE.*"

HURRY UP, WILLYA?!

HE'S LYING.

UH-HUH.

INTERDEPENDENT COMBINATIONS AREN'T ALWAYS AN *EQUAL BALANCE* THOUGH AND MAY FALL *ANYWHERE* ON A SCALE BETWEEN TYPES ONE AND TWO.

GENERALLY SPEAKING, THE MORE IS SAID WITH *WORDS,* THE MORE THE PICTURES CAN BE FREED TO GO EXPLORING AND *VICE VERSA.*

155

156

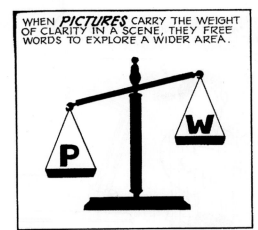

WHEN *PICTURES* CARRY THE WEIGHT OF CLARITY IN A SCENE, THEY FREE WORDS TO EXPLORE A WIDER AREA.

LET'S SAY I SHOW YOU A WOMAN WALKING ACROSS THE STREET IN THE RAIN, BUYING A PINT OF ICE CREAM AND EATING IT IN HER APARTMENT--

--ALL IN *PICTURES.*

157

IT COULD BECOME AN *INTERNAL MONOLOGUE.*

(INTERDEPENDENT)

PERHAPS SOMETHING WILDLY *INCONGRUOUS*

(PARALLEL)

MAYBE IT'S ALL JUST A BIG *ADVERTISEMENT!*

(INTERDEPENDENT)

OR A CHANCE TO RUMINATE ON *BROADER TOPICS.*

(INTERDEPENDENT)

158

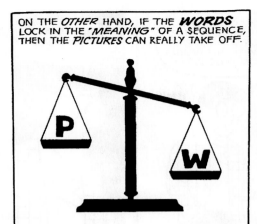

ON THE *OTHER* HAND, IF THE **WORDS** LOCK IN THE *"MEANING"* OF A SEQUENCE, THEN THE *PICTURES* CAN REALLY TAKE OFF.

P | W

SAME SCENE NOW, BUT THIS TIME ALL IN *WORDS!*

I CROSSED THE STREET TO THE CONVENIENCE STORE. THE RAIN SOAKED INTO MY BOOTS.

I FOUND THE LAST PINT OF CHOCOLATE CHOCOLATE CHIP IN THE FREEZER.

THE CLERK TRIED TO PICK ME UP. I SAID *NO THANKS.* HE GAVE ME THIS CREEPY LOOK...

I WENT BACK TO THE APARTMENT--

--AND FINISHED IT ALL IN AN HOUR.

ALONE AT LAST.

159

NOW, ONE COULD JUST *COMBINE* THE *PICTURES* FROM PAGE 157 WITH THE WORDS FROM PAGE 159--

--BUT WHAT ARE SOME *OTHER* OPTIONS?

IF THE ARTIST WANTS TO, HE/SHE CAN NOW SHOW ONLY *FRAGMENTS* OF A SCENE.

(WORD SPECIFIC)

OR MOVE TOWARD GREATER LEVELS OF *ABSTRACTION* OR *EXPRESSION*.

THE CLERK TRIED TO PICK ME UP. I SAID *NO THANKS*. HE GAVE ME THIS CREEPY LOOK...

(AMPLIFICATION)

PERHAPS THE ARTIST CAN GIVE US SOME IMPORTANT *EMOTIONAL* INFORMATION.

I WENT BACK TO THE APARTMENT--

(INTERDEPENDENT)

OR SHIFT AHEAD OR BACKWARDS IN TIME.

--AND FINISHED IT ALL IN AN HOUR.

ALONE AT LAST.

(WORD SPECIFIC)

160

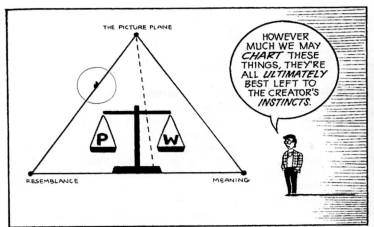

THE PICTURE PLANE

P W

RESEMBLANCE | MEANING

HOWEVER MUCH WE MAY *CHART* THESE THINGS, THEY'RE ALL *ULTIMATELY* BEST LEFT TO THE CREATOR'S *INSTINCTS.*

THE MIXING OF WORDS AND PICTURES IS MORE *ALCHEMY* THAN SCIENCE.

SOME OF THE SECRETS OF THOSE *FIRST* ALCHEMISTS MAY HAVE BEEN LOST IN THE ANCIENT PAST.

BUT WE HAVE SOME POWERFUL MAGIC RIGHT HERE IN THE *20TH CENTURY, TOO!*

THE RICHNESS OF MODERN LANGUAGE IS AN *IRREPLACEABLE COMMODITY!*

THIS IS AN *EXCITING TIME* TO BE MAKING COMICS, AND IN MANY WAYS I FEEL VERY *LUCKY* TO HAVE BEEN BORN WHEN I WAS.

STILL, I DO FEEL A CERTAIN *VAGUE LONGING* FOR THAT TIME OVER *50 CENTURIES AGO* --

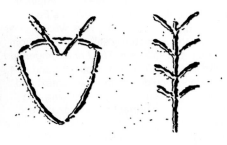

-- WHEN TO TELL WAS TO *SHOW* --

-- AND TO SHOW WAS TO *TELL.*

161

Appendix B
On Reading Visual and Verbal Texts

Many writers create a picture with words; many artists convey a complicated idea in a single image; and, increasingly, words and images are combined to create meaning. As you become better readers of the diverse texts in *Seeing & Writing 4* and more effective writers, we hope that you also will become more conversant with the distinctions between types of texts as well as with the different genres. The following eight groups of suggestions offer strategies for approaching a range of verbal and visual texts: images, essays, advertisements, poetry, paintings, photographs, short stories, and mixed media.

READING AN IMAGE

Seeing & Writing 4 features many types of images, including photographs, ads, paintings, prints, and film stills. We recommend that you use the following guidelines for reading and interpreting various kinds of images.

Determine the initial type of image.

It's easy to assume that most images we encounter on a daily basis are photographs. In some cases, however, images that appear to be photos may be paintings – for example, the advertisements in the World Wildlife Fund portfolio (p. 616). In other cases, what appear to be photos are actually stills or frames from films (e.g., the stills from *The Lone Ranger* and *Smoke Signals* in Chapter 5, pp. 431 and 434.)

Viewers should consider the context and construction of each image. In looking at a movie still, it is important to have an understanding of the film. You should also be aware of the different limitations and opportunities available to photographers as opposed to painters. Photographers can enhance and transform their shots, but they always begin with an image that captures a specific moment in time. Painters may capture the mood of a moment, but not with the click of a shutter.

A photographer is expected, on some level, to be "true" to his or her subject; a painter is not. When a photographer alters an image, the reader should ask why – as she should when a painter attempts to re-create life exactly.

Determine the "figure" and the "background."

These terms, which are drawn from Gestalt theories of visual organization, are useful in determining the most important object in an image. The figure is what draws the viewer's attention; the background is its immediate context. Just as a story might have a protagonist, a visual image has a figure – what the viewer should follow throughout the narrative of the image. This figure might be a building, a person, or an object. Everything else is background.

Often the viewer's eye works almost unconsciously to find the figure in a visual image. For example, it is fairly easy to determine that the figure in Mark Peterson's *Image of Homelessness* (p. 169) is the homeless man lying in the appliance box. The viewer intuits this information because in many ways the photo is a standard, centered portrait. However, in an image like one of Camilo José Vergara's photographs of 65 East 125th Street, Harlem (pp. 156–57) it might take a moment to think through what the figure is. Depending on how a given viewer defines the figure, he or she may read the photo quite differently from the way another viewer reads it.

Determine the narrative of the image.

Every image communicates something to the viewer. Our culture is driven by narrative, driven by a desire to draw connections and to create – or imply – a story. So the easiest way to begin reading an image is to determine its story. What are the denotative and connotative meanings of the objects, people, and places within the image? Where are the items in the image placed in relationship to one another? In our drive to make meaning, we often connect elements that are in close proximity and establish relationships between or among them. This is as true for objects (e.g., the items in Peter Menzel and Faith D'Aluisio's photos in Chapter 1, beginning on p. 30) as it is for people (e.g., the people standing around a table in Tina Barney's photo on p. 555). Viewers, like readers, prefer an interpretation that offers closure.

Because viewers come from varying backgrounds and read with different perceptions, many may perceive the narrative of an image differently. In some cases, such as with images we think of as art, these varying perspectives add depth to a reading. However, in other cases, such as advertisements, the varying perspectives can weaken the sales appeal of the ad. For example, Martin Parr might be quite pleased if a variety of viewers were to find a variety of narratives in his photos of tourists (pp. 236–39). But if some viewers were to read the advertisements for the male body (pp. 000–00) as a parody of masculinity rather than as an endorsement of it, the ad agencies' sales objectives might fail.

Some aspects of an image draw our attention, while others recede.

A viewer's initial impulse is to focus on the center of an image because it offers balance, but often an artist shifts the viewer's focus through the use of color, light, or line. Locating the composition's focal point can help the viewer to interpret the image. A good first step is to divide the image by finding its horizontal or diagonal line. Sometimes this line is self-evident, as in Mark Peterson's *Image of Homelessness* (p. 169). At other times the line is less obvious but still present, as in Tracy Baran's photograph *Mom Ironing, 1997* (p. 60), where the horizontal line of the ironing board directs the viewer's attention and also balances the implied movement within the image.

If the viewer's initial reaction is to stare at the center of an image, then the artist might try to counter this impulse by drawing attention elsewhere. The viewer should think about how the focal point (its position, its composition, its identity) helps to construct the meaning of the image. For example, in Martin Parr's photo *Greece, Athens, Acropolis* (p. 237) the viewer can try to focus on the crowd that is slightly in the foreground, but the crowd at the left edge of the picture competes for attention, creating a sense of movement and pulling the viewer into the activity.

Look for patterns of color, shape, or shadow in the image.

Viewers organize information by establishing relationships of similarity, by looking for patterns. And patterns may be established by repeating a color or a shape, by repeating the use of light or dark. Just as a writer might use alliteration or rhyming to draw a reader's attention to connections in a poem, a visual artist uses repetition to draw a viewer's attention. The question is "Why is my eye being drawn in this way?" The pattern may suggest the image's meaning (or part of that meaning), or it may be wholly imposed by a viewer seeking closure.

Advertising images rely on repeated patterns to convey and then underscore their message. Yet patterns are not exclusively the domain of commercial art. See, for example, Roger Shimomura's piece *24 People for Whom I Have Been Mistaken* (pp. 422–23). The photographs, despite showing very different individuals, are all the same size and all are set in the same frame. Such repetition highlights the inclination of some Americans to stereotype people instead of focusing on each individual's distinctive characteristics.

Patterns may also be traced within one painting, such as the blue tones in Edward Hopper's *House by the Railroad* (p. 143), or across a series of images to determine an artistic style, like the heavy shadows on the faces of Nancy Burson's *He/She* series (pp. 360–65).

Visual artists employ many of the same devices that verbal artists use.

When considering an image you should look for visual examples of metaphor, metonymy, or symbolism. While readers of prose texts frequently find metaphor, viewers of images often find metonymy – the concept of "a part substituting for the whole." Metonymy is particularly well suited to a visual medium, as when an artist shows a fragment of a larger object in order to send a message to the reader. For example, James Nachtwey's photograph *Crushed Car* (p. 284) and Frank Fournier's photograph *Omayra Sanchez, Colombia, 1985* (p. 590) focus on only one object and one person affected by a much larger catastrophe. By focusing on detail these photographs bring the viewer's attention to what cannot be seen; the viewer is left to imagine how horrific the event outside of the frame must be.

Viewers might well also look for symbolic images, often referred to as cultural icons. A culture often has a visual shorthand language, and within this language certain images have specific, shared meanings: for example, the

American flag, a cowboy, Elvis Presley, Marilyn Monroe. These symbolic images may be used in a way that is true to their accepted cultural currency or in a way that subverts this cultural meaning. For example, the Retrospect on *American Gothic* (pp. 526–27) illustrates a few of the many reincarnations this iconic image has undergone over the past several decades. What do these versions say about American art and culture? How is the meaning of each version different from the meaning of the original?

Remember that all images are composed and that a complete reading should account for all design elements that were within the control of the artist.
The elements within an image are much like the elements in a poem. When a reader analyzes a poem, she accounts not merely for its language but also for its use of capitalization, punctuation, arrangement into lines and stanzas, and so on. When a viewer analyzes an image, she should think about it in essentially the same way, asking the following questions about its design:

> What is the size of the image? Is it a miniature or a magnification? How does this design aspect relate to its message?
>
> What is the perspective of the image? Is the viewer placed above the image, below it, or at the same level? How does this perspective help shape the overall meaning of the image?
>
> Is there anything only partially within the frame of the image? Why might the artist have chosen this type of framing?
>
> Is there any obvious distortion in the image (things taller, smaller, flatter, fatter, brighter, darker, etc.)? How does this distortion relate to or shape the meaning of the image?

An active reader explores how the artist has chosen to present his or her final image: photo or painting, watercolor or oil, black and white or color. These statements hold true for painters, graphic designers, and photographers. For example, one of the most popular contemporary photographers, Lorna Simpson, often dramatically enlarges her photos and has them printed on feltboard. In this case a viewer seeking to read the images must also account for the manner in which a photo printed on felt is very different from a photo printed on glossy paper. So, too, each of the images reproduced in this book is of necessity relatively small; but in a museum or gallery space each would appear much larger.

READING AN ESSAY

Each essay in *Seeing & Writing 4* is part of a larger whole – a textbook – composed of written and visual texts. Each essay should be read not only for what it says but also for how it is structured, how it is laid out (how words and images are distributed on the page), and how it fits into the entire chapter. What inferences can you make about *Seeing & Writing 4* from the way the texts are presented? Looking at essays as physical objects can be an important step in seeing (and developing one's own) written texts with a fresh eye.

The core activity of reading an essay involves being a careful observer, first establishing the evidence of your reading through a series of precise observations.

> Exactly what happens in the essay? What process occurs (what decisions does the writer make?) between the opening and the closing paragraphs?
>
> What type of voice speaks in the essay? Who is speaking? In what tone? In what kind of language?
>
> Within what context is the essay located? What details does the writer give to help the reader visualize the essay's broader context?
>
> What ideas and/or images predominate? What patterns or shifts in ideas and/or images occur during the course of the essay? With what effect(s)?
>
> What is the purpose of the essay? Is it to describe, to tell a story, to explain, to argue – or some combination of these?

The more accurate and plentiful a reader's observations are about a given text, the more opportunities there will be to establish and validate significant inferences.

READING AN ADVERTISEMENT

There are many examples of advertisements in *Seeing & Writing 4*, spanning a wide range of products and appeals throughout the twentieth century and into the twenty-first. The advertisement as a genre has existed for as long as the market economy has; a combination of words and pictures serves a single purpose, no matter the product – to persuade consumers to purchase a product or service. Because ads often must make their points in a compact manner, they combine visual and verbal strategies to shape the most effective message possible in the briefest amount of space. Most of us encounter more advertisements in a day than any other kind of text; recent research suggests that most Americans encounter nearly two thousand commercial appeals each day. The following questions will facilitate critical reading of advertisements.

What is the viewer's eye drawn to first in the advertisement?

In the Bell System advertisements presented in the Retrospect in Chapter 1 (pp. 54–58), the telephones are often paired with images of families, and the ad's language reminds us how easily the telephone can put us in contact with loved ones. As a result the association of Bell telephones with the importance of maintaining family relationships is underscored visually.

How much of the advertisement's message is delivered through words and how much through images? What is the proportion of one to the other?

In the U.S. Military advertisement (p. 386) most of the message is conveyed through the image: A woman first appears as a rock 'n' roll musician, but then we notice her combat boots. The text appeals to an American woman's desire to be strong and independent.

Are the connotations of the language consistent with the connotations of the images?

The image of children holding guns dominates the Collaborate/Amnesty International *Imagine* campaign ad on page 585. The word "imagine" draws our eye, and the text continues in smaller print with "nothing to kill or die for." In this case the contradiction between the text and the image lends the message a sense of urgency.

In what ways does the advertisement appeal to a specific type of reader/viewer?

The purpose of advertisements is to market something to a specific audience on the basis of particular values and aspirations. The 1980 ad for Bell System featured in the Retrospect in Chapter 1 (p. 56) appeals to people who live far from their family.

What is the underlying "logic" of the advertisement?

What does it suggest? This type of logic is created by pairing an image and a product. For example, in the ads presented in the Retrospect in Chapter 4 on "Building the Male Body" (pp. 354–57) the underlying logic is that men must maintain a powerful physique in order to succeed.

READING A POEM

Poetry is one of the oldest, most imaginative, and most intense forms of verbal communication. In *A Handbook to Literature* Hugh Holman and William Harmon define poetry as "a term applied to the many forms in which human beings have given rhythmic expression to their most imaginative and intense perceptions of the world, themselves, and the relation of the two" (p. 384). These definitions underscore the point that imagination, emotions, and aesthetic values – along with such characteristics as rhythm and the use of intense and concrete images – mark the experience of reading poetry. So, too, the language of poetry is, as the celebrated English poet John Milton noted, "simple, sensuous, and impassioned." Poetry is also a form of communication that accentuates the sound of the speaker's voice, his or her tone of voice. To read poetry effectively, one might well follow the suggestion of Robert Frost and read with what he calls the "hearing imagination." The poet, much like other artists and musicians, is especially sensitive to artistic expressions of states of consciousness. One teacher, Charles Hood of Antelope Valley College, defines poetry as "a tango with death."

Because we generally expect the language of poetry to be more economical than that of prose, every word in a poem bears the pressure of meaning and significance. So, too, many readers argue that poetry is meant to be experienced as much as it is meant to be read. The questions that follow will help readers, especially those who are unfamiliar with the genre, to reach a better understanding and appreciation of this ancient form of verbal art.

Who is the speaker of the poem? How would you characterize the speaker?

In Jacinto Jesús Cardona's "Bato con Khakis" (p. 324) the speaker remembers how, as a younger man, he admired the elusive cool of the other boys in his neighborhood. Recalling his desire to emulate them, the poet evokes his feelings at the time, even switching to the present tense to admit, "cool bato I am not." But by writing the poem Cardona has already answered his youthful question, "Could I be the bookish bato?"

What kinds of images are present in the poem?

The images in poems can be literal (capturing a moment, a scene, a person, an action, or a perception as they are) or figurative (representing a moment, a scene, a person, an action, or a perception as it resembles something else). In "The Waitress" (p. 501) Billy Collins imagines a night in which all the waitresses and waiters who have ever served him gather "for one night in a vast ballroom / where they have removed their jackets, / their aprons and bowties, / and now they are having a cigarette / or they are dancing with one another, / turning slowly in each other's arms / to a five-piece syncopated band." At the end of the poem Collins's fantasy of the ballroom "is made of nothing but autumn leaves – / red, yellow, and gold – / just waiting for a sudden gust of wind / to scatter it all." By taking the waitress out of her restaurant and placing her in a crowded ballroom, Collins encourages us to look more closely at the woman he positions at the center of his poem.

What does the poem sound like?

Reading poems aloud invariably helps in understanding how they work. This can be a way to discover and characterize the tone of a poem, one of the most important aspects of its meanings. For example, reading aloud from Pablo Neruda's "Ode to Things" (p. 112) will call attention to the effect of his many fragments.

By using short stanzas and common language Neruda's verse mirrors the commonality of his subject.

What is the setting of the poem? Is it in a landscape? Does it have characters?

Different poems foreground different elements. Jane Yolen's "Grant Wood: American Gothic" (p. 523) takes its setting from the painting, but she mentions details of the house and of the character's dress only to instruct the reader to ignore them. The "brooch at the throat, / the gothic angel wing / of window" is unimportant; what is essential to Yolen is the character of these two people, which she imagines "looks out at you" from their eyes.

How does the poem look on the page?

A reader doesn't need a detailed knowledge of poetics to make careful observations about a poem's shape – its length, the arrangement of its lines, or any other visual detail. In "Edward Hopper and the House by the Railroad (1925)" by Edward Hirsch (p. 142), the length of the stanzas and their placement on the page suggest a balanced structure, which is fitting since the poem describes a house.

READING A PAINTING

Each painting in *Seeing & Writing 4* is part of a visual genre that shares certain conventions and goals. Painting, along with sculpture, has historically been associated with high art and the individual style and vision of the artist. One of the oldest visual genres, painting has developed through many schools of representative and abstract styles of expression. The following questions will help you read paintings in a meaningful way even if you have never studied the conventions of painting.

What is the style of painting?

Viewers don't need to be well versed in art history to determine whether a painting is more or less realistic. To begin reading a painting, they should seek to understand what the painter wants to convey: a realistic depiction of a person, place, or thing; a purely personal impression of it; or something in between. For example, Edward Hopper's *House by the Railroad* (p. 143) is recognizable as exactly what its title states – even though Hopper imbues the painting with a haunting feeling and a strong sense of isolation.

What is the focal point of the artist's attention in the painting? How does the subject of the painting relate to the manner in which the artist depicts it?

Like all art, paintings can affect the way their viewers see the world. For example, through his depiction of *Li'L Sis* (p. 328) William H. Johnson reveals expectations placed on this child as a girl growing up in the rural South. Pierre-Auguste Renoir paints a waitress (p. 500) in a straightforward manner and thereby underscores his respect for both the woman and her profession, an appreciation he wants his viewers to share.

What perspective is used in the painting?

Perspective situates the viewer and can highlight or minimize a sense of depth. For example, in *House by the Railroad* (p. 143) Edward Hopper relies on perspective to create a sense of isolation. In contrast, many primitive or folk art styles of painting, such as the one used by César A. Martínez (p. 325), avoid highlighting perspective and offer instead simple, flat images. These images underscore a sense of primitive purity and honesty. Readers should also be alert to paintings that add depth where one might not expect it (e.g., the view of the curtains in the top window in Grant Wood's *American Gothic*, p. 516) or deny depth where one does expect it (e.g., the flat-looking image by James Rosenquist, p. 640). Often these works use perspective to add nuance to the meaning and significance of the painting.

What is the tone of the painting?

As a writer uses words, a painter uses color and light. A painting might be inviting, with little shading and bright colors. An example is Pierre-Auguste Renoir's *A Waitress at Duval's Restaurant* (p. 500), which conveys a sense of the personal warmth of the waitress and the comfortable atmosphere of the restaurant. Alternatively a painting might be rich, bright, and confrontational, with many bold colors. An example is William H. Johnson's *Li'L Sis* (p. 328).

READING A PHOTOGRAPH

Like the paintings, the photographs in *Seeing & Writing 4* are part of a genre that shares certain conventions and goals. This genre has existed for a more than a century. It is commonly recognized as setting the standard for realistic representation, replacing painting as the most accurate means of recording an image. Generally photographs can be divided into two broad categories: (1) documentary photographs, such as those that accompany a news story, that seek to accurately show what a person, place, or event looks like; and (2) creative photographs, such as artistic photos and advertisements, in which the person, place, event, or photograph has been staged to achieve a specific effect. The Looking Closer section for Chapter 7, "Altering Images" (pp. 663–86), examines the blurring of the distinctions between these two types of photographs. The following questions will help you understand and appreciate photographs even if you are unfamiliar with the genre conventions of photography.

Is the photo meant to convey an artistic purpose, or is it presented for a commercial purpose or as news?

The distinctions are becoming increasingly blurred, but a reader should still understand the overarching purpose of the photo. Doing so will also help you to understand its context. For example, viewers may be expected to spend only a few seconds scanning a newspaper photo but minutes or even a longer time studying an art photo in a gallery. A photographer's beliefs about how an audience will perceive an image will affect the way in which he or she composes the image. Viewers might consider how Lauren Greenfield's *Ashleigh, 13, with Her Friend and Parents, Santa Monica* (p. 378) differs dramatically from James Nachtwey's photo of Ground Zero (p. 284), largely because of their contexts and purposes. The former presents an oblique commentary; the latter presents a historic moment.

Is the photo in black and white or color?

Black and white photos, such as Andrew Savulich's snapshots (pp. 278–81), hold a documentary connotation. Often these may be news photos, and the simplicity of black and white (initially a limitation of the printing press) conveys a sense of straightforward presentation of information. Other photos may not be news images but carry the same connotations, such as Brook Jensen's photographs in the opening portfolio in Chapter 6 (pp. 493–97).

Does the image in the photo seem to have been altered in any way?

Photographs seem to capture exactly what the photographer sees: a moment in time. However, it is easy to edit an image, rearrange subjects in it, enhance colors and shading, or add digital effects. Often these changes are difficult to discern. Viewers should consider the purpose of the photo when asking whether effects might have been added and how to interpret their use. For example, most readers understand that the image of a model in an advertisement or a fashion feature might be modified before it is published. However, fewer readers expect that news images, such as that of the flag raising on Iwo Jima (p. 308), will be altered.

How is the image framed in the photo?

An image in a photo might be centered, offset to the left, or offset to the right. Traditionally a straight, centered photograph is used for portraits. Offset photos are often used to suggest motion by drawing the viewer's eye along a horizontal or diagonal line, as in Martin Parr's *Paris, 18th District* (p. 236). Sometimes these images also suggest entrapment by crowding the subject against one of the photo's edges. In addition, photos have a vertical axis that can either open up or close down an image. If a photographer heavily shades the top of an image, then it can appear to be pressing down on the photo subject; if the image is bright, then the opposite effect results. For example, the Cuban flag in Jon Lowenstein's photograph *Protest in Humboldt Park against Bomb Testing on the Island of Vieques, Puerto Rico* (p. 216) offers an imposing element that crowds the composition.

How is the photo cropped?

Often what is left out of a photo is as important as what is included. A photo may have been cropped (or cut) to eliminate elements that would distract from the subject or to refocus the subject. For example, Joe Rosenthal's picture (p. 308) has focused the viewer's attention on the flag raising as a symbol of victory by eliminating any distracting elements.

READING A SHORT STORY

The short story spans works such as biblical narratives, Chaucer's tales, and contemporary fiction, and it gained recognition in the twenti-eth century as a very important literary genre. Generally a short story can be defined as a brief fictional prose narrative; the term is often applied to any work of narrative prose fiction that is shorter than a novel. A short story usually has an identifiable plot, structure, characters, setting, and point of view. The following questions will help you think critically about the elements of a short story.

What is the point of view of the story? Who is the narrator, and from what perspective (point of view) is he or she speaking?

In "Girl" (p. 329) Jamaica Kincaid tells the story from two first-person points of view. One voice gives commands to a young girl and offers opinions, and the young girl speaks in another voice, offering a contradictory view. The narrative reads somewhat like an argument that we, as readers, overhear. This treatment makes readers feel as if they are the girl wishing to defend herself. As a result the girl is presented as a sympathetic character.

What is the setting of the story? Where does it take place?

What are the characteristics of that place? Eudora Welty's "The Little Store" (p. 147) takes place in Jackson, Mississippi, and as the title suggests, the store is the setting. This location becomes emblematic of the lives that play out in the small community during the narrator's childhood. As Welty states, "We weren't being sent to the neighborhood grocery for facts of life, or death. But of course those are what we were on the track of, anyway" (para. 31).

Who are the characters in the story? To whom is the story happening? How are the characters affected?

The very short story "Vivian, Fort Barnwell" by Ethan Canin (p. 242) has few characters — primarily the narrator and his wife. However, it is about characters that are not present — his mother and grandmother. The story is about the narrator's realization that a photograph he has always treasured is not of his mother but of his grandmother. What he thought was his clear memory of the day and place in the photograph turns out to be faulty. He questions, "My God, you're right. How could that have happened?" (para. 5). Indeed, the family history embodied in family snapshots may not be "true" as we remember.

What happens in the story? What is the main action?

What happens in "I Stand Here Ironing" by Tillie Olsen (p. 62) is simple and profound. As she irons a dress, the narrator's thoughts dwell on her troubled daughter and on how her family has arrived at its present situation. The story's action does not move beyond the woman's ruminating as she irons.

What are the significant images in the story? How do things look?

Eudora Welty's "The Little Store" (p. 147) is about what a child sees and fails to see. Although Welty's descriptions utilize all five senses, some of the most revealing involve sight. The description of the cheese being "as big as a doll's house" (para. 16) firmly puts readers in the child's point of view. The narrator's descriptions provide readers with a sense of character as well as a sense of place.

What changes or transformations occur (or fail to occur) during the course of the narrative?

Amy Tan's "Fish Cheeks" (p. 218) is a narrative of a young Chinese American girl who struggles to come to terms with her Chinese heritage because she wants to assimilate completely into American culture. She describes the evening when an American family came to her childhood home for dinner and, to her horror and embarrassment, her family boldly displayed aspects of their Chinese culture. By the end of the narrative she gains a sense of what would become an important lesson – that she must be proud of who she is.

READING MIXED MEDIA

The term *mixed media* generally describes the work of contemporary artists who employ unusual combinations of material to achieve a desired effect (sometimes appealing to senses of smell, taste, and touch as well as sight). Materials used in the texts in *Seeing & Writing 4* that are labeled as mixed media include wood, "found" ordinary objects, photographs, newspapers, videos, and other unusual or unexpected building blocks combined and presented in extraordinary ways. (*Mixed media* is often used to characterize a piece when it doesn't fall into a "pure" category such as painting or photography.)

What material has been used in the creation of the work?

Why might the artist have used this particular combination of materials? Often the original source of some part of the artwork – text from a newspaper, for example – has been deliberately chosen to make a particular point and must be considered in reading the work as a whole. The artist Sally Mankus (not represented in *Seeing & Writing 4*), for example, lifts rust, carbon, and marking from charred surfaces (mainly bakeware). She writes that "objects (pans, pot lids, napkins, etc.) and materials (rust, carbon) used are so common they become symbols in a universal language."

Is any part of the work a "found" object?

Mixed media works often include "found" objects, that is, things that have been incorporated into an original piece or simply appropriated for art. When artists use found objects they are commenting on the role of these products within our culture. For example, Pepón Osorio's *Badge of Honor* (pp. 92–93 and 95) includes actual posters of basketball players and suggests how such figures can become father figures.

Is the work realistic, or is it abstract and impressionistic?

Any work of art falls along this spectrum, and its degree of realism is in part a message. For example, in *Badge of Honor* (pp. 92–93, 95) the exaggerated opulence of the boy's room invites viewers to contrast it with the father's stark cell.

If the work is three dimensional, what does the third dimension add to the piece?

Unless otherwise enhanced, photography and painting are primarily two-dimensional media. Most mixed-media pieces offer viewers a third dimension, which might make the work tactile or might add realism.

If the work includes text, what is the relationship between the text and the image/body of the piece?

Mixed-media pieces sometimes take the form of a collage of image and text. The text comments on the work, helping to frame the viewer's reading.

Glossary

abstract art Visual art that explores meaning through shape, color, and texture rather than through a realistic representation of scenes or objects.

abstract expressionism An abstract art movement in which the act of expressing emotions was considered as important as the resulting work. Abstract expressionists applied paint rapidly to the canvas, believing that the spontaneity of this technique released their creativity.

allusion An indirect, brief, or casual reference to a person, place, event, object, or artwork. Allusion draws on a body of images or stories shared by the audience and allows a short phrase to bring up a whole set of associated information.

ambiguity The potential for being understood in more than one way. Both literature and the visual arts use ambiguity to express the inherent richness and complexity of the world. In advertising, ambiguity can be used to deceive without actually lying.

analogy The use of a comparison to extend knowledge of something new by means of its similarity to something already known. Analogy can be explanatory, as in comparing ice skating with in-line skating. Comparing the "war on drugs" with Prohibition is an example of using analogy to further an argument.

analysis The process of breaking something complex into its parts, examining each part and the relations among the parts, and coming to a better understanding of the whole. An analytical essay reconstructs the whole in an orderly way to facilitate understanding.

argument A claim advanced with its supporting reasons, or evidence. The claim addresses a single point ("the town should fund a night school"). The reasons may be facts ("25 percent of high school students in this town drop out without graduating") or values ("everyone deserves equal treatment"), but they must lead logically to the conclusion without intellectual dishonesty. In an argument essay the claim is the thesis statement; it is presented early and followed by a summary of the argument. Then each of the reasons is developed, with supporting information where it is needed. In addition to advancing sufficient reasons to support its claim, a good argument assesses and refutes claims opposed to it. An effective argument essay takes into account the audience's values and knowledge base.

assertion A claim or statement of belief. To be useful in discourse, an assertion needs supporting evidence. An unsupported assertion is merely an expression of opinion.

assumption A claim accepted without the necessity of proof or other support. While assumptions are necessary devices in all arguments, many faulty arguments depend on assumptions that, once accepted, require the acceptance of the conclusions. Analysis of an argument should always include a clear statement of its assumptions.

audience The intended recipient of a communication or work of art. Audiences differ in their values, assumptions, knowledge bases, needs, desires, tastes, and styles. Having an accurate sense of the intended audience is essential for a writer. See "Visualizing Composition: Audience" (p. 439) for examples.

brainstorming The recording of thoughts as they occur, with no regard for their relation to each other. When writers brainstorm they leap from one thought to another without exploring the connections among ideas. Brainstorming unleashes creativity by temporarily removing the censor or editor that restricts us to considering only what we already know.

cause and effect An analysis that focuses on why something happens (cause) and what occurs as a result (effect). Explorations of cause and effect can be quite complex since some events have many contributing causes, not all of them close to the event itself. Unless the writer demonstrates a causal mechanism, the mere association of events (coincidence) is not grounds for concluding a cause and effect relationship.

character The combination of features or qualities that distinguishes a person, group, or object from another; a person (or, occasionally, an animal or inanimate object) in a literary or dramatic work.

claim A statement made with the intention that it be accepted as true. In an argument essay the thesis statement expresses the claim.

classification The act of sorting things on the basis of shared characteristics. The characteristics can be physical ("the class of all round things"), social ("the class of middle-income people"), personal ("the class of things I don't like"), and so on. The items in one class may or may not also belong to other classes.

cliché A figure of speech or a graphic expression that fails to communicate effectively because of overuse. A cliché fails in two ways: (1) because the point of figurative language is to convey something more richly than literal words can, and (2) because the empty phrase is like a dead space. To avoid cliché, use figures of speech that arise from concrete, specific experience. Picture what you want the reader to see, and make sure your language calls up that picture effectively.

color Literally, the ranges of the electromagnetic spectrum that are reflected by pigments or transmitted by light. In art, the use of color is a deliberate choice. In writing, adding color involves adding emotional content to a factual account.

comic A story told in drawings, hand-lettered dialogue, and short bits of written narrative. Not all comics are intended to be funny; Marjane Satrapi's "The Veil," from *Persepolis* (p. 343) is a comic tale based on her experience as a child growing up in Iran.

compare and contrast A systematic exploration of the ways in which two or more things are alike and different. A writer might use this technique to show that two apparently dissimilar things are alike in some important way or to point out crucial differences between two related things.

composition The act of arranging parts so that they form a meaningful or pleasing whole. A written or graphic composition requires careful planning of the sequential or spatial relationship of its elements to produce this meaningful unity. See each chapter's "Visualizing Composition" for explanations and illustrations of these elements of composition: "Slowed-Down Reading" (p. 71), "Tone" (p. 188), "Structure" (p. 277), "Purpose" (p. 359), "Audience" (p. 439), "Metaphor" (p. 558), and "Point of View" (p. 649).

connotation The associations and emotional impact carried by a word or phrase in addition to its literal meaning. A minivan, an SUV, and a Volkswagen Bug are all vehicles, but specifying one of them as a character's means of transportation conveys meaning beyond the literal cubic feet of interior capacity.

context The part of a text or statement that surrounds a particular word or image and helps determine its meaning; the interrelated conditions within which something exists or occurs (historical, cultural, and environmental setting). Context is essential to the full understanding of a text or event. See each chapter's "Context" for further illustration and explanation of context.

contrast The use of strong differences in art or in argument. Advertising often uses contrast by pointing out the differences between a product and its competitors.

critical reading The act of analyzing, interpreting, and evaluating verbal or graphic text. A critical reading of a text includes close reading, note-taking, contextualizing, rereading, and connecting. Most texts provoke some emotional response; a critical reader explores this emotional response rather than simply accepting it as valid.

critical thinking The practice of subjecting claims to close examination and analysis.

cropping Making a photograph smaller by trimming it so that some of the original photo is removed. Cropping is part of the photographer's act of framing an image.

deduction In logic, a form of argument in which *if* the premises are true, then the conclusion *must be* true as well. To dispute a conclusion derived through deduction, a writer must show that at least one of the premises is false. (Compare with *induction*.)

definition An explanation of the meaning of a word, phrase, or concept. A definition essay is an extended exploration both of the class to which something belongs and of the ways it differs from other things in that class.

demographic The statistical characterization of a population by age, marital or household status, education, income, race, ethnicity, and so on.

denotation The direct and explicit meaning of a specific word; in contrast to *connotation*, which means to suggest or convey what is not explicit.

description An account of an event, object, person, or process. A writer uses description to convey a vivid and accurate image to the reader. Description requires attention to sensory details – sights, smells, sounds, tastes, touch. *Subjective description* includes an account of the writer's inner experience of the thing being described.

design The plan for an event, object, or process. Design combines purpose with an understanding of the ways things work. It marks the difference between a random collection and a purposeful composition.

diction Stylistic choice of words and syntax, as between high (educated and formal) and low (ordinary and popular), between abstract and concrete, between specific and general. In "Cool Like Me" (p. 415), Donnell Alexander alternates street diction – "I'm the kinda nigga who's so cool that my neighbor bursts into hysterical tears whenever I ring her doorbell after dark" – with more conventional usage – "But her real experience of us is limited to the space between her Honda and her front gate."

digital imaging Creating or altering images electronically. Before the use of digital imaging, photographic evidence was considered a reliable record of events. Since digital technology can generate realistic images of things that have no real-world counterpart, photographs have lost this status.

documentary photography Photography that pays close attention to factual detail. Although it captures an image of what actually is, it still uses such compositional techniques as framing and cropping. Documentary photography sometimes implies social commentary. The photographer James Nachtwey (pp. 284–88) has a particularly effective sense of the form.

draft A preliminary or intermediate version of a work. A first draft forges the results of research, planning, note-taking, brainstorming, and freewriting into the beginning of a cohesive whole. Further drafts refine the thesis, improve the organization, add transitions, and strengthen the conclusion.

emphasis The bringing of increased attention to a point or element to convey its importance. Repetition and prominent placement add emphasis, as do the use of italics, large type, color, and bold contrast.

euphemism An expression used in place of a word or phrase that is considered harsh or unpleasant – for example, using *passed away* for *died*.

evidence Information presented in support of a claim. To be convincing, the information must be from a reliable source and adequately documented.

exposition An essay that explains difficult material. In addition to analysis, exposition uses familiar illustrations or analogies. K. C. Cole's "A Matter of Scale" (p. 85) is an example of exposition.

figurative language Language that is not literally true but that expresses something more richly and effectively than literal language can. In "Seeing" (p. 96) Annie Dillard calls an island *tear-shaped*, conveying in two words an image that would require a much longer description in literal terms.

font The design of lettering used in text. Fonts can be formal, elegant, traditional, modern, casual, silly, or purely functional. Choice of font is a subtle but critical design element.

found objects Ordinary objects, not originally intended as art, that are found, chosen, arranged, and exhibited by an artist.

framing Constructing by fitting parts into a whole; designing; shaping; putting into words, formulating; enclosing in, or as if in, a frame. Framing is one of the compositional elements of a photo or other graphic image.

freewriting A strategy in which the writer writes without pausing to consider grammar, sentence structure, word choice, and spelling. Also called *nonstop writing*. Freewriting is a technique writers can use to get started with thinking and writing.

graphic design The application of design principles to articles intended for commercial or persuasive purposes. Virtually every printed or broadcast item – packaging, signage, sets and backdrops, book covers, magazines – has been graphically designed to maximize the effectiveness of its message.

graphic elements Separate pieces that are assembled into a whole in a graphic composition.

high art Art whose techniques require formal education and whose purpose is primarily aesthetic. In contrast, *craft* may be decorative but is mainly functional, and *folk art* or *popular art* requires little formal training.

hyperbole An obvious and intentional exaggeration – for example, using *starving* for *hungry*.

hypothesis An explanation that accounts for the known facts and makes further predictions that logically must be true if the explanation is true. These predictions can be tested, and the hypothesis is disconfirmed if they are false.

iconic Widely accepted as a symbol.

identity A unified, persistent sense of who a person uniquely is; the inner experience of one's self.

idiom A style of expression peculiar to an individual or a group. Idiomatic expressions may make no sense literally – for example, "to have it in for someone" or "to give someone a piece of your mind."

illustration A picture or design in a print medium used to explain a point in the text.

illustration / exemplification One of the methods of discourse; a process in which writers use specific examples to represent, clarify, and/or support either general or abstract statements. For an example of illustration, see Annie Dillard's essay "Seeing" (p. 96).

image A thing that represents something else; a symbol, an emblem, a representation. Also, the picture called into a reader's mind by a writer's use of descriptive or figurative language.

induction A method of reasoning from experience, from observed facts to a generalized pattern; scientific reasoning is inductive. *Inductive generalization* is the conclusion that the next item in a series will be like the items already observed. The strength of an inductive conclusion depends on the size of the sample observed and the uniformity of the sample. (Compare with *deduction*.)

inference An intellectual leap from what one sees to what those details might suggest; a conclusion drawn from available facts. An interpretation of a text is an inference, a conclusion about what the text means based on detailed observations about it.

installation A planned, deliberate arrangement of artworks in a space.

invention The development of a device or process not previously in use.

irony An often-humorous aspect of writing that calls attention to the difference between the actual result of a sequence of events and the expected result; an expression that says one thing while intending to convey its opposite.

layout The process of arranging printed or graphic material on a page; the overall design of a page, including such elements as type size, typeface, titles, and page numbers.

media The methods by which things are transmitted; in particular, the mass media – newspapers, magazines, movies, television and radio broadcasts, and recordings – that transmit ideas and images to the culture at large.

medium The material or technique used by an artist; by extension, the material or technique that carries a message, including print and airwaves.

metaphor A word or phrase that means one thing but is used to describe something else in order to suggest a relationship between the two; an implied comparison. Sarah Vowell is using metaphor when she says in "The First Thanksgiving" (p. 245), "We are heading into uncharted and possibly hostile waters, pioneers in a New World. It is Thanksgiving. The pilgrims had the *Mayflower*. I buy a gravy boat." See "Visualizing Composition: Metaphor" (p. 558) for more examples.

metonymy A figure of speech in which one word or phrase substitutes for another closely associated with it – for example, *Washington* for *U.S. government*.

mixed media A composition using two or more media, as in a collage, a sound and light show, or a combination of sculptures and paintings.

narrative A verbal or graphic account of events.

narrator The person telling a story, from whose point of view it has cohesive unity. The narrator can be a character in the story or an observer who takes no part in the action.

oblique Neither perpendicular nor parallel; indirect.

observation The act, practice, or power of noticing; a comment or remark based on something observed. In rhetoric, an observation is a neutral statement supported by specific evidence about something in a text.

ode A formal poem in praise of something noble.

parody A mocking imitation that exaggerates some quality in the original. Parody is used to entertain – unlike satire, whose purpose is to stimulate reform.

personification The attribution of human qualities to an object or an idea; often used as a poetic device.

perspective The physical or figurative point from which the artist or writer sees the subject; also, the effect of that standpoint on what the writer or artist sees and conveys. The size, relation, and even existence of both physical and conceptual things seem different depending on the observer's literal or figurative relation to a scene.

persuasion The act or process of moving someone to a decision or an opinion.

photoessay A collection of photographs composed to develop a point or a theme in the manner of a written essay.

photojournalism The reporting of events through the use of photographs.

point of view The perspective, or angle of vision, from which writers and artists see and present a subject. This perspective may be expressed – simply and literally – as the physical stance they establish in viewing a subject. In writing, point of view may also be revealed through the tone of voice, or attitude, that the writer expresses in addressing a subject. See "Visualizing Composition: Point of View" (p. 649) for examples.

pop art An art movement that uses familiar images from the mass culture to blur the distinction between high art and popular expression. James Rosenquist (p. 640) is a pop artist.

portfolio A representative collection of an artist's work; in particular, a collection of closely related images. See "Portfolio" features on

Gueorgui Pinkhassov (p. 72), Joel Sternfeld (p. 132), Andrew Savulich (p. 278), Nancy Burson (p. 360), and Nikki S. Lee (p. 397) for examples.

portraiture The making of a posed representation of a person or group of persons. In addition to showing a physical likeness, a portrait conveys the subject's personality. Historically, portraits included clothing, jewelry, and settings that showed the subject's social standing.

premise A statement that forms the basis of an argument and leads to the conclusion; one of the reasons why a claim should be accepted.

public art Art that is paid for with tax dollars, installed in public places, and intended for a wide audience. The Vietnam Veterans Memorial in Washington, D.C., is an example of public art.

purpose The goal a writer has in mind; the effect a writer intends to have on the audience. See "Visualizing Composition: Purpose" (p. 359) for examples.

representation A depiction, portrayal, or reproduction that brings to mind a specific thing or person.

revision The act of rewriting an initial draft of a text, working toward a final version. Revising includes both large-scale changes such as restructuring or rewriting and smaller-scale changes such as editing for grammar and syntax.

rhetoric Writing or speaking for the purpose of communication or persuasion, with attention to audience and purpose; the principles, technical terms, and rules developed for the practice of rhetoric.

satire A form of literary composition that criticizes through the use of ridicule; a form of political speech whose intent is to provoke change.

simile A figure of speech that compares two unlike things using the words *like*, *as*, *as if*, or *as though*. In "Fish Cheeks" (p. 218), Amy Tan uses simile when she writes of "tofu, which looked like stacked wedges of rubbery white sponges."

staged photography A work in which the photographer arranges the elements of a picture deliberately, in contrast to a candid shot or a documentary photograph.

stereotype A generalization that can be either positive or negative. The word *stereotype* comes from the form or mold used by artisans to create a repeating pattern. To hold a stereotyped idea of a population is to believe all of its members are alike instead of being highly variable individuals.

still life A form of painting that represents a composed arrangement of ordinary objects. The act of making art out of the ordinary challenges the viewer to look more carefully at the everyday.

structure The way in which the parts of a system are put together; the planned framework of a piece of writing. See "Visualizing Composition: Structure" (p. 277) for more examples.

style The way in which something is said, done, performed, or expressed. The poet Robert Frost defined style as "the way [a person] carries himself [herself] toward his [her] ideas and deeds."

syllogism A valid argument containing two premises and a conclusion. If both premises are true, then the conclusion is true. But if one of the premises is false, there is no way to judge the conclusion.

symbolism The use of something tangible, material, or visible to stand for and express what is intangible, spiritual, or invisible – for example, the eagle symbolizes the qualities that make up U.S. national culture.

syntax The study of the rules whereby words or other elements of sentence structure are combined to form grammatical sentences; the pattern of formation of sentences or phrases in a language. Syntax implies a systematic, orderly arrangement.

texture As an element of art, the surface or visual feel – smooth, rough, soft, and so on. The texture may be actual or simulated.

thesis statement An explicit statement of the purpose of an essay; in an argument essay, the claim that the writer is advancing and that the text will support.

tone The feelings conveyed by the writer's choice of words. In "No Place Like Home" (p. 158) David Guterson conveys disapproval with his choice of descriptive words – "expensive mountain bikes," "conspicuously devoid of gas stations." See "Visualizing Composition: Tone" (p. 188) for more examples.

typography The design, style, and arrangement of printed material. Careful choice of fonts establishes tone. The relative sizes of fonts; the use of color, italics, and bold; and the arrangement of blocks of text and white space guide a reader's attention. Digital technology has expanded typography options and has increased the effectiveness of text as a vehicle for communication.

values The ideals, customs, and institutions of a society toward which its people have an emotional reaction. These values may be positive (such as cleanliness, freedom, or education) or negative (such as cruelty, crime, or blasphemy).

visual literacy The ability to read and write in a purely visual medium; the ability to decode the meaning delivered by visual texts through design, typography, and images.

voice The sound of the text in the reader's mind as well as the sense of the person it conveys. Voice results from the distinctive blend of diction and syntax, the resulting rhythms and sounds, and the use of images and idioms. A voice that is natural and authentic sounds consistent to the reader, but a voice that is "put on" gives itself away in false notes.

Rhetorical Table of Contents

Description

Acknowledgments

Chapter 1
Verbal Texts
Akiko Busch. "Introduction." Originally published in *The Uncommon Life of Common Objects: Essays on Design and the Everyday*. New York: Metropolis Books, 2005. Reprinted by permission.

K. C. Cole. "A Matter of Scale." From *The Universe and the Teacup: The Mathematics of Truth and Beauty*. Copyright © 1998 by K. C. Cole. Reprinted by permission of Harcourt, Inc.

Annie Dillard. "Seeing." From *Pilgrim at Tinker Creek*. Copyright © 1974 by Annie Dillard. Reprinted by permission of HarperCollins Publishers, Inc.

Brian Doyle. "Joyas Volardoras." From T*he American Scholar*, Volume 73, No. 4, Autumn 2004. Copyright © 2004 by the author. Reprinted by permission of The American Scholar.

Siri Hustvedt. "Unknown Keys." From *How I Write*, by Dan Crowe, et al. Copyright © 2007 by Dan Crowe. Reprinted by permission of the author and Rizzoli International Publishers, Inc.

Pablo Neruda. "Ode to Things." From *Odes to Common Things* by Pablo Neruda and Fundacion Pablo Neruda (Odes in Spanish). Copyright © 1994 by Ferris Cook (Illustrations and Compilation). By permission of Little, Brown & Company.

Annalee Newitz. "My Laptop." From *Evocative Objects: Things We Think With*, edited by Sherry Turkle. MIT Press.

Tillie Olsen. "I Stand Here Ironing." From *Tell Me A Riddle*. Copyright © 1961 Tillie Olsen. Reprinted by permission of The Francis Goldin Literary Agency.

Larry Woiwode. "Ode to an Orange." Two pages from *The Paris Review*, 1985 by Larry Woiwode. Reprinted by permission of Donadio & Olson, Inc.
Visual Texts
Hungry Planet, 2005. Peter Menzel. © Peter Menzel / menzelphoto.com

Penelope Umbrico (with Her Daughters), Monday, February 3, 2003, 7–7:30 p.m. Matthew Pillsbury / Courtesy of Matthew Pillsbury and Bonni Benrubi Gallery, NYC.

Orange Crate Labels. Courtesy of California Orange Growers.

Have One Brand. Sequoia Citrus Association. Courtesy the Bancroft Library, University of California, Berkeley.

Retrospect: Phone Home. Gaslight Advertising Archives. *T-Mobile Google Phone.* REUTERS / Mike Segar.

Mom Ironing, 1997. Tracey Baran. © Tracey Baran, Courtesy Leslie Tonkonow Artworks + Projects, NY.

Visualizing Composition: Slowed-Down Reading. Peter Arkle. © Peter Arkle, 2009.

Gueorgui Pinkhassov Portfolio. *Pregame Prayer, Billy Ryan High School, Denton, Texas; Salat-ul-Zuhr (Noon) Prayers, Mardigian Library, University of Michigan–Dearborn; Day of Miracles Ceremony, Land of Medicine Buddha, Soquel, California; Satnam Waheguru Prayer, Minar's Taj Palace, New York.* Courtesy Gueorgui Pinkhassov / Magnum Photos.

Badge of Honor, 1995. Pepón Osorio. © Pepón Osorio. Courtesy Ronald Feldman Fine Arts, New York / www.feldmangallery.com

Unknown Keys. Siri Hustvedt. "Unknown Keys." From *How I Write,* by Dan Crowe, et al. Copyright © 2007 by Dan Crowe. Reprinted by permission of the author and Rizzoli International Publishers, Inc.

Magic Money Boxes. George Skelcher. Courtesy of George Skelcher.

Story of Stuff screenshot. Courtesy of Annie Leonard / Story of Stuff.

This is Daphne and those are her things, 2007. Trujillo Paumier. Courtesy of Trujillo Paumier.

Chapter 2
Verbal Texts
Julia Alvarez. "Neighbors." First published in *Double-Take* magazine, Spring 2000. Copyright © 2000 by Julia Alvarez. Reprinted by permission of Susan Bergholz Literary Services, New York, NY, and Lamy, NM. All rights reserved.

Angela M. Balcita. "Americano Dream." From *Red Mountain Review*, Fall 2005. Reprinted in *Utne Reader*, July / August 2006. Also published in *Elysian Fields Quarterly* (Vol. 23, #1). Reprinted by permission of the author.

Richard Ford. "At Home. For Now." From *Smithsonian Magazine*, December 2007. Copyright © 2007 by Richard Ford. Reprinted by permission of the author.

David Guterson. "No Place Like Home: On The Manicured Streets of a Master-Planned Community." Originally published in *Harper's Magazine*. Copyright © 1991 by David Guterson. Reprinted by permission of Georges Borchardt, Inc., for David Guterson.

Edward Hirsch. "Edward Hopper and the House by the Railroad (1925)." Poem from *Wild Gratitude* by Edward Hirsch. Copyright © 1985 by Edward Hirsch. Used by permission of Alfred A. Knopf, a division of Random House, Inc.

Kenji Jasper. "The Streets Change, But Memories Endure." Originally published in *Newsweek* magazine, August 13, 2007, "My Turn" column. Reprinted by permission of the author.

Norman Mailer. From "Three Minutes or Less." Copyright © Norman Mailer. Reprinted by permission of Norman Mailer Licensing, LLC.

Pat Mora. "Immigrants." Copyright © 1986 Arte Publico Press–University of Houston. Reprinted with permission from the publisher of *Borders* by Pat Mora.

Bharati Mukherjee. "Imagining Homelands." Originally published in *Letters of Transit: Reflections on Exile, Identity, Language, and Loss*, ed. by André Aciman. Copyright © 1999 by Bharati Mukherjee. Reprinted by permission of the author.

Scott Russell Sanders. "Homeplace." First published in *Orion* (Winter 1992). Copyright © 1992 by Scott Russell Sanders. Reprinted by permission of the author.

Amy Tan. "Fish Cheeks." First published in *Seventeen Magazine*. Copyright © 1987. Reprinted by permission of the author and the Sandra Dijkstra Literary Agency.

Eudora Welty. "The Little Store" and excerpt from "Storekeeper, 1935." From *The Eye of the Story*. Copyright © 1978 by Eudora Welty. Used by permission of Random House, Inc.

Visual Texts

Joel Sternfeld Portfolio. Courtesy of the artist and Luhring Augustine, New York.

House by the Railroad, 1925. Edward Hopper, House by the Railroad, 1925. Digital Image © The Museum of Modern Art/Licensed by SCALA/Art Resource, NY.

Storekeeper, 1935. Eudora Welty. Reprinted by permission of Russell & Volkening as agents for the author. © 1989 by Eudora Welty.

65 East 125th Street, Harlem series. Camilo Jose Vergara. Courtesy of Camilo Jose Vergara/ http://invinciblecities.camden.rutgers.edu/intro.html

Image of Homelessness. Mark Peterson. Courtesy of Mark Peterson/Redux Pictures.

Visualizing Composition: Tone. Peter Arkle. © Peter Arkle, 2009.

The Road to Success. Artist Unknown. From Katharine Harmon's *You Are Here*, courtesy of Princeton Architectural Press, Inc.

Flickr Portfolio. *At University, Take Two*, Julie Mierwa. *MC's Dorm Room*, Patrick Moberg. *Clutter*, Adrienne X. Shon. *My Space*, Matt Weir.

Camino a Manabao, 1993. Pobilio Diaz.

A Mexican American Family Celebrates a Quinciniera, 2007. Samantha Appleton. Courtesy of Samantha Appleton/Noor Images.

A Mother Walks Home with Her Children after School in Dearborn, Michigan, 2002. Monica Almeida. Courtesy of Monica Almeida/The New York Times/Redux.

Protest in Humboldt Park against Bomb Testing on the Island of Vieques, Puerto Rico. Jon Lowenstein/ Noor Images.

Little India, 2005. Alex Webb. Courtesy of Alex Webb/ Magnum Photos, Inc.

What Is America? Jesse Gordon. From New York Times Op-Art, July 3, 2000.

Chapter 3

Verbal Texts

Dorothy Allison. "This Is Our World." From *DoubleTake* magazine (Summer 1998). Copyright © 1998 Dorothy Allison. Reprinted by permission of the Francis Golden Literacy Agency.

Ethan Canin. "Viewfinder." From *Vivian, Fort Barnwell*. First published in *DoubleTake*. Copyright © 2001 by Ethan Canin. Reprinted by permission of William Morris Agency, LLC on behalf of the author.

Bill McKibben. "Year One of the Next Earth." From *In Katrina's Wake*, by Bill McKibben. Copyright 2006 by Princeton Architectural Press, Inc. in the format Textbook via Copyright Clearance Center.

N. Scott Momaday. "The Photograph." From *The Man Made of Words* by N. Scott Momaday. Copyright © 1998 by N. Scott Momaday. Reprinted with the permission of the author.

James Nachtwey. "Ground Zero." From *American Photo*, 13.1 January/February 2002. Reprinted with permission of American Photo Magazine.

Joe Rosenthal. Extract from *Faces of the Twentieth Century: Master Photographers and Their Work* by Mark Edward Harris. Copyright © 1998 by Mark Edward Harris. Reproduced by permission of Abbeville Press.

Will Self. Quotation originally published in *How I Write: The Secret Life of Authors*, edited by Dan Crowe. Copyright © 2007 by Will Self. Reprinted with permission of The Wylie Agency, LLC.

Susan Sontag. "On Photography." Excerpt from *On Photography* by Susan Sontag. Reprinted by permission of Farrar, Straus & Giroux, LLC.

Clive Thompson. "This Just In: I'm Twittering." First appeared in *Wired* magazine, June 26, 2007. Copyright © 2007–2009 Clive Thompson. Reprinted by permission of David Wallis as agent for Clive Thompson.

Sarah Vowell. "The First Thanksgiving." From *The Partly Cloudy Patriot*, pp. 9–15. Reprinted with the permission of Simon & Schuster Adult Publishing Group. Copyright © 2002 by Sarah Vowell.

Visual Texts

Martin Parr Portfolio. Courtesy of Martin Parr/Magnum Photos, Inc.

Vivian, Fort Barnwell. From *Vivian, Fort Barnwell* by Ethan Canin. First published in *DoubleTake*. Copyright © 2001 by Ethan Canin. Reprinted by permission of William Morris Agency, LLC on behalf of the author.

Yearbook Photos. Courtesy of Classmates Yearbook, Inc.

Sharbat Gula, 1985; *Sharbat Gula*, 2002. Steve McCurry. Courtesy of Steve McCurry/Magnum Photos, Inc.

National Geographic cover, June 1984. © 2008 National Geographic.

USA Today cover, 2008. © 2008, USA TODAY. Reprinted with permission.

Anchorage Daily News cover, 2008. Courtesy of the Anchorage Daily News.

The Commercial Appeal cover, 2008. Courtesy of the Commercial Appeal.

The Oregonian cover, 2008. © 2008 The Oregonian. All rights reserved. Reprinted with permission.

Visualizing Composition: Structure. Peter Arkle. © Peter Arkle, 2009.

Andrew Savulich Portfolio. Courtesy of Andrew Savulich.

Crushed Car. James Nachtwey. James Nachtwey/ VII Photo Agency LLC.

Lakeview Sign among Debris; Remains of a Home, Ninth Ward, New Orleans; Remains of a Home with Canal and Levee in Background, Chalmette; Refrigerator in a Tree near Port Sulphur, 2005. Chris Jordan. Courtesy of Chris Jordan.

Marines Raising the Flag on Mount Suribachi, Iwo Jima. Joe Rosenthal. Courtesy of Joe Rosenthal / AP / Wide World.

Three-cent Iwo Jima Stamp, 1945. U.S. Postal Service. AP / Wide World Photos.

Flag Raising, World Trade Center, 2001. Associated Press photograph by Thomas E. Franklin. © 2001 The Record (Bergen County, N.J.), photograph by Thomas E. Franklin.

Superbowl XXXVI, 2002. Photograph by David J. Phillip. Courtesy Associated Press / Wide World Photos.

Memorial Day, 1994. Mark Zingarelli / The New Yorker, © Condé Nast Publications.

Chapter 4
Verbal Texts
Susan Bordo. "Never Just Pictures." From *Twilight Zones: The Hidden Life of Cultural Images from Plato to O. J.* by Susan Bordo. Copyright © 1979 by The Regents of the University of California.

Jacinto Jesús Cardona. "Bato con Khakis." From *Heart to Heart: New Poems Inspired by Twentieth Century American Art*, edited by Jan Greenberg. Copyright © 2001 by Jacinto Jesús Cardona. Reprinted by permission of the author.

Judith Ortiz Cofer. "The Story of My Body." From *The Latin Deli: Prose and Poetry*. Copyright © 1993 by Judith Ortiz Cofer. Reprinted by permission of the University of Georgia Press.

Jamaica Kincaid. "Girl." From *At the Bottom of the River* by Jamaica Kincaid. Reprinted by permission of Farrar, Straus & Giroux, LLC.

Katha Pollitt. "Why Boys Don't Play with Dolls." From *The New York Times Magazine*, October 8, 1995 by Katha Pollitt. Reprinted by permission of the author.

Marjane Satrapi. "Introduction" and "The Veil" from *Persepolis: The Story of a Childhood*, translated by Mattias Ripa and Blake Ferris, translation copyright © 2003 by L'Association, Paris, France. Used by permission of Pantheon Books, a division of Random House, Inc.

Visual Texts
Self-Portrait, 1980 (masculine/feminine). Robert Mapplethorpe. © The Estate of Robert Mapplethorpe. Used by Permission.

Self-Portrait, 1980 (masculine/feminine). Robert Mapplethorpe. © The Estate of Robert Mapplethorpe. Used by Permission.

Bato con Khakis, 1982. César A. Martínez. From *Heart to Heart*, ed. Jan Greenberg and Harry N. Abrams, 2001. Courtesy of César A. Martínez.

Li'L Sis, 1944. William H. Johnson. Smithsonian American Art Museum, Washington, D.C., U.S.A. Photo Credit: Smithsonian American Art Museum, Washington, D.C. / Art Resource, NY.

"The Veil," from *Persepolis: The Story of a Childhood* by Marjane Satrapi, translated by Mattias Ripa and Blake Ferris, © 2003 by L'Association, Paris, France. Used by permission of Pantheon Books, a division of Random House, Inc.

How Joe's Body Brought Him Fame Instead of Shame, 1944. © Charles Atlas, Ltd. Reprinted with permission.

Asics ad. © Asics America Corporation, 1998. Reprinted with permission.

Visualizing Composition: Purpose. Peter Arkle. © Peter Arkle, 2009.

From the *He / She* series. Nancy Burson. © 1996–97 by Nancy Burson.

Pirelli tire ad featuring Carl Lewis. Courtesy of the Advertising Archive.

Ashleigh, 13, with Her Friend and Parents, Santa Monica. Lauren Greenfield. Courtesy of Lauren Greenfield / VII Photo Agency LLC.

Nature vs. Nurture cartoon. Art Spiegelman. Copyright © 1997 Art Spiegelman. First appeared in *The New Yorker*, September 8, 1997. Reprinted with permission of The Wylie Agency, Inc.

Untitled (Cheerleading #81), 2002; *Untitled (Football #75),* 2002. Brian Finke. © Brian Finke. Courtesy of ClampArt, New York City.

Today's Military ad featuring Valerie Vigoda, 2003. © John Huet.

Chapter 5
Verbal Texts
Donnell Alexander. "Are Black People Cooler than White People? Dumb Question." Copyright Donnell Alexander. Reprinted by permission of Featherwell.com

Ta-Nehisi Coates. "This Is How We Lost to the White Man." Reprinted by permission of Ta-Nehisi Coates and the Watkins-Loomis Agency. © 2008 The Atlantic Monthly.

W. E. B. Du Bois. "Double Consciousness." Original title, "Of Our Spiritual Strivings." Reprinted with permission of The Permissions Company, Rights Agency for The David Graham Du Bois Trust.

Michael Hsu. "The Squint and the Wail." From *I.D.* magazine. www.id-mag.com/article/The_Squint_and_the_Wail/. Reprinted by permission.

James McBride. "What Color Is Jesus? When Your Mother Is White and Your Father Is Black, the Questions Never Stop." Published in the *Washington Post*, July 31, 1988 issue, W24. Copyright by Jadel Publishing Inc. Reprinted by permission of SLL / Sterling Lord Literistic, Inc.

Naomi Schaefer Riley. "The Risks of Multiracial Identification." From *The Chronicle of Higher Education*, November 10, 2006. Reprinted by permission of the author.

Luc Sante. "Be Different! (Like Everyone Else!) From *The New York Times Magazine*, October 17, 1999. Copyright © 1999, Luc Sante. Reprinted by permission.

Visual Texts
Nikki S. Lee Portfolio. © Nikki S. Lee, Courtesy Sikkema Jenkins & Co., NY.

The Chin Family. Photograph by Thomas Porostocky.

24 People for Whom I Have Been Mistaken, 1999. Roger Shimomura. Courtesy of Private Collection of David E. Schwartz.

Party; Ich, 2003–2004. Yang Liu. Courtesy of Yang Liu Design www.yangliudesign.com.

The Life of Buffalo Bill film poster, 1910. Museum of the American West, Autry National Center of the American West, Los Angeles; 87.29.2.

Redskin film poster, 1929. Redskin starring Richard Dix. Paramount Pictures. Courtesy of the Everett Collection, Inc.

The Indians Are Coming, 1938. Courtesy of the Everett Collection, Inc.

Lone Ranger and Tonto film still. Courtesy of Photofest.

Peter Pan film still, 1953. Courtesy of Photofest.

Death Valley Days film still. Death Valley Days starring Ronald Reagan. Courtesy of the Everett Collection, Inc.

Smoke Signals film still. © Miramax films. Jill Sabella / Everett Collection. Screenplay by Sherman Alexie. Chris Eyre, director; actors: Adam Beach and Evan Adams. Reprinted by permission.

"Arnold Schwarzenegger"; "Queen Elizabeth II", 1993. Tibor Kalman. From Colors magazine, #4, "Race." Reprinted by permission.

Visualizing Composition: Audience. Peter Arkle. © Peter Arkle, 2009.

Carlton Davis Portfolio. Courtesy of Carlton Davis.

Authentic Cuban Santera,1993. Reprinted with permission by Cristina Taccone photography.

Part Asian 100% Hapa. Portraits by Kip Fulbeck. From the book Part Asian 100% Hapa.

Chapter 6

Verbal Texts

Billy Collins. "The Waitress." From Sailing Alone Around the Room. Copyright © 2001 by Billy Collins. Used by permission of Random House, Inc.

Guy Davenport. "The Geography of the Imagination." From The Geography of the Imagination: Forty Essays. Copyright © 1981 by Guy Davenport. Reprinted by permission of the Estate of Guy Davenport.

William Deresiewicz. "The Dispossessed." From The American Scholar, Volume 75, No. 1, Winter 2006. Copyright © 2005 by the author. Reprinted by permission of the publisher.

Barbara Ehrenreich. "This Land Is Their Land." From The Nation, June 30, 2008. Reprinted by permission of International Creative Management as agents for the author.

Paul Fussell. "A Touchy Subject." From Class: A Guide Through the American Status System. Copyright © 1983 by Paul Fussell. Reprinted with the permission of Simon & Schuster Adult Publishing Group.

Woody Guthrie. "This Land Is Your Land." Words and music by Woody Gutherie. © 1956 (renewed) 1958 (renewed) 1970 (renewed) Ludlow Music, Inc., New York, NY. Reprinted by permission.

Sally Stein. "Passing Likeness: Dorothea Lange's 'Migrant Mother' and the Paradox of Iconicity." From Only Skin Deep: Changing Visions of the American Self, edited by Coco Fusco and Brian Wallis. Copyright © 2003 Sally Stein and the International

Center of Photography. Published by Harry N. Abrams, Inc. Reprinted by permission of the author.

Jane Yolen. "Grant Wood: American Gothic." Copyright © 2001 by Jane Yolen. First appeared in Heart to Heart. Published by Harry N. Abrams, Inc. Reprinted by permission of Curtis Brown, Ltd.

Visual Texts

Brooks Jensen Portfolio. Standing Drill Bits, Ellensburg, Washington, 1986; Three Drills, Hockinson, Washington, 1987; Felix Muñoz, Cuero, Texas, 1988; Vernon Barrow and Grandson, Denison, Kansas, 1989; Joe Sasak, Leroy, Wisconsin, 1989. Brooks Jensen / www.brooksjensenarts.com, LensWork Publishing.

A Waitress at Duval's Restaurant. Auguste Renoir. The Metropolitan Museum of Art, New York, NY U.S.A.

The Louisville Flood, 1937. Courtesy Margaret Bourke White / Getty Images.

Billboard on U.S. Highway 99. Courtesy Dorothea Lange, Library of Congress.

American Gothic. Painting by Grant Wood. Photography © The Art Institute of Chicago.

American Gothic. Gordon Parks. Courtesy Gordon Parks / Corbis.

Counter Culture American Gothic. Personality Posters, Inc. Library of Congress.

Post-9/11 American Gothic. © The New Yorker Collection 2001 Marisa Acocella from cartoonbank.com. All rights reserved.

The Simple Life. Courtesy of the Everett Collection.

The Advocate cover. The Advocate, Courtesy of Regent Media.

Workers Leaving Pennsylvania Shipyard. Courtesy John Vachon / Library of Congress.

Pike County. Courtesy National Archives.

Hurricane Katrina Evacuees. Courtesy Getty Images.

Class Matters Portfolio. By the New York Times 2005 by Macmillan Books.

The Reunion. Tina Barney © Tina Barney, Courtesy of Janet Borden, Inc.

Visualizing Composition: Metaphor. Peter Arkle. © Peter Arkle, 2009.

Migrant Mother, Nipomo, California, 1936. Dorothea Lange American, 1895–1965. © The Dorothea Lange Collection, Oakland Museum of California, City of Oakland. Gift of Paul S. Taylor.

Florence Thompson and her daughters, Modesto, CA. By Bill Ganzel, http://www.ganzelgroup.com. From Dust Bowl Descent, by Bill Ganzel, 1984.

Hopi Indian Man, 1926. Dorothea Lange, Oakland Museum of California, City of Oakland. Gift of Paul S. Taylor.

The Vanishing Race, 1907. Edward S. Curtis. National Anthropological Archives. Smithsonian Institution, Washington, D.C.

Down and Out in Discount America cover. By The Nation magazine, January 3, 2005. Reprinted with permission from the issue of The Nation. http://www.thenation.com

Eloy, Arizona. Dorothea Lange. Courtesy National Archives.

Chapter 7

Verbal Texts

Isabel Allende. "Omayra Sanchez." From *Talking Pictures: People Speak about the Pictures That Speak to Them* by Marvin Heiferman (Chronicle Books). © 1994 Isabel Allende. Reprinted by permission of the author.

Frank Fournier. "Interview on the Photograph of Omayra Sanchez." Reprinted by permission of the author.

Steven Johnson. "Watching TV Makes You Smarter— *The New York Times Magazine*, 04/24/2005." From *Everything Bad Is Good for You*. Copyright © 2005 by Steven Johnson. Used by permission of Riverhead Books, an imprint of Penguin Group (USA) Inc.

Michael Lewis. "Serfs of the Turf." From *The New York Times Op-Ed*, November 11, 2007. Reprinted by permission of the author.

John Long. "Ethics in the Age of Digital Photography." Reprinted by permission of the author.

Rev. John P. Minogue. "The Twentieth-Century University Is Obsolete." From *Inside Higher Ed*, September 5, 2006. Reprinted by permission of the author.

Michael Pollan. "Farmer in Chief." From *The New York Times Magazine*, October 12, 2008. Copyright © 2008 by Michael Pollan. Reprinted by permission of International Creative Management, Inc.

Virginia Postrel. "The Politics of the Retouched Headshot." From *The Atlantic Monthly*, October 16, 2008. Copyright © 2008. Reprinted by permission.

Susan Sontag. Excerpt from "Plato's Cave." From *On Photography* by Susan Sontag. Copyright © 1977 by Susan Sontag. Excerpt from *Regarding the Pain of Others*. Copyright © 2003 by Susan Sontag. Reprinted by permission of Farrar, Straus and Giroux, LLC.

Mitchell Stephens. "Expanding the Language of Photographs." From *Media Studies Journal*, 1997. Copyright © 1977. Reprinted by permission of Freedom Forum.

Visual Texts

Imagine series. Collaborate. Courtesy of Collaborate / Citizen Group, San Francisco © 2003 for Amnesty International. Creative Director / Copywriter: Robin Raj; Art Director: Kurt Lighthouse; Photography: Magnum.

Rodolfo Monteil (Defend the Earth). Courtesy of Collaborate, San Francisco, for Amnesty International and Sierra Club. Creative Director / Copywriter: Robin Raj; Art Director: Kurt Lighthouse; Photography: Keba Konte.

Death Penalty Y/N (Yes/No). Courtesy of Collaborate, San Francisco, for Rock the Vote. Creative Director / Copywriter: Robin Raj; Art Director: Kurt Lighthouse / Daniel Jung; Photography: Getty Images.

Omayra Sanchez, Colombia, 1985. Frank Fournier. © 1985 Frank Fournier / Contact Press Images.

Frank Fournier. Michelle Poire. © 2004 Michelle Poire / World Picture News.

World Wildlife Fund Portfolio. Courtesy EuroRSCG.

Wiretaps and Privacy Rights. Clay Bennett. Used with the permission of Clay Bennett and the Washington Post Writers Group in conjunction with the Cartoonist Group. All rights reserved.

Professional Courtesy, 1996. James Rosenquist. © James Rosenquist / Licensed by VAGA, New York, NY.

Missing the Target. Robert Unell. Courtesy Robert Unell / The Kansas City Star.

I'm Taking a Poll, Sir. Wayne Stayskal. Reprinted by permission of the artist.

Visualizing Composition: Point of View. Peter Arkle. © Peter Arkle, 2009.

Home of a Rebel Sharpshooter, Gettysburg, July, 1863. Alexander Gardner. From *Gardner's Photographic Sketchbook of the American Civil War 1861–1865*. Courtesy of the Division of Rare & Manuscript Collections, Cornell University Library.

The Men of the 308th, the "Lost Battalion," April 28, 1919. © Corbis.

Omaha Beach, June 6, 1944. Robert Capa. © Robert Capa / Magnum Photos.

Greenhouse Dog. VIP's view DOG detonation from Officer's Beach Club patio. Enewetak Island, April 7, 1951. Courtesy of the National Archives.

Children Fleeing a Napalm Strike, Vietnam, 1972. Nick Ut. AP / Wide World Photos.

Iraqi Man at a Regroupment Center for POWs, Najaf, Iraq, March 31, 2003. Jean-Marc Bouju / AP / Wide World Photos.

Image of Kwakiutl Woman. George Hunt. Courtesy of the Museum of Natural History.

Members of the 129th Rescue Squadron, Moffitt Federal Airfield, CA. Photo by Lance Cheung.

Breaching Great White Shark. Charles Maxwell. © Charles Maxwell, reprinted with permission.

The Politics of Fear. Barry Blitt / The New Yorker, © Conde Nast Publications.

Bootiful. Rankin. Courtesy Rankin / Icon International.

Appendix A

Verbal Texts

John Berger. "Chapter 1." From *Ways of Seeing* by John Berger. Copyright © 1972 by John Berger. Used by permission of Viking Penguin, a division of Penguin Group (USA) Inc.

Visual Texts

The Key of Dreams. René Magritte. © 2006 C. Herscovici, Brussels / Artists Rights Society (ARS), New York. *Le Clef des Songes (The Key of Dreams)*. Coll. Wormland, Munich, Germany. Photo credit: Bridgeman-Giraudon / Art Resource, NY.

Regents of the Old Men's Alms House. Frans Hals. © Hals Museum. Reprinted by permission of Frans Halsmuseum.

Regentesses of the Old Men's Alms House. Frans Hals. © Hals Museum. Reprinted by permission of Frans Halsmuseum.

Still Life with Chair Caning, 1912. Pablo Picasso. © Copyright ARS / NY. Photo Credit: Bridegeman-Giraudon / Art Resource, NY.

Virgin of the Rocks. Leonardo da Vinci. c. 1491–1508. National Gallery, London, Great Britain. Photo Credit: Art Resource, NY.

Virgin of the Rocks. Leonardo da Vinci. c. 1483. Louvre, Paris, France. Photo Credit: Scala / Art Resource, NY. Photo credit: Alinari / Art Resource, NY.

Virgin and Child with St. Anne and St. John the Baptist. Leonardo da Vinci. National Gallery, London, Great Britain. Photo Credit: Art Resource, NY.

Venus and Mars. Sandro Botticelli. National Gallery, London, Great Britain.

Procession to Calvary, 1546. Pieter Brueghel, the Elder. Kunsthistorisches Museum, Vienna, Austria. Photo Credit: Erich Lessing / Art Resource, NY.

Wheatfield with Crows. Vincent Van Gogh. Van Gogh Museum, Amsterdam, The Netherlands. Photo Credit: Art Resource, NY.

Woman Pouring Milk. Jan Vermeer. © Raymond Schoder / CORBIS.

Scott McCloud. From *Understanding Comics* by Scott McCloud. Copyright © 1993, 1994 by Scott McCloud. Reprinted by permission of HarperCollins Publishers.

Index of Verbal and Visual Texts

A Note on the Type

Seeing & Writing 4 was designed at 2x4 by Erica Deahl and Fabienne Hess, using a mixture of typefonts. Chapter heads, headnotes, and questions appear in Akzidenz Grotesk (1896), released by the H. Berthhold AG type foundry. The primary text font is Sabon (1964–67), drawn by the German designer Jan Tschichold

A Note about Peter Arkle

Freelance illustrator Peter Arkle lives in New York City. When he's not producing ads and creating illustrations for the country's leading magazines and newspapers, he publishes *Peter Arkle News*, a newspaper containing stories and drawings about everyday life. Check out his work at *www.peterarkle.com*.

More help online

Student Center for Seeing & Writing
bedfordstmartins.com/seeingandwriting

Students

Try a tutorial on analyzing images

Read interviews with writers and artists

Watch videos of real writers

See reliable research links

Find help with citing sources

Build a bibliography

Instructors

Download sample syllabi

Browse tried-and-true assignments

Share your best teaching ideas

Upgrade to *VideoCentral: English*

Package *ix: visualizing composition* tutorials and models